RUSSIA
CAUCASUS MOUNTAINS
GEORGIA
T'bilisi (Tiflis)
Lesser Caucasus
Kür
AZERBAIJAN
Baki (Baku)
ARMENIA
Yerevan
Aras
CASPIAN SEA
KAZAKHSTAN
UZBEKISTAN
Garabogaz Aylagy
TURKMENISTAN
Aşgabat (Ashgabat)
Köpetdag Mts.
Mount Ararat 5,137 m 16,854 ft
URARTU
Van Gölü (Lake Van)
Daryācheh-ye Orūmīyeh (Lake Urmia)
Dijlah (Tigris)
Al Furāt (Euphrates)
Reshteh-ye Alborz (Elburz Mountains)
Tehrān
MEDIA
PARTHIA
ASSYRIA
MESOPOTAMIA
SYRIA
ARAM
KŪHHĀ-YE ZĀGROS (ZAGROS MOUNTAINS)
BABYLONIA
Baghdād
IRAN
SYRIAN DESERT
IRAQ
AKKAD
SUMERIA
An Nāşirīyah (Nasiriyah)
ELAM
CHALDEA
PARSA (PERSIA)
Al Kuwayt (Kuwait)
KUWAIT
PERSIAN GULF
An Nafūd
ARABIAN PENINSULA
Strait of Hormuz
Gulf of Oman
BAHRAIN
Al Manāmah (Manama)
QATAR
Ad Dawḩah (Doha)
Abū Zaby (Abu Dhabi)
UNITED ARAB EMIRATES
OMAN
Ar Riyāḑ (Riyadh)
SAUDI ARABIA
Ar Rub' al Khālī (Empty Quarter)
0 100 200 300 kilometers
0 100 200 300 miles
Present-day drainage, coastlines, and country boundaries are represented.
40°E
50°E
60°E
40°N
30°N

The BIBLICAL WORLD

An ILLUSTRATED ATLAS

By JEAN-PIERRE ISBOUTS

FOREWORD *by* BRUCE CHILTON

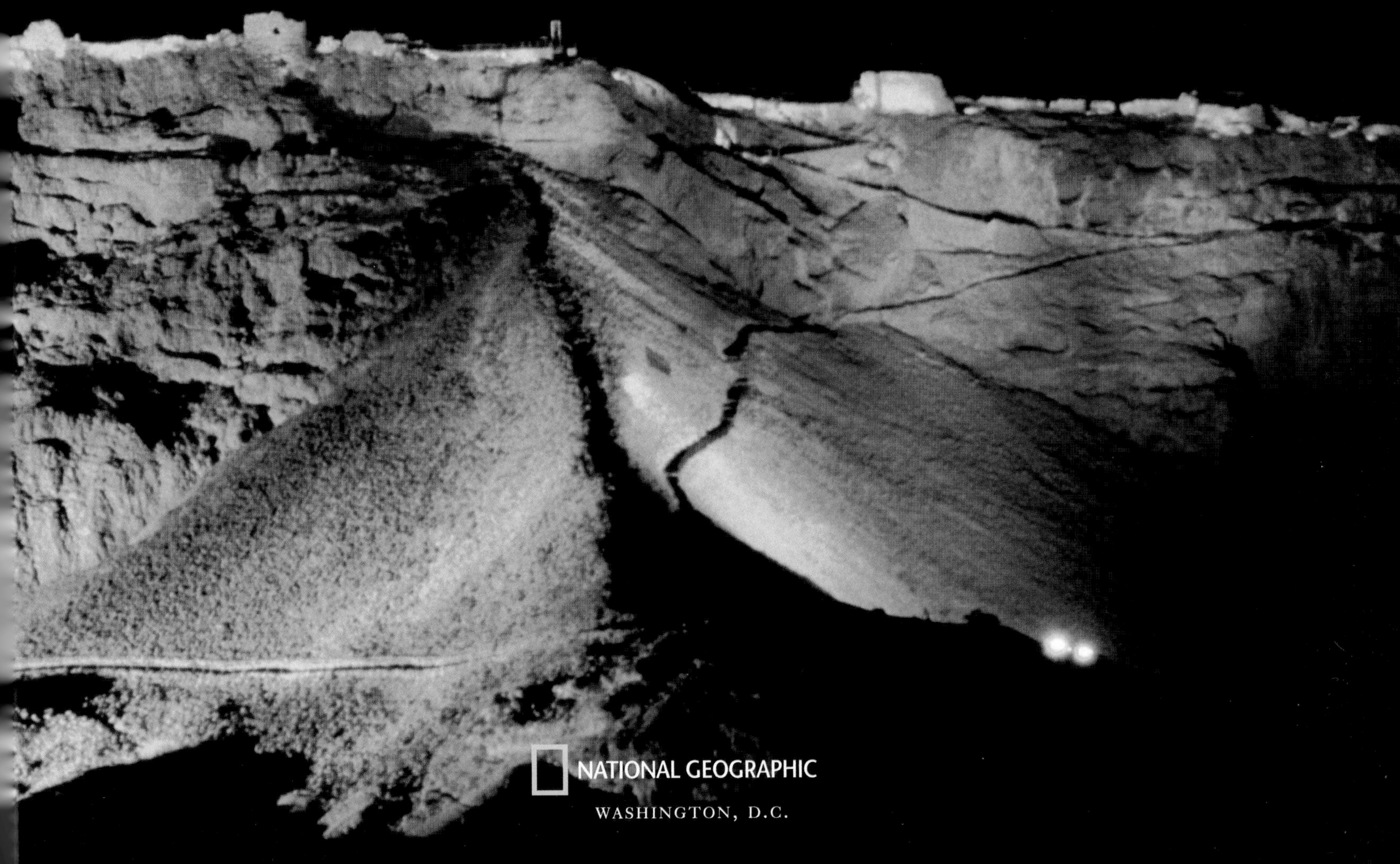

NATIONAL GEOGRAPHIC

WASHINGTON, D.C.

BOARD OF ADVISERS

CONTENTS

OPPOSITE: Growing near the Dead Sea, green acacia trees are able to survive in the rocky sands of the desert.

PREVIOUS PAGES 2–3: A full moon rises over the ancient fortress of Masada, seated on the eastern edge of the Judean desert.

PREVIOUS PAGE 1: Created by a 10th-century Spanish artist, this illustration depicts "The Dream of Nebuchadnezzar" and appears in "Bible Mozarabe."

FOREWORD

THE BIBLE IN ALL ITS VARIETY—as embraced by the continuous traditions of Judaism and Christianity, and honored within Islam—persistently refers to its lands, both the places individual texts came from and the places biblical authors longed to see. Each of the writings comes from a specific location, with its own geography and culture; evidence usually points directly or indirectly to the times and localities, as well as the circumstances, that brought a book to birth.

Yet readers of the Bible often have trouble imagining the physical, pragmatic conditions that have left indelible traces on the texts. What did it mean for Abraham to leave his native Mesopotamia and to take up the seminomadic ethos of earliest Israel? How could Moses have prompted an escape of slaves from Egypt, who sought a land flowing with milk and honey? In addition to understanding the political circumstances of these and subsequent times, readers who want to enter into the epic stories of the Bible need to have a sense of the wildlife, the dangers, the beauties, and the productivity of the biblical lands.

This atlas brings together maps, photographs, time lines, and artifacts in a way that adds dimensions too often lacking in assessments of the Bible and its associated literatures. A sense of place and time helps us to appreciate the meaning, tone, and emotional resonance of any writing, and that applies all the more to biblical literatures, which were written in differing locations, periods, and circumstances. Deep attachment to the significance of biblical lands even survived national catastrophe.

With Israel at the edge of annihilation, during the Exile in Babylonia after 587 B.C.E., the Bible began to emerge as a written whole. Israelites held the memory of the land that had been lost within their hearts, and cherished the dream of a return to it as if to Eden. Their aspirations, which increasingly included the hope that God would reshape the course of all human history, involved a literal return to their land, but also an expectation that the land itself would blossom in a way not seen since the beginning of Creation.

Christianity was born in the matrix of that promise of a new fulfillment. Its story begins in territorial Israel, but then fans out into the lands around the Mediterranean world, which the prophecies of Jesus—and of Israelite prophets before Jesus—predicted would join the worship of Israel. The New Testament opens the story of how the Roman Empire transformed itself to worship an executed rabbi as the Son of God, instead of its all-powerful emperor.

Just as the lands of the Bible do not stop at the edge of territorial Israel in late antiquity, so the resonance of biblical texts reaches beyond the period of the Old and New Testaments. The story of this atlas embraces the interpretation of these writings during the Byzantine and Muslim periods, and shows how people, east as well as west of Jerusalem, not only looked to the Bible to explain the meaning of their lives and to express their hope for a blessed future, but also looked *through* the Bible, making its images and promises and visions and warnings into the lens that made sense of human existence.

—BRUCE CHILTON

OPPOSITE: **The shimmering waters of the Nile River reflect the last rays of daylight as the sun sets near Luxor.**

INTRODUCTION

NO BOOK HAS BEEN OF GREATER INFLUENCE on the development of Western civilization than the Bible. It is the foundational text of Judaism and Christianity and is accepted as divinely inspired Scripture by Islam. But the Bible is also a superbly geographical narrative. Its stories take place across the full breadth of the ancient Near East, particularly the crescent-like territory curving from Egypt and Israel to Syria and Mesopotamia (today's Iraq), which scholars refer to as the Fertile Crescent. At the center of this crescent lies a narrow strip of land, squeezed between the Syrian Desert and the Mediterranean Sea, which was alternatively known as Canaan, Israel, Judea, and Palestine. A bottleneck in the principal trade routes between Egypt and Mesopotamia, this narrow ribbon became the Holy Land where both Judaism and Christianity would sink roots.

THE BIBLE IS NOT ONE COHESIVE NARRATIVE but a collection of highly diverse works, including prose, poetry, hymns, prayers, and codes of law, which were originally contained on individual scrolls—known as *biblia* in Greek. In fact, the word "Bible" itself has different meanings to Jews and Christians.

The Bible of Judaism, which we will refer to as the Hebrew Scriptures, is organized in three divisions:

- **The Law** (*Torah*), or Five Books of Moses, which consist of Genesis, Exodus, Leviticus, Numbers, and Deuteronomy; these are often referred to by their Greek name, Pentateuch, meaning "Five Scrolls";
- **The Prophets** (*Nevi'im*), including the former prophets (Joshua, Judges, Samuel, and Kings) and the latter prophets (including Isaiah, Jeremiah, Ezekiel, and the Twelve Minor Prophets); and
- **The Writings** (*Ketuvim*), which include the Psalms, Proverbs, the Book of Job, the Book of Daniel, the Book of Chronicles, and others.

THE HEBREW INITIALS of these three names (*Torah–Nevi'im–Ketuvim*) form the acronym TaNaKh, the collective name for the Hebrew Scriptures in Judaism. Some scholars have argued that the Book of Deuteronomy should be considered part of a second grouping, consisting of the Books of Joshua, Judges, Samuel, and Kings, given this group's consistent treatment of Israel's history through the prism of Covenant theology, and Israel's ability (or failure) to abide by it. Scholars refer to this grouping as the Deuteronomistic History and believe it was edited during the reign of King Josiah in the seventh century B.C.E., only to reach its final form during or immediately after the Babylonian Exile (586–537 B.C.E.). A parallel history, known as the Chronicle History and including the Books of Chronicles (I and II), Ezra, and Nehemiah, covers the same time period, though from a different perspective, continuing well into the Persian era (537–332 B.C.E.). Chronicles generally is believed to have been composed between 450 and 435 B.C.E.

OPPOSITE: **As night falls, bright lights illuminate the Jerusalem City Museum of Citadel of David and Jaffe Gate in Jerusalem, Israel.**

In addition, there are a some 13 religious works, written by Jewish authors between 300 B.C.E. and the late first century C.E., which for various reasons were not included in the final canon or composition of the Hebrew Scriptures. Called Apocrypha by Christian authors, these books include wisdom sayings, poetry, prayers, and histories that were included in the Septuagint, the Greek translation of the Hebrew Scriptures. In turn, the Septuagint (including the Apocrypha) was adopted by Christians as the Old Testament, so called to distinguish these works from the New Testament, the principal Christian Scripture, which includes the four Gospels of Matthew, Mark, Luke, and John; the Book of Acts of the Apostles; the Epistles (or Letters) attributed to Paul; additional apostolic letters; and the Book of Revelation.

To understand the Bible, it is instructive to understand how its individual books came about. Even conservative scholars would agree that the Bible did not originate overnight, but that its stories emerged over many centuries, transmitted through oral history—as well as individual written sources. Since the 17th century, scholars have tried to identify and reconstruct these separate strands of biblical tradition by looking for distinctive patterns in language, style, or theological focus.

One prominent example are the different sources that, scholars believe, were woven together by ancient editors or redactors to form the Pentateuch, the Five Books of Moses. Proponents of this theory, which is known as the documentary hypothesis, suggest that four distinct sources were used. Regardless of the validity of this theory, it is a testament to the skill of the ancient redactors that they were able to integrate these traditions into a cohesive, and for many readers almost seamless, biblical narrative.

The same techniques of literary, source, and form criticism have been used to analyze the underlying sources of the New Testament. For example, early critics readily acknowledged the similarities between the Gospels of Mark, Matthew, and Luke, even though these probably originated in different locations and time periods. This led to the dual source hypothesis, which argues that Mark is the oldest gospel, and that both Matthew and Luke borrowed large segments from Mark, while also incorporating material from another source, known as Q, which has not survived. We refer to these various sources in our narrative, albeit with the caveat that these and other hypotheses continue to be challenged.

Any attempt to match the Bible with the history of the ancient Near East inevitably faces the question to which extent its narrative may be treated as history writing. No one will question the Bible's moral and religious significance and its use as a beacon of moral values in everyday life. Whether the Bible is also a reliable source of historical information continues to be a subject of considerable scholarly debate. In recent decades specifically, biblical archaeologists have often been divided between those who accept the intrinsic historical value of the Bible and those who fundamentally question the Bible's historicity—particularly pertaining to the Late Bronze and Early Iron Ages. This debate is particularly intense given the relative dearth of archaeological material from these periods in the Holy Land. Some have attributed this lack of evidence to the relative illiteracy of Israel's predominantly agricultural society, the modest scope of its culture, and the frequency of military invasion. In order to afford the reader a balanced perspective, therefore, this book has sought to present many different views, so that readers may judge for themselves.

ONE OTHER CONTROVERSIAL ASPECT OF BIBLICAL SCHOLARSHIP is the very chronology of biblical events and the historicity of dates presented in the Bible. Here, too, there is no consensus, and attempts to establish a chronology in reference to Egyptian or Assyrian king lists often vary by several hundred years.

The linchpin of any attempt at creating a biblical chronology is the dating of the Israelite settlement in Canaan—the Promised Land. Although many different dates (and theories) have been offered, this book follows the opinion that the first appearance of distinctly Israelite settlements in Canaan probably took place in the Early Iron Age, certainly by 1200 B.C.E. This assumption is based on a number of factors, including the reference, in the Book of Exodus, to the construction of the cities of Pithom and Pi-Ramses (arguably built during the reign of Pharaoh Seti I (1290–1279 B.C.E.) and Ramses II (1279–1213 B.C.E.). This anchor, then, helps determine the preceding chronology, though this identification continues to be a subject of considerable debate. Given the many difficult questions surrounding the historical attestation of biblical figures featured in Genesis through the Book of Judges, this book only offers specific dates for the reigns of Israel's leaders beginning with Saul. Unless noted otherwise, dates provided for political leaders such as kings and emperors denote the term of their reign. In the case of Egyptian pharaohs, this book follows the standard National Geographic chronology of ancient Egypt.

For the purpose of this book, all biblical quotations have been taken from the 1989 New Revised Standard Version translation (NRSV) of the Old and New Testament. In addition, this book also features a number of excerpts from the Koran (Qur'an), the Holy Book of Islam. While the Koran originated much later, in the seventh century C.E., it often includes interesting material about figures and events described in the Bible that are typically informed by a uniquely Arab perspective. Quotes from the Koran have been taken from the English translation by Muhammad Zafrulla Khan (1970). Translations of Sumerian, Babylonian, Ugaritic, Egyptian, and other Near Eastern literary sources have been quoted from a standard work on the subject, James B. Pritchard's multivolume series, *The Ancient Near East* (1958).

As has become common practice, this atlas of the biblical world uses the non-denominational temporal indicators of B.C.E. (Before the Common Era) instead of the traditional B.C. (Before Christ), and likewise C.E. (Common Era) rather than A.D. (Anno Domini) to identify key dates in history.

The text often refers to the God of Israel by using the tetragrammaton YHWH, meaning Yahweh. In quotations from the Koran, we will follow the example of several recent Muslim and non-Muslim authors and adapt the Islamic name of biblical figures to the one most familiar to a Western audience. Hence, Allah is translated as God; Ibrahim is Abraham, Musa is Moses and Isa is Jesus. The purpose of this translation is to enhance the accessibility of the text for the English-speaking reader.

Thus equipped, let us embark on our journey through the biblical world.

JEAN-PIERRE ISBOUTS
Fielding Graduate University
Santa Barbara, California

About this Book

The Biblical World: An Illustrated Atlas depicts the key stories of the Bible on the canvas of contemporary cultures in Canaan (Israel), Mesopotamia, Syria, Egypt, and the eastern Mediterranean. The book's ten chapters cover from the dawn of civilization to the era of the Islamic conquest, with a sharp focus on events in the Fertile Crescent and specifically, the Holy Land. Each chapter summarizes the biblical narrative within a set time period and compares it to insights provided by modern geographical, archaeological, and literary research. Sidebars highlight aspects of daily life, such as marriage, childbirth, food supply, dress, trade, language, art, and burial practices.

More than 350 remarkable photographs of geographical locations, archaeological sites, and artifacts illustrate the atlas. Time lines on each section opener offer a global overview of events during the period in question. At the end of each chapter, the time lines are reiterated in a comparative matrix to show the variety of historical, cultural, and political developments in the Near East.

The atlas features more than 50 stunning maps developed by the National Geographic Society and concludes with a visual essay of ancient maps of Palestine and Jerusalem from crusader times through the 19th century. The Holy Land is perhaps one of the most mapped regions in the world because of its religious and historical significance. Several areas have changed little from biblical times.

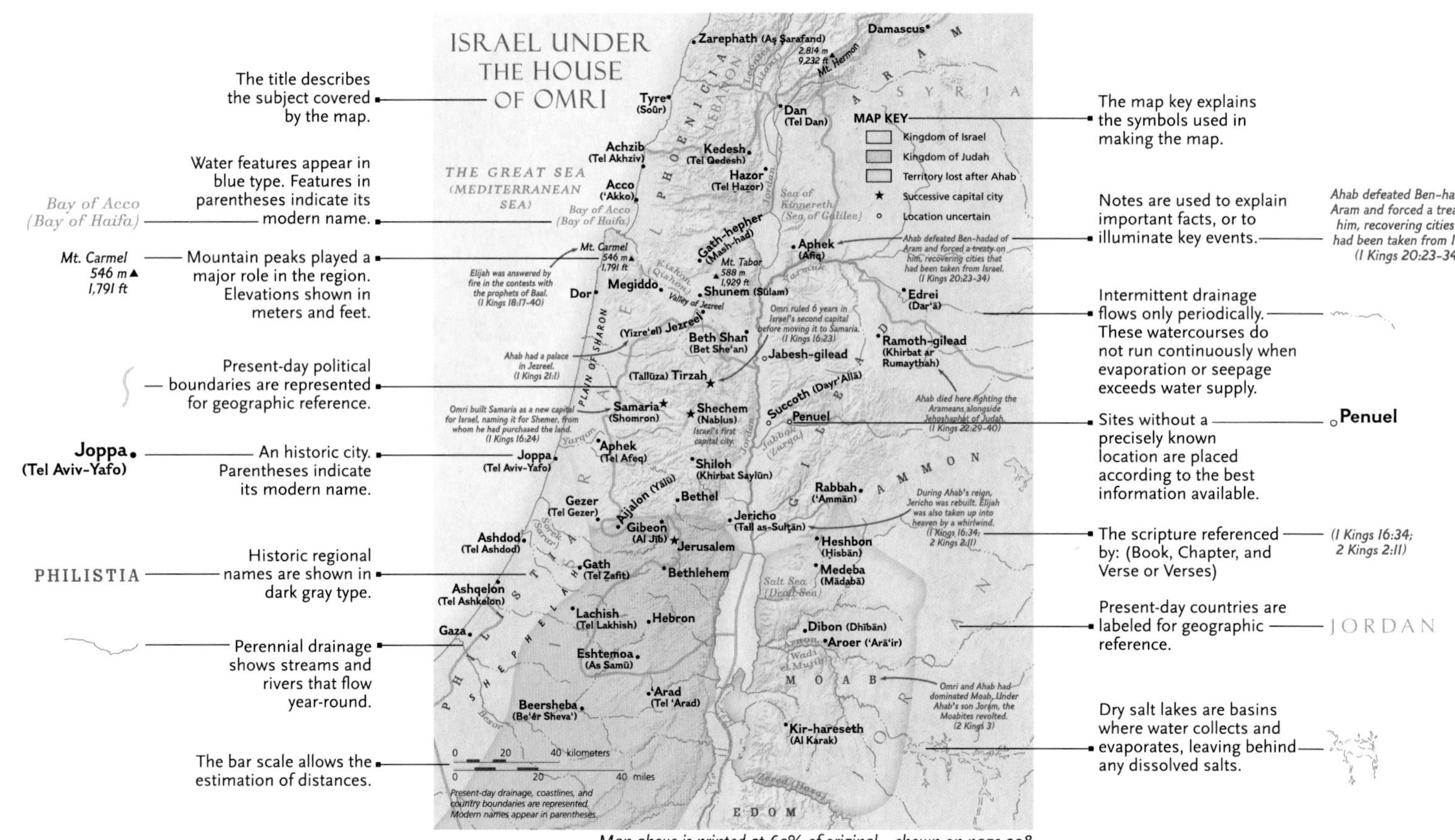

Map above is printed at 60% of original—shown on page 208.

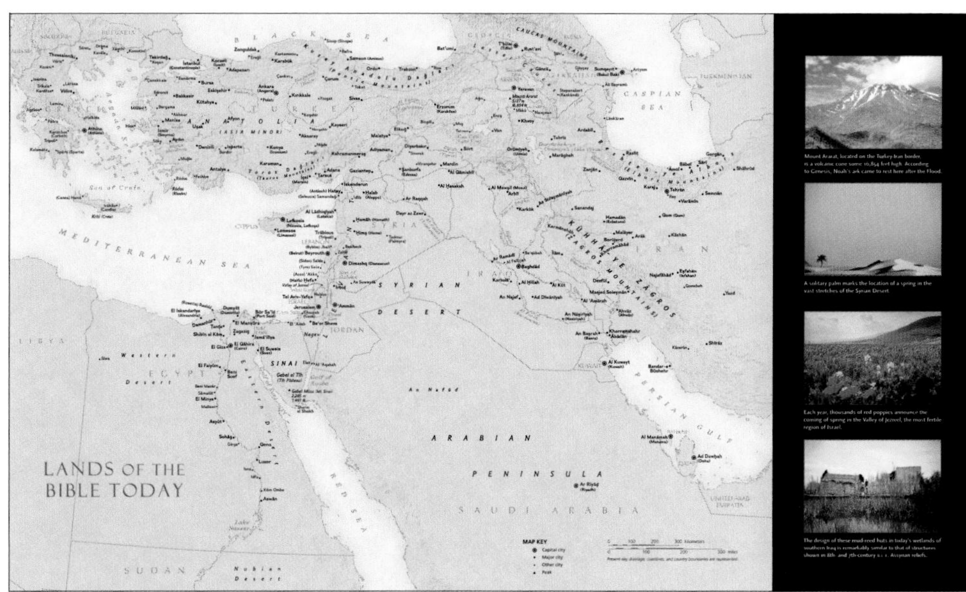

MAP SPREAD

The events of each chapter are located geographically by way of several individual maps, each prepared specifically for this book by the staff of the National Geographic Society. In addition, each chapter also includes one large double-page map showing major cities, regions, and trade routes, while a separate column of photographs illustrates key sites or events.

ERA INTRODUCTION SPREAD

Each chapter opens with a brief summary that introduces the principal characters and events of the period, which are then described in detail in subsequent sections. A time line at the bottom of the page highlights the most important events of the era, while a pull quote defines a key theme in the Bible or other ancient texts.

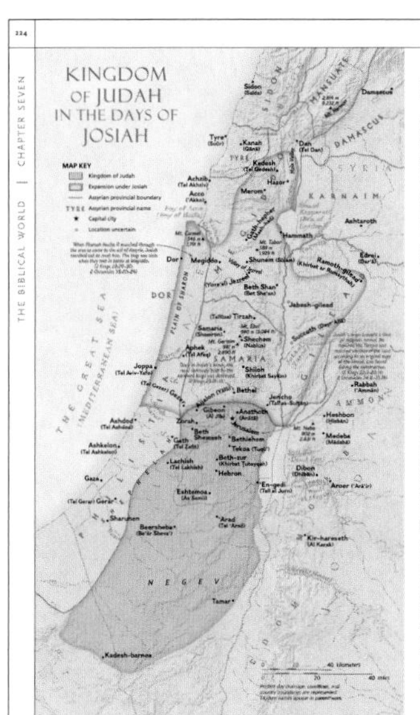

SIDEBAR SPREAD

Throughout each chapter, special sidebars describe what life was like for peoples of the Near East. These sidebars focus on farming, trade, dress, food, childbirth, burial customs, architecture, and other fascinating aspects of daily life in ancient lands.

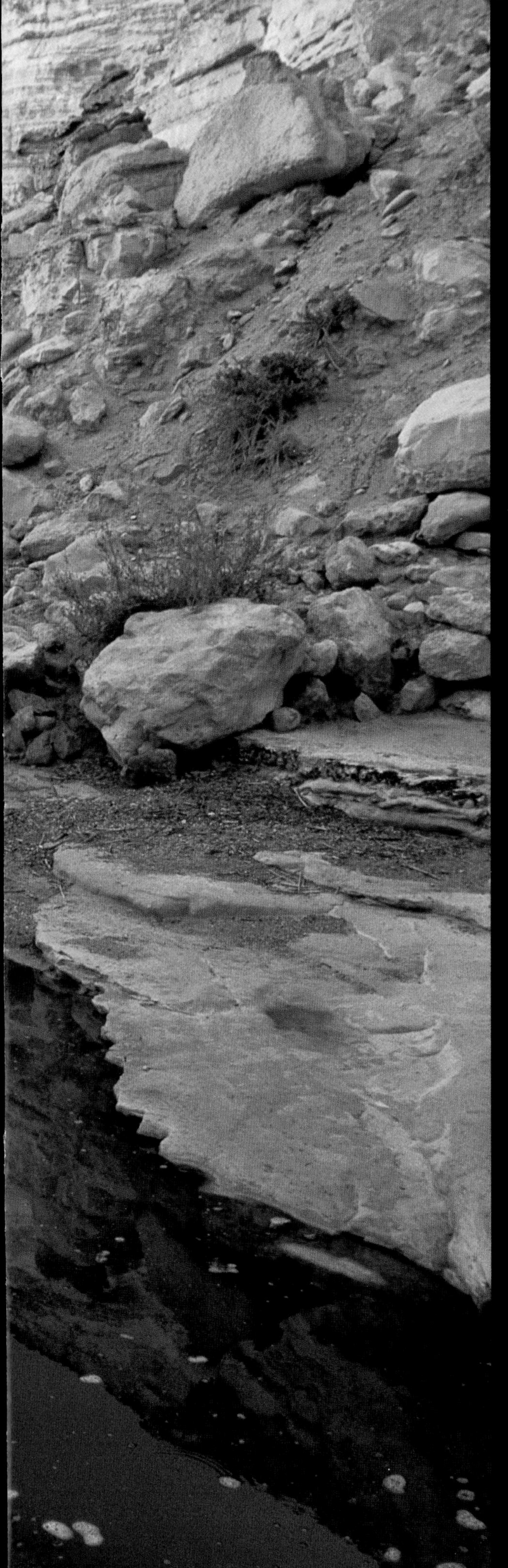

CHAPTER ONE

The World Before Abraham

THREE OF THE WORLD'S GREAT RELIGIONS—JUDAISM, Christianity, and Islam—were born in the same crescent-shaped swath of land that today we recognize as the cradle of Western civilization. From the confluence of the Euphrates and the Tigris Rivers in southern Mesopotamia to the alluvial plains of Canaan and the rich Nile River Delta beyond, this area known as the Fertile Crescent is the canvas on which stories in the Scriptures of Judaism, Christianity, and Islam unfold. Today, this crescent encompasses the modern states of Iraq and Iran in the east; Turkey and Syria in the north; Lebanon, Israel, and Jordan at the center; and Egypt to the south.

Here, in the heart of the Near East, we first witness an epochal change in human psychology. For thousands of years, man had hunted animals and birds to provide food for his family. However, sometime near the end of the Epipaleolithic period (Middle Stone Age), around 10,000 B.C.E., prehistoric man moved from a destructive strategy for procuring sustenance to a productive one. He learned how to grow crops and domesticate animals. This act in turn encouraged the development of primitive settlements, laying the foundation for the rise of the first cities of human civilization.

The ancient riverbed of Wadi Zin, in the Ein Avdat Canyon of the Negev, is fed by rainfall as well as mysterious subterranean springs.

LANDS OF THE BIBLE

A grove of palm trees in Iraq stir in the gentle breeze along the Euphrates River, one of the two main rivers that nurtured ancient Mesopotamia.

THE UNIQUE SHAPE and character of the large, bountiful area known as the Fertile Crescent is the result of two factors: the specific orientation of major rivers and tributaries, and the effects of high mountain ranges that trap and release moisture in the prevailing winds, channeling rainfall down into lands on their windward side. To the north, for example, the crescent is shielded by the towering ranges of the Zagros Mountains in western Iran and the Taurus Mountains of southwestern Turkey, where peaks can soar as high as 6,000 feet. Mount Ararat in eastern Turkey rises as high as 15,000 feet; not surprisingly, the Bible identifies this impressive peak as the resting place of Noah's ark.

Just beneath these high mountains is a flat alluvial plain known as Mesopotamia, a Greek word meaning "[the land] between the two rivers." The waters of these two rivers, the Euphrates and the Tigris, ensured that this land would be the place where humans could begin the development of civilization. To the north of Mesopotamia, the crescent curves back south into a narrow strip of fertile land, squeezed between the Mediterranean Sea and the Syrian Desert, to form the ancient territory of Syria-Damascus in the north and Israel, known as Canaan in Genesis, to the south. Here the deserts

ca 300,000 B.C.E.
Early evidence of modern humans present near the Sea of Galilee

ca 40,000 B.C.E.
Stone tools in use in ancient Israel

ca 15,000–8500 B.C.E.
Hunter-gatherers present in ancient Near East

ca 12,000 B.C.E.
Numerous cereal crops grow wild in Fertile Crescent

Then God said: "Let the earth put forth vegetation: plants yielding seed, and fruit trees of every kind on earth that bear fruit with the seed in it." And it was so; ... and God saw that it was good. (Genesis 1:11-12)

of Syria and Arabia push closest to the Mediterranean coast, pressing the crescent up into its characteristic shape.

In many ways, this narrow stretch of land offers a microcosm of the sharp geophysical contrasts found in the Near East. Its coastal region, from Byblos and Tyre down to the Sinai Peninsula, is either steep and craggy or covered with sand dunes, offering few inlets that can serve as natural harbors—perhaps a reason why neither the Canaanites nor the later Israelites were a seafaring people. Farther inland, the terrain rises to limestone highlands at the center of this area. The high plateau is dramatically carved in two by a deep crevasse known as the Jordan River Valley. This depression is part of the so-called Great Rift Valley, a deep fault in the terrestrial surface running from Turkey through the Orontes Valley in Syria, the Bekaa Valley in Lebanon, and on along the Jordan River to the Dead Sea and into the Gulf of Aqaba. Through much of its course, the Jordan River is flanked by the Judean hills in the west and the Jordanian hills in the east, which form the final bulwark against the infinite wastes of the Syrian Desert. These mountain ranges screen the moisture carried by prevailing winds from the Mediterranean Sea, channeling most rainfall into the fertile valleys of Canaan while withholding this moisture from the great Syrian Desert beyond. Fed by three small streams—the Banyas, the Dan, and the Hazbani—the Jordan flows through the Sea of Galilee down south, traveling more than 200 miles before expending itself into the lowest lake on Earth, the Dead Sea, which lies 1,300 feet below sea level.

At the southwestern tip of the crescent lays Egypt, blessed by a fertile ribbon of land along the Nile River. Believed to be the longest river on Earth, the Nile originates in the great lakes of central Africa and Ethiopia and opens, like a lotus flower, into the Nile River Delta along the Mediterranean coast.

Much of the topography of ancient Israel was more suitable for pastoral nomads than farmers. Such nomads are small communities of people who raise herds of domesticated animals and move with them from one pasture to the next in search of fresh land on which flocks can graze. One area of ancient Israel welcoming to nomads is the Valley of Jezreel, a stretch of land between the coast and the Sea of Galilee. Numerous springs as well as two small rivers, the Kishon and the Harod, water the Jezreel, which the Bible sometimes calls the Plain of Esdraelon. It is the largest and most fertile valley in all of Palestine, hotly contested by the Canaanites and the Israelites, following the settlement of the Israelites in the Promised Land. Because of its easy accessibility, the Jezreel is also a natural crossroads of caravan routes between East and West, between the markets of Mesopotamia and the wealthy buyers of Egypt. Not surprisingly, the valley would therefore be the arena of countless battles, from the dash of chariots in Old Testament times to the clash of armor in the 20th century.

This 7th-century B.C.E. clay figure possibly represents a Canaanite fertility goddess. It was found near Tell Duweir, the ancient city of Lachish, in Israel.

Early History

THE BEGINNINGS of human existence in the Near East, as everywhere on Earth, were marked by a constant search for food. While some stayed behind to care for their offspring, others explored the steppes, forests, and marshes. They

ca 10,000 B.C.E.
Glaciation period ends, marking end of the Epipaleolithic or Middle Stone Age

ca 9000 B.C.E.
Proto-villages in Palestine

ca 8000–7700 B.C.E.
Cultivated wheat and barley are grown in the Fertile Crescent

ca 8000–7500 B.C.E.
Sheep, cattle, and goats are domesticated

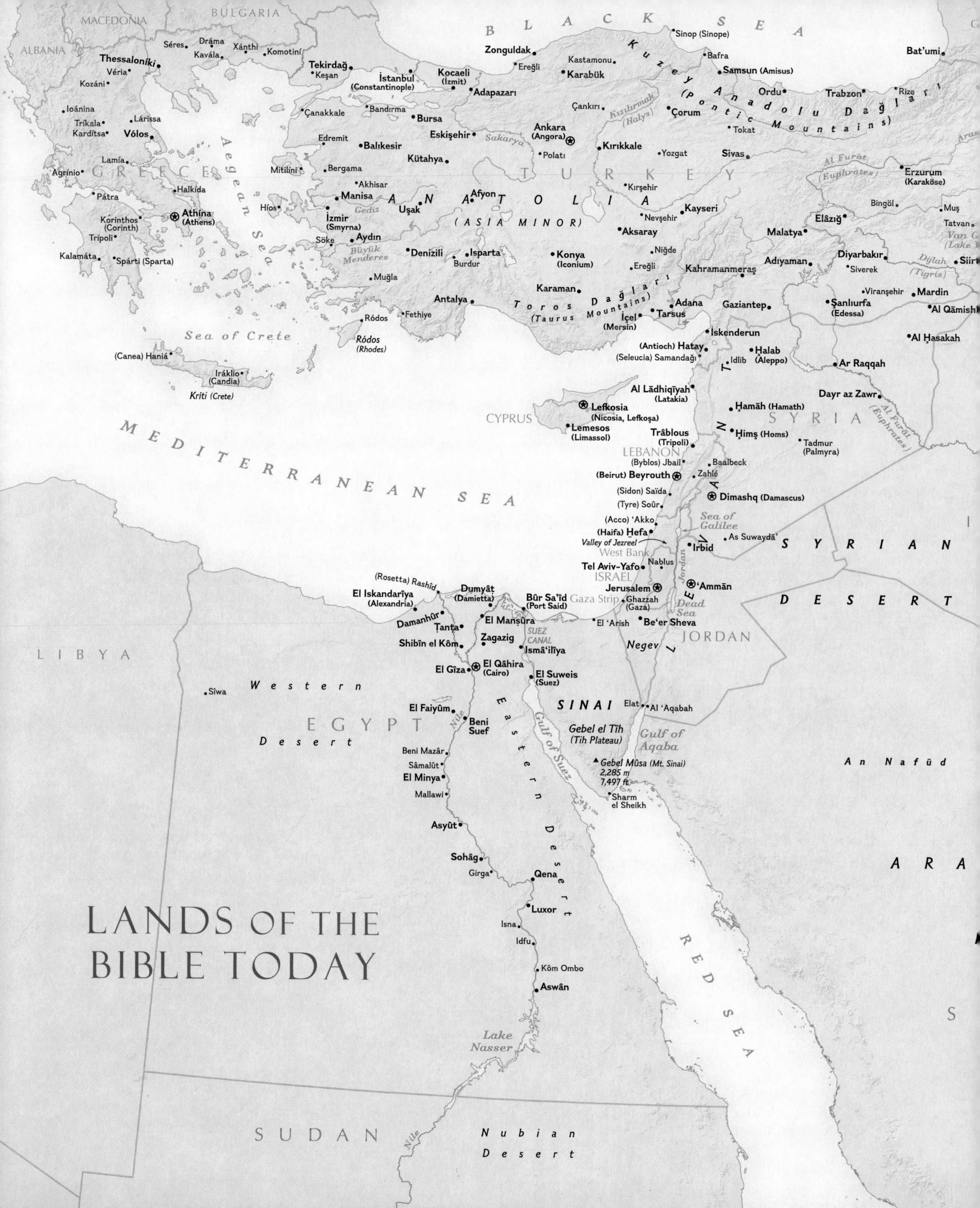
LANDS OF THE BIBLE TODAY
BLACK SEA
MEDITERRANEAN SEA
RED SEA
Aegean Sea
Sea of Crete
MACEDONIA
BULGARIA
ALBANIA
GREECE
TURKEY
ANATOLIA
(ASIA MINOR)
CYPRUS
SYRIA
LEBANON
ISRAEL
West Bank
Gaza Strip
JORDAN
EGYPT
LIBYA
SUDAN
LEVANT
SINAI
SYRIAN DESERT
Western Desert
Eastern Desert
Nubian Desert
An Nafūd
Negev
Kuzey Anadolu Dağları (Pontic Mountains)
Toros Dağları (Taurus Mountains)
Kızılırmak (Halys)
Sakarya
Gediz
Büyük Menderes
Al Furāt (Euphrates)
Dijlah (Tigris)
Van Gölü (Lake Van)
Sea of Galilee
Jordan
Dead Sea
Valley of Jezreel
Suez Canal
Gulf of Suez
Gulf of Aqaba
Gebel el Tîh (Tih Plateau)
Gebel Mûsa (Mt. Sinai) 2,285 m 7,497 ft
Nile
Lake Nasser
Kriti (Crete)
Ródos (Rhodes)
Thessaloníki
Séres
Dráma
Kavála
Xánthi
Komotiní
Véria
Kozáni
Ioánina
Tríkala
Kardítsa
Lárissa
Vólos
Lamía
Agrínio
Halkída
Pátra
Athína (Athens)
Kórinthos (Corinth)
Trípoli
Kalamáta
Spárti (Sparta)
(Canea) Haniá
Iráklio (Candia)
Tekirdağ
Keşan
İstanbul (Constantinople)
Kocaeli (İzmit)
Adapazarı
Zonguldak
Ereğli
Kastamonu
Karabük
Sinop (Sinope)
Bafra
Samsun (Amisus)
Ordu
Trabzon
Rize
Bat'umi
Çanakkale
Bandırma
Bursa
Eskişehir
Çankırı
Çorum
Tokat
Ankara (Angora)
Kırıkkale
Yozgat
Sivas
Erzurum (Karaköse)
Edremit
Balıkesir
Kütahya
Polatlı
Mitilíni
Bergama
Akhisar
Manisa
Afyon
Uşak
Kırşehir
Kayseri
Nevşehir
Bingöl
Muş
Tatvan
Híos
İzmir (Smyrna)
Aydın
Söke
Denizli
Isparta
Burdur
Muğla
Aksaray
Niğde
Konya (Iconium)
Ereğli
Elâzığ
Malatya
Diyarbakır
Siverek
Siirt
Adıyaman
Kahramanmaraş
Karaman
Antalya
Fethiye
Ródos
Adana
Tarsus
İçel (Mersin)
Gaziantep
Şanlıurfa (Edessa)
Viranşehir
Mardin
Al Qāmishlī
Al Ḩasakah
İskenderun
(Antioch) Hatay
(Seleucia) Samandağı
Idlib
Ḩalab (Aleppo)
Ar Raqqah
Al Lādhiqīyah (Latakia)
Dayr az Zawr
Lefkosia (Nicosia, Lefkoşa)
Lemesos (Limassol)
Ḩamāh (Hamath)
Ḩimş (Homs)
Trâblous (Tripoli)
Tadmur (Palmyra)
(Byblos) Jbail
Baalbeck
(Beirut) Beyrouth
Zahlé
(Sidon) Saïda
(Tyre) Soûr
Dimashq (Damascus)
(Acco) 'Akko
(Haifa) Hefa
As Suwaydā'
Irbid
Nablus
Tel Aviv-Yafo
Jerusalem
'Ammān
Ghazzah (Gaza)
Be'er Sheva
El 'Arîsh
(Rosetta) Rashîd
El Iskandarîya (Alexandria)
Dumyât (Damietta)
Bûr Sa'îd (Port Said)
Damanhûr
El Manṣûra
Ṭanṭa
Zagazig
Shibîn el Kôm
Ismâ'ilîya
El Gîza
El Qâhira (Cairo)
El Suweis (Suez)
Sîwa
El Faiyûm
Beni Suef
Elat
Al 'Aqabah
Beni Mazâr
Sâmalût
El Minya
Mallawi
Sharm el Sheikh
Asyût
Sohâg
Girga
Qena
Luxor
Isna
Idfu
Kôm Ombo
Aswân

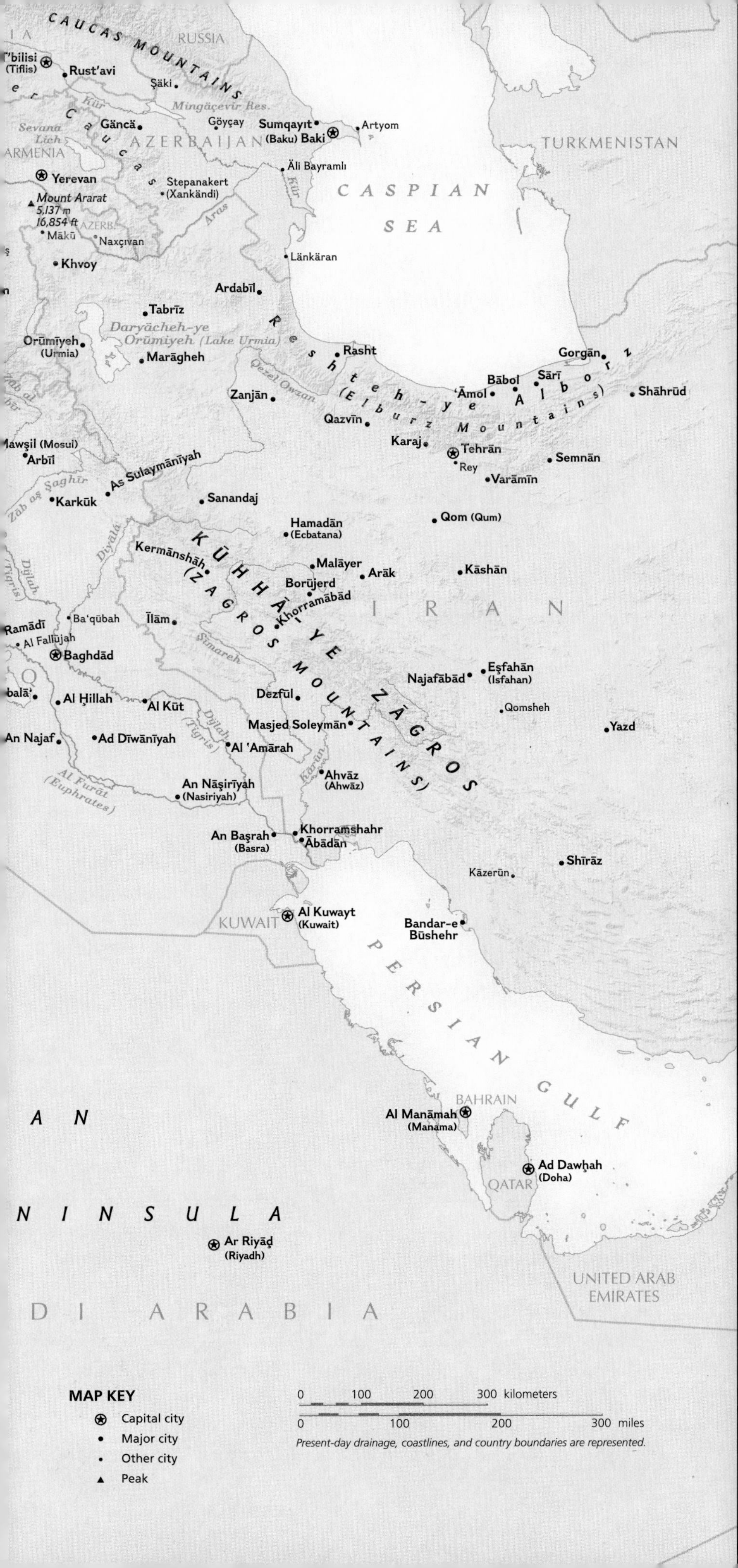

CAUCASUS MOUNTAINS
RUSSIA
T'bilisi (Tiflis)
Rust'avi
Şäki
Mingäçevir Res.
Kür
Gäncä
Göyçay
Sumqayıt
Artyom
(Baku) Baki
AZERBAIJAN
TURKMENISTAN
Sevana Lich
ARMENIA
Yerevan
Stepanakert (Xankändi)
Äli Bayramlı
CASPIAN SEA
Mount Ararat 5,137 m 16,854 ft
AZERB.
Mākū
Naxçıvan
Aras
Länkäran
Khvoy
Ardabīl
Tabrīz
Daryācheh-ye Orūmīyeh (Lake Urmia)
Orūmīyeh (Urmia)
Marāgheh
Reshteh-ye Alborz (Elburz Mountains)
Rasht
Qezel Owzan
Gorgān
Bābol
Sārī
Āmol
Shāhrūd
Zanjān
Qazvīn
Karaj
Tehrān
Rey
Semnān
Varāmīn
Mawşil (Mosul)
Arbīl
As Sulaymānīyah
Zāb aş Şaghīr
Karkūk
Sanandaj
Hamadān (Ecbatana)
Qom (Qum)
Kūhhā-ye Zāgros (Zagros Mountains)
Diyālá
Kermānshāh
Malāyer
Arāk
Kāshān
Borūjerd
Khorramābād
Dijlah (Tigris)
IRAN
Ramādī
Ba'qūbah
Īlām
Al Fallūjah
Baghdād
Simareh
Najafābād
Eşfahān (Isfahan)
Karbalā'
Al Ḩillah
Al Kūt
Dezfūl
Qomsheh
An Najaf
Ad Dīwānīyah
Masjed Soleymān
Yazd
Al 'Amārah
Kārūn
Ahvāz (Ahwāz)
Al Furāt (Euphrates)
An Nāşirīyah (Nasiriyah)
An Başrah (Basra)
Khorramshahr
Ābādān
Kāzerūn
Shīrāz
KUWAIT
Al Kuwayt (Kuwait)
Bandar-e Būshehr
PERSIAN GULF
BAHRAIN
Al Manāmah (Manama)
Ad Dawḩah (Doha)
QATAR
ARABIAN PENINSULA
Ar Riyāḑ (Riyadh)
SAUDI ARABIA
UNITED ARAB EMIRATES

MAP KEY

- Capital city
- Major city
- Other city
- Peak

0 100 200 300 kilometers
0 100 200 300 miles

Present-day drainage, coastlines, and country boundaries are represented.

Mount Ararat, located on the Turkey-Iran border, is a volcanic cone some 16,854 feet high. According to Genesis, Noah's ark came to rest here after the Flood

A solitary palm marks the location of a spring in the vast stretches of the Syrian Desert.

Each year, thousands of red poppies announce the coming of spring in the Valley of Jezreel, the most fertil region of Israel.

The design of these mud-reed huts in today's wetlands o southern Iraq is remarkably similar to that of structures shown in 8th- and 7th-century B.C.E. Assyrian reliefs.

God sent him forth from the Garden of Eden to till the ground … At the east of the Garden of Eden he placed the cherubim, and a sword flaming and turning to guard the way to the tree of life. (Genesis 3:23-24)

hunted animals that could provide their families with meat for eating, skins for making clothing, and bones for fashioning tools. Their prey ranged from deer, gazelles, wild cattle, and boar to migratory birds, which they felled with bows and arrows or small sharp blades. Often, people would also scour the fields for wild cereals and fruits, including almonds, acorns, and pistachios—hence the term "hunter-gatherer." During the cold winter months, prey as well as crops became scarce. Thus, for thousands of years, mankind was doomed to live in small groups that moved from one area to the next, hugging the Fertile Crescent's rain shadows, the relatively wet regions that in most years produced harvests sufficient to sustain life.

No one knows the exact time when prehistoric humans moved away from the hunt and devoted themselves to growing crops for food or raising domesticated animals. Scholars usually place this development near the end of the Middle Stone Age, around 10,000 B.C.E. This change was not an instant revolution. It is believed that the hunter families gradually began to rely on crops of wild wheat and barley that grew naturally in the alluvial plains of Canaan and Mesopotamia. Before long, these protofarmers discovered that they could somewhat control the cycle of crop growth by careful tilling and seeding, creating domesticated varieties of cereals in the process, including hulled wheat with strong spiked husks like emmer and einkorn wheat, as well as barley. With the use of a millstone, these kernels could be ground up fine to produce flour, which was then mixed with water to create dough that could be baked in an oven.

The advantages of farming over hunting were obvious. With a fairly predictable source of food, people could live in settlements and be spared the dangers and difficulties of treks through unknown territory. The production of surplus crops allowed people to feed and raise animals such as sheep, goats, and cattle. Adapting animals to a controlled life serving the needs of humans is called "domestication." Domesticated animals were a reliable source of milk, meat, wool, and hide, and also worked as draft animals in the field. After forgoing their reliance on hunting, humans had greater control over their destinies and that of their families.

The tree of life is a prominent symbol in Assyrian reliefs, such as this panel showing two portraits of King Ashurnasirpal worshipping a deity, possibly the sun god Shamash.

Still, choosing cultivation over the hunt was not as obvious as it may seem. Vegetation depends on rainfall, which is scarce in the Near East. Climatologists have determined that the climate of the region has changed surprisingly little over the past 10,000 years. Even today, western Palestine and the northern elevations of Mesopotamia receive rainfall only in winter and early spring, after westerly winds are cooled by the high mountain plateaus. Beyond these favored regions, agriculture simply would have been impossible—but for the presence of rivers, springs, and oases, with their groves of figs and date palms.

As a result, prehistoric settlements developed, albeit gradually, near rivers and other natural sources of fresh water such as springs, often considered a precious gift from the gods. The earliest settlement found in ancient Palestine dates from around 9000 B.C.E. Such protovillages enabled early farmers to share tools, seeds, and draft animals, while women also found shared support in raising their offspring. As these villages prospered, eventually numbering in the hundreds, tribal bonds began to develop among the people.

A PLACE CALLED EDEN

On the sixth day of Creation, says Genesis, God creates humankind "in the image of God, male and female" (Genesis 1:27). These first humans are called Adam and Eve. And then the Lord plants a garden in Eden, with "every tree that is pleasant for the sight and good for food," and in this garden "he put the man whom he had formed" (Genesis 2:8-9). This garden, evocative of the lush groves of Sumer, is watered by a river split into four branches: the Tigris, Euphrates, Pishon, and Gihon (Genesis 2:10-14). The Euphrates and the Tigris are well known, but the courses of the Pishon and the Gihon are uncertain. Using satellite photography, some scholars claim to have detected traces of the Pishon in the ancient dry riverbed of the Wadi Batin—a claim supported by a cuneiform tablet from the Babylonian palace of Nippur that refers to Eden as the Sumerian word for "uncultivated plain." Others suggest that Eden may be linked to the Sumerian legend of a utopian land called Dilmun, which is sometimes identified with the region of present-day Bahrain. Regardless of location, the biblical description of Eden leaves little doubt about the site's significance: It was everything that the harsh Syrian Desert was not.

Man's sojourn in this idyllic garden is short. A serpent persuades Adam and Eve to eat from the forbidden "tree of the knowledge of good and evil," after which they are evicted and forced to sustain themselves by "tilling the ground" (Genesis 3:23)—a biblical reference to the moment when agriculture became the mainstay of human existence. The tree as a symbol of life figured prominently in Mesopotamian mythology, while the role of the serpent is reminiscent of the Mesopotamian Epic of Gilgamesh, in which a serpent steals a plant that confers immortality. For the Bible, however, the Eden story underscores how human existence is merely an "exile" from a primordial state of divine perfection.

These scenes of Adam and Eve in Paradise as envisioned by Lucas Cranach the Elder (1472–1553) were painted around 1530.

Dawn of Civilization

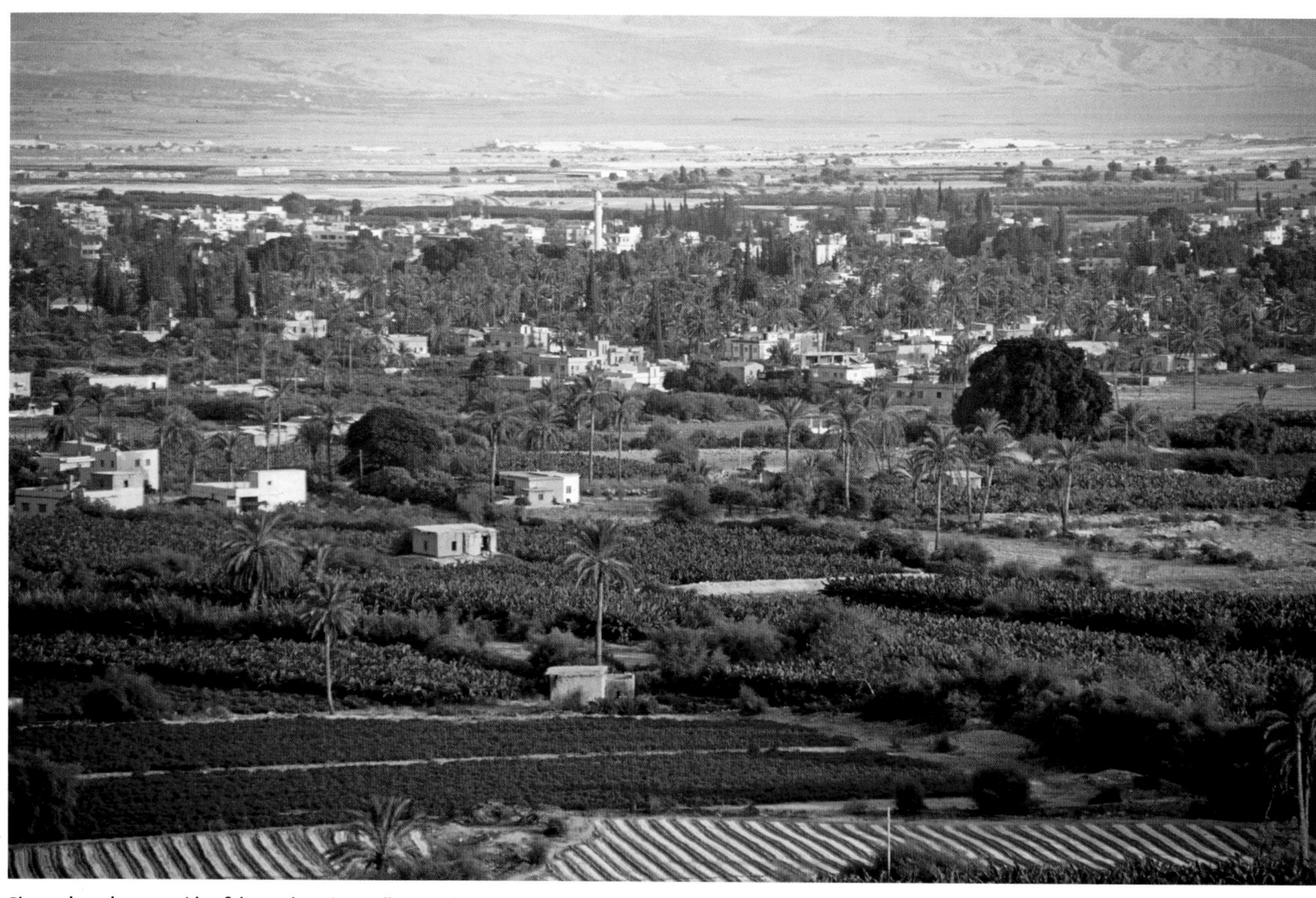

Situated on the west side of the Jordan River valley, Jericho is one world's oldest cities. Human settlements there date as far back as 9000 B.C.E.

ANCIENT JERICHO, located about 15 miles northeast of Jerusalem on a mound known as Tell es-Sultan, is perhaps the most impressive of the early settlements in the ancient Near East, dating as far back as 9000 B.C.E. Archaeologists call this time the Pre-Pottery Neolithic Period (New Stone Age), which spans a time from about 8500 to 5500 B.C.E. Ancient Jericho may have sprawled across as many as 75 acres. No doubt, the reason for its growth was the presence of not one but several large springs, including the Fountain of Elisha, which still provides the farmers of modern Jericho with upward of a thousand gallons of water a day. During extensive excavations in the 1950s, the British archaeologist Kathleen Kenyon uncovered the remains of round huts, made not with reeds but with mud bricks—the earliest known use of mud baked in the sun. Even more remarkable is that this village, home to a thousand souls or more, was surrounded by a stone wall and a ditch, anchored by a mysterious tower. Thirty feet in diameter, the tower featured an internal staircase of stone steps that presumably led to its summit for observation, sacrifice, or some other type of religious rite.

In and around Jericho, Kenyon discovered numerous fragments of sickle blades, which suggest that its inhabitants

ca 9000 B.C.E.
Earliest settlement at Jericho

ca 7000 B.C.E.
Ain Ghazal flourishes

ca 5000 B.C.E.
Metal tools appear; earliest evidence of copper in Mesopotamia

ca 5000 B.C.E.
Clay pottery becomes widespread

Now Abel was a keeper of sheep, and Cain a tiller of the ground. In the course of time Cain brought to the Lord an offering of the fruit of the ground, and Abel for his part brought of the firstlings of his flock, their fat portions. (Genesis 4:2-3)

were farmers, cultivating such crops as barley, flax, einkorn and emmer wheat. Nevertheless, the discovery of arrowheads may indicate that these villagers also hunted to complement their diet.

Jericho prospered throughout the Stone Age and then suffered a catastrophe of unknown origin—perhaps an earthquake. The city was abandoned, only to be built up again in the fourth millennium B.C.E.

Up to this point, the early villagers had experimented with various forms of vessels to store their foodstuffs. These primitive pots were made of stone, burnt lime, or gypsum—with varying results. In the course of the sixth millennium B.C.E., however, the technique of molding and firing vessels of clay became increasingly widespread. Clay pottery was relatively cheap to produce; what's more, once baked, this pottery became extremely durable. As pottery manufacture was taken up by particular artisans and became more consistent in its characteristics, each region began to develop distinctive patterns of production and decoration. Clay vessels broke easily, but the sherds themselves, once discarded and buried in a settlement's debris, were virtually indestructible. The recovery of such potsherds in a prehistoric stratum, a layer laid bare during excavations, is extremely valuable to archaeologists, for these fragments allow excavators to date the layer to a particular era.

Jericho was considered one of the oldest and largest human settlements of the Neolithic period until the discovery of Ain Ghazal, near today's Amman in Jordan. The oldest excavated stratum at Ain Ghazal dates to about 7200 B.C.E., but this settlement was almost three times larger than Jericho. Its inhabitants raised a variety of crops and kept domesticated animals, including dogs, cattle, and pigs. But the most astonishing feature of Ain Ghazal is its domestic structures. Unlike the mud-brick huts of Jericho, these are square houses made of stone, and each dwelling is divided by walls to separate areas for various purposes. These walls were plastered to protect the family against moisture in winter and excessive heat in summer; in later centuries, the floors were plastered as well. This archetype of a farmer's home would remain common in the Near East for many thousands of years.

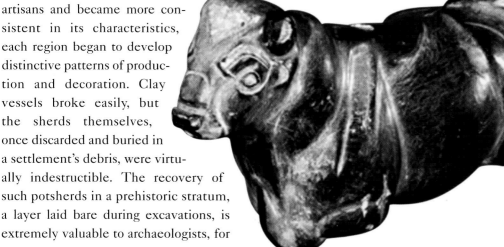

Some thousand miles to the east, in Mesopotamia, we see a similar development during the rise of the Ubaid culture (5200–3500 B.C.E.), named after the artifacts found at Tell el Ubaid in southern Mesopotamia. Among these are pottery samples that show a consistent and elegant geometric pattern applied with brown or black paint. Some of these vessels are equipped with handles and spouts. Even more advanced is the layout of Ubaid villages. Until this time, settlements were a relatively haphazard affair. But Ubaid habitations show evidence of some form of planning. The houses, built of mud brick, are grouped around a shared courtyard and separated from other blocks by small alleyways. Strategically placed throughout the village are larger structures that may have provided storage for the villagers. In the center of the settlement is a mound, surmounted by what some scholars presume is a large shrine, dedicated to the patron god of the village. If this presumption is true, it indicates the emergence of a faith system: The shared belief that man's fate is controlled by otherworldly and vastly more powerful beings. Such sacred mounds in the heart of the settlement

Limestone bull from the late Uruk period (3450–3100 B.C.E.), found near Uruk, Iraq, and dated between 3300 and 3100 B.C.E.

ca 5200–3500 B.C.E.
Ubaid culture flourishes in Mesopotamia

ca 5000 B.C.E.
Sanctuary complex present in Eridu

ca 5000 B.C.E.
Earliest evidence of human burial at Eridu

ca 4500–3300 B.C.E.
"Professional" classes emerge

would become common in communities throughout southern Mesopotamia.

The Growth of Settlements

For the next two millennia, these early human settlements continued to grow as farming methods improved and the yield of domesticated crops increased. In time, the growing surplus of food allowed some members of the community to abandon farming and to focus instead on crafts for which there was a growing demand. A distinct class of craftsmen emerged, engaged in either the production of pottery, tools, farming implements, and textiles, or the processing of farming products. Such diversification naturally made communal life more complex. Before long, villagers understood that a central administrator was needed to set common values for barter and to rule over any disputes that might arise. A leader was chosen. As the village grew, the power and influence of this tribal chieftain increased as well. Thus, the foundation was laid for the emergence of city-states during the next millennium, led by a king, who also served as chief priest of the city's patron god.

In this early stage of human development, villages and their central shrines were relatively modest. An exception is the highly sophisticated central sanctuary found at the site of ancient Eridu, often considered the world's first urban development. Originally Eridu was located close to the mouth of the Euphrates River, but over the millennia deposits of riverborne silt increased the distance between the city and the Persian Gulf. Today's location is near Abu Shahrain in

THE WALLS OF JERICHO

Jericho is considered both the lowest and the oldest continuously occupied city in the world. Located 846 feet below sea level, the settlement built a succession of defensive walls near the end of the eighth millennium B.C.E. Originally modest, the walls eventually rose to a grand height of some 20 feet, anchored by a massive, 30-foot-high round tower. This tower may have served as a high place for observation, for sacrifice, or some other type of religious rite.

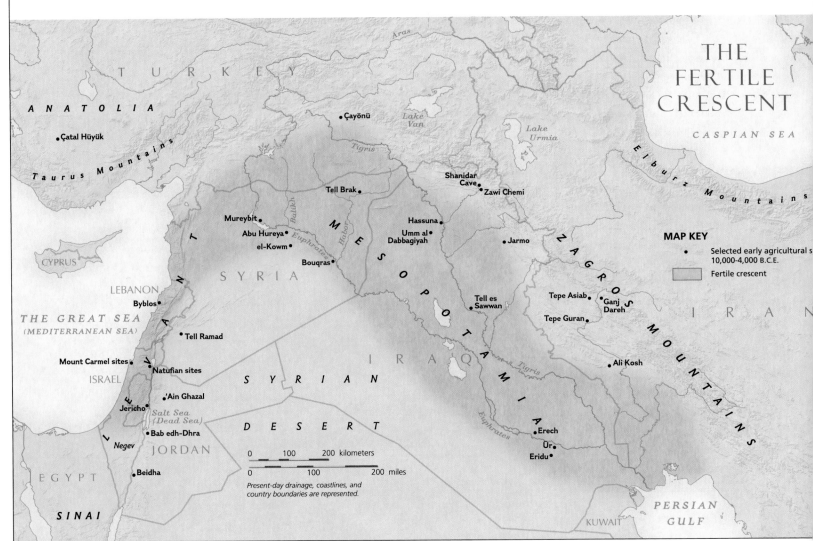

THE FERTILE CRESCENT

MAP KEY

• Selected early agricultural s 10,000-4,000 B.C.E.

Fertile crescent

0 100 200 kilometers

0 100 200 miles

Present-day drainage, coastlines, and country boundaries are represented.

DIGGING THROUGH TIME

After a settlement in the ancient Near East was destroyed or abandoned—as a result of earthquake, drought, or act of war—it was often rebuilt by successive generations. These new arrivals typically built their mud-brick or stone structures on top of the ruins of the preceding epoch. Across the centuries a city could thus rise to form a veritable mound—called a *tell* in Arabic, or *tel* in Hebrew.

When digging through such a tell, archaeologists have in many cases been able to identify successive periods of habitation as individual strata, or layers, of debris, almost like layers in a cake. Distinguishing and studying these layers is called stratigraphy; archaeologists typically use a numerical system to catalog the successive layers, which is then used to create a three-dimensional, computer-generated graph of the mound. Jericho, for example, boasts no less than 21 layers of human occupation, built up by successive generations. To distinguish one layer from the other, however, is often a daunting task, particularly since the material may have shifted as a result of earthquakes, storms, or other natural disturbances.

The role of pottery in stratigraphy is crucial for modern archaeologists, since after around 6000 B.C.E., the craft of making pottery became the domain of trained artisans. As a result, the decoration and firing process of clay pots and jars became stylistically consistent, and each region developed a distinct style of shapes, paints, and decorative patterns that would differentiate their product from vessels produced elsewhere. The classification of these styles—using the distinguishing features of color, material, and decoration, and the shapes of the rim, handle, and sometimes spout—has become a crucial archaeological discipline, for the presence of such potsherds in the layers of a tell allows excavators to identify a given stratum in terms of date and culture. Fortunately, while earthenware breaks easily, once it has been broken, the individual sherds are extremely durable.

Potsherds—referred to by archaeologists as *ostraca* when they bear notations or figures—had a great variety of subsequent uses in ancient times. Large pieces became scoops to fetch water or measure corn. In the Bible, Job used a potsherd to scrape the sores on his body. Potsherds also served as notepaper, a common material on which to write messages or make notes.

During excavations in the late 1960s at Saqqara in Egypt, archaeologists discovered a treasure trove of ostraca with text in Demotic (a cursive script based on hieroglyphics and developed in Lower Egypt between 650 and 400 B.C.E.). It turned out that these sherds were written on by a scribe dispensing advice and prophesies, based on his dreams.

During the invasion by Babylonian forces of Judah, the hill country between Jerusalem and Hebron, Jewish field posts would communicate with their military commanders in the city of Lachish by notes scratched in Hebrew on bits of pottery. For archaeologists, therefore, the presence of a potsherd in an excavated layer is a prized possession. Until the Persian period, when coins make the dating process much easier, the changing styles of broken pieces of pottery are often the only markers of time on which archaeologists can rely.

Archaeologists place markers to identify each separate layer of human habitation in this excavation of a typical tell, or mound. Potsherds, particularly those with writing (known as *ostraca*), help to date each layer as it is uncovered.

Iraq, some 12 miles southwest of Ur. Eridu was home to a large population of both farmers and fisher-hunters, living in huts made of reeds or mud brick. At one end rose what is perhaps the very first monumental structure in human history: a temple complex on a stepped terrace, accessible via stairways and dedicated to Enki, the Sumerian god of fresh water and wisdom. Inside, excavators found bone fragments of fish and other small creatures that may have been offerings to the deity. The Eridu shrine was destroyed and rebuilt at least 12 times over the centuries; archaeologist Fuad Safar, who began to excavate the site in 1946, estimated that the oldest sanctuary dates to before 5000 B.C.E.

Close to the sanctuary, Safar and fellow archaeologist Seton Lloyd found a vast cemetery of individual mud-brick tombs, many well stocked with pottery, food, jewelry, and other artifacts. This necropolis may have been intended for the nobility of Eridu, who wished to be buried in the shadow of the city's great temple. Many of the tombs' 6,500-year-old bones were still in excellent condition. Men, women, and children had been carefully laid on their backs, accompanied by what appear to be personal items. In one instance, a small boy had been buried with his dog, a bone still in its jaws.

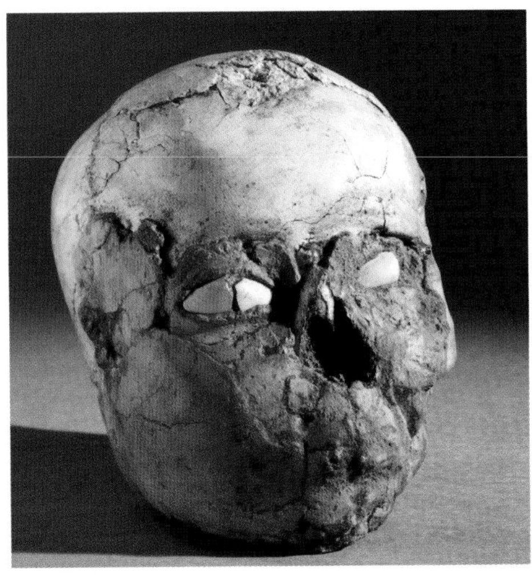

Neolithic plastered skulls from Jericho, like this one from around 7200 B.C.E., were often found beneath dwellings, where families buried them perhaps to ensure that the deceased could guide the living.

The Sumerian King List, an ancient genealogy of Mesopotamian rulers compiled around 2100 B.C.E., describes Eridu as the first city-state on Earth. "After kingship was lowered from heaven," it reads, "kingship was first established in Eridu. In Eridu, Alulim became king and ruled for 28,800 years." Indeed, Eridu would remain the center for the worship of Enki for centuries to come.

The primary source of Eridu's wealth was its crop surplus, which could be sold to other village communities. An informal trade network began to develop, with people exchanging foodstuffs for highly prized raw materials such as copper, seashells, or obsidian. Obsidian is a natural glass found in volcanic areas, particularly in southeastern Turkey. It is much prized for its use in blades and tools. Other important city centers began to

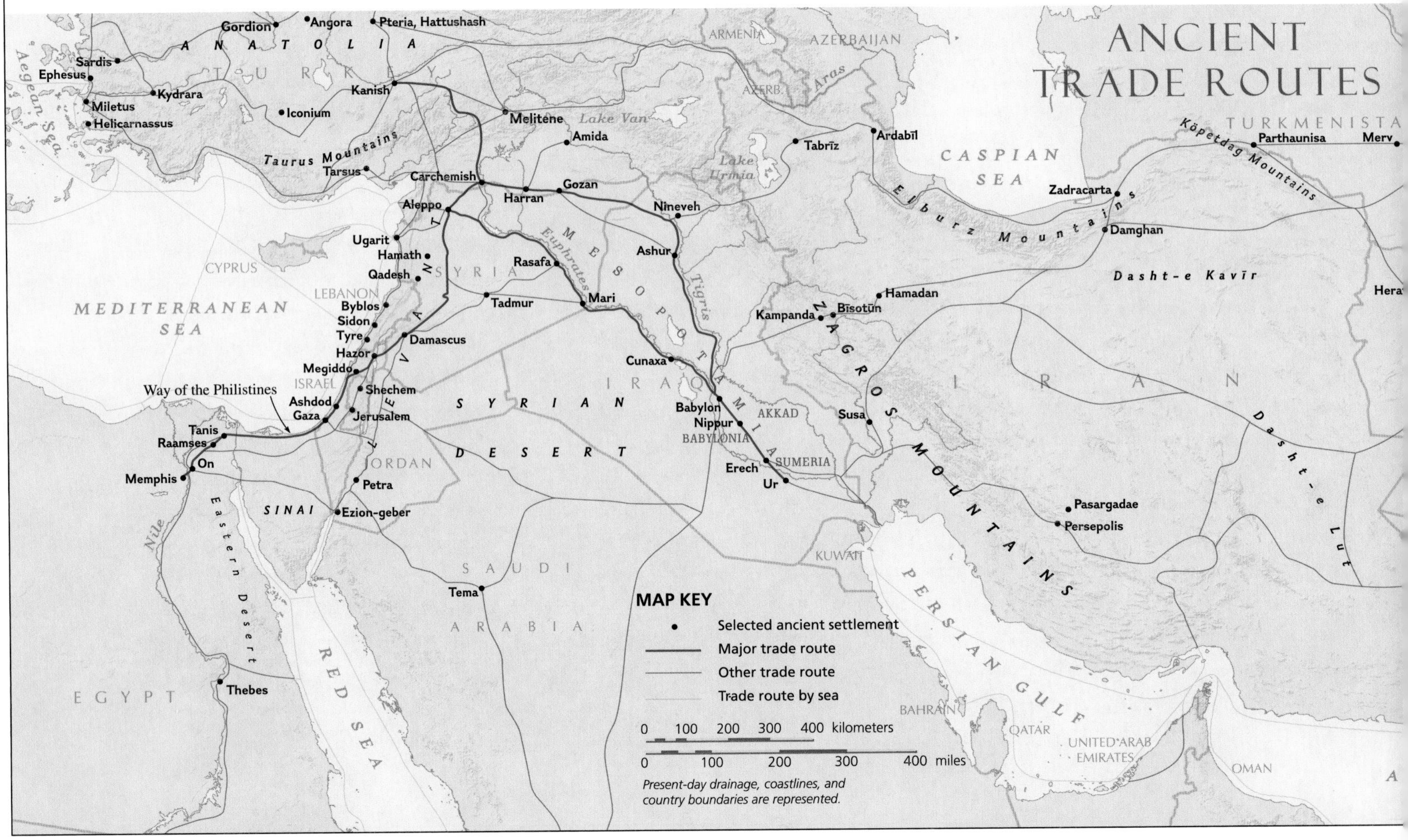

ANCIENT TRADE ROUTES

MAP KEY

- Selected ancient settlement
- Major trade route
- Other trade route
- Trade route by sea

0 100 200 300 400 kilometers

0 100 200 300 400 miles

Present-day drainage, coastlines, and country boundaries are represented.

emerge, including Uruk, Lagash, Kish, Nippur, and Ur.

Inevitably, these prosperous communities aroused the envy of other, less fortunate, settlements. The villages began to compete over such things as water rights, trade concessions, or fertile swaths of land. This interaction spurred the development of another profession: the military. Affluent settlements began to throw up walls and other defensive works to protect themselves against marauders, which in turn encouraged others in outlying areas to come and settle inside the relative safety of these fortifications.

The emergence of defensive walls was not limited to southern Mesopotamia. A telling example was excavated on the site of ancient Arad in the Negev desert of Canaan. Arad's stone wall was buttressed by medieval-style, semicircular bastions that offered the defending archers a greater field of fire. Interestingly, this unusual feature is faithfully represented on a wall painting in an Egyptian tomb of the 5th dynasty. The castlelike layout of Arad has led researchers to suggest that it was the residence of a king, similar to the nascent city-states of Mesopotamia, with a palace, administrative facilities, and a large water reservoir in which to collect the winter rains. A similar arrangement has been found on the ancient site of Megiddo in the heart of Israel's Valley of Jezreel. Here, too, the mud-brick dwellings of the Chalcolithic period (4500–3150 B.C.E.) were laid out in a rectangular grid pattern, similar to that of the communities of the Ubaid culture, and surmounted by an ancient shrine.

Naturally, the development of proto-cities like Eridu, Arad, and Megiddo did not occur overnight; they evolved over many centuries. Nevertheless, by the beginning of the fourth millennium B.C.E., a handful of prosperous communities had become so large, and architecturally so sophisticated, that they became true cities.

BURIAL PRACTICES

In prehistoric Canaan and Mesopotamia, villagers typically buried the head of a deceased family member beneath their dwelling, perhaps so that the spirit would continue to serve the family after death. After all tissue had decomposed, the facial features often were restored with clay. During the Chalcolithic period, a new custom emerged: The entire body was interred until fully decomposed, then the bones were buried in a ceramic box, called an ossuary, which often resembled a house. The practice of burial in ossuaries continued well into the New Testament era.

EARLY TRADE

THE PRINCIPAL COMMODITIES OF TRADE IN the Chalcolithic period were copper and turquoise (Egypt), incense and ivory (Arabia and India), wine (Canaan and the Aegean), wood (Lebanon), cereals (Mesopotamia and Syria), and carnelian and obsidian (central Turkey). Goods were traded for silver throughout the region.

In Sumer, trade fostered the development of mathematics based on a decimal system, as well as the emergence of a written language. To facilitate the complex calculations in trading goods, the Akkadians developed the abacus. The Babylonians continued to develop the Sumerian mathematical tables by using a sexagesimal system, based on the value of 60. The system survives to this day in the division of one hour into 60 minutes, one minute into 60 seconds, and a circle into 360 degrees.

Tablets from Old Babylon (1900–1200 B.C.E.) document flourishing trade throughout Mesopotamia. Goods traveled along a variety of "highways," each skirting the Syrian Desert. Egypt traded with the Levant (the region east of the Mediterranean Sea) via the Way of the Philistines, a route that hugged the eastern Mediterranean all the way to Byblos and Ugarit, where the road turned inland toward either Aleppo and Harran, or Mari. From here, a route running just below the Euphrates brought goods to the Sumerian capital cities of Nippur, Uruk, and Ur. Ur, which at the time was closer to the Persian Gulf, was the way station to trade with the Indus River Valley. Another route ran just north of the Tigris and connected Harran with Ashur and Hamadan, where it then branched off toward Bactria and the markets of the East.

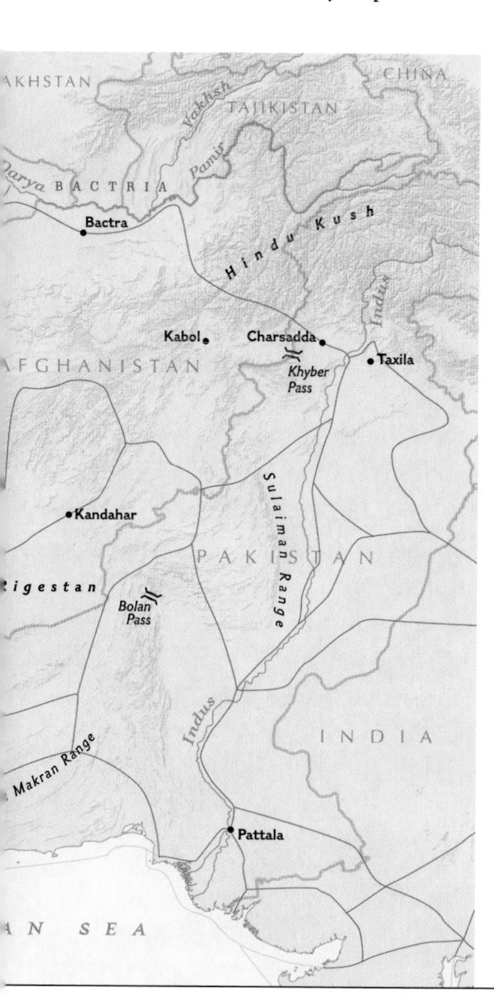

RISE OF CITY-STATES

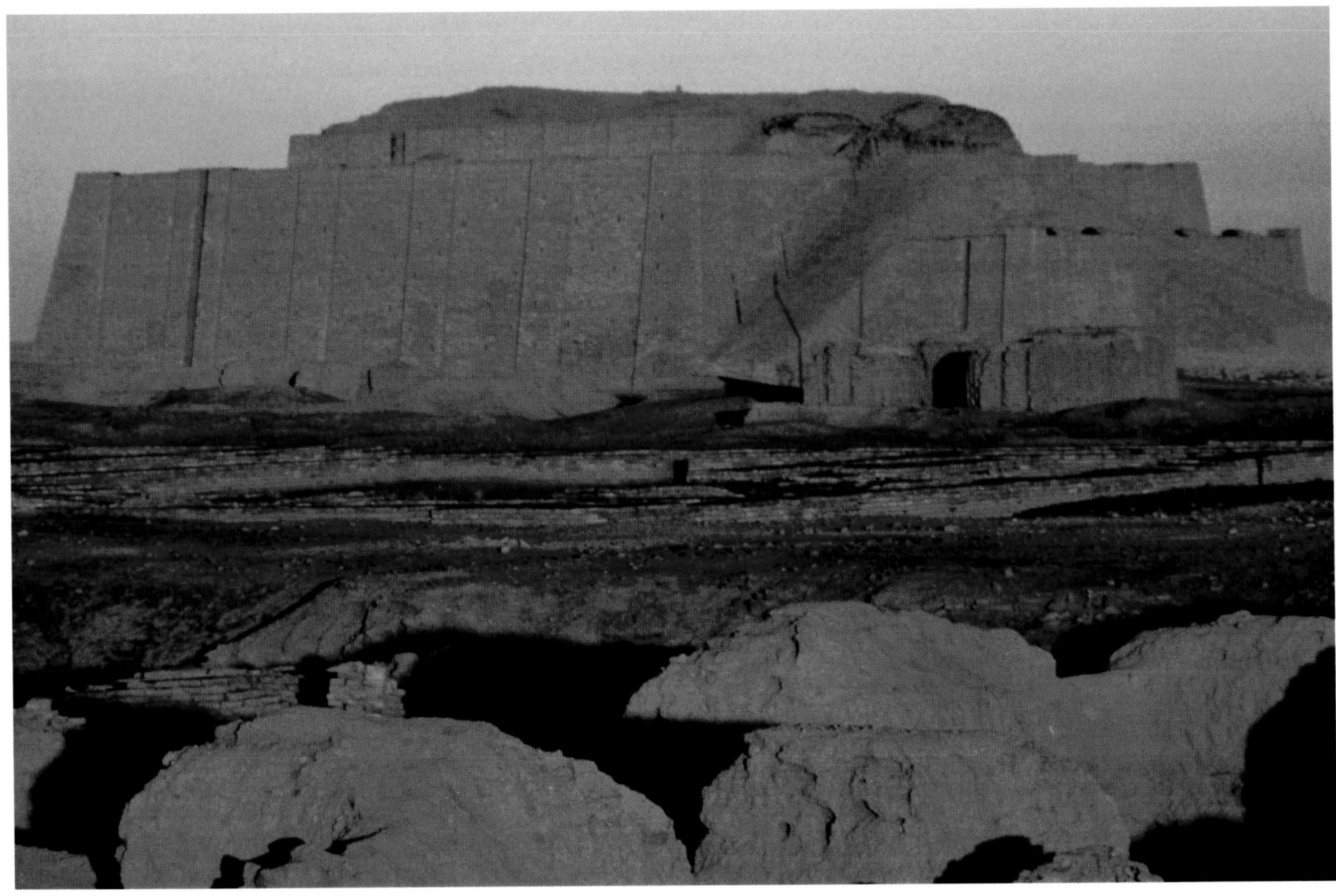

The partially reconstructed ziggurat of Ur, built of mud bricks, rises over the ancient site of Ur in Iraq. It may have been dedicated to Nanna, the moon god.

THE MOST DRAMATIC urbanization took place in southern Mesopotamia between about 3300 and 2600 B.C.E., in the territory that archaeologists refer to as Sumer. This urban revolution spawned a culture that can truly be considered the foundation of human civilization. It bequeathed mankind such critical innovations as writing, wheeled transport, legislation, literature, monumental architecture, and fine arts.

The secret of this great flowering of civilization in Sumer lay, once again, in its agricultural wealth. Unlike the Nile, the Euphrates and Tigris Rivers do not flood the countryside in predictable cycles. A field could bear fruit in abundance one year, only to be parched and dry the next. Near the end of the fourth millennium B.C.E., Sumerian farmers devised a sophisticated system to control the watering of the alluvial soil bordering the two rivers. They began to dig a network of canals that could carry the water from the rivers far inland.

Naturally, such an ambitious and labor-intensive irrigation system could not be built and maintained by even a handful of farmers. It required planning, equipment, and resources—in sum, it required organization. To accomplish this, the Sumerians formed a farmers' cooperative, which after 3000 B.C.E. was

ca 3500 B.C.E.
Sumerian farmers develop a sophisticated irrigation system

ca 3200 B.C.E.
Uruk emerges as a complex society

ca 3000 B.C.E.
Copper and tin are combined to form bronze

ca 2900 B.C.E.
A destructive flood sweeps Sumer

The beginning of his kingdom was Babel, Erech, and Accad, all of them in the land of Shinar. From that land he went into Assyria, and built Niniveh, Rehoboth-ir, Calah, and Resen between Niniveh and Calah; that is the great city. (Genesis 10:10-12)

in charge of a vast irrigation network across the Sumerian plains. So lush were Sumer's vineyards and so fertile its groves that it was easy to imagine Sumer as the Garden of Eden on Earth.

This growing wealth spurred the development of agricultural markets, which soon burgeoned into city-states. Led by a king and covering a territory of several hundred square miles, these city-states developed a growing bureaucracy to regulate and administer the expanding initiatives of public life. Thus a hierarchical political system was born in which professional bureaucrats mediated between the populace and their supreme ruler.

The Emergence of Uruk

FROM 3000 TO ABOUT 2700 B.C.E., Uruk—known as Erech in the Bible (Genesis 10:10)—emerged as the dominant city-state of Sumer. According to the Sumerian King List, Uruk was founded by a mythical ruler named Enmerkar, whose successor—the famous King Gilgamesh—erected the city's defensive walls. "Look at it still today," says the poet of the Epic of Gilgamesh, first recorded around 2100 B.C.E.; "the outer wall where the cornice runs, it shines with the brilliance of copper; and the inner wall, it has no equal." These famed walls remained shrouded in legend until 1912, when a German team uncovered the remains of Uruk some 150 miles southeast of Baghdad, in Iraq. Some scholars believe that the name "Iraq" derives from Uruk. The excavations proved that the description in the Epic of Gilgamesh was not poetic license. The walls of the ancient city ran for more than five miles in circumference. At its peak, Uruk covered some 250 acres—by far the largest city-state of Sumer in this period.

At the core of the city lay an elaborate temple complex. One of the shrines, the White Temple, stands on a raised mound 40 feet high. It is believed to be the first of Sumer's most distinctive architectural archetype: the ziggurat. A ziggurat, derived from the Babylonian word *ziqqurrat*, is a rectangular tower that tapers vertically by successively receding stories connected by stairways. At Uruk, the ziggurat formed a large raised platform on which the shrine was built. Presumably ziggurats were designed to raise officiating priests—and all those who were privileged to be present during rituals—closer to the heavens.

This small gypsum statue of an embracing couple was found beneath the shrine of Inanna in Nippur and dates around 2600 B.C.E.

From the very beginning, Mesopotamian culture was closely intertwined with a collective belief in unseen supernatural powers, which, it was thought, exerted control over events on Earth but could, in turn, be influenced or appeased by cultic practice, including sacrifice. In Sumer, religious practice was driven primarily by the needs of agriculture. Drought, flooding, or climatic changes could doom the farmer's yield and jeopardize the economy of the city-state. In an effort to better understand and control their agricultural cycles, the Sumerians evolved a pantheon of regional gods, each of whom was believed to be responsible for one key element in the harvest—sun, moon, water, earth, fertility, and so on.

Typically, each city adopted a particular deity as its patron god or goddess. In Uruk, the dominant gods were Inanna, the goddess of fertility, love, and war, who was worshipped in the Pillar Temple of Eanna; and An, the god of heaven and ruler of the constellations, who was venerated in

ca 2280 B.C.E.
Akkadian Empire reaches its height

ca 2150 B.C.E.
Akkadian period comes to an end

ca 2100 B.C.E.
Epic of Gilgamesh is recorded

ca 2000 B.C.E.
Amorites conquer Ur and establish Babylon as their capital

the ziggurat of the White Temple. The mythology of Inanna, An, and other gods was anchored in a creation epic that would influence many later chronicles of the beginning of time—including Genesis.

The Mesopotamian gods were represented in the form of small sculpted pieces, which rank as history's first instances of statuary. The earliest figurines are rather primitive depictions of males and females, often with the genitals sharply emphasized—possibly for use in fertility rituals. As time wore on, the Sumerian sculptors became more confident in shaping larger and more realistic depictions of the gods as well as their worshippers. One example is the beautifully carved face of a female, known as the Warka Head, excavated in Uruk and tentatively dated to 3100 B.C.E. The limestone head, which features inlaid eyes and eyebrows, would have been topped with a wig. Though the rest of the statue is lost, scholars believe that it probably stood in one of the temple precincts of Uruk.

This 7th-century B.C.E. Assyrian tablet from Nineveh relates a part of the famous Epic of Gilgamesh, including the story of a great flood that echoes the story of Noah.

These sanctuaries contained not only statues representing the gods, but also the human faithful—perhaps to assure these gods that they were attended with round-the-clock worship. Excavations throughout Mesopotamia have yielded a veritable hoard of these votive statues, called *orants*. They typically depict a male or female worshipper dressed in fringed skirts or gowns, their hands tightly clasped in front of them—presumably a Sumerian gesture of worship and piety. The eyes are large and exaggerated, often still marked with a thin trace of paint. The men invariably wear long and carefully stylized beards. Some of the oldest of these figures date from around 2900 B.C.E.

As Uruk's culture expanded, deities like Inanna, An, and Utu became recognized as gods throughout the Sumerian realm. When Babylon, a major city-state, absorbed the Sumerian commonwealth after 2000 B.C.E., these deities were simply taken over and renamed—akin to the way in which the Romans would adopt the gods of Greek mythology. Thus, Inanna became the Babylonian Ishtar, and Utu became Shamash.

The petitioning of the Sumerian gods was probably driven by the sheer unpredictability of the Tigris and Euphrates. No one could foretell when the rivers would rise, or whether floods would come and destroy much of the carefully built irrigation networks. Not surprisingly, stories of great floods began to circulate very early in Mesopotamian history.

Found at Tell el Ubaid, this relief from the early dynastic period (2900–2350 B.C.E.) shows Sumerian dairy farmers storing milk in large vessels.

LEGENDS OF THE FLOOD

In Genesis, God is repelled by the "wickedness of humankind," and the "evil inclination" of their hearts (Genesis 6:5). So the Lord resolves to wipe out humanity with a massive flood, but he does not wish to kill everyone. Only a man called Noah and his family are to be saved. God gives Noah detailed instructions to build an ark (literally, a "chest") that will rise upon the floodwaters. Since the Genesis description does not refer to rudder or sails, this ark was apparently a boat without any means of navigation. Nevertheless, Noah had to build the ark large enough to accommodate a "male and female" of every kind of living being (Genesis 6:19).

The Bible story of the great Flood bears a strong similarity to events in Sumerian and Babylonian myths. One such myth is called the Epic of Atrahasis and dates from the second millennium B.C.E. According to this epic, man was molded from clay by a goddess named Mami. When the humans became too noisy for the gods to bear, the earth and air god, Enlil, resolved to destroy mankind with a great flood. Fortunately, the hero of this story, a man named Atrahasis, is fore-

warned by the god Enki, who orders him to build a boat and fill it with all of his possessions, as well as a stable of animals and birds.

Another version, preserved on a tablet found in the palace of King Ashurbanipal in Nineveh, relates the epic of the legendary warrior-king Gilgamesh and the immortal Utnapishtim. "In those days," Utnapishtim says, "the world teemed, the people multiplied, the world bellowed like a wild bull." The gods decided to do away with these noisy, meddlesome humans. The god Ea, however, had vowed to protect Utnapishtim, and so Ea tells him to build a boat. "These are the measurements of the barque as you shall build her," he says; "let her beam equal her length, let her deck be roofed like the vault that covers the abyss; then take up into the boat the seed of all living creatures." The verse shows similarities to the instructions Noah receives in Genesis: "Make yourself an ark of cypress wood; ... This is how you are to make it: the length of the ark three hundred cubits, its width fifty cubits, and its height thirty cubits. Make a roof for the ark, and finish it to a cubit above; ... And of every living thing, of all flesh, you shall bring two of every kind" (Genesis 6:14-19).

What these and other stories suggest is that the oral tradition of Genesis was very familiar with and possibly informed by the myths of ancient Mesopotamia.

Found in the Monastery of Kykkos, located in the highlands of Cyprus, this 12th-century mosaic (above) shows Noah's ark and the great Flood.

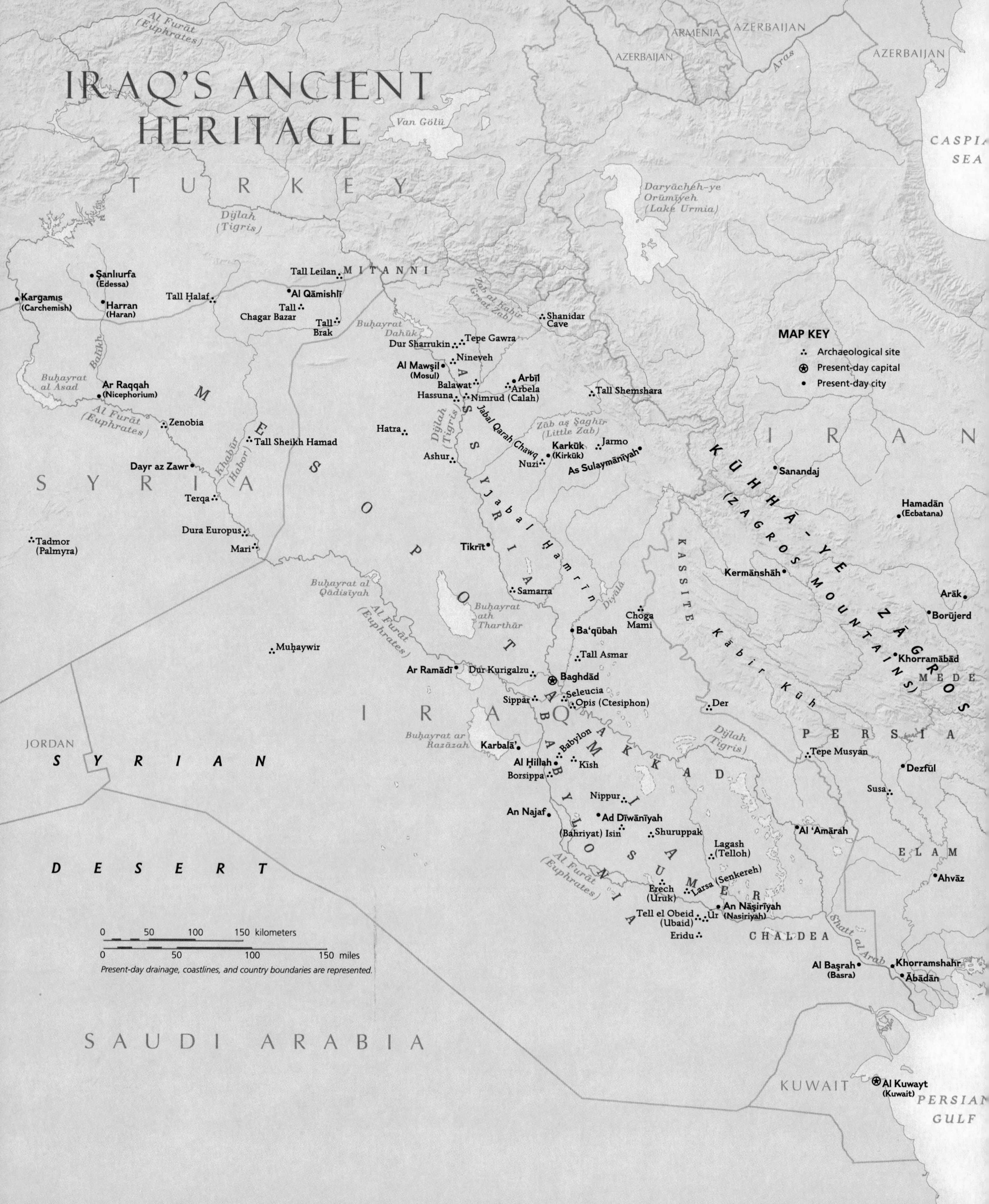

IRAQ'S ANCIENT HERITAGE
TURKEY
SYRIA
IRAQ
IRAN
JORDAN
SAUDI ARABIA
KUWAIT
ARMENIA
AZERBAIJAN
AZERBAIJAN
AZERBAIJAN
CASPIAN SEA
PERSIAN GULF
SYRIAN DESERT
MESOPOTAMIA
ASSYRIA
AKKAD
BABYLONIA
SUMER
CHALDEA
MITANNI
MEDE
PERSIA
ELAM
KASSITE
Al Furāt (Euphrates)
Dijlah (Tigris)
Van Gölü
Daryācheh-ye Orūmīyeh (Lake Urmia)
Aras
Balīkh
Buḩayrat al Asad
Khābūr (Habor)
Buḩayrat Dahūk
Zab al Kabīr (Great Zab)
Zāb aş Şaghīr (Little Zab)
Jabal Qarah Chawq
Jabal Ḩamrīn
Diyālā
Buḩayrat al Qādisīyah
Buḩayrat ath Tharthār
Buḩayrat ar Razāzah
Kabīr Kūh
KŪHHĀ-YE ZĀGROS (ZAGROS MOUNTAINS)
Shaţţ al 'Arab
Şanlıurfa (Edessa)
Kargamıs (Carchemish)
Harran (Haran)
Tall Ḩalaf
Tall Leilan
Al Qāmishlī
Tall Chagar Bazar
Tall Brak
Ar Raqqah (Nicephorium)
Zenobia
Tall Sheikh Hamad
Dayr az Zawr
Terqa
Dura Europus
Mari
Tadmor (Palmyra)
Muḩaywir
Dur Sharrukin
Tepe Gawra
Nineveh
Al Mawşil (Mosul)
Balawat
Hassuna
Nimrud (Calah)
Arbīl
Arbela
Shanidar Cave
Tall Shemshara
Hatra
Ashur
Karkūk (Kirkūk)
Nuzi
Jarmo
As Sulaymānīyah
Tikrīt
Samarra
Choga Mami
Ba'qūbah
Tall Asmar
Ar Ramādī
Dur Kurigalzu
Baghdād
Sippar
Seleucia
Opis (Ctesiphon)
Karbalā'
Babylon
Al Ḩillah
Kīsh
Borsippa
Nippur
An Najaf
Ad Dīwānīyah
(Bahriyat) Isin
Shuruppak
Lagash (Telloh)
Erech (Uruk)
Larsa (Senkereh)
An Nāşirīyah (Nasiriyah)
Tell el Obeid (Ubaid)
Ur
Eridu
Der
Tepe Musyan
Al 'Amārah
Susa
Dezfūl
Ahvāz
Sanandaj
Hamadān (Ecbatana)
Kermānshāh
Arāk
Borūjerd
Khorramābād
Al Başrah (Basra)
Khorramshahr
Ābādān
Al Kuwayt (Kuwait)
MAP KEY
Archaeological site
Present-day capital
Present-day city
0 50 100 150 kilometers
0 50 100 150 miles
Present-day drainage, coastlines, and country boundaries are represented.

After, for seven days [and] seven nights, the flood had swept over the land, ...
Utu came forth, who sheds light on heaven [and] earth. The Sumerian Myth of the Deluge

The Early Dynastic Period of Ur

In 1922, the British archaeologist Sir Leonard Woolley was excavating the royal tombs of Ur near Tell al Muqayyar, north of Basra in today's Iraq. His workmen, digging through several strata of rubbish and potsherds, suddenly struck "perfectly clean clay, uniform throughout, the texture of which showed that it had been laid there by water." As Woolley wrote in 1930, this clay layer "continued without change" through a depth of eight feet, when it ended as suddenly as it had appeared. It was, he declared, unmistakable evidence of a great flood, for "no other agency could possibly account for it." Woolley's discovery produced a surge of excitement. At last, it was claimed, tangible proof of the great Flood, the first great catastrophe described in the Bible, had been found.

But as excavations continued across Mesopotamia, other signs of greater and lesser flooding were brought to light. It became clear that the ancient "land between the two rivers" had repeatedly suffered mild to severe flooding. One rather catastrophic flood can be dated to 3000 or 2900 B.C.E. So traumatic was this experience that it was enshrined in Sumerian mythology; even the Sumerian King List distinguishes between antediluvian rulers and those who came "after the flood."

The great flood of circa 2900 B.C.E. did not destroy the population centers, but it may have accelerated a power shift between the competing city-states. Uruk, which up to then had been the dominant city, slowly yielded to Ur's growing strength and influence. The Sumerian King List faithfully records that after "Erech (Uruk) was defeated, its kingship was carried off to Ur." Ur was an ancient city as old as Uruk, with settlements that dated back to the Ubaid period. Today, Ur lies ten miles distant from the Euphrates, surrounded by bare desert; but in Ur's heyday, the Euphrates flowed much closer, and Ur's surrounding fields were lush and fertile. By 2750 B.C.E., Ur had become the dominant city-state in all of southern Mesopotamia and the main center of its trade, including links with faraway territories like Egypt. In 2560, the new ruler of Ur, Mesannepadda (2560–2525 B.C.E.) assumed authority over all of Sumer.

Ur became a cultural center without parallel. During his excavations on Tell al Muqayyar, Woolley uncovered a group of royal tombs containing the remains of 74 people, 68 of them female. The bodies were arranged as if participating in a funerary procession. One tomb had a gold dagger, "its hilt of lapis lazuli decorated with gold studs"; other tombs held elaborate headdresses, a lovely harp trimmed in gold, as well as cups and vessels of the finest materials. Woolley theorized that these tombs contained the bodies of King Abargi and Queen Puabi—and their complete retinue. All the groomsmen, the ladies-in-waiting, the soldiers, and the courtiers may have been put to death at the time of the funeral so as to continue to serve the royals in the afterlife.

Ur also boasted many magnificent buildings; the most impressive was the 80-foot-high ziggurat dedicated to the moon god Nanna. This ziggurat, partly restored, still stands today near the excavations at Tell al Muqayyar. Sumer's architectural talents were not limited to the building of temples alone, however. The royal tombs, for example, featured fully developed arches some 3,000 years before their reappearance in Roman architecture. The so-called Standard of Ur, a block of wood decorated on both sides with scenes in red limestone, shell, and lapis lazuli, shows us another Sumerian invention: the wheel-borne chariot. It was an awkward contraption, with solid wooden wheels (the spoked wheel did not appear until 1800 B.C.E.), but with it the Sumerians had invented a key element in the development of transportation that endures to this day.

SUMERIAN SCRIPT

After 3500 B.C.E., Sumerian merchants began to record trade by using soft clay tablets that they impressed with small symbols representing the type and quantities of goods. These small symbols eventually led to a primitive script of pictures, or pictograms, that were essentially abbreviated icons for a product, number, or value. People eventually grasped that sequences of these icons could become abstractions of complete thoughts, with various objects linked by an action symbol—somewhat as in a sentence. Through daily use, these sets of pictograms were organized into a set of about 600 symbols, known as cuneiform script. Cuneiform refers to the wedgelike shape made by the pen or stylus that impressed the symbols, or "letters," into the soft clay. So successful was the revolution of cuneiform script, and so sophisticated its grammar, that virtually all other developing language groups in greater Mesopotamia, including Akkadian, Hittite, and Elamite, adopted it.

Royal Treasures of Ur

ca 2600–2400 B.C.E.

Two goats face one another in this shell-and-lapis-inlaid plaque from the tomb of Queen Puabi in Ur.

This bull's head of gold and lapis lazuli formed part of the sounding box of a lyre, found in the tomb of Queen Puabi in Ur.

An exquisitely chiseled helmet made of hammered gold, found in the tomb of Meskalamdug in Ur.

THIS EAGLE WITH WINGS OF LAPIS LAZULI AND THE GOLD HEAD OF A LION FORMED PART OF THE TREASURE OF UR, FOUND IN MARI.

THE TREASURES FROM THE ROYAL TOMBS of Ur offer a glimpse of the Sumerian upper classes during the early dynastic period. The ornaments worn by the women suggest a flair for fashion and skilled artistry. One necklace combines carnelian beads with lapis lazuli and gold pendants. One skeleton, believed to be Queen Puabi, was crowned with a headdress of gold leaves interspersed with delicate flowers, made from precious gems. Noblewomen were highly regarded in Sumerian society; they were often educated and allowed to have property. Woolley's discovery of a game board, made of shell, bone, lapis lazuli, and red limestone, gives a view of home life. This game, somewhat similar to checkers, was known throughout the ancient Near East.

MANY WOMEN IN THE TOMB OF QUEEN PUABI WERE BURIED WITH SPLENDID DIADEMS, EARRINGS, AND NECKLACES MADE OF GOLD LEAVES, LAPIS LAZULI, AND CARNELIAN.

THE TOWER OF BABEL

Genesis relates how human beings decide to build a huge tower that will reach as high as possible—almost as far as heaven itself (Genesis 11:3-4). Before the construction is completed, however, God strikes back by sowing confusion among mankind; from one moment to the next, everyone suddenly "babbles" in different languages (in Hebrew, the verb *bala'* means "to confuse"). The Bible says that this accounts for why the tower is called Babel. Scholars believe the word may also be derived from the Akkadian root of the name Babylon: *bab-ili,* gate of the god.

In fact, most of the leading cities of southern Mesopotamia built tall, stepped pyramids, or ziggurats, to raise their shrines ever closer to the heavens. One of the best-preserved ziggurats, which has now partly restored, is the one at Ur, which was excavated by the British archaeologist Sir Leonard Woolley from 1922 onward near Tell al Muqayyar in southern Iraq.

This ziggurat was constructed by Ur-Nammu, king of Ur from 2112 to 2095 B.C.E. The stucture was later expanded by Nabonidus (555–539 B.C.E.), the last Babylonian king. The ziggurat was built on three levels, each accessible via stairways, and topped by a shrine dedicated to the moon god Nanna. The ziggurat was erected inside an elaborate enclosure that included temple facilities, a treasury, and residences for the priestly caste.

As elsewhere, the Ur ziggurat was built of mud brick and mortar made of bitumen. The description in Genesis echoes this process closely: "And they said to one another, 'Come, let us make bricks, and burn them thoroughly.' And they had brick for stone, and bitumen for mortar. Then they said, 'Come, let us build ourselves a city, and a tower with its top in the heavens' " (Genesis 11:3-4). This, Genesis tells us, occurred in the land of Shinar, a term elsewhere used to denote Babylon.

Dutch painter Pieter Brueghel the Elder (ca 1525–1569) created this depiction of the Tower of Babel's construction.

Perhaps the greatest contribution of Sumerian civilization was its development of writing. Scholars believe that the earliest forms of writing date to around 3300 B.C.E., when trade in surplus crops first became a major intrastate economic activity. Traders, needing to keep track of who bought what, pressed small symbols representing the type and quantities of goods purchased into soft clay tablets. Over time and daily use, these pictograms became stylized into a form of alphabet, now known as cuneiform script.

What made the development of the cuneiform script so significant is that it was used on clay. Baked clay is extremely durable and virtually impervious to the effects of time. Entire libraries from the ancient world, filled with papyrus scrolls, have been lost to fire or floods; but clay endures. A fire only serves to harden the material further. The 3,000 years in which cuneiform script was used offers us an invaluable window on the history of Mesopotamia.

The Akkadian Empire

DESPITE UR'S political and cultural preeminence, competition with 11 other city-states continued. The rivalry between Ur, Kish, and Uruk was particularly intense. This internecine strife abruptly ended when a common enemy invaded: the Akkadians, a group of people from the north. The Akkadians are characterized as Semites because their language, different from that of Sumerians, belongs to a family of languages that evolved not only into Hebrew but also into Aramaic, Assyrian, and Syriac.

The Akkadian armies were led by a king whose fame would later achieve mythical proportions: Sargon of Akkad (2334–2279 B.C.E.). The quarrelsome city-states were no match for Sargon's battle-hardened veterans. What's more, excessive evaporation of scarce water in the region's far-flung irrigation network had led to increased saline levels. Cuneiform records from the period show a dramatic drop in crop yields. Having already vanquished the kingdom of Mari, Sargon turned on Uruk, Lagash, Eridu, and Ur, defeating them in short order. Sargon then joined these city-states into one political unit, the first unified body politic the region had ever known. By 2280 B.C.E., this Akkadian Empire stretched from the Taurus Mountains in today's southern Turkey to Lebanon in the west and the Persian Gulf in the east.

King Naram-Sin of Akkad, wearing a horned tiara, towers over his vanquished enemies. This pink sandstone stela dates to around 2250 B.C.E. and was found in Susa, Iran.

Sargon's grandson Naram-Sin (2254–2218 B.C.E.) fought hard to keep the empire intact. Some of the city-states had risen in open rebellion upon the death of Sargon, while foreign tribes were pressing at the borders. In the ancient Near East, a tribe (such as the Elamites and Gutians) constituted a group of people with a shared ancestry, culture, and language but often with fluid political or geographic affiliations. Initially, Naram-Sin's campaigns against the Gutians were successful, a fact attested to by a magnificent limestone slab, or stela, that is now in the Louvre in Paris. It shows the triumphant king at the top of a mountain summit under the protection of two astral deities, reveling in his victory over the Lullubi (a group of people who lived at the border between today's Iraq and Iran).

The stela marks only one of Naram-Sin's victories. By 2218 B.C.E., at the end of his reign, the Akkadian Empire still controlled all of Assyria, Syria, and major parts of Turkey. The orientation of these conquests was no accident, for it followed the direction of the main international caravan routes.

The Akkadian period ended approximately around 2150 B.C.E., when Naram-Sin's son, Shar-kali-sharri, was no longer able to resist the Gutians, who captured major parts of southern Mesopotamia. The central government system established by Sargon dissolved. The Gutians delegated regional authority to native governors, provided their tribute was paid on time. An ambitious viceroy named Gudea governed the city of Lagash; he ordered his sculpted likeness to be placed in strategic locations throughout Lagash-controlled territory. These statues, made of a black stone called diorite, can be found today in museums from London to New York.

The governors' powers steadily grew, and by the beginning of the 21st century B.C.E., much of the territory of Sumer was again in native hands. King Ur-Nammu of Ur presided over a brief but glorious restoration known as the third dynasty of Ur (ca 2113–2006 B.C.E.). But soon, other threatening invaders appeared, including the Amorites. Their appearance may have set the stage for the story of Abraham.

LAND OF THE NILE

A felucca plies the waters of the Nile near Aswan, Egypt.

AS THE SUMERIAN civilization reached its apogee in Mesopotamia, similar developments were taking place in ancient Egypt, though with different results. Egypt's civilization, too, first stirred along the banks of another great river—in its case, the Nile. But unlike the Euphrates and the Tigris, the Nile rose dependably each year to deposit mineral-rich alluvial sediment all across the fields bordering the river, which the Egyptians referred to as *kemet*—black land. In Egypt, therefore, there was no need for a complex irrigation system like the one developed by the Sumerians—the river provided all the irrigation the soil required.

Climatologists suggest that before the Neolithic period, Egypt was far greener than today. Archaeologists have discovered rock drawings that indicate the presence of nomadic shepherds in the Sahara desert as early as the ninth millennium B.C.E., when the world was just recovering from the last ice age. When the ice retreated, the seas rose, as did the temperatures—some believe by as much as 15 degrees Fahrenheit. Consequently, the desert—which the Egyptians called *deshret,* red land—began to encroach on the moist swamps and steppes of northern Egypt. Were it not for the great Nile, all of Egypt may have been reduced to

ca 4000 B.C.E.
Early farming settlements present in Egypt

ca 3100 B.C.E.
Unification of Upper and Lower Egypt

ca 3000 B.C.E.
Egyptians develop mummification to preserve the dead for the afterlife

ca 2700 B.C.E.
Hieroglyphic writing emerges in Egypt

For any who sees Egypt, without having heard a word about it before, must perceive, if he has only common powers of observation, that the Egypt to which the Greeks go in their ships is an acquired country, the gift of the Nile. Herodotus, *The Histories*

sand dunes, absorbed in one unbroken desert across northern Africa and into the Arabian Peninsula. But then, in the words of the Greek historian Herodotus, Egypt was "the gift of the Nile," fed by spring rains in the African highlands. Without the Nile, Egyptian civilization would never have emerged.

By the fifth millennium B.C.E., when human settlements had sprung up along the Euphrates River in Mesopotamia, a comparable evolution took place in the Nile River Valley. Much of the local population consisted of nomadic herders, moving their sheep and goats from one pasture to the next. Excavations in the marshy Faiyum area west of the Nile and north of present-day Cairo have uncovered fragments of spears that suggest a significant local involvement with hunting and fishing. Elsewhere, the remnants of emmer wheat and barley indicate the development of farming communities, possibly using crop seeds imported from as far away as Mesopotamia.

During the later Neolithic period, there is increasing evidence of trade with both Mesopotamian and Aegean civilizations. Copper, discovered in Egyptian mines, became a sought-after commodity that was smelted and fabricated in numerous villages along the Nile. These prehistoric villages consisted of homes and workshops built with mud brick, often grouped around a central shrine, as in Eridu. In time, the communities began to coalesce into regions, or nomes, each run by a tribal chieftain. By 3300 B.C.E., these nomes had allied themselves into two distinct separate kingdoms.

The first, known as Lower Egypt, encompassed a territory, bisected by the Nile, from the Mediterranean to an area roughly near today's Cairo. This region was the Nile River Delta, permeated with tributaries of the Nile that over the centuries had deposited layers of rich alluvial sediment. It was a fertile land filled with green pastures and shaded by date palms that, in times of drought, would attract nomadic tribes from as far as Canaan and Syria—including the Israelites. Here, amid the subtropical groves and palm forests, the invading Hyksos, and later the Ramessides, would build their capitals of Avaris and Tanis. And here, in the northeastern region known as Goshen, the Israelites would toil, according to the Bible, on the construction of the twin cities, Per Atum and Ramesses.

The other kingdom was referred to as Upper Egypt. It ran along the narrow ribbon of fertile land bordering the Nile, past its cataracts into Nubia to a line just north of present-day Khartoum. In this far more forbidding landscape, sustained by the life-giving artery of the river, the pharaohs would build some of their greatest monuments, including Abydos, Thebes, and Abu Simbel.

The Kingdoms Unite

THE THIRD-CENTURY B.C.E. Egyptian historian Manetho tells us that around 3100 B.C.E.—just as Uruk gained ascendancy in the delicate framework of city-states of Sumer—a mythical king named Menes (perhaps Narmer) gathered sufficient strength to unify the two lands of Upper and Lower Egypt. This unification is celebrated by a ceremonial plaque, known as the Narmer Palette, discovered near the ancient city of Kom el-Ahmar. On one side, King Narmer wears the white miter or *hedjet* of Upper

The Narmer Palette, dated around 3000 B.C.E., marks the victories of King Narmer (or, possibly King Menes), who unified the kingdoms of Upper and Lower Egypt.

ca 2630 B.C.E. Construction of the stepped pyramid at Saqqara begins

ca 2575 B.C.E. Egypt's Old Kingdom period begins with the 4th dynasty

ca 2575–2450 B.C.E. Great Pyramids of Khufu, Kafre, and Menkaure are built

ca 2150 B.C.E. Egypt's Old Kingdom ends

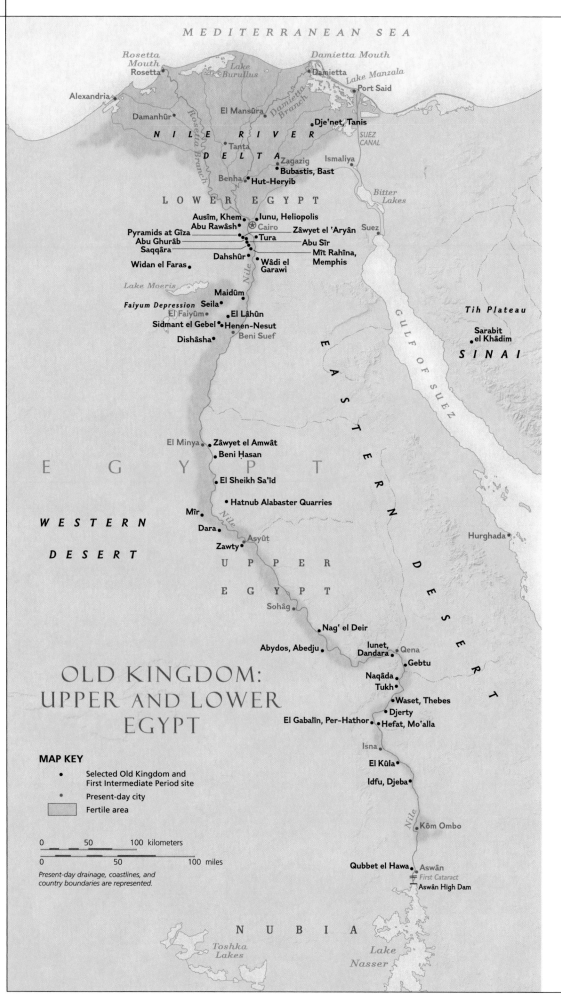

OLD KINGDOM: UPPER AND LOWER EGYPT

MAP KEY

- • Selected Old Kingdom and First Intermediate Period site
- • Present-day city
- Fertile area

0 50 100 kilometers
0 50 100 miles

Present-day drainage, coastlines, and country boundaries are represented.

Egypt; on the other, the red crown or *deshret* of Lower Egypt. Later, the pharaohs would combine both crowns into one headdress, known as the *pschent.*

Narmer founded the 1st dynasty of the Early Dynastic period of Egypt (ca 3100–2575 B.C.E.), the beginning of 31 dynasties over a span of 3,000 years. Each king or pharaoh was revered as a god, the living descendant of the sun god Re on Earth.

Narmer's son Aha solidified the unified kingdom by building a capital city at Memphis, not far from modern Cairo. According to Herodotus, Narmer himself had marked the spot by constructing a dam in the Nile, thus enabling his son to

This painted limestone statue of King Djoser, found in the funerary complex of Saqqara, is believed to be the oldest life-size statue from the Old Kingdom (ca 2575–2150 B.C.E.).

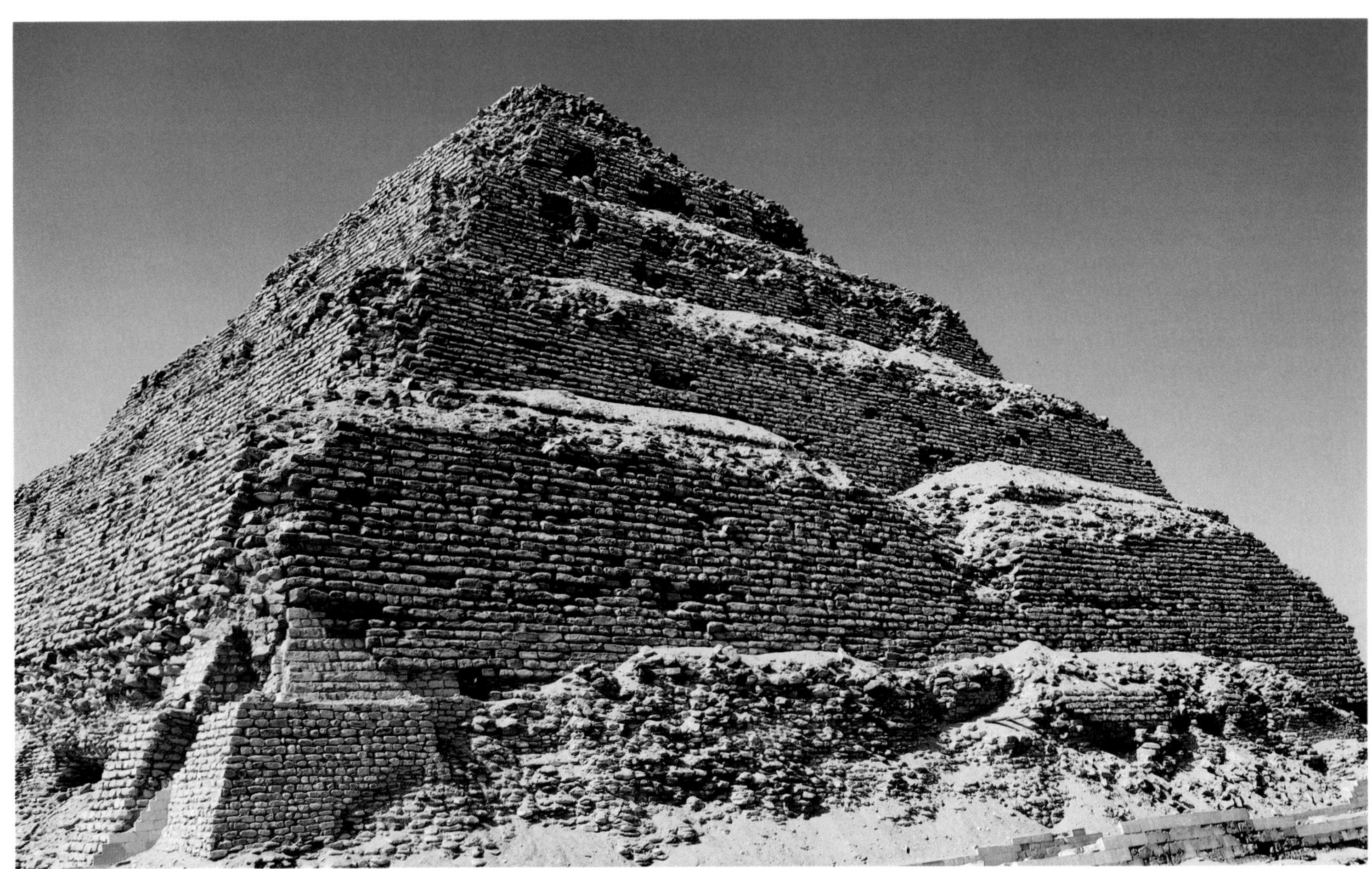

The stepped pyramid of Djoser in Saqqara survives as the oldest structure built entirely of stone. It set the precedent for the use of pyramids as a place of royal burial.

build on the reclaimed land. Under the leadership of Memphis, Egypt's cultural development soon began to rival the great cities of Sumer in architecture, literature, sculpture, and science, including medicine. Memphis traded its copper and turquoise for raw materials such as wood, gold, and the myriad chemicals needed in its mortuary temples, the center of Egypt's cult of the dead.

Monumental Architecture

ONE OF THE EARLIEST mortuary shrines of the Old Kingdom can still be seen in Saqqara, which served Memphis as the necropolis for its noblemen. Here King Djoser of the 3rd dynasty began what is possibly the oldest example of a planned architectural complex still in existence today. Its purpose was to create a mortuary facility where the pharaoh, long after his death, would continue to be worshiped in a series of religious festivals. As such, the city would have to withstand the test of time; like its king, it would have to be immortal. Therefore, it was built of stone rather than mud brick, which would not last as long.

BIBLICAL MEASUREMENT

Units of measurement often appear in the Bible to describe important buildings and objects. Both Noah's ark and Solomon's Temple are measured in cubits; God tells Noah to build the ark 300 cubits long, 50 cubits wide, and 30 cubits high (Genesis 6:14-19). Solomon's Temple measured 60 cubits long and 30 cubits high (I Kings 6:2). Scholars estimate that a cubit equals approximately 18 inches. Other measures include a "finger" (three-quarters of an inch), a "palm" (3 inches), and a "span" (9 inches).

To achieve this daunting task, Djoser turned to an architect named Imhotep—it is the first time in history that we hear of an architect by name. Imhotep did not disappoint his monarch. In laying out this city, he created many of the architectural elements that would later return in the architecture of Greece and Rome: fluted columns with capitals adorned with lotus or papyrus leaves; ornamental friezes decorated with reliefs; false doors; and galleries paved entirely in marble and limestone.

The tour de force of Imhotep's design is a massive, stepped pyramid, which in its heyday rose to 180 feet. Imhotep achieved this stupendous height by stacking a series of limestone blocks of diminishing size. Deep inside this massive structure was the burial chamber for the pharaoh, hacked out of bedrock.

Why Djoser chose a pyramid to mark his tomb remains a subject of debate. Some scholars believe that the design represents the hierarchical arrangement of Egypt's society under the beneficence of Djoser. Others associate the pyramid with astronomical observations or with the projection of sunlight, since Re was the greatest god in the Egyptian pantheon. Others seek to link the pyramid to the ziggurats in Mesopotamia.

The Saqqara pyramid did set the trend for Pharaohs and help establish one of the most well-known symbols of Egyptian culture. In subsequent pyramids, the stepped structure would be clad with a veneer of limestone to create a smooth surface on all four sides. A small access way, designed with several false turns to confuse thieves, led to the chamber in which the pharaoh's sarcophagus was placed. Smaller pyramids and tombs were built nearby to house the royal family and the pharaoh's closest advisers.

And so Ptah rested, after
he had made everything …
he had formed the gods,
he had made cities,
he had founded nomes,
he had put the gods
in their shrines.

The Memphite Theology of Creation

The greatest examples of Egyptian pyramids are those still standing in Giza, near Cairo, including the Pyramids of Khufu (Cheops, 2589–2566 B.C.E.) and Khafre (Khephren, 2558–2532 B.C.E.).

The task of building so vast a mortuary complex consumed a Pharaoh's attention throughout much of his reign—as well as his treasury. During the Middle Kingdom (ca 1975–1640 B.C.E.) and New Kingdom (ca 1539–1075 B.C.E.), the practice was gradually abandoned in favor of tombs carved deep into the mountains west of Thebes. Architects shifted their attention to building monumental temples to Egypt's principal gods, such as the massive Temple of Amun at Karnak.

By the end of the Old Kingdom, after the long reign of Pepi II (ca 2278–2184 B.C.E.), Egypt lay exhausted from the burden of building massive pyramids, compounded by a downturn in international trade and the failure of harvests. The power of the central administration crumbled. The nobles withdrew to their various nomes to husband their estates. Only by the beginning of the 11th dynasty, around 1975 B.C.E., was pharaonic power able to reunify the country and enter the Middle Kingdom period. Shortly thereafter, the first of Israel's patriarchs, the Bible says, would embark on a journey to the borders of Egypt.

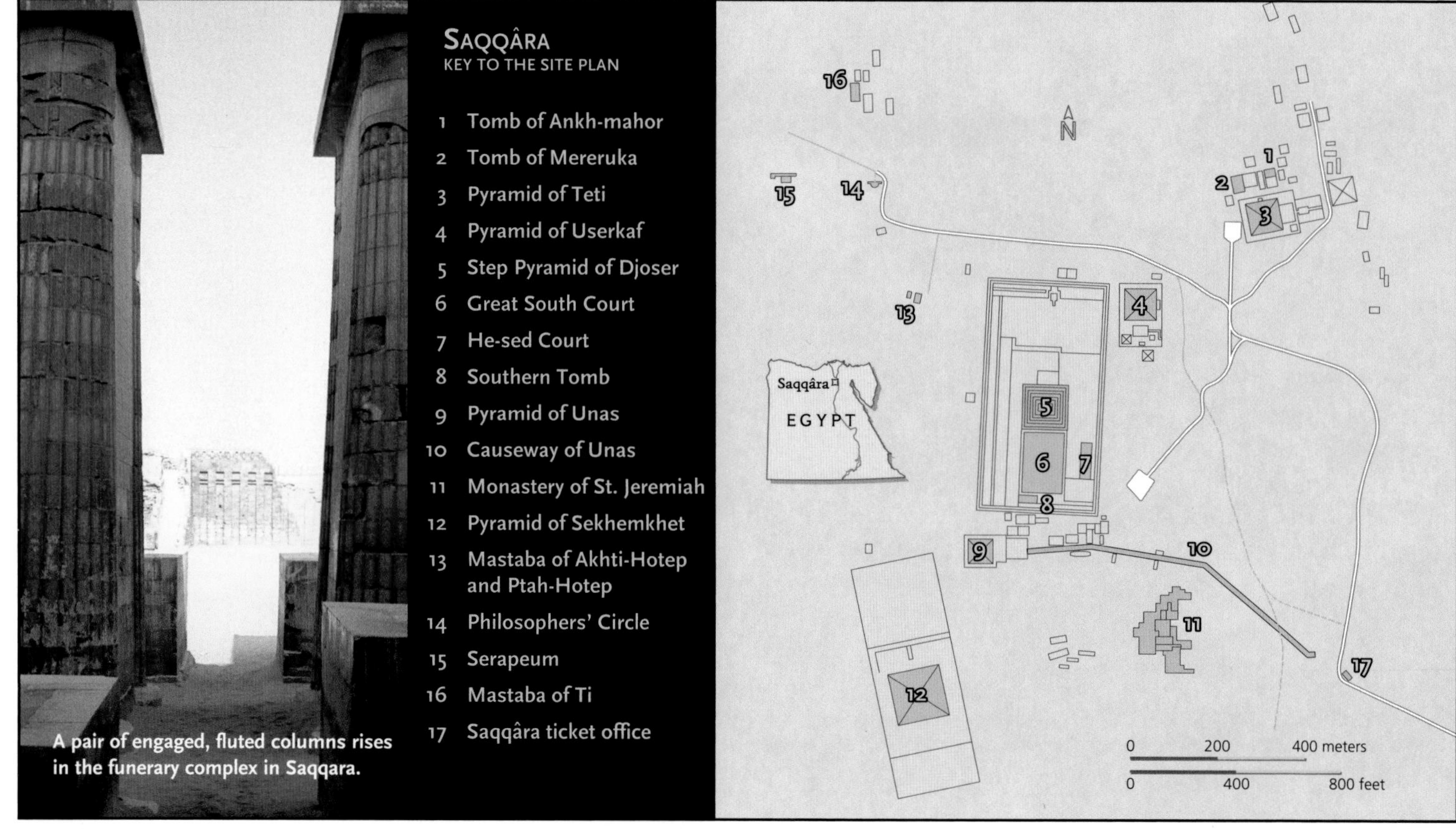

A pair of engaged, fluted columns rises in the funerary complex in Saqqara.

EGYPT	MESOPOTAMIA	CANAAN
ca 6000 B.C.E. Evidence of weaving is present in Neolithic settlements in Egypt	ca 8000 B.C.E. Cultivated wheat and barley are grown in the Fertile Crescent	ca 9000 B.C.E. Protovillages in Canaan and throughout the Near East
ca 4000 B.C.E. Presence of early farming settlements in Egypt	ca 5200 B.C.E. Ubaid culture emerges	ca 7500 B.C.E. Earliest evidence of domesticated animals in Syria
ca 3100 B.C.E. Unification of Upper and Lower Egypt	ca 5000 B.C.E. First metal tools appear; clay pottery becomes widespread	ca 7200 B.C.E. Earliest settlement at Ain Ghazal
ca 2700 B.C.E. Hieroglyphic writing present in Egypt	ca 3500 B.C.E. Sumerian farmers develop complex irrigation systems to aid and control agriculture	ca 6000 B.C.E. Obsidian trade spreads throughout ancient Near East
ca 2630 B.C.E. Construction of the stepped pyramid at Saqqara begins	ca 3300 B.C.E. Clay tablets document trade in Mesopotamia	ca 3000 B.C.E. Megiddo is likely the most powerful city-state in northern Canaan
ca 2575 B.C.E. Pharaoh Snefru leads expeditions to the south (Nubia) and west (Libya)	ca 3200 B.C.E. Uruk emerges as a complex society	ca 3000 B.C.E. Phoenician settlements present along the Syrian coast
ca 2550 B.C.E. At Giza, Great Pyramids are built	ca 2280 B.C.E. Akkadian Empire reaches its height	ca 3000 B.C.E. The abacus, a counting device that employs beads and string, is in use throughout the Middle East and Mediterranean
ca 2175 B.C.E. Pharaoh Pepi II ends 90-year reign, marking the end of the Old Kingdom in Egypt	ca 2000 B.C.E. Amorites invade Syria and Mesopotamia and establish Babylon as their capital	ca 2500 B.C.E. Semitic Canaanite tribes settle along the coast of Palestine
		ca 2675 B.C.E. Lebanon is exporting cedar wood to Egypt and Sumeria
		ca 2300 B.C.E. The Egyptian Army under King Pepi I campaigns in Canaan
		ca 2000 B.C.E. Hittite immigration into Asia Minor

CHAPTER TWO

The Journey of Abraham

GENESIS, THE FIRST OF THE FIVE BOOKS OF MOSES (also known as the Pentateuch, or Torah), begins with the story of God's creation of Earth and its inhabitants. It then continues with other stories, including that of the Garden of Eden and the tree of the knowledge of good and evil, whose fruit, though forbidden, tempts Adam and Eve. Later, the book describes the great Flood brought by God upon his creations. Genesis then introduces the lives of the patriarchs, including Abraham, Isaac, and Jacob, the ancestors of the Israelites, who through God's covenant with Abraham will become God's chosen people. This covenant affirms that the Lord will make of Abraham "a great nation" and lead him "to the land that I will show you"—the Promised Land.

According to Genesis, Abraham was called upon to forsake his many ancestral gods and commit himself to the worship of one true God—a concept without parallel in any of the religions practiced at that time in the Fertile Crescent. With God's guidance, Abraham traveled the full breadth of the Fertile Crescent on a journey in search of the land promised to his people. This journey, which ends in the land of Canaan, is well described in Genesis, and this chapter will examine that story in relation to a number of recent archaeological discoveries.

A Bedouin shepherd watches his flock in the hills of the Negev, not far from ancient Beersheba.

Family History

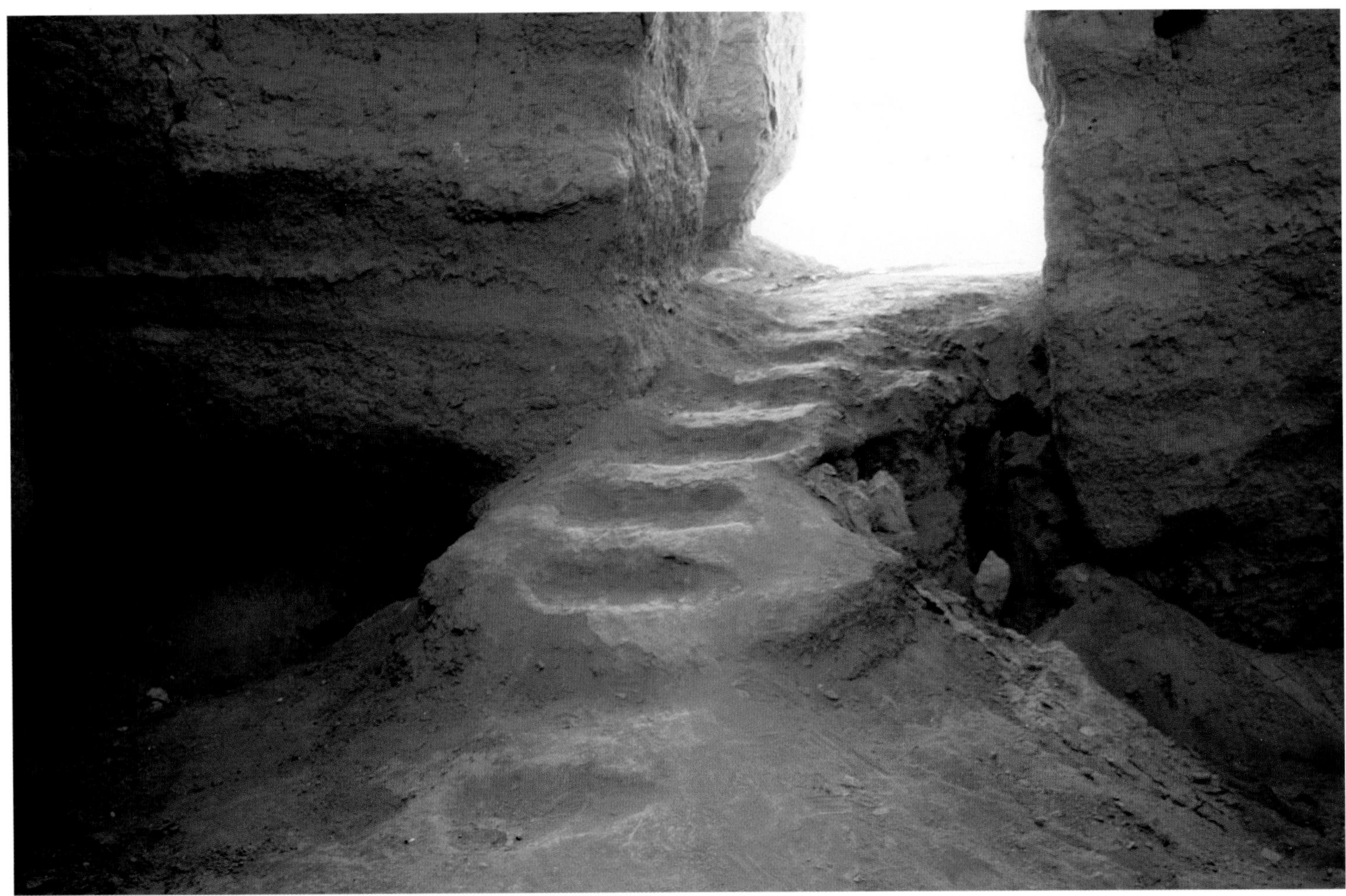

Stairs ascend inside the royal palace of Mari. Around the year 1760 B.C.E. Babylonian King Hammurabi destroyed the palace, located near today's Tell Hariri, in Syria.

The Book of Genesis anchors the story of the birth and growth of the people of Israel within the context of the great civilizations of its time. The book also provides the principal thesis of the Hebrew Bible: that throughout their history, the Chosen People were led, admonished, and ultimately saved by the power of one God, the Creator of the universe, a Being passionately devoted to moral and social justice.

Although at the beginning of Genesis the scope of the story embraces all living creatures on earth, the narrative progressively narrows down to the lives of several individuals, the patriarchs, whose heirs will become the 12 tribes of Israel. Genesis depicts the great events of creation, the calamitous destruction from the Flood, and the dispersal of the wicked people of Babel. But when the story turns to Abraham, the first of the patriarchs, Genesis shifts lenses, focusing on the intimate setting of one family.

The Family of Abraham

Genesis describes Abraham (at first called Abram) as the son of a man named Terah, who in turn is identified as a descendant of Noah, the righteous man saved by God from the great Flood. Next, Genesis introduces us to Abraham's

ca 2250 B.C.E.
Early Bronze Age settlements begin to decline

ca 2100 B.C.E.
Amorites (nomadic Semitic tribes) move into parts of southern Mesopotamia

ca 2000 B.C.E.
Urban centers reemerge in Canaan

ca 2000 B.C.E.
Special drills are used to plant seeds in Egypt. A separate device, the shadoof, lifts water to irrigate fields

Go from your country and your kindred, and your father's house, to the land that I will show you. And I will make of you a great nation. (Genesis 12:1-2)

family, including his brothers Nahor and Haran; his sister-in-law Milcah; his nephew Lot, and Abraham's own wife, Sarah (at first called Sarai). Abraham's brother Haran, however, "died before his father Terah in the land of his birth, in Ur of the Chaldeans" (Genesis 11:28).

Is this the Ur rediscovered by Sir Leonard Woolley in the 1920s? Several scholars have tried to dispute this attribution, arguing that the "Chaldeans" are a tribe that in later centuries inhabited a region not far from Haran, where Terah ultimately will take his family. Modern scholarship, however, has shown that tribal names in the Bible are sometimes applied anachronistically, from the viewpoint of the sixth- and fifth-century B.C.E. scribes who codified the Hebrew Bible. It is therefore possible that, at least in the eyes of the Bible's authors, Abraham's family came from Ur of Sumer, the cradle of civilization.

We are, however, left to speculate about the source of Terah's livelihood. Was he an aristocrat or a merchant? Did he ply a trade? Or had he originally been a nomad, as Abraham chose to become, moving from field to pasture to graze his flocks? How could a family from a city as sophisticated as Ur readily adapt to the rigors of a nomadic life—forever in search of water for their herds? And why, indeed, did Abraham decide to break with his ancestral Mesopotamian deities to heed the word of one God?

Some answers to these questions may be found in a number of important archaeological finds uncovered in just the last few decades. While these discoveries do not provide evidence that Abraham was a historic figure, they do indicate that the Bible's account of Abraham's life meshes well with much of what we know of ancient life in the Fertile Crescent.

The Ugaritic Texts

THE DISCOVERY of ancient texts in the royal palace of Mari and in the vast palatial tract of the age-old city of Ugarit, both in present-day Syria, greatly increased our knowledge of early life in the Near East. Mari was located on the Euphrates near today's Tell Hariri, some 30 miles north of the Syria-Iraq border. Centrally located, Mari was heavily involved in trade between north and south, between Egypt and Babylon, as well as in the movement of goods to the tribal kingdoms of today's Iran and Syria. Dedicated to its patron god Dagan, god of the grain harvest, Mari reached its zenith as the capital of King Zimri-Lim in the 18th century B.C.E., before it was overrun by the Babylonian King Hammurabi around 1760 B.C.E. In his zeal to extinguish every vestige of this former rival, Hammurabi ordered Zimri-Lim's 300-room palace destroyed. Drifting sand gradually covered the ruins, hiding them until their discovery by French archaeologists in the 20th century. Deep inside these ruins was a cache of more than 20,000 clay tablets, only a quarter of which have been translated to date. These cuneiform tablets provide detailed information about the economic, cultural, and political affairs of Zimri-Lim's realm and stretch back some 200 years earlier—quite possibly coinciding with the story of Abraham's journey to Haran, which some scholars place between 2000 and 1800 B.C.E.

The second trove of ancient material was found in Ugarit, first excavated in 1929 near Ra's Shamrah, on Syria's

Found near Tello (ancient Girsu) in today's Iraq, this diorite statue is known as the "Lady with the Shawl." It probably depicts a princess from Gudea (ca 2140 B.C.E.).

ca 1975 B.C.E. Middle Kingdom begins in Egypt

ca 1950 B.C.E. Building of Great Temple and palace begins at Mari

ca 1950 B.C.E. Decline of Ur

ca 1900 B.C.E. Elamites migrate from Persia to southern Mesopotamia

Mediterranean coast. French archaeologist Claude Schaeffer laid bare a huge two-story palace complex that covered some two acres, containing not only the private residence of the king but also his administrative center. Nearby, the excavators found a storage room packed with clay tablets. Surprisingly, many tablets were not inscribed in the Akkadian cuneiform common in this region since the days of King Sargon, but were in a 30-character Ugaritic cuneiform, which bears some resemblance to North Semitic alphabets and may be one of the precursors of the Hebrew alphabet.

The tablets provide insights into the religious myths and practices of Canaan and its surrounding region. Their information gives some understanding of the cultural and religious context of the era of Abraham and subsequent patriarchs, right up to the Israelite settlement of Canaan, following the return from Egypt.

This statue of Ebih-Il, superintendent of Mari, was found in the temple of Ishtar at Mari and dated to around 2400 B.C.E.

So why would the head of a presumably urban family like Terah's choose the life of a nomad? The Mari Tablets may give us answers, since they show the division between sedentary and nomadic lifestyles as not so rigid in Abraham's day as we would expect. The boundaries between agricultural and pastoral clans were fluid; people adapted to their condition as the situation warranted. For example, while clearly a nomad, Abraham's son Isaac does not hesitate to "sow seed in that land, and reap a hundredfold" (Genesis 26:12). Some scholars believe that Terah was the descendant of a tribal group known as the Amorites (or Amurru in Akkadian), who after 2100 B.C.E. began to inhabit parts of southern Mesopotamia and ultimately controlled the entire region. These tribes, Semitic in origin, had strong pastoral roots but eventually

Herders tend to their sheep near the village of Haran (Harran), in modern-day Turkey, known for its beehive-shaped houses made of stone and brick.

adapted to the ways of Sumerian civilization. Indeed, some of the Mari texts contain Amorite references similar to such names from Genesis as "Terah," "Nahor," "Serug," and "Haran."

The question that remains is why would a man like Terah move his family up north, to an uncertain future in the city of Haran? Here, too, archaeological insights may prove useful. The steady immigration of Amorite tribes from the margins of the desert was destabilizing. Eventually, Ur's control of the region all but collapsed, and southern Mesopotamia was once again plunged into civil strife, further exacerbated by the arrival of the Elamites from Persia around 1900 B.C.E. All these factors could have prompted a family from Ur to flee the political upheaval in their city-state, in search of a safer haven.

Genesis has told us that Terah headed north, to the city of Haran (Genesis 11:31). This would have made good sense under the circumstances. South of Ur was the sea; to the east lay the heartland of the feared Elamites, and westward was nothing but desert. In addition, all of the main caravan routes led northward, following the Euphrates across the Fertile Crescent. Haran, located today in Turkey, was one of the principal Sumerian trading posts in the north, established in the days of King Sargon.

The Journey to Haran

TERAH'S FAMILY might have reached the city of Mari about one month after departing from Ur. Just then reaching its peak, Mari was a major trading terminus of grain, olive oil, pottery, and Lebanese timber, and the center of the cult of the gods Dagan, Ishtar, and Shamash, all of Sumerian origin. From there, Terah's family would have traveled the remaining 250 miles to Haran by following a tributary of the Euphrates, the Balikh River, which led them straight into the city.

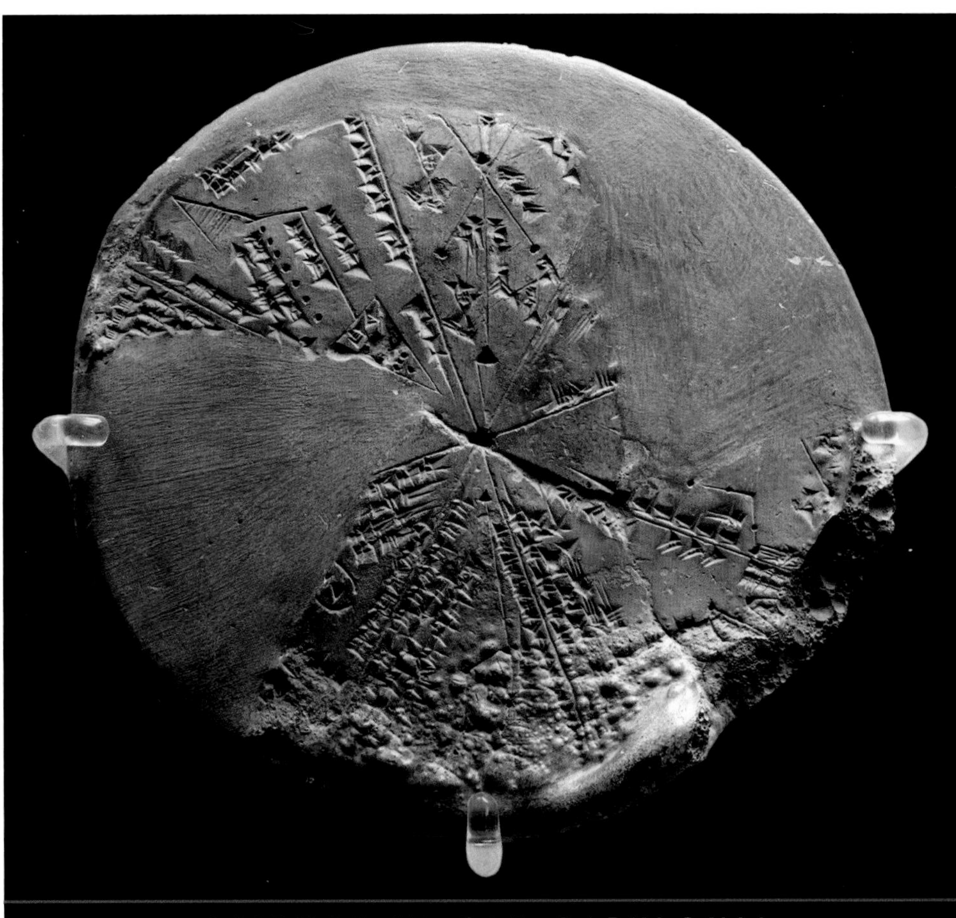

SCIENCE IN OLD BABYLONIA

THE CITY OF UR IN THE 20TH AND 19TH centuries B.C.E. witnessed a flowering of science and literature even as the alliances between city-states dissolved into civil strife. Old Sumerian texts were adapted and translated into Akkadian, the Semitic language introduced into the region by Amorite tribes. Myths, poems, and epics of gods and heroes from the Dynastic and Predynastic periods were updated and copied.

At the same time, sciences—including mathematics, medicine, and astronomy—flourished. Excavators have found tablets that record observations of the planet Venus or project the constellation of stars on circular planispheres or star charts. Another tablet, now in the British Museum in London, discusses problems of geometry. At this time in Babylonian history, astronomical observations were still pure science; astrology did not become a major preoccupation until after 1000 B.C.E. By 500 B.C.E., Babylonian scientists could accurately predict the position of the sun, moon, planets, and various bright stars.

In these exploits, Babylonian scientists and artisans drew heavily from the legacy of Sumerian science. The Royal Tombs in Ur, for example, feature fully developed arches some 3,000 years before their appearance in Roman architecture. Another Sumerian invention was the wheel, as shown on chariots depicted on the so-called Standard of Ur, which was found in the Royal Cemetery of Ur and dated to around 2600 B.C.E.

Found at Nineveh, Assyria, this Babylonian planisphere, inscribed with cuneiform text, shows a schematic representation of constellations in eight separate segments.

Haran, or *harranu* in Akkadian, means crossroads. Indeed, the city was located at the junction of the great Mesopotamian highway and the road from Charchemish to Amida and Nineveh. As in much of Mesopotamia, Haran was populated by Amorites who spoke a local Akkadian dialect and worshipped many gods of Sumerian origin, including the moon god Sin. It was a fertile place at the time, with vast stretches of cedar forests that were the envy of the ancient world. The Bible says Terah settled his family in Haran. The climate was temperate, and the meadows were green. But then, one day, Terah failed to rise from his bed.

Terah's death would have changed everything for the family. In a Mesopotamian clan, the father was the patriarch; he ruled over the fate of his family, his servants, and his slaves. He chose where to pitch tents, planned the daily routines of herding and grazing, and supervised the men. He also was responsible for dealing with traders and vendors and maintaining friendly relations with neighboring nomadic groups. Now, these responsibilities would have fallen on the shoulders of Abraham. According to the Bible, Abraham felt a stirring in his soul: a whisper of the voice of God, telling him that Haran was not his destiny. He must head farther south, to the land of Canaan, where rivers flowed and the grass was moist and fresh. "Go from your country and your kindred and your father's house to the land that I will show you. I will make of you a great nation, and I will bless you, and make your name great" (Genesis 12:1-2). This is God's covenant with Abraham, the divine promise of a land, a nationhood, and prosperity that would be the guiding principal throughout the story of Genesis.

El in Canaan

ABRAHAM OBEYS the voice of God without question; he "went, as the Lord had told him." But how familiar was Abraham with the voice of God? Was this the first time God revealed himself to the patriarch? Significantly, this segment of Genesis uses the word *El* or *Elohim* to denote God—as "the Lord." God will continue to be known as El until he reveals himself as YHWH to Moses in the Book of Exodus.

The Ugaritic tablets allow us to place the Abrahamic El in the context of other deities worshiped in Syria (and presumably in Canaan as well). In Ugaritic mythology, a deity named El was the supreme head of the pantheon of gods, father of creation, not unlike the role of the pagan Allah in pre-Islamic Arabia. Although Baal is by far the most visible god in the Canaanite pantheon, he, too, was subservient to the divine authority of El.

Found in the Mari palace, this rare fragment of painted plaster from approximately 1800 B.C.E. depicts two attendants leading a bull, probably to a place of sacrifice.

Seen in this context, Abraham's obedience to the pre-Israelite El may be less a break with the past than was previously assumed. It is also noteworthy that God does not order Abraham to burn the effigies of other ancestral gods that were almost certainly on display in a typical Mesopotamian household. He does not, as yet, inform Abraham that he is the only God, as YHWH will insist much later in the biblical narrative. What makes the El of Genesis different, however, is that Abraham's God deigns to deal directly with a single human being. With this simple act, Abraham's El signals that he is unlike any of the deities that Abraham may have worshipped before.

Not everyone travels with Abraham to Canaan. "Get you from your kindred," Genesis 12:1 says, and so it is only his wife and his nephew Lot, together with their servants and their flocks, who accompany Abraham on his journey south. The other members of Terah's family remain in Haran. Much later, when the Bible recounts the search by Jacob, Abraham's grandson, for a wife among his kinsmen, it says he travels back to Haran.

Genesis does not say how Abraham journeyed to Canaan, except to say that his first significant stop was the city of Shechem. Most scholars assume that a man like Abraham would have taken the main caravan route south, later known as the King's Highway, which led through Aleppo, Ebla, and Damascus. At Damascus, the main route pushed down into the Transjordan plateau until the road curved west toward Shechem. While this route is fine for men and animals accustomed to the desert, someone making the journey for the first time would probably have taken a more circuitous route into northern Canaan through Dan and Hazor, keeping close to pastures and the sweet waters of the Jordan River.

ANCIENT MESOPOTAMIA
TURKEY
SUBARTU
Haran
Tall Halaf
Abraham settled here with his father. He later left to continue on to Canaan. (Genesis 11:31-12:4)
Tigris
Euphrates
AMURRU
SYRIA
MESOPOTAMIA
Temple dating from about 4,000 B.C.E. discovered here under 12 layers of later settlement.
Tepe Gawra
Nineveh
Great Zab
Village of farmers, builders, and craftsmen that flourished about 4,400 B.C.E. A sickle made from flint chips glued together was found here.
Hassuna
Nimrud (Calah)
Ekallatum
Little Zab
Ashur
Nuzi
Small clay tablet from about 2,300 B.C.E. found here displays a map, one of the oldest known.
Referred to as the "Land of Shinar," where people first settled after the flood. (Genesis 11:2)
Some 25,000 cuneiform tablets were unearthed from a royal archive here.
Mari
Simurrum
Diyala
Eshnunna
IRAQ
Sippar
Der
Urua
AKKAD
Agade
Sargon's capital, the actual location of the city remains unknown.
Babylon
Kish
Borsippa
Dilbat
Mashkan Shapir
Nippur
Isin
Adab
Shuruppak
Umma
Lagash
Erech (Uruk)
Larsa
Tell el Obeid (Ubaid)
Ur
Eridu
SUMER
CHALDEA
The ancient Sumerian King List, a chronological roll of early rulers, traces its lineage from "heaven." It lists "Ku-Baba, a barmaid," who reigned here after the flood.
Stela of the Vultures found here; this stone slab pictures armed Sumerian soldiers marching in a phalanx, the birth of military discipline about 2,500 B.C.E.
Gave its name to the earliest Babylonian culture. Clay pins reinforcing mud walls formed primitive mosaics.
The native city of Terah and his son Abraham. From here the family departed for Canaan. (Genesis 11:31)
Susa
ELAM
IRAN
ZAGROS MOUNTAINS
GUTIUM
Kābir Kūh
Lake Van
Lake Urmia
ARMENIA
AZERBAIJAN
Aras
CASPIAN SEA
Elburz Mts.
SYRIAN DESERT
DAN
SAUDI ARABIA
KUWAIT
PERSIAN GULF
Shatt al Arab
MAP KEY
Approximate extent of Sargon's dynasty, ca. 2230 B.C.E.
Babylonian control, 1750 B.C.E.
Third dynasty of Ur, main kingdom, ca. 2047 B.C.E.
Location uncertain
0 50 100 150 kilometers
0 50 100 150 miles
Present-day drainage, coastlines, and country boundaries are represented.

THE ENTRY INTO CANAAN

A cult mask and two halves of a potter's wheel lie exactly as they were found in the Canaanite stronghold of Hazor, dated around the 15th century B.C.E.

THE LAND OF CANAAN that Abraham would have entered, possibly around 1850 B.C.E., had only recently emerged from a long period of "slumber." The growth of settlements during the Early Bronze Age (3150–2200 B.C.E.) had suffered a reversal sometime after 2250 B.C.E. The reasons for this decline are not clear, but it is possible that the region experienced a prolonged drought. In addition, Canaan's economy was closely linked to that of its great neighbor to the southwest, Egypt, since international trade inevitably passed through Canaan. This trade had slowed considerably as a result of political upheaval during what is called Egypt's First Intermediate period (2125–1975 B.C.E.). Many Canaanite settlements had simply been abandoned as the country's population returned to pastoral life. Then, in 1938 B.C.E., came a turning point when the Egyptian King Amenemhet I (1938–1908 B.C.E.) acceded to the throne and initiated a reunification of Egypt's provinces. The result was a rapid economic recovery that would continue throughout the 12th dynasty. A renewed demand for goods destined for temples and palaces throughout Egypt revitalized the trade with Syria, the Levant, and Mesopotamia. The Canaanite towns fortunate enough to

ca 2100 B.C.E.
Ur-Nammu founds the third dynasty of Ur

ca 1960 B.C.E.
Egypt invades Nubia and extends its borders to the Nile's Second Cataract

ca 1950 B.C.E.
Egyptian army invades Canaan

ca 1938 B.C.E.
Under Amenemhet I's reign, Egypt begins a period of rapid economic growth

At that time the Canaanites were in the land. Then the Lord appeared to Abram, and said, "To your offspring I will give this land."

(Genesis 12:6-7)

straddle the principal trading routes revived as their storage facilities and provisioning services were once again in demand.

This new economic boom, however, also led to increased regional strife. Almost every Canaanite town of substance now found itself compelled to buttress its precincts with stout defensive works, lest its wealth attract the attention of marauders. A good example is the very first Canaanite settlement that Abraham may have encountered, the city of Hazor, some ten miles north of the Sea of Galilee. By contemporary standards, Hazor was vast, covering some 200 acres. In the mid-19th century B.C.E., the city may have comprised as many as 20,000 people, who were supplied water from springs in nearby Nahal Hazor. According to the Book of Joshua, Hazor was considered "the head of all those kingdoms" (Joshua 11:10). Not surprisingly, Hazor also appears in 17th-century tablets from Mari as well as in some Egyptian texts of magic and execration from the 19th century B.C.E.

The only access to the heavily fortified city was through massive gates in the Lower City. These gates anchored a defensive system that was repeatedly restored and expanded for centuries to come. According to the Bible, Hazor would later be a thorn in Joshua's side as the Israelite commander tried to conquer the region north of the Sea of Galilee. The remains of ancient Hazor were first identified in 1875, but its mound wasn't fully excavated until a campaign, from 1955 through 1958 and again in 1968, brought the Israeli archaeologist Yigael Yadin to the site. Excavations continue to this day.

In the biblical account, Abraham did not stay at Hazor: his first principal objective was Shechem. A wary traveler in a foreign land, Abraham avoided most of the settlements of the coastal region and stuck to the Samarian highlands, where grazing lands were sparse but a wandering nomad raised few eyebrows.

Like Hazor, Shechem was a prosperous place, and the Bible notes that Abraham paused to erect an altar to El. God rewarded him by reiterating his promise: "To your offspring I will give this land" (Genesis 12:7). Ancient Shechem has been excavated at Khirbat Balatah, just southeast of the city known today as Nablus, straddling the strategic pass between the hills of Mount Gerizim and Mount Ebal. A large temple platform is still visible today, but it dates from the 13th century B.C.E., and is most likely dedicated to Baal, the preeminent fertility god of Canaan.

Unlike Hazor, Shechem in the mid-19th century B.C.E. was not fortified. Its prominence, however, is attested to by an Egyptian stone monument, or stela, dedicated to a warrior named Sobkkhu. This officer boasts of his participation in the military campaigns of Senusret III, the pharaoh whose rule (1836–1818 B.C.E.) spanned the time in which Abraham may have dwelled in Canaan. Senusret not only expanded Egypt's territory southward into Nubia, he also marched east to reaffirm Egypt's political influence over Canaan and Syria. Along the way, the monument states, the king invested Shechem, or Sekmem. Whether this involved an actual conquest by battle or merely a show of force is not known. In years to come, many of Egypt's pharaohs would periodically venture out from their palaces at

This 12th-dynasty pectoral shows Amenemhet III smiting an enemy beneath the Nekhbet, a patron goddess of the Pharaohs.

ca 1918 B.C.E.
Senusret I becomes Pharaoh

ca 1900 B.C.E.
Assyrians set up trading centers throughout the Middle East

ca 1876 B.C.E.
Amenemhet II comes to power in Egypt

ca 1800 B.C.E.
Hebrew clans begin migrating to Egypt

THE LAND OF CANAAN

Abraham's Canaan, or Kena'an in the Bible, was a sliver of land squeezed between the Jordan River and the Mediterranean Sea, a narrow corridor of fertile valleys and dry highlands that connected the Old Babylonian Empire in Mesopotamia with the Egypt of the 12th and 13th dynasties. Small wonder, then, that the chief source of wealth for the people of Canaan was the sale of goods and services to the large caravans that trekked through their land on their way to the markets of Thebes and Babylon.

Egyptian records of the time refer to Canaan as Retenu; its nomadic tribes are contemptuously described as Abiru or Habiru—translated as "sand-dwellers" or "migrants"—which may or may not be the root of the word "Hebrew." The words *eres-kena'an* (land of Canaan) are found in a cuneiform inscription dated as early as the 16th century B.C.E. Nevertheless, the Canaan of the early second millennium B.C.E. was a sparsely populated place. Most of the urban settlements were located closer to the coast. The principal cities were Hazor in the north; Megiddo in the Valley of Jezreel; Beth Shan in the northern Jordan Valley; and Socoh, Aphek, and Joppa in the coastal region. Nomads and their flocks kept mainly to the central hills, moving from Hazor to Shechem (the Egyptian Sekmem), Ai, and Bethel in the Samarian mountains before they descended to Hebron and the desert farther south, near Beersheba.

The Jordan River Valley and the Transjordan plateau stretch beneath the ancient fortress of Beth Shan.

Thebes to march down the dusty roads of Canaan, ensuring that everyone still understood who was in charge.

Abraham's journey, the Bible says, was far from over. He traveled farther south, to Bethel and Hebron, where there were pastures to be found in the Judean hills. At each major city along the way, Abraham erected an altar to the glory of El. In wintertime, the Bible notes, he led his herd to the rim of the Negev, where grass and shrubs would sprout during the winter rains. This movement between the mountains and the Negev continues throughout the Bible's account of Abraham's story, and quite possibly reflects the seasonal migrations of nomadic clans and their herds in ancient Canaan. During the hot summer, the herdsmen would have looked for pastures at higher elevations, either in the southern highlands around Hebron or farther north, between Bethel and Shechem. During the winter, clans moved their herds south to the Negev, where grazing lands were sustained by winter rains.

Abraham's Sojourn in Egypt

AND THEN, SAYS GENESIS, "there was a famine in the land; so Abram went down to Egypt to reside there as an alien" (Genesis 12:10). Abraham had little choice but to follow the other nomadic tribes into "refugee camps" just across the border with Egypt, lest his flocks perish. Usually their journey led to the Nile Delta, where there was water and pasture aplenty. Indeed, we may have a vivid record of just such a caravan of refugees in a tomb found near the hamlet of Beni Hasan, some 200 miles south of Cairo. In 1890, British excavators discovered a set of rooms belonging to a local governor named Khnumhotep II. The tomb was decorated with brightly colored scenes typical of an Egyptian nobleman's life—hunting in the marshes, overseeing the harvest, and heading out for a night of celebration. Hieroglyphics reveal that the governor was appointed to his position by "the King of Upper and Lower Egypt," Nubkaure, also known as Amenemhet II, who reigned from 1876 to 1842 B.C.E.

I loved the corn god.
I have grown the grain
in every golden valley
where the Nile entreated me;
none hungered in my day,
none thirsted, and all men
were well content.
They praised me, saying,
"Wise are his commands."

Instruction of Pharaoh Amenemhet

HOW A CHIEFTAIN MIGHT LOOK

During the time associated with Abraham, how might a Semitic chieftain have looked? This copper portrait of a man gives us an idea. Its highly realistic features—heavy-lidded eyes, distinctive nose and lips, and carefully coiffed beard—indicate that this piece most likely represents a prominent person, not an idealized image of a god. Despite its almost Hellenistic realism, the head is still very much the craftsmanship of a third-millennium B.C.E. artisan; it is cast as an almost solid piece of copper.

One of the tomb's wall paintings shows something else entirely. It depicts a long train of people, surrounded by their livestock, who are strikingly different from the lithe and elegantly dressed Egyptian figures. They use awkward, thick woolen coats to cover their light skin. The women's hair is long enough to cover their shoulders, while the men sport pointed beards. Despite their formidable appearance, they appear quite humble—almost as if they are pleading with the Egyptian men in the scene.

Accompanying hieroglyphs note that these are the Abiru, which literally means "sand-dwellers" and should probably be translated as "migrants." The term Abiru, or Habiru, which returns quite often in both Egyptian and Akkadian texts, may be the root of the word "Hebrew," though this notion is contested. What is clear, however, is that the figures in the painting are nomads whom famine has once again driven to the portals of the Egyptian Empire. At this very moment, they are pleading with the Egyptian border guards to let them in. The leader of the tribe is identified as Abishai. He was no relation to Abraham's tribe, even though there is a tantalizing reference to "Abishai, the son of Zeruiah" in I Samuel, many hundreds of years later.

This snapshot of a Semitic tribe from Canaan, appealing to the Egyptian authorities for temporary asylum, presents an interesting question. Why would such a painting exist in the tomb of so august a figure as Khnumhotep? Arguably, his duties included the command of one or several border garrisons

he remains of ancient Ugarit were first excavated in 929 near its former port, Ra's Shamrah, on Syria's Mediterranean coast.

rom this view of the funerary complex in aqqara, Egypt, the stepped pyramid of King Djoser ca 2650–2631 B.C.E.) rises in the distance.

Ancient Beersheba was excavated near Tel es-Sheba in he southern Negev, with the remains of city dwellings rom the Middle Iron Age (1000–900 B.C.E.).

he Canaanite temple complex of Hazor, in northern Galilee, is believed to have been destroyed in the 13th century B.C.E. at the time of the Israelite settlement in Canaan.

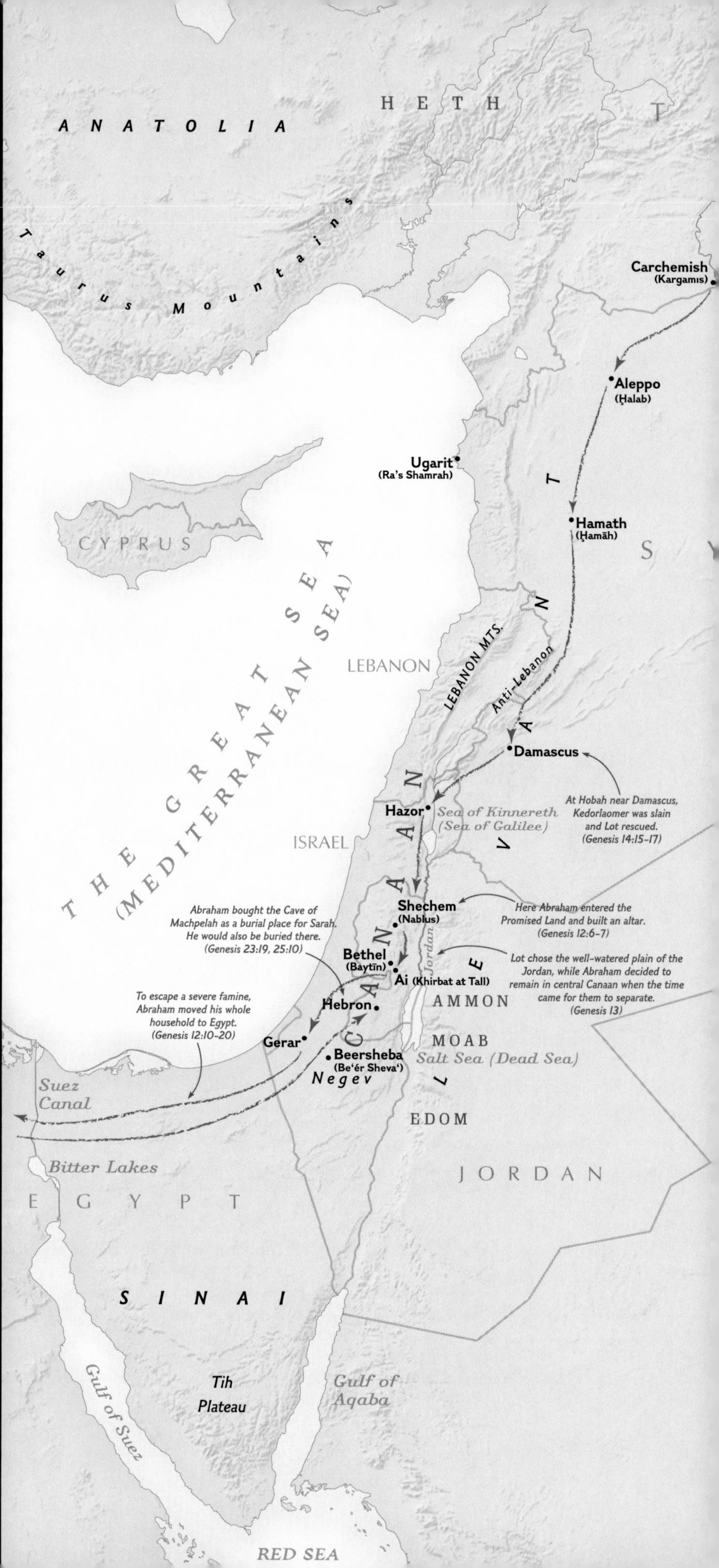

ANATOLIA
HETH
Taurus Mountains
Carchemish (Kargamış)
Aleppo (Ḥalab)
Ugarit (Ra's Shamrah)
CYPRUS
Hamath (Ḥamāh)
THE GREAT SEA (MEDITERRANEAN SEA)
LEBANON
LEBANON MTS.
Anti-Lebanon
Damascus
At Hobah near Damascus, Kedorlaomer was slain and Lot rescued. (Genesis 14:15-17)
Hazor
Sea of Kinnereth (Sea of Galilee)
ISRAEL
CANAAN
LEVANT
Shechem (Nablus)
Here Abraham entered the Promised Land and built an altar. (Genesis 12:6-7)
Abraham bought the Cave of Machpelah as a burial place for Sarah. He would also be buried there. (Genesis 23:19, 25:10)
Bethel (Baytīn)
Ai (Khirbat at Tall)
Jordan
Lot chose the well-watered plain of the Jordan, while Abraham decided to remain in central Canaan when the time came for them to separate. (Genesis 13)
AMMON
Hebron
To escape a severe famine, Abraham moved his whole household to Egypt. (Genesis 12:10-20)
Gerar
Beersheba (Be'ér Sheva')
MOAB
Salt Sea (Dead Sea)
Negev
Suez Canal
EDOM
Bitter Lakes
JORDAN
EGYPT
SINAI
Tih Plateau
Gulf of Aqaba
Gulf of Suez
RED SEA

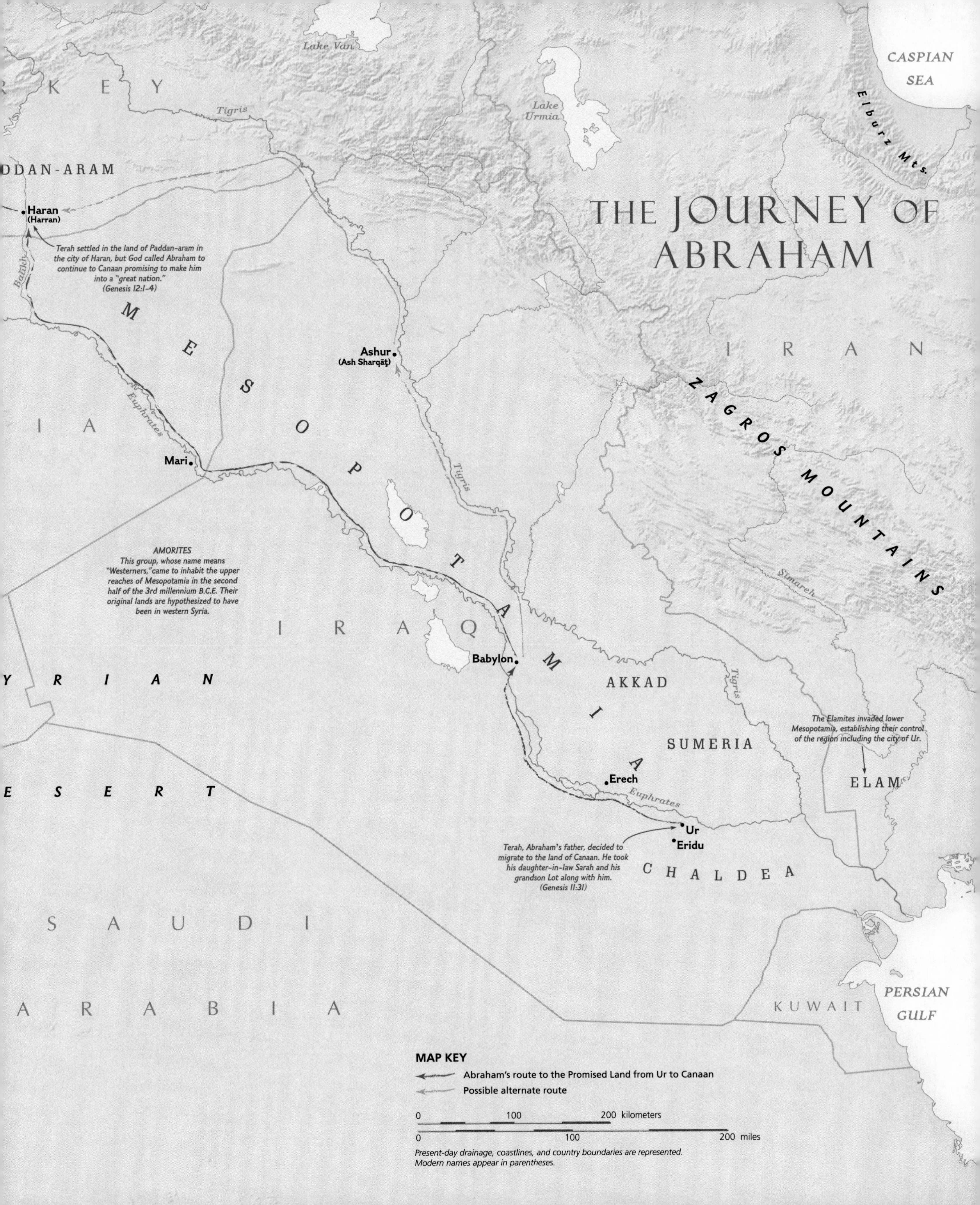

THE JOURNEY OF ABRAHAM
CASPIAN SEA
Elburz Mts.
Lake Van
Lake Urmia
Tigris
DDAN-ARAM
Haran
(Harran)
Terah settled in the land of Paddan-aram in the city of Haran, but God called Abraham to continue to Canaan promising to make him into a "great nation." (Genesis 12:1-4)
Balikh
MESOPOTAMIA
Euphrates
Ashur
(Ash Sharqāṭ)
IRAN
ZAGROS MOUNTAINS
Mari
Tigris
AMORITES
This group, whose name means "Westerners," came to inhabit the upper reaches of Mesopotamia in the second half of the 3rd millennium B.C.E. Their original lands are hypothesized to have been in western Syria.
Simareh
IRAQ
Babylon
AKKAD
Tigris
YRIAN
SUMERIA
The Elamites invaded lower Mesopotamia, establishing their control of the region including the city of Ur.
ELAM
Erech
Euphrates
ESERT
Ur
Eridu
Terah, Abraham's father, decided to migrate to the land of Canaan. He took his daughter-in-law Sarah and his grandson Lot along with him. (Genesis 11:31)
CHALDEA
SAUDI ARABIA
KUWAIT
PERSIAN GULF
MAP KEY
Abraham's route to the Promised Land from Ur to Canaan
Possible alternate route
0 100 200 kilometers
0 100 200 miles
Present-day drainage, coastlines, and country boundaries are represented.
Modern names appear in parentheses.

THE SCOURGE OF FAMINE

The Bible often refers to famine; the word appears no less than 24 times in the Book of Genesis alone. As Egyptian records attest, famine was by no means a rare occurrence, often leading to social disorder and wholesale migrations. The uncertainty of rainfall, on which all agriculture in Canaan depended, was the principal factor, but other calamities—such as wind, hail, mildew, disease, and insect pests—could also cause a harvest to fail. In addition, farmers often had to cultivate on rocky terrain or loose topsoil that was vulnerable to the elements.

Since grain was the principal crop, a poor harvest had an immediate impact on Canaan's food supply. Even Egypt was not immune. Archaeologists have found evidence of an extensive drought that may coincide with the period of Abraham's sojourn into Egypt. Some climatologists have linked this drought to persistent low flooding levels of the Nile during the Old Kingdom. The spread of iron plows after 1200 B.C.E. improved crop yields since farmers could now break the hard soil more deeply and effectively prior to seeding; but the uncertainty of rain cycles remained.

In the Book of Genesis, famine is a weapon often wielded by God to punish people for wickedness or disobedience. Later, the prophets use the threat of famine to bring rebellious people to heel (Jeremiah 14:15).

Dating from the 5th dynasty (ca 2450–2325 B.C.E.), during Egypt's Old Kingdom, this relief is believed to represent Bedouin dying of hunger in the desert.

that guarded the sovereign soil of Egypt. As such, he would be charged with issuing temporary permits to foreign tribes desperate to reach the watered plains of the delta. Perhaps this painting was meant to depict him as a man of power and compassion, not averse to turning a sympathetic ear to peaceful nomads who came to his door in times of crisis. And indeed, one of the officials in the painting is clutching a scroll that may be a visa, allowing the tribes to pass.

Clearly the wall painting suggests that caravans from the east were bound to arouse the interest of high officials. Genesis tells us that "When Abram entered Egypt the Egyptians saw that [Sarah] was very beautiful. When the officials of Pharaoh saw her, they praised her to Pharaoh" (Genesis 12:14-15).

And Pharaoh, Genesis says, is taken with Sarah's beauty. Abraham had anticipated this, and had urged his wife to "say you are my sister," so that "my life may

be spared on your account" (Genesis 12:12-13). Thus ensues a liaison between Sarah and the ruler of Egypt. Abraham is well compensated, receiving livestock and slaves in return.

Nevertheless, the Bible, foreshadowing what will come to pass in the Book of Exodus, says Egypt was visited by plagues. Pharaoh discovers the truth—the object of his desire belongs to someone else. He summons Abraham and asks, "Why did you not tell me that she was your wife?" (Genesis 12:18). Genesis does not record what Abraham said in his defense, but Pharaoh is mollified—and more so than Abraham could have dared hope for. The couple is allowed to leave Egypt unmolested; Abraham is also permitted to keep the many gifts that the pharaoh had bestowed upon him and his wife—including a young female slave who will soon become a key figure in the story.

And so, Genesis continues, Abraham departs from the Nile Delta—unaware that his great-grandson, Joseph, will return one day to this very region to become the second most powerful figure in the land.

Depicting a Semitic tribe asking permission to enter Egypt, this mural was copied from a Beni Hasan tomb that belonged to a servant of Pharaoh Amenemhet II (ca 1876–1842 B.C.E.).

EGYPT IN THE TIME OF ABRAHAM

AT THIS STAGE OF THE BIBLICAL STORY, Egypt rather than Mesopotamia exerts a powerful influence on Canaan. Compared to the more basic culture of the Canaanites, Egypt's Middle Kingdom civilization dazzled the world, even as its economic and political power entered a period of steady decline. The quality of Egypt's art remained unchallenged, exemplified by a magnificent black granite statue of Pharaoh Senusret III of the 12th dynasty. The work was executed around 1830 B.C.E., which is roughly contemporary with the putative journey of Abraham into Egypt. The heavy eyelids, the somber expression, and the firm mouth of the king suggest a weariness with power that stands in stark contrast to the formalized portraits of the Old Kingdom. Another exquisite work from this period is the statue of the official Ankhrekhu. Though the features are realistic, the hair, hands, and vestments are stylized in an almost modern manner.

Senusret III exemplifies the 12th-dynasty kings who, of necessity, turned away from grandiose funerary monuments to concentrate on the economy and infrastructure of Egypt. Senusret pushed through a number of agricultural initiatives, including the digging of the Bahr Yusef canal in the Faiyum and the broadening of a bypass canal at the First Cataract of the Nile. He also expanded Egypt's territory south, at the expense of Nubia, and conducted a punitive campaign against Syria. During the latter, he passed through the Canaanite town of Shechem, where the Bible says Abraham would build the first altar to God.

The black statue of Pharaoh Senusret III (ca 1836–1818 B.C.E.) offers a vivid contrast to the quartzite figure of the official Ankhrekhu created during the same period.

SARAH AND HAGAR

The Jordan River runs through lush terrain in northern Israel, near the lands Lot claimed for his own in the biblical story.

IN GENESIS 13, ABRAHAM returns to Bethel, in Canaan. Pharaoh's gifts have made him a wealthy man (Genesis 13:2). His family and their herds have multiplied to a size that is well beyond the normal capacity of local wells and pastures. Abraham decides that his tribe should split into two clans, one under his leadership and the other following Lot, his nephew. Lot gets to pick the region in which he would like to dwell. With a keen eye for good land, Lot chooses the irrigated plains of Jordan, running all the way down to the Dead Sea, and settles in a place called Sodom. Abraham accepts his choice and retraces his steps, back to the hill country where he had camped earlier.

But, as Genesis recounts, the travels and travails of Lot are not over. The fertile land of the Transjordan is fought over by four kings. In one battle, the city of Sodom falls and Lot is taken prisoner. His kinsmen flee back to Abraham and plead his nephew's case. Abraham doesn't think twice. He rallies his slaves and "trained men," some 300 strong, and attacks the enemy's encampment near Dan by night. Lot and all "his goods, and the women and the people" are set free (Genesis 14:16).

Duly impressed, one of the principal leaders in the region, the priest-king Melchizedek of Salem (quite possibly

ca 1900 B.C.E.
Cuneiform script is streamlined to about 600 characters

ca 1894 B.C.E.
Sumu-Abum establishes a new dynasty with Babel at its center, thus beginning the Babylonian Era

ca 1850 B.C.E.
Egyptians undertake irrigation projects in Faiyum and other regions

ca 1842 B.C.E.
Reign of Pharaoh Amenemhet II ends

[The Lord] brought him outside and said, "Look toward the heaven and count the stars, if you are able to count them." Then he said to him, "So shall your descendants be." (Genesis 15:5)

Jerusalem), returns to pay homage to Abraham. He prays that Abraham be blessed "by God Most High," or El Elyon. This appellation was customary for the Canaanite god El (Genesis 14:19).

The Bible then tells of Abraham's return to the city of Hebron. Hebron is one of the oldest sites in Canaan, perched some 3,000 feet above sea level on a picturesque hill of vineyards and olive trees. "Hebron" is derived from the Hebrew word *haver*, or friend, as Abraham is often called by the Bible "a friend of God." Interestingly, the Arabic name for Hebron, Al Khalil, has the same meaning. Archaeologists have uncovered evidence of a settlement on the site dating from the 19th or 18th century B.C.E.—roughly the time when a family like Abraham's may have come down to settle on its fertile hills.

Abraham and Sarah are childless. Abraham is troubled. If he dies without a son, how will the great nation that God had promised him come about? Faced with this quandary, a Mesopotamian chieftain such as Abraham had several options. As numerous ancient texts, including the Code of Hammurabi, indicate, his first option was divorce. The husband needed only to return "the full amount of her marriage-price and … the dowry which she brought from her father's house" (Laws 138). A second option was to take one of his wife's female slaves and designate her as a "surrogate mother." In Sumer as well as in Babylonia, this practice was well established. An Assyrian marriage contract from the 19th century B.C.E. stipulates that if the bride cannot bear children within two years of the wedding, she must purchase a slave woman to produce a child for her husband. In Genesis, too, it is Sarah who suggests this arrangement to her husband, and who picks one of her maids to perform this service. The name of this girl is Hagar.

The selection of Hagar will have significant consequences for the future history of three great faiths. Genesis is careful to note that Hagar is not a Hebrew but an Egyptian slave girl, whom Pharaoh gave to Abraham when it was Sarah who served as "surrogate wife" to the Egyptian king (Genesis 16:1). Abraham agrees to the arrangement, and Sarah takes Hagar to her husband's tent "as a wife." The term in Hebrew is *'ishshâ*, which can mean either "wife" or "concubine."

This eighth-century-B.C.E. stone relief from Susa, in present-day Iran, depicts a woman being waited on by her female slave.

As the Bible's narrative continues, Hagar is shown to be with child. The slave girl now knows she controls the very future of Abraham's tribe. In fact, says Genesis, Hagar "looked with contempt on her mistress" (Genesis 16:4). The 18th-century B.C.E. Code of Hammurabi anticipates such a situation. "If a female slave has claimed equality with her mistress because she bore children," it stipulates, "her mistress may not sell her," but she may put the girl in her place by marking her "with the slave-mark" (Laws 146). In Genesis, too, Sarah knows that she cannot dismiss Hagar, but she retaliates for Hagar's behavior by "[dealing] harshly with her, and so [Hagar] ran away from her" (Genesis 16:6).

At this moment, Genesis says, God intervenes—the first of two such interventions to save the life of Hagar and her son—by sending an angel to Hagar at an oasis "on the way to Shur," which we assume was somewhere on the road between Beersheba and the Egyptian frontier. The angel of the Lord orders her to return to Sarah and tells her that she "shall bear a son; you shall call him Ishmael, for the Lord has given heed to your affliction" (Genesis 16:11). The name Ishmael, a contraction of *El* (God) and *shama'* (hears), means "God hears (me)." In addition, the angel holds out the promise that God will

ca 1822 B.C.E.
Rim-Sin is the last Sumerian king to rule

ca 1800 B.C.E.
Assyrians use a series of signal fires to communicate across long distances

ca 1800 B.C.E.
Settlements in Canaan begin to fortify themselves

ca 1763 B.C.E.
Hammurabi establishes the Babylonian Empire

POLYGAMY IN THE BIBLE

Throughout the Old Testament we read of patriarchs taking several wives. One of the first instances is when Genesis tells us that Lamech, a descendant of Cain, took two wives: "the name of the one [was] Adah, and the name of the other Zillah" (Genesis 4:19). Such polygamy was most likely motivated by the need to produce sufficient children to control the tribe's principal asset: the herd of domesticated livestock. For farmers, too, one's harvest could be limited by the number of children able to help till and reap the fields.

Childbirth was fraught with danger for both new mothers and infants. Many children were carried away by disease while still in their infancy, and many women died during childbirth. Tribes practiced polygamy as a way of sustaining themselves and ensuring the survival of the clan.

If a wife were infertile, as in the case of Abraham and his first wife, Sarah, the husband was entitled to take a female servant or slave in order to maintain his progeny. This motive is why Abraham could take Hagar as a second wife, lest his family line become extinct.

However, a man's ability to take multiple wives was not without boundaries. The conclusion of a marriage required the payment of a dowry to the bride's family, meaning the number of wives a man could take was often limited by his financial means.

The practice of polygamy would continue well into the age of the monarchy, when both David and Solomon took many foreign wives as a way of solidifying an alliance with a tribe or state. The Bible alleges that Solomon's harem included 700 princesses and 300 concubines (I Kings 11:3), a likely exaggeration. After the Babylonian Exile, polygamy fell into disfavor and monogamy became the ideal.

A Royal Palace in Morocco, painted by the French artist Benjamin Jean Joseph Constant (1845–1902), shows how Western minds imagined polygamy in ancient times.

"so greatly multiply your offspring that they cannot be counted for multitude" (Genesis 16:10). With this the battle lines are drawn, for the Lord will soon give a very similar pledge to Sarah's future son, Isaac.

And so, says Genesis, Hagar returns. Abraham somehow keeps the warring factions apart, and the young slave girl bears a son, whom Abraham names Ishmael. The years pass, and Ishmael grows up to be a fine lad, the pride of his father.

When the boy is 13, Genesis 17 recounts, God reappears before Abraham and reaffirms his covenant that Abraham shall be "the ancestor of a multitude of nations." To seal this covenant, God asks Abraham to circumcise himself as well as Ishmael and all the male members of his household. From that day forward, every male baby born to Jewish parents is circumcised on the eighth day after birth. Then God makes another promise, miraculous though it may seem, and tells Abraham that his wife will have a son of her own.

Abraham, says Genesis, "fell on his face and laughed, and said to himself, 'Can a child be born to a man who is

This clay tablet from Ugarit, dated to around 1250 B.C.E., is a royal decree confirming the divorce of King Ammistomru from Benteshina, the daughter of the King of Amurru.

a hundred years old?'" (Genesis 17:17). The episode is reminiscent of a Ugaritic text called the Epic of Aqhat. It tells the story of an elderly king named Danel, who is left without a son and heir. He fervently prays for his wife to conceive, and Baal, the god of storms and rain, pleads to El, the supreme god of Canaan, on his behalf. El responds, "Let him kiss his wife, and she will conceive; in her embracing she will become pregnant." Danel's wife then gives birth to a son, who is named Aqhat. The young child is then presented with a bow, with which he will soon become an expert—a small detail that will also appear in the biblical story.

Soon after God's promise of a son, Genesis 18 places Abraham in the Plain of Mamre, near Hebron, in a wide and fertile valley where his servants are tending to his many flocks. He is dozing in the heat of the afternoon, sitting in the shade of an oak tree, when three mysterious strangers appear. Abraham hospitably offers them water, "a little bread," and the shade of his tree. The humble piece of bread is actually a magnificent feast of meat from a freshly slaughtered calf, sweet cakes, and milk. Thus refreshed, the three guests also predict that Sarah shall bear Abraham a son. This time it is Sarah who bursts out laughing, saying, "After I have grown old, and my husband is old, shall I have pleasure?" "Is anything too wonderful for the Lord?" is the reply (Genesis 18:12-14).

True enough, Genesis says, Sarah conceives and presents Abraham with a son. Abraham calls him Isaac (or Yishaq), which means, appropriately, "he who laughs."

Now one question looms large in the biblical story: Which son shall succeed the father as chieftain? Hagar claims it rightfully should be Ishmael: He is Abraham's firstborn, and he is 13 years older than Isaac and will soon be mature enough to take over the leadership from his aging father. Sarah insists that Isaac should be the one: As the issue of Abraham and his first wife, regardless of his age or position, Isaac has the greater legitimacy.

That such disputes often arose among Mesopotamian clans is underscored by certain edicts in the Code of Hammurabi. Such laws state that if the father "during his lifetime ever said 'My children!' to the issue whom the slave bore him," thus treating them on an equal level with the children of his wife, then the slave's children shared equally in the inheritance (Laws 170). Genesis makes it clear that Abraham named the boy right after birth, thereby accepting him as his legitimate heir. Nevertheless, the Code of

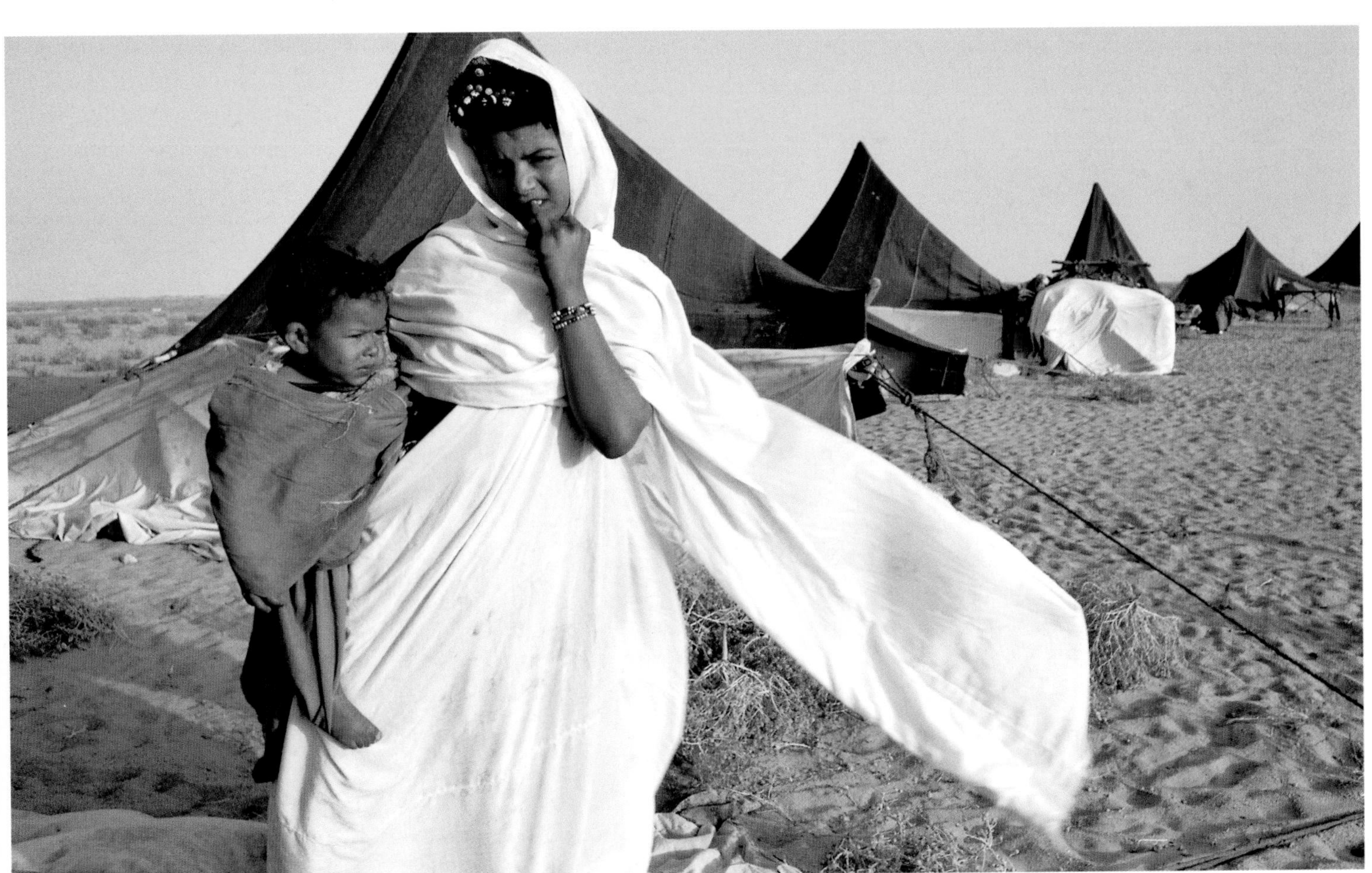

Facing challenges that Hagar and Ishmael might have confronted, this modern-day Bedouin mother and child return to their tent before a sandstorm hits.

BAKING BREAD

THREE STRANGERS APPROACH ABRAHAM while he sits in the shade of an oak tree. In the biblical account, these are three messengers who who predict the future birth of Abraham and Sarah's son Isaac.

In the story, Abraham puts on a display of hospitality for the three visitors. As they approach his tent, he offers them a meal. Though he warns the repast will be simple (water and "a little bread"), the servings are quite elaborate: fresh bread, milk, and above all, the meat from a slaughtered calf—a rare luxury. He even specifies to his wife Sarah how she should make the bread: "Make ready quickly three measures of choice flour, knead it, and make cakes" (Genesis 18:6).

Abraham's instructions accurately describe the practice of making bread in Canaan. The women would take kernels of grain (translated as "corn" in the King James Bible) and grind them into flour using a stone mill. The flour was mixed with water and sometimes leavened with yeast, using the spoiled baking from days before.

The resulting dough was then kneaded into thin, round cakes to decrease cooking time. The cakes were fed into a simple oven of baked earth or stone, which were heated by coals or fire. An effective process, this baking method would remain largely the same in Canaan well into the era of the New Testament. In the cities and larger villages, however, bread was often baked and sold at community ovens by professional bakers.

This diagram shows a common floorplan for ancient bakeries in Egypt. Baking methods changed very little for thousands of years.

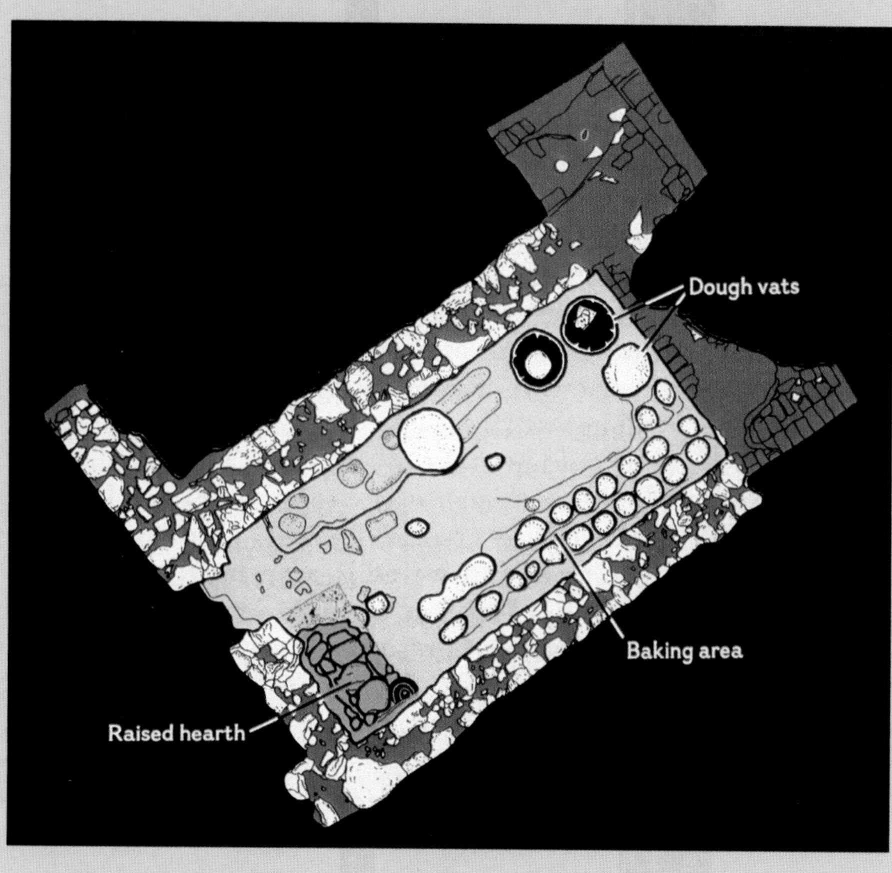

Hammurabi allows that the firstborn of the first wife could be entitled to preferential treatment.

According to the Bible, this is also God's intent. "As for Ishmael, I have heard you," God assures Abraham, playing on the meaning of the name Ishmael; "he shall be the father of twelve princes, and I will make him a great nation. But my own covenant I will establish with Isaac" (Genesis 17:20-21).

Thus emboldened, Sarah makes her move. She tells her husband to "cast out this slave woman with her son" (Genesis 12:10). Dismissing a surrogate mother and her offspring without compensation was a serious matter, however. The Laws of Lipit-Ishtar, which precede the Code of Hammurabi by some 200 years, state that "if a man's wife has not borne him children but a harlot from the public square has borne him children, he shall provide grain, oil, and clothing for that harlot." In the Bible story, however, Abraham merely gives bread and water to Hagar, "along with the child," and sends her away (Genesis 21:14).

Before long, Hagar is lost. After several days of aimless wandering in the Negev, south of Beersheba, she collapses near some shrubs. Hagar cannot bear to see her son die, so she gently places him in the shade of a nearby tree, then falls to her knees and cries. Fortunately, God takes pity on her. "Do not be afraid," says an angel of the Lord. "Come, lift up the boy and hold him fast with your hand, for I will make a great nation of him" (Genesis 21:17-18). God then opens Hagar's eyes and she sees a well nearby. They rush over and drink their fill. Thus fortified, Genesis assures us, the boy "lived in the wilderness, and became an expert with the bow. He lived in the wilderness of Paran" (Genesis 21:20-21). Paran was the

OPPOSITE: This view of an escarpment in the Negev, in the southern part of modern Israel, is the setting for Hagar's journey.

[T]he angel of God called to Hagar from Heaven, and said, … "Come, lift up the boy, and hold him fast with your hand, for I will make a great nation of him." (Genesis 21:17-18)

northeastern region of the Sinai Peninsula, centered on the oasis of Kadesh-barnea. Kadesh was a seven-day march from the Egyptian border at Pelusium (now Tell el Farama), using the ancient trade route along the Mediterranean coast. Hagar went there, says Genesis 21:21, when the boy reached maturity, and she "got a wife for him from the land of Egypt."

Two Traditions Diverge

"I WILL MAKE of you a great nation." The Israelite, Christian, and Muslim traditions diverge here, though many centuries will separate the compilations of their scriptures. The three faiths acknowledge Abraham as their spiritual father, but Genesis continues its story through Isaac, Jacob, and the 12 tribes of Israel, which carries through into the writings of Christianity. Much later, Islamic scripture follows the lineage of Ishmael, arguing that since Ishmael was born before Isaac, he is the legitimate heir of his father and thus the true object of God's covenant.

Indeed, Genesis confirms that Ishmael will become the progenitor of many Arab peoples. His sons are named "Nebaioth, the firstborn of Ishmael; and Kedar, Adbeel, Mibsam, Mishma, Dumah, Massa, Hadad, Tema, Jetur, Naphish, and Kedemah" (Genesis 25:13-15). Many of these names reappear as the names of Arab tribes in Assyrian as well as in Muslim texts. The Nebaioth, for example, are called Nabat in Arabic; in Roman times they would be known as the Nabataeans. Kedar will become the leader of the Qedarites (Qaydhar in Arabic), while Tema may be linked to the great oasis of Tayma in northwest Arabia. What's more, it is a caravan of "Ishmaelites" that later in Genesis carry off Isaac's grandson Joseph to Egypt.

The Muslim tradition also continues the story of Hagar, just as Genesis continues the narrative of Abraham and Sarah.

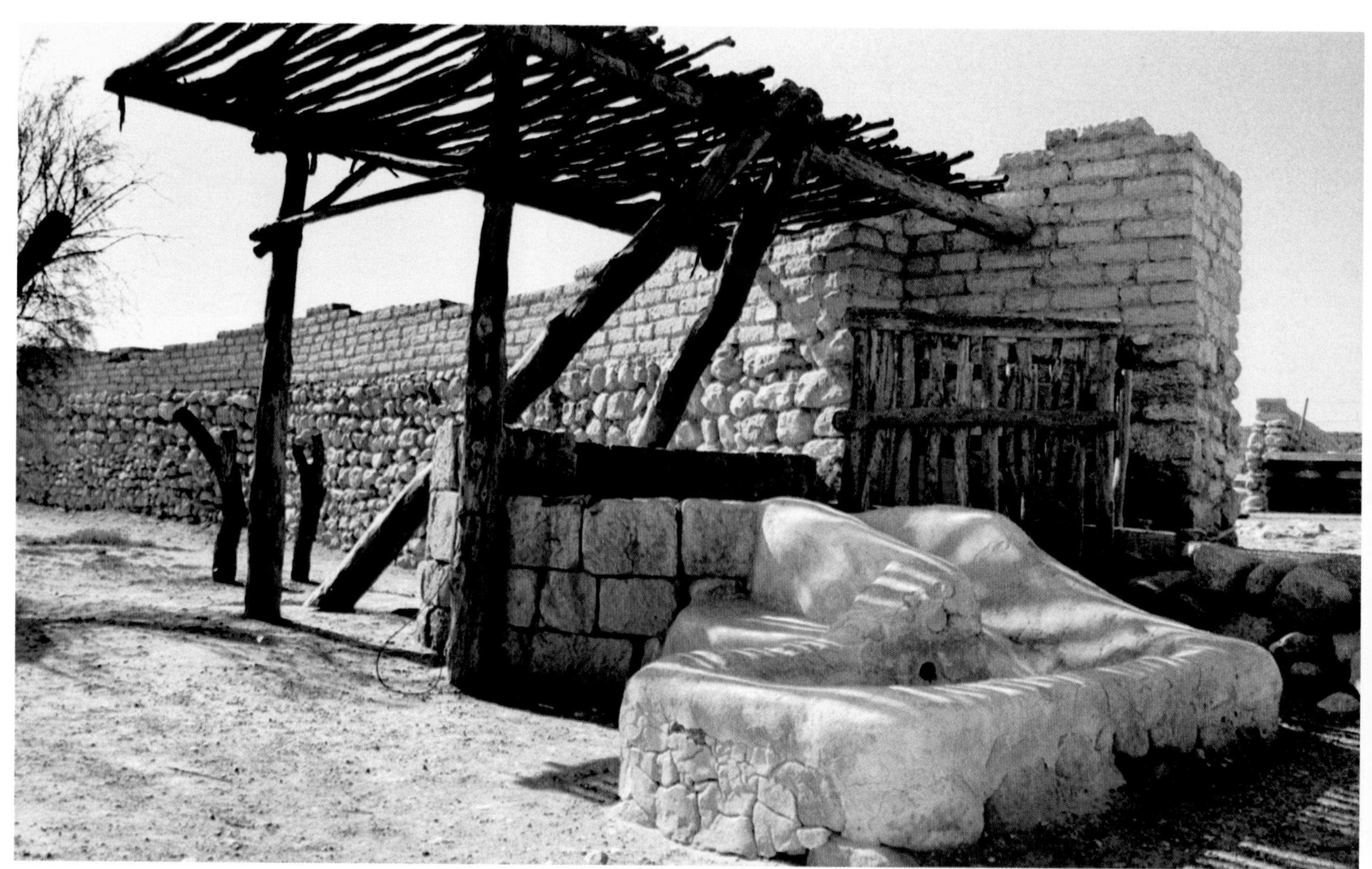

Located outside the city walls of ancient Beersheba, this partial reconstruction shows what a deep well might have looked like in Abraham's time.

THE IMPORTANCE OF WELLS

In a land such as Canaan, which was mostly dependent on rainfall, a spring-fed well was a prized possession. Such a well could provide a steady water supply for humans and animals alike through all seasons and facilitated the growth of crops. However, they required constant maintenance and sometimes rationing. Water rights were fiercely defended. Village chieftains like Laban often chose to close off the well with a stone (Genesis 29:2-3) or to keep its location secret. Abraham secured his access to a well in Beersheba by offering the local chieftain "seven ewe lambs." A village well was also the center of social life. Women congregated there to fill their skins and vessels, and hear the latest gossip.

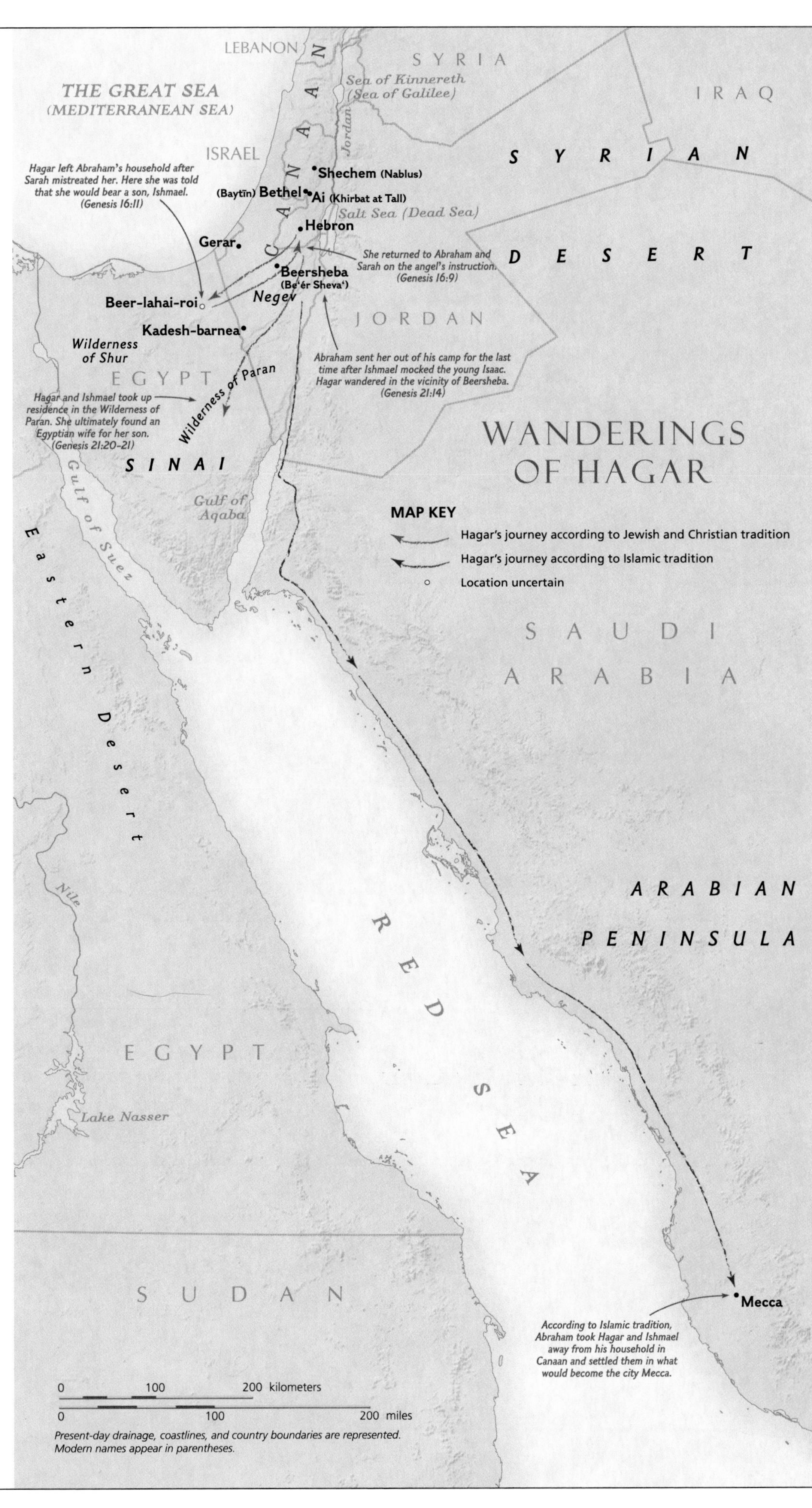

According to Muslim authors, Abraham (or Ibrahim in the Koran) accompanies Hagar (Hajar) and their infant son, Ishmael (Ishmail), on their journey into the desert, crossing over the Transjordan plateau into the Hijaz region of the Arabian Peninsula. Once in the desert they soon run out of water. Abraham leaves Hagar and his son to search for a well. Hagar searches for water as well, moving from the mountain of As Safa to the hill of Al Marwa. She runs back and forth seven times—a ritual commemorated by Muslims during the annual hajj, or pilgrimage, in Mecca. Suddenly, water gushes forth from the ground. This well is called Zam-zam, and its discovery ultimately led to a settlement named Mecca. God then orders Abraham and Ishmael to build a "House of Pilgrimage for men and a place of security" (Koran 2:125). The sacred Ka'bah, the holiest place in Islam, still stands in the center of Mecca.

Though the Abraham narratives in the Bible and Koran go their separate ways, the two books periodically intersect. Unlike the Bible, the Koran is not one continuous, linear narrative. Time and again, the Holy Scripture of Islam harks back to leading figures like Ibrahim, Yusuf (Joseph), Mûsa (Moses), and Isa (Jesus).

THE FINAL TEST

These tree trunks in the vicinity of 'En-gedi are encrusted with salt from the Dead Sea, which has a 22 to 30 percent saline content.

MANY OTHER GREAT events take place in the Bible while the tragedy of Sarah and Hagar is played out. In the Cities of the Plain, where Abraham's nephew Lot settled, the inhabitants engage in such depravity that God, deeming them beyond redemption, orders them destroyed. Genesis never quite elaborates on the nature of the sinful ways of these cities, but it mentions two by name. "How great is the outcry against Sodom and Gomorrah ... !" laments the Lord (Genesis 18:20). Abraham then sits down with God to bargain, since he wants to save the city of his nephew Lot. In the end, God offers that if just ten righteous citizens can be found in Sodom, he will relent.

But the city's fate is sealed when the men of Sodom attack two angels sent by God to investigate. For Abraham's sake, the angels attempt to save Lot and his family. Lot, his wife, and two daughters are rushed out into the plain, toward the city of Zoar. They are under strict orders not to turn and look back. But as the Lord proceeds to shower fire and brimstone from the heavens, Lot's wife cannot contain her curiosity. She looks back—and is instantly turned into a pillar of salt.

Where were Sodom and Gomorrah? There is no consensus among scholars.

ca 1800 B.C.E.
Babylonians adopt the lunar calendar

ca 1790 B.C.E.
Rise of the Hittites in Asia Minor

ca 1782 B.C.E.
Semitic immigration into Egypt increases

ca 1770 B.C.E.
Babylon is the region's largest city

Then the Lord rained on Sodom and Gomorrah sulfur and fire ... he overthrew those cities, and all the Plain, and all the inhabitants of the cities, and what grew on the ground. But Lot's wife, behind him, looked back, and she became a pillar of salt. (Genesis 19:24-26)

An earlier reference to "bitumen pits" (Genesis 14:10), suggests the southern end of the Dead Sea, which was devastated by an earthquake between 1900 and 2100 B.C.E. This upheaval could have unleashed showers of steaming tar—and thus inspired the Bible's account of the two cities' destruction. Gomorrah is sometimes associated with the ancient settlement of Numeira, and Sodom with Bab edh-Dhra. Both of these settlements along the Dead Sea were excavated from the 1970s onward by archaeologists of Harvard University. Perhaps the image of Lot's wife frozen into a salt pillar was suggested to the Bible's authors by actual piles of salt that, in fact, are present in the region to this day. The memory of Sodom also lives on in a nearby salt massif called Har Sedom (or *Jabal Usdum* in Arabic).

Abraham, the Bible continues, then drifts farther south, to the city of Beersheba, where he decides to settle his family. Springs and wells are a precious rarity in the desert, and the arrival of Abraham's herd of thirsty goats and sheep is reported with alarm to the local ruler, King Abimelech. Abraham is summoned, resulting in another bargaining session. In the end, Abraham and Abimelech swear an oath by which Abraham grants the king seven ewe lambs in return for the right to use the well. This, Genesis explains, is the meaning of Beersheba: "the well of seven," or alternatively, "the well of the oath."

In 1969, ancient Beersheba was discovered at Tel Sheva, some three miles east of modern Be'er Sheva', the major city of Israel's Negev. According to the archaeologist Yohanan Aharoni, the settlement was first inhabited as early as the fourth millennium B.C.E., though the remains that are visible today probably date from the late 12th century B.C.E., some 600 years after the putative arrival of Abraham. Nevertheless, near an impressive three-pillared gate, the excavators discovered an ancient well, now restored, which may be much older and quite possibly reach back to the age of Abraham.

Here, in Beersheba, Abraham pitched his tent, wondering whether he would live out his last years in peace. It was not to be. God, the Bible tells us, resolves to put Abraham to a horrific test. This passage is undoubtedly one of the most dramatic in Genesis. God orders Abraham to take his son, "your only son Isaac, whom you love," and to go north into the land of Moriah. There, God told him, you will "offer him ... as a burnt offering" (Genesis 22:2). Genesis does not give details of Moriah other than to say that it is a three-day march from Beersheba. A reference in II Chronicles (II Chronicles 3:1) places Mount Moriah in the city of Jerusalem. This identification is upheld by some Muslim traditions, which locate the site on Jerusalem's Temple Mount, or Haram esh Sharif in Arabic, a spot marked today by the Dome of the Rock.

As Abraham sets out with his son on this journey, young Isaac soon begins to wonder about the purpose of this surprise outing. His father, the Bible says, cannot bring himself to reveal the true reason. In the Koran, on the other hand, Abraham says, "O my son! Surely I have seen in a dream that I should sacrifice you," to which his son calmly replies, "O my father! do what you are commanded" (Koran 37:102). As preparations are made for the sacrifice, Genesis describes in detail how Abraham builds a pyre, binds his son, and lays the young boy on top of the kindling.

This horned Canaanite altar was discovered in Beersheba. Altars like this one are typical of those used in the the 9th and 10th centuries B.C.E.

ca 1760 B.C.E.
Babylonian forces under Hammurabi's command conquer Mari

ca 1755 B.C.E.
Egypts powerful 12th dynasty comes to an end

ca 1739 B.C.E.
Southern Mesopotamia suffers an economic downturn

ca 1630 B.C.E.
Middle Kingdom ends and Second Intermediate period begins in Egypt

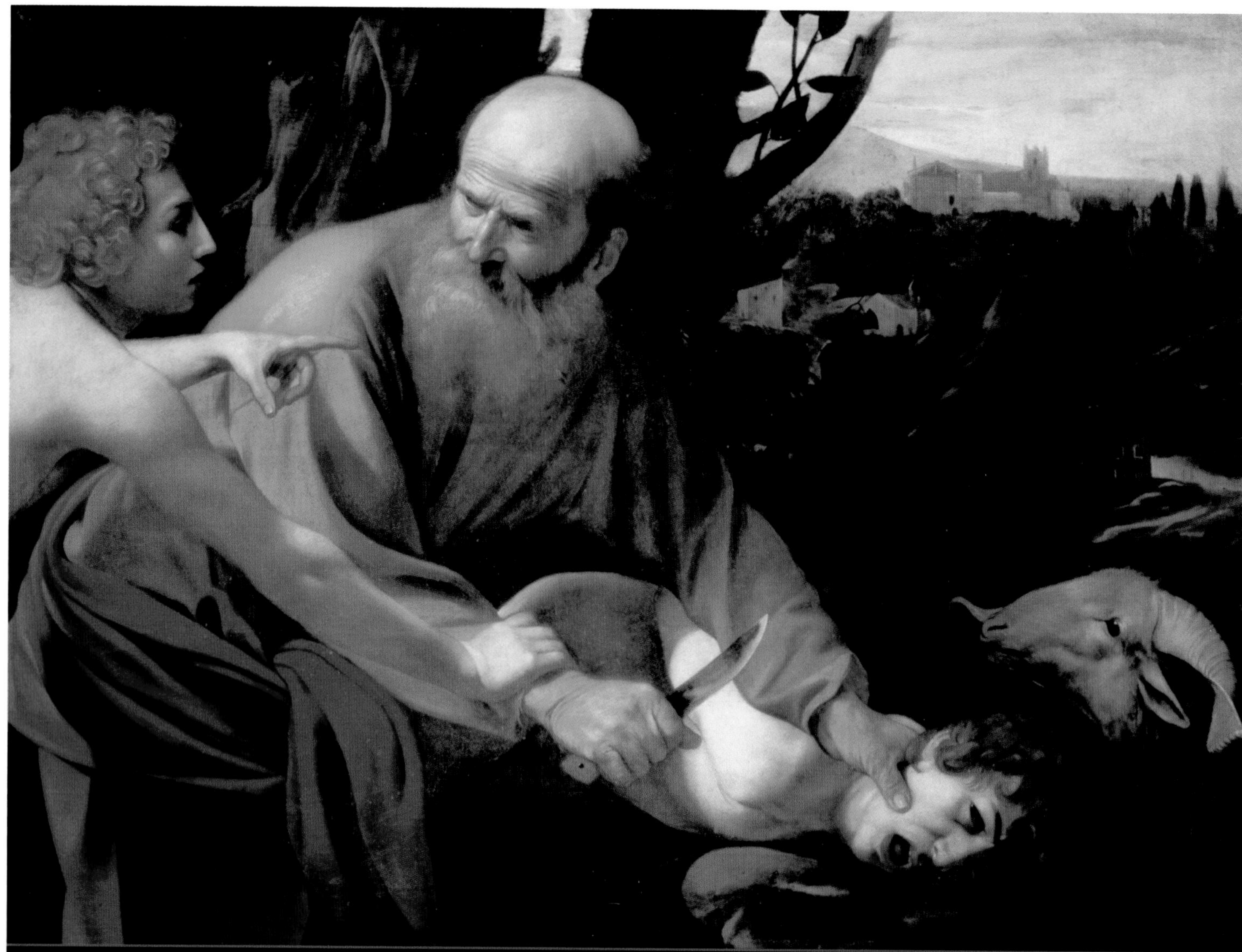

FATHER OF THREE FAITHS

ABRAHAM (AVRAHAM IN HEBREW, IBRAHIM IN Arabic) is revered by Jews, Christians, and Muslims alike. Each of the three faiths considers him the founder of monotheism, the man who harkened to only a single God. For Jews, Abraham is the man of God's first covenant, the progenitor of the people of Israel, whom God will lead into nationhood.

As such Abraham is also revered in Christendom. Christians, however, identify with another aspect of the story. They see in Abraham's willingness to offer up his own son a foreshadowing of God's sacrifice of his own son, Jesus, for the redemption of mankind. For them, the depiction of Isaac carrying the kindling wood for his own pyre to the top of Mount Moriah anticipates the image of Jesus carrying his cross to Calvary.

Muslims venerate Abraham as the first Muslim (meaning, "he who submits himself [to God]"). He is also one of Islam's principal prophets. The Koran calls Islam "the religion of Abraham" (Koran 2:135). Islam and Judaism each commemorate Abraham's near-sacrifice of his son on Mount Moriah. In Judaism, the event is marked during the Jewish festival of Rosh Hashanah by the blowing of the shofar, the traditional ram's-horn trumpet, because God had allowed Abraham to sacrifice a ram in the place of Isaac.

For Muslims, the event is celebrated each year during the Islamic festival of Eid al-Adha. For Eid, which comes at the end of the annual pilgrimage of the hajj, Muslim families around the world will sacrifice a cow or ram, of which they only eat a third; the rest is given to friends and shared with the poor.

Italian artist Michelangelo Merisi da Caravaggio (1573–1610) painted the climax of the Abraham story in his 1591 *The Sacrifice of Isaac*.

Then, he pulls out his dagger and raises it, ready to plunge it into the heart of his son. But suddenly an angel cries out, "Abraham! ... Do not lay your hand on the boy ... for now I know that you fear God" (Genesis 22:11-12).

We are left to wonder about the purpose of this account in Genesis. Why would Abraham's God ask him to destroy the one thing he loves more than himself—his own flesh and blood? Countless students and scholars of the Bible have pondered the significance of the Akedah (the Binding of Isaac). In Genesis, the story is a test of Abraham's absolute obedience to God. Christians see a foreshadowing of the sacrifice on the cross of Jesus, God's only son, in their view. Others, notably Rabbi J. H. Hertz, interpret the Akedah as God's demonstration that he will not tolerate the ancient practice of human sacrifice. In this view, the Hebrew God is passionately involved with the course of humanity, unlike the haughty nature gods of Babylonian and Canaanite origin who remain largely indifferent to the fate of man.

After these things God tested Abraham. He said to him, "Abraham! ... Take your son, your only son Isaac, whom you love, and go to the land of Moriah, and offer him there as a burnt offering on one of the mountains that I shall show you."

(Genesis 22:1-2)

Abraham's God, however, will soon demand exclusivity; this becomes the guiding theme throughout the unfolding of the Bible's story. Many of Abraham's children will submit themselves to God, but see no reason why they cannot worship other deities as well. The later Israelites, too, will pay homage to YHWH, then rush to appease other gods lest they become jealous and spoil the harvest out of spite. Well into the days of the latter prophets,

GODS OF CANAAN

Tablets uncovered in the Royal Palace of Ugarit, on the Syrian coast, provide a wealth of information on Canaanite gods from the period of the patriarchs. After the Israelite conquest of Canaan, too, the Hebrew cult of a single god, El, would clash with deities worshipped by the Canaanites, the most influential of whom was Baal. Of Mesopotamian origin, Baal is alternatively revered as "Lord of the Earth" or as "Lord of Rain and Dew," the prerequisites for a successful harvest. The Babylonian mother goddess, Ishtar, was equally prominent; Canaanite farmers would visit her shrines and mate with cult prostitutes to secure the fertility of their new crops. Ishtar, known as Inana in Sumer, was also revered as the goddess of sexual love and is believed by some to be the patron goddess of prostitutes. In a curious coincidence, she may have been associated with the planet Venus, named after the Roman goddess of love.

The clay relief known as the "Queen of the Night" portrays a Babylonian goddess; it was probably made between 1792 and 1750 B.C.E., during the reign of King Hammurabi.

The British Museum owns an intriguing plaque of baked clay, known as the "Queen of the Night," which may represent Ishtar or her sister and rival, Ereshkigal, queen of the underworld. Made in the first half of the 18th century B.C.E. during the reign of King Hammurabi, the clay goddess wears a horned cap, symbol of divinity, while clutching the rod and ring of justice in her hands. The association with the night is probably suggested by the presence of an owl on either side of her, combined with the dark painted background. Her full nudity makes the identification of Ishtar likely.

While worship of Canaanite deities usually included chants and offerings of animals or crops, in times of drought desperate villagers would sometimes sacrifice their firstborn children. The Genesis story of Abraham's aborted attempt to sacrifice Isaac may be seen as a signal to Canaanite communities that El will not tolerate such horrific practices.

many Israelites felt that to worship Abraham's God and no one else needlessly placed the tribe and its holdings at risk.

The Binding of Isaac story ends with Abraham sacrificing a ram and returning to Beersheba. In due course, the family returns to the gentler climate of Hebron. When Sarah dies, Abraham decides that Hebron will be where Sarah and all his family will be put to rest. He finds a cave that suits his needs. It is called the Cave of Machpelah. In Genesis 23, Abraham must barter for the rights to the tomb, because the owner, Ephron the Hittite, immediately understands that the old man in front of him is a man of means. Abraham pays the agreed-upon price. Shortly thereafter, Sarah is buried in the cave.

Genesis concludes the story of Abraham by noting that he takes another wife, Keturah, and has many children by her. Isaac is designated as his heir, although "to the sons of his concubines Abraham gave gifts, while he was still living" (Genesis 25:5-6). These sons, however, are sent away to the East, "away from his son Isaac," so that no one can contest Isaac's rightful inheritance.

And then, Abraham "breathed his last and died in good old age, an old man and full of years" (Genesis 25:8). He is put to rest in the Cave of Machpelah, close to Sarah. According to the biblical account, Abraham's son Isaac and his wife Rebekah, his grandson Jacob and his wife Leah will all find their final resting place here, making the Cave of Machpelah truly the family tomb of the patriarchs.

Religious tradition holds that this tomb still exists. It is one of very few archaeological sites associated with the figure of Abraham, and therefore

OPPOSITE: **An illuminated "A," from the late 12th-century Bible de Souvigny, depicts Abraham and his progeny.**

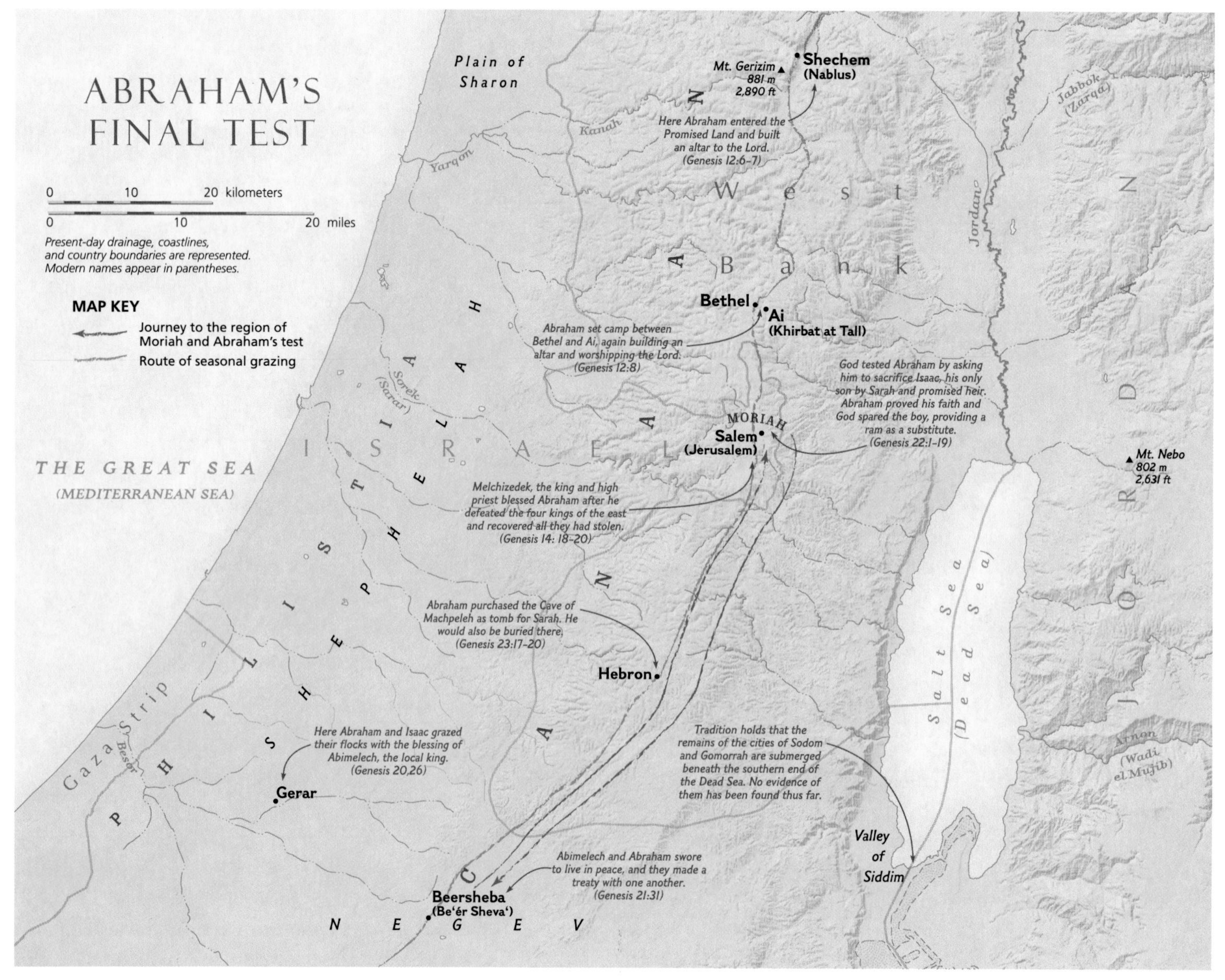

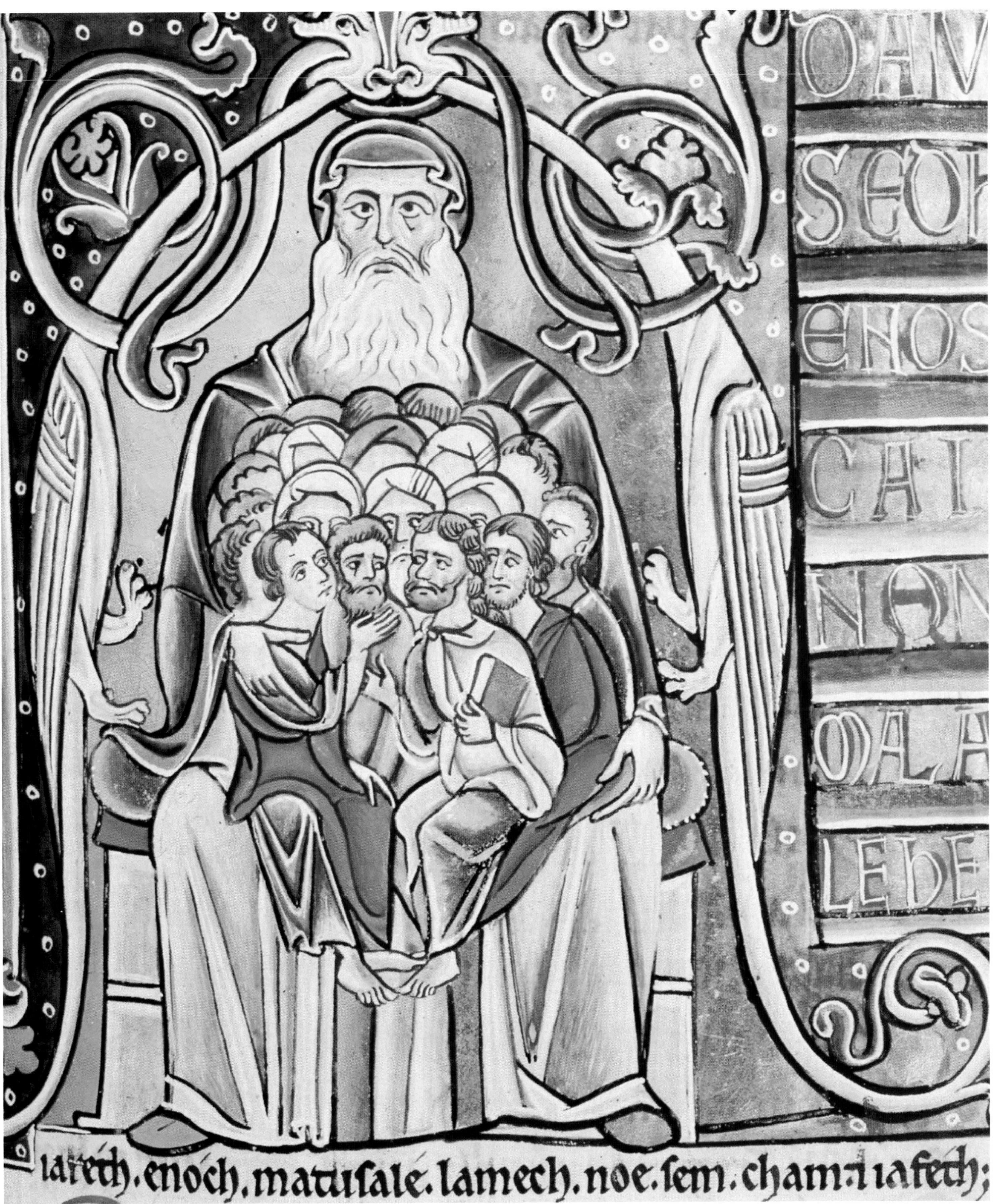
iareth. enoch. matusale. lamech. noe. sem. cham. 7 iafeth;

the oldest shrine in Judaism. It was venerated for many centuries until, in the first century B.C.E., Herod the Great built a vast mausoleum over the site. Allowing for various additions, this Herodian structure has remained largely intact to this day. Herod conceived the shrine as a vast and open-walled enclosure. The entire compound originally measured some 215 feet by 115 feet, its walls adorned with flat Hellenistic pilasters reminiscent of those on the walls that surrounded the Second Temple in Jerusalem. The same finely chiseled masonry can be seen on the walls of the Herodian platform on the Temple Mount.

Under the Byzantine Empire, the mausoleum became a Christian basilica. After the Islamic conquest, it was converted into a mosque. In the ninth century C.E., the Fatimid caliph built a new entrance in the northeastern wall; he also added domes to cover the tombs of Abraham and Sarah and built a large hostel to house the flood of pilgrims. During the Crusades, the inner shrine was again made a church. After Salah al-Din reconquered Hebron, the crusader columns and capitals were used to build an Islamic pulpit. The cave became a mosque once again, and it remains an Islamic site. It is still equally revered by Jews, Christians, and Muslims. In Arabic, it is known as Haram el Khalil, the "shrine of the man who was a friend of God."

In Jerusalem, Abraham is remembered. An inscription at the Jaffa Gate, where the road between Hebron and Jerusalem ends, quotes the Koran: "There is no God but Allah, and Abraham is beloved of him."

Abraham in Genesis

IN THE WORLDVIEW of Genesis, the progress of human history is not subject to the laws of nature or the socioeconomic evolution of man, but to the will of God. Good things happen because God's power is allowed to manifest itself through faith; bad things happen because men neglect their duties to God and allow themselves to be seduced by evil. In this context, Abraham is a key figure. Until Abraham, human beings dealt only empirically with divine beings, who were callous figures capable of acts of great cruelty toward mankind. God, by contrast, is a source of moral good who reveals himself to Abraham in Haran and continues to guide him—directly or through the agency of angels—throughout the rest his life.

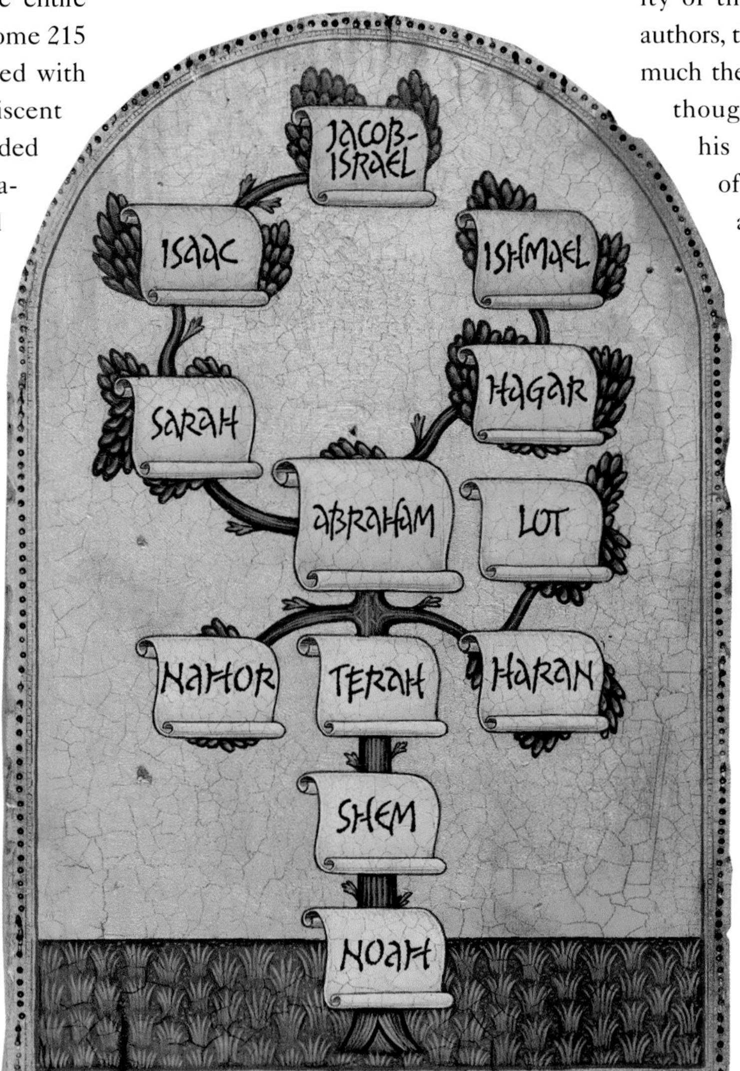

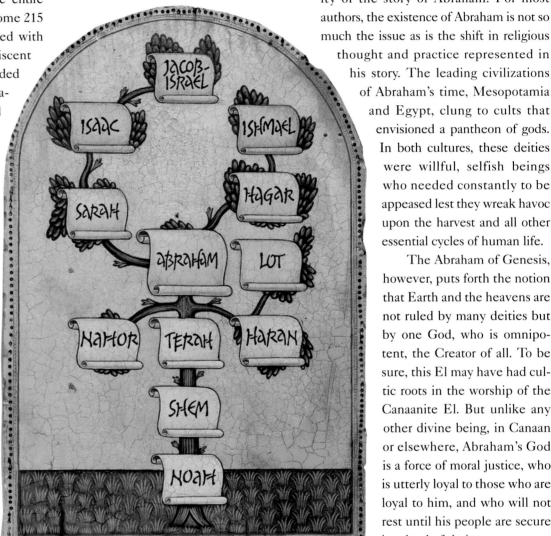

A modern rendering of Abraham's family tree traces his ancestors from Noah as well as his descendants through Sarah and Hagar.

From the point of view of history, scholars continue to debate the authenticity of the story of Abraham. For most authors, the existence of Abraham is not so much the issue as is the shift in religious thought and practice represented in his story. The leading civilizations of Abraham's time, Mesopotamia and Egypt, clung to cults that envisioned a pantheon of gods. In both cultures, these deities were willful, selfish beings who needed constantly to be appeased lest they wreak havoc upon the harvest and all other essential cycles of human life.

The Abraham of Genesis, however, puts forth the notion that Earth and the heavens are not ruled by many deities but by one God, who is omnipotent, the Creator of all. To be sure, this El may have had cultic roots in the worship of the Canaanite El. But unlike any other divine being, in Canaan or elsewhere, Abraham's God is a force of moral justice, who is utterly loyal to those who are loyal to him, and who will not rest until his people are secure in a land of their own.

The question that remains is why the idea of monotheism did not occur to the vaunted intelligentsia of Sumer or to the sophisticated elites in Egypt. Why did this paradigm shift take place among nomadic men and women in search of a permanent home? Did being unmoored and unfettered create the psychological precondition for a man to look upon his universe afresh? Was it only in primitive

Canaan, where there was no central authority bolstered by elaborate religious stagecraft, that the idea of monotheism could find fertile ground?

By the same token, however, the worship of pagan gods remained firmly entrenched in settlements throughout Canaan. As the story of the Bible unfolds, Abraham's children are tempted to worship both El and the local gods that are so closely associated with agriculture in the region. But the message of Abraham's story remains: Abraham's legacy is a monotheism of many peoples. "Walk before me," the Lord says, "be blameless ... and you shall be the ancestor of a multitude of nations" (Genesis 17:1-4); "in you all families of the earth shall be blessed" (Genesis 12:3). Today, with Muslims, Christians, and Jews all acknowledging Abraham as the father of their faiths, the Genesis prophecy can be said to have come true.

This 19th-century Jewish rug depicts the Tomb of the Patriarchs, also known as the Cave of Machpelah, in Hebron.

EGYPT	MESOPOTAMIA	CANAAN
ca 2125 B.C.E. First Intermediate period begins	ca 2100 B.C.E. Amorites move into parts of southern Mesopotamia	ca 2000 B.C.E. Reemergence of urban centers
ca 2000 B.C.E. Special "drills" are used to plant seeds in Egypt. A separate device, the shadoof, helps farmers lift water to irrigate fields	ca 1950 B.C.E. Building of Great Temple and palace at Mari begins	
		ca 1950 B.C.E. Egyptian army invades Canaan
ca 1975 B.C.E. Middle Kingdom begins	ca 1900 Assyrians set up trading centers throughout the Middle East	ca 1900 B.C.E. Hazor is the prominent city-state of the region
ca 1991 B.C.E. Amenemhet initiates rapid economic growth in Egypt	ca 1800 B.C.E. Babylonians invent lunar calendar	ca 1800 B.C.E. Hebrew clans begin migrating into Egypt
ca 1836 B.C.E. Senusret III becomes pharaoh and extends Egypt's territory		
ca 1755 B.C.E. Egypt's powerful 12th dynasty comes to an end		ca 1800 B.C.E. Use of bronze becoming widespread
ca 1630 B.C.E. Middle Kingdom ends and Second Intermediate period begins	ca 1792–1750 B.C.E. Reign of Hammurabi	ca 1800 B.C.E. Egyptian texts lists Canaanite city-states, including Jerusalem

Scholars date the time of the story of Abraham to the first part of the Middle Bronze Age, a period that spans between 2000 and 1750 B.C.E.

CHAPTER THREE

Joseph in Egypt

IN TELLING THE STORY OF JOSEPH, THE BOOK of Genesis goes to an entirely different setting: the splendid halls of Egypt's capital. It would be difficult to imagine a greater contrast than that between a dusty tent in Jacob's camp at Beersheba and the elegant, incense-filled home of one of Pharaoh's leading lieutenants. Strikingly different, too, are the tone and scope of the narrative. In previous chapters Genesis has been mostly occupied with tales of humble shepherds and their womenfolk, but Joseph's story thrusts us into the epicenter of the most sophisticated civilization on Earth, to witness Joseph's meteoric rise to the second highest office in the land.

The ultimate intent of the account is for the clan of Abraham, Isaac, and Jacob to find themselves in Egypt. Here, in the Nile Delta region called Goshen, their enslavement awaits—a trial that will unite their strengths and forge in them the will to return to Canaan and build a nation of their own. The story of Joseph concludes the Book of Genesis; it is quite literally the pivot point between the primeval history of Abraham's offspring and the foundation of Israel.

Watered by several tributaries, the Nile Delta is Egypt's most fertile region. According to Genesis, Pharaoh settled the tribe of Jacob here.

THE CHILDREN OF JACOB

A Turkish girl stands in the center of the village of Haran (Harran), Turkey, where Jacob went to look for a bride from his kinsmen.

SOME SCHOLARS HAVE characterized the story of Joseph as a novella within the oral traditions of Genesis. The story is expertly crafted and told, filled with dramatic turns and cliffhangers. Nevertheless, it recapitulates themes we have encountered before: the conflict between faith and ambition, the love and envy between brothers, and the struggle to put down roots in a foreign land. All of these themes propel us inexorably to the grand finale, the heart-stopping scene in which Joseph is reconciled with his brothers, thus restoring the path of Israel to its destiny.

Before Joseph's journey into Egypt can be traced, we must pick up the thread of the clan's story in Canaan. By now, Abraham and Sarah have passed away. Their son Isaac is the head of the clan and heir to God's covenant with Abraham. Before his death, says Genesis 24, Abraham had sent a trusted family servant back to Haran to find a bride for Isaac, lest his son be forced to marry a local Canaanite. In Haran, the servant encounters Rebekah, and Isaac subsequently marries her. However, as the years pass, Rebekah does not conceive, and Isaac fears that his young bride may be barren. He appeals to God, who rewards him with the birth of twin

ca 1850 B.C.E.
Hittite presence is widespread in Canaan

ca 1755–1630 B.C.E.
13th-dynasty Pharaohs build mud-brick pyramids at Saqqara

ca 1740
Trade relations between Mesopotamia and South Asia end

ca 1740 B.C.E.
Many cities in southern Mesopotamia are abandoned

When her time to give birth was at hand, there were twins in her womb. The first came out red, all his body like a hairy mantle; so they named him Esau. Afterward his brother came out, with his hand gripping Esau's heel; so he was named Jacob. (Genesis 25:24-26)

brothers: Esau and Jacob. Red-haired, with his body covered in what was "like a hairy mantle," Esau is the first to be born (Genesis 25:25), though only by mere seconds. Jacob is a skinny little thing who lacks the strength to leave his mother's womb except by holding on to his brother's heel. Hence he is called Ya'akov, based on the Hebrew root *ekev,* or heel.

Esau, according to Genesis, grows up to be a strong and muscular young man. His father's favorite, Esau is a "skillful hunter, a man of the field"; by contrast, Jacob is "a quiet man, living in tents" (Genesis 25:27). This gentle soul soon becomes the favorite son of his mother, Rebekah.

In a replay of the rivalry between Ishmael and Isaac, the question arises: Which of the twins will receive Isaac's birthright? Even during pregnancy, Rebekah felt the boys struggling in her womb. When they are teenagers, things come to a head. One day, Genesis says, while Jacob is stirring a tasty stew, Esau returns from the field without any game in his bag. Smelling the aroma of his brother's bubbling red stew, he eagerly runs to the tent to partake of the meal. "Let me eat some of that red stuff," he barks at his brother (Genesis 25:30). It is another one of Genesis's double entendres, for *edom,* red stuff, is also Esau's nickname and the name of the land where he will dwell in the future. Jacob, sensing a sudden advantage, offers his brother a deal. "First sell me your birthright," he says. Esau's stomach is growling. "If I don't eat right away," he muses, "I will starve to death; and what good is a birthright then?" (Genesis 25:32). So the two young men make the pact. Esau eats and drinks to his fill, then realizes what he has done. He walks away, embittered.

Of course, such an arrangement would never have held up in the eyes of Isaac: The father decides who inherits the birthright and the leadership of the clan. The remarkable aspect of this story, however, is that Jacob resorts to deception—a theme that will run throughout the Jacob story as well as the journey of Joseph.

Times passes; in Genesis 26, a famine drives Isaac's family to Gerar in the territory of Abimelech, where his father, Abraham, had once dwelt many decades earlier. Here, Isaac reopens the wells that Abraham had dug, before moving back to Beersheba. He builds an altar to the Lord, as his father had done before him. Esau marries, but his wives are Hittites (Semites from Anatolia, modern Turkey). This doesn't sit well with Isaac, nor with the boy's mother.

Isaac, however, is growing old. His boys were born when Isaac was already 60 years old. As he lies in bed, virtually blind, he decides the time has come to settle the issue of the birthright—and God's covenant. For Isaac, there is no question of who is best qualified. It is Esau. He is Isaac's favorite son, strong as an ox, and a skillful hunter of the game that his father loves so much. Isaac summons Esau and tells him to go shoot some venison. "Bring it to me to eat," Isaac says, "so that I may bless you before I die" (Genesis 27:4). Flushed with excitement, Esau grabs his bow and runs to the nearby wilderness.

Rebekah overhears her husband. She quickly tells Jacob to slaughter two goats, so she can make Isaac's favorite meat stew before Esau returns. She then dresses Jacob in one of Esau's sweat-stained tunics. She covers his hands and neck with the rough wool of the goats, and tells him to carry the meal to his father. Isaac questions

A rare Egyptian ostracon (painted potsherd), excavated in Deir el Medineh. New Kingdom, 19th dynasty (ca 1292–1190 B.C.E.).

ca 1738 B.C.E.
Kim Suen II of Larsa is the last Mesopotamian king to claim to be a god

ca 1720 B.C.E.
Semitic immigrants in Egypt sack Memphis

ca 1630 B.C.E.
Egypt's Second Intermediate period begins

ca 1600 B.C.E.
Canaanites begin using alphabetic script

how his son has found his prey so quickly. Jacob replies, "Because the Lord your God granted me success" (Genesis 27:20). Isaac believes he can feel Esau's furry hands as his son sits beside him. He can even smell Esau's masculine scent. But the voice he hears is that of Jacob. "Are you really my son Esau?" Isaac asks. "I am," is the answer (Genesis 27:24). The meat stew is delicious, and Isaac blesses Jacob. It is he who will continue the Lord's covenant and become the head of a great nation.

As soon as Isaac has finished blessing him, Jacob leaves his presence—and not a moment too soon. In strides Esau with his savory dish. His old father is shocked when he realizes he's been deceived. But what is done is done, and the transfer of the birthright cannot be taken back. Overcome with rage, Esau rushes out of the tent, hell-bent on killing his deceitful brother. But Rebekah, aware of everything, quickly tells Jacob to pack and head for her kinsmen in Haran before Esau finds him. Ever resourceful, she secures Isaac's consent for Jacob's hasty departure by presenting it as a quest for securing a bride from Haran. The idea of having another Hittite bride in the family is too much to bear—something that Isaac can only agree with wholeheartedly (Genesis 27:46).

Jacob in Haran

AND SO, Jacob sets out for Paddan-aram, literally the "road of Aram" leading to Haran, the same road that, according to Genesis, Jacob's grandfather Abraham took so many years earlier. It is a journey of some 700 miles, taking him north through Hebron, Salem (Jerusalem), and Ai. Along the way, says Genesis 28:10-22, he stops in a settlement called Luz. Here, Jacob has a dream in which he sees a ladder rising up into heaven. At its top stands the Lord, who reaffirms his promise to Abraham that his offspring will one day become a mighty nation. The next morning, Jacob marks the sacred place where he has slept by building an altar. He renames the settlement Bethel—*Beth-el*, meaning "the house of the Lord." Jacob then continues his journey, traveling from Shechem through the Valley of Jezreel, past the fortified settlement of Megiddo and on to Hazor, Damascus, Aleppo, the great caravan city of Carchemish, and ultimately to Haran.

A LADDER TO HEAVEN

JACOB'S VISION OF A LADDER THAT REACHED into heaven (Genesis 28:10-22) is a popular motif in the Near East. The idea of a celestial stairway inspired the people of Babel to build their gigantic tower. The motif also appears in Sumerian mythology. It may, in fact, be the driving force behind the multiplatform pyramids, or ziggurats, built by both the Sumerians and Babylonians. The idea endured into Assyrian times. In the tale of Nergal and Ereshkigal, "Queen of the Underworld," the queen's vizier is invited to ascend "the long staircase of the heavens" in order to bring his queen a dish from a banquet of the gods.

Jacob sees angels traveling up and down the ladder in order to convey messages between mankind and God (the Hebrew word for angel, *malak,* literally means "messenger"). Similar ideas also appear in Akkadian and Egyptian writings of the period. "Now let the Ladder of the God be given to me," intones one of the Pyramid Texts from the Old Kingdom, "Let the Ladder of Seth be given to me, so that I may ascend on it to the sky."

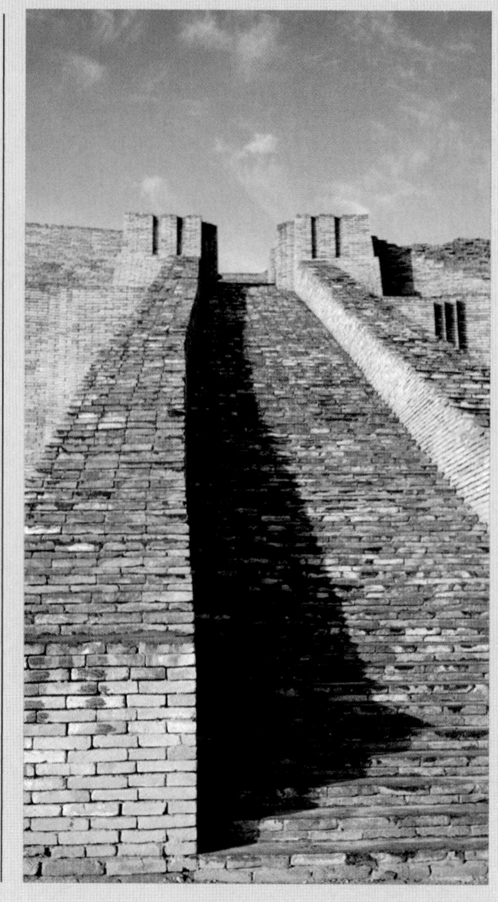

Later, rabbinic scholars interpreted Jacob's ladder as the long and arduous journey of Israel before the coming of the Messiah. The Midrash (rabbinic commentaries on the Bible) sees Jacob's ladder as the attribute of a man lifelong surrounded by angels: some ascending into heaven, others descending to accompany Jacob on his journeys. Other traditions place the location of the ladder (or *sulam*) on Mount Moriah in Jerusalem, the future location of the First Temple, which will become the most sacred connection between Earth and heaven. For these rabbinic sages, Jacob's ladder symbolized the *Seder Hishtalshalut,* the ladder of the worlds, the link between our physical world and the ethereal sphere of God.

The reconstructed mud-brick staircase of the ziggurat of Ur, Mesopotamia, rebuilt by King Ur-Nammu during the third dynasty of Ur (ca 2113–2006 B.C.E.).

Here still reside many relatives of the family of Terah, Abraham's father. Jacob straightaway heads for the town well, where he meets a beautiful young woman named Rachel. As it turns out, she is the daughter of Laban, the brother of his mother, Rebekah (Genesis 29:1-12). But Laban exacts a stiff price for the hand of his daughter: Jacob must work in his pastures for seven years.

Jacob has little choice. In Mesopotamia, the average price a groom's family was expected to pay the father of the bride was around 40 shekels of silver. This payment was held in trust by the father on his daughter's behalf, in case the marriage ended prematurely through the husband's death or divorce. If however the groom was unable to pay this amount up front, he could agree to perform compensatory work for his future father-in-law until the bride price was covered. The annual wage for a shepherd was about ten shekels; hence, four years of labor would have sufficed for the average bride. On the other hand, Genesis tells us that Rachel is exceptionally lovely; moreover, Jacob, a fugitive from Esau, is in no position to bargain. Laban does not hesitate to exploit the situation. He's experienced in such matters, for it was he who participated in negotiating the marriage contract between his sister Rebekah and Isaac.

When Jacob completes the seven-year term, Laban hatches a plan. He is aware that if Rachel does marry, this will diminish the chances for her older sister, Leah, to find a husband. Traditionally, it is the elder daughter who marries first. Leah is not as beautiful as Rachel; Genesis remarks that "Leah's eyes were lovely," but that "Rachel was graceful and beautiful" (Genesis 29:17).

Nevertheless, the wedding is scheduled. As darkness falls and Jacob prepares to spend the night with his bride, Laban stealthily smuggles Leah, rather than

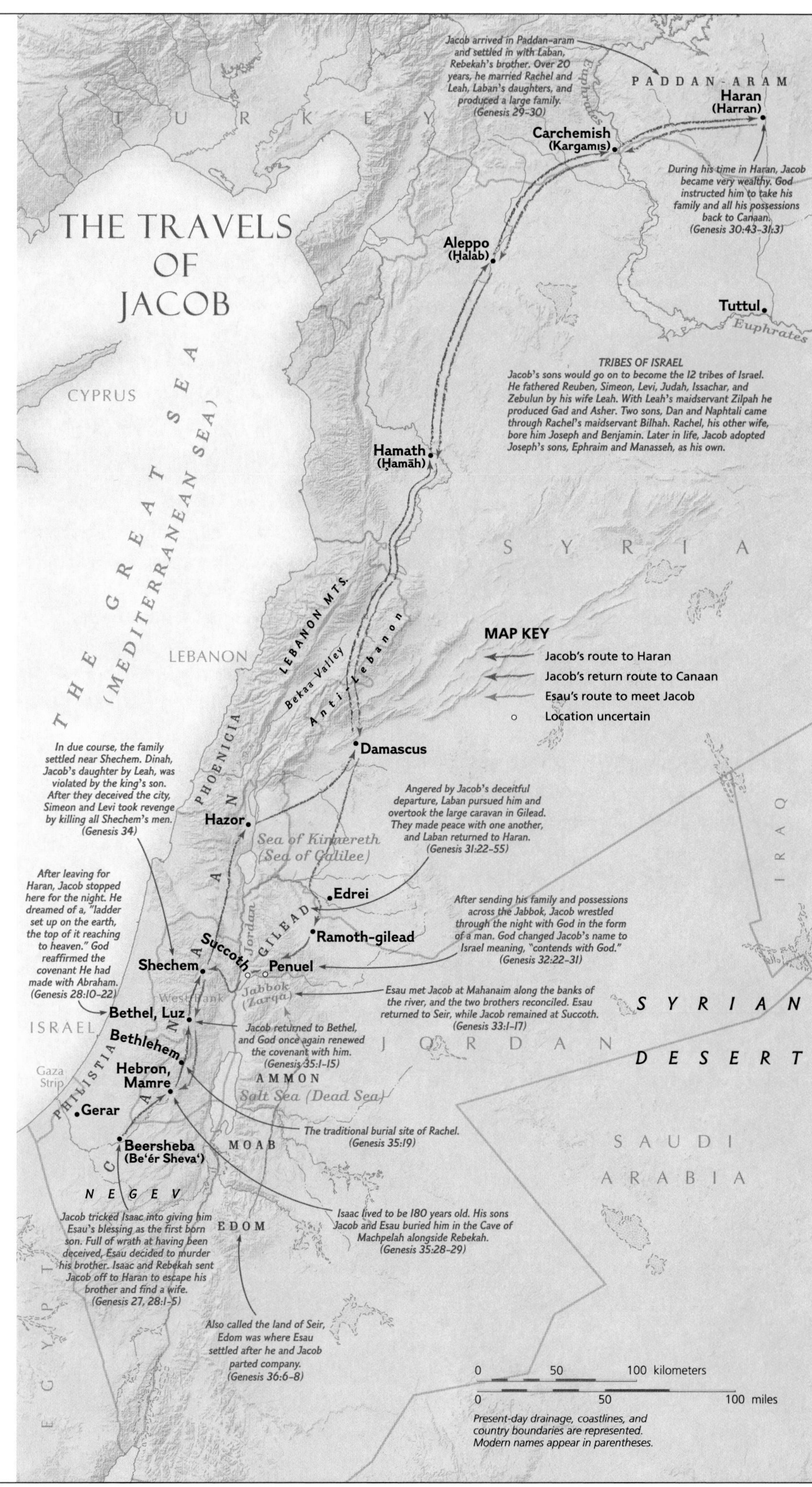
THE TRAVELS OF JACOB
T U R K E Y
CYPRUS
THE GREAT SEA (MEDITERRANEAN SEA)
Jacob arrived in Paddan-aram and settled in with Laban, Rebekah's brother. Over 20 years, he married Rachel and Leah, Laban's daughters, and produced a large family. (Genesis 29-30)
Euphrates
PADDAN-ARAM
Haran (Harran)
Carchemish (Kargamıs)
During his time in Haran, Jacob became very wealthy. God instructed him to take his family and all his possessions back to Canaan. (Genesis 30:43-31:3)
Aleppo (Ḥalab)
Tuttul
Euphrates
TRIBES OF ISRAEL
Jacob's sons would go on to become the 12 tribes of Israel. He fathered Reuben, Simeon, Levi, Judah, Issachar, and Zebulun by his wife Leah. With Leah's maidservant Zilpah he produced Gad and Asher. Two sons, Dan and Naphtali came through Rachel's maidservant Bilhah. Rachel, his other wife, bore him Joseph and Benjamin. Later in life, Jacob adopted Joseph's sons, Ephraim and Manasseh, as his own.
Hamath (Ḥamāh)
S Y R I A
LEBANON MTS.
Bekaa Valley
Anti-Lebanon
LEBANON
MAP KEY
Jacob's route to Haran
Jacob's return route to Canaan
Esau's route to meet Jacob
Location uncertain
PHOENICIA
CANAAN
Damascus
In due course, the family settled near Shechem. Dinah, Jacob's daughter by Leah, was violated by the king's son. After they deceived the city, Simeon and Levi took revenge by killing all Shechem's men. (Genesis 34)
Hazor
Sea of Kinnereth (Sea of Galilee)
Angered by Jacob's deceitful departure, Laban pursued him and overtook the large caravan in Gilead. They made peace with one another, and Laban returned to Haran. (Genesis 31:22-55)
IRAQ
After leaving for Haran, Jacob stopped here for the night. He dreamed of a, "ladder set up on the earth, the top of it reaching to heaven." God reaffirmed the covenant He had made with Abraham. (Genesis 28:10-22)
Edrei
GILEAD
Jordan
Ramoth-gilead
After sending his family and possessions across the Jabbok, Jacob wrestled through the night with God in the form of a man. God changed Jacob's name to Israel meaning, "contends with God." (Genesis 32:22-31)
Succoth
Shechem
Penuel
Jabbok (Zarqa)
West Bank
Esau met Jacob at Mahanaim along the banks of the river, and the two brothers reconciled. Esau returned to Seir, while Jacob remained at Succoth. (Genesis 33:1-17)
Bethel, Luz
ISRAEL
Bethlehem
Jacob returned to Bethel, and God once again renewed the covenant with him. (Genesis 35:1-15)
J O R D A N
SYRIAN DESERT
Gaza Strip
PHILISTIA
Hebron, Mamre
AMMON
Salt Sea (Dead Sea)
Gerar
The traditional burial site of Rachel. (Genesis 35:19)
Beersheba (Be'ér Sheva')
MOAB
SAUDI ARABIA
NEGEV
Jacob tricked Isaac into giving him Esau's blessing as the first born son. Full of wrath at having been deceived, Esau decided to murder his brother. Isaac and Rebekah sent Jacob off to Haran to escape his brother and find a wife. (Genesis 27, 28:1-5)
EDOM
Isaac lived to be 180 years old. His sons Jacob and Esau buried him in the Cave of Machpelah alongside Rebekah. (Genesis 35:28-29)
EGYPT
Also called the land of Seir, Edom was where Esau settled after he and Jacob parted company. (Genesis 36:6-8)
0 50 100 kilometers
0 50 100 miles
Present-day drainage, coastlines, and country boundaries are represented. Modern names appear in parentheses.

Rachel, into the marriage bed. In the darkness of the tent, the marriage is consummated. Genesis here continues the theme of deceit: Jacob deceived his father in order to obtain his birthright; now his father-in-law has deceived him with the woman who will bear his progeny.

The morning dawns, the newlyweds awake, and Jacob is startled to find Leah lying beside him. He marches off to his father-in-law, but Laban is unruffled: "This is not done in our country—giving the younger before the firstborn" (Genesis 29:26). If Jacob is still interested in Rachel, the young man will simply have to work another seven years to secure her as his bride (Genesis 29:26-27). "Complete the week of this one," he adds solicitously, "and we will give you the other."

"The week," in ancient parlance, was the honeymoon when both bride and groom were excused from chores in the camp and the fields. They could remain

This bronze mirror, with a handle in the shape of a girl, was found near Acre in Israel. It dates to the Late Bronze Age (1550–1200 B.C.E.).

undisturbed in their tent, increasing the chances of an early pregnancy and thus validating the marriage. Jacob dutifully acquits himself of his marital obligations toward Leah before he can take his beloved Rachel into his arms at last. As the husband of two wives, Jacob returns to his labors as a shepherd of Laban's flocks for the next seven years.

The description in Genesis emphasizes that Jacob is crazy about Rachel, whereas his first wife Leah is "unloved." However, the Bible tells us, "the Lord ... opened [Leah's] womb; but Rachel was barren" (Genesis 29:31). It is a harsh verdict, for Jacob would want nothing more than to have children with Rachel. Nevertheless, it is Leah who conceives and gives Jacob children. So do the handmaidens given him in lieu of Rachel, echoing the tragic surrogate motherhood of Hagar. Together, these women present Jacob with a string of sons, each of whom will be the progenitor of a future tribe of Israel. Leah is the mother of Reuben, Simeon, Levi, Judah, Issachar, and Zebulun. Rachel's maid Bilhah gives

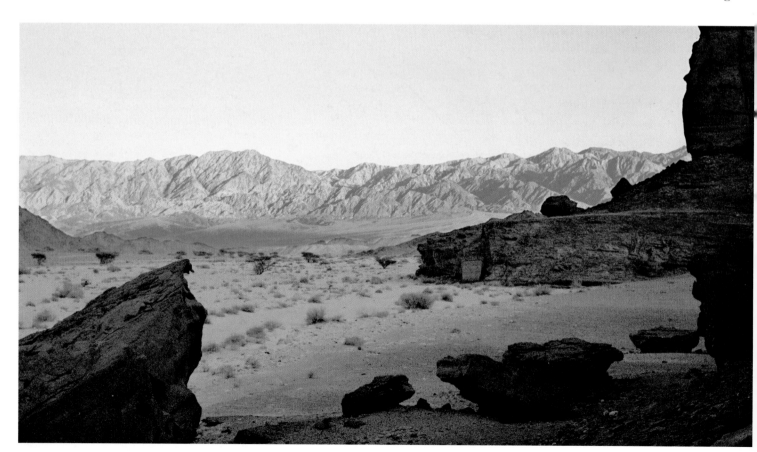

A view of the Wadi al 'Arabah Valley, located between the Dead Sea and the Gulf of Aqaba, with the mountains of Edom in the distance.

birth to Dan and Naphtali, whereas Leah's maid Zilpah presents Jacob with Gad and Asher. Echoing the fate of Sarah, it is only late in life that Rachel is finally granted the blessing of having her own son. Thus, Genesis has set the stage for the drama that is soon to unfold—the tale of Joseph, son of Rachel, who is as despised by his brothers as Leah once was by their father, Jacob.

A Move to Canaan

THE TIME HAS COME for Jacob and his extended family to return to Canaan. Despite Laban's crafty efforts to deny him his legitimate share of the flocks, Jacob sets out, in Genesis 31, with a large retinue of herds, slaves, and donkeys. But Jacob decides to take a route back to Canaan that is different from the one he traveled decades before. He crosses the Euphrates River toward Damascus, then turns westward toward Gilead—a route that will take him into the Transjordan and the region that will later be known as Edom (or Udumi in Assyrian)—the desert country southeast of the Dead Sea. This is where Esau lives; in fact, the Bible presents Esau as the forefather of the Edomites.

Deep in his heart, Jacob still cherishes the hope that he and his twin brother may reconcile. In due course, his large entourage approaches the Jabbok River, a tributary that flows westward into the Jordan. Then, word reaches Jacob that Esau is marching toward him with 400 men in tow. Jacob hastily dispatches his wives, slaves, and herds to safer havens. When all are gone and Jacob is left alone in camp, a mysterious figure appears who wrestles with Jacob until daybreak, when he finally desists. It is an angel who changes Jacob's name into Israel, "he who has struggled with the Lord," thus confirming Jacob as the heir of God's covenant (Genesis 32:28).

JOSEPH'S COAT

"NOW ISRAEL LOVED JOSEPH MORE THAN any of his children," says Genesis, "and he had made him a long robe" (Genesis 37:3). Traditionally, the garment given by Jacob to his son Joseph is translated as a multicolored or "striped" coat. This description is borne out by the depiction of Semitic nomads in Egyptian wall paintings at Beni Hasan, who all wear colorful robes adorned with tassels. Nevertheless, the exact translation of the Hebrew word *passim* is not "multicolored stripes" but "a garment of strips," implying that Joseph's coat is long sleeved, cut from the finest strips of cloth. Most shepherds wore sleeveless flax tunics, and covered themselves with rough woolen coats to protect against the chill at night and cold and rain in winter. Joseph's coat was special not because of its colors but because it was long and hemmed, a garment usually worn by persons of wealth and authority. Later in the story, Genesis confirms this interpretation when it describes how the brothers strip Joseph "of his robe, the long robe with sleeves that he wore" (Genesis 37:23), before throwing him into a dry cistern.

Found in Egypt, this long-sleeved linen tunic reflects a style popular for 1,500 years. It is one of the oldest intact garments ever discovered.

This divine intervention is a counterpoint to the earlier episode, in which Jacob in a dream saw a stairway with angels ascending and descending from heaven. The intervention of angels shows that his sojourn in Haran, where the fathers of the 12 tribes of Israel are born, is bracketed by God's blessing. What's more, "Israel's" contest near the Jabbok River, on the threshold of Canaan, foreshadows the great struggle by which the children of the Exodus will reach the borders of the Jordan River.

Jacob and Esau finally meet, and Jacob's fears are unfounded. All of his earlier ruses are forgiven. Esau embraces his brother and weeps, says Genesis 33:4, and they part in peace.

At last Jacob reenters Canaan. Here, according to Genesis 33:17, he builds a house for his family and sheds for his cattle near the village of Succoth (a variation on *sukkot*—booths). This town has been tentatively identified with a site near Tell Deir 'Alla, north of the Jabbok River and east of the Jordan. Jacob's family and his herds are exhausted from the long trek through the desert. What's more, Rachel is pregnant with her second child. A few weeks later, near the city of Bethlehem just outside Salem, she gives birth to Jacob's 12th son, Benjamin. But the ordeal of childbirth is too much for Rachel, and she dies. Jacob erects a pillar on her grave, and then leads his family down to Hebron, where he meets his aged father shortly before Isaac's death. In Hebron, Jacob and Esau reunite to bury their father in the family tomb of Machpelah (Genesis 35:29).

Sibling Rivalry

As Genesis 37 begins, Jacob's sons are grown men. They spend much of their

In 1630, Spanish painter Diego Rodríguez de Silva y Velázquez (1599–1660) painted this dramatic scene, *Jacob Receives the Bloody Coat of Joseph*.

time in the field, tending to their father's herds of sheep, goats, and cattle. Observing the common seasonal migrations, the brothers regularly move from one valley to the next. It is obvious that Joseph is his father's favorite, the first-born of his beloved wife, Rachel, for Jacob has given him a magnificent "long robe with sleeves." This is an unheard-of luxury in a family of shepherds, who usually take to the field in sleeveless tunics, patched and torn, that are not likely to catch the eye of any passing Canaanite girls. The brothers are therefore understandably jealous and firmly resolve that their brother needs to be taught a lesson. They quietly await an opportunity to put him in his place.

To make matters worse, Joseph starts to have some very strange dreams. "Listen to this dream that I dreamed," Joseph tells his brothers in Genesis 37:6. "There we were, binding sheaves in the field. Suddenly my sheaf rose, and stood upright; then your sheaves gathered around it, and bowed down to my sheaf." These visions suggest that Joseph's station is high above that of his brothers, who are not amused; indeed, they hate him even more (Genesis 37:6-8).

But Joseph is oblivious to this. In fact, when his father tells him that his brothers have taken the flocks up north, to pastures near Shechem, Joseph is eager to follow them. As it turns out, the shepherds have moved on to Dothan, some 20 miles distant. Dothan was a major city that straddled the main route leading through the Valley of Jezreel to Esdraelon, and from there to the coastal road known as the Way of the Philistines, which led into Egypt. Located some 15 miles north of Shechem, just southeast of Megiddo, Dothan was excavated in the early 1950s at Tel Dotha. The wealth it must have accumulated from servicing passing caravans is illustrated by the ancient remains, which cover some 25 acres, surrounded by a stout wall.

He recognized it, and said, "It is my son's robe! A wild animal has devoured him; Joseph is without doubt torn to pieces." Then Jacob … mourned for his son many days. All his sons and all his daughters sought to comfort him; but he refused to be comforted, and said, "No, I shall go down to Sheol to my son, mourning." Thus his father bewailed him.

(Genesis 37:33-35)

CURRENCY IN CANAAN

Genesis notes that Joseph was sold for 20 shekels or "silver pieces." Egyptian inscriptions from the early second millennium B.C.E., as well as the Code of Hammurabi, reveal this was the fair rate for a mature male slave. It equaled roughly two years of paid labor. Most of Canaan used Egyptian silver as currency, but the northern region increasingly adopted Babylonian currency, reflecting then-current trade practices. Coins were not yet in use. Merchants would value measure the silver (or other precious metals) ingots, rings, or other jewelry on a balance equipped with ceramic weights. Some of the oldest scales found in Palestine date to 3000 B.C.E.

Joseph's brothers, seeing Joseph appear on the horizon, mutter, "Here come this dreamer" (Genesis 37:19). They know that their father Jacob is far away, back in the main camp, so they can do as they please. Joseph is stripped of his long robe and unceremoniously thrown into a dry cistern, whereupon the brothers debate what to do with him. At that moment, on the main road abutting the field, a caravan of "Midianite traders" is passing by. Joseph's brothers watch the passing caravan with keen interest. Everyone knows where the caravan is headed: to Egypt. They also know that the Egyptian nobility is always looking for an able-bodied slave from Canaan. "Come," says Judah, "let us sell him to the Ishmaelites, and not lay our hands on him" (Genesis 37:26).

"Midianites" were tribes from the Midian, the region just east of the Gulf of Aqaba, in what today is southern Jordan. The term "Ishmaelites" refers to descendants of Ishmael, so both "Ishmaelites" and "Midianites" denote Arab tribes. With its keen sense of justice, Genesis makes the subtle point that, just as Ishmael was sent away as a fugitive to Egypt, so too do his descendants now take Joseph as a slave to the great kingdom on the Nile.

But what will Joseph's brothers tell their father? They decide that Joseph has had an unfortunate accident. A goat is slaughtered, and its blood is spilled on the precious ribbons of Joseph's garment. This piece of evidence is rushed to Jacob forthwith. They tell him a wild animal has attacked and killed Joseph. Jacob wails and collapses in grief. He is inconsolable. "No," he says gravely, "I shall go down to Sheol [the grave] to my son, mourning" (Genesis 37:35).

JOSEPH'S JOURNEY

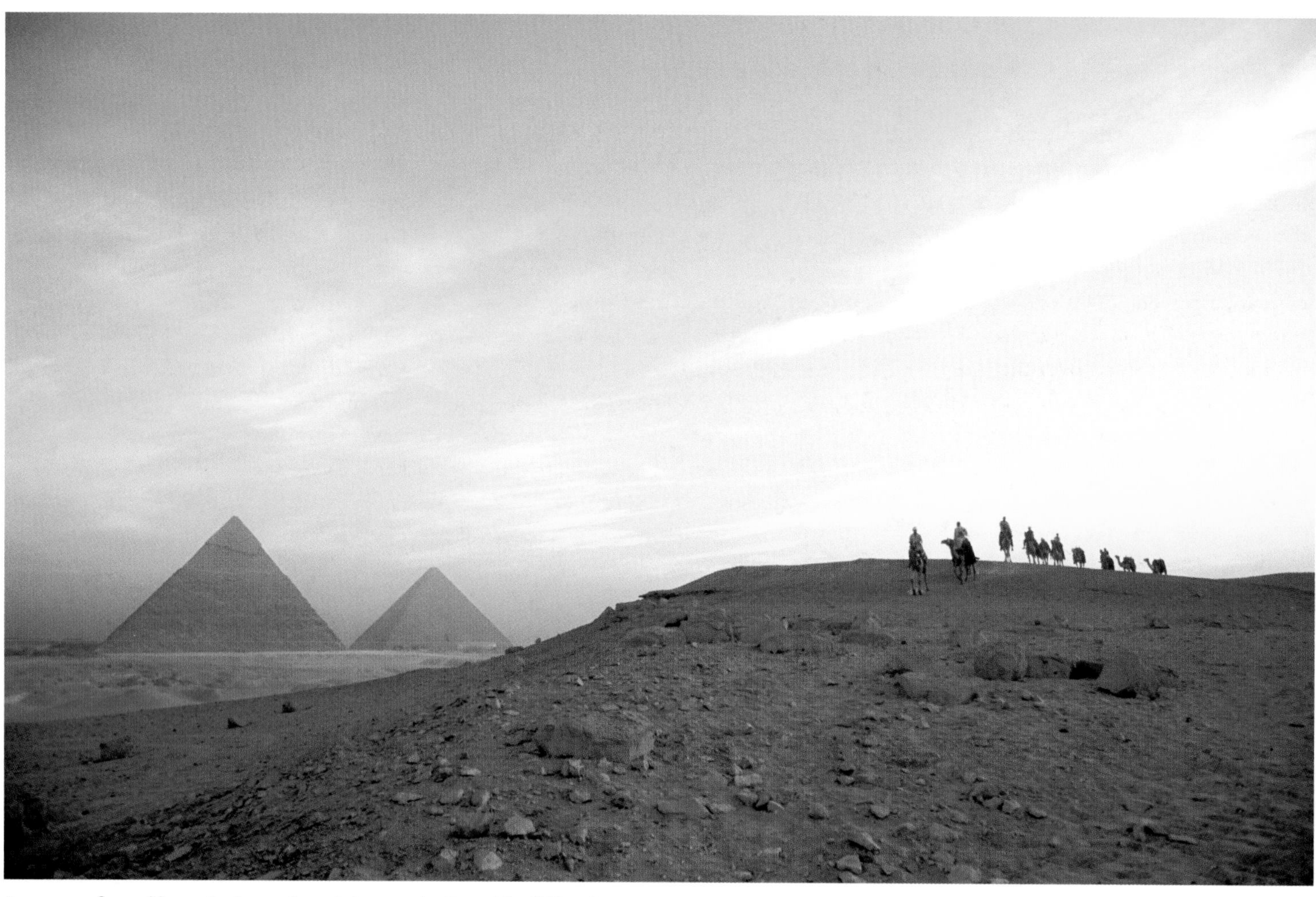

A caravan of camel-borne traders arrives at dawn at the Pyramids of Giza, Egypt.

JOSEPH, MEANWHILE, is stumbling along in the train of the Midianite merchants. Genesis conjures up an exotic image of "a caravan of Ishmaelites ... with their camels carrying gum, balm and myrrh" (Genesis 37:25). The description rings true. Commodities from southern Arabia and Africa were always in great demand in Egypt. The mention of camels in the Ishmaelite caravan, however, is an anachronism. Archaeological evidence has shown conclusively that camels were not domesticated in the Near East until around 1200 B.C.E. and only became the preferred mode of long-distance transport after the Davidic monarchy. In reality, the traders would have used donkeys. The sixth- and fifth-century B.C.E. scribes who compiled the Pentateuch, however, could not imagine risking a voyage to faraway Egypt on any conveyance other than a camel.

Though spices were their main trade item, it was not unusual for Arab traders to carry along a batch of slaves. Egypt, like other great civilizations of antiquity, depended on slaves for constructing and maintaining its vast temples and facilities. Slaves who showed above-average abilities were put to work in the vast household staffs that ran the estates of the nobility.

Such slaves were usually acquired en masse during military campaigns, when

ca 1800 B.C.E.
Assyrian kingdom comes to power in Northern Mesopotamia

ca 1715 B.C.E.
Nineveh is established near near the confluence of the Tigris and Khosr rivers

ca 1700 B.C.E.
Windmills are used in Babylon

ca 1650 B.C.E.
Babylonians record appearances of the planet Venus

The Lord was with Joseph, and he became a successful man; he was in the house of his Egyptian master. His master saw that the Lord was with him, and that the Lord caused all that he did to prosper in his hands. (Genesis 39:2-3)

both foreign prisoners and civilian captives would be hauled off to servitude in Egypt. Egyptian records show that at the beginning of the 4th dynasty (ca 2575–2450 B.C.E.), Pharaoh Snefru was able to carry off 7,000 slaves (as well some 200,000 head of cattle) following his spectacular victory over the Nubians. But Egypt had not conducted a major war for quite some time. Hence, the slave markets relied on private enterprise to obtain the "product," usually as a result of raids on unsuspecting villages.

And so, the Arab traders continue their journey to Egypt. Genesis reports that they had come from Gilead, possibly using a route close to the one taken by Jacob many years before. Their bags filled with spices, such traders would have traveled the King's Highway from Mari to Qatna and on to Damascus, moving across the Transjordan plateau before crossing into Canaan through the lowlands of the Valley of Jezreel. The King's Highway proper led straight south to the ports of today's Gulf of Aqaba (or Elat), where ships would have been waiting to carry cargo to Upper (or southern) Egypt.

The Joseph story implies that the Ishmaelites favored the coastal road, the Way of the Philistines, which led to Lower (northern) Egypt. After Dothan, the road skirted the Mediterranean all the way to Ashkelon. During the time in which the Joseph story appears to be set, Ashkelon was already a large city. Egyptian records from the 18th century B.C.E. describe it as a thriving port. From Ashkelon, the trail ran through the territory of Gaza and on to the border of the Sinai Peninsula.

Today, the coastal road along the Mediterranean follows the original caravan trail closely. It leads from Gaza City through Khan Yunis to Rafah at the entrance to the Sinai. Unlike the dramatic peaks and sharp crevices that mark the southern Sinai, the northern part of the peninsula is a barren landscape of dunes and salt marshes. For a young lad like Joseph, not used to long desert marches, it would have been tough going. After a day or two, the caravan would have crossed the Wadi el 'Arish, which in Joseph's time was already an oasis, for here stood a border outpost manned by Egyptian soldiers.

From the wadi, a caravan would have traveled some 90 miles through another stretch of sand dunes before reaching the border of Egypt. This trail would gain infamy during Egypt's New Kingdom as the highway of Egyptian military campaigns against Canaan, Syria, and the Hittites. Traders chose such well-traveled trails because they typically featured a number of watering holes, located strategically at a travel distance of no more than two days—the maximum time a man on a donkey could travel without replenishing his water bags. The maintenance of such trails was entrusted to local governors. According to a stela in Kubban from 1270 B.C.E., an official of Egypt's desert mines had to report to Pharaoh that "only half of the caravans arrive safely, for they die of thirst on the road, together with the asses they drive before them." The reason, the official explains, is "that the necessary supply of drink for their water skins is not available."

The next destination on the coastal road was a small fishing port known today as Flusya; from there it was a two-day march to Bir el 'Abd, a small Bedouin hamlet that even today jealously guards its wells. Appropriately enough, Bir el 'Abd means "the well of the slave." The village also marks the boundary of the Nile Delta. Here, the forbidding landscape of sand and dunes is gradually replaced by the more pleasant vista of green pasture, bordered by small groves of palm trees.

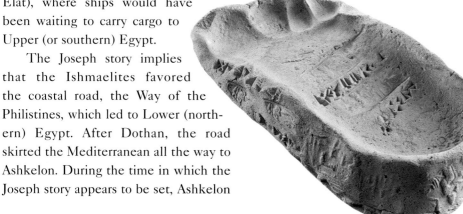

This clay footprint from Mesopotamia contains a cuneiform inscription accounting for an indebted couple's being forced to sell their children into slavery.

ca 1630 B.C.E.
Egypt's nobility relocates the 17th dynasty south to Thebes after Hyksos invasion

ca 1630 B.C.E.
The first king of the Hyksos, Sheshi, establishes the 15th dynasty in Egypt

ca 1600 B.C.E.
Egyptians write a medical book showing workings of the heart, stomach, bowels, and blood vessels

ca 1595 B.C.E.
Hittites sack Babylon, and the first Babylonian Empire comes to an end

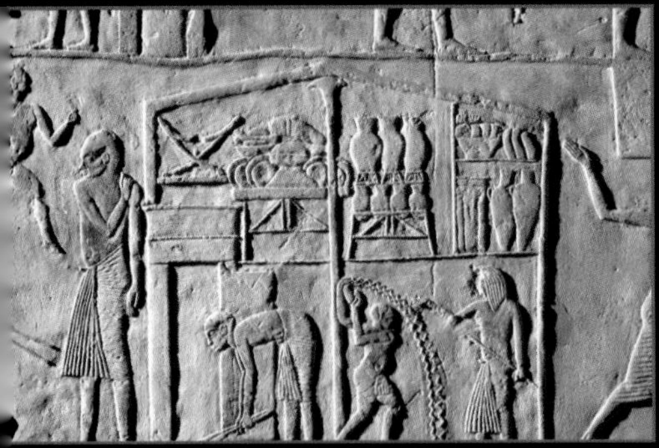

The caravan carrying Joseph would have also been bearing goods to trade. Here, in this limestone relief from an 18th-dynasty tomb, workers store them.

The traders who brought Joseph to Egypt would not have relied on camels. They relied on donkeys, as shown in the 1st-dynasty Libyan Palette from Abydos.

Agriculture plays a large role in the Joseph story. This 18th-dynasty mural from the tomb of Mennah, shows Egyptian methods of farming.

Traders also brought slaves, like Joseph, to Egypt, who relied on forced labor. Warfare provided another source of slaves, like these Libyan prisoners of war, as depicted in Ramses III's temple at Medinet Habu.

JOSEPH'S JOURNEYS

MAP KEY

- Migration route for grazing livestock
- Joseph's journey into Egypt
- Route taken by Joseph's family into Egypt and on their return to Canaan to bury Jacob
- Historic trade route
- Historic city
- Present-day city
- Point of interest

0 20 40 kilometers

0 20 40 miles

Present-day drainage, coastlines, and country boundaries are represented. Modern names appear in parentheses.

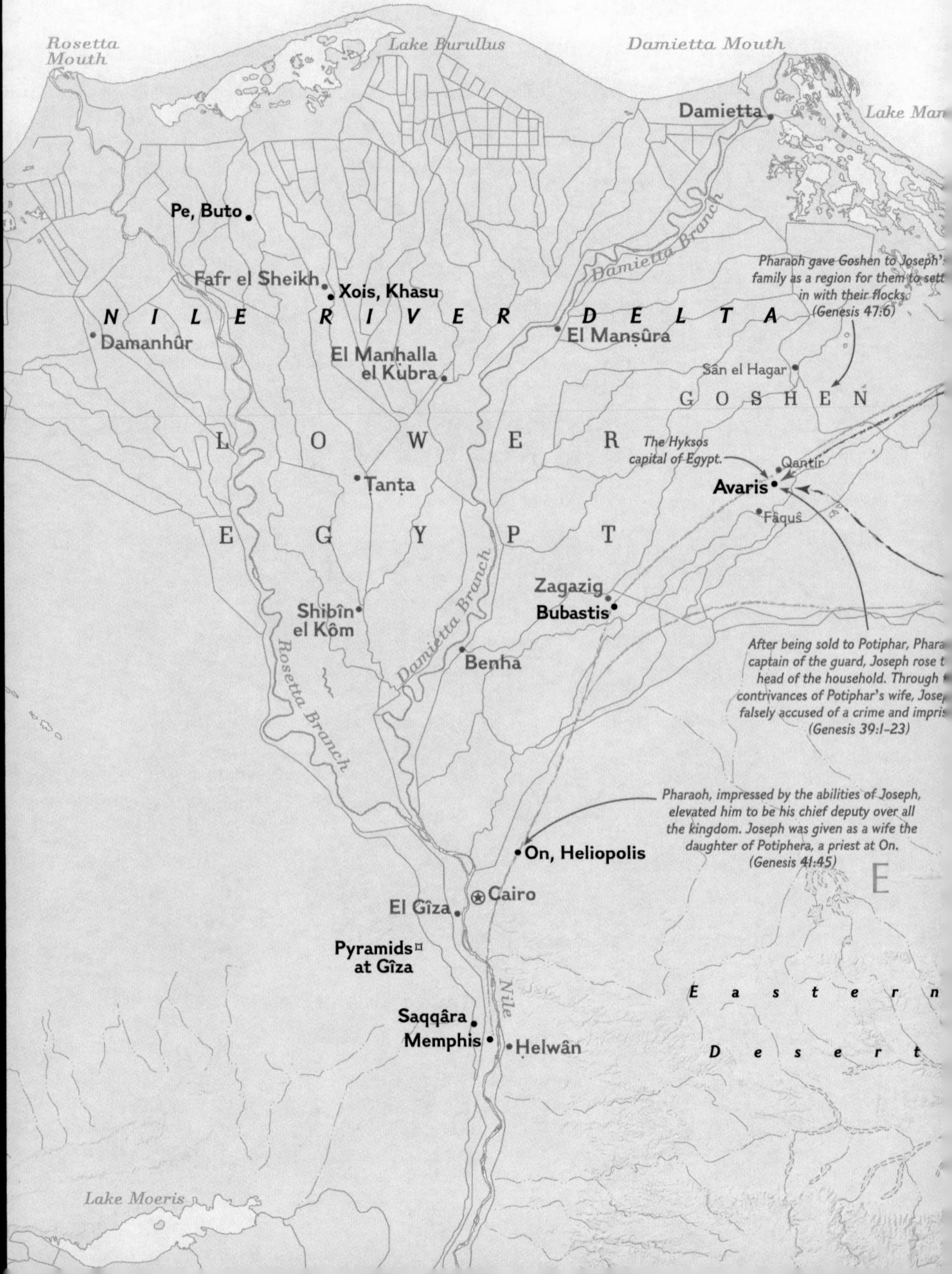

Rosetta Mouth
Lake Burullus
Damietta Mouth
Damietta
Lake Man
Pe, Buto
Kafr el Sheikh
Xois, Khasu
NILE RIVER DELTA
Damanhûr
El Manhalla el Kubra
El Manṣûra
Damietta Branch
Sân el Hagar
GOSHEN
LOWER EGYPT
Tanta
Qantir
Avaris
Fâqûs
Zagazig
Bubastis
Shibîn el Kôm
Benha
Rosetta Branch
On, Heliopolis
Cairo
El Gîza
Pyramids at Gîza
Nile
Saqqâra
Memphis
Helwân
Eastern Desert
Lake Moeris

Pharaoh gave Goshen to Joseph's family as a region for them to settle in with their flocks. (Genesis 47:6)

The Hyksos capital of Egypt.

After being sold to Potiphar, Pharaoh's captain of the guard, Joseph rose to head of the household. Through the contrivances of Potiphar's wife, Joseph was falsely accused of a crime and imprisoned. (Genesis 39:1–23)

Pharaoh, impressed by the abilities of Joseph, elevated him to be his chief deputy over all the kingdom. Joseph was given as a wife the daughter of Potiphera, a priest at On. (Genesis 41:45)

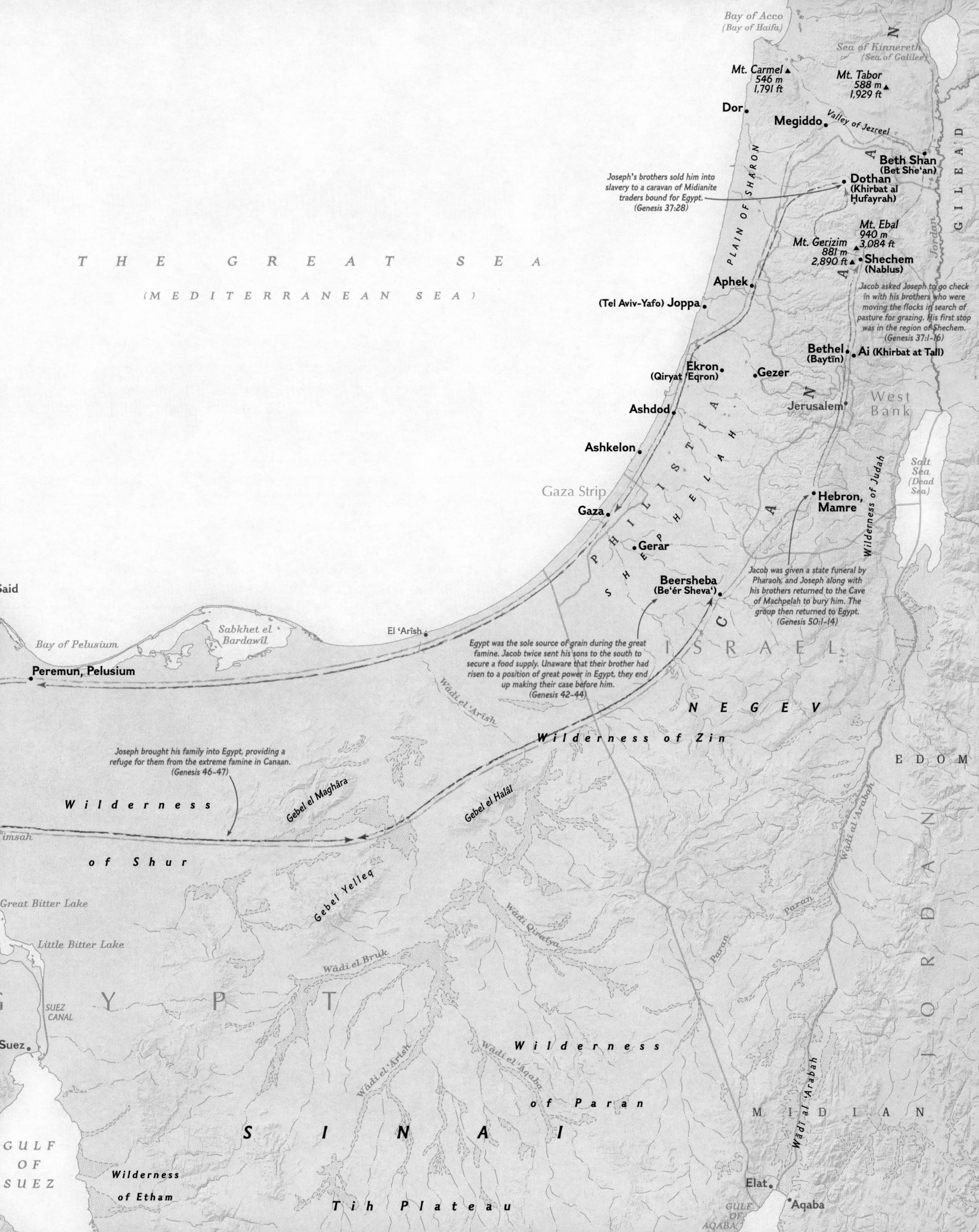

Bay of Acco
(Bay of Haifa)
Sea of Kinnereth
(Sea of Galilee)
Mt. Carmel
546 m
1,791 ft
Mt. Tabor
588 m
1,929 ft
Dor
Megiddo
Valley of Jezreel
Beth Shan
(Bet She'an)
Dothan
(Khirbat al Ḥufayrah)
Joseph's brothers sold him into slavery to a caravan of Midianite traders bound for Egypt.
(Genesis 37:28)
PLAIN OF SHARON
GILEAD
Jordan
Mt. Ebal
940 m
3,084 ft
Mt. Gerizim
881 m
2,890 ft
Shechem
(Nablus)
THE GREAT SEA
(MEDITERRANEAN SEA)
Aphek
(Tel Aviv-Yafo) Joppa
Jacob asked Joseph to go check in with his brothers who were moving the flocks in search of pasture for grazing. His first stop was in the region of Shechem.
(Genesis 37:1-16)
Bethel
(Baytīn)
Ai (Khirbat at Tall)
Ekron
(Qiryat 'Eqron)
Gezer
Jerusalem
West Bank
Ashdod
Ashkelon
PHILISTIA
SHEPHELAH
CANAAN
Salt Sea
(Dead Sea)
Gaza Strip
Gaza
Hebron,
Mamre
Wilderness of Judah
Gerar
Beersheba
(Be'ér Sheva')
Jacob was given a state funeral by Pharaoh, and Joseph along with his brothers returned to the Cave of Machpelah to bury him. The group then returned to Egypt.
(Genesis 50:1-14)
t Said
Sabkhet el Bardawîl
Bay of Pelusium
El 'Arîsh
Egypt was the sole source of grain during the great famine. Jacob twice sent his sons to the south to secure a food supply. Unaware that their brother had risen to a position of great power in Egypt, they end up making their case before him.
(Genesis 42-44)
ISRAEL
Peremun, Pelusium
Wâdi el 'Arîsh
NEGEV
Wilderness of Zin
EDOM
Joseph brought his family into Egypt, providing a refuge for them from the extreme famine in Canaan.
(Genesis 46-47)
Wilderness
of Shur
Gebel el Maghâra
Gebel el Halâl
Timsah
Wādī al 'Arabah
Gebel Yelleq
Great Bitter Lake
Wâdi Qiraiya
Paran
Little Bitter Lake
Wâdi el Bruk
EGYPT
SUEZ CANAL
JORDAN
Suez
Wâdi el 'Arîsh
Wâdi el 'Aqaba
Wilderness
of Paran
Wādī al 'Arabah
MIDIAN
SINAI
GULF OF SUEZ
Wilderness
of Etham
Tih Plateau
Elat
Aqaba
GULF OF AQABA

Another two-day journey by foot and Joseph's caravan would have reached the border of Egypt at the ancient city of Peremun, "the city created by Amun," later known as Pelusium. Its remains are located close to the modern village of Tell el Farama. At Peremun, the traders would have stopped to request their transit visas, no doubt offering some of their silver or spices to expedite the proceedings.

Joseph Enters Egypt

WHAT KIND OF AN Egyptian society would Joseph have encountered? Many scholars have argued that the story of Joseph appears to be set in the mid-17th century B.C.E., a time when the unity of Egypt's Upper and Lower Kingdoms had crumbled once again. A number of local princes had gained control of the northern part of Egypt. What provoked this disintegration is hard to ascertain. It is possible that flooding levels of the Nile had remained low for many seasons, sharply curtailing the harvests of the largely agrarian economy of the unified kingdom. The pyramids built by the rulers of the 13th dynasty (ca 1755–1630 B.C.E.) at Saqqara are small, pitiful affairs built of mud brick, with only a thin veneer of limestone. The pyramid of Khendjer (or Userkare), built around 1747 B.C.E., is but a shadow of the grand pyramids of Khufu and Khafre in Giza, which by this time were more than 800 years old. Under pressure from regional warlords, the power in the country had shifted to the new capital in the north: the city of Avaris, located on one of the tributaries of the Nile.

The gradual disintegration of Egypt's central authority invited a wave of immigration from the east, including a large number of peoples from Canaan, Syria, and Anatolia. Already in 1991 B.C.E., the author of the so-called Prophesy of Neferti complained that "the land [is] being cast away ... [by] Asiatics who pervade the land. ... [They] have come down into Egypt, for a fortress lacks another beside it, and no guard will hear." Now, at the onset of the so-called Second Intermediate period in Egypt (ca 1630–1520 B.C.E.), the wave of poor immigrants pressing at Egypt's borders became overwhelming. Once in the country, most rushed to the fertile fields of the Nile Delta, where farmers were always in need of cheap labor. Hence, the group of slaves dragged along by the Ishmaelites would hardly have raised an eyebrow.

It is not clear from Genesis to which city Joseph is taken. We are told that he is put to work in the household of Potiphar, "one of Pharaoh's officials, the captain of the guard" (Genesis 37:36). Joseph is thus spared the fate of ending his life in the hellish work pits or in the fields. In Potiphar's house, a slave like Joseph would have encountered many Semites like himself, pulled from the ever abundant pool of cheap immigrant labor. An 18th-century B.C.E. roster of an upper-class household from Thebes lists 80 servants, of which no less than 40 names

POTIPHAR'S WIFE

WHEN JOSEPH FIRST ENTERS POTIPHAR'S household, his good looks catch the attention of the Egyptian's wife. Genesis calls him "handsome and goodlooking" (Genesis 39: 6). In the Bible, Potiphar's wife tries to seduce Joseph, but he refuses her; to cover her tracks, she accuses Joseph of attempting to lie with her despite her resistance. Potiphar believes his wife and sends the innocent Joseph to prison.

The Bible does not tell us the name of Potiphar's wife, but the Islamic tradition does: She is called Zulaikha, later adopted as Zelikah in rabbinic texts. The Koran relates how with a handsome lad like Joseph in the house, Zulaikha knew that tongues in the city were bound to wag. In retribution, she invites the local women to a banquet to see the young man in person.

When they are all busy cutting up their food with knives, she summons Joseph to the dining room. The women look up, stunned. They "cut their hands (in amazement), and they said: how far from God is imperfection; this is not a mortal; this is a noble angel!" (Koran 12:31-32). In rabbinic texts, notably the 12th-century Sefer ha-Yashar, the women cut their fingers while peeling oranges, and Zelikah says triumphantly, "What would you do if, like myself, you had him every day before your eyes?"

This 15th-century Islamic print from Afghanistan portrays the attempted seduction of Joseph by Potiphar's wife, Zulaikha, as described in the Koran.

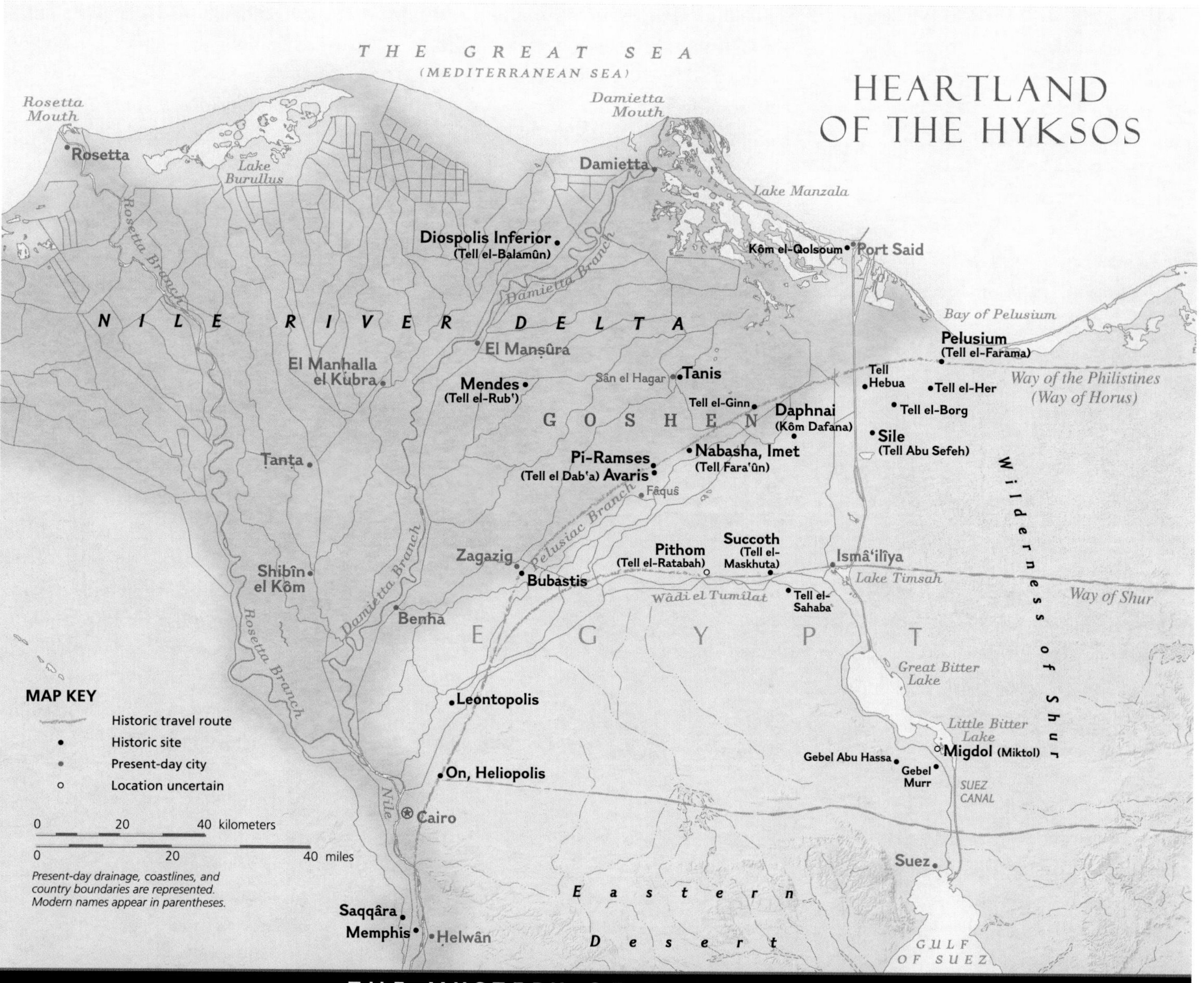

THE MYSTERY OF THE HYKSOS

WHO WERE THE HYKSOS, THE "RULERS OF foreign lands" who took control of the Nile Delta around 1630 B.C.E. and ruled it for more than a century as the 15th dynasty? Scholars have offered theories identifying the Hyksos as either Hittites, Hurrians, Aryans, Syrians, or Canaanites. Others, seeing a Minoan influence in some of the decoration of pottery retrieved from 16th-century B.C.E. Avaris, believe Greeks from Crete or Mycenae were involved. While as a group, the Hyksos may have numbered many immigrant tribes, some scholars now believe the Hyksos were of Canaanite origin. One telling clue is the names of the five Hyksos kings, which betray a Canaanite influence. One king is even called Yakob-her, which one scholar identified as a "commemoration" of the patriarch Jacob. This suggestion would bolster the hypothesis that Joseph was, in fact, a high official in a Hyksos administration. Others caution that the names of Hyksos kings were invariably Egyptianized and are therefore altered beyond recognition. They argue for an identification of the Hyksos with the Hittites, since it was most likely the Hittites who introduced the iron chariot and the composite bow to the Near East. The widespread presence of Hittites in Canaan as early as the 19th century B.C.E. is attested to in Genesis. Abraham bought the Cave of Machpelah from Ephron the Hittite (Genesis 23:10), while Esau married two Hittite women (Genesis 26:34).

are of Semitic origin. The list includes female weavers and spinners with such names as Aqaba, Haiimmi, and Menahem. Since Egyptians had trouble pronouncing these foreign names, "guest workers" from Canaan or Syria were promptly given Egyptian names, which rolled more easily off the local tongues.

Like most ancient peoples, the Egyptians did not bother to learn much about the cultures of bordering territories, which they considered barbarian. To them, all peoples to the east were considered "Asiatics" or, in the case of tribal people, "sand-dwellers." "Their tongues are separate in speech, and their natures as well," reads a 14th-century B.C.E. hymn. "Their skins are distinguished ... [Yet everyone] has his food, and his time of life is reckoned." Since few Egyptians bothered to learn a foreign tongue, immigrant workers and slaves, like Joseph, were expected to adopt the language of the land and assimilate as best they could.

In the Genesis story, where did Joseph's master live? The name "Potiphar" does not appear in any Egyptian records until the New Kingdom, but the position of captain of the guard is eminently plausible. Since Potiphar is described as being close to Pharaoh himself, it is reasonable to assume that he would have been the commander of an elite guard, possibly Pharaoh's own company of royal bodyguards, rather than an officer serving in Egypt's regular army. This would imply that Genesis placed Potiphar close to the royal palace of Pharaoh.

The question is important, because at the presumed time of Joseph's journey to Egypt, the Nile River Delta went through another political convulsion that would have a major impact on Egypt's subsequent history.

The Hyksos Period

AS FAR AS WE CAN GLEAN from a third-century B.C.E. Egyptian historian named Manetho and from archaeological findings, the influence of Semitic immigrants became so great that some of their tribal chiefs overthrew the Egyptian sheikhs and established their own fiefdoms. By 1720 B.C.E., the power of these fiefdoms had grown to the point that they marched on the ancient capital of Memphis and sacked the city. The ancient nobility was stunned by this coup d'état. In response, the Egyptian aristocracy withdrew to Thebes, there to establish the 17th dynasty. The northern part of the country was now completely controlled by foreign chieftains, the leader of whom did not hesitate to arrogate to himself the title of Pharaoh. Manetho calls these Semitic usurpers "Hyksos" or Hikau-khoswet, which means "desert princes." Their first king was Sheshi, who established the 15th dynasty (ca 1630–1520 B.C.E.).

Joseph receives from Pharaoh a golden collar, like this vulture-shaped one recovered in the tomb of King Tutankhamun (ca 1332–1322 B.C.E.), which were Egyptian symbols of power.

In view of subsequent developments described in Genesis, it is possible that the Joseph story is set in the Northern Kingdom, at the court of the Hyksos Pharaoh, rather than in the court of the Egyptian king in Thebes. The Hyksos established their royal court in Avaris, which had already been the northern capital for quite some time. Avaris has been identified with the site of Tell el Dab'a, though very little remains of the city today (or of any other Egyptian monuments in the region for that matter), due to continuous flooding. Austrian archaeologist Manfred Bietak, who has conducted extensive excavations in the area, believes that Avaris was expanded by the Hyksos to a size of almost two square miles. His most recent excavation at Tell el Dab'a is uncovering a vast 200-foot mud-brick palace of the 16th century B.C.E. If confirmed, this discovery would be the largest Hyksos palace structure ever found in the Nile Delta. Though Avaris was much smaller than the sprawling crown cities of Memphis or Thebes, the luxury of its temples and residences would have made a deep impression on a shepherd boy from Canaan.

Joseph resolves to make the best of his predicament, Genesis tells us. He is diligent and resourceful, and Potiphar takes a liking to him. The captain "made him overseer of the house and put him in charge of all that he had" (Genesis 39:4).

And Pharaoh said to Joseph, "I had a dream, and there is no one who can interpret it. I have heard it said of you that when you hear a dream you can interpret it." Joseph answered Pharaoh, "It is not I; God will give Pharaoh a favorable answer." (Genesis 41:15-16)

Joseph, moreover, is an attractive lad, "handsome and good-looking" (Genesis 39:6). This fact is not lost on Potiphar's wife. She tries to seduce him, but Joseph steadfastly refuses her advances.

One day, she cannot contain herself. She grabs him by his garment and cries, "Lie with me!" But Joseph brushes her off and runs, leaving her standing with his tunic in her hand. Now, Potiphar's wife has to do some quick thinking. If anyone sees her with the incriminating evidence, it would be only a matter of time before her husband finds out. Taking the initiative, the wife calls out to the servants and declares loudly that the "[Hebrew] came in to me to lie with me ... and when he heard me raise my voice and cry out, he left his garment beside me and fled outside" (Genesis 39:15). The woman's words were readily believed. Potiphar promptly sends Joseph to prison.

Such a story is almost as old as Egypt itself. Time and again, we will see that the narrative tradition of the Bible is rooted in the lore of the region in which the stories evolved. One famous example is the Egyptian fable of "The Tale of Two Brothers," found in the Papyrus d'Orbiney. Once, the story goes, there was a man named Bata who lived with his older brother, Anubis, and his wife. One day, when they were both working in the fields, they ran out of seed, so Anubis promptly dispatched Bata to fetch some. Bata arrived at Anubis's house just as his sister-in-law was finishing her toilette. "There is [great] strength in you," she purred. "I see your vigor daily. Come, let's spend an hour lying together. It will be good for you. And I will make fine clothes for you."

The loyal Bata was shocked. "What is this great wrong you said to me?" he asked. "Do not say it to me again! But I will not tell it to anyone." And Bata stomped off to the fields, leaving the wife fretting whether he would tell his brother after all. Planning a preemptive defense, she covered herself with paint and mud. When Anubis came home, she lay prostrate in their bedroom, crying that Bata had tried to force himself on her. Naturally, the poor Bata protested his innocence, but inevitably it was the woman, her dress strategically torn, who was thought to tell the truth.

The Pharaoh's Dream

In prison, Genesis continues, Joseph is remanded not to a punitive colony but to a detention center for "the king's prisoners" (Genesis 39:20). Soon, two new prisoners from Pharaoh's immediate circle arrive: the king's personal sommelier, or cupbearer, and the royal baker.

THE EGYPTIAN DIET

Genesis refers to large granaries built by Joseph. Egypt was one of the largest grain-producing regions in the Near East. The two main crops were emmer (or spelt) wheat and barley, used to bake bread and brew beer, staples of the Egyptian workers' meals. This diet was complemented with lentils, beans, cabbage, and, occasionally, fish. Only the very wealthy families were able to eat meat on a regular basis; they dined principally chicken and oxen beef.

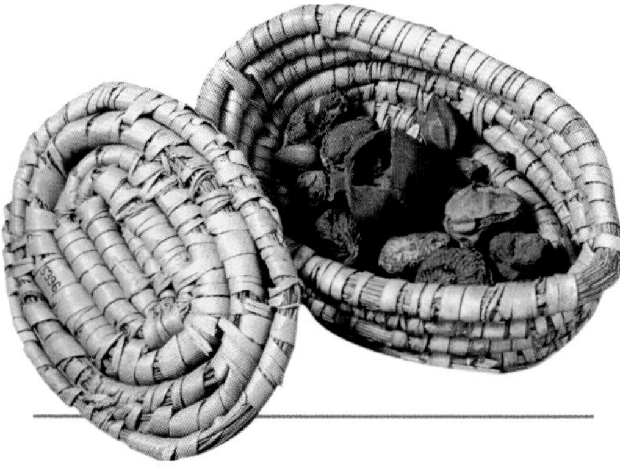

Joseph's good conduct wins him considerable freedom inside the prison. One day, he is surprised to find the baker and the cupbearer sitting on the ground, dejected. Both just had vivid dreams. The problem for them is that there is no one to interpret the dreams.

For an Egyptian, this dilemma was bad news indeed. As elsewhere in antiquity, dreams were considered the medium by which the gods revealed a glimpse of the future to mere mortals. The interpretation of dreams was a critical science, avidly resorted to by kings and commoners alike. In Egypt alone, hundreds of "dream books" were written about the meaning of sleep-induced visions, as these typically foretold either good fortune or disaster. People sometimes went to sleep (or to "incubate") in the temple of their favored deity, hoping that the god would reveal an answer to their worries. Given the disjointed and surreal nature of most dreams, it was readily acknowledged that their meaning was often hidden, and therefore in need of decoding. In the book *Teachings for Merikare*, written by King Kheti for his son, the king warns that dreams typically mean the exact opposite of their surface meanings. An activity as mundane as eating or drinking, for example, often portended great and ominous events. If one saw himself leading his cattle home from the fields, it was considered an excellent omen, for it meant that the dreamer would "shepherd" the spirit of his family. Glimpsing oneself in a polished mirror, however, was considered tantamount to seeing one's imminent death.

We now understand the long faces of the baker and the cupbearer. Talented dream interpreters, like sorcerers and magicians, moved in high circles and were unlikely to be found in prison. But then Joseph appears and tells them, "Do not interpretations belong to God?" (Genesis 40:8). Impressed by this reply, the cupbearer begins to tell his dream. "There were three branches," he says, "Pharaoh's cup was in my hand; and I took the grapes and pressed them into Pharaoh's cup" (Genesis 40:10-11).

Joseph reflects on this and says: "This is its interpretation: the three branches are three days; within three days Pharaoh will lift up your head and restore you to your office." The delighted cupbearer nods and smiles. "But ... do me the kindness," Joseph adds, "to make mention of me to Pharaoh, and so get me out of this place" (Genesis 40:12-14).

This papyrus from the reign of Ramses II (ca 1279–1213 B.C.E.) provides a list of both "good" and "bad" dreams and their interpretations.

Now the baker, too, is keen to hear Joseph's interpretation of his dream. He has dreamt that three cake-baskets were on his head, and birds were eating from them. In his case, however, the future is not so bright. In three days, Joseph says, "Pharaoh will lift up your head—from you!" (Genesis 40:19).

The days pass. On the third day, Pharaoh wakes up and decides to overturn the sentence of the cupbearer. He is promptly restored to his office. And just as Joseph foretold, the baker is hanged for his offense.

Joseph waits for a reprieve, or a token of gratitude from the cupbearer, but nothing is forthcoming. Two long years must pass. Joseph slowly withers away in prison.

Then, one night, it is Pharaoh himself who has a vision. He dreams that he is standing by the Nile, "and there came up out of the Nile seven sleek and fat cows, and they grazed in the reed grass. Then

GUM, BALM, AND MYRRH

EGYPT'S CREATIVE ENDEAVORS REVOLVED around its cult of the dead. Its rituals required raw materials not available in Egypt: timber, marble, granite, and countless precious metals and gems. In addition, the mummification process involved the use of various exotic chemicals and spices, most notably natron. However, the "gum, balm and myrrh" carried by the Ishmaelites to Egypt were luxury items, used in temples as well as in the homes of the rich, rather than in the mortuary of the embalmer.

Balm was the gum of the balsam tree *(Commiphora opobalsamum)* that grew in southern Arabia and was mostly used for its medicinal qualities. According to the Bible, this tree was introduced to Palestine by the Queen of Sheba.

Myrrh is the resin of a bush of thorns *(Commpihora myrrha)* that grew along the Arabian and African coasts on the Red Sea. It was used as a perfume agent in oils and as incense in the temple. In Roman Palestine, myrrh (mixed with oil) was used for purification of the deceased prior to burial (as in the case of Jesus). Myrrh was also an adhesive and therefore only applied as the last and final step of burial preparation before the body was wrapped in linen. Egypt's high society used myrrh to "aromatize" their homes, while the priesthood burned vast quantities of incense in the temples. A relief in the mortuary temple of Queen Hatshepsut (ca 1473–1458 B.C.E.), the female pharaoh, records one of many expeditions to Punt (possibly Somalia) to procure ships loaded "heavily with ... all goodly fragrant woods of God's-Land, heaps of myrrh-resin, with fresh myrrh trees ... ihmut incense, sonter-incense, [and] eye-cosmetic ... Never was brought the like of this for any king ... since the very beginning."

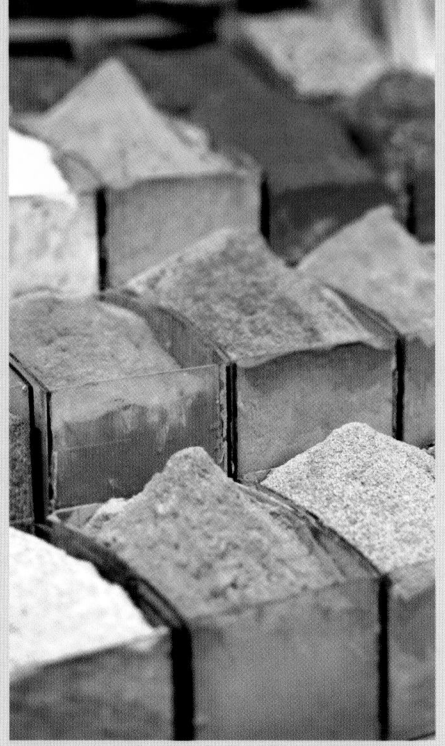
Just as merchants have purveyed them for centuries, colorful and exotic spices await buyers in the souk of Aswan, Egypt.

seven other cows, ugly and thin, came up. … The ugly and thin cows ate up the seven sleek and fat cows" (Genesis 41:1-4).

Pharaoh instantly summons his sorcerers and interpreters, to no avail, as no one can decipher the dream. But then, the cupbearer remembers his time in prison. "A young Hebrew was there with us," he says. "He interpreted our dreams to us" (Genesis 41:9-12). The young Hebrew is summoned from prison and told of Pharaoh's mysterious dream. Joseph pauses, and says, "The seven good cows are seven years … of great plenty throughout all the land of Egypt. After them there will arise seven years of famine" (Genesis 41:26-30). Joseph's interpretation highlights a recurring problem for Egyptian society: famine. In the decades preceding the Hyksos rule, Egypt's law and order, its *maat*, had been torn asunder by the repeated failure of the harvest. Its royal house fell because of it. A prophecy of prolonged famine not only spelled great economic hardship, but also, quite possibly, a repetition of great political upheaval.

This wall painting from Nebamun's tomb at Western Thebes, created during the 18th dynasty of the New Kingdom, depicts a scene that recalls Pharoah's mysterious dream.

Fortunately, Joseph has a strategy to thwart this great catastrophe. "[Let] Pharaoh select a man who is discerning and wise," he says. "Let Pharaoh proceed to appoint overseers over the land, and … [let] them gather all the food of these good years that are coming" (Genesis 41:33-35).

Pharaoh ponders the young man in front of him. "You shall be over my house," the king replies, "and all my people shall order themselves as you command; only with regard to the throne will I be greater than you" (Genesis 41:40). With one stroke, Pharaoh has appointed Joseph to grand vizier, a powerful position akin to that of prime minister, second only to Pharaoh himself.

Joseph As Grand Vizier

AND SO, the son of a tribal chieftain in Canaan, a sand-dweller, an Abiru, is appointed to the second-highest office in the most powerful empire of his time. Scholars, naturally, have taken issue with this aspect of the story. In all of Egypt's literature, there is no record of an Asiatic slave rising to the position of grand vizier. Such a powerful position only was granted after many years of service, and typically went to a person of unquestionable loyalty to the crown. To offer such authority to an unknown foreigner, an alien, runs counter to everything we know about ancient Egypt. For these scholars, the story of Joseph's rise to power is a myth. Its purpose is to underscore the moral superiority of God's people over the bankrupt polytheism of Egypt: Despite the great test by enslavement in the years to come, Israel will emerge as a nation in being for all time, whereas Egypt's might will turn to dust.

There are, nevertheless, some tantalizing clues in Joseph's story that betray, at the very least, an intimate knowledge of Egyptian history and culture. "Seven years" as a distinct unit of time is found in several Egyptian texts, particularly in the Book of the Dead. A text purporting to be a decree from King Djoser, builder of the stepped pyramid of Saqqara (27th century B.C.E.), states that "all in the palace were afflicted by a great evil, since the Nile had not come [i.e., inundated the land] in my time for seven years." As a result, the text continues, "grain was scant, fruits were dried up, and everything people eat was in short supply." This document was actually written during the Ptolemaic period (ca 2nd century B.C.E.), but its iteration of a seven-year famine is noteworthy.

The method of Joseph's installation as the grand vizier is equally intriguing. "Removing his signet ring from his hand," says Genesis, "Pharaoh put it on Joseph's hand; he arrayed him in garments of fine linen, and put a gold chain around his neck" (Genesis 41:42). The Egyptian Museum in Cairo and the Metropolitan Museum of Art in New York have several such breathtaking collars of office. They are strung together with tubular beads of feldspar, carnelian, or lapis lazuli, and topped with two large falcon heads of gold. As a mark of divine power, collars like these had no parallel in their time. The Pharaoh's "signet ring," is also an important detail in the story, for it gives

THE SECRET OF THE WHEELED CHARIOT

THE ABILITY OF THE HYKSOS MILITARY TO vanquish the armed might of Egypt was in no small measure due to their secret weapon, the horse-drawn chariot. These light chariots, pulled by twin horses, revolutionized the battlefield of the mid-second millennium B.C.E.

Wheeled wagons had been used before, notably by the Sumerians, but the development of the spoked wheel made the chariot a lightning-fast vehicle with great maneuverability. The Hyksos used their desert chariots to devastating effect, decimating the Egyptian infantry with their skilled archers and missileers while proving too fast for Egyptian return fire.

The chariot was possibly developed by the Hittites in their home territory of Anatolia (modern Turkey) and subsequently introduced in the Near East. The first reference to a chariot in Near Eastern texts appears in an 18th-century B.C.E. Hittite Anitta text, where a chariot is drawn by up to 40 teams of horses.

The exiled Egyptian royals in Thebes took heed and began to build chariots of their own. They ultimately used them to to evict the Hyksos invaders. Later in the Bible, Egyptian-built chariots figure prominently in the story of the Exodus. They also appear in Egyptian accounts, such as the climactic Battle of Qadesh, where Ramses II deployed thousands of chariots against an equal number in the Hittite army. The battle between the two armies ended in a draw. After fighting had ceased, Ramses and the Hittite King Hattusilis III entered into a nonaggression pact, the first such agreement in recorded history.

Terra-cotta model of a four-wheeled chariot from Mesopotamia, dated to the third and early second millennium B.C.E.

Joseph the royal seal with which to authenticate his decrees.

But perhaps the most intriguing reference in Genesis is that Pharaoh allows Joseph to "ride in the chariot of his second-in-command" (Genesis 41:43). Naturally, Joseph would have had to travel many miles throughout the kingdom to supervise the gathering of surplus grain. Before the advent of the Hyksos, however, no one in Egypt had ever seen a horse, let alone ridden in a chariot. The iron chariot with spoked wheels, pulled by two fast horses, was introduced by the Hyksos. At the very least, the explicit chariot reference suggests that the story of Joseph and the period of the Hyksos in Egypt are closely intertwined. It is certainly tempting to think that the new Hyksos government would welcome ambitious young men who, like themselves, were "Asiatics" from the east.

Another authentic detail is Pharaoh's decision to give Joseph an Egyptian name. This practice was common for Asiatic immigrants in Egypt. Joseph was henceforth known as Zaphenath-paneah, which some commentators believe may mean "he deciphers the concealed" (Genesis 41:45). What's more, Genesis tells us that Pharaoh gives Joseph the daughter of a priest from On in marriage. This move would have been exceedingly shrewd. Even in the Egypt of the Hyksos, the priesthood still exerted considerable political power. By marrying Joseph into a priestly family from the city of On, Pharaoh would have preempted whatever potential resistance may have arisen among the clergy against Joseph's extraordinary powers.

As grand vizier of the realm, Joseph's duties would have been legion. A text describing the daily schedule of Rekhmire, vizier to Tuthmose III, notes that "the overseers of hundreds ... shall report to him their affairs." It is the vizier, the author of the text notes, who "dispatches the official staff to attend to the water-supply in the whole land," who "arranges the hearing of mayors and village sheikhs who go forth in his name," and who receives reports on "the rising of the Nile." Having thus been counseled by his vast staff, it is the vizier who then makes his personal report to Pharaoh.

The Bible describes Joseph as an able and talented executive. "He stored up in every city the food from the fields around it," says Genesis, suggesting that the local functionaries set aside their regional strife and gave Joseph their full assistance (Genesis 41:48). In each of the key cities, large beehive-type granaries would have been built and filled to the rafters with grain. Many such granaries have survived, in miniature form, in tombs throughout Egypt.

On, later called Heliopolis, lies just five miles north of Cairo, near the city of Matariyeh. A major city during the Old and Middle Kingdoms, On was chiefly known as a center for the worship of the sun god Atum. Since it was located at the apex of the Nile Delta, On was the obvious place to create a central depository of grain. Indeed, in the Book of the Dead, On (or Iunu) is described as the place of "multiplying bread," based on an ancient myth by which the god Horus fed the multitudes with only seven loaves of bread, symbolic for the seven souls of the god Re. From On, Joseph could travel north to oversee the harvesting of grain, or west across the Nile to supervise the gathering of dates, figs, and other fruits from the nearby fields of the Faiyum.

Today, the fields of the Faiyum are as green and fertile as they were then. Driving along one of the many waterways in the region, a traveler may stumble upon a canal that is called Bahr Yusef, the Canal of Joseph, to this day.

British painter Sir Lawrence Alma-Tadema (1836–1912) depicted Joseph in all his finery as a vizier in *Joseph, Overseer of the Pharaohs.*

THE CLAN MOVES TO EGYPT

According to Genesis, in times of famine caravans would travel from all over the Near East to Egypt in search of food amid the bounty of the Nile Delta.

FEEDING ITS PEOPLE was the principal responsibility of Egypt's rulers. "I gave bread to all the hungry of the Cerastes-Mountain," boasts Henku, the governor of the 12th province, or nome, around 2390 B.C.E. Pharaoh's ability to sustain the people depended on the annual flooding of the Nile. If the inundation was too deep, seeds could not germinate; if it was too shallow, there was insufficient silt deposited to support a full harvest. Each year, kings and commoners alike prayed fervently for a perfect Nile flooding. "Hail to thee, O Nile!" reads a hymn to the Nile from the late second millennium B.C.E. "You create the grain, you bring forth the barley, assuring perpetuity to the temples. If you cease your toil and your work, then all that exists is in anguish."

But after seven years, the Nile refused to rise, denying the parched land its rich fertile silt. The royal compact between Pharaoh and his people, assuring his subjects access to grain, was threatened. This is why, "when all the land of Egypt was famished, the people cried to Pharaoh for bread" (Genesis 41:55). Not only Egypt was affected; all over the Near East, the harvest failed. "There was famine in every

ca 1600 B.C.E.
A small group of Aryan-speaking peoples, the Mitanni, rule northern Mesopotamia

ca 1600 B.C.E.
Glass is molded into various types of vessels and objects in Canaan

ca 1600 B.C.E.
Mycenaean civilization emerges in the south of Greece

ca 1550 B.C.E.
Middle Bronze Age ends

The seven years of plenty that prevailed in the land of Egypt came to an end; and the seven years of famine began to come, just as Joseph had said. There was famine in every country, but throughout the land of Egypt there was bread. (Genesis 41:53-54)

country," says the Bible (Genesis 41:54), and nowhere more so than in Joseph's native land. Canaan's principal vegetation was nourished not by rivers and streams, but by annual rainfall. After seven years of drought, the situation would have been infinitely worse than in Egypt. Shepherds and farmers had little choice but to pack up their families and trek west, to Egypt. "[All] the world came to Joseph in Egypt to buy grain," says Genesis, "because the famine became severe throughout the world" (Genesis 41:57).

Jacob, too, summons his sons. "[There] is grain in Egypt," he says; "go down and buy grain for us there, that we may live and not die" (Genesis 42:2). The brothers prepare for the long journey along the coast to the gates of Peremun. All of Jacob's sons are sent to Egypt—except one. Benjamin, Jacob's other son by his beloved, Rachel, stays home. The patriarch cannot bear the thought of possibly losing his youngest son as well.

The journey to Egypt takes almost a month. The main route, the Way of the Philistines, would have been packed with refugees from the famine, some hailing from as far as Byblos and Damascus. Long lines form in front of the border checkpoints as people desperate for relief clamor to enter. A letter from an Egyptian border official named Inena, dating from the 13th century B.C.E., may describe such a scene. "We have finished letting the Bedouin tribes of Edom pass the Fortress of Mer-ne-Ptah Hotep-hir-Maat," Inena notes, and then adds, "to keep them alive, and to keep their herds alive."

After a long journey, according to Genesis 42:6, the brothers come at last into the presence of Joseph. The grand vizier is fully decked out in the ornamental garb of his high office, so naturally his brothers do not recognize him. But Joseph has noticed them, and in his mind a plan begins to form. When his brothers make their obeisance and offer their petition, he cuts them off. "You are spies," he declares. "[You] have come to see the nakedness of the land!" The brothers protest their innocence. "We ... are twelve brothers, the sons of a certain man in the land of Canaan," they proclaim loudly. "[The] youngest, however, is now with our father, and one is no more." Lies! Joseph rails. "Here is how you shall be tested: as Pharaoh lives, you shall not leave this place unless your youngest brother comes here!" (Genesis 42:9-15). The brothers are conveyed to prison; there, Joseph lets them languish for three days while he perfects his plan.

This stone slab shows Mentuwoser, a high official at the court of Senusret I (ca 1918–1875 B.C.E.), presiding over his funeral banquet.

The brothers are summoned back to the palace, where Joseph offers them a compromise: One of them shall remain in Egypt as hostage; the others shall return to Canaan with their grain and fetch the youngest son, Benjamin. "Thus your words will be verified," says Joseph ominously, "and you shall not die" (Genesis 42:20). And with that, Joseph points to Simeon. The guards promptly bind him.

When the brothers return home minus Simeon, they present Jacob with the alarming news that his son will be killed unless they all return with Benjamin. In Genesis, as well as in the much later telling in the Koran, Jacob is

ca 1550 B.C.E.
The Hittites capture Aleppo, in modern-day Syria

ca 1502 B.C.E.
The Mitanni and the Hittites threaten Egypt's borders in Syria and Canaan

ca 1500 B.C.E.
Musical instruments, including the lyre and guitar, are used in Hittite religious dances

ca 1473–1458 B.C.E.
Reign of Queen Hatshepsut in Egypt

ORIGIN OF THE 12 TRIBES

THE BIBLE ARGUES THAT THE POLITY OF ancient Israel developed as a conglomeration of 12 distinct pastoral tribes—groups of clans and families bound together by blood. Though deeply autonomous, tribes usually deferred to the authority of a tribal chieftain or sheikh in matters such as where to find fresh pastures, how to secure access to village wells, and how to defend the tribe against hostile marauders.

In the Bible, the Promised Land is settled by 12 tribes, each of which descended from a son or grandson of Jacob. Jacob was renamed "Israel," which is why the 12 tribes are collectively referred to as "Israelites." Reuben, Simeon, Judah, Issachar, and Zebulun, all sons of Jacob and his first wife, Leah, became fathers of tribes named after them. The tribes of Gad and Asher traced their lineage to sons of Jacob and Zilpah, Leah's servant. Jacob's second wife, Rachel, also bore two sons: Benjamin and Joseph. Only Benjamin became the father of a tribe, though Joseph's sons, Manasseh and Ephraim, each had a tribe named after him. Lastly, the tribes of Dan and Naphtali descended from the union of Jacob and Rachel's maidservant, Bilhah.

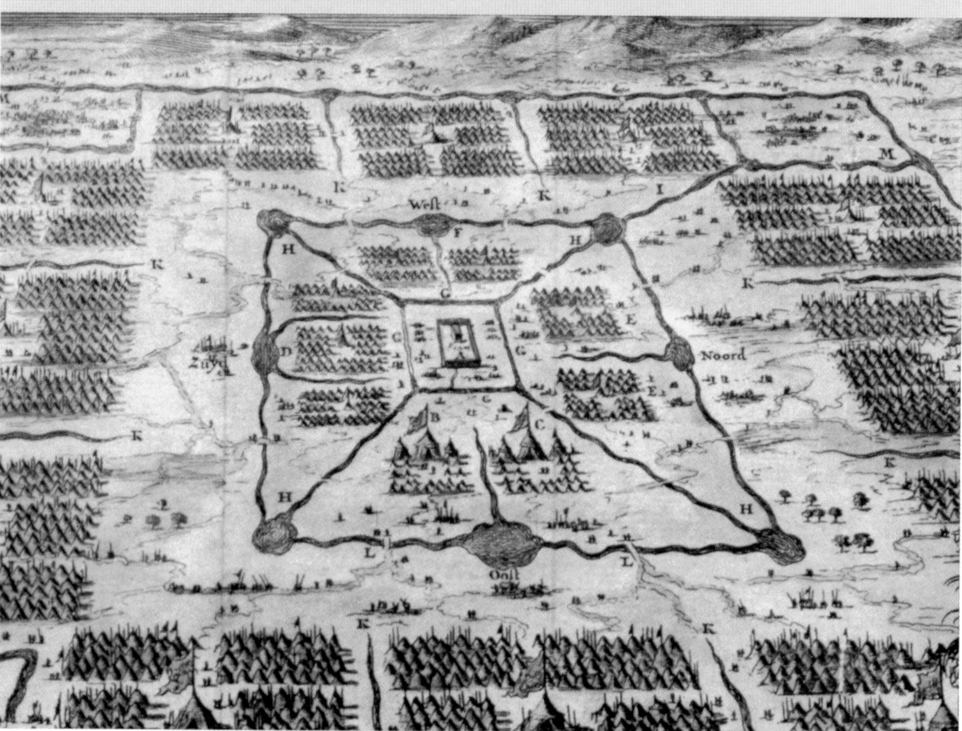

A Dutch colored etching from 1705 imagines the tents of the 12 tribes as pitched around the tabernacle containing the Ark of the Covenant.

desperate. He beseeches his sons, "How can I trust you with him, and expect anything different from what happened the last time when I entrusted you with a brother of yours?" (Koran 12:65).

But the famine persists, and Jacob has no choice but to send his sons back—Benjamin included. Anticipating that the release of Simeon will come at a steep price, Jacob instructs his sons to "take some of the choice fruits of the land in your bags, and carry them down as a present to the man—a little balm and a little honey, gum, resin, pistachio nuts, and almonds" (Genesis 43:11).

A silver cup with a gold handle in the form of a goat, discovered near Bubastis (Zagazig) in 1909 and dated to around 1200 B.C.E.

Joseph Reveals Himself

JOSEPH HAS NOT forgotten his captivity in the dry cistern in Dothan. He is determined to make his brothers suffer, to have them experience the same sense of betrayal they once inflicted upon him. He calmly awaits the return of his brothers, with Benjamin in tow. When they arrive, Genesis describes how Joseph unfolds the last act in his devious plan. He invites them to his house so that he can wine and dine his guests as the refined man of the world that he is. The next day, the brothers—who still have no clue why this grand vizier is so friendly—are packed off to Canaan. Huge bushels of grain strain the straps on the backs of their donkeys. To their amazement, the brothers discover that the money with which they paid for the supplies has been returned to them. But what they do not know is that Joseph has hidden his own silver goblet in one of the bags—in the sack that belongs to Benjamin.

Just as the brothers approach the border, they are overtaken by Joseph's steward, who announces that one of the grand vizier's precious goblets is missing. He searches the sacks, and sure

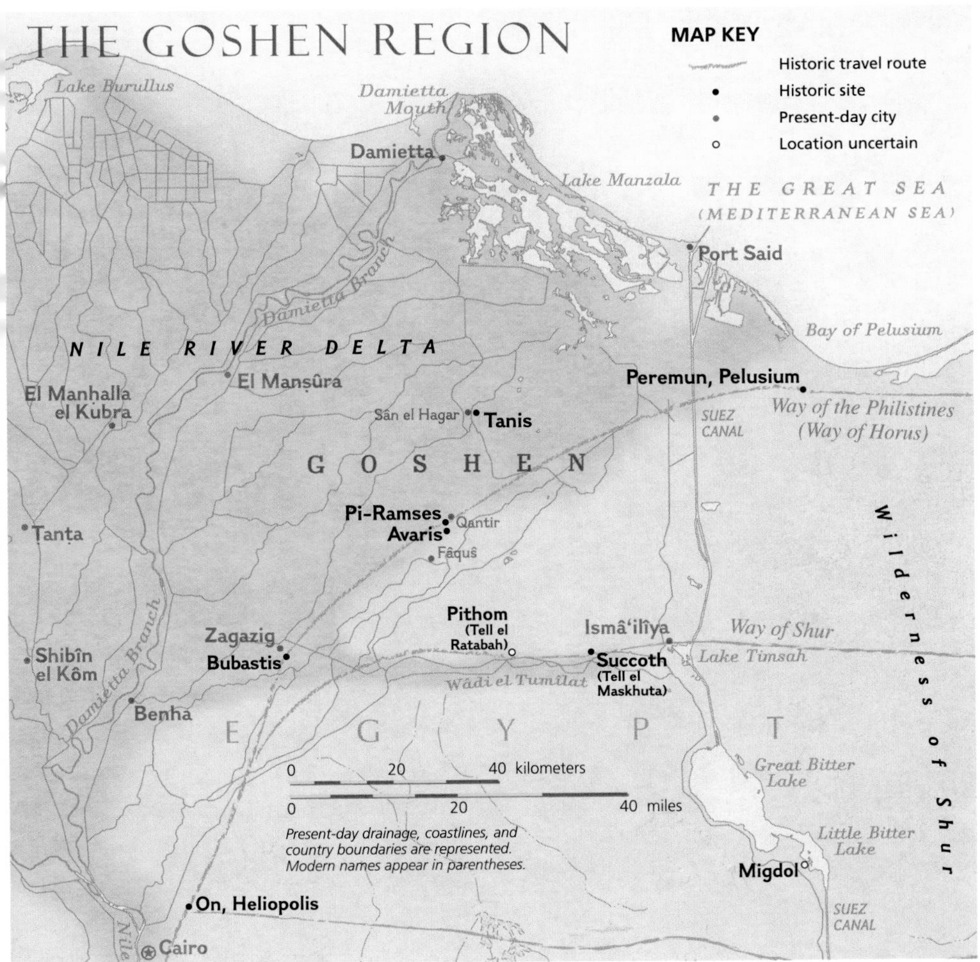

enough, Benjamin's bag contains the missing item. The young boy is promptly arrested and hauled back to the capital. His brothers follow in despair. They ask to speak to Joseph personally.

This time, it is Judah who appeals to Joseph; Judah, the very man who saved Joseph's life but sold him into slavery for a fistful of silver. "What can we say to my lord? ... How can we clear ourselves?" he asks. "[The] one in whose possession the cup was found," Joseph orders, "shall be my slave; but as for you, go up in peace to your father" (Genesis 44:16-17). But, says Judah, "when I return to my father, your servant, and the boy is not with us, then, as his life is bound up in the boy's life, he will die" (Genesis 44:30-31). Judah offers himself as a slave instead, "for how can I go back to my father if the boy is not with me?"

When Joseph sees the torment in his brothers' eyes, he can no longer restrain himself. All the servants are dismissed. Then he turns to his brothers and cries out:

I am your brother, Joseph,
whom you sold into Egypt. And now do not
be distressed, or angry with yourselves,
because you sold me here; for God sent me
before you to preserve life. ...
Hurry and go up to my father and say to
him, "Thus says your son Joseph,
God has made me lord of all Egypt;
come down to me, do not delay.
You shall settle in the land of Goshen, and
you shall be near me, you and your children
and your children's children, as well as your
flocks, your herds, and all that you have.
I will provide for you there"

(Genesis 45:4-11).

THE PASTURES OF GOSHEN

Joseph's decision in Genesis to settle his tribal family in the land of Goshen makes sense given what is known of the region (Genesis 45:9-11). Goshen (Qosem in a 12th-dynasty papyrus) was located in the northeastern part of the Nile Delta near Wâdi el Tumîlat, between the easternmost channel of the Nile and the Bitter Lakes. Well irrigated, it offered plenty of pastureland. Today, many of the Nile channels that existed in Joseph's day have disappeared, but the region is still one of the most fertile in Egypt. Since, according to Genesis, Joseph assures his family that they "shall be close" to his house, possibly Joseph lived in the Hyksos capital of Avaris (associated today with Tell el Dab'a), in the heart of the eastern delta. The Book of Exodus returns to Goshen to find Joseph's descendants, the Israelites, in bondage.

Jacob's Family Settles in Egypt

AND THUS, according to Genesis, the clan of Abraham, Isaac, and Jacob moves to Egypt. As Joseph has promised, they are invited to settle in the emerald pastures of the plain of Goshen. Joseph, says Genesis, "made ready his chariot and went up to meet his father Israel in Goshen." He presented himself, and "wept on his neck a good while" (Genesis 46:29). With Pharaoh's permission, the family is granted "a holding in the land of Egypt, in the best part of the land, the land of Rameses" (Genesis 47:11). Though the name of the city is an anachronism (it would not be built until some 400 years after the time in which the Joseph story seems to be set), Genesis has thus pinpointed the location of their new home in the eastern part of the delta, close to the Hyksos capital of Avaris. Since Joseph assured his brothers that "you shall be near me" (Genesis 45:10), perhaps Joseph himself has also moved to Avaris. Located this close to the border, he would be well positioned to receive foreign delegations petitioning for food.

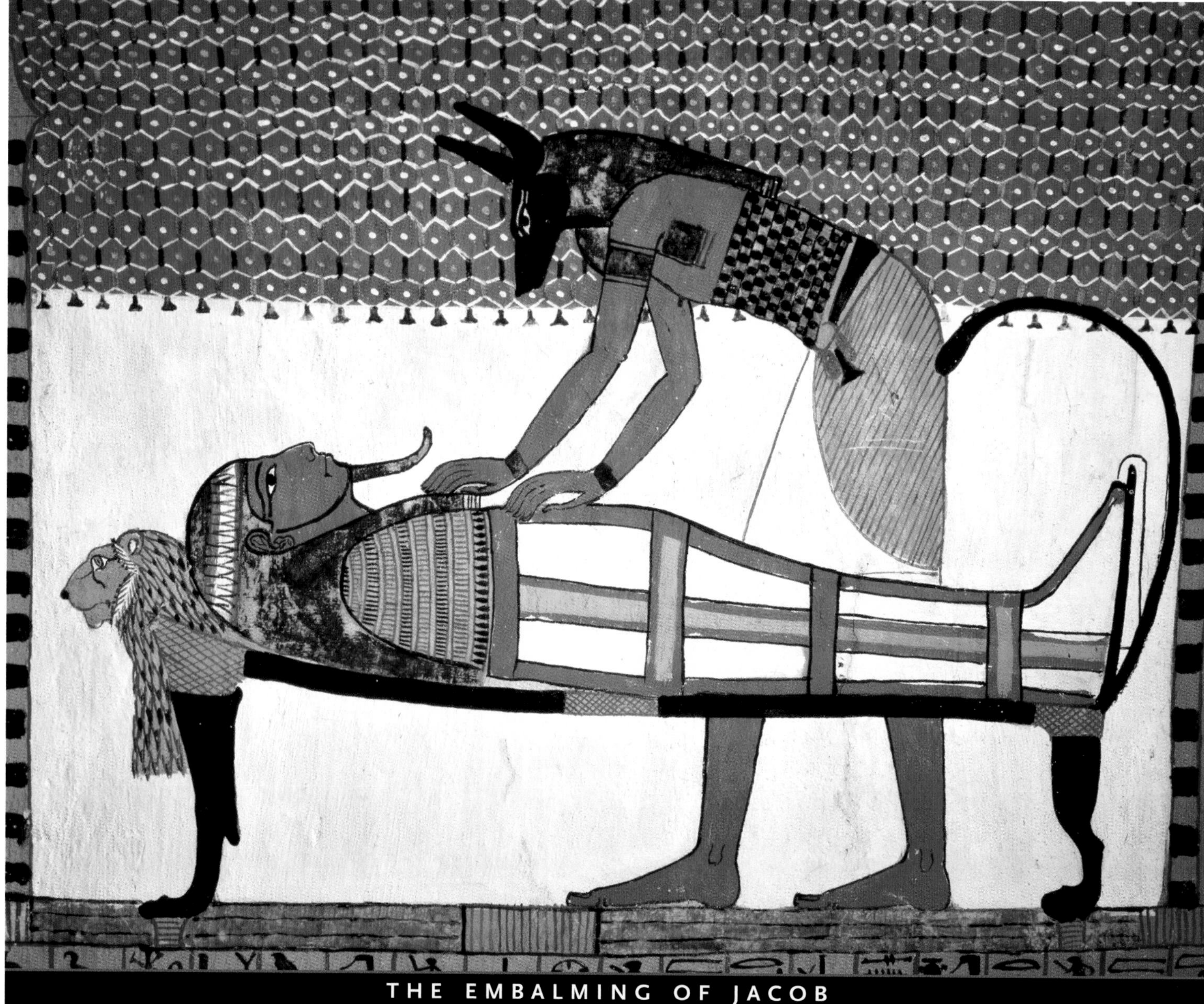

THE EMBALMING OF JACOB

Much of Egypt's religious cults revolved around mortuary procedures, principally the embalming of the deceased to prepare it for existence in the afterlife. Embalming was standard procedure for affluent Egyptians, as it was thought to preserve the integrity of a man's soul and body, his *ka* and *ba*. By keeping the exterior appearance of the body physically intact, the soul would recognize the body, and return to it time and again.

The secret to embalming is to remove all moisture from the body, thus eliminating the principal promoter of decay. Egyptian embalmers used a salt compound called natron—a mixture of sodium carbonate, bicarbonate, sodium chloride, and sodium sulfate, which were recovered from the Nile. Internal organs, prone to rapid decay, were removed and stored in canopic jars, the lids of which were shaped in the form of the divinity consigned to protect the organs. Scientists believe that the embalming cult may have originated with witnessing the natural dessication of corpses interred in Egypt's dry desert sands.

Jacob and Joseph are the only biblical figures whose bodies are embalmed (Genesis 50:2). Usually, Egyptian embalmers required 70 days, but Genesis says it only took 40 days to prepare the body of Jacob, possibly because the primary purpose of the mummification was to preserve the body during the long journey to the Cave of Machpelah in Hebron.

Anubis, the Egyptian god who served as guardian of the dead, leans over the mummy of Sennutem, a necropolis official of the 18th dynasty, ca 1539–1292 B.C.E.

Today, the fields of Avaris, just outside the village of Qantîr, are planted with the grain that foreigners once traveled from Canaan to obtain. Hardly any ruins remain; anything of value has long since been carted off to the Egyptian Museum in Cairo. Over time, the Nile channel that was Avaris's reason for existence filled with silt, and the royal court was forced to move elsewhere. According to the archaeologist Manfred Bietak, the city of Tanis, capital of the 21st dynasty (ca 1075–945 B.C.E.), was built at this time; but by then, the name of Joseph was only a memory.

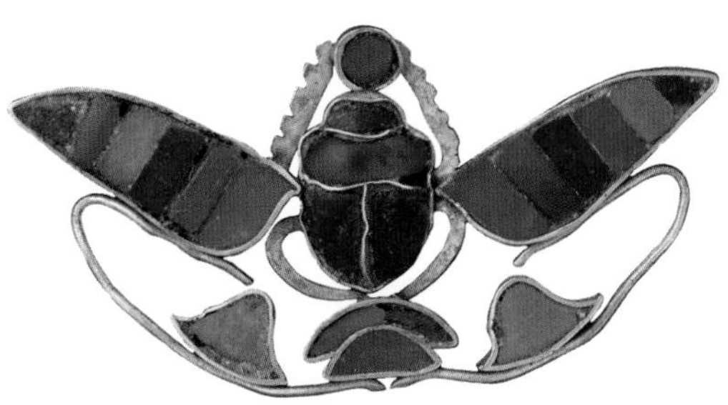

This scarab pendant made of gold and silver and inlaid with carnelian and lapis lazuli dates to the reign of Pharaoh Senusret II (ca 1842–1837 B.C.E.).

As far as Jacob is concerned, the Bible tells us that he lived his final years surrounded by the love of Joseph and his family. Seventeen years he resided in Egypt, says Genesis; and when at last he died, Joseph prepared him for burial in true Egyptian fashion. He had Jacob embalmed, after which the body was escorted back to Canaan. Conforming to his wishes, Jacob was buried in the Cave of Machpelah, alongside his father, Isaac, and his paternal grandfather, Abraham.

EGYPT	MESOPOTAMIA	CANAAN
ca 1640 B.C.E. Egypt's Middle Kingdom ends when the north is overtaken by the Hyksos, a nomadic group	ca 1700 B.C.E. One of the first locks is found in use at the Assyrian palace of Khorsabad in Nineveh	ca 1750 B.C.E. Hittite presence is widespread in Canaan
ca 1630 B.C.E. Egypt's nobility relocates the 17th dynasty to Thebes, while the Hyksos establish their capital at Avaris in the north	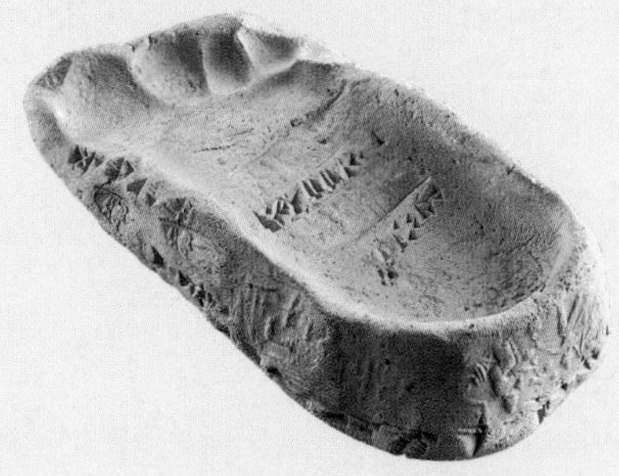	ca 1600 B.C.E. Glass is molded into objects and vessels in Phoenicia
ca 1600 B.C.E. Domesticated cats are present in Egypt	ca 1650 B.C.E. Babylonians first record the appearance of the planet Venus	ca 1530 B.C.E. Hyksos establish a temporary base in southern Canaan
ca 1600 B.C.E. Egyptians record a remarkably accurate medical text detailing the workings of the body	ca 1600 B.C.E. A small group of Aryan-speaking peoples, the Mitanni, rule northern Mesopotamia	
	ca 1595 B.C.E. The first Babylonian Empire ends with Hittite sack of Babylon	ca 1500 B.C.E. Kingdom of Mitanni rules parts of northern Syria in an empire stretching from the Mediterranean through to northern Mesopotamia
ca 1530 B.C.E. Pharaoh Ahmose drives the Hyksos from Egyptian soil	ca 1500 B.C.E. Instruments including the lyre and guitar in use in Hittite religious dances	ca 1468 B.C.E. Pharaoh Thutmose III defeats a coalition of Canaanite and Syrian kings near Megiddo in Canaan
ca 1520 B.C.E. The Hyksos 15th dynasty comes to an end		

Many scholars date the story of the Joseph's Egyptian sojourn to the Second Intermediate Period (ca. 1630-1520 B.C.E.) and, specifcally, the reign of the 15th dynasty of Hyksos kings in the north.

CHAPTER FOUR

The Exodus

If the focus of Genesis is to affirm God's covenant through the generations of Abraham, Isaac, and Jacob, then it is in Exodus that this divine covenant is made a tangible reality. Jacob's children, living in the land of Goshen, have been reduced to slaves, working in the construction pits of Pharaoh. Their newborn males are hunted down and massacred. In a very real sense, the Hebrew tribes face extinction, unless they can be rescued from the clutches of the most powerful empire on Earth. Their amazing escape from bondage lies at the core of Exodus, and indeed of the Old Testament altogether. Time and again, future generations of Jews and Christians will point to the story of Exodus as living proof of the immense saving power of God.

But, the Bible asserts, this rescue comes at a price. God expects the people of Israel to reciprocate by honoring the terms of the covenant. These will be spelled out in the covenant law, which takes up the remainder of the Pentateuch. These laws pertain to virtually every aspect of life—including birth, marriage, trade, family and tribal relations, and social justice. Exodus, in sum, marks the moment when the ancestral belief of Abraham matures into a national faith—that of Judaism.

The top of Mount Sinai, where many believe Moses received the Ten Commandments, bears the names of those who have scaled it.

THE HEBREW TRIBES ENSLAVED

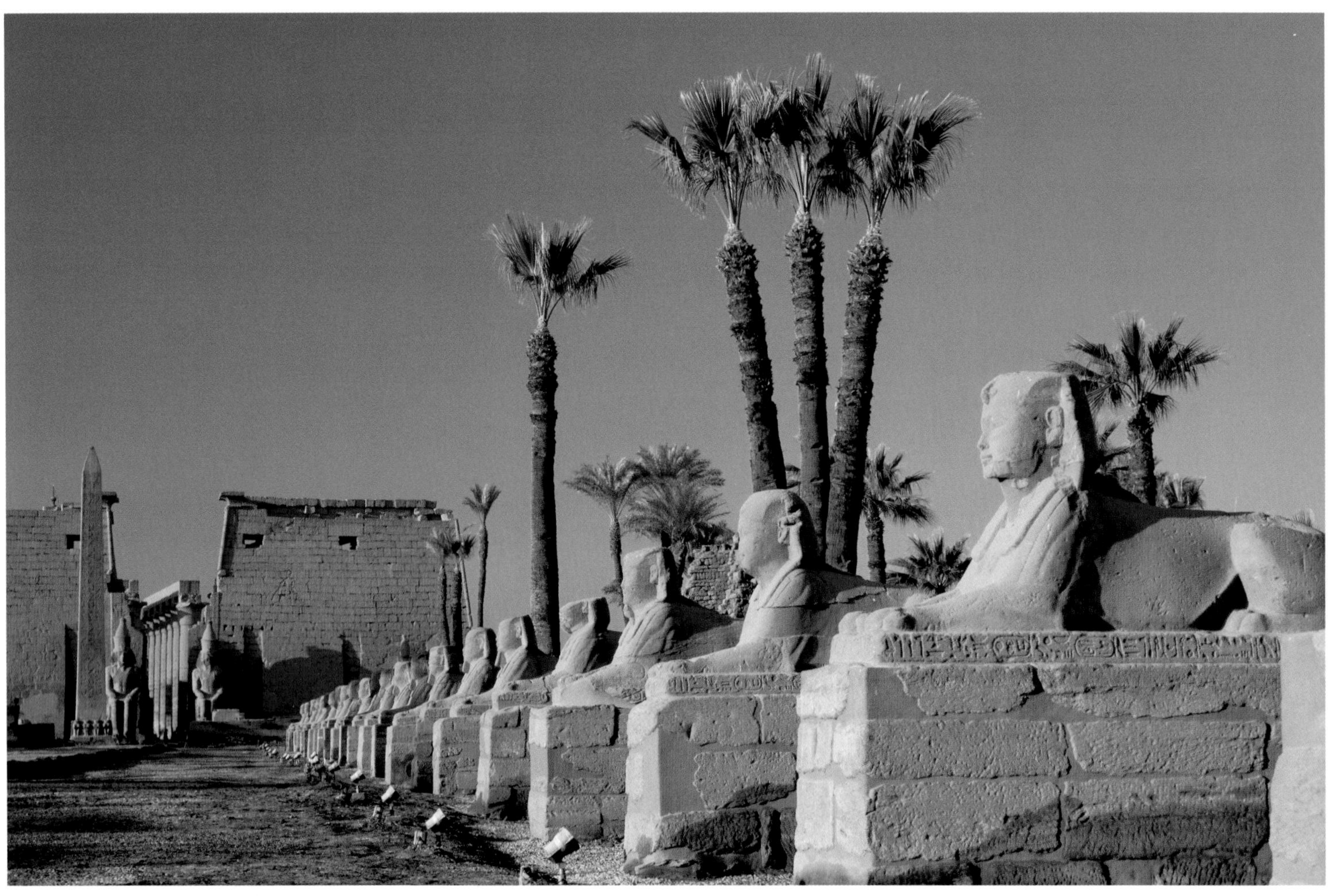

An impressive row of sphinxes flank the Processional Way to the temple precinct of Luxor in Egypt, symbol of the might of the New Kingdom.

AS THE BOOK OF EXODUS begins, the children of Jacob have lived peacefully for nearly a century in the land of Goshen. If it is true that the story of Joseph coincides with the reign of a Hyksos king, possibly that of King Sheshi or King Yakub-her, then Joseph's successors would have served under kings with Canaanite-sounding names such as Khyan and Apepi. Indeed, a stele in Karnak refers to Apepi, or Apophis, as "the Prince of Retenu," the Egyptian name for the greater region of Canaan and Syria. We do not know exactly when each of these Hyksos kings ruled, only that the 15th dynasty of Avaris lasted from approximately 1630 to 1520 B.C.E.

In the Book of Exodus, Jacob's children are "fruitful and prolific; they multiplied and grew exceedingly strong" (Exodus 1:7). We can imagine that their herds grew as well, while the tribe enjoyed the bounty of Goshen. They may have turned to farming and learned to till the land in the Egyptian fashion, planting crops after the floods of the Nile receded and the soil was plump with fertile nitrates. They may have gone fishing in the nearby lakes or hunted for ducks and geese in the marshes. They assimilate to Egyptian ways because, as Joseph once said, "all shepherds are abhorrent to the Egyptians" (Genesis 46:34).

ca 1550 B.C.E.
Egyptian influence in Canaan continues

ca 1539–1292 B.C.E.
18th dynasty rule begins in Egypt, ushering in the powerful New Kingdom

ca 1532 B.C.E.
Pharaoh Ahmose, the first ruler of the 18th dynasty, successfully drives out the Hyksos

ca 1530 B.C.E.
Hyksos court flees to Canaan

Joseph died and all his brothers and that whole generation. But the Israelites were fruitful and prolific; they multiplied and grew exceedingly strong, so that the land was filled with them. (Exodus 1:6-7)

Goshen is a paradise on Earth. It is the "best part of the land," assures Pharaoh in the final chapters of Genesis (Genesis 47:6). A papyrus from the 19th dynasty (ca 1292–1190 B.C.E.), written by a student named Pai-Bes to his instructor, Amenemopet, praises the "wealth of good things" in Goshen. "The pools are filled with fish, the lagoons are thick with birds; the meadows are covered with succulent grass; the fruits from the cultivated fields all taste like honey ... People are glad to be living here." The bounty of the land is illustrated by a wall painting from the Old Kingdom that shows adolescents like Pai-Bes at play in the marshes.

However, the Hyksos regime soon came under attack. In the southern capital of Thebes, the disenfranchised 17th dynasty of Egypt had never given up hope for the reunification of the country under its leadership. Around 1570 B.C.E., a fleet led by Pharaoh Ta'o II floated down the Nile. The great war of liberation, pitting "Old Egypt" against the Asiatic Hyksos, had begun. The battle did not end well for Ta'o II. Excavators found his mummified body in a tomb near Deir el Bahri in 1881; examinations performed years later found indications that his head had been slashed by swords. His son, Kamose, took up the torch and continued the battle. The conflict became the Sixty Years' War—a war of attrition that caused untold havoc upon the placid fields of the Nile.

As in any other war of national survival, victors became heroes. One such hero was Ahmose, a captain of a Theban war galley. As the proud hieroglyphics in his tomb in El Kab near Aswan tell us, he fought under three successive princes of the 18th dynasty: Ahmose (ca 1539–1514 B.C.E.), Amenhotep I (ca 1514–1493 B.C.E.), and Thutmose I (ca 1493–? B.C.E.). The soldier Ahmose's account indicates that the Hyksos armies put up a stiff resistance as the Theban phalanx moved deeper into the Nile Delta. "There was fighting on the water in the canal of Pa-Djeku in Avaris," Ahmose's text relates. "I captured a man, and made off with his hand." Severing the hand of a vanquished foe was an established custom by which Egyptian officers could ascertain the total body count of the fallen enemy.

As the armies of Ahmose steadily advanced northward, panic must have spread among the Hebrew tribes. Generations earlier, they would have simply pulled the pegs of their tents and moved back to Canaan. But by now, the Hebrews were settlers, harvesters, and fishermen—not desert nomads. And so we assume they stayed in Goshen and awaited the outcome. Eventually, the Hyksos forces started to give way. After a clash of arms that left thousands dead or dying in the hot sand, a bloodied Ahmose emerged victorious. The war was won. Old Egypt had triumphed.

The Hyksos court gathered its treasure and fled back east to Canaan. Pharaoh Ahmose entered their capital, Avaris, and allowed his troops to go on a rampage. "I carried off one man and three women from there," Captain Ahmose reports; "His Majesty gave them to me as slaves." Only in 1999 did archaeologist Manfred Bietak uncover a complex of buildings near Tell el Dab'a, the presumed site of Avaris, which revealed a thin layer of burned earth—testimony to the fury of King Ahmose's wrath.

But Pharaoh did not stop there. Knowing that he had the Hyksos on the run, Ahmose decided to pursue them, determined to erase this foreign threat from Egypt's borders. Once in Canaan, the retreating Hyksos soldiers formed a defensive line at Sharuhen, which scholars believe may be modern Tell al Far'ah, in the southern Negev. Only after the city was besieged and sacked did the king

Young Egyptian men joust over a bridge in this painted limestone relief from Saqqara, ca 2450 B.C.E. Old Kingdom, 5th dynasty.

ca 1514–1493 B.C.E. Egypt expands its territory into Libya during the reign of Amenhotep I

ca 1500 B.C.E. The Egyptian Empire extends from Nubia to present-day Syria

ca 1473 B.C.E. Senenmut, the court architect to Queen Hatshepsut, begins work on her splendid mortuary temple

ca 1468 B.C.E. Thutmose III defeats the Hittites in Canaan

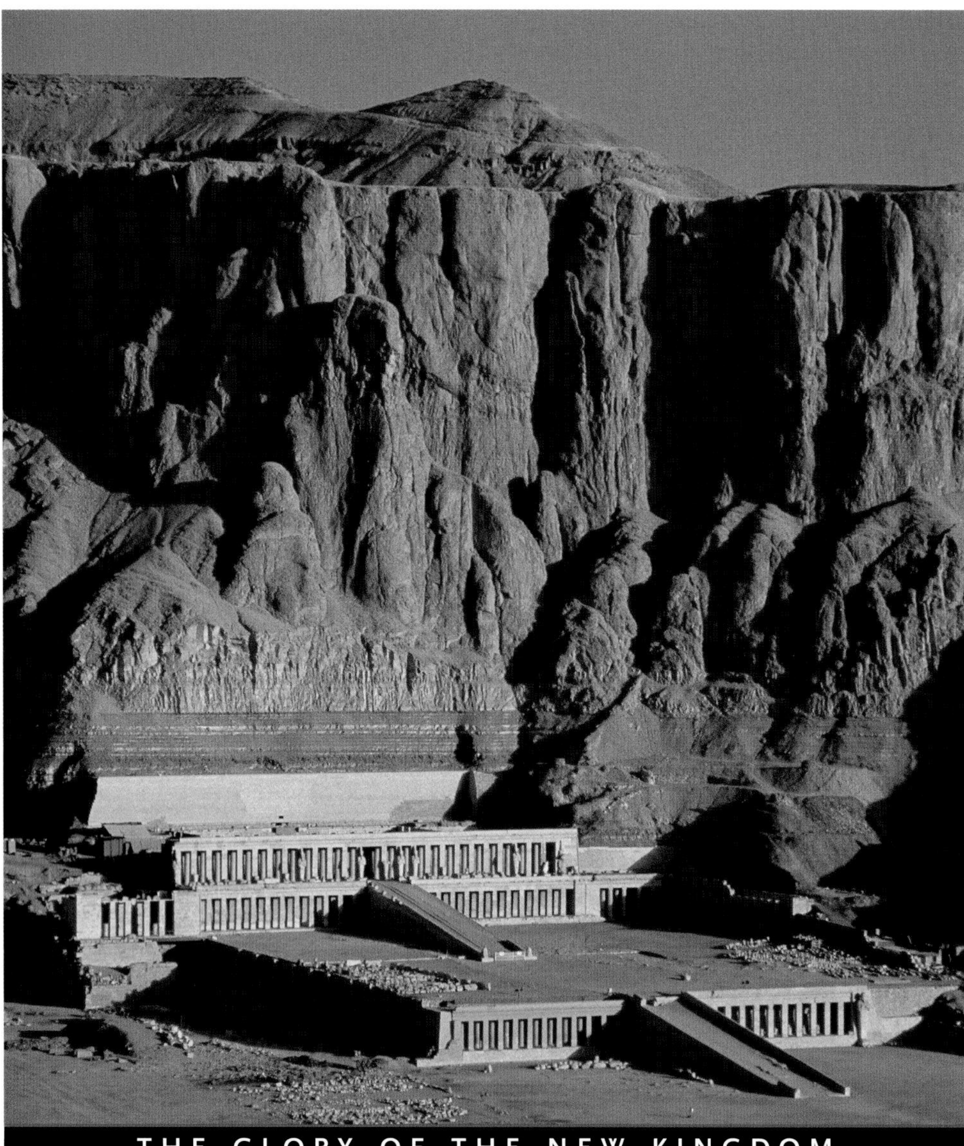

THE GLORY OF THE NEW KINGDOM

THE CITY OF THEBES CHANGED DRAMATICALLY during the New Kingdom (1539–1075 B.C.E.). With war booty flowing into the state coffers, the city became a beehive of new construction. One of the most spectacular new projects was initiated by the spouse and co-regent of Thutmose II, the mysterious Queen Hatshepsut (ca 1473–1458 B.C.E.). Designed by her court architect and senior adviser Senenmut, Hatshepsut's splendid mortuary temple—built near the towering cliffs of Deir el Bahri—rises as a large three-floor esplanade supporting a sanctuary cut deep into the rock. This daring feat of engineering is aligned with another major project on the opposite bank of the Nile, the great Temple of Amun in Karnak. Under the New Kingdom, Amun assumed the status of Egypt's principal deity. Thutmose III claimed that the campaign to extend the borders of imperial Egypt was "at the command of his divine father, Amun-Re." Amun's great temple in Karnak would become the nucleus of a vast priestly administration that soon would vie for secular power.

Queen Hatshepsut's grand mortuary temple, designed by the architect Senenmut, was partially carved from limestone cliffs near Luxor.

finally return to Egypt—there to contemplate an offensive against the Nubians.

This tale clearly reveals that a new kind of Pharaoh had emerged: the warrior kings of the 18th (ca 1539–1292 B.C.E.) and 19th (ca 1292–1190 B.C.E.) dynasties, forged by battle, vowing never again to suffer the humiliation of foreign occupation. Ahmose and his descendants of the Thutmosides dynasty raised new, professional armies and built strongholds along the eastern border, the Upper Nile, and the frontiers with Nubia. They further bolstered Egypt's national security by creating a buffer zone of vassal states—including Canaan, Edom, Moab, and Syria—that were ruled by proxy through local governors. The era of a new Egypt, the imperial Egypt of the New Kingdom, had begun.

Back in the Nile River Delta, every vestige of the Hyksos occupation was methodically erased. Collaborators with the former regime were prosecuted. Royal cartouches of Hyksos kings on public buildings were stamped over with the royal markings of the 18th dynasty.

What happened to the Hebrew tribes after the Hyksos left? Most likely, the Egyptians relegated them to second-class status, as "Asiatics," who would never again occupy positions of power. Perhaps they were left alone to pursue their harvests and raise their cattle—though always under a cloud of suspicion.

Egypt's 19th Dynasty

SIXTY-FIVE YEARS after the fall of Avaris, Thutmose III (ca 1479–1425 B.C.E.) received word of renewed unrest in the Eastern territories. Various tribal kingdoms, notably the Mitanni and the Hittite (located in today's Turkey and Syria), were pressing against the borders of Egypt's buffer zone, challenging its sphere of influence in Syria and Canaan. According to stone inscriptions at Karnak, the king promptly moved to the heart of Canaan and in 1468 B.C.E. met the rebellious Hittites near the old Canaanite shrine and fortress of Megiddo. Riding "in a chariot of fine gold, adorned with his accoutrements of combat," the pharaoh and his troops executed a complex pincer movement around the fortress to rout the enemy. "Thou hast smitten the Sand-dwellers as living captives!" exult the annals in Karnak, carved around 1460 B.C.E. "Thou has made captive the heads of the Asiatics of [Canaan]." From that point on, virtually every pharaoh of the 19th and 20th dynasties would find himself leading an army east into Canaan and Syria, to remind the vassal states who was in charge.

All this wealth and glory nearly came to naught when Amenhotep IV assumed power in 1353 B.C.E. Shocking the nation, Amenhotep renounced the traditional Egyptian deities and ordered his people to venerate the sun god, Aten. He changed his name to Akhenaten and moved his court from Thebes to a new capital city in central Egypt named Akhetaten ("the horizon of Aten"), now identified with Tell el Amarna. There he ruled with his wife, Nefertiti. Artwork from this era shows the king and his family in a new style, one emphasizing a pear-shaped body, protruding stomach, heavy eyelids, and elongated skull.

The king's almost complete devotion to religious affairs threatened Egypt's control of the vassal states of the east. Once again, Hittite forces began to foray into Egyptian-held territory. The small Egyptian garrisons stationed in Canaan and Syria were powerless against them. "Please, my King," wrote the Egyptian governor of Jerusalem, Abdiheba, "send archers against the men who are committing these crimes ... The Habiru are taking the cities of the king!" But Akhenaten had little interest in Egypt's foreign affairs. When he died in about 1336 B.C.E., the court promptly abandoned Amarna and returned to Memphis. There, Akhenaten's ultimate successor, the boy-king Tutankhaten became pharaoh. He soon changed his name to the now famous Tutankhamun ("the living image of

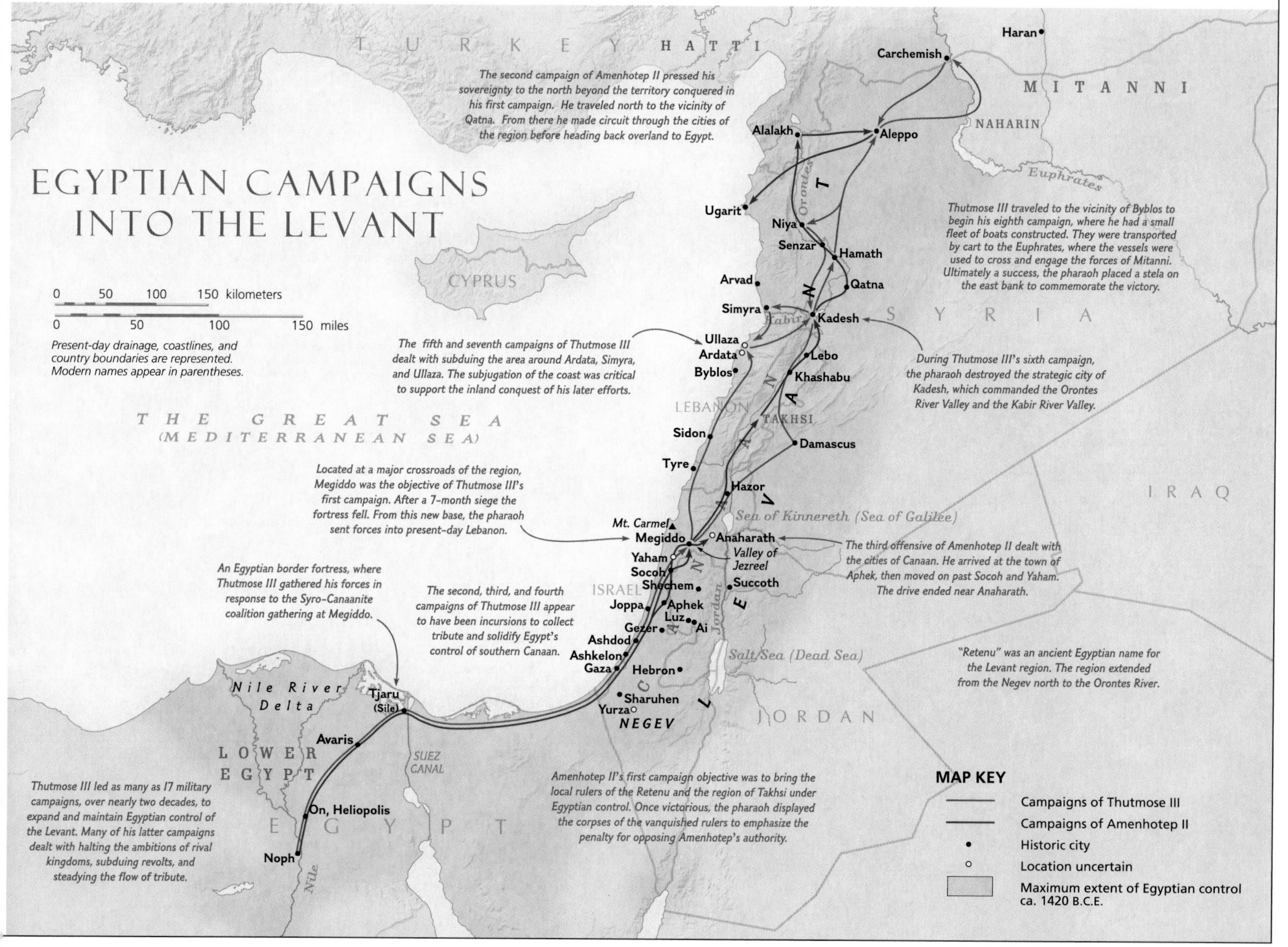

THE ROYAL LINE

THE NEARLY 500-YEAR PERIOD of New Kingdom rulers (1539–1075 B.C.E.) brought ancient Egypt to the peak of its power and wealth. Vowing never to suffer foreign occupation again, these kings created a buffer zone of vassal states including Canaan, Edom, Moab, and Syria. Many of the New Kingdom rulers also built monumental works throughout Egypt and ordered elaborate tombs for themselves in the Valley of the Kings.

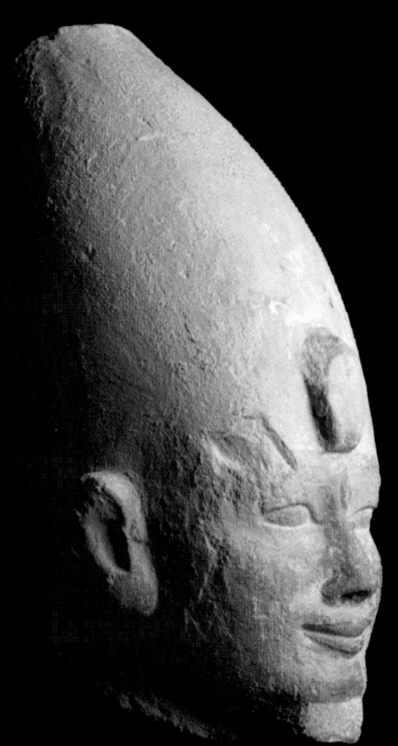

2 AMENHOTEP I
ca 1514–1493 B.C.E.

Amenhotep I continued Ahmose's conquest of Nubia and extended Egypt's territory into Libya. His mummy was located in 1881.

3 THUTMOSE III
ca 1479–1425 B.C.E.

Thutmose III, the "Napoleon of Egypt," conducted 17 campaigns into the Levant, consolidating Egyptian control from Nubia to Syria.

Ahmose succeeded in evicting the Hyksos from Lower Egypt and drove them deep into Canaan. He also launched a conquest of Nubia.

1 AHMOSE
ca 1539–1514 B.C.E.

Queen of Thutmose II and co-regent with her son Thutmose III, she briefly ruled as pharaoh and built an elaborate mortuary complex.

4 QUEEN HATSHEPSU
ca 1473–1458 B.C.E.

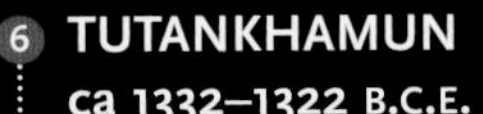

6 TUTANKHAMUN
ca 1332–1322 B.C.E.

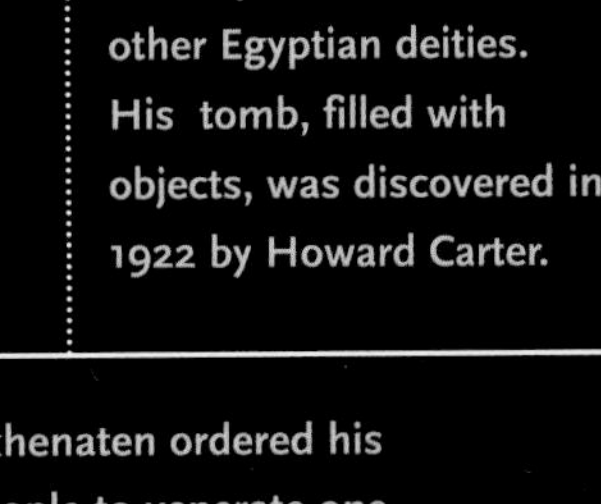

Tutankhamun restored the worship of Amun and other Egyptian deities. His tomb, filled with objects, was discovered in 1922 by Howard Carter.

8 RAMSES II
ca 1279–1213 B.C.E.

Greatest of New Kingdom kings, Ramses II stemmed the Hittite invasions at the Battle of Qadesh in 1274 B.C.E. and left many great monuments to his reign.

Akhenaten ordered his people to venerate one god: the sun god, Aten. He moved his court from Thebes to a new capital city near Amarna.

AKHENATEN
5 ca 1353–1336 B.C.E

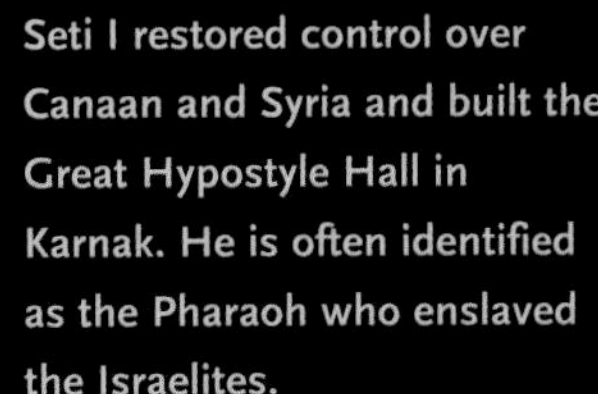

Seti I restored control over Canaan and Syria and built the Great Hypostyle Hall in Karnak. He is often identified as the Pharaoh who enslaved the Israelites.

SETI I
7 ca 1290–1279 B.C.E.

Amun"), and the old priesthood and worship of Amun was reinstated.

The military-minded 19th dynasty (1292–1190 B.C.E.) realized that only a massive effort could fully restore Egypt's power in the East. Seti I (ca 1290–1279 B.C.E.) saw the need for new military garrisons near the vulnerable eastern border. The ideal place, as the Hyksos kings had discovered centuries earlier, was the eastern Nile Delta. The Hyksos capital of Avaris, however, had fallen into ruin.

Consequently, Seti I began to build a new garrison city. In later years it would become known as Pi-Ramses-Meri-Imen ("the house of Ramses the beloved of Amun"), the city the Bible calls Raamses. Though hardly a stone remains, Pi-Ramses has been identified with a mound near Qantir, a village just north of the provincial capital of Faqus, some 70 miles north of Cairo.

There was only one problem: labor. Who would build these wonderful works? Pharaoh only had to look outside the balcony of his new palace in Pi-Ramses. There, in the fields of Goshen, were people of a vaguely Asiatic origin. No Egyptian may have known where they came from, or their legal status. Any records about their grant of asylum, assuming these ever existed, would have been lost when Ahmose destroyed Avaris and other Hyksos structures in the Goshen area.

It is at this time, says the Book of Exodus, that "a new king arose over Egypt, who did not know Joseph." Quite possibly, the king that Exodus has in mind is Seti I. "Look," says Pharaoh, "the Israelite people are more numerous and more powerful than we" (Exodus 1:8-9). This statement is surely an exaggeration; but as we have seen, the Nile Delta had always attracted vast numbers of immigrant workers from Canaan. To enlist these foreign workers into the construction pits of Pi-Ramses seemed a logical next step. "Come," the pharaoh of Exodus continues, "let us ... set taskmasters over them" (Exodus 1:10-11).

In 1279, Seti's third child, a son named after Seti's father, Ramses I, succeeded to the throne and began an astounding 67-year reign. His impact on Egypt as well as the world of biblical history would be profound. Ramses II harbored even more ambitious plans than his father. Already, he had seen that the new capital city of Pi-Ramses, begun by his father, was too small. He commissioned a second city, dedicated to the patron god of his family and dynasty, Per-Atum, or Pithom as the Bible calls it. And so, says Exodus, "they built supply cities, Pithom and Ramses, for Pharaoh. ... The Egyptians became ruthless in imposing tasks on the Israelites, and made their lives bitter hard service in mortar and brick" (Exodus 1:11-14).

It was then that a baby was set adrift on the river in a basket made of papyrus and sealed with bitumen and pitch.

OPPOSITE: The Great Hypostyle Hall at Karnak, begun by Ramses I (ca 1292–1290 B.C.E.), was once supported by 134 giant columns.

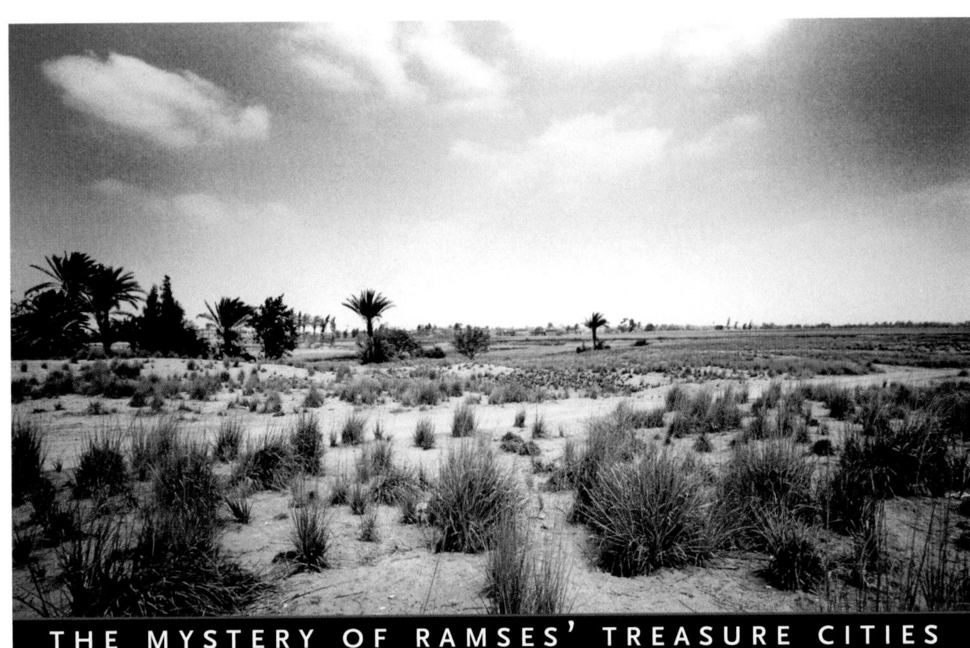

THE MYSTERY OF RAMSES' TREASURE CITIES

THE EXISTENCE OF THE BIBLICAL CITIES of Raamses (Pi-Ramses-Meri-Imen) and Pithom (Per-Atum) are well attested in ancient texts, but their locations have remained a mystery for centuries. Archaeologist Manfred Bietak believes he has identified Pi-Ramses near the village of Qantir, close to Tell el Dab'a, about 70 miles north of Cairo. If he is right, it would bolster the belief that Pithom once stood near Tell el Maskhuta, south of the village of Qassasin on the Suez Canal, for the two locations are not more than 20 miles apart. Very little of Pi-Ramses remains; most of it lies buried under fields where today farmers use ox-drawn plows similar to the ones used by their forebears thousands of years ago. Dr. Bietak believes that the city was dismantled when Pharaoh Siamun (ca 978–960 B.C.E.) chose to rebuild Tanis as the new capital of the 21st dynasty (ca 1075–945 B.C.E.). If the city remained unfinished at the time of the Exodus, its use as a quarry for nearby construction would have been logical.

This mound near the Nile Delta village of Qantir covers what archaeologists believe was the location of Pi-Ramses.

The Mystery of Moses

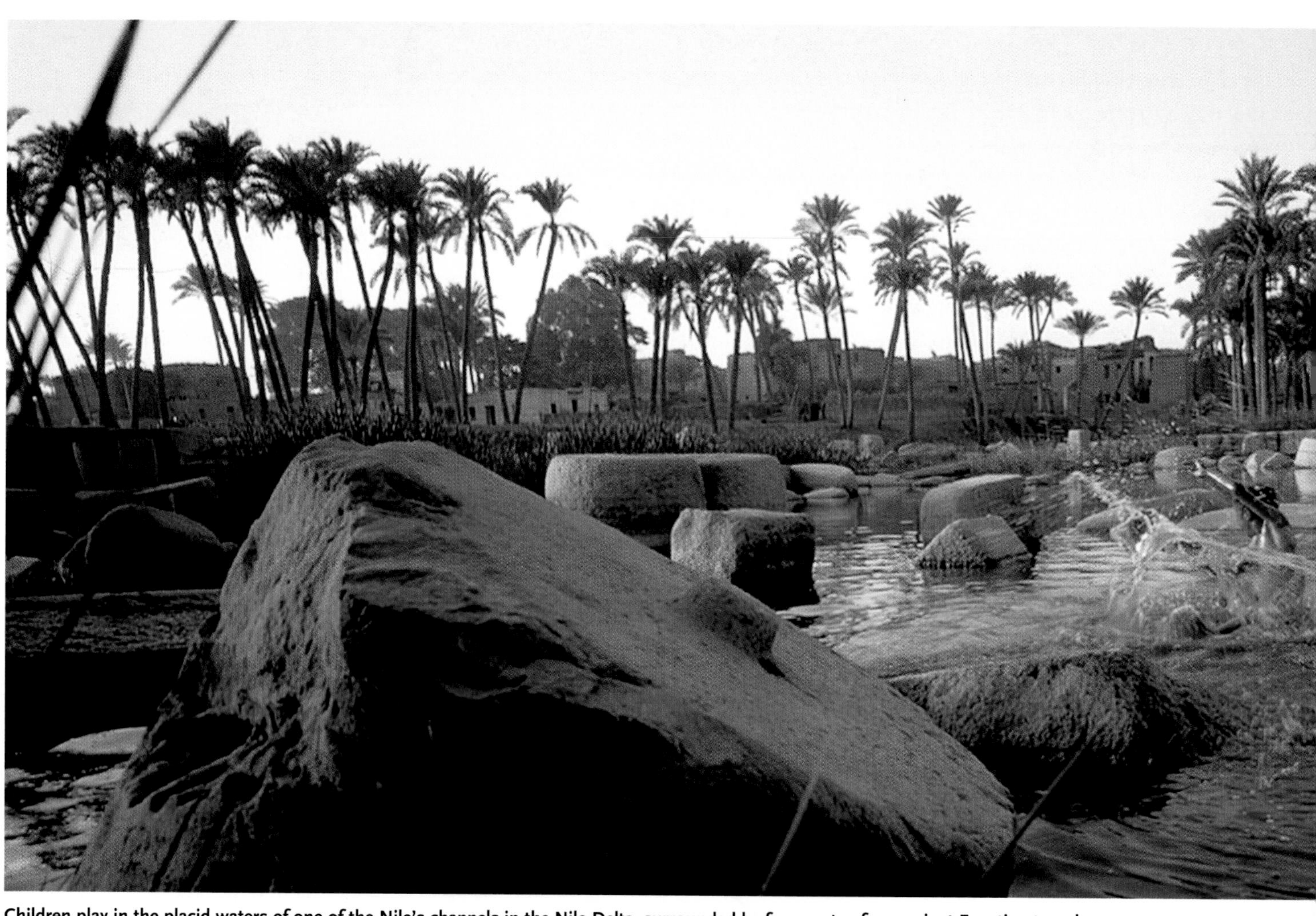

Children play in the placid waters of one of the Nile's channels in the Nile Delta, surrounded by fragments of an ancient Egyptian temple.

Moses is a cardinal figure in the Jewish faith; no other mortal person so encapsulates the history, the law, and the being of the Jewish people. He is the quintessential figure, the communicator with the divine, the giver of Law. Moses is also held in great reverence by Christians and Muslims. Christians view Moses as the receiver of the covenant that, in Christian eyes, was ultimately fulfilled by the birth of Jesus, who often referred to Moses in his teachings. Muslims also acknowledge Moses, or Mûsa, as God's Lawgiver. In fact, the Koran features more stories of Mûsa than of any other prophet.

But who was Moses? The key figure of the Book of Exodus is a mysterious character and the subject of considerable scholarly research and debate. Although we know much about the history of Egypt in the period in which the story of Moses is set, historical attestation of Moses himself does not exist. Indeed, the information in Exodus is sometimes contradictory. For example, Moses is a Hebrew, but is raised at the court of Pharaoh as an Egyptian prince. Though a pampered aristocrat, he is somehow able to make his way, all by himself, across the Sinai desert and survive—an amazing feat, even for the hardiest of Bedouin. He feels a kinship with the Israelites of

ca 1600 B.C.E.
Alphabetic script replaces Minoan hieroglyphic script

ca 1550 B.C.E.
Mycenaeans trade throughout the Mediterranean

ca 1500 B.C.E.
Kassites rule Babylon and adopt local customs

ca 1500 B.C.E.
Iron weapons and tools in use in most of the Near East

God called to him out of the bush, "Moses, Moses!" And he said, "Here I am." Then he said, "Come no closer! Remove the sandals from your feet, for the place on which you are standing is holy ground." (Exodus 3:4-5)

Goshen, but they consider him an outsider. In Egypt as well as during the long trek across the desert, Hebrew children will constantly heckle and conspire against him. Though raised in luxury, Moses only finds true happiness while living as a shepherd in the Midian desert with his Kenite wife, Zipporah.

Many scholars have suggested that Moses is a composite figure, a blend of tribal traditions originating in Goshen, the Midian community, and the later experience of Israel itself. Some have gone so far as to suggest that the entire Exodus episode, though rooted in some ancient Egyptian experience, is largely the work of skillful seventh- and sixth-century B.C.E. scribes. Exodus, however, points us to real names and places, many of which have been corroborated by Egyptian documents or by modern archaeology. By using these signposts, we may be able to reconstruct the story of Moses and the incredible saga of the liberation of Israel from Egypt.

Moses in Egypt

MOSES' INTRODUCTION in the Bible bears all the hallmarks of ancient lore. According to Exodus, Pharaoh is so concerned by the high birthrate among the Hebrew slaves that he orders every newborn male to be cast into the river (Exodus 1:22).

Around this time, the Book of Exodus continues, a Hebrew slave marries a young woman from his tribe. Exodus notes that both of these young people come from the tribe of Levi, no doubt with the intent of establishing a Levitical pedigree for Moses. The third son of Jacob and Leah, Levi accompanied Jacob during the migration into Goshen, where he settled with his sons Gershon, Kohath, and Merari. Many years later, after Moses received the Laws on Mount Sinai, the descendants of Gershon and Merari were designated as a class unto themselves and given the task of serving the Temple as priestly servants—the Levites. Moses, who with his brother Aaron descended from Kohath, thus chose his kinsmen for this high honor.

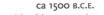

The young Hebrew bride, named Jochebed, soon conceives and gives birth to a son. Though elated, Jochebed fears that Pharaoh's patrols will discover her baby and kill him. She waits three months to ensure that the baby is healthy and strong. Then she places the baby in a papyrus basket, plastered with "bitumen and pitch" (Exodus 2:3). The choice of papyrus was an obvious one: Most Egyptian skiffs were made of tightly bound bundles of papyrus reeds and coated with bitumen to make the craft watertight. Jochebed takes one last look, and then gently floats the basket into the current of the Nile.

Jochebed and her husband, Amram, also have an older daughter. Though she is unnamed in this part of the story, we assume it is Miriam, who later appears in Exodus to compose a hymn of praise after Pharaoh's chariot forces are destroyed crossing the "Red Sea." As instructed by her mother, the girl strategically positions herself on the banks to ensure that no harm will come to her infant brother. At that moment, the daughter of Pharaoh comes down to the river with her ladies-in-waiting to bathe. She spots the floating basket and orders one of her servants to retrieve it. When she sees the crying babe, the Bible says that

Found in a tomb at western Thebes, this hunting scene dates to the 18th dynasty of the New Kingdom, around 1356 B.C.E.

ca 1500 B.C.E. Ugaritic ships control commerce in the eastern Mediterranean

ca 1450 B.C.E. Mycenaeans take control of Crete, ending Minoan civilization

ca 1400 B.C.E. City of Jericho, destroyed by the Hittites, is rebuilt and prospers

ca 1353–1336 B.C.E Akhenaten (Amenhotep IV) rules Egypt, shifting the capital from Thebes to Amarna

"she took pity on him. 'This must be one of the Hebrews' children,' she said" (Exodus 2:5-6). Miriam immediately rushes to the scene. "Shall I go and get you a nurse from the Hebrew women to nurse the child for you?" she asks. Pharaoh's daughter accepts her offer, so Miriam fetches her mother to serve as the child's nurse. Moses and his mother are thus reunited until the baby is weaned and his education can begin. At that time, Moses is brought to the palace, and Pharaoh's daughter raises him as her son (Exodus 2:10).

A NASA photograph clearly shows the lotus-shaped green zone of the Nile Delta as well as the vast desert expanse of the Sinai Peninsula.

This magnificent overture to the Moses story raises some questions. If Pharaoh were in such a rush to build his new cities, why would he want the male issue of his slaves killed? Why keep the slaves from multiplying, depriving the state of free labor? Perhaps the answer is twofold. For one, the episode of the Hebrew infanticide will, in a subsequent chapter, justify the terrible retribution of the tenth plague, when it is the Egyptian firstborns who are slain. The second reason may be that, as elsewhere in the Pentateuch, the Bible does not hesitate to borrow familiar motifs from Mesopotamian or Egyptian traditions to make a point. The story of Moses' narrow escape in a basket of papyrus, for example, closely mirrors the miraculous survival of King Sargon I as an infant.

As we have seen, Sargon I (2334–2279 B.C.E.) was the founder of the Akkadian Empire. According to Babylonian tradition, when Sargon was an infant his mother feared for his life. She herself was a foreign princess named Enitu, and the legitimacy of her son was in doubt. Consequently, as Sargon told his story, "She put me in a box made of reeds, and closed the lid with bitumen. She cast me in the river, which did not submerge me. The river carried me along and brought me to Akki the water

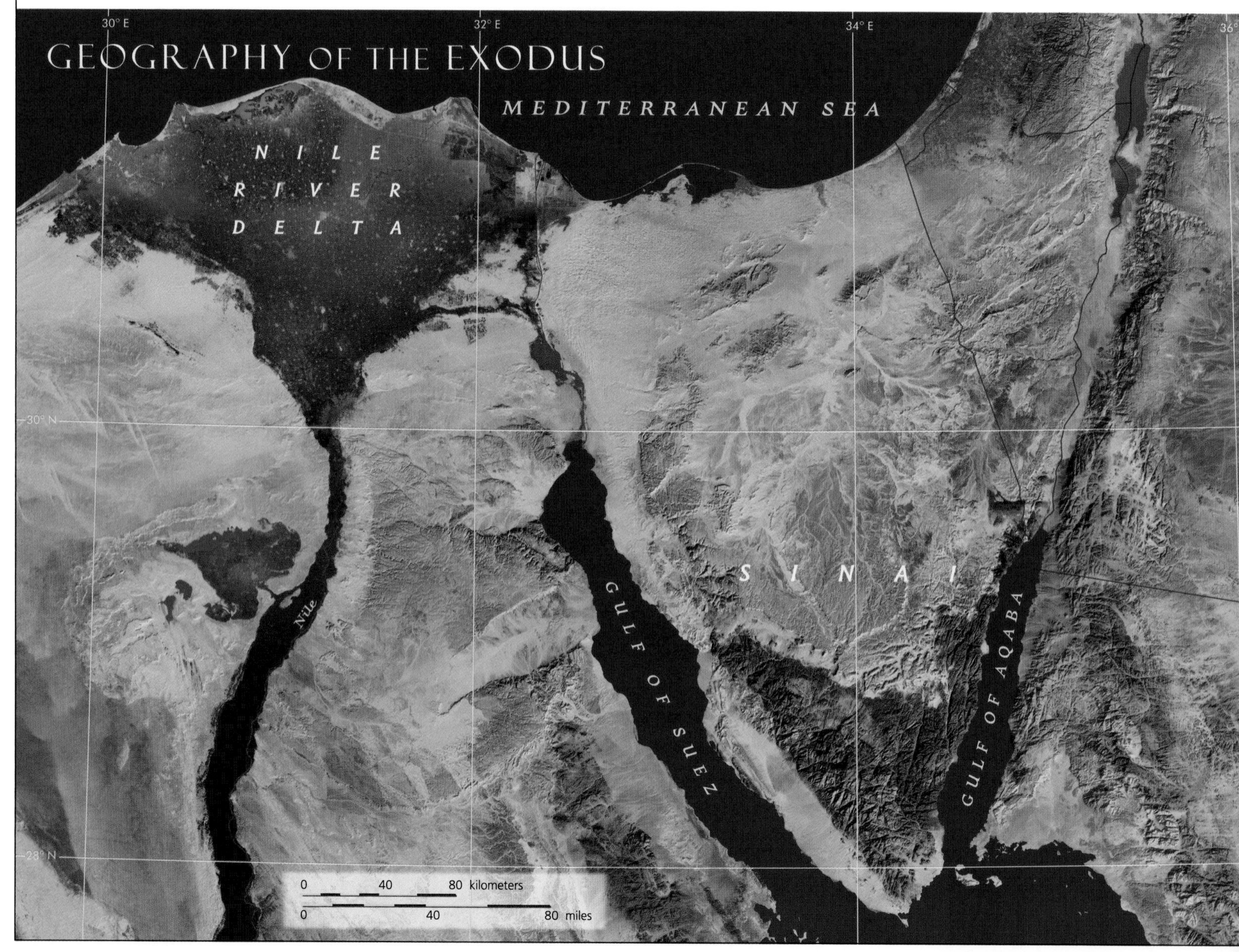

***The Finding of Moses*, by the British painter Sir Lawrence Alma-Tadema (1836–1912), was created in 1904 at the occasion of the opening of the Aswan Dam.**

drawer ... Akki took me up and raised me as a son." Another comparison can be drawn with the Hittite myth "The Queen of Kanesh and the Tale of Zalpa," in which the queen bears no less than 30 sons. She sets them afloat in baskets down the river, where the gods will ultimately save them. The point of borrowing from such traditions may be to demonstrate that Moses, like Sargon, enjoyed divine protection from the very beginning of his life.

Moses Strikes the Overseer

EXODUS GIVES US little information about Moses' youth. Any prince raised at the court of the pharaoh, however, would have been given a thorough education. Egyptian literature abounds with wisdom and moral instructions to those destined to lead. The Instructions of Amenemopet, found on a hieratic papyrus manuscript now in the British Museum, which dates to about 1000 B.C.E. and is based on an older original, makes an important point. "Guard yourself from preying on the oppressed," it counsels the future princes, "or against overbearing those who are powerless."

If Moses did ever hear those words, he must have taken them to heart. According to Exodus, one day Moses comes to the construction pits to watch the Hebrews toiling away. The wall decorations from the tomb of Rekhmire confirm that there were always plenty of taskmasters about, ready to lash with a whip if a slave sought a moment's rest. As Moses approaches, one of these supervisors is giving a thorough beating to a slave, "one of his kinfolk." Incensed, Moses

SHE CALLED HIM MOSES

According to the Book of Exodus, the name "Moses" means "drawn from the water." Egyptologists note that Moses or Mose was a common name in ancient Egypt. Derived from the Egyptian *ms(w)*, it was used to create a patronymic; it means "son of" or "gave birth to." The name of Pharaoh Thutmose, for example, means "begotten by Thut." That the founder of the Jewish faith retained his Egyptian name through the centuries suggests, some scholars believe, that he was a historical figure.

"looked this way and that, and seeing no one he killed the Egyptian and hid him in the sand" (Genesis 2:12). The next day, he again ventures out into the construction zone. Two Hebrew slaves are fighting. Moses rushes over and asks, "Why do you strike your fellow Hebrew?" The man replies, "Who made you a ruler and judge over us? Do you mean to kill me as you killed the Egyptian?" (Exodus 2:11-14).

This response is interesting, for it suggests that the slaves do not reciprocate Moses' feelings of kinship. To the Hebrews, he remained just another Egyptian nobleman in fancy dress, a member of the ruling caste. Here we find the theme of alienation that runs throughout the Moses saga. Moses never truly belongs; though he is respected, perhaps even revered, no one embraces him with the intimate bond of tribal affection that is so prominent elsewhere in the Bible.

The encounter with the quarreling Hebrews exposes another fact: The killing of the taskmaster had been observed. And indeed, "when Pharaoh heard of it, he sought to kill Moses" (Exodus 2:15). And so Moses fled—into the wilderness of Sinai.

Moses Encounters Jethro

The Sinai Peninsula is, in the words of the Bible, a "great and terrible place," covering some 20,000 square miles. Its stark landscape, surrounded by dark crevices and looming mountains, has its own unique sense of majesty. Water wells, even today, are scarce. Nevertheless, somehow Moses is able to make his way to Midian, just east of the Gulf of Aqaba, in what today is southern Jordan.

The Bible now cuts to a favored location for people to meet, a well. Moses, exhausted by the long journey, sits down to drink from one when seven girls appear. They have come to haul water for the flock of their father, a man named Jethro, the "priest of Midian" (Exodus 2:16). At that very moment, several boorish shepherds arrive and start to bully the girls. Moses comes to their defense, and the girls rush back to their father with a breathless account of the Egyptian who has saved them. Moses is received as the hero of the hour, and Jethro gives him his daughter Zipporah as his wife. Before long, Zipporah presents Moses with a son, Gershom, whose name is word play on the Hebrew *gersham*, meaning "an alien [in the land]." The idle life of luxury in Pi-Ramses is but a distant memory. With his young wife, Zipporah, and his infant son, Moses is happy.

Moses was afraid and thought, "Surely this thing is known." When Pharaoh heard of it, he sought to slay Moses. But Moses fled from Pharaoh. He settled in the land of Midian, and he sat down by a well.

(Exodus 2:14-15)

Sandal soles from the New Kingdom (ca 1539–1075 B.C.E.) depict a Nubian and an Asiatic prisoner.

The story would have been familiar to Egyptians of the second millennium B.C.E. One of the well-known tales in Egyptian literature is the "Story of Sinuhe," which has survived on a number of papyri and ostraca (inscribed potsherds), all dating from 1800 B.C.E. to well after 1000 B.C.E. As the story goes, in the turmoil following the death of Pharaoh Amenemhet I (ca 1938–1908 B.C.E.) an Egyptian named Sinuhe is accused of a crime (for reasons never quite fully explained). He promptly decides to flee the royal court and head east, through the land of Canaan and on to Syria. Eventually he enters the region near Byblos, which is ruled by a sheikh named Ammi-enshi. The sheikh welcomes him warmly and gives him the hand of his daughter in marriage. "There I spent many years," Sinuhe relates, "and my children grew up to be strong men."

But there is a difference. Sinuhe traveled through Canaan using the well-trodden caravan routes, secure in the knowledge that a well or an inn could never be far off. In Exodus, on the other hand, Moses journeys across the breadth of Sinai, one of the most daunting deserts on Earth. A journey like his would be tantamount to suicide unless the traveler were well equipped with water bags, a donkey, and an intimate knowledge of the locations of oases along the way. Even if Moses had been a commander of Pharaoh's elite guards, he would not have learned how to survive alone in the desert for weeks or months on end. So how is it that Prince Moses, in his royal finery, is able to travel from Pi-Ramses to the Gulf of Aqaba, straight across the Sinai Peninsula? After all, in the Bible's account of the Exodus from Egypt, the Hebrews will suffer terribly in the desert, unaccustomed as they are to the harsh terrain, the heat, and the lack of food and water. There is no indication in the text that Moses was ever initiated into the rigors of desert survival. And yet, if we accept the account in the Book of Exodus, this former prince is able to complete the journey, all by himself.

Moses in Midian

ONCE AGAIN, it is possible that the biblical story seeks to integrate multiple sources, combining the Moses of Midian with the Moses of Egypt. An alternate theory suggests a more radical scenario. As we have seen, the kings of the 18th and 19th dynasties maintained a ring of buffer states, ruled by vassal governors, to serve as a trip wire for any threat of invasion. By necessity, these governors were local chieftains who understood the native language and customs, and could be relied upon to pay annual tribute to the crown. It follows that these sheikhs were also in a perfect position to organize and launch a rebellion. Egypt therefore engaged in various strategies to ensure that each local viceroy maintained his loyalty to the pharaoh.

One such practice was to "invite" the oldest son of a provincial governor to be educated at the royal court. Such an education was not without benefits, as it exposed the provincials to Egyptian language, writing, literature, architecture, and the arts. In the process, these young princes were groomed (or perhaps indoctrinated) to be the next vassal kings—politically reliable and fully conversant with Egyptian language, customs, and worldview. What's more, their presence in Pi-Ramses, under the watchful eyes of Pharaoh's guard, sent a powerful message to the governor back home. If any trouble arose in the land, the first act of the pharaoh would be to kill the son of the transgressor in question.

According to this theory, Moses may originally have been such a hostage student, quite possibly the son of a Midianite chieftain. It would explain why Moses would be intimately familiar with the routes to and from Midian. It would also explain why Moses had to flee after the murder of the taskmaster.

A modern Bedouin woman from Madaba, Jordan, wears a traditional headdress adorned with gold coins from her dowry.

The Lord said, "... The cry of the Israelites has now come to me ... So come, I will send you to Pharaoh to bring my people, the Israelites, out of Egypt." (Exodus 3:7-10)

Guest student or not, such a heinous crime certainly would have been punished severely.

Be that as it may, there are several indications in the Bible of the special role played by the people of Midian. The Midianite tribe, according to Genesis, traced its origins to a son of Abraham's second wife, Keturah, whom he married after Sarah's death (Genesis 25:1-2). Later, in the Book of Numbers, we learn that Midianites were referred to as Kenites by a prophet named Balaam. "Enduring is your dwelling place," says the prophet, "and your nest is set in the rock" (Numbers 24:21). The word "Kenites" is related to the word *qain*, coppersmith in Arabic. The tribe of Midian, in short, was famous for its work in copper, which was found in richly veined mountain ores nearby. The presence of these copper ores also explains why Midian would be a prized possession of the Egyptian Empire.

The key to this theory is that, like Jacob's clan, the Midianites were descendants of Abraham. It is not unreasonable to assume that they, too, had continued to worship the El of Abraham. This would explain why Moses, though not a true son, felt a kinship with the Hebrew slaves in Pi-Ramses, even though such sentiments were unrequited by the slaves. Their customs, their hymns, and their prayers may not have been dissimilar from those a Midianite such as Moses would have been taught at home.

The Lord Reveals Himself

THEN, one day, Exodus says, Moses "led his flock beyond the wilderness" into the canyons of the lower Sinai Peninsula. There, in the shade of Mount Sinai (also referred to as Mount Horeb), a strange phenomenon catches his eye: "He looked, and the bush was blazing, yet it was not consumed." God calls out to him, "I have observed the misery of my people who are in Egypt; I have heard their cry on account of their taskmasters" (Exodus 3:1-7). The same story is told later in the Koran. "Now," God says, "Go you and your brother with My Message and be truthful; Go you both to Pharaoh, ... and say: we are apostles of the Lord; therefore send the children of Israel with us and do not torment them any longer!" (Koran, Sura Ta-Ha, 20:42-43, 47). This charge from the God who speaks from a burning bush fills Moses with ambivalence. Why should these Hebrew slaves accept him as their leader? Why, indeed, would Pharaoh even deign to receive him? Whose authority would Moses be able to invoke? "I am who I am," says God. "Thus you shall say to the Israelites, 'I am has sent me to you' " (Exodus 3:13-14).

Ehyeh asher ehyeh—I am that I am. From this point forward, El, the God of Abraham, will be known to Moses and all the congregation of Israel by the tetragrammaton, the four Hebrew consonants of YHWH. What does it mean? Some scholars have suggested that God's full title is Yahweh-Asher-Yahweh—He Brings Into Existence Whatever Exists. Or, YHWH may simply be an expression of wonderment and awe at the majesty of the Lord—an abstract abbreviation precisely because the magnificence of God cannot be captured in the words of mortals.

This new vision of the Lord propels the Exodus narrative from this point forward. He is not a remote God, this YHWH, but a God who takes a passionate interest in the fate of the Hebrew tribes. The long period of silence in Goshen is over. YHWH will not rest until the children of Israel are safely out of Egypt and settled in the land of Canaan.

Moses, reluctantly, does as God orders him. Since Moses is unsure of his rhetorical powers, God asks him, "What of your brother Aaron the Levite? I know that he can speak fluently" (Exodus 4:14). And so Aaron initiates the tradition of the Levites as servants of the Lord, culminating in their role as Temple servants.

EGYPT'S TASKMASTERS

Wall paintings in the tomb of Grand Vizier Rekhmire, near Thebes, show Egyptian taskmasters forcing pale-skinned Semitic foreigners to labor. "I have fed these Abiru tribes with bread, beer, and every good thing," the text invokes Rekhmire as saying, "but the rod is in my hand; be not idle." The Abiru, whose name some scholars believe is related to the word *Hebrew*, had been reduced to slavery. This practice was common in ancient Egypt, particularly in the New Kingdom. Major construction projects were painstakingly built by thousands of slaves, usually young men taken captive during Egyptian raids into neighboring Canaan, Gaza, Edom, and Syria.

SAINT CATHERINE'S MONASTERY

TODAY THE MASSIVE WALLS OF ST. Catherine's Monastery, officially the Monastery of the Transfiguration, still rise in the shadow of Mount Sinai. In C.E. 337, the mother of the Roman Emperor Constantine, Queen Helena, commissioned a chapel built near the reputed site of the burning bush from which God spoke to Moses. A group of monks settled at the site. From the sixth century on, it developed into a center of learning that followed the Greek Orthodox rites but otherwise claimed to be independent. When desert bandits continued to harass the small shrine, Emperor Justinian built a fortified enclosure around the place, which was completed in C.E. 565. He also expanded the living quarters, populating the shrine with 200 monks and guards. Over time, the monastery's library accumulated a treasure trove of icons and early codices that is second only to the Vatican Library.

The site is sacred to Jews, Christians, and Muslims. A Muslim tradition holds that the Prophet Muhammad visited the monastery. After the Muslim conquest of Sinai, the Prophet decreed that the monastery would always be under the protection of Islam, one reason why it has escaped destruction throughout its long history. A copy of this decree is still on display. In the 11th century, the monks even built a mosque inside the monastery, opposite the church, which dates from C.E. 542. Today, only a handful of Greek Orthodox monks remain.

Saint Catherine's Monastery can claim to be the only structure in the world inhabited without interruption since the time of Constantine.

The Ten Plagues

Swarms of locusts obscure the Pyramids of Giza near Cairo on November 17, 2004, recalling the eighth plague of the Bible.

Moses, accompanied by his brother Aaron, returns to Egypt and appears in front of Pharaoh with his petition. Seeking refuge in a bit of subterfuge, he asks that Pharaoh grant the Israelites a brief furlough so that they may celebrate a festival to their God in the desert. And Pharaoh replies, "Who is the Lord, that I should heed him and let Israel go? I do not know the Lord, and I will not let Israel go" (Exodus 5:1-2).

In fact, Moses' good intentions have quite the opposite effect. Enraged by Moses' request, Pharaoh orders his taskmasters to "no longer give the people straw to make bricks, as before." Instead, he says, "let them go and gather straw for themselves. But you shall require of them the same quantity of bricks as they have made previously; do not diminish it, for they are lazy" (Exodus 5:7-8).

The Hebrew slaves are very upset over this failed rescue attempt. It is they who will pay the price for Moses' poorly prepared venture. Moses, in turn, lays the failure of his mission at the Lord's feet, accusing God of doing "nothing at all to deliver your people" (Exodus 5:23). But YHWH replies that this outcome has been his intention all along: The Egyptians shall experience the full brunt of his wrath and know "that

ca 1400 B.C.E.
Tyre, Byblos, and Sidon thrive as centers of Phoenician trade

ca 1350 B.C.E.
Suppiluliuma I, king of the Hittites, conquers Syria and ends the powerof the Mitanni

ca 1332–1322 B.C.E.
Reign of King Tutankhamun

ca 1300 B.C.E.
The Hittite Empire spans the region from northern Mesopotamia to Anatolia

The Lord said to Moses, "Stretch out your hand toward heaven so that hail may fall on the whole land of Egypt, on humans and animals and all the plants of the field in the land of Egypt." (Exodus 9:22)

I am the Lord when I stretch out my hand against Egypt" (Exodus 7:5).

God then sends a series of plagues throughout the land of Egypt to bend Pharaoh's will. The Nile turns to blood, killing its fish and making its water undrinkable. Thousands of frogs cover the land, followed by invasions of gnats and flies. These epidemics strike man and animals alike. Hailstorms ravage the fields and destroy the harvest; whatever remains is devoured by locusts.

At first glance, these plagues may seem random. But these afflictions actually follow a plausible sequence of events. The waters of the Nile River turning the color of blood—becoming undrinkable and killing the fish (Exodus 7:17-21)—is a phenomenon that has been observed in modern times and must also have occurred in antiquity. Scientists have linked this mysterious coloring to either sedentary deposits from the Abyssinian lakes or to a toxic excess of algae and bacteria in the water. The Admonitions of Ipuwer, a papyrus document from the Hyksos period now in the collections of the National Museum of Antiquities in Leiden, describes several natural disasters, including the Nile "turning into blood."

If indeed the Nile had become undrinkable in places, exacerbated by the presence of dead and decomposing fish, animals living along its shores would have fled in search of fresh water—thus perhaps explaining why swarms of frogs suddenly covered the land (Exodus 8:5-6). At the same time, the heaps of dead fish along the banks would have become a natural breeding ground for bacteria and flies. Since the fifth plague is an outbreak of "pestilence" among the livestock (Exodus 9:3-6), scholars have theorized that this disease may be anthrax *(Bacillus anthracis)*, carried by the flies and gnats feeding on the carcasses of dead fish and other animals. During the sixth plague, the disease may have spread to humans and caused "boils," a description that may refer to the black lesions caused by skin anthrax (Exodus 9:9-11).

A second sequence of related events is initiated by the advent of hail (Exodus 9:22-25). Even in Egypt, severe weather in the winter months is not uncommon. In February 2004, a vast winter storm dumped over two feet of snow on large areas of Jordan and Israel, causing some masonry in the retaining walls on Jerusalem's Temple Mount to crumble under the weight.

The incidence of unusually high levels of hail and rain can encourage the breeding of a variety of insects, including locusts, which Exodus identifies as the eighth plague (Exodus 10:12-15). Desert locusts *(Schistocerca gregaria)* are very common in the Middle East, notably in the Sudan. Locusts typically travel in large swarms that can devastate a field in a short period of time. In the December 1915 issue of NATIONAL GEOGRAPHIC, the American vice-consul in Jerusalem, John Whiting, described a locust plague in Palestine that lasted almost eight months and stripped large swaths of land of all vegetation. The locusts were so voracious that they even attacked small infants.

Exodus tells us that the plague was lifted only when the Lord "changed the wind into a very strong west wind," which in turn may have carried the next plague. We read that a darkness settled over the land (Exodus 10:21-22), possibly caused by a type of sandstorm known as a khamsin, which ravages North Africa to this day. Blowing from the southwest across the Sahara, a khamsin can travel from Libya across Egypt and down toward the Arabian Peninsula, reaching temperatures of significantly more than 100 degrees Fahrenheit. The large amounts of sand and dust particles carried by this storm can literally turn day

This colored, New Kingdom limestone relief shows Ramses II (1279–1213 B.C.E.) holding his enemies by their hair before smiting them.

ca 1292 B.C.E. 19th dynasty begins in Egypt with rule of Ramses I

ca 1290–1279 B.C.E. Seti I rules Egypt

ca 1285 B.C.E. The Assyrian Empire begins under the rule of King Adadnirari I

ca 1279 B.C.E. Reign of Ramses II begins

LET THEM GATHER STRAW

ENRAGED BY MOSES' REQUEST TO LET HIS people go, Pharaoh orders his taskmasters to "no longer give the people the straw to make brick, as before." Instead, he says, "let them go and gather straw for themselves. But the tally of the bricks, which they made before, will not be any less" (Exodus 5:7-8).

As archaeological finds have borne out, straw was used as a binding agent for creating mud bricks throughout Egypt. Only certain temples were made of stone; homes, public buildings, and even the pharaohs' palaces were built with mud bricks, called *debet* by ancient Egyptians. Sometimes, bricks were stamped with a cartouche of the ruling king; one such brick, stamped with the mark of Ramses II, is now in the collection of the Oriental Institute in Chicago.

According to an Egyptian account, *Satire on the Trades*, brickmaking was a dirty, exhausting process. Separate teams were ordered to gather and cut straw, to shape the mud by hand or with molds, and to supervise the drying process, which could take about three weeks. The bricks were then carried by slaves to the construction sites. Each of these separate tasks has been represented by miniature figures found in tombs throughout Egypt.

Modern experts have suggested that the life span of unfired mud brick, when exposed to the elements, is about 30 to 50 years. This fact would explain why dwellings in the ancient Near East were often rebuilt in situ, on top of the rubble of the preceding structure, and why settlements often rose to become vertiable mounds over time.

A wall painting of brickmakers was found in the tomb of Rekhmire, vizier under the 18th dynasty's Thutmose III and Amenhotep II.

into dusk, or even night. The frequency of this phenomenon is underscored by its name, *khamsin*, which is the Arabic word for "fifty" and denotes the number of days that this terrible Saharan wind can occur in any given year.

But it is the tenth and last plague that finally breaks Pharaoh's will. As YHWH explains to Moses, he intends to go throughout Egypt and kill all of the country's firstborns (Exodus 11:4-5). It is a calculated strike of terror, conceived not only to shock Pharaoh out of his recalcitrance, but also to exact a heavy retribution for the killing of the Hebrews' firstborn sons a generation earlier.

To ensure that the Hebrew slaves themselves shall be safe, God tells Moses and Aaron that each Hebrew family must slaughter a lamb, "without blemish, a year-old male"; its blood they must "put on the two doorposts and the lintel of the houses in which they eat it." Then each family must roast the lamb and eat it with staffs in hand (Exodus 12:6-11). This supper is the first Passover, an event that will be annually remembered to celebrate the Lord's rescue of the people of Israel.

At midnight, the Book of Exodus asserts, the tenth plague strikes.

> *At midnight the Lord struck*
> *down all the firstborn in the*
> *land of Egypt, from the firstborn*
> *of Pharaoh who sat on his throne*
> *to the firstborn of the prisoner*
> *who was in the dungeon, and all*
> *the firstborn of the livestock.*
> *Pharaoh arose in the night, he and*
> *all his officials and all the Egyptians;*
> *and there was a loud cry in Egypt,*
> *for there was not a house*
> *without someone dead.*
>
> (Exodus 12:29-30)

More than 3,000 years later, in May 1995, a team of archaeologists from the

American University in Cairo discovered a huge underground tomb in the Valley of the Kings near Luxor—possibly the largest underground burial chamber in all of Egypt. From the names and cartouches inscribed on the walls, the scholars determined that this tomb belonged to the family of Pharaoh Ramses II. In all, the archaeologists uncovered 50 mummies—all sons of the pharaoh, who fathered 52 sons.

Among the mummified bodies is a man named Amon-er-khe-peshef. He was the crown prince, the oldest son of the pharaoh, who died while Ramses was still alive. It is a tantalizing thought: Could this be the son who perished during the ravages of the tenth plague? Or, conversely, did the premature death of Amon-er-khe-peshef inspire the story of the death of the firstborn?

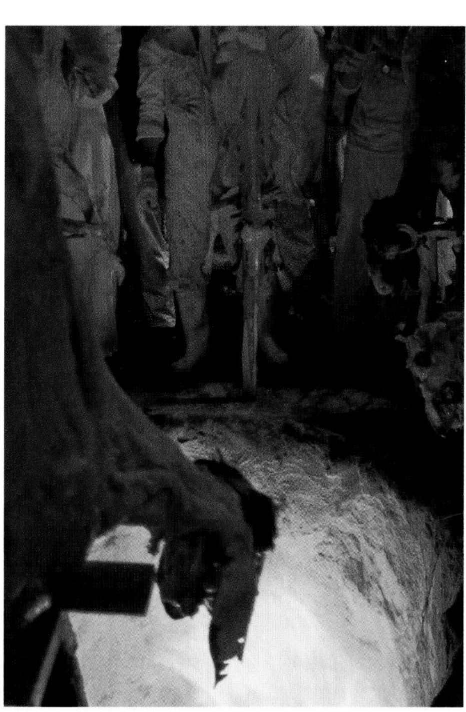

Samaritans offer sheep as a sacrifice on the eve of the Passover celebration on their holy mountain of Gerizim, near the West Bank city of Nablus.

Whatever the case may be, the death of his oldest son is too much for Pharaoh to bear. He summons Moses and Aaron and says, "Rise up, go away from my people, both you and the Israelites. ... Take your flocks and your herds, as you said, and be gone" (Exodus 12: 31-32). And so, under the leadership of Moses, the Israelites depart at last. They journey from the city of Pi-Ramses to Succoth and from there to Etham, "on the edge of the wilderness" (Exodus 12:37; 13:20).

The city of Succoth may be identical to Pithom or Per-Atum, which as we have seen was the second city built by the Israelites. It was probably located at the southeastern rim of the Nile Delta, near today's hamlet of Tell el Ratabah. Moses, having rallied the slaves in Pi-Ramses, would likely have journeyed

In the West African nation of Mali, a shepherd and his flock rush to their village of Kamaka before a huge sandstorm, or khamsin, can overtake them.

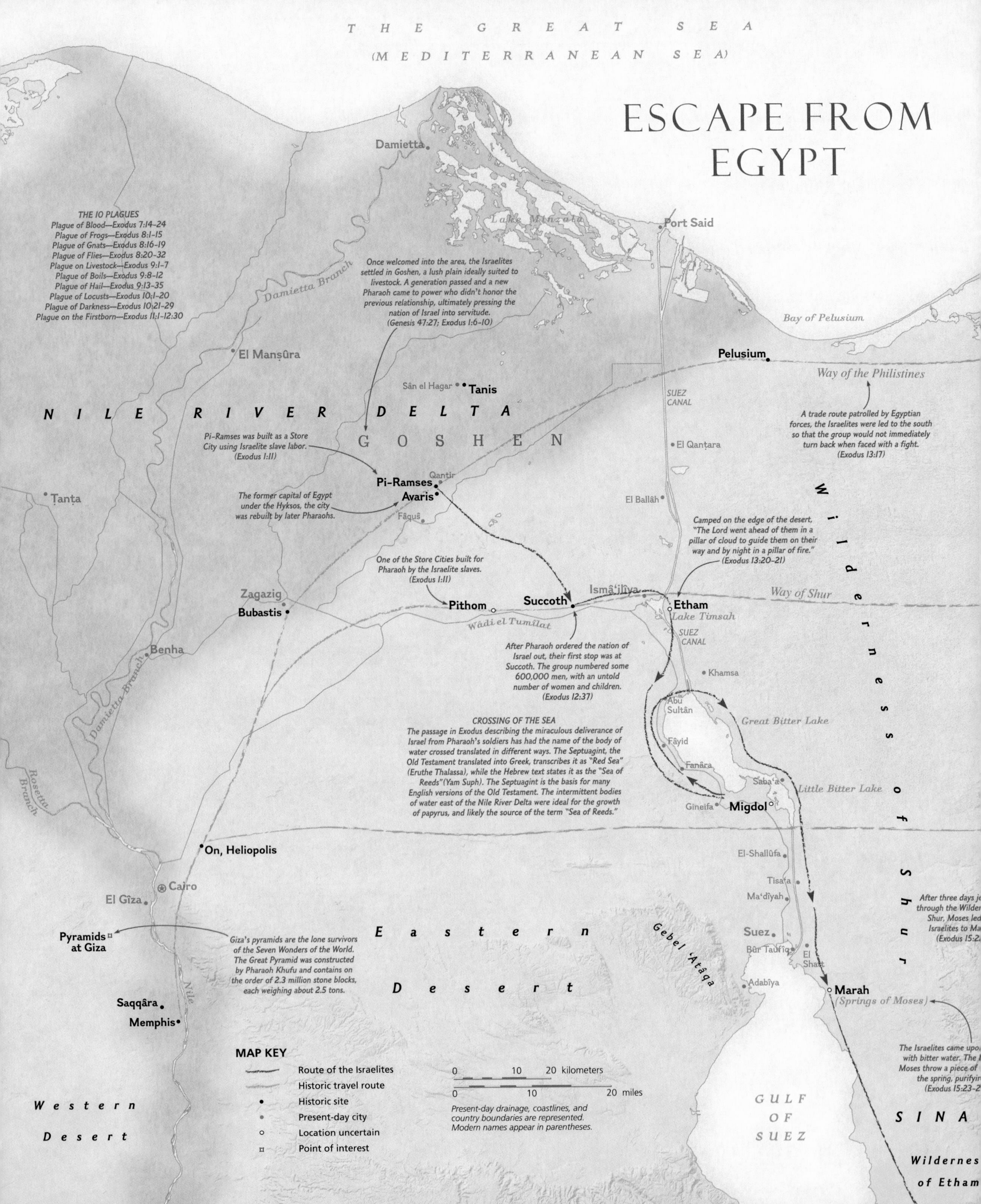

THE GREAT SEA
(MEDITERRANEAN SEA)
ESCAPE FROM EGYPT
THE 10 PLAGUES
Plague of Blood—Exodus 7:14–24
Plague of Frogs—Exodus 8:1–15
Plague of Gnats—Exodus 8:16–19
Plague of Flies—Exodus 8:20–32
Plague on Livestock—Exodus 9:1–7
Plague of Boils—Exodus 9:8–12
Plague of Hail—Exodus 9:13–35
Plague of Locusts—Exodus 10:1–20
Plague of Darkness—Exodus 10:21–29
Plague on the Firstborn—Exodus 11:1–12:30
Once welcomed into the area, the Israelites settled in Goshen, a lush plain ideally suited to livestock. A generation passed and a new Pharaoh came to power who didn't honor the previous relationship, ultimately pressing the nation of Israel into servitude. (Genesis 47:27; Exodus 1:6–10)
Damietta
Lake Manzala
Port Said
Damietta Branch
Bay of Pelusium
El Manşûra
Pelusium
Way of the Philistines
Sân el Hagar
Tanis
SUEZ CANAL
NILE RIVER DELTA
GOSHEN
A trade route patrolled by Egyptian forces, the Israelites were led to the south so that the group would not immediately turn back when faced with a fight. (Exodus 13:17)
Pi-Ramses was built as a Store City using Israelite slave labor. (Exodus 1:11)
El Qanţara
Qantir
Pi-Ramses
Avaris
Ţanţa
The former capital of Egypt under the Hyksos, the city was rebuilt by later Pharaohs.
El Ballâh
Fâqûs
Camped on the edge of the desert, "The Lord went ahead of them in a pillar of cloud to guide them on their way and by night in a pillar of fire." (Exodus 13:20–21)
Wilderness of Shur
One of the Store Cities built for Pharaoh by the Israelite slaves. (Exodus 1:11)
Zagazig
Bubastis
Pithom
Succoth
Ismâ'îlîya
Etham
Way of Shur
Wâdi el Tumîlat
Lake Timsah
SUEZ CANAL
After Pharaoh ordered the nation of Israel out, their first stop was at Succoth. The group numbered some 600,000 men, with an untold number of women and children. (Exodus 12:37)
Benha
Khamsa
Abu Sultân
Great Bitter Lake
Damietta Branch
CROSSING OF THE SEA
The passage in Exodus describing the miraculous deliverance of Israel from Pharaoh's soldiers has had the name of the body of water crossed translated in different ways. The Septuagint, the Old Testament translated into Greek, transcribes it as "Red Sea" (Eruthe Thalassa), while the Hebrew text states it as the "Sea of Reeds" (Yam Suph). The Septuagint is the basis for many English versions of the Old Testament. The intermittent bodies of water east of the Nile River Delta were ideal for the growth of papyrus, and likely the source of the term "Sea of Reeds."
Fâyid
Fanâra
Saba'a
Little Bitter Lake
Rosetta Branch
Gineifa
Migdol
On, Heliopolis
El-Shallûfa
Cairo
Tisa'a
El Gîza
Ma'dîyah
Pyramids at Giza
Giza's pyramids are the lone survivors of the Seven Wonders of the World. The Great Pyramid was constructed by Pharaoh Khufu and contains on the order of 2.3 million stone blocks, each weighing about 2.5 tons.
Eastern Desert
Gebel 'Atâqa
Suez
Bûr Taufîq
El Shatt
Adabîya
Marah
(Springs of Moses)
Saqqâra
Memphis
Nile
MAP KEY
Route of the Israelites
Historic travel route
Historic site
Present-day city
Location uncertain
Point of interest
0 10 20 kilometers
0 10 20 miles
Present-day drainage, coastlines, and country boundaries are represented. Modern names appear in parentheses.
Western Desert
GULF OF SUEZ
SINA
Wildernes of Etham

to Pithom to liberate the Hebrews in that city as well. Some experts accept the location of Pithom near Tell el Ratabah but argue that Succoth was another city farther east, close to the present-day site of Tell el Maskhuta. Both sites lie along today's Wadi el Tumilat, a dry bed that leads east toward the Sinai, passing between Lake Timsah (or Crocodile Lake) in the north and the Bitter Lakes in the south. This location is very important, for it is here, according to the Bible, that the most spectacular manifestation of the Lord's power takes place.

Back in Pi-Ramses, the Book of Exodus recounts, Pharaoh is having second thoughts. "What have we done, letting Israel leave our service?" he asks. Pharaoh thereupon summons "six hundred picked chariots and all the other chariots of Egypt with officers over all of them" (Exodus 14:7). Egypt's great army gives chase and catches up with the fleeing slaves near a place the Bible refers to as the "Red Sea" (Exodus 13:18). Among the Hebrews, the mood promptly turns to despair. "Is this not the very thing we told you in Egypt?" the people cry out, blaming the hapless Moses for their state of affairs (Exodus 14:12). YHWH and Moses provide a miraculous solution:

Then Moses stretched
out his hand over the sea.
The Lord drove the sea back
by a strong east wind all night,
and turned the sea into dry land;
and the waters were divided.
The Israelites went into the sea
on dry ground, the waters forming
a wall for them on their
right and on their left.

(Exodus 14:21-22)

Moses said to the people, "Do not be afraid, stand firm, and see the deliverance that the Lord will accomplish for you today; for the Egyptians whom you see today you shall never see again. The Lord will fight for you." (Exodus 14:13-14)

The brush-covered sandbanks on the Bitter Lakes may have been the "dry land" by which the Israelites made their escape from Egypt.

Pharaoh's men follow in close pursuit. The moment the last slave is across, Moses stretches out his hands once again and the waters close, burying the Egyptians in a watery grave. The Koran allows Pharaoh one final cry of atonement: "And when he was drowning, Pharaoh said: 'Now I believe that there is no God but He in Whom the Children of Israel believe'" (Koran, Yunus 10:90).

It is a magnificent miracle, but could this remarkable crossing have a basis in fact? Virtually everyone now agrees that the Bible did not intend to place the destruction of Pharaoh's forces at the Red Sea, as was originally thought. The Hebrew words *Yam Suph*, translated as "Red Sea" in the King James Bible, actually means "Sea of Reeds." There are no reeds on the shores of the Red Sea. But sandbanks, sometimes covered with brush or reeds, continue to grow in the marshes of the Bitter Lakes to this day.

What's more, the Bitter Lakes lie directly in the path from Goshen to Sinai. It is possible that this spot is where Exodus places the crossing of the Israelites, during low tide, when the sandbanks were exposed. Of course, the bottom of this marshland would be mud—solid enough for a person, but certainly too soft to support Pharaoh's heavy armored chariots. Their wheels would have gotten stuck in the sandy bottom. Other chariots may have been sucked under the wet earth altogether.

With this miraculous crossing, the Hebrews are able to continue their journey out of bondage in Egypt. The next phase of their journey will be no easier than the first. Turning away from the remnants of Pharoah's forces, the Hebrews face the harsh wilderness of the Sinai Peninsula. It is through here that Moses will continue the route of the Exodus, as he guides his people to the Promised Land.

The Journey to Freedom

Visitors to the summit of Mount Sinai are treated to a spectacular view from an altitude of some 7,500 feet above sea level.

WITH THE CROSSING at the sea, the Hebrews began the Exodus from Egypt—their long journey through the wilderness to a new beginning in the Promised Land. The Books of Exodus and Numbers name a variety of places along their route, usually based on the presence of oases. Verifying these locations remains difficult because the descriptions in Exodus and Numbers do not always agree. Today there is little scholarly agreement in identifying these specific places in the modern topography of the Sinai.

There is consensus, however, that Moses did not seem to be directly heading for Canaan, the Promised Land, at all. If he were, he would have taken the exact same road that brought Joseph to Egypt. Since the days of the Middle Kingdom, this coastal highway, later known as the Way of the Philistines, had been vastly expanded and modernized to accommodate the long columns of military traffic heading toward the Egyptian buffer states of Canaan, Edom, and Syria. It was the most direct road to and from Canaan.

As we have seen, Thutmose III and his army of trained foot soldiers only took ten days to move from the Nile Delta to Gaza, at the border of Canaan. A month or less should certainly have

ca 1290 B.C.E.
Heavily defended city of Troy is destroyed, possibly by the Mycenaeans

ca 1275 B.C.E.
Hittite forces threaten Canaan and Syria

ca 1274 B.C.E.
Ramses II battles Hittites near Kadesh

ca 1259 B.C.E.
The Hittites agree to a peace treaty with Egypt

On the third new moon after the Israelites had gone out of the land of Egypt, on that very day, they came into the wilderness of Sinai ... Israel camped there in front of the mountain. (Exodus 19:1-2)

sufficed for the Hebrew slaves to make the entire trip to Canaan. But Moses did not guide his people along this route.

Why does Moses not lead his people to Canaan along the more direct coastal road? Exodus offers an explanation. "God did not lead them by way of the land of the Philistines, although that was nearer; for God thought, 'If the people face war, they may change their minds and return to Egypt' " (Exodus 13:17). This statement implies that taking the coastal road would have led to an armed clash. It is certainly true that since Seti I's reign, most oases along this road had been constantly guarded and patrolled by roving Egyptian soldiers looking for deserters, foreign infiltrators, and other misfits.

But there may be another reason why Exodus does not have Moses taking the shortest route to Canaan: He may have been unsure of its location. He chooses to follow the only road through Sinai with which he is most familiar. This southern road along the rim of the Red Sea ultimately led back to Midian—the same route Moses may have taken as a fugitive. Moses simply may not have known where this Promised Land is supposed to be. Certainly, none of the Hebrew slaves would have remembered. But if there is anyone who knows the way to Canaan, it is Moses' father-in-law, Jethro. And so to Jethro Moses goes.

Path to the Promised Land

FIRST, ACCORDING to Exodus, Moses leads his people from Pi-Ramses to Succoth, near today's Wadi el Tumilat. From there, he moves around Lake Timsah to the presumed site of Etham, "on the edge of the wilderness." Here, God commanded Moses to encamp "in front of Pi-hahiroth, between Migdol and the sea, in front of Baal-zephon ... by the sea" (Exodus 14:2). *Migdol* means "tower" in Hebrew, but it may also refer to the Egyptian fortress of Miktol, which guarded the beginning of a second caravan route into Egypt that cut straight across the desert of Sinai. Today, the remains of Miktol have been identified at a dig near Abu Hasan, some ten miles north of Suez, which strongly supports the claim that "the sea" was, in fact, the area of the Bitter Lakes.

Naturally, this fortress would have held plenty of soldiers, so the Book of Exodus has Moses double back and loop around the Bitter Lakes, perhaps looking for a sandbank area at low tide. His followers cross just as the Egyptian cavalry catches up with them. Once across, they would have been greeted by the forbidding sight of Sinai's limestone plateau rising high in front of them. But Moses doesn't plan to lead his people across these heights. Instead, Exodus says, he makes an immediate right turn and follows the southern route, which hugs the Sinai coast all the way down the peninsula.

Today's road from Isma'iliya to Sharm el Sheikh traverses much of the same ground that the children of Israel may have taken. Leading along the western rim of the Great Bitter Lake, the road now moves past El Shallufa into the vast Ahmed Hamdi Tunnel under the Suez Canal, which connects Cairo with all points east in the Sinai. From there, the road turns south, running along the deep blue waters of the Red Sea.

According to Exodus, Moses and his people travel for three days without finding any water until they

This early 19th-century Seder plate of pewter shows Moses being taken from his basket of pitch; the rim bears a Hebrew inscription from Exodus (2:24).

ca 1250 B.C.E.
An earthquake in Nineveh damages the Temple of Ishtar

ca 1213 B.C.E.
Pharaoh Ramses II dies

ca 1200 B.C.E.
Hittite Empire ends

ca 1200 B.C.E.
Egyptians begin to use flax to make linen

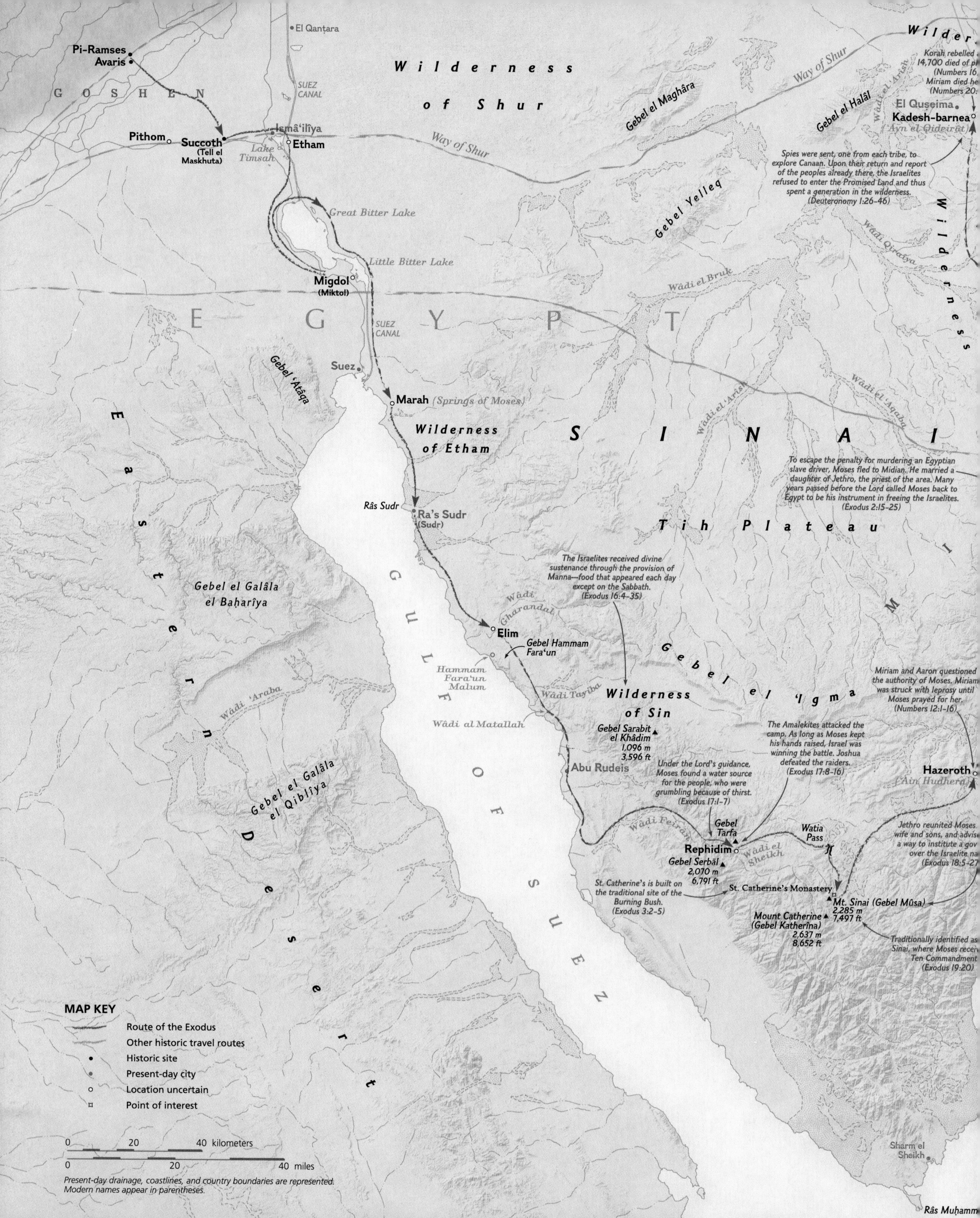

El Qantara
Pi-Ramses
Avaris
GOSHEN
Wilderness of Shur
SUEZ CANAL
Way of Shur
Gebel el Maghâra
Gebel el Halâl
El Quseima
Kadesh-barnea
('Ayn el Qudeirat)
Korah rebelled
14,700 died of pl
(Numbers 16
Miriam died he
(Numbers 20
Pithom
Succoth
(Tell el Maskhuta)
Ismâ'ilîya
Etham
Lake Timsah
Spies were sent, one from each tribe, to explore Canaan. Upon their return and report of the peoples already there, the Israelites refused to enter the Promised Land and thus spent a generation in the wilderness.
(Deuteronomy 1:26-46)
Gebel Yelleq
Great Bitter Lake
Little Bitter Lake
Wâdi Qiraiya
Wâdi el Bruk
Migdol
(Miktol)
EGYPT
SUEZ CANAL
Gebel 'Atâqa
Suez
Marah (Springs of Moses)
Wâdi el 'Arish
Wâdi el 'Aqaba
Wilderness
Wilderness of Etham
SINAI
Eastern Desert
To escape the penalty for murdering an Egyptian slave driver, Moses fled to Midian. He married a daughter of Jethro, the priest of the area. Many years passed before the Lord called Moses back to Egypt to be his instrument in freeing the Israelites.
(Exodus 2:15-25)
Râs Sudr
Ra's Sudr
(Sudr)
Tih Plateau
The Israelites received divine sustenance through the provision of Manna—food that appeared each day except on the Sabbath.
(Exodus 16:4-35)
Gebel el Galâla el Bahariya
GULF OF SUEZ
Wâdi Gharandal
Elim
Gebel Hammam Fara'un
Hammam Fara'un Malum
Gebel el 'Igma
Wâdi Tayiba
Wilderness of Sin
Miriam and Aaron questioned the authority of Moses. Miriam was struck with leprosy until Moses prayed for her.
(Numbers 12:1-16)
Wâdi 'Araba
Wâdi al Matallah
Gebel Sarabit el Khâdim
1,096 m
3,596 ft
The Amalekites attacked the camp. As long as Moses kept his hands raised, Israel was winning the battle. Joshua defeated the raiders.
(Exodus 17:8-16)
Abu Rudeis
Under the Lord's guidance, Moses found a water source for the people, who were grumbling because of thirst.
(Exodus 17:1-7)
Hazeroth
('Ain Hudhera)
Gebel el Galâla el Qiblîya
Wâdi Feiran
Gebel Tarfa
Watia Pass
Jethro reunited Moses wife and sons, and advise a way to institute a gov over the Israelite na
(Exodus 18:5-27
Rephidim
Wâdi el Sheikh
Gebel Serbâl
2,070 m
6,791 ft
St. Catherine's is built on the traditional site of the Burning Bush.
(Exodus 3:2-5)
St. Catherine's Monastery
Mt. Sinai (Gebel Mûsa)
2,285 m
7,497 ft
Mount Catherine (Gebel Katherîna)
2,637 m
8,652 ft
Traditionally identified as Sinai, where Moses recei Ten Commandment
(Exodus 19:20)
MAP KEY
Route of the Exodus
Other historic travel routes
Historic site
Present-day city
Location uncertain
Point of interest
0 20 40 kilometers
0 20 40 miles
Present-day drainage, coastlines, and country boundaries are represented. Modern names appear in parentheses.
Sharm el Sheikh
Râs Muhamm

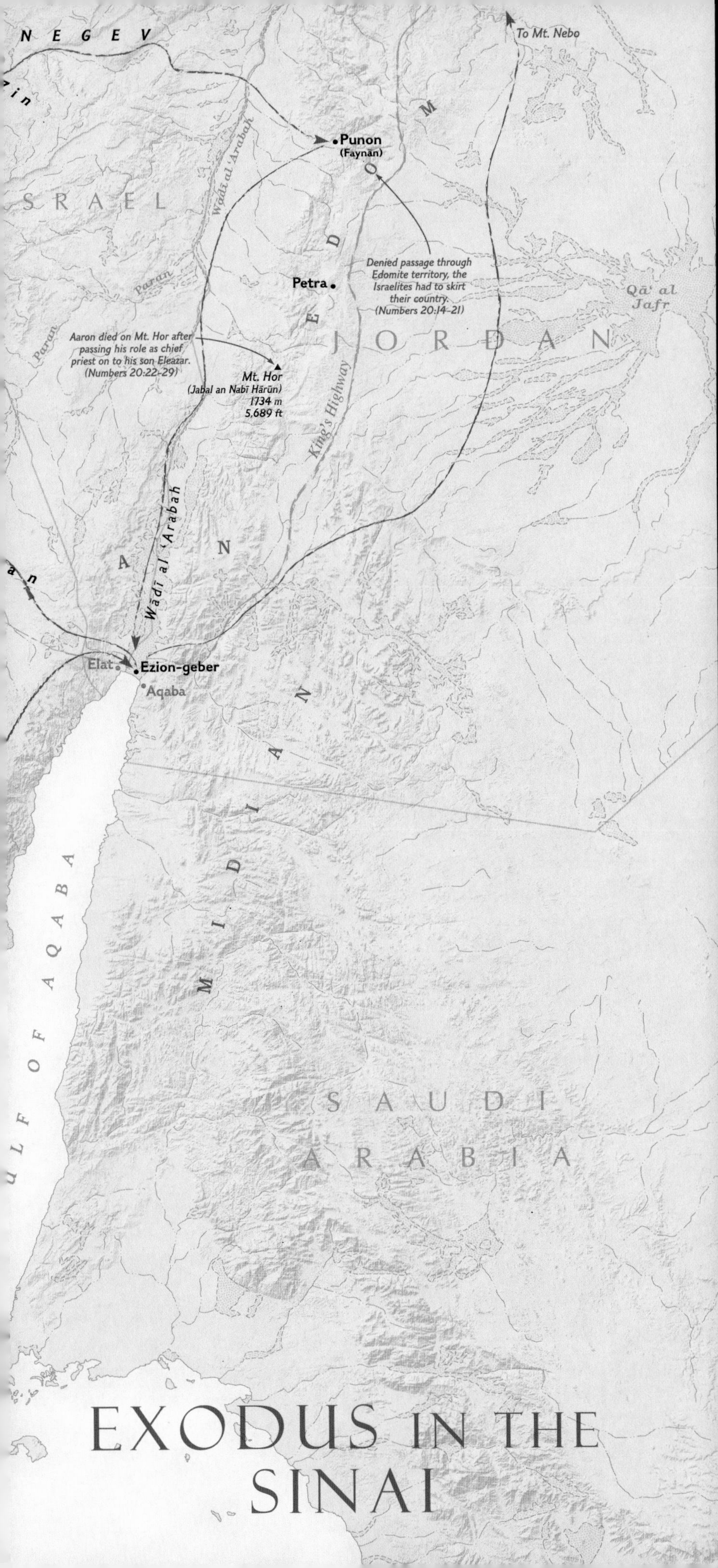

EXODUS IN THE SINAI

NEGEV

ISRAEL

JORDAN

EDOM

MIDIAN

SAUDI ARABIA

GULF OF AQABA

To Mt. Nebo

Punon (Faynān)

Wādī al 'Arabah

Paran

Petra

Qā' al Jafr

Denied passage through Edomite territory, the Israelites had to skirt their country. (Numbers 20:14–21)

Aaron died on Mt. Hor after passing his role as chief priest on to his son Eleazar. (Numbers 20:22–29)

Mt. Hor (Jabal an Nabī Hārūn) 1734 m 5,689 ft

King's Highway

Elat

Ezion-geber

Aqaba

Mount Sinai (Gebel Musa in Arabic) is traditionally associated with the location in the Bible, where Moses receives the Tablets of the Law from YHWH.

The palm grove in the oasis of Wadi Feiran is often associated with Rephidim, the place in Exodus where Moses strikes a rock, causing water to flow from it.

The oasis of 'Uyun Musa (Springs of Moses) is identified by some as the oasis of Marah, described in Exodus as the first Israelite campsite in Sinai.

Placed "between Elim and Sinai," the Wilderness of Sin is the location in Exodus where the Lord miraculously delivers quail and manna to the hungry Israelites

come to the oasis of Marah, where the water is "bitter" (Exodus 15:22-23). Moses, however, makes the water sweet. Tradition has identified Marah with the small oasis of 'Uyun Musa (Springs of Moses), located some 25 miles from the Bitter Lakes. Most scholars accept that the Hebrews, untrained in desert survival and weakened by a slave's poor diet, would not have been able to travel much more than eight or ten miles per day. A three-day march would therefore have brought them not much farther than 'Uyun Musa. Even today this hamlet, sheltered in a clump of date palms, derives its water from a warm thermal well. Packed with minerals, the water tastes somewhat metallic and may have appeared bitter to a people reared on the sweet water of the Nile.

Miracles in the Desert

From 'Uyun Musa, the coastal road travels some 23 miles to Ras el Sudr. This 1,500-foot rock juts up toward the azure sky above the Bible's Red Sea, today's Gulf of Suez. According to local legend, the rock represents Pharaoh, struggling to come up for air after the Prophet Mûsa has thrown him into the Red Sea. Just beyond lie the hot springs of Hammam Fara'un Malun ("baths of the cursed pharaoh").

About ten miles past Hamman Fara'un, a small trail leads left through the Wadi al Matallah and up across the soft limestone plateau of Debbet el Qerai. Just above the trail is the ancient mining complex of Sarabit el Khadim—quite literally, "the heights of the slave." Farther south are the old mines of Wadi el Maghara, where malachite and turquoise were culled from the soil and rock in the days of Khufu, builder of the Great Pyramid in Giza in the 4th dynasty. Moses' route in the Bible, in other words, followed the ancient Egyptian road to the copper mines of Sinai.

Meanwhile, the search for water continues. According to Exodus, Moses meets with success after the Hebrews "came to Elim, where there were twelve springs of water and seventy palm trees; and they camped there by the water" (Exodus 15:27).

When Michelangelo Buonarroti (1475–1564) sculpted Moses, he added horns to the head based on an erroneous Latin translation of *karan*, rays of light, from St. Jerome's version of the Latin Bible.

MIRACLE OF THE QUAIL

In Exodus, the Hebrew slaves, accustomed to a steady diet of bread and beer, grow hungry and turn against Moses. Moses appeals to YHWH, and the Lord promises to "rain bread from heaven." Miraculously, quail "come up and cover the camp." The presence of quail may not be as astounding as it seems. Sinai lies on the annual spring migratory path of several birds, including quail, from Africa to cooler northern climates. Exhausted by the long flight, the quail would not have been hard to catch. To this day, the Bedouin of northern Sinai set nets to capture quail. In 2005, the practice had become so widespread that the Egyptian government intervened, insisting the Bedouin obtain quail-hunting licenses and prohibiting hunting after September 1, to protect the birds on the return journey to their breeding grounds. In response, several Bedouin tribes have turned to quail breeding.

Where was Elim? Some scholars associate it with 'Uyun Musa, suggesting that Marah should be identified with the oasis farther north called Bir Marah. Others, however, place Elim some five miles from Sarabit el Khadim, in a small grove known as Wadi Gharandal. Elim means "tamarisks," which are shrubs found throughout the Sinai landscape. Even today there is a well under a copse of date palms and tamarisks, often used by local Bedouin. From there, Moses turns inland, "and Israel came to the wilderness of Sin, which is between Elim and Sinai" (Exodus 16:1). Though their water bags were filled, at this

Say to them, "At twilight you shall eat meat, and in the morning you shall have your fill of bread; then you shall know that I am the Lord your God." (Exodus 16:12)

moment the Israelites begin to complain of hunger.

These slave-workers are no longer the robust "sand-dwellers" that their forefathers had been. Having likely been raised on a daily diet of bread and beer, their hunger turns them, once again, against Moses. Some cry that they were better off sitting by the "fleshpots" in the land of Egypt (Exodus 16:3)—an exaggeration to be sure, for no slave in Egypt was fortunate enough to eat cooked meat. But the Lord promises Moses that he will "rain bread from heaven." The Bible describes how first, "quails came up and covered the camp." Then, in the morning, "there was a layer of dew around the camp. When the layer of dew lifts, there on the surface of the wilderness is a fine, flaky substance, as fine as frost on the ground" (Exodus 16:13-14). The Israelites do not know what it is. They call it "manna," which some scholars believe to be Aramaic for "What is it?" They gather it and knead it into dough, from which they are able to bake bread.

Bedouin tribes of the Sinai, such as the Awarma, Sawalha, and Muziena, have been familiar with the manna phenomenon for centuries. For them, manna is the sap from tamarisks *(Tamarix mannifera)*, which is extraced from the bark by a small scale insect *(Coccus manniparus)*. The sweet, sticky secretion drops to the ground, where it can be collected and used as a sweetener, or made into wafers. Whether these droplets would have sufficed to feed the Israelite multitudes is open to question. Nevertheless, the existence of manna even to this day underscores that the narrative of the Book of Exodus is often based on actual occurrences witnessed in the ancient Near East.

Thus fortified, the children of Israel face the long journey through the wasteland of Sin. Moses turns southeast, Exodus says, away from the Red Sea. Here, the ancient road east plunges into the mountains, coiling around the towering escarpments of the Gebel Serbal and the Gebel Tarfa before running down the Watia Pass. Along the way stands a rock that the Bedouin call Hesi el Khattatin ("spring hidden by the scribes"). In Bedouin lore, the scribes are Moses and Aaron.

Here is the next major station along the route. As Exodus tells us, "the whole

Italian Renaissance artist Ercole de' Roberti (1450–1496) of Ferrara shows *The Israelites Gathering Manna* during their time in the Sinai.

congregation of the Israelites journeyed by stages, as the Lord commanded. They camp at Rephidim" (Exodus 17:1). Rephidim is the vast palm grove known today as Wadi Feiran, an immense stretch of trees surrounded on all sides by the majestic rise of the Sinai massif. It is still the largest oasis in all of Sinai, productive enough to water a large flock of sheep—and people. This place is where, according to Exodus, Moses struck a rock and caused water to come from it (Exodus 17:6). But the Amalekites, a local tribe, took offense and attacked the Israelites, probably to defend their water rights. A bitter battle ensued, but eventually the Israelites prevailed.

From here it is but a short distance, a five-day march, to Mount Sinai. Moses brings his people to the place where his mission started. In the shadow of the great mountain, Jethro the priest waits; with him are Moses' wife, Zipporah, and their two sons.

Once again, the enigmatic Jethro guides Moses to the next phase of his great task. That Jethro is a priest of YHWH (though, perhaps, not exclusively) is attested by the verse in which Jethro "brought a burnt offering and sacrifices to God" (Exodus 18:12). A keen observer, Jethro sees how Moses fritters away his attention in countless disputes. You must learn to delegate, Jethro tells Moses, for his principal task is to "represent the people before God" (Exodus 18:19). With these words, Jethro prepares Moses for his penultimate task.

The Ten Commandments

MOUNT SINAI is a craggy, forbidding mass of gray and pink granite that rises some 7,500 feet above sea level. From its summit, a breathtaking panorama of desert and mountain peaks stretches far beyond Sinai to the Gulf of Aqaba. According to biblical tradition, Moses received the Ten Commandments from the Lord here:

I am the Lord your God, who brought
you out of the land of Egypt, out of the
house of slavery; you shall have
no other gods before me.
You shall not make for yourself an idol,
whether in the form of anything that
is in heaven above, or that is on the
earth beneath, or that is in the water
under the earth. …
You shall not make wrongful use of the
name of the Lord your God. …
Remember the sabbath day, and keep it holy.
Six days you shall labor and do
all your work. But the seventh day is
a sabbath to the Lord your God;
you shall not do any work. …
Honor your father and your mother. …
You shall not murder.
You shall not commit adultery.
You shall not steal.
You shall not bear false
witness against your neighbor.
You shall not covet your neighbor's
house; you shall not covet your neighbor's
wife, or male or female slave, or ox,
or donkey, or anything that belongs
to your neighbor.

(Exodus 20:2-17)

THE GOLDEN CALF

During Moses' long absence on Mount Sinai, the Book of Exodus says, the Israelites grew impatient and asked of Aaron, "Come, make gods for us, who shall go before us" (Exodus 32:1). Aaron cast a golden calf, to which the Israelites made offerings. When Moses returned, he was so incensed by this idolatry that he smashed the stone tablets of the Law and ordered 3,000 males put to death. Some modern scholars argue that the image of a calf or bull, symbol of virility and strength, had often been associated with the Canaanite El. They note that Moses' disappearance may have prompted the Israelites to seek a "restoration" of their link to YHWH by building a golden icon that would serve as an attribute of YHWH, and thus as his representative, not as his replacement. Centuries later, King Jeroboam I of the Northern Kingdom of Israel would likewise commission two golden calves for the sanctuaries of YHWH in Bethel and Dan, to serve as the Lord's attendants.

On the summit of Mount Sinai, the covenant between Abraham and El is ratified into a pact, a formal treaty between YHWH and his people. That day, the rabble of former slaves and bricklayers, of herdsmen and shepherds, truly becomes a nation. The Ten Commandments outline a moral code that will reverberate throughout Western civilization. As a formal covenant between God and man, it is without parallel in ancient history; as a code of human behavior, it will inspire Jews, Christians, and Muslims up to our times.

The remainder of the Book of Exodus, as well as the Books of Leviticus, Numbers, and Deuteronomy, lays out the Covenant Law, the Laws of Moses that will henceforth define the practice of Judaism. As some scholars have claimed, there are similarities between these laws and the Babylonian tradition of social justice that had earlier produced the Code of Hammurabi and other legal works. There are also parallels between the Ten Commandments and Egyptian law, with which the Hebrew people in Goshen were undoubtedly familiar. In the Book of the Dead, for example, we hear of the Negative Confession through which each Egyptian, after death, has to defend the actions of their lives before a panel of judges in the underworld: "I have not killed. I have not caused pain; I have not caused tears. I have not deprived cattle of their pasture."

But in all other aspects, the Mosaic laws are unique, for they move well beyond mere ritual to spell out an entire code of conduct by which humanity shall abide. "You must not distort justice; you must not show partiality," Deuteronomy admonishes the future judges and officials of Israel (Deuteronomy 16:19). Merchants and traders are told to be fair and just: "You shall have only a full and honest measure" (Deuteronomy 25:15). Each man and woman should show compassion to the downtrodden and marginalized. "You shall not strip your vineyard bare, or gather the fallen grapes of your vineyard," warns Leviticus. "[You] shall leave them for the poor and the alien" (Leviticus 19:10). After all, Deuteronomy reminds Moses' followers of how they were once like the "poor and alien." "You shall also love the stranger, for you were strangers in the land of Egypt" (Deuteronomy 10:19).

The Death of Moses

THE STORY OF Exodus does not end here. Soon after the events on Mount Sinai, the people of Israel are once again on the move, this time heading toward another Egyptian mining center, Ezion-geber, near today's Elat. Exodus states that guides from Midian are now plotting the route. These guides take the caravan past the oasis of Hazeroth to the great oasis of Kadesh-barnea.

Hazeroth has been associated with the oasis of Ain Hudhera. It is the only oasis of note in this part of Sinai, so remote that even today it can only be reached by camel provided by local Bedouin. From here to Kadesh-barnea,

DATING THE EXODUS

ACCORDING TO THE BIBLE, THE EXODUS occurred exactly 430 years after the arrival of Jacob's tribe in Egypt under the protection of Joseph. If we assume that the story of Joseph is placed at the time of King Sheshi, the founder of the 15th (Hyksos) dynasty (ca 1630–1520 B.C.E.), then the Bible cannot be too far off the mark, for 430 years later we find ourselves in the middle of the reign of Ramses II (ca 1279–1213 B.C.E.). Many scholars therefore tend to date the story of the Exodus to the mid-13th century, between 1260 and 1220 B.C.E. This dating appears to conflict with a reference in Kings (I Kings 6:1), in which we read that by the fourth year of Solomon's reign, 480 years had passed since the Israelites came out of Egypt. Solomon's reign is usually pegged from 970 to 931 B.C.E. Calculating our way back from Solomon's fourth year on the throne (967 B.C.E.), that would place the Exodus further back, around 1447 B.C.E. Scholars have sought to explain this apparent conflict by suggesting that the Book of Kings is referring to "480 years" in a symbolic sense, as 12 generations (12 x 40 years)—12 being a favored number for its reference to the 12 tribes of Israel. The dating of the mid-13th century is usually upheld because of the references in the Book of Exodus to the cities of Pithom and Raamses, both cities built by Ramses II, and by the mention of Israel on the famous Victory Slab of Merneptah, Ramses' successor.

The Victory Slab of Merneptah (1213–1204 B.C.E.), found in Thebes, contains the only reference to Israel in ancient Egyptian sources.

on the threshold of Canaan, is a mere 60 miles. But Moses knows that his exhausted people are not ready to fight their way into the Promised Land. An army must be assembled first, an army born in the desert and hardened by its harsh conditions. Only then can the great conquest of Canaan begin. Only then will the long journey home come to an end.

For Moses, it was not to be. On the eve of the Hebrews' entry into the Promised Land, Deuteronomy records, he went up Mount Nebo to cast one last gaze upon the Promised Land. And there, he died. The Bible tells us:

> *Moses was one hundred twenty years old when he died; his sight was unimpaired and his vigor had not abated. …*
>
> *Never since has there arisen a prophet in Israel like Moses, whom the Lord knew face to face. He was unequaled for all the signs and wonders that the Lord sent him to perform in the land of Egypt, against Pharaoh and all his servants and his entire land, and for all the mighty deeds and all the terrifying displays of power that Moses performed in the sight of all Israel.*
>
> (Deuteronomy 34:7-12)

Moses was not granted a magnificent burial, nor a tomb filled with golden objects. He was put to rest in a grave in "a valley in the land of Moab" that remains unknown to this day (Deuteronomy 34:6), further adding to the mystery that will forever shroud this hallowed figure of the Old Testament.

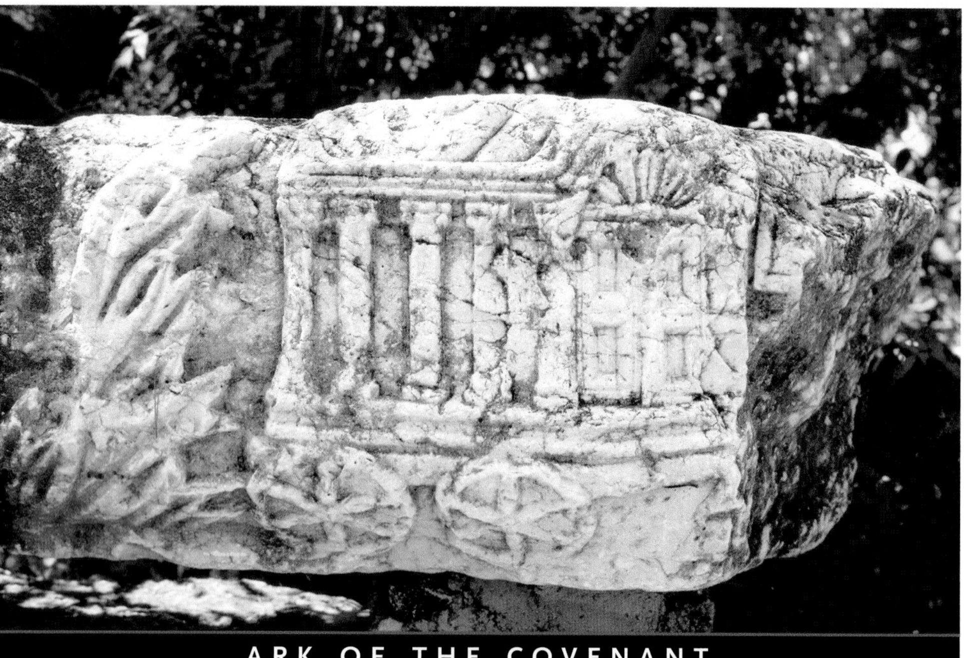

ARK OF THE COVENANT

THE ARK OF THE COVENANT, AS DESCRIBED in the Bible, is the physical link between the Israelites and YHWH, the "footstool of God's throne." As the box that contained the stone tablets given by God to Moses, the Ark became the Hebrews' holiest shrine. The Book of Exodus describes it as about three feet long, about two feet wide and high, gilded inside and out with gold, and sealed with a gold lid topped by two cherubim. It is carried by inserting two poles through the golden rings at each corner.

In its design, the Ark (perhaps not surprisingly) follows the Egyptian model for barques, sanctuaries that could be carried during religious processions. A similar chest with rings was discovered as part of the treasure of Tutankhamun.

During the wanderings in the desert, priests carried the Ark in advance of the people. After the settlement of Canaan, according to the Bible, it was kept in a variety of shrines and often carried into battle, which enabled the Philistines to capture it (it was returned seven months later). The Ark was ultimately enshrined in Jerusalem, in Solomon's Temple. When the Babylonian King Nebuchadnezzar captured Jerusalem in 587 B.C.E., the Ark was presumably lost. Various texts, however, insist that the Ark was hidden in a secret location, which remains to be discovered.

This rare depiction of a wagon, possibly the Ark of the Covenant, was found on a fragment of a lintel from the synagogue of Capernaum, built in the third century C.E.

Pharaoh's Fate

HISTORY TELLS US that Ramses II enjoyed a long and prosperous reign while Pharaoh, and his subjects worshipped him as a deity. Egypt enjoyed great wealth during this time, as evidenced by the countless temples and collossal statues commissioned by Ramses II throughout the kingdom. One of the best known and most impressive of his projects is the temple at Abu Simbel in southern Egypt. There, carved out of a sandstone cliff on the banks of the Nile River, four massive, 66-foot-tall statues of the Pharaoh himself sit at the entrance to the temple.

Ruling for 66 years, Ramses II outlived most of his sons and even his first,

OPPOSITE: In the Bible, Mount Nebo is where Moses dies. To honor Moses, 6th-century-C.E. Christians constructed a basilica here. Today, this modern structure protects its ruins.

Pharaoh's chariots and his army he cast into the sea;
his picked officers were sunk in the Red Sea. The floods covered them:
they went down into the depths like a stone. (Exodus 15:4-5)

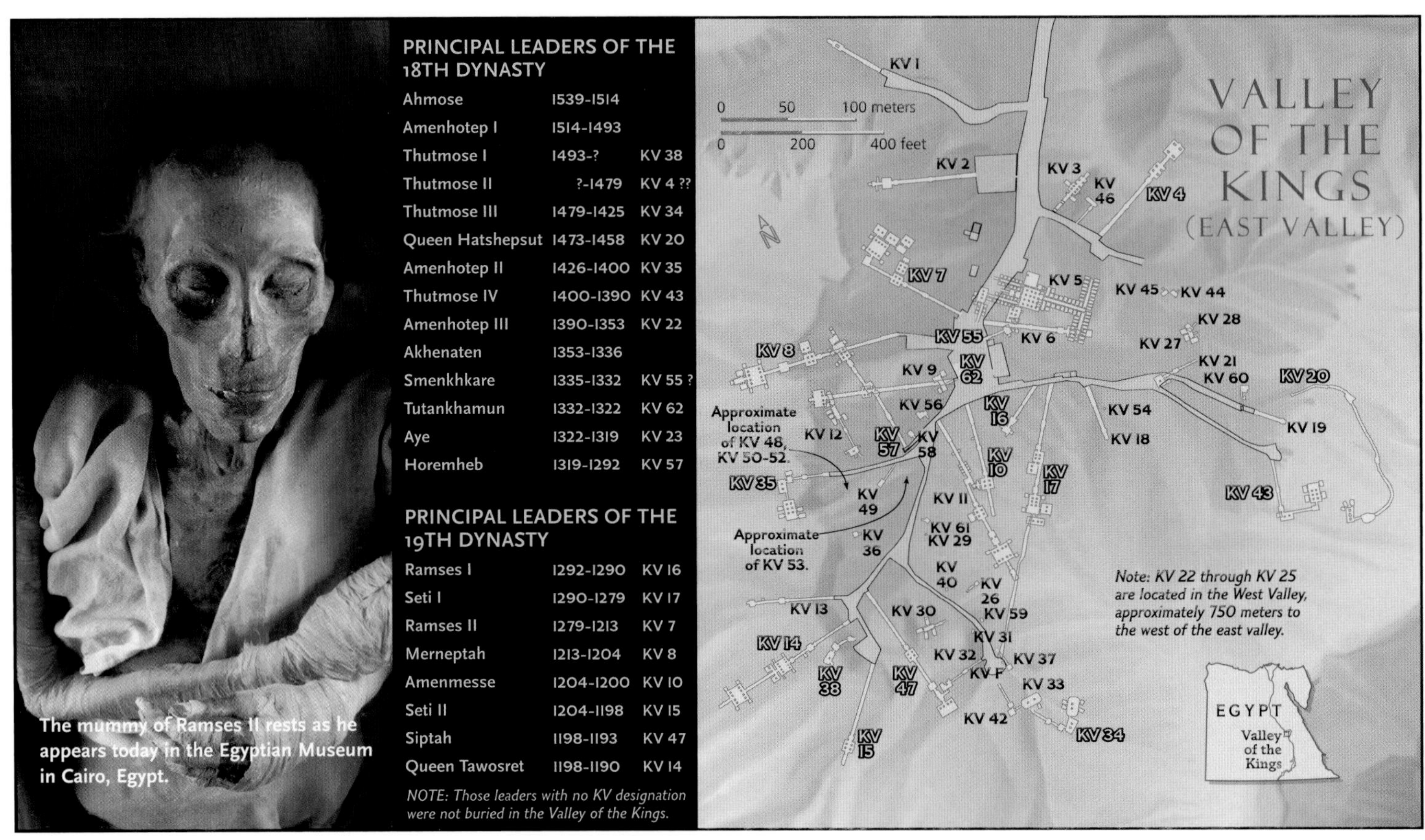

PRINCIPAL LEADERS OF THE 18TH DYNASTY

Ahmose	1539-1514	
Amenhotep I	1514-1493	
Thutmose I	1493-?	KV 38
Thutmose II	?-1479	KV 4 ??
Thutmose III	1479-1425	KV 34
Queen Hatshepsut	1473-1458	KV 20
Amenhotep II	1426-1400	KV 35
Thutmose IV	1400-1390	KV 43
Amenhotep III	1390-1353	KV 22
Akhenaten	1353-1336	
Smenkhkare	1335-1332	KV 55 ?
Tutankhamun	1332-1322	KV 62
Aye	1322-1319	KV 23
Horemheb	1319-1292	KV 57

PRINCIPAL LEADERS OF THE 19TH DYNASTY

Ramses I	1292-1290	KV 16
Seti I	1290-1279	KV 17
Ramses II	1279-1213	KV 7
Merneptah	1213-1204	KV 8
Amenmesse	1204-1200	KV 10
Seti II	1204-1198	KV 15
Siptah	1198-1193	KV 47
Queen Tawosret	1198-1190	KV 14

NOTE: Those leaders with no KV designation were not buried in the Valley of the Kings.

The mummy of Ramses II rests as he appears today in the Egyptian Museum in Cairo, Egypt.

and some say favorite, wife, Nefertari. He ultimately lost his battle with immortality in 1213 B.C.E., dying at age 90. His tomb lies in the Valley of the Kings. The location of this burial site has been known since antiquity; the entrance has long been accessible to the outside world. Like most other burial sites in the Valley of the Kings, his magnificent grave was later robbed. Today, much remains to be learned about the final resting place of Ramses II. Thick layers of flood debris, mud, and silt have obscured a lot of the original artwork and architectural detail.

After the tomb had been broken into and looted, Ramses's sarcophagus was moved to another location. It remained hidden until 1881, when archaeologists were finally able to locate his mummified body at Deir el Bahri. His mummy offers several facts about the man who had dominated Egypt for so long. Standing five feet eight, Ramses would have been considered tall by most Egyptians. Skeletal evidence reveals that arthritis eventually caused the pharaoh to stoop as he aged.

Since much of Egyptian art is idealized, archaeologists can only speculate as to what Ramses II might have looked like. Thanks to his mummy, a more realistic picture of the pharaoh has emerged. He had red hair (a rare trait in Egyptian men at that time), high cheekbones, big ears, a narrow chin, and a hooked nose. His teeth were riddled with cavities as well. Today, the man who once may have come face to face with Moses rests in a temperature-controlled room in the National Museum in Cairo.

The Mystery of the Exodus

THE EVENTS OF EXODUS continue to confound scholars in search of the historical proof behind the story. As many have pointed out, no archaeological evidence has ever been found in Sinai of a mass migration in the 13th century B.C.E. Despite numerous excavations, most of the sites mentioned in this chapter have failed to yield any visible proof of occupation during the Late Bronze Age.

Some scholars suggest that the Exodus was, in reality, a gradual emigration of Asiatic immigrant workers, including the Hebrews, out of Egypt because of discriminatory policies under the New Kingdom. Still others believe the story of Exodus was inspired by the eviction of the Hyksos—a suggestion bolstered by the fact that the Hyksos initially settled in southern Canaan.

Unfortunately, Egyptian records make no reference to an event fitting the description of the Exodus. This absence is not surprising, for Egyptian kings seldom made a habit of recording their defeats. But perhaps, a corroboration of the Exodus account can be inferred from the so-called Victory Slab of Pharaoh Merneptah, the son of Ramses II. The monument dates to around 1207 B.C.E.—two or three decades after the Hebrews may have entered the land of Canaan.

Like his father before him, Merneptah liked to parade his armies through Canaan to ensure that the tribute was paid on time. His Victory Slab describes the event in a boastful inscription, "Canaan is pacified and all its evil with it; the people of Israel are desolate, without offspring, Palestine has become Egypt's widow." Of course, the opposite is true. After the Egyptian army had its fill of looting, it moved on and the locals—including the Israelites—were left to live in peace.

What Merneptah did not realize is that with his stela, he immortalized the memory of the Hebrew slaves by recording the first reference to their new nation: Israel. It is a truly remarkable accomplishment that in such a short time, the slaves of Goshen were able to create a body politic worthy of mention in a royal Egyptian monument.

Work on the cities of Pi-Ramses and Per-Atum, where the Hebrews had slaved for so long, was suspended after the death of Ramses II. Many of the structures were ultimately torn down and reused in the construction of a vast new city, Tanis, which would serve the pharaohs of the Third Intermediate period (ca 1075–715 B.C.E.). The Temple of the Ramesseum, which Ramses built on the western bank of the Nile as a shrine to his own cult, was destroyed by an earthquake. The giant statue of the pharaoh, calculated to intimidate all who came upon it, fell to the ground, shattered, and has remained in pieces ever since. The land of Goshen would never reclaim its former glory.

EGYPT	MESOPOTAMIA	CANAAN
ca 1473 B.C.E. Hatshepsut becomes Egypt's first female Pharaoh and begins construction of a mortuary complex	ca 1500 B.C.E. Domesticated chickens widespread in Mesopotamia	ca 1500 B.C.E. Mitanni and Hittites challenge Egypt's influence in Canaan and Syria
ca 1353 B.C.E. Akhenaten rules Egypt; shifts capital from Thebes to Akhetaten (Amarna)	ca 1500 B.C.E. Kassites rule Babylon and adopt local customs	ca 1500–1250 B.C.E. Hebrews live in bondage in Egypt
ca 1322 B.C.E. Tutankhamun dies	ca 1350 B.C.E. Suppiluliuma I, king of the Hittites, conquers Syria and ends the power of the Mitanni	ca 1400 B.C.E. Tyre, Byblos, and Sidon thrive as centers of trade in the region
ca 1279–1213 B.C.E. Ramses II rules Egypt	ca 1300 B.C.E. The Hittite Empire reaches from northern Mesopotamia to Anatolia	ca 1340 B.C.E. The Egyptian governor in Jerusalem appeals to Akhenaten for reinforcements to fight mauraders
	ca 1285 B.C.E. In northern Mesopotamia, King Adadnirari I founds Assyrian Empire	
	ca 1250 An earthquake damages the Temple of Ishtar at Nineveh	

Though opinions vary, most scholars date the story of the Exodus to the end of the Late Bronze Age, a period spanning from 1300 to 1200 B.C.E.

CHAPTER FIVE

The Settlement in Canaan

THE LAST WORD OF THE BOOK OF DEUTERONOMY, the concluding volume of the Pentateuch, is "Israel." As the biblical narrative continues in the Book of Joshua, the Israelites are indeed standing on the threshold of the Promised Land. Moses' successor, a field commander named Joshua, is poised to invade Canaan with his newly trained Israelite army. This commander will initiate a lightning campaign, relying on stealth and speed to take the Canaanite cities by surprise. Within a few years, much of the highland territory, the spinal column of Canaan, will be in Israel's hands.

Archaeologists, however, have failed to find conclusive evidence of an Israelite campaign in the Early Iron Age (1200–1000 B.C.E.). As such, many scholars suggest that the settlement in Canaan was, in reality, a gradual process of immigration over a long period of time. Rebuffed by strong Canaanite communities in the fertile valleys and along the coast, the Hebrew tribes had no choice but to settle in the central highlands. There, too, the tribes found themselves in continuous conflict over water wells, pastures, arable land, and other resources. But the greatest upheaval was yet to come: the arrival of superbly armed predatory hordes, collectively known as the Sea Peoples.

The aquamarine Sea of Galilee spreads out below the Canaanite fortress of Hazor, one of the cities conquered by Joshua.

CONQUERING CANAAN

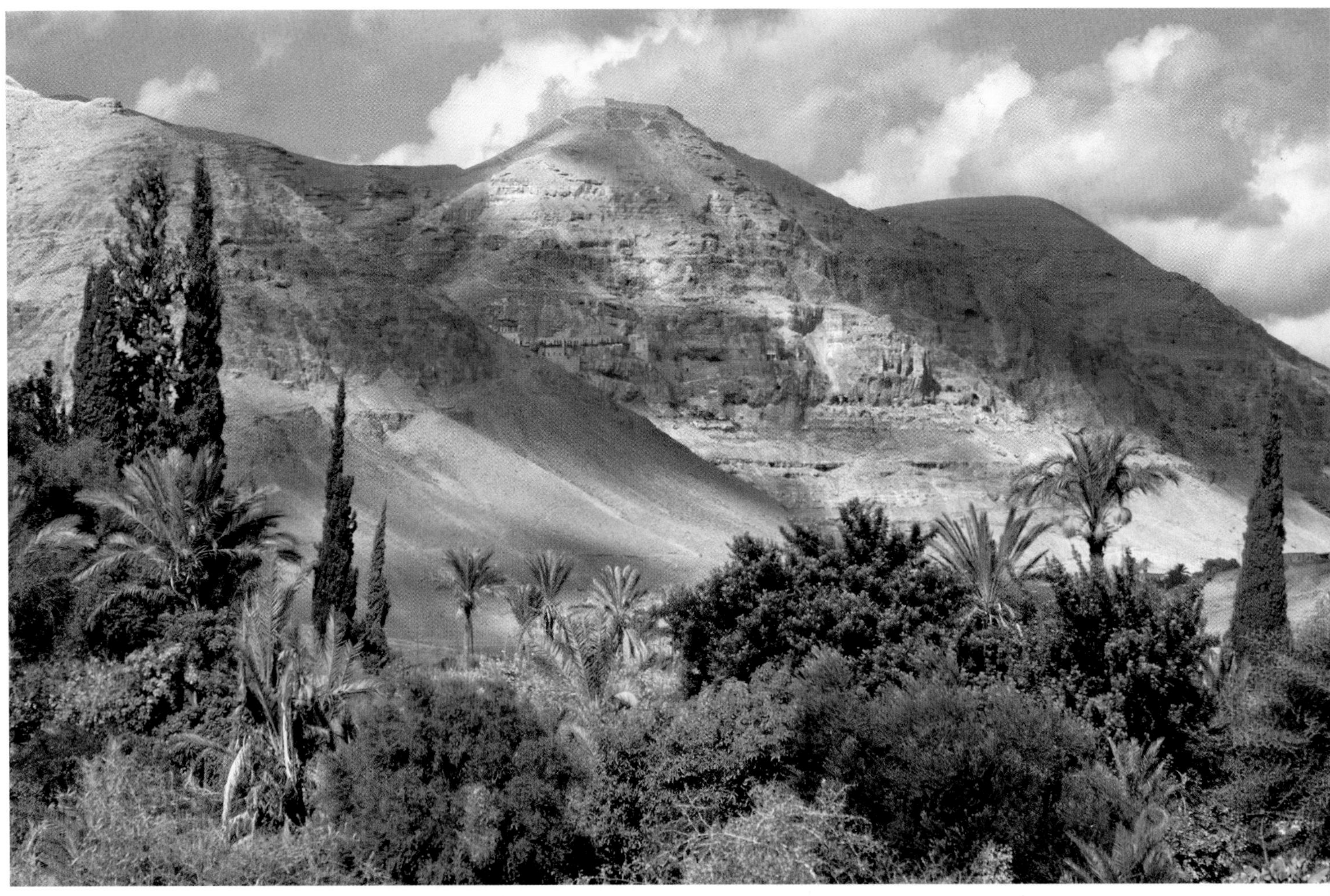

The barren Judean hills contrast with the lush olive and palm groves of Jericho, one of the first Canaanite cities taken by Joshua and the Israelite forces.

THE BOOK OF JOSHUA opens the Hebrew Bible's second grouping of Scripture, known as Nevi'im or The Prophets. Joshua is the first of four "Israelite history" works: Joshua, Judges, Samuel, and Kings. Joshua and Judges are devoted to the story of the Israelite conquest and settlement in Canaan. Joshua describes the original offensive against Canaanite settlements in the highlands; Judges narrates the constant struggle the settlers faced against nearby communities as well as foreign invaders, such as the Philistines, who almost succeeded in bringing the young Israelite commonwealth to its knees. Hard-pressed by enemies, the Hebrew tribes reluctantly accepted the rule of ad hoc supreme commanders—judges—thus preparing the way for Israel's monarchy.

The Books of Joshua and Judges narrate a history that is increasingly being attested by both literary and archaeological testimony. Particularly since the founding of Israel in 1948, Israeli archaeologists have conducted extensive excavations at ancient sites mentioned in the Bible to determine whether the biblical narrative can be corroborated by historical evidence.

The results have been uneven, however. There are clear signs of military conquest during the early Iron Age in places such as Hazor, but no evidence elsewhere

ca 1244 B.C.E.
Tukulti-Ninurta becomes king of Assyria

ca 1230 B.C.E.
Israelites destroy Hazor

ca 1207 B.C.E.
Assyria defeats Babylon

ca 1200 B.C.E.
Mesopotamian craftsmen perfect iron tools; start of the Iron Age throughout Near East

[The Lord said,] "Be strong and courageous; for you shall put this people in possession of the land that I swore to their ancestors to give them." (Joshua 1:6)

dentifies the type of destruction described n Joshua. Indeed, much of the debris found at large settlements dates to a later phase, to when the Philistines invaded Canaan. This lack of evidence has led scholars to two important conclusions. First, the "conquest" of Canaan may have been a process of gradual settlement over many generations that was only completed during the monarchies of David and Solomon in the tenth century B.C.E. Second, as a majority of scholars agree, the Book of Joshua was originally edited as part of a larger literary effort that produced not only the Books of Judges, Samuel, and Kings, but also its theological anchor, the Book of Deuteronomy (the last of the Five Books of Moses). Taken together, scholars refer to this oeuvre as the Deuteronomistic History, possibly compiled by scribes and scholars during and after the reign of King Josiah in the seventh century B.C.E.

According to this theory, the Book of Joshua was pieced together from several different oral traditions related to the settlement of ancient Israel in Canaan, spanning a period of some 200 years. In the seventh century B.C.E., Israel had shrunk to an enclave of Judah, a mere vassal of Assyria. Jewish scribes, eager to emphasize the invincibility of Joshua and his army, may have compressed the gradual integration of Israelite tribes in Canaan into one comprehensive hero saga to stress the immediate role of YHWH in the fortunes of "prehistoric" Israel—just as the figure of Moses may have been used to rally the different traditions related to the Exodus from Egypt. Viewed in this context, the disparity between Joshua's tales of conquest and the archaeological record of the Late Bronze and Early Iron Ages is less puzzling.

Regardless of the historicity of Joshua's military activity, however, the overriding purpose of the Book of Joshua is to demonstrate that the Israelites are able to take possession of the Promised Land under direct orders of YHWH through his intermediary, Joshua, so that they may build an indigenous society governed by the laws and rule of the Lord.

The Fall of Jericho

WE FIRST ENCOUNTER Joshua in the Book of Exodus, during the battle against the Amalekites over the use of the wells at Rephidim. Moses notices this young man's bravery and promotes him to serve as his aide-de-camp. Joshua next appears during the approach to Mount Sinai (Exodus 24:13) and after the construction of the tabernacle, the tent of worship. Joshua also participates in a special reconnaissance team, which reports that Canaan is a land that "flows with milk and honey." However, the men emphasize, its cities are heavily fortified and virtually impregnable.

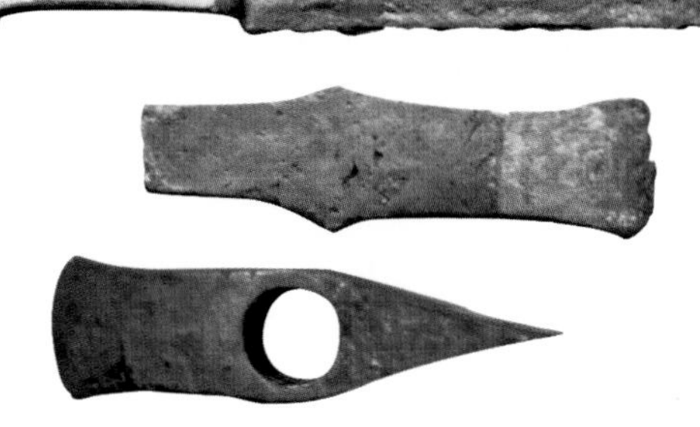

The choice, in the Bible, of Joshua as Moses' successor reflects the urgent need for a bold, imaginative, and inspiring military commander. Apparently Joshua is well aware of his desert army's handicaps. Though highly motivated, the Hebrews, the Bible says, lack the necessary weaponry, such as long-range composite bows or a battering ram, to take a city by force. The composite bow, introduced by the Philistines, used laminated layers of different wood, glued together with tree sap or boiled hide, to create a bow of terrific resiliency that far outranged traditional bows. Nor were the Israelites equipped with the heavy armor of the 13th century B.C.E., the iron war chariots that some of the Canaanite forces were able to put in the field. Joshua thus knows he cannot take a city by frontal assault or meet a Canaanite army in a head-on clash.

The original reconnaissance, as recorded in Numbers 13, reveals that the Valley of Jezreel and other fertile areas in the north are heavily defended. The flat plains were perfectly suited for chariots, which could maneuver at will. What's more, this "breadbasket of Canaan" was protected by a ring of fortresses that included Megiddo, Beth-Shan, and Hazor, which explains why Joshua chose to focus on the more sparsely defended hill country in the center, where chariots offered little advantage. Here, after all, were places such as Shechem,

This short, bone-handled sword and two axe-heads date to the Early Iron Age (1200–1000 B.C.E.), the putative period of the Israelite settlement in Canaan.

ca 1200 B.C.E.
The four-room pillared house begins to appear throughout Canaan

ca 1187 B.C.E.
Ramses III takes the throne in Egypt

ca 1180 B.C.E.
The Sea Peoples attempted invasion of Egypt is repulsed by Ramses III

ca 1173 B.C.E.
Elamites sack Babylon

where Abraham had built his first altar to El; Bethel, where Jacob had pitched his tents; and Hebron, where many of the patriarchs had been laid to rest. What's more, the Bible says, Joshua opts for tactics that avoid direct confrontation and favor stealth, guile, and deception.

Joshua, the Bible says, first focused on the city of Jericho. It was an inevitable choice, for Jericho sat astride the main path between the Transjordan and Joshua's ultimate objective: the spine of the high country running across the length of Canaan. A squad sent by Joshua reports that Jericho is surrounded by massive walls—so thick, in fact, that people actually live in them. One of these people is a prostitute named Rahab, who offered to shelter the squad (Joshua 2:15). And indeed, no sooner does the Israelite army show itself than Jericho's inhabitants hunker down behind their formidable defenses.

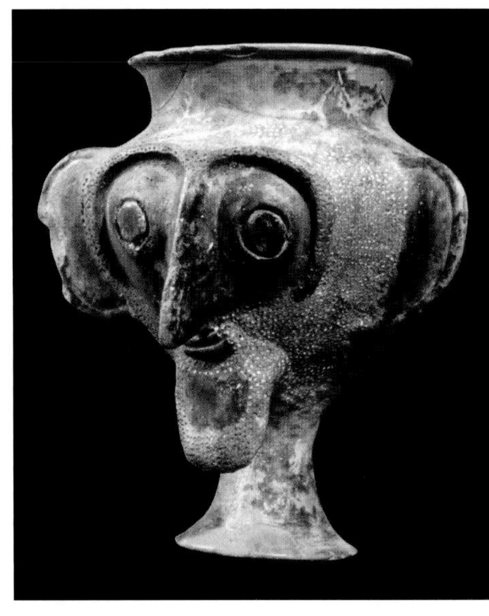

Occupied for 11,000 years, Jericho has yielded thousands of artifacts, including this drinking cup from the Middle Bronze Age (1750–1550 B.C.E.).

For six days, Joshua and his troops march around the walls of the city seven times. In the middle of their column is the Ark of the Covenant, containing the sacred tablets of Moses, accompanied by seven priests blasting their war horns. The Ark has become Israel's war standard, a proud token of God's power and presence that, Joshua calculates, would bolster his soldiers' morale and enlist YHWH's awesome power. In the ancient Near East, this belief was not unusual. Babylonian reliefs show that it was common practice in Mesopotamia to carry the totem of a warlord. Assyrian kings in particular made a habit of riding at the head of their troops with a statue or symbol of their dynasty's patron god, thus assured of his protection.

On the seventh day, the Book of Joshua continues, the Israelite army repeats the military parade around Jericho. But as the soldiers finish their seventh turn, and as the priests blow the shofars, Joshua rallies his people to a mighty war cry. The walls, says the Bible, "fell down flat" (Joshua 6:20). Some have suggested that the horns could have created an acoustic concussion

THE TRUMPETS OF JOSHUA

ACCORDING TO THE BOOK OF JOSHUA, THE Israelites laid siege to the walled city of Jericho under specific instructions of YHWH. "You shall march around the city," says the Lord, "... for six days, with seven priests bearing seven trumpets of rams' horns before the ark." On the seventh day, the priests are to "make a long blast with the ram's horn," and all the people are to "shout with a great shout; and the wall of the city will fall down flat" (Joshua 6:3-5).

Long before the time of the settlement, trumpets were used by the Egyptians to direct the movement of units during battle. Some of these trumpets were made of silver and bronze with mouthpieces of silver or gold; a magnificent specimen was found in the tomb of Tutankhamun.

Adorned with bands of gold, this shofar comes from Megiddo and dates to Late Bronze Age IIA (1400–1300 B.C.E.).

As the Bible indicates, Joshua's trumpets were made from a ram's horn (or shofar) that had been flattened and twisted into a bell shape after immersion in hot water.

The shofar eventually became a priestly instrument. According to the Book of Numbers, the shofar is blown to mark the new moon and solemn feasts. The Mishnah, the Rabbinic text that first recorded the Oral Law, states that two different horns were used in the Second Temple in Jerusalem. One, made of the horn of an ibex and equipped with a gold mouthpiece, was used to mark the New Year; another, made of a ram's horn, was sounded on fast days. Indeed, the ram's horn is probably the only Hebrew instrument to have survived from biblical times until today.

that smashed against the walls, loosening the mortar and causing them to crumble. Joshua's troops, the Bible continues, climb over the rubble and devote themselves "to destruction," which involved the massacre of "all in the city, both men and women, young and old, oxen, sheep, and donkeys" (Joshua 6:21). All of Jericho is burned to the ground, but Joshua first forbids looting; artifacts of silver and gold and vessels of bronze and iron are deposited in the "treasury of the house of the Lord" (Joshua 6:24).

The site of ancient Jericho is well known, having been found by Charles Warren in 1868. It is some 20 miles east of Jerusalem and nine miles north of the Dead Sea, near an oasis called Tell es-Sultan. Its wells still pump fresh water. As the British archaeologist Kathleen Kenyon revealed during her excavations in the 1950s, the massive, six-foot-thick walls that were the marvel of the Pre-Pottery Neolithic Period (8500–5500 B.C.E.) had all but crumbled in the early seventh millennium B.C.E., possibly as a result of an earthquake. On these ruins rose a succession of smaller settlements that, at times, were protected by a rampart of pressed earth—a mere shadow of the formidable walls of old. According to Kenyon, these mud walls were destroyed and rebuilt no less than 17 times. Finally, a new settlement arose around 2000 B.C.E. This city was surrounded by a modest wall made of packed earth, a demarcation to be sure, but nothing that could withstand an assault by a determined foe. This barrier was destroyed sometime near the end of the Middle Bronze Age, around 1550 B.C.E.—several centuries before the presumed time that Joshua would have marched on the city. Arguably, the fame of Jericho's ancient walls must have lived on through the centuries and perhaps inspired the story of Israel's unique military "weapon," the blasts of the horns.

The Capture of Ai

THE ISRAELITE COMMANDER, the Book of Joshua continues, next targets the hill country. Two roads wound their way westward from Jericho, slowly moving up to the high desert plateau of the Judean hills. One, rising some 4,000 feet, led to Jerusalem, the redoubt of the Jebusites. A more manageable route steered to the settlement of Ai, a city through which both Abraham and Jacob had passed. The less stoutly defended Ai was 12 miles north of Jerusalem.

***The Fall of Jericho* by Jean Fouquet (ca 1420–1480) appears in the illuminated manuscript *Antiquities of the Jews* by Flavius Josephus.**

Joshua opts to take Ai. After the victory at Jericho, he likely feels that a small force will suffice to take the city. Unexpectedly, this group of soldiers is defeated, but God gives Joshua a new plan. Joshua detaches a regiment of roughly 5,000 men and orders them to hide in the brush just west of the city during the night. After daybreak, his main force launches a mock attack on the city's northern gates. As Ai's troops stream out of the city, Joshua and the Israelites pretend to flee, luring the enemy away. At that moment, the stealth troops hidden in the brush surge forward. They occupy the city unopposed, then rush after Ai's forces, attacking them from the rear while Joshua's men turn to attack from the front, a classic pincer movement. Ai and its citizens are destroyed. This time, however, with the Lord's consent, Joshua takes the city's livestock and spoils, before burning it to the ground, making it "forever a heap of ruins" (Joshua 8:27-28).

Ai has been identified with a mound near Khirbat at Tall. It is close to the ancient city of Bethel, which was excavated by the American scholar William F. Albright in the late 1930s. A distinguished line of archaeologists have surveyed Khirbat at Tall, including John Garstang in the 1920s, Judith Marquet-Krause in the early 1930s, and Joseph Callaway in the 1970s. All found that Ai had been a prosperous city in the Early Bronze Age (3150–2000 B.C.E.), but saw no evidence of a large settlement, or massive destruction, during the period of Joshua's conquest in the late 13th century B.C.E. Some scholars believe that the earlier prominence of Ai was incorporated

The Bible describes how Joshua's forces leveled ericho's walls. These fortifications of Jericho date from he Middle Bronze Age IIA and IIB (1950–1550 B.C.E.).

n the Bible, Joshua uses stealth to conquer the city of i. The location of Ai has been linked to a mound near Khirbat at Tall, close to the ancient city of Bethel.

Al Jib, the site of ancient Gibeon, is according to the Bible, where the Lord makes the sun stand still so Joshua can defeat the forces of King Adonizedek.

The green slopes of Mount Tabor are where the Bible says Deborah musters her Israelite army before facing he Canaanites in the Battle of Jezreel.

JOSHUA AND THE CONQUEST OF CANAAN

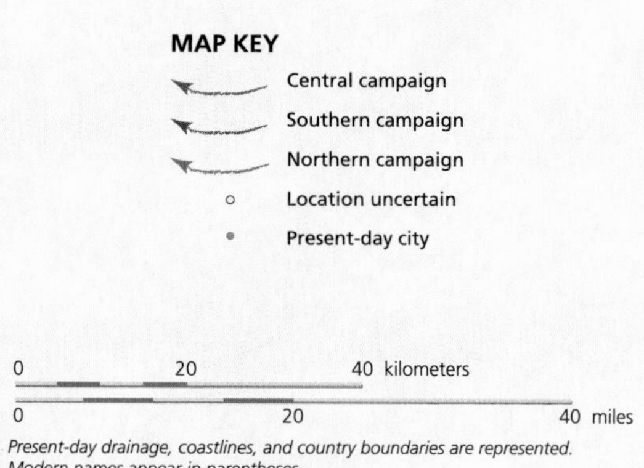

THE GREAT SEA
(MEDITERRANEAN SEA)

E G Y P T

Sidon
(Saïda)
Damascus
ARAM
2,814 m
9,232 ft
Mt. Hermon
Leontes
(Līṭāni)
PHOENICIA
LEBANON
Tyre
(Soûr)
Dan
(Tel Dan)
SYRIA
Joshua attacked and defeated the combined armies of several northern Canaanite cities. The victors chased the fleeing forces northward into the region of Sidon. (Joshua 11:7–8)
Kedesh
(Tel Qedesh)
Hazor
(Tel Ḥazor)
BASHAN
Achzib
(Tel Akhziv)
Merom
Jordan
Hazor, the main Canaanite city of the north, was taken and burned. (Joshua 11:11)
Acco
('Akko)
Achshaph
(KafrYasīf)
Bay of Acco
(Bay of Haifa)
Sea of Kinnereth
(Sea of Galilee)
Kishon
(Qishon)
Madon
Hammath
(Ḥammat)
Ashtaroth
Mt. Carmel
546 m
1,791 ft
Shimron Meron
(Semunieh)
Mt. Tabor
588 m
1,929 ft
Jabneel
Yarmuk
Joshua continued attacking and taking the rest of the Canaanite cities that had sent their armies to fight at Merom. (Joshua 11:12)
Jokneam
(Yoqne'am)
Shunem
(Sūlam)
Endor
('En Dor)
Edrei
(Dar'ā)
Dor
Megiddo
(Tel Megiddo)
Valley of Jezreel
Ta'anach
(Ta'annuk)
Beth Shan
(Bet She'an)
Ramoth-gilead
(Khirbat ar Rumaythah)
En-gannim
(Janīn)
PLAIN OF SHARON
Dothan
(Khirbat al Ḥufayrah)
Jabesh-gilead
GILEAD
West Bank
Joshua brought all the tribes together to renew the covenant with the Lord, and remind the people to stay faithful. (Joshua 24:1–27)
Mt. Ebal
940 m
3,084 ft
Tirzah
(Tallūza)
Succoth (Dayr'Allā)
Penuel
The inheritance of Joshua where he was buried. (Joshua 24:30)
Mt. Gerizim
881 m
2,890 ft
Shechem
(Nablus)
Jabbok
(Zarqa)
Yarqon
Aphek
(Tel Afeq)
Shiloh
(Khirbat Saylūn)
After an initial defeat, the Hebrews took Ai with a well planned ambush. (Joshua 7–8)
AMMON
Joppa
(Tel Aviv-Yafo)
Joshua, after a forced march from Gilgal, attacked an army of Amorites in defense of the allied city of Gibeon. The battle became a rout and the Hebrews pursued the remaining force. (Joshua 10:9–10)
Timnath-serah
The Hebrews crossed the Jordan and established their first permanent camp in Canaan. (Joshua 4:19)
Rabbah
(Amman)
Bethel
Ai (Khirbat at Tall)
Ambushing Force
Main Force
Gilgal
Joshua sent spies to evaluate the land, especially Jericho, a key Canaanite city. (Joshua 2:1)
One of the 5 city-states of the Philistines. Others were Ashkelon, Ekron, Gath, and Gaza.
Upper Beth-horon
(Bayt 'Ūr al Fawqā)
Jericho
(Tall as-Sulṭān)
Jericho
(Arīḥā)
Abel-shittim
Gezer
(Tel Gezer)
Gibeon
(Al Jīb)
Sorek
(Sarar)
Ekron
(Tel Miqne)
Heshbon
(Ḥisbān)
Beth Shemesh
(Tel Bet Shemesh)
Jerusalem
Ashdod
(Tel Ashdod)
Mt. Nebo
802 m
2,631 ft
Medeba
(Mādabā)
Jarmuth
(Tel Yarmut)
Gath
(Tel Ẕafit)
Bethlehem
Jericho was taken after the walls collapsed before the Ark of the Covenant, opening the way into all Canaan. (Joshua 6:20)
Ashkelon
(Tel Ashkelon)
Ashqelon
Adullam
(Ḥorbat 'Adullam)
Lachish
(Tel Lakhish)
Beth-zur
(Khirbat Ṭubayqah)
Salt Sea
(Dead Sea)
(Qiryat Gat) Libnah
SHEPHELAH
CANAAN
Wilderness of Judah
Makkedah
Hebron
Dibon
(Dhībān)
Gaza
(Tuffuh) Tappuah
Gaza Strip
'En-gedi
(Tell el Jurn)
Aroer
('Arā'ir)
Arnon
(Wadi el Mujib)
Eglon
Debir
Eshtemoa
(As Samū)
Gerar (Tel Gerar)
PHILISTIA
The defeated Amorite kings hid themselves in a cave. Joshua trapped, then executed them. (Joshua 10:26)
'Arad
(Tel Arad)
'Arad
Sharuhen
(Tel Sharuḥen)
Beersheba
(Be'ér Sheva')
MOAB
Besor
JORDAN
After he took the key cities, Joshua captured several more in the Negev. He then returned to the camp at Gilgal. (Joshua 10:41–43)
Zered (Hasa)
NEGEV

THE BREADBASKET OF ISRAEL

THE VALLEY OF JEZREEL, SCENTED BY CITRUS and mimosa, was and still is the most fertile region in Canaan. Its name in Greek, Esdraelon, means "may God sow fertility." The Valley of Jezreel is a triangular plain sheltered from the ocean winds by the protruding Carmel mountain range to the northwest and the Gilboa mountain range in the south. These ranges give the valley the appearance of a three-fingered hand; the central finger is known as the Harod Valley, which drops some 400 feet to connect with the Jordan River Valley near Bet She'an (Beth Shan). The Kishon River runs through much of the Valley of Jezreel, providing it with a continuous supply of water for local irrigation. The valley's principal crops in Canaanite times were wheat, olives, figs, and grapes.

Running northwest to southeast, the wide, 18-mile-long Valley of Jezreel has always been a prime battlefield, from Thutmose III's famous battle at Megiddo during the 15th century B.C.E. to the clash between the judge Deborah and the Canaanites at Mount Tabor and subsequent battles between Saul and the Philistines. Here, as well, King Jehu of Israel would vanquish King Ahaziah of Judah, and in turn, Pharaoh Neco would smite King Josiah. As the valley's principal fortress, Megiddo became the Har Megiddo, or Armageddon, in the Book of Revelations—the site of the final battle between Good and Evil at the end of time.

A modern view of the Valley of Jezreel and Mount Tabor reveals what was the most fertile region of ancient Canaan.

nto the Joshua story, or that Ai was confused with Bethel, its neighboring city. Then again, perhaps Khirbat at Tall is not the site, and the biblical Ai is yet to be discovered.

In the Book of Joshua, however, the fall of Ai marks a pivotal narrative moment. Up to this point, the leading cities of Canaan have largely ignored the Israelites. But the dramatic taking of Ai unnerves them. Believing their town to be next, the elders of Gibeon, a settlement six miles northwest of Jerusalem, offer Joshua a pact. To ensure that the Hebrew commander will agree not to loot their communities, the elders enact a ruse. Dressed in rags, the Gibeonites enter the Israelite camp, pretend to be from far away, secure their treaty, and leave. Three days later, Joshua discovers that the Gibeonites "were [really] their neighbors and were living among them" (Joshua 9:16). But honor-bound by the treaty, he is powerless to break it.

A reconstruction of the Shrine of the Steles, a Canaanite temple believed to have been destroyed around C.E. 1230, as it was found in Hazor by Yigael Yadin in 1955.

With the northern route secured, Joshua turns south to face his enemies. The Bible describes how King Adonizedek of Jerusalem forms a military alliance with troops from leading cities, including Lachish and Hebron, against the Hebrews. Adonizedek decides to make an example of Gibeon and attacks their city. The Gibeonites ask Joshua for help. Joshua promptly orders his army back to Gibeon, where he routs the forces of the enemy. They retreat down the hills into the valley of Aijalon, where the Lord batters them with huge stones from heaven. As darkness begins to fall, Joshua fears that they could escape, so he prays for the sun to stand still over Gibeon, and his wish is granted (Joshua 10:12-13). Joshua's forces swarm over the southern hill country, capturing Azekah, Lachish, Hebron, and Debir. He then turns north, toward the city of Hazor.

The Conquest of Hazor

HAZOR, a leading trading site, is often mentioned in Egyptian and Ugaritic tablets. From its position just north of the Sea of Galilee, Hazor controlled the principal trading routes joining up with the Way of the Philistines along the Mediterranean coast. In one of the Amarna Letters (diplomatic dispatches on tablets recovered from the capital of Pharaoh Akhenaten), King Ashtaroth of the Transjordan complains to the Egyptian king that the ruler of Hazor "took from me three cities." Not without reason, the Book of Joshua refers to Hazor as "the head of all those kingdoms" (Joshua 11:10). It also says that Jabin, King of Hazor, rallies the northern kingdoms into a defensive coalition against the Israelites (Joshua 11:1-3). But, the Bible claims, Joshua defeats them, captures Hazor, and burns it to the ground (Joshua 11:10-11).

Many years later, during the time of a judge named Deborah, the Lord "sold [the Israelites] into the hand of King Jabin of Canaan, who reigned in Hazor" (Judges 4:2). This phrasing suggests that either the king was still alive, or that his successor had the same name. Either way, the reference implies that Hazor is far from "burned by fire" by Deborah's time. In 1955, the Israeli archaeologist Yigael Yadin uncovered Hazor's fate. He exposed the northwest corner of a large building, which bore clear traces of soot. Yadin identified the building as the palace of King Ibni-Addu—quite possibly, the Jabin of the Bible—and concluded that Hazor had been razed by the Israelites around 1230 B.C.E. His assertion came under heavy attack from the scholarly community, leading to a new excavation by an Israeli team in the 1990s. They uncovered a throne room buttressed by wooden beams of Lebanese cedar—an unheard-of luxury. The plaster near the walls still carried traces of ash.

The palace also contained pieces of Canaanite pottery, while fragments of smashed Egyptian and Canaanite figurines were found throughout the stratum. These sherds date the building to the Late Bronze Age, at the beginning of the presumed period of Israelite settlement. The broken Egyptian statuary suggests that Egyptians did not raze the city. The site also lacks the distinctive geometric pottery that could indicate the Sea Peoples, the Philistines in particular. But plenty of idolatrous Canaanite cult statues had been deliberately destroyed. On the strength of this evidence, the excavators agreed with Yadin's original conclusion. Still, the suggestion that Hazor is the only Canaanite city with evidence of Israelite military activity during this period continues to be debated.

THE HEBREW SETTLEMENT

Modern workers use iron tools to break down the hard soil near the ancient city of Avdat in Israel.

WITH THE FORTRESS OF Hazor destroyed, the Book of Joshua turns to the important question of where the 12 tribes of Israel will settle. This issue was deeply charged, for Canaan was not the vast swath of fertile land that Goshen had been. The hills of Galilee, the Carmel, and northern Samaria were green and lush with forests, but the central highlands were hot and dry, covered with soil that was hardly suited for agriculture. Water was also a key problem. Only the coastal regions enjoyed a predictable amount of rainfall, while the Valley of Jezreel and the Jordan Valley were irrigated by rivers and streams. By contrast, the highlands were only suitable for dry farming, and pastures were few.

Joshua strives to be fair. The Bible relates how he takes "all that land: the hill country and all the Negeb ... from Mount Halak, which rises toward Seir, as far as Baal-gad in the valley of Lebanon below Mount Hermon" (Joshua 11:16-17) and sets about to divide it among the tribes. Mount Halak is usually identified as today's Jebel Halaq, some 40 miles south of the Dead Sea in an area the Bible calls Edom (a territory stretching from today's southern Jordan to the Negev). Baal-gad is associated with the area of Upper Galilee north of Hazor. It may be identified with Banyas, a

ca 1156 B.C.E.
Reign of Ramses III ends

ca 1150 B.C.E.
Mycenaean civilization declines

ca 1143 B.C.E.
Under Nebuchadnezzar I, Babylon briefly rises to power and defeats the Elamites

ca 1125 B.C.E.
Israelites and Canaanites meet at the Battle of Megiddo

[Joshua said,] "If you transgress the covenant of the Lord your God ... and go and serve other gods and bow down to them, then the anger of the Lord will be kindled against you, and you shall perish quickly from the good land that he has given to you." (Joshua 23:16)

village some eight miles east of modern Qiryat Shemona on the Banyas River. As the city of Caesarea Philippi, it would gain some renown as the place where, according to the Gospel of Matthew, Jesus calls Peter his "rock" on which he would build his church. In sum, the land to be assigned to the Israelite tribes stretched all the way from the Negev in the south to the Hula Valley in the north, even though many parts of this territory were still in Canaanite hands.

Honoring a promise once given by Moses, Joshua settles the tribes of Reuben and Gad in the former Amorite possession of Sihon, on the Transjordan plateau (Joshua 13:15-28). One part of the large Manasseh tribe is granted half the land of Gilead, between the Jabbok and Yarmuk Rivers (Joshua 13:29-32), while the other Manasseh clans go to the foothills between Shechem and the Valley of Jezreel. The tribe of Joseph is settled in the central highlands near Ephraim; Judah is given the land south of Jerusalem, centered on Hebron, though Hebron itself becomes the possession of Caleb (Joshua 14-15).

For the remaining seven tribes, Joshua first conducts a detailed survey of the remaining territory. He then orders lots to be drawn. Benjamin's tribe receives the hill country north of Jerusalem (Joshua 18:11-28). Immediately to the west comes the tribe of Dan, which is given the coastal plain (Joshua 19:40-48). Simeon's tribe moves south to the Negev region around Beersheba (Joshua 19:1-9). The north is apportioned to the four other tribes. Asher settles in western Galilee (Joshua 19:24-31), Zebulun in central Galilee (Joshua 19:10-16), and Naphtali in eastern Galilee (Joshua 19:32-39). The tribe of Issachar is moved to the valley between Beth Shan and the Jezreel (Joshua 19:17-23).

The tribe of Levi is not given any particular region, for its members are a priestly caste, destined to serve all the tribes of Israel. Instead, the Levites are placed in various towns throughout the land. Recognizing the potential for blood feuds between clans and tribes, Joshua also reserves six cities (including Hebron, Kedesh, and Shechem) as "cities of refuge" for those who had inadvertently killed a man, so as to protect them from undue revenge.

The Bible acknowledges that the allocation was not fully satisfactory. Many tribes find their boundaries surrounded by hostile states that do not look kindly on the Israelite invasion. Reuben and Gad are threatened by the kingdoms of Moab and Edom. Asher, Zebulun, and Naphtali live in close proximity to the kingdoms of Geshur and Maachah, while the northernmost tribes butt against the Amorite kingdom. The tribe of Dan finds itself squeezed by the hill country and the coastal cities proper, all of which remain undefeated. Meanwhile, the fortified cities of Jerusalem, Beth Shan, and Megiddo remain in Canaanite hands, as do the fertile northern plains.

The problems that ensue from this arrangement are documented in the Book of Judges, whose narrative spans a period from around 1200 to 1020 B.C.E. The name "Judges" refers to a number of ad hoc Israelite leaders to whom the tribes often turned to unify the Hebrews against a common threat. As such, the book is, in the truest sense of the word, a collection of disparate folk stories about heroes of

This sickle handle, decorated with an animal's head, was found in a cave in the Carmel and dates to the Middle Bronze Age IIB (1750–1550 B.C.E.).

ca 1115 B.C.E.
Tiglath-Pileser I becomes king of Assyria

ca 1103 B.C.E.
Phoenicians develop an alphabetic script

ca 1100 B.C.E.
The "Tale of Wen-Amon" tells of an Egyptian official passing through Canaan to buy cedars in Lebanon

ca 1100 B.C.E.
Mesopotamian scholar compiles a medical diagnostic textbook

CLIMATE AND VEGETATION

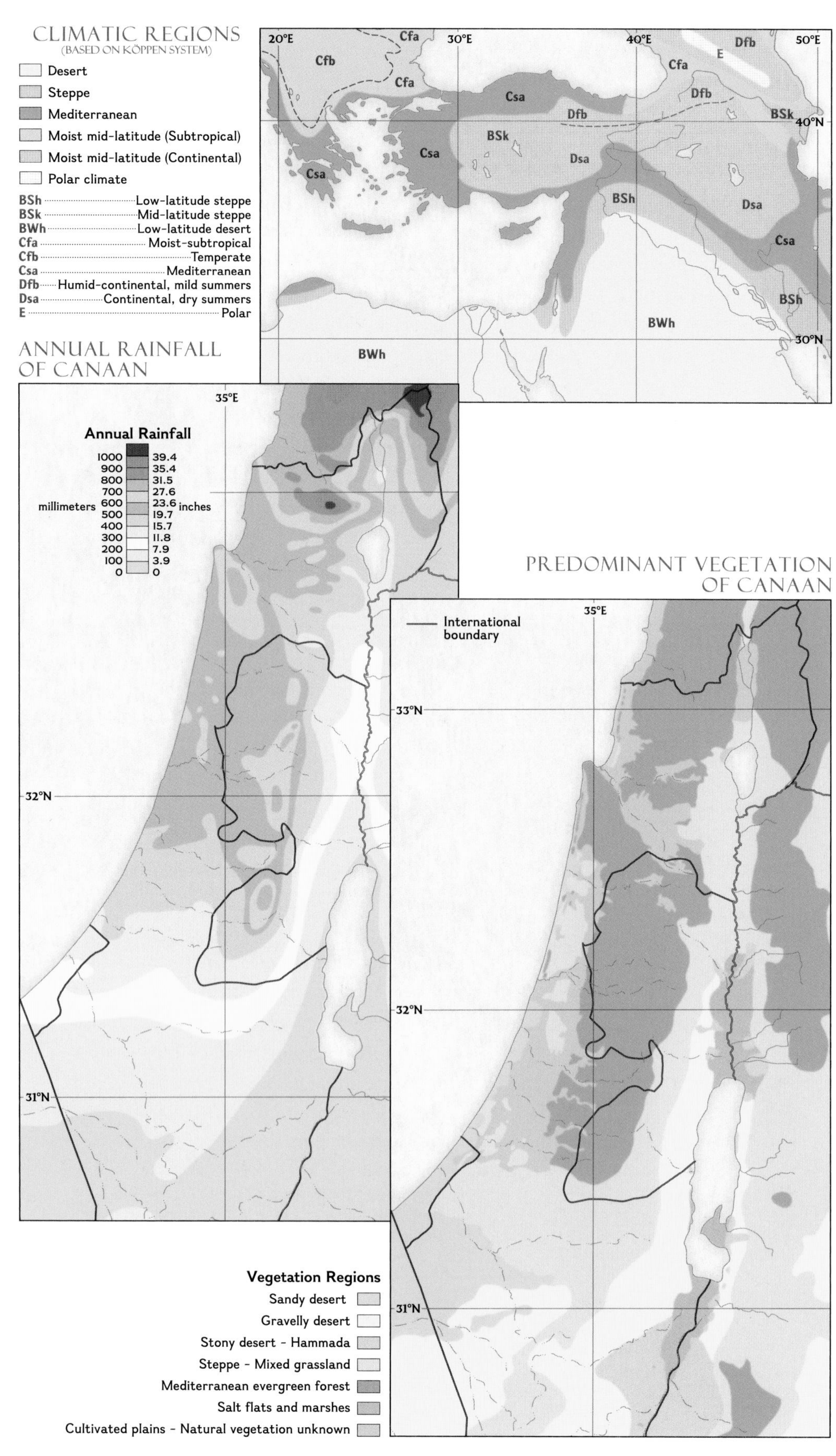

DECLINE OF EGYPTIAN POWER

Until the end of the Bronze Age, Canaan (Retenu in Egyptian inscriptions and literature) had been in the Egyptian sphere of influence, with many communities paying tribute to the Egyptian crown. After the 13th century B.C.E., Egyptian hegemony began to crumble under the weight of internal unrest, brought on by harvest failures and famine throughout Upper and Lower Egypt. Some scholars believe that the settlement of the Israelites, sometimes by force of arms, would not have succeeded if Egypt had still been the dominant power in Canaan, keen to protect its interests. The emerging power vacuum would soon be filled by the rising colossus in the East: Assyria.

Israel's prehistory, preserved by oral tradition until their codification in the seventh or sixth century B.C.E. More often than not, these heroes were up against impossible odds. "The Lord was with Judah," says Judges; "[but he] could not drive out the inhabitants of the plain, because they had chariots of iron" (Judges 1:19).

The Evidence of Israelite Settlement

WHETHER BY CONQUEST, immigration, or otherwise, there is no doubt that the Early Iron Age (1200–1000 B.C.E.) saw a remarkable population increase in northern Canaan. In the fall of 1991, archaeologist Adam Zertal concluded a 12-year study of the very region that, according to the Bible, Joshua had allocated to the tribe of Manasseh. This area is bordered by the Jordan on the east, the Valley of Jezreel on the north, and Shechem to the south. Zertal's survey identified the remains of some 116 Canaanite settlements dating from the Middle Bronze Age IIB (1750–1550 B.C.E.). Excavations show that during the next 300 years this region saw a steep decline in population, leaving only 39 sites still inhabited. But in the years following 1200 B.C.E., the population rose precipitously to a total of 136 sites.

Even more remarkable was the location of these new settlements. Whereas during the earlier period most communities were located in the fertile valleys and the plains, during the Early Iron Age many of the new settlements had shifted to the mountainous areas of the foothills and highlands. Here, the land is covered with terra rossa topsoil, which is far more difficult to cultivate. This shift would have made no sense, were it not for the narrative of Joshua, which admits that in many places the Israelites were driven from the fertile valleys by the better-armed Canaanite natives.

Fortunately for the Israelites, the hardship of dry farming on the stubborn highland soil was alleviated by the advent of farming tools made of iron. This metal only became available in quantity throughout the Near East after 1200 B.C.E. (hence the name Iron Age). With these new implements, which were far more effective in working the hard ground, the Israelites were presumably able to eke out a living, high above the rich alluvial plains below.

What's more, the Hebrews only controlled certain enclaves within Canaan. Key fortified cities—including Beth Shan, Megiddo, and Jerusalem—and strategic regions, including the Valley of Jezreel—were not in Israelite hands at all. And as the subsequent narrative in Judges will show, it was in these places where the conflict between Israelites and Canaanites would erupt in the future.

Nevertheless, whether by sword or by stealth, by the early 12th century B.C.E. Israelite communities had begun to successfully stake out a presence in Canaan. In the decades to come, they would devote themselves to building their settlements, raising their herds, and gathering their crops. The two cultures, Canaanite polytheism and Israelite monotheism, entered a period of wary coexistence.

The Emergence of Hebrew

AS THE ISRAELITES TOOK ROOT, the first signs of a distinct culture began to emerge. The most important development was a distinct language, both in oral and written form. Up to this point, Canaan itself had been largely bereft of a literary tradition of its own. For centuries, the two dominant languages in the region were Akkadian, which used the Babylonian cuneiform script, and

A waterfall on the Banyas, a tributary of the Jordan River, near Mount Hermon. The town of Banyas was renamed Caesarea Philippi in New Testament times.

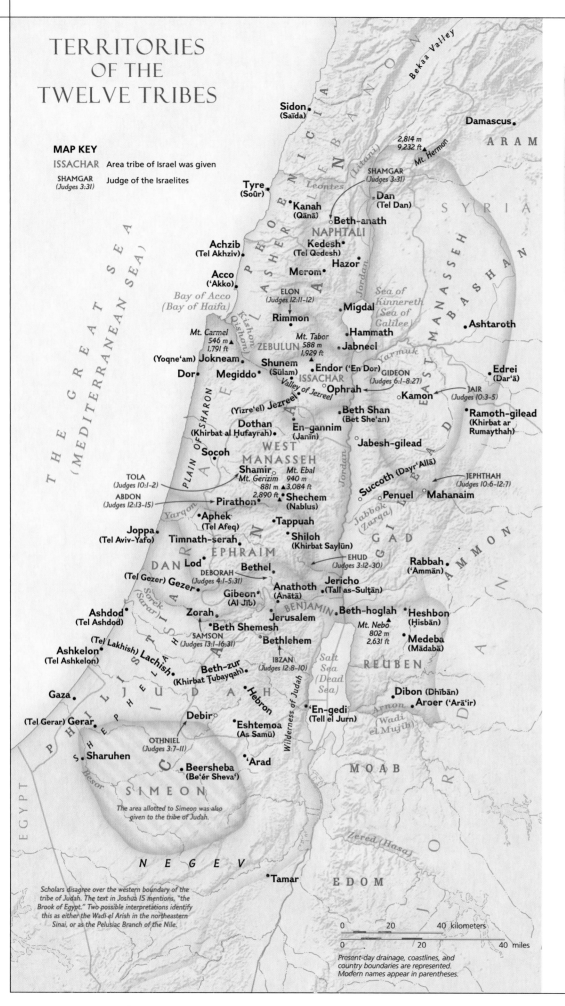

TERRITORIES OF THE TWELVE TRIBES

MAP KEY

ISSACHAR Area tribe of Israel was given

SHAMGAR (Judges 3:31) Judge of the Israelites

Sidon (Saïda)
Damascus
ARAM
Bekaa Valley
2,814 m 9,232 ft Mt. Hermon
SHAMGAR (Judges 3:31)
Tyre (Soûr)
Leontes
Litani
Dan (Tel Dan)
Kanah (Qānā)
Beth-anath
NAPHTALI
SYRIA
Achzib (Tel Akhziv)
Kedesh (Tel Qedesh)
Hazor
Acco (ʻAkko)
Merom
BASHAN
EAST MANASSEH
ASHER
Bay of Acco (Bay of Haifa)
ELON (Judges 12:11-12)
Rimmon
Sea of Kinnereth (Sea of Galilee)
Migdal
Ashtaroth
Jordan
Kishon (Qishon)
Mt. Carmel 546 m 1,791 ft
Mt. Tabor 588 m 1,929 ft
ZEBULUN
Hammath
Jabneel
Yarmuk
(Yoqneʻam) Jokneam
Shunem (Sūlam)
Endor (ʻEn Dor)
GIDEON (Judges 6:1-8:27)
Edrei (Darʻā)
Dor
Megiddo
ISSACHAR
Valley of Jezreel
Ophrah
JAIR (Judges 10:3-5)
Kamon
(Yizreʻel) Jezreel
Beth Shan (Bet Sheʻan)
Ramoth-gilead (Khirbat ar Rumaythah)
THE GREAT SEA (MEDITERRANEAN SEA)
PLAIN OF SHARON
Dothan (Khirbat al Ḩufayrah)
En-gannim (Janīn)
Jabesh-gilead
Socoh
WEST MANASSEH
GILEAD
TOLA (Judges 10:1-2)
Shamir
Mt. Ebal 940 m 3,084 ft
Mt. Gerizim 881 m 2,890 ft
Succoth (Dayr ʻAllā)
JEPHTHAH (Judges 10:6-12:7)
ABDON (Judges 12:13-15)
Pirathon
Shechem (Nablus)
Penuel
Mahanaim
Yarqon
Aphek (Tel Afeq)
Tappuah
Jabbok (Zarqa)
Joppa (Tel Aviv-Yafo)
Timnath-serah
Shiloh (Khirbat Saylūn)
GAD
EPHRAIM
AMMON
DAN
Lod
EHUD (Judges 3:12-30)
Rabbah (ʻAmmān)
DEBORAH (Judges 4:1-5:31)
Bethel
(Tel Gezer) Gezer
Jericho (Tall as-Sulţān)
Anathoth (ʻAnātā)
Gibeon (Al Jīb)
Sorek (Sarar)
BENJAMIN
Beth-hoglah
Heshbon (Ḩisbān)
Ashdod (Tel Ashdod)
Zorah
Jerusalem
Mt. Nebo 802 m 2,631 ft
Beth Shemesh
SAMSON (Judges 13:1-16:31)
Bethlehem
Medeba (Mādabā)
(Tel Lakhish) Lachish
Ashkelon (Tel Ashkelon)
IBZAN (Judges 12:8-10)
Salt Sea (Dead Sea)
REUBEN
Beth-zur (Khirbat Ţubayqah)
PHILISTIA
SHEPHELAH
JUDAH
Hebron
Gaza
Dibon (Dhībān)
Aroer (ʻArāʻir)
ʻEn-gedi (Tell el Jurn)
Arnon (Wadi el Mujib)
(Tel Gerar) Gerar
Debir
Eshtemoa (As Samū)
Wilderness of Judah
OTHNIEL (Judges 3:7-11)
Sharuhen
ʻArad
Beersheba (Beʻér Shevaʻ)
MOAB
Besor
SIMEON
EGYPT
The area allotted to Simeon was also given to the tribe of Judah.
Zered (Hasa)
JORDAN
NEGEV
Tamar
EDOM

Scholars disagree over the western boundary of the tribe of Judah. The text in Joshua 15 mentions, "the Brook of Egypt." Two possible interpretations identify this as either the Wadi el Arish in the northeastern Sinai, or as the Pelusiac Branch of the Nile.

0 20 40 kilometers
0 20 40 miles

Present-day drainage, coastlines, and country boundaries are represented. Modern names appear in parentheses.

The Gezer Calendar, a limestone tablet discovered in the early 1900s in Tel Gezer, is believed to be the oldest example of Hebrew writing. It dates to the late tenth century B.C.E.

Egyptian hieroglyphics (although some Egyptian correspondence, particularly the Amarna Letters, was conducted in cuneiform as well). By 1100 B.C.E., about a century after the apparent biblical date of the settlement, evidence of a language that can be tentatively identified as ancient (or Old) Hebrew begins to emerge in Canaan. This language had evolved from a common northwestern Semitic root that, by varying degrees, was also spoken in Phoenician, Ugaritic, Moabite, and Edomite dialects.

It is tempting to think that Old Hebrew only crystallized after the immigration into Canaan, as a result of the growing communication within and between tribal communities, although there is no evidence to support this line of thought. Some scholars believe that Old Hebrew originated earlier, possibly during the wanderings in the desert or even in Egypt. Scholarly analysis has shown that the oldest written texts in the Bible are poetic passages found in the Books of Genesis, Exodus, and

Judges. It is probably safe to say that the settlement of Israelite communities in Canaan accelerated the development of indigenous Hebrew.

In adopting a writing system for Hebrew, the settlers chose neither the cuneiform script nor the Egyptian hieroglyphic or hieratic (cursive) systems. In fact, an early pictographic form of writing, arranged in alphabetic order, had emerged in the region as early as 1150 B.C.E., known as Proto-Canaanite. Next came the first instance of a truly alphabetic script, the Phoenician alphabet, which is documented in a royal monument from Byblos around 1050 B.C.E. The Phoenician dialect owed much to the same northwestern Indo-Semitic dialect that formed the basis of Hebrew and Aramaic. It was only natural, therefore, that when the Israelite settlers began to record their transactions in writing, they would turn to the Phoenician script. The oldest example of written Hebrew is a small tablet from Gezer, dated around 925 B.C.E., describing a calendar of agricultural seasons.

The key challenge presented by any form of writing is to accurately grasp the phonemes (significant sounds) by which spoken language communicates its meaning. Latin (as well as modern English) uses vowels to indicate the difference between, say, "cat" and "cot." Semitic scripts such as Old Hebrew and Phoenician used a different strategy, by accentuating the different pronunciation of consonants; vowels were usually not written down. For example, an inscription on a bronze arrowhead from the 11th century states that the weapon belongs to "d" (meaning "Ada"), who was the son of "b'l' " (meaning "Bala").

Many years later, around 800 B.C.E., the Greeks adopted the Phoenician alphabet as well. Classic Greek, however, places a greater emphasis on vowels, so the Greeks adopted separate symbols for *a*, *e*, *i*, *o*, and *u* that, by and large, we continue to use today. The alphabet of Old Hebrew, by contrast, continued to evolve as a separate branch of the Phoenician alphabet until it became a clearly distinct script by the seventh century—the time when, scholars believe, the Pentateuch (the Five Books of Moses), was first committed to writing in its current form.

Then the Lord raised up judges, who delivered them out of the power of those who plundered them. Yet they did not listen even to their judges; for they lusted after other gods and bowed down to them.

(Judges 2:16-17)

TRACING ISRAELITE SETTLEMENTS

On archaeological sites, pottery is the most commonly found artifact; it has been used to identify a nascent Israelite culture during the period of the Israelite settlement. The finds include a remarkable tall jar, or pithos, with a distinctive rim collar, capable of holding some 15 gallons of water, oil, or wine. In fact, some 30 percent of all excavated Early Iron Age sites in the hill country settled by the Israelites often contained these rim-collared jars. Most of these sites were concentrated around the Jordan River Valley and the rivers and tributaries in the east. Based on this evidence, archaeologists believe that the Israelite immigrants entered Canaan in the north, hugging the Jordan River Valley, before percolating down to the southern hill country and the plains beyond.

Israelite Dwellings

ANOTHER EXPRESSION of a distinct Israelite culture was architecture. Clearly, the climate of Canaan was very different from what the nomadic Israelites were used to in the desert. Pitched tents would not do, not if the Israelites were to create and maintain a permanent presence in the land—making a living as settled farmers rather than nomads. Canaanite dwellings were rather straightforward: a small courtyard, flanked on two sides by a single covered room. Though easy to build, this plan was ill suited for the multifunctional type of farms that the Hebrew settlers required. Many archaeologists believe the requirements of farming may be the reason why a very different type of one-family dwelling appears during the Early Iron Age—a house, moreover, that could be built quickly and cheaply with the soft and porous limestone found throughout the highlands.

This new dwelling is the distinctive four-room pillared house that begins to appear throughout the central hills of Canaan after 1200 B.C.E. This simple design uses pillars supporting the roof beams to divide the house into four separate function areas, all grouped around a small central courtyard for air and light. A low wall, or a curtain, hung between the pillars, dividing the house into a stable for farm animals, a central storage for supplies, living space, and the family's sleeping quarters.

A close corollary of the four-room pillared house was the house cistern. Living in the highlands, many Israelites did not have access to water wells or streams in Canaanite territory. Instead, they had to learn to preserve the precious rainfall during winter months by using iron-tipped tools to quarry cisterns in the chalky limestone rock. The cisterns were then lined with plaster to create a watertight seal. In a later phase, the farmers developed an interlocking system of household cisterns, not only to increase storage capacity, but also to filter the water by allowing the sediments to settle during transfer between multiple basins. Another phenomenon of this period, often associated with the Israelites, are tall earthenware jars called pithoi, notable for a distinctive rim around the collar. Roughly three feet tall, the jars were probably used to haul water from cisterns or to store precious commodities like oil and wine.

Some scholars have challenged the view that the introduction of the four-room house and the rim-collared jars was exclusively Israelite, pointing to examples found well outside the radius of Israelite territory. Nevertheless, their appearance closely coincides with the putative period of the biblical settlement and, at the very least, reflects a new emphasis on multifunctional habitats—combining agriculture, husbandry, and crafts—that biblical accounts also describe. These innovations certainly further served to cement the presence of the Israelites in the region, to sustain the stable growth of their settlements, and to make the Hebrew community a dominant cultural force in the years to come.

FROM BRONZE TO IRON

The growth of the Israelite settlement in Canaan coincided with the growing use of iron in western Asia. Iron was mined in the northern hills of Hittite country (now Turkey) and traded throughout the region by the Phoenicians. Small quantities of iron had been used before, notably by the Egyptians, but it remained rare. Now iron flooded the market, becoming a powerful new commodity—so much so that scholars mark this time as the end of the Bronze Age and the beginning of the Iron Age.

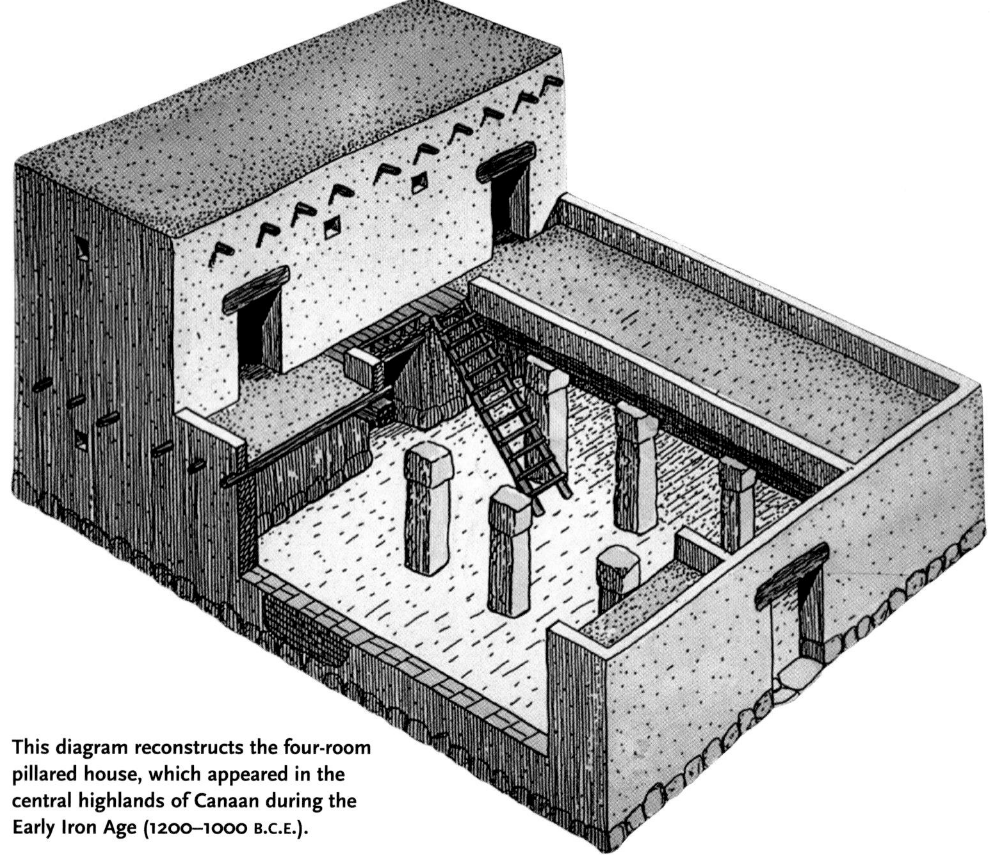

This diagram reconstructs the four-room pillared house, which appeared in the central highlands of Canaan during the Early Iron Age (1200–1000 B.C.E.).

The Period of the Judges

INEVITABLY, as the new Israelite communities grew, tension with the Canaanites increased. In many places, there was a renewal of hostilities. The author of the Deuteronomistic History depicts these cyclical clashes as God's punishment for tribes that had neglected their religious duties to YHWH in favor of the worship of local cults (Judges 2:11-13).

More often than not, if a Hebrew settlement comes under attack, a neighboring tribe will rally to its cause. Sometimes, if large swaths of Israelite land are threatened by Canaanite aggression, the tribes elect a temporary leader, or judge, and, with God's help, resist the aggression. The biblical narrative presents 12 such judges (a figure doubtlessly inspired by the 12 tribes), each of whom is given temporary jurisdiction over tribal territory. These leaders are not judges in the modern, legal sense. Rather, they are charismatic figures selected for their military and strategic acumen; some are even described as "savior" (or *moshia'* in Hebrew). As noted in Judges, judging (or *shofet* in Hebrew) is strictly reserved for YHWH (Judges 11:27).

The largest problem facing the judges is the lack of sophisticated weaponry. A century will pass before this imbalance will be made up for by the number of soldiers the Israelite judges can field. One example is the battle against King Jabin of Hazor in the Valley of Jezreel. For a long time, the Israelite tribes located in the north have been forced to pay tribute to Jabin as the dominant Canaanite power in the area (Judges 4:1-3). The judge who inspires the Israelites into revolt is not a man, but a woman. She is a prophetess named

Deborah, determined to establish Israelite power in the fertile Valley of Jezreel once and for all.

To do so, she needs troops, not only from local clans but also from all the tribes in the Israelite commonwealth—a difficult enterprise even in the best of times. Deborah, the Book of Judges says, is up to the task, however. Whenever her appeal for military assistance falls on deaf ears, she cleverly questions the tribe's bravery. "Why did you tarry among the sheepfolds," she scoffs at one reluctant chieftain, "to hear the piping for the flocks?" (Judges 5:16). Clearly, this woman brooks no argument, and in the end, she gets the troops she needs.

Deborah and her commander, Barak, the Book of Judges continues, muster the Israelite army on high ground, on the slopes of Mount Tabor, overlooking the Valley of Jezreel. The Canaanites are unruffled. They know they can rely on their mighty chariot force, which stands under the command of a general named Sisera. But Sisera has not reckoned with the power of YHWH. God unleashes a rainstorm that swells the waters of the Kishon River and promptly floods the Valley of Jezreel, turning the soft earth to mud (Judges 5:20-21). Before long, the heavy chariots are mired in the muck, echoing the fate of the chariots of Pharaoh at the Red Sea. When Barak sees that the Canaanite forces are marooned, he throws his infantry into battle and defeats the Canaanite soldiers. At last, the Valley of Jezreel is in Israelite hands. It is a turning point in the war for Canaan.

After the battle, according to the Book of Judges, Deborah rises with a song of triumph that will inspire Israel for centuries to come—a battle cry of freedom for a young and vibrant nation, sheltered and nurtured by an all-powerful divinity:

Hear, O kings; give ear,
O princes;
to the Lord I will sing,
I will make melody to the
Lord, the God of
Israel.

(Judges 5:3)

ARROWHEAD OF ADA

Hebrew developed out of a common Indo-Semitic language that was, by varying degrees, also spoken in Phoenician, Moabite, and Edomite dialects. The settlement of the Israelites in Canaan helped to accelerate the development of an indigenous Hebrew as a distinct branch. Canaan itself had been slow to adopt its own written language (though Babylonian cuneiform tablets and Egyptian hieroglyphics have been found in abundance there). The Israelites adopted the linear alphabet developed by the Phoenicians, whose alphabet was widely used along trade routes throughout the Mediterranean Basin, including Greece.

That such an alphabet existed as early as the 11th century B.C.E. is clear from a remarkable bronze arrowhead, inscribed with a dedication: "arrowhead of Ada son of Ba'la." "Arrowhead" is written as *hs*—which is quite similar to the Hebrew word for "arrowhead." The Hebrew word, spelled as *hes*, appears in both the books of Isaiah and Jeremiah.

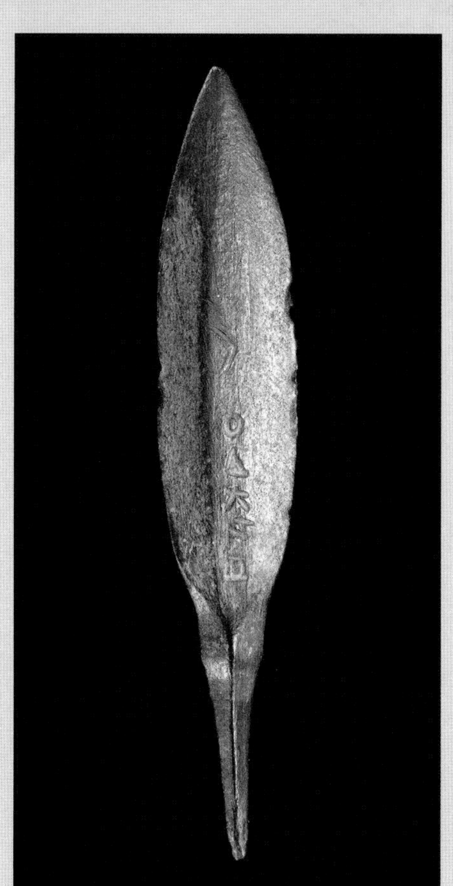

A projectile head inscribed with the words *arrowhead of Ada* written in the Phoenician alphabet and dating from the 11 century B.C.E.

Several other arrowheads with similar inscriptions have also been recovered. In the mid-1950s, Frank Cross and Abbé J. T. Milik published their discovery of three other bronze heads from javelins or arrows. These additional findings bore almost identical inscriptions, written in the Phoenician alphabetic script. The projectile heads had been uncovered in a cache near Al Khidr, three miles west of Bethlehem. Each of the inscriptions reads as *hs* (arrowhead) followed by a name. One of the names is 'bdlb't (pronounced as 'abdulabi't), which means "servant of the lioness." Another arrowhead, discovered by Abbé Milik in Lebanon, bears the name Zakkur bin Bin'ana.

The names on these arrowheads appear to correlate with the names on a Ugaritic list of bowmen. This discovery has prompted some scholars to suggest that the arrowheads might be an indication of the presence of a dedicated "archer class" that operated in Canaan during the 11th century B.C.E.

THE SEA PEOPLES

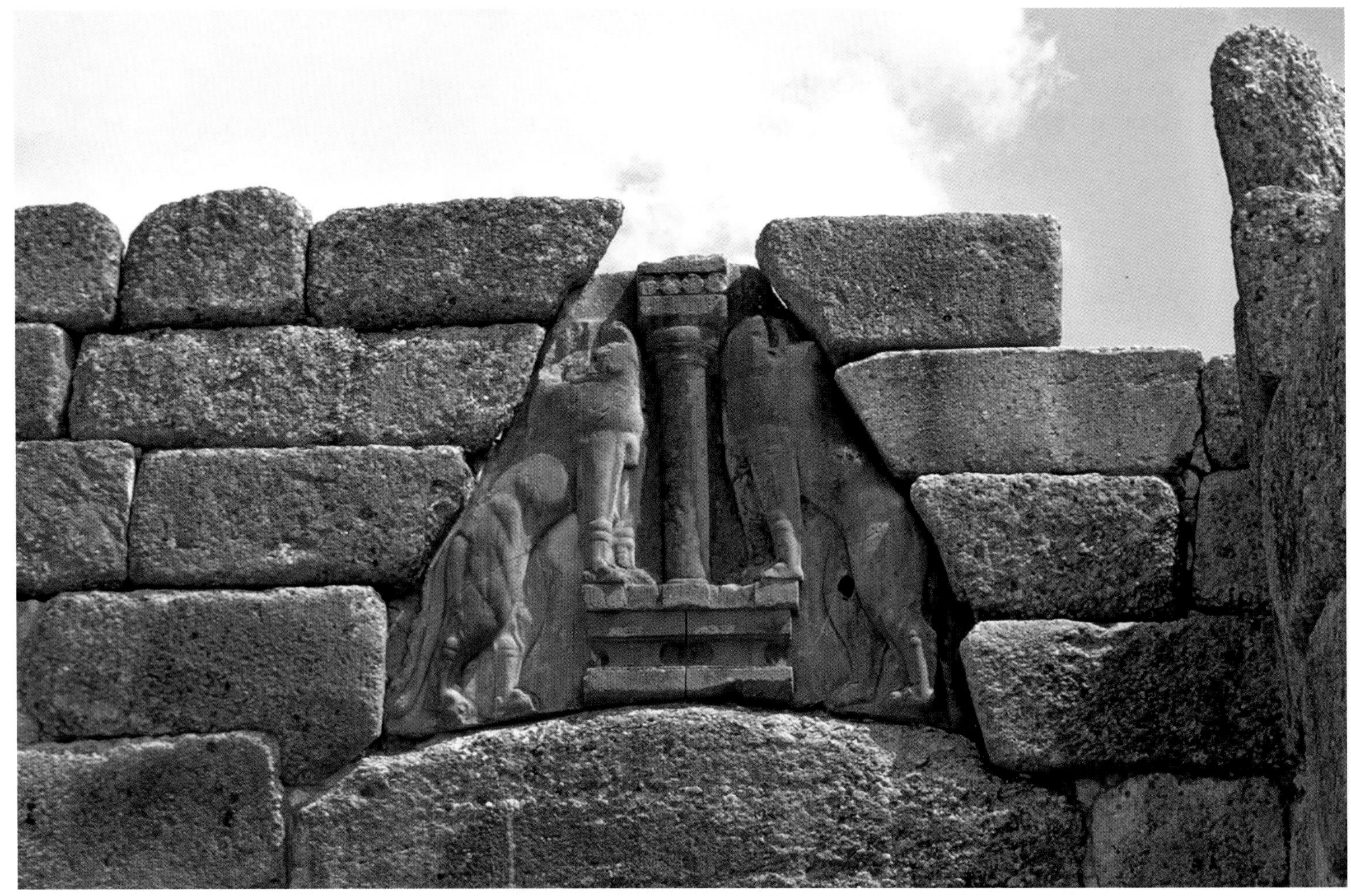

Discovered in 1841, the Lion Gate of ancient Mycenae dates to around 1250 B.C.E. It belonged to the fortress walls and featured two lions guarding the city entrance.

SOME 800 MILES WEST OF Canaan, across the Mediterranean Sea, lies a landmass called the Peloponnesus, a large peninsula attached to the mainland of Greece. By 1600 B.C.E., just as the Hyksos were consolidating their rule in the Nile Delta, the city of Mycenae was emerging there as the dominant power in Greece. Even today, after excavations conducted in 1876 by Heinrich Schliemann, the site of ancient Mycenae is impressive to behold. Its capital enclave was surrounded by a wall of huge stones in the center of which stood the Lion Gate, a massive portal covered by a 12-ton lintel and topped by sculptures of twin lions guarding a Minoan-style column, symbol of the sacred earth of Greece.

One of Mycenae's rulers was the legendary King Agamemnon of Homer's *Iliad*, which recounts a long war between Mycenae and Troy—inspired by the very real economic competition between the two cities. After a cataclysmic volcanic eruption on the Aegean island of Thera around 1500 B.C.E., which destroyed many Minoan cities, Mycenae emerged as the preeminent culture in the Mediterranean Basin. By the 14th century, pieces of Mycenaean earthenware pottery could be found throughout Egypt and Mesopotamia. These vessels

ca 1150 B.C.E.
Philistines consolidate their presence in Canaan

ca 1100 B.C.E.
Hittites and Arameans found city-states in Syria, northern Mesopotamia, and Anatolia

ca 1075 B.C.E.
Egyptian New Kingdom ends; the Third Intermediate period begins

ca 1025 B.C.E.
Saul becomes king of Israel

The Israelites again did what was evil in the sight of the Lord, and the Lord gave them into the hand of the Philistines for forty years. (Judges 13:1)

probably contained commodities from the prosperous international trade of the time, either tin (necessary to turn copper into bronze), wheat, wool, or wine. The growing importance of Mycenae was due in no small measure to the growing tension between Egypt and the Hittite Empire, which the Greek city was able to exploit as a "neutral party," able to do business with both.

But by the 12th century B.C.E., the proud walls of Mycenae lay in ruins. The maritime trade that propelled the Greek city-states to untold wealth had all but disappeared. A shadow of death was stealing across the Mediterranean Basin, destroying everything in its path. Eventually, this wave reached Anatolia, obliterating the Hittite Empire (which not even Ramses II had been able to bring to heel) before turning its sights on Syria and Canaan. One of the Ugaritic tablets records a frantic plea from Ammurapi, the king of Ugarit, to the king of Cyprus. "Enemy boats have arrived," the king exclaims, "the enemy has set fire to the cities and wrought havoc."

The main culprits of this upheaval were groups of marauding tribes that scholars group together as the Sea Peoples. Ugaritic texts refer to them as the Shiqalaya, meaning "they who live on boats." They were not an organized army, but a motley band of predatory raiders whose origins have never been firmly ascertained. Contemporary records speak of different tribes such as the Teresh or Tyrsenoi, who may have originated in Anatolia; the Sherden, sometimes identified with Sardinia; and the Shekelesh, who may have been of Sicilian origin. The group also included a tribe called the Peleset, more commonly known as the Philistines, possibly with roots in Crete.

The motive for the Sea Peoples' destructive swath across the ancient Near East is not clear. There are indications, however, that a vast famine swept the northern part of Asia Minor in the 13th century. So dire was this famine that it prompted an international relief effort, including the dispatch of grain ships from Egypt. Perhaps this famine jolted the great mass of poor and marginalized folk into a desperate search for food that, once bolstered by success, soon degenerated into a naked quest for loot and plunder.

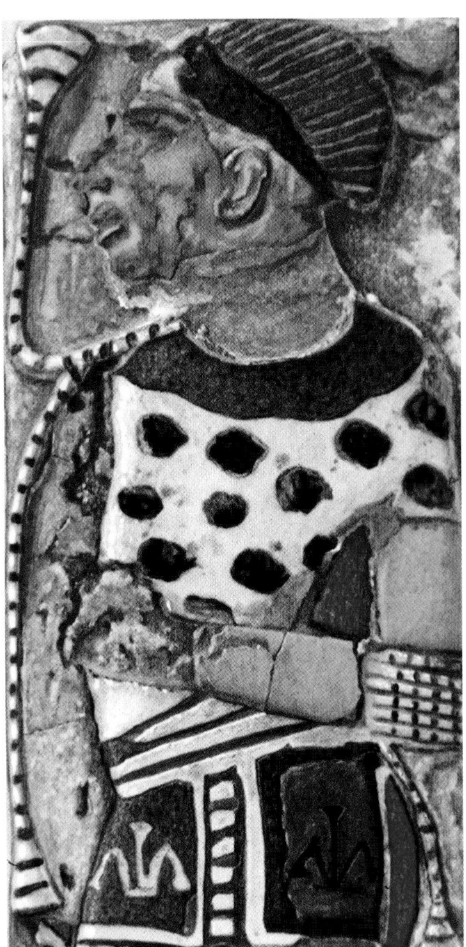

By 1175 B.C.E., the Sea Peoples had conquered most of the coastal regions of modern Syria and Lebanon. They next turned their attention to the last great power in the region: the land of Egypt, with its countless temples and treasures. As it happened, Egypt at the time was ruled by Ramses III, an able king and highly accomplished military commander. A series of reliefs on Ramses's funerary temple in Medinet Habu, west of Thebes, give us a detailed account of what happened next. "They came with fire prepared before them, forward to Egypt," the hieroglyphics reveal. Ramses III, however, was ready: "The chiefs, the captains of infantry, the nobles, I caused to equip the harbor-mouths, like a strong wall, with warships, galleys, and barges." Hardly were these defenses in place than the Sea Peoples appeared on the horizon. As was their habit, they divided their forces into a two-pronged assault: The infantry attacked on land, while the naval force staged an amphibious assault along the coast to deliver the final blow. The strategy had

This relief from the mortuary temple of Ramses III (ca 1187–1156 B.C.E.) from Medinet Habu depicts a prisoner wearing a typical Philistine headdress.

ca 1010 B.C.E.
Hebrew alphabet begins to develop

ca 1000 B.C.E.
Second period of Iron Age begins

ca 1000 B.C.E.
Phoenicians establish colonies throughout the Mediterranean

ca 1000 B.C.E.
Greeks migrate across the Aegean Sea and colonize parts of present-day Turkey

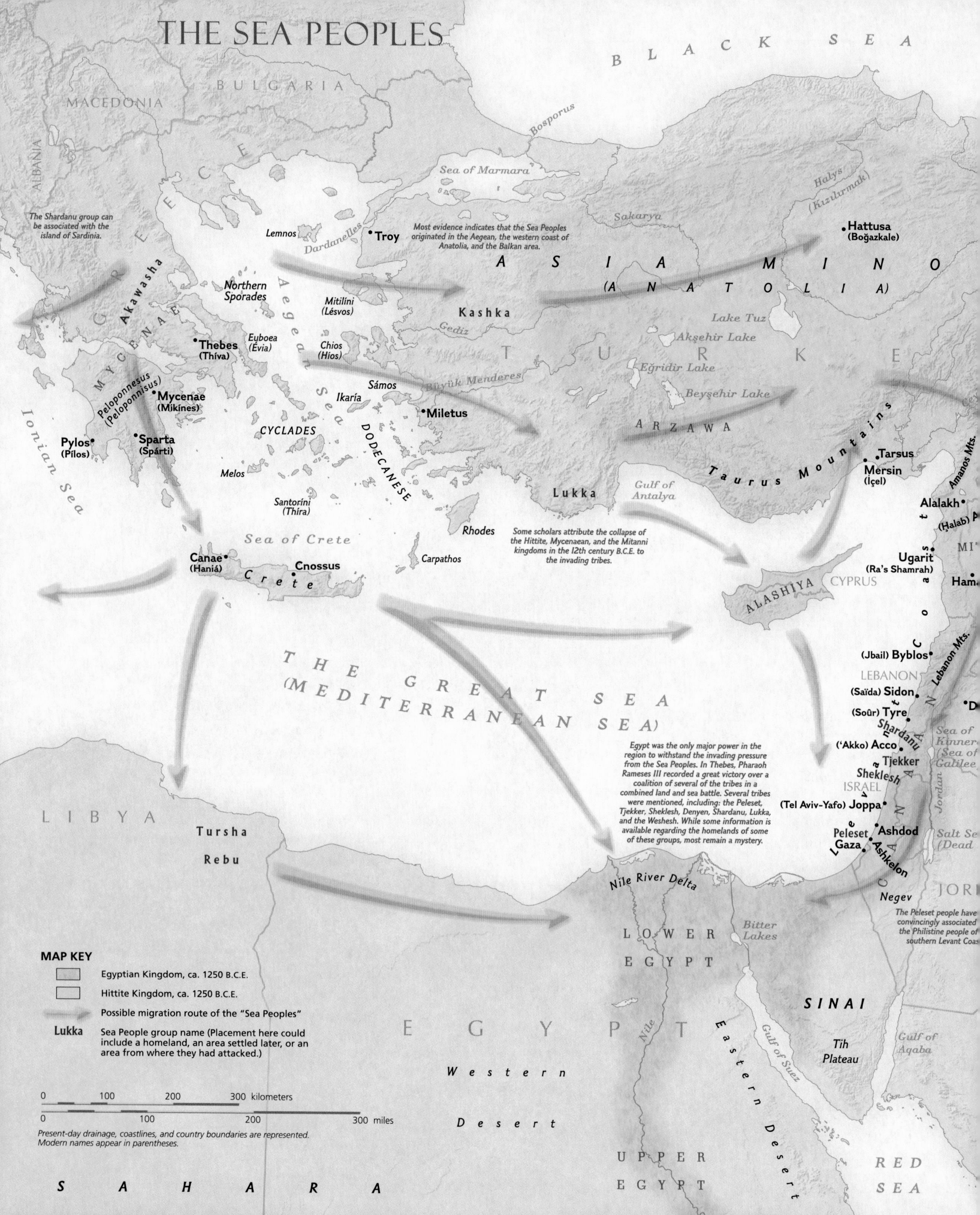

THE SEA PEOPLES
BLACK SEA
BULGARIA
MACEDONIA
ALBANIA
GREECE
Bosporus
Sea of Marmara
Halys (Kızılırmak)
Sakarya
The Shardanu group can be associated with the island of Sardinia.
Lemnos
Dardanelles
Troy
Most evidence indicates that the Sea Peoples originated in the Aegean, the western coast of Anatolia, and the Balkan area.
Hattusa (Boğazkale)
ASIA MINOR (ANATOLIA)
Akawasha
Northern Sporades
Aegean Sea
Mitilíni (Lésvos)
Kashka
Lake Tuz
Gediz
Akşehir Lake
MYCENAE
Thebes (Thíva)
Euboea (Évia)
Chios (Híos)
TURKEY
Eğridir Lake
Büyük Menderes
Peloponnesus (Peloponnisus)
Mycenae (Mikínes)
Sámos
Ikaría
Beyşehir Lake
Miletus
Ionian Sea
Pylos (Pílos)
Sparta (Spárti)
CYCLADES
DODECANESE
ARZAWA
Taurus Mountains
Tarsus
Mersin (Içel)
Amanos Mts.
Melos
Lukka
Gulf of Antalya
Santoríni (Thíra)
Alalakh
(Halab)
Rhodes
Sea of Crete
Some scholars attribute the collapse of the Hittite, Mycenaean, and the Mitanni kingdoms in the 12th century B.C.E. to the invading tribes.
Canae (Haniá)
Cnossus
Crete
Carpathos
Ugarit (Ra's Shamrah)
ALASHIYA
CYPRUS
Coast
THE GREAT SEA (MEDITERRANEAN SEA)
(Jbail) Byblos
LEBANON
Lebanon Mts.
(Saïda) Sidon
(Soûr) Tyre
Shardanu
Sea of Kinneret (Sea of Galilee)
Egypt was the only major power in the region to withstand the invading pressure from the Sea Peoples. In Thebes, Pharaoh Rameses III recorded a great victory over a coalition of several of the tribes in a combined land and sea battle. Several tribes were mentioned, including: the Peleset, Tjekker, Sheklesh, Denyen, Shardanu, Lukka, and the Weshesh. While some information is available regarding the homelands of some of these groups, most remain a mystery.
('Akko) Acco
Tjekker
Sheklesh
ISRAEL
CANAAN
Jordan
LIBYA
(Tel Aviv-Yafo) Joppa
Tursha
Levant
Ashdod
Peleset
Gaza
Ashkelon
Salt Sea (Dead
Rebu
Nile River Delta
Negev
The Peleset people have convincingly associated the Philistine people of southern Levant Coas
Bitter Lakes
LOWER EGYPT
MAP KEY
Egyptian Kingdom, ca. 1250 B.C.E.
Hittite Kingdom, ca. 1250 B.C.E.
Possible migration route of the "Sea Peoples"
Lukka
Sea People group name (Placement here could include a homeland, an area settled later, or an area from where they had attacked.)
SINAI
EGYPT
Nile
Eastern Desert
Gulf of Suez
Gulf of Aqaba
Tih Plateau
Western Desert
0 100 200 300 kilometers
0 100 200 300 miles
Present-day drainage, coastlines, and country boundaries are represented. Modern names appear in parentheses.
UPPER EGYPT
RED SEA
SAHARA

Egyptian ships, with their distinctive lion-head–shaped prows, launch their attack on the Sea Peoples, from a relief at the mortuary temple of Ramses III at Medinet Habu.

confounded cities all along the coasts of Turkey, Syria, and Canaan, but in Ramses the invaders would face a far more capable opponent.

As the illustrations at Medinet Habu testify, Ramses rallied his troops to meet the Peleset infantry on Egypt's eastern border. The Philistines were a robust lot: tall, white-skinned, and ferocious-looking in their curiously horned hats and short skirts. Seeing the Egyptian ranks, they attacked with gusto, and a bloody battle ensued. Ramses quickly moved from one place to the next, rallying his troops whenever his infantry threatened to give way. After the Philistine land army had been defeated, the battle shifted to the Nile Delta, where Egypt's defense was weakest. Egypt had never fought a naval battle in home waters. It feared the unpredictable Mediterranean and preferred to keep its vessels on the tranquil Nile.

Ramses, however, had manned his river galleys "from bow to stern with valiant warriors bearing their arms, soldiers of the choicest of Egypt, being like lions roaring upon the mountaintops." As soon as the Philistine ships came within range, clouds of Egyptian arrows rained down upon them, and the Philistines withdrew. Ramses proudly posted monuments of his spectacular victory throughout his realm; one statue found its way to the residence of the Egyptian governor in Beth Shan.

Repulsed from Egyptian shores, the Philistines pointed their ships back east, probing for a safe place to land. They chose the southern coast of Canaan. Up to this point, the coastal cities here—

SEA TRADE BEFORE THE SEA PEOPLES

Around 1300 B.C.E., a midsize cargo vessel was slowly working its way up along the littoral of Asia Minor when, just off Uluburun on the southern coast of Turkey, it sank, taking its rich, ten-ton cargo to the murky depths of the Mediterranean Sea. This ship was discovered in 1982. After excavation began in 1984, archaeologists were dazzled by the the goods it carried: ingots of tin and copper (used to make bronze); one ton of terebinth resin, possibly used as incense, contained in nearly 150 Canaanite amphorae; tusks of elephant ivory and hippopotamus teeth; priceless logs of ebony, as well as the earliest known intact ingots of glass. These commodities gave archeologists important evidence of a strong international trade in the Late Bronze Age. Two centuries later, maritime trade routes were destroyed by the Sea Peoples, who ravaged the Mediterranean before settling along the coast of Syria and Palestine.

Ashkelon, Ekron, Ashdod, Gath, and Gaza—had rebuffed any Israelite infiltration attempts. The Philistines, however, conquered the cities with ease and quickly consolidated their power. They turned the five cities into a confederacy that became known as Philistia (from which the Greeks later derived the word "Palestine" to denote all of Canaan). Soon, Philistine earthenware coffins with their anthropoid lids began to appear throughout the region.

And so, by the middle of the 12th century B.C.E., a third major group of people began to compete for the scarce water and land resources of Canaan. It was only a matter of time before these headstrong people would come into conflict with the equally headstrong and determined Israelite settlers, and it is this conflict that takes up the latter part of the Book of Judges. Whereas Deborah was concerned with battling the Canaanites around the Valley of Jezreel, and a later judge, Gibeon, rallied against invading Midianites and Amalekites from the Transjordan, a folk hero named Samson would become the hero of the Philistine Wars.

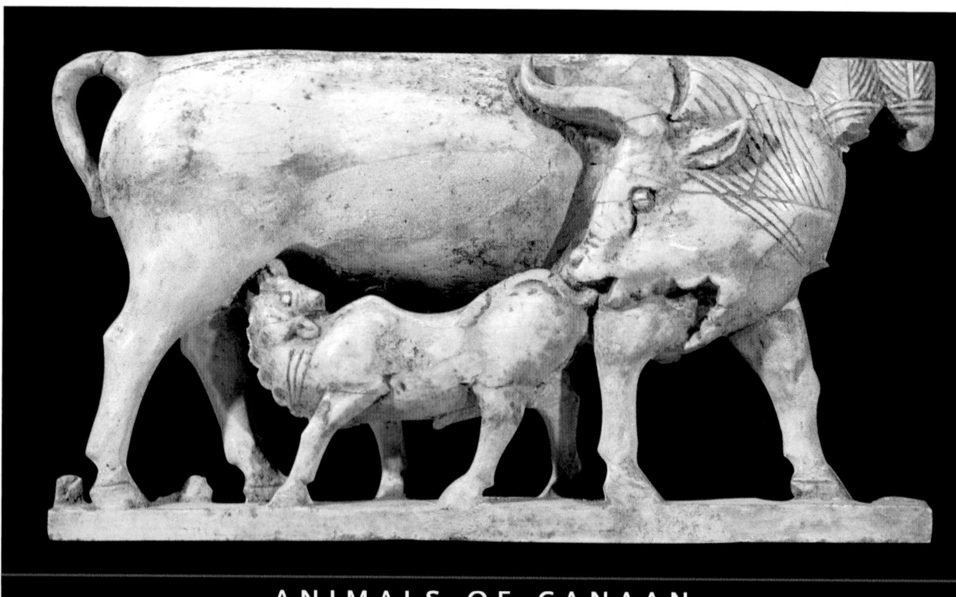

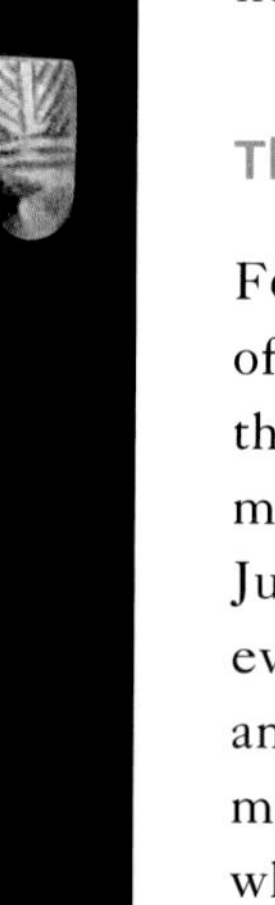

ANIMALS OF CANAAN

FAUNA FLOURISHED IN ANCIENT CANAAN, numbering some 100 mammal and 200 bird species, including boars, deer, gazelles, leopards, eagles, peacocks, and storks. The Bible often refers to animals to illustrate its story, though many have since disappeared from the region. Isaiah says the lame will leap like deer in welcoming the return to Jerusalem (Isaiah 35:6). The description of a dragon in Job is clearly inspired by a crocodile (Job 41). Proverbs calls the lion the "mightiest among wild animals" (Proverbs 30:30). Hosea mentions a leopard (Hosea 13:7), which was thought to be extinct in the Levant until one was seen near 'En Gedi in 1974. In the highlands, wild bears were particularly feared (II Samuel 17:3, II Kings 2:24). The sparrow is mentioned some 40 times, notably in Psalms (84:3) and by Jesus (Matthew 10:29 and Luke 12:6). Vipers are often referred to as poisonous snakes (arguably the *Vipera xanthina*), as in Isaiah's "viper and flying serpent" (Isaiah 30:6) and the New Testament's "brood of vipers" (Matthew 3:7, 12:34, and elsewhere). For nomadic tribes, the most important animal was the sheep. Psalms uses sheep as a metaphor for the congregation of Israel (Psalms 77:20), as does John (21:16). The Torah considers all beasts of prey unclean; only cud-chewing animals with cloven hooves can be slaughtered and eaten. Birds thought to be carnivorous also are held to be unclean.

This delicate ivory from northern Syria depicts a cow suckling her calf and was probably carved between 850 and 650 B.C.E.

The Story of Samson

FOLLOWING THE NOW familiar paradigm of divine premeditation that appears in the Bible as well as in Mesopotamian mythology, the birth of Samson in Judges is anticipated by a wondrous event. Samson's parents, like Abraham and Sarah, are without child, but his mother receives a visit from an angel who brings her the promise of a son. This boy, the angel adds, shall be a Nazarite, a person consecrated to God, who will "deliver Israel from the hand of the Philistines" (Judges 13:5). The word "deliver" suggests that, at the time, the Israelite settlers (in this case, the tribe of Dan) are already under Philistine control.

The tribe of Dan had been given the narrow territory between the Judean highlands around Jerusalem and the coastal region. Already squeezed by Canaanite power, the tribe's position was further exacerbated when the coastal strip was conquered by the Philistines. It was only a matter of time before the Philistines initiated hostile raids into Danite territory, pushing the settlers ever eastward, into the dry Judean foothills. Judges confirms that at the time of Samson's birth, Philistia has "dominion over Israel" (Judges 14:4).

Samson himself is born in the village of Zorah, nestled in the foothills of Shephelah, a strategic barrier between the Philistine plain and the Israelite-held highlands, located some 13 miles west of Jerusalem. It may not have been the most pleasant of locales: Zorah, or Zoh'ruh', means "wasps."

The Philistines were well organized, well trained, and well armed; they had razor-sharp swords made of iron. They were also harnessed by the most potent weapon of all: absolute unity. Unlike the loose affiliation of tribes that typified the Israelite alliance, the Philistines were centrally ruled by a council of lords (or *seranim*) that left little room for internal debate or dissent.

As the Bible presents the story, however, Samson has an asset of his own: great physical strength. As a young man, Samson came across a lion in the vineyards of Timnah and killed it with his bare hands, not unlike the ancient Greek hero, the demigod Herakles or Hercules, who as one of his 12 labors once choked the Nemean Lion in his powerful arms. Yet, like Hercules, Samson has a weakness: a love of women, particularly the exotic, white-skinned Philistine girls. Soon he is betrothed to a young woman from Timnah, originally a Danite town that had fallen to the Philistines. Timnah is tentatively identified with Tel Batash, about four miles northwest of Bet Shemesh. Samson, says the Book of Judges, sponsors a wedding feast, but the guests harass his young bride over a riddle. Incensed, Samson kills a group of Philistines in the city of Ashkelon, after which he flees to his father's house. A longing for his bride, however, drives Samson back to Timnah, only to learn that his wife has been given to his best man. This time, Samson takes revenge by capturing 300 foxes, lighting their tails with fire, and chasing them across the fields and vineyards of Philistine-held territory to destroy the harvest (Judges 15:4-5). The feud escalates further when the aggrieved farmers burn the bride and her father. Samson retaliates by striking them "hip

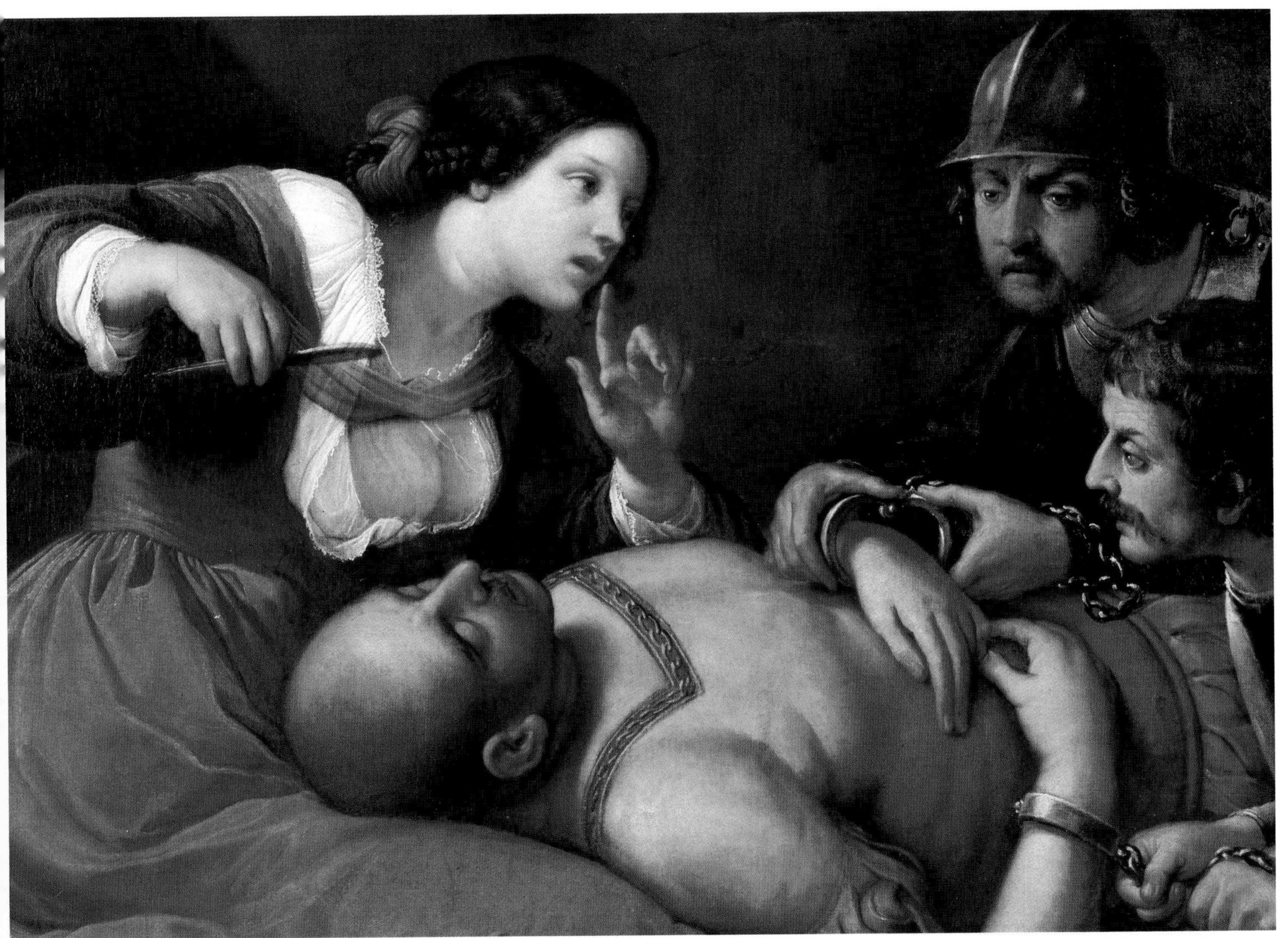

Italian artist Michelangelo Merisi da Caravaggio (1573–1610) depicts Delilah's betrayal and Samson's newly shorn head in *Samson and Delilah*.

and thigh with great slaughter," before vanishing into the hills (Judges 15:8).

Belatedly, the Hebrew settlers rush to intervene. "Do you not know that the Philistines are rulers over us?" they chide Samson (Judges 15:11). Chastened, Samson agrees to surrender himself to their custody. As fate would have it, the Hebrew party then encounters some Philistines. Samson, however, receives "the spirit of the Lord." The Bible says the ropes that bind Samson melt off (Judges 15:14); he then picks up a donkey's jawbone and proceeds to smite the Philistines—one thousand of them.

Soon, the Bible continues, Samson once again finds himself entranced by another Philistine lady—Delilah, from the Valley of Sorek. Sorek, which means "red grape," denotes the plain between the foothills of Jerusalem and the coastal region. When word of the relationship between the Philistine and the Israelite spreads, the Philistines see an opportunity. They start to devise a plot to capture this dangerous Israelite. They offer Delilah a vast treasure of silver shekels if she can conjure a way to disable the source of Samson's great strength.

Using all the charms at her disposal, Delilah sets about to learn his great secret. Samson, who loves riddles and games, plays along with her, feeding her a number of false leads that put all the Philistine designs to naught. After three unsuccessful attempts, Delilah decides to take a different approach. "How can you say 'I love you,'" she pouts. "You have mocked me three times now and have not told me what makes your strength so great" (Judges 16:15). She steadily builds the pressure until Samson relents. "If my head were shaved," the hero finally confides, "then my strength would leave me" (Judges 16:17).

With this confession, Samson seals his fate. While he sleeps, the faithless Delilah calls in an accomplice, who stealthily cuts his hair. The Philistines then fall upon him, gouge out his eyes, and throw him in prison in Gaza, sentenced to end his days as a draft animal turning a mill.

Bringing the story of Samson to a climax, the Book of Judges claims that the Lord has not forgotten the Israelite hero. While in prison, his hair begins to grow back. A short while later, the seranim of Philistia welcome some 3,000 Philistines for a grand celebration in their temple, which is dedicated to the god Dagon. After the party is in full swing and "their hearts were merry," Samson is brought up to entertain them. Standing between the "two middle pillars" of the hall, Samson appeals to the Lord to give him back his strength. Immediately, he feels his old power surge through his veins and muscles. He grips the columns and says "Let me die with the Philistines." Pushing with all his strength, he heaves against the columns. Slowly, the massive stone pillars give way, bringing the roof down on all who are gathered in the temple, killing every last soul (Judges 16:29-30).

The Philistines created coffins that resembled people. This human-shaped one comes from Tel Rehov, dating from the Iron Age II (1000–800 B.C.E.).

In 1971, a team of excavators led by the Israeli archaeologist Amihai Mazar explored and documented the remains of three Philistine temples on Tel Qasila, located on the northern fringe of modern Tel Aviv–Yafo. Each temple was built on the ruins of its predecessor from about 1150 to 1050 B.C.E. Mazar determined that the last temple, measuring 46 by 26 feet, was destroyed by fire around 980 B.C.E., possibly as a result of the last and ultimately successful campaign against the Philistines led by King David. Interestingly enough, its roof was supported by a huge crossbeam, running along an east-west axis, which in turn rested on two large pillars of cedar wood, each planted on a round limestone base.

It is not exactly clear to which deity the temple was dedicated, though the god Dagon cannot be excluded as a possibility. The principal god of the Philistine pantheon, Dagon had originated in Mesopotamia during the third millennium B.C.E. Since *dgn* (dagon or dagan) means "grain" in both Hebrew and Ugaritic, scholars have associated this deity with the harvest of wheat. In Syria, Dagon was considered the father of Baal and second only to the supreme god, El. It is possible that the Philistines first encountered Dagon during their conquest of Syria and then adopted him as their chief god.

The Legacy of Samson

AS IS THE CASE WITH other stories from the Book of Judges, the Samson episode is quite possibly a self-contained saga without any immediate connection to other events of the Israelite settlement. For all its gripping plot and rich detail, however, the story of Samson is unique.

A rather unusual name, Samson or Shimshon means "[man] of the sun." As we have seen, he hailed from the city of Zorah or Tsorah, located in close proximity to Bet Shemesh. Bet Shemesh means "house of Shemesh," which some scholars believe indicates that this township was devoted to the cult of Shamash, the Mesopotamian god of the sun. According to one theory, Samson may have been a mythological figure amalgamated from Mesopotamian and possibly even Greek sources, though others steadfastly believe in the story's roots in biblical history.

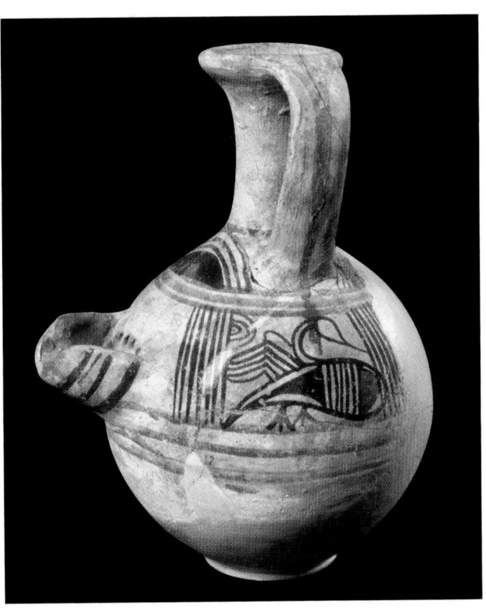

The elegantly stylized birds and ducks of this 12th-century B.C.E. Philistine jug, found near Ashdod, betrays clear Aegean influences.

Samson's great courage and fantastic strength notwithstanding, the folk hero's exploits ultimately contribute little to the Israelite cause. In the Bible, the Philistines continue to grow in strength, further marginalizing the Hebrew settlers. Some may have hoped for an accommodation, similar to the understanding that some tribes have reached with their Canaanite neighbors. But when the Philistines launch a massive invasion of the Judean highlands, the heart of Israelite territory, the tribes realize their very survival is at risk. How can they counter this threat, this massive army of chariots and swift swords of iron?

Reluctantly, the elders of the 12 tribes agree that all of the Israelite militias need to submit to a supreme commander, who will have overall authority for conducting their defense. They settle on the son of Kish, of the tribe of Benjamin, who has distinguished himself by liberating the city of Jabesh-Gilead in a war against the Ammonites. His name is Saul.

EGYPT	MESOPOTAMIA	CANAAN
ca 1180 B.C.E. Ramses III repulses an invasion of the Sea Peoples in Egypt	ca 1207 B.C.E. Assyria defeats Babylon	ca 1230 B.C.E. The Israelites destroy Hazor
ca 1075 B.C.E. New Kingdom of Egypt ends; Third Intermediate period begins	ca 1200 B.C.E. Mesopotamian craftsmen perfect iron tools; start of Iron Age throughout Near East	ca 1200 B.C.E. The four-room pillared house begins to appear throughout Canaan
	ca 1173 B.C.E. Elamites sack Babylon	ca 1175 B.C.E. Philistines conquer Canaan's coastal cities, creating Philistia
	ca 1143 B.C.E. Under Nebuchadnezzar I, Babylon briefly rises to power and defeats the Elamites	ca 1150 B.C.E. The Philistines build the first of several Dagon sanctuaries at Tell Qasile
	ca 1115 B.C.E. Tiglath-Pileser I becomes king of Assyria	

Many scholars date the settlement of the Israelites in Canaan to around 1200 B.C.E. It is after this period that scholars have noted an increase of human habitation accompanied by artifacts that indicate a distinctly Israelite culture in the region.

CHAPTER SIX

Kingdom of David and Solomon

THE TWO BOOKS OF SAMUEL (WHICH APPEAR AS ONE volume in the Hebrew Scriptures) cover the hundred-year period of Israel's monarchy and the reigns of David and Solomon, kings of a unified Israel. Samuel is the last judge as well as the first of the prophets who will minister to Israel's kings. For centuries afterward, this golden age of political unity and economic prosperity will rank as Israel's finest moment. It will gain almost mythical status after the Assyrians destroy the kingdom. Indeed, the guiding theme of the subsequent books of the Deuteronomistic History (notably, I and II Kings) is that the Davidic kingdom can only be restored if the people of Israel abide by the Covenant Law, abstain from the worship of pagan gods, and hearken to the word of prophets sent by God.

Some scholars suggest that the monarchical period had its challenges. Tribal jealousies still fomented tension and even rebellion. And Solomon's ambitious building program came at the expense of forced labor practices and heavy taxes. Nevertheless, David and Solomon are rightfully remembered for great achievements: the unification of the 12 tribes of Israel and the construction of the First Temple dedicated to YHWH—built in the nation's new capital, Jerusalem.

In Jerusalem the Al 'Aqsa Mosque (left) and the Dome of the Rock (right) today sit where Solomon's Temple once was on Temple Mount

Battles of Saul

The bounty of Galilee is evident in this springtime photo of a Galilean olive grove.

During the first two centuries following the settlement, the Israelites, according to the biblical account, are able to strengthen their presence in Canaan. The constant need to defend their homesteads against marauders, both Canaanite and Philistine, breeds a sense of solidarity and shared identity. Surrounded by hostile territory and always engaged in a struggle to cultivate their land, the settlers find solace and comfort in cultic practices centered on the worship of YHWH. This period, some scholars argue, is the time when many of the Deuteronomistic laws were defined. One example is the dietary practices described in the Bible, which balanced food production in the highlands of Canaan with cultic beliefs. Excavations in modern Israel have recovered a great number of pig bones from Iron Age settlements in Philistine-held territory as well as in Transjordan, but there are no such remains in the Israelite-held highlands. This evidence shows that in Israelite farming communities, pigs were neither raised nor eaten and that a distinctly Hebrew culture had taken root.

The Israelites had grown in numbers as well. Archaeological evidence has shown that during the early 12th century B.C.E. there were fewer than 250 new settlements in the entire Israelite territory,

ca 1200 B.C.E.
The city of Ugarit is destroyed, possibly by the Sea Peoples

ca 1200–1025 B.C.E.
Israel is ruled by a series of judges

ca 1187–1156 B.C.E.
Reign of Ramses III in Egypt

ca 1168 B.C.E.
Babylon is sacked by the Elamites

[Samuel] said: "The Lord has anointed you ruler over his people Israel. You shall reign over the people of the Lord and you will save them from the hand of their enemies all around." (I Samuel 10:1)

the equivalent of a population of 45,000 or less. Over the next 200 years, this number would triple to about 150,000 people in more than 500 villages and communities. At the same time, agricultural output rose dramatically, notably in the production of olive oil and wine, which, unlike cereals, flourished on the terraced hills of the high country. A relatively great incidence of animal bones from this era suggests that the farms continued to be multifunctional, with settlers growing crops while also raising sheep, goats, and cattle.

Throughout this period, however, the Israelite territories continued to face threats from surrounding communities. Their orchards, sprawling vineyards, and bursting stock pens became even more irresistible targets.

The Prophet Samuel

It is presumably during this time that, according to the Bible, a man named Samuel is born in a town in the hill country of Ephraim. His mother, Hannah, during a pilgrimage to the shrine at Shiloh, vows to God that if he will grant her a son, she will dedicate him to God's service (I Samuel 1:11). A child is born, and Hannah names him Shmu'el, which means "God heard [me]." After Samuel is weaned, his mother takes him to the shrine at Shiloh to be raised by the priests.

"In those days," says the Bible, "the word of the Lord was rare; visions were not widespread"; yet it is at Shiloh that the Lord speaks once again. He chooses Samuel to be his channel, warning him that he will punish the house of Eli, high priest of the sanctuary of Shiloh, because of the sins of his sons (I Samuel 3:4-11). With this revelation, Samuel became the first of Israel's major prophets.

Samuel is serving the shrine at Shiloh, the biblical account continues, when the Philistines launch an offensive against the Israelites. They start at Aphek, opposite the Hebrew village of Ebenezer, which sits astride the strategic highway that links the coastal plain with the highlands and trade routes beyond. Some scholars place the location of Aphek just east of modern Tel Aviv, near Tell Ras el-Ain on the Yarqon River, not far from the Philistine remains of Tel Qasila. The Philistines kill roughly four thousand men on the battlefield (I Samuel 4:2). As the survivors stumble back into the Israelite camp of Ebenezer, the elders of Israel debate "why the Lord put us to a rout today." They resolve to "bring the ark of the covenant of the Lord here from Shiloh, so that he may come among us and save us from the power of our enemies" (I Samuel 4:3). The priests of Shiloh consent, and before long the gold-plated chest appears in the camp. But not even the Ark can save the embattled garrison, the Bible says. The Israelites succumb during the next Philistine offensive. In the melee, the Philistines capture the Ark and triumphantly carry it to Ashdod, where it is prominently displayed in the Temple of Dagon. When apprised of the Ark's capture, Eli, the high priest in Shiloh, dies on the spot. Meanwhile, the Philistines consolidate their gains by building garrisons in the hill country of the Ephraim and Benjamin tribes, including one at Geba (I Samuel 13:3).

According to the Book of Samuel, the Philistines soon feel the "heavy hand" of the Lord. The statue of Dagon is toppled; Ashdod itself is struck with an outbreak of disease, possibly the plague. The Philistines try to relocate the Ark to another city, but the plague follows the Ark.

This sherd showing a man holding the legs of an animal is from an incense stand dated to the tenth century B.C.E., the putative period of King David.

ca 1114–1076 B.C.E. King Tiglath-pileser I rules Assyria

ca 1050 B.C.E. Philistines destroy the sanctuary of Shiloh

ca 1050 B.C.E. Samuel, the last of the judges, becomes the leader of Israel

ca 1025 B.C.E. Samuel anoints Saul as the new king of Israel

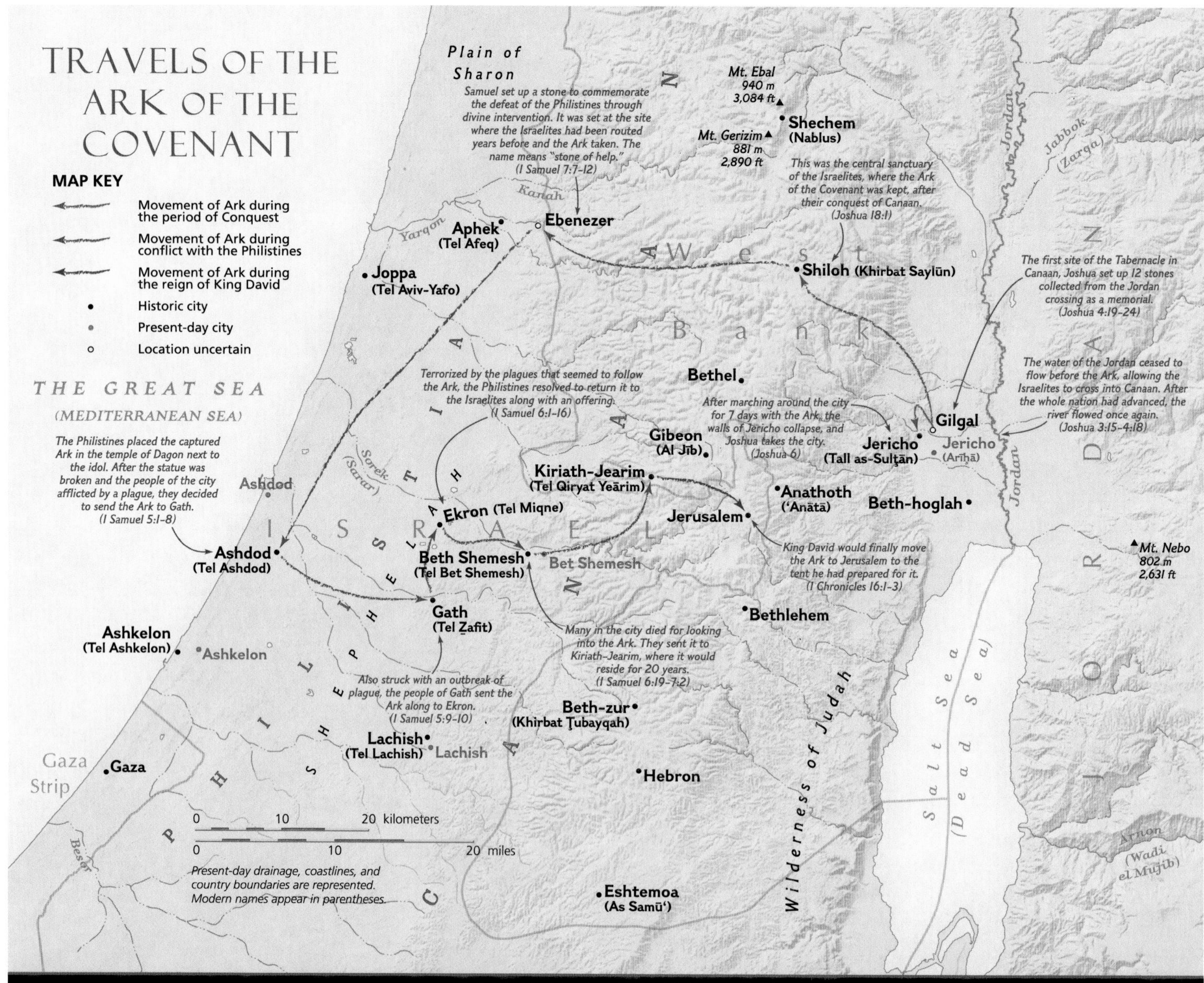

TRAVELS OF THE ARK OF THE COVENANT
MAP KEY
Movement of Ark during the period of Conquest
Movement of Ark during conflict with the Philistines
Movement of Ark during the reign of King David
Historic city
Present-day city
Location uncertain
THE GREAT SEA
(MEDITERRANEAN SEA)
Plain of Sharon
Samuel set up a stone to commemorate the defeat of the Philistines through divine intervention. It was set at the site where the Israelites had been routed years before and the Ark taken. The name means "stone of help." (I Samuel 7:7-12)
Mt. Ebal 940 m 3,084 ft
Mt. Gerizim 881 m 2,890 ft
Shechem (Nablus)
This was the central sanctuary of the Israelites, where the Ark of the Covenant was kept, after their conquest of Canaan. (Joshua 18:1)
Jordan
Jabbok (Zarqa)
Kanah
Yarqon
Aphek (Tel Afeq)
Ebenezer
Joppa (Tel Aviv-Yafo)
WEST BANK
Shiloh (Khirbat Saylūn)
The first site of the Tabernacle in Canaan, Joshua set up 12 stones collected from the Jordan crossing as a memorial. (Joshua 4:19-24)
The water of the Jordan ceased to flow before the Ark, allowing the Israelites to cross into Canaan. After the whole nation had advanced, the river flowed once again. (Joshua 3:15-4:18)
Terrorized by the plagues that seemed to follow the Ark, the Philistines resolved to return it to the Israelites along with an offering. (I Samuel 6:1-16)
Bethel
After marching around the city for 7 days with the Ark, the walls of Jericho collapse, and Joshua takes the city. (Joshua 6)
Gilgal
Jericho (Tall as-Sulṭān)
Jericho (Arīḥā)
Gibeon (Al Jīb)
The Philistines placed the captured Ark in the temple of Dagon next to the idol. After the statue was broken and the people of the city afflicted by a plague, they decided to send the Ark to Gath. (I Samuel 5:1-8)
Ashdod
Sorek (Sarar)
Kiriath-Jearim (Tel Qiryat Yeārim)
Anathoth (ʻAnātā)
Beth-hoglah
Ekron (Tel Miqne)
Jerusalem
King David would finally move the Ark to Jerusalem to the tent he had prepared for it. (I Chronicles 16:1-3)
ISRAEL
Ashdod (Tel Ashdod)
Beth Shemesh (Tel Bet Shemesh)
Bet Shemesh
Mt. Nebo 802 m 2,631 ft
JORDAN
Gath (Tel Ẓafit)
Bethlehem
Ashkelon (Tel Ashkelon)
Ashkelon
Many in the city died for looking into the Ark. They sent it to Kiriath-Jearim, where it would reside for 20 years. (I Samuel 6:19-7:2)
Also struck with an outbreak of plague, the people of Gath sent the Ark along to Ekron. (I Samuel 5:9-10)
Beth-zur (Khirbat Ṭubayqah)
Salt Sea (Dead Sea)
Wilderness of Judah
PHILISTIA
SHEPHELAH
CANAAN
Lachish (Tel Lachish)
Lachish
Gaza Strip
Gaza
Hebron
Besor
Arnon (Wadi el Mujib)
0 10 20 kilometers
0 10 20 miles
Present-day drainage, coastlines, and country boundaries are represented. Modern names appear in parentheses.
Eshtemoa (As Samūʻ)

TRAVELS OF THE ARK

The Ark of the Covenant is the sacred, gold-plated chest of acacia wood that, according to the Bible, contains the stone tablets of the Ten Commandments that God presented to Moses. The Ark is the symbol of the Lord's presence on Earth. Priests carry the Ark on the subsequent journey of the Israelites in the desert, preceding their caravan. To transport the Ark, poles would have to be inserted through two rings on either side of the Ark, since no one is allowed to touch it directly.

During the crossing of the Jordan River into the Promised Land, the "waters flowing from above stood still," and the riverbed runs dry as soon as the feet of the priests carrying the Ark touch the water (Joshua 3:15-16). The Bible describes how Ark is brought into battle, most notably during the fall of Jericho.

When the Philistines defeat the Israelites at Ebenezer, the Ark is brought from the shrine at Shiloh to bolster the troops. The Philistines capture it, unfortunately, and carry it in triumph to the Temple of Dagon in Ashdod. The Bible recounts how, in retaliation, the Lord topples Dagon's statue and spreads disease when the Ark travels to the Philistine cities of Gath and Ekron. The Philistines thereupon return the Ark to the Israelites near Beth Shemesh (I Samuel 6:1-12), and eventually it lodges in the village of Kiriath-jearim, "in the house of Abinadab on the hill" (I Samuel 7:1). There it remains until David carries it to a tabernacle built as its shrine in the newly conquered city of Jerusalem.

At last, the exasperated Philistines place the Ark on a cart pulled by two milk cows, which carry it unguided to the Israelite settlement of Bet Shemesh (I Samuel 6:1-12). The Ark is later moved to the settlement of Kiriath-jearim (I Samuel 7:1).

The Bible interprets the growing threat of Philistine aggression as God's punishment for the worship of other gods by the Israelites. This belief becomes the guiding theme of Deuteronomistic History: The people of Israel will prosper as long as they observe the Covenant Law and worship only YHWH. As soon as they allow themselves to be seduced by other cults, or ignore the warnings of his prophets, the Lord will strike them down, using hostile forces as his proxy.

The Choice of a King

As I Samuel unfolds, the tribes reach a consensus that their political structure needs revision. Their enclaves are dispersed over a large territory, hemmed in by hostile nations on virtually all sides. The situation had worsened over the preceding decades. Enemy salients had pressed into the meandering demarcations between Israelite and foreign-held territory, providing convenient jumping-off points for raids such as the Battle of Ebenezer. Though each tribe fiercely prized its independence—no one wished to be ruled by a king—it became clear that in military matters and foreign policy, the tribes had to act together. To direct their efforts, they needed, if not a king, then at least a chieftain. The word used in I Samuel, *melekh,* can mean both.

How the tribes arrive at this decision is a matter of debate. Even within I Samuel, several different scenarios illustrate the Israelites' apprehension to submitting to a king. One source, often called the pro-monarchic strand, suggests that the creation of the monarchy is the will of YHWH, as communicated by Samuel (I Samuel 9:15-16). The other, referred to as the anti-monarchic source, indicates that the choice of kingship originates with the tribal elders, against Samuel's will (I Samuel 8:4-6).

The profile of a captured Philistine decorates the mortuary temple of Ramses III (ca 1187–1156 B.C.E.) at Medinet Habu.

What brings matters to a head, however, is a resumption of hostilities in the eastern part of Canaan: The kingdom of Ammon launches an unprovoked attack on Jabesh-gilead. The Ammonites lived in a region to the northeast of the Dead Sea, where they were engaged in a constant struggle with the tribes of Gad and Reuben for possession of local water resources. Jabesh-gilead itself lay east of the Jordan, some 20 miles south of the Sea of Galilee; today it is alternatively identified with Tell Maklub or Tell Abu Kharaz. As one of the easternmost cities of Hebrew-held territory, Jabesh was an alluring prize for the Ammonites, who could look down on the Jordan River Valley from the heights of the Transjordan plateau.

The king of the Ammonites was Nahash, who had a habit of gouging out the right eye of those who crossed him (I Samuel 10:27). Nahash, says the Bible, besieges Jabesh, forcing the frightened inhabitants to sue for terms (I Samuel 11:1). These, however, are daunting. Nahash insists that once the city surrenders, every man, woman, and child must lose his or her right eye.

In desperation, the elders of Jabesh send runners to neighboring tribes. One reaches Gibeah, some 40 miles south of Jabesh, on the other side of the Jordan. Here, a young man named Saul, who stands "head and shoulders above anyone else" (I Samuel 9:2), is spurred into action by Jabesh's predicament. He slaughters two oxen and sends their bloody remains throughout Israelite territory. The pieces of flesh are a reminder of the animal sacrifice that had sealed the tribes' mutual defense pact. Saul's message is clear. Before long, all of the Israelite militia mobilize and dispatch their troops to Gibeah (I Samuel 11:7-9). Saul deploys the soldiers around the siege works of the Ammonites. A daring attack at dawn catches the opposing forces by surprise. "They cut down the Ammonites until the heat of day," says the Bible, "and those who survived were scattered" (I Samuel 11:11). The tribes are jubilant. At long last, the people of Israel celebrate a victory.

The nomination of Saul as an ad hoc commander of Israelite troops was not unusual; many biblical judges, such as Deborah and Gideon, had served in that role before. But Samuel goes a step further because the Lord reveals to him,

"I will send a man ... from the land of Benjamin, and you shall anoint him to be ruler over my people Israel." When Samuel meets Saul, the Lord says, "Here is the man of whom I spoke" (I Samuel 9:16-17). So Samuel anoints Saul as melekh to rule "over the people of the Lord and ... save them from the hand of their enemies all around" (I Samuel 10:1).

Other strands in the Book of Samuel, however, resist this headlong rush to kingship. In these strands, Samuel counsels against placing such awesome power in the hands of one man. "[A king] will take the best of your fields," one version warns. "He will take your male and female slaves, and the best of your cattle and donkeys, and put them to his work" (I Samuel 8:14-16).

No one can deny, however, that Saul has demonstrated his mettle as a military leader. Together with his son Jonathan, he now rallies the Israelite tribes for an all-out offensive that, inch by inch, drives the Philistines from the highlands. But the offensive is not a rout. Saul's inability to inflict a decisive defeat creates an impasse. Both Israelites and Philistines dig in and prepare for a long war.

Saul's failure to eliminate completely the Philistine threat is, scholars believe, the real reason, why Saul is depicted as a man of flawed character in the Bible . To the Deuteronomistic redactors, this inability is unforgivable. Any man truly filled with the spirit of the Lord would have made short shrift of the foe. In the Bible, Saul's inconclusive campaigns begin to erode his self-confidence and, ultimately, his mental stability. Increasingly, he retreats to the comforting shadows of a military fortress in his hometown of Gibeah.

This stronghold's location remained a mystery until 1922, when William Albright and a team of archaeologists from the American Schools of Oriental Research uncovered the remnants of a fortified residence near Tall al Ful, a short distance from Jerusalem. Pottery sherds date the building to around 1020 B.C.E. The complex is grouped around a wide-open courtyard and surrounded by a thick wall, anchored by turrets. Perhaps this open area could have been used to muster Saul's royal guard. It is a simple layout, barren but functional, without any concern for luxury or decoration.

But, the Bible says, there is one exception in Saul's otherwise spartan life—he likes music. Up to this point, the Bible has given us little information about the music of Israel. We suspect that during their sojourn in Egypt, the Hebrew tribes may have sung songs of the old country. After Moses closes the waters over the phalanx of Pharaoh's charioteers, he and the Israelites burst into song, which scholars believe is an authentic ancient hymn (Exodus 15:1-18). The Bible also tells us that the walls of Jericho are shaken by the blast of trumpets, and that Deborah rallies her troops with an anthem so powerful that people still sang it years after her death. But this music was in the service of the nation—hymns sung in praise of the glory of YHWH, the Lord of Israel. Music made for private pleasure, as pure entertainment, was a different matter.

The origins of an indigenous Israelite musical tradition are not clear. The Egyptians were fond of music, and no banquet was complete without the attendant chamber ensemble. It is possible that the Israelites adopted Egyptian instruments (the tambourine and the lyre among others) as well as some of their secular thematic material. Other experts believe the Israelites borrowed from the Canaanite musical repertoire, such as it was. What we do know is that a young man in Saul's retinue from the tribe of Judah was known for his talent on the harp. His name was David.

THE MUSIC OF ANCIENT ISRAEL

The oldest musical instruments in antiquity are Egyptian flutes (ca 4000 B.C.E.). Harps, flutes, and lyres were found in the Mesopotamian Royal Palace of Ur (ca 2100 B.C.E.). Jubal, a descendant of Cain, is credited with the invention of music (Genesis 4:21). The shofar (ram's horn) had only a limited range but was used at religious festivals. Later, long-necked trumpets were used in the Temple. In the Bible, the most common instruments are stringed, like the harp and the lyre (like the Egyptian one below), and percussive, such as the tambourine and cymbals (Genesis 31:27).

The King and the Shepherd

ONCE AGAIN, the Book of Samuel uses different strands to relate David's early years. One tradition presents David as a young and promising warrior who is brought to Saul's court to lift Saul's dark moods with his music. The young soldier plays the lyre so skillfully that Saul appoints him as his armor-bearer (I Samuel 16:16-21). Another source says David is a shepherd boy whose singing lifts the spirits of all those toiling in the fields. David's introduction to the story is also when a hamlet named Bethlehem is mentioned for the first time.

David's Bethlehem was close to today's city of Bethlehem, six miles south of Jerusalem and perched on the fault line

Singers, musicians, and dancers enliven a banquet scene in this wall painting from the reign of Thutmose IV (ca 1400–1390 B.C.E.).

between the fertile Bayt Jala region and the Judean desert. Some scholars argue that the earliest reference to Bethlehem (Bit-Lahamu or Beth-Lahamu, meaning "house of Lahamu") is in one of the Amarna Letters written by the ruler of Jerusalem, Abdiheba. Lahamu may have been a Canaanite deity, though others believe the etymology of Bethlehem is rooted in *beth lehem*—house of bread.

One day, the Lord directs Samuel—now a respected prophet bent by age—to fill his "horn with oil" and go to "Jesse the Bethlehemite, for I have provided for myself a king among his sons" (I Samuel 16:1). When Samuel appears before Jesse and his sons, the Lord points Samuel's eyes to David, Jesse's youngest son. The prophet duly anoints the lad with oil, so that "the spirit of the Lord came mightily upon David from that day forward" (I Samuel 16:13).

Meanwhile, the Philistines are again preparing for battle. This time, they choose a battlefield inside the territory of Judah, "between Socoh and Azekah, in Ephes-dammim" (I Samuel 17:1). Socoh, or Sokoh, is identified with an excavation site close to modern Khirbet 'Abbad, some 14 miles west of Bethlehem. The site has yielded several distinctive jar handles stamped with the figure of a four-winged scarab and the Hebrew letters *lmlk—Lamed Mem Lamed Kaf,* which means "belonging to [the] king." This inscription, however, does not refer to Saul or David, but to King Hezekiah (727–697 B.C.E.). The vessels may have been used to collect agricultural products for the exclusive use of the Judean king. Azekah, on the other hand, has been associated with an ancient fortress that Israeli archaeologists excavated near Zekharya, at the entrance to the strategic HaEla Valley. The Philistine choice of the dry plain between these two cities was astute, for it offered the most direct gateway from Philistine territory into the Israelite-controlled highlands.

As the battle begins in the biblical account, the Philistines deploy a new and terrifying weapon—a giant named Goliath. Fully clad in armor, this fearsome man emerges with an immense bronze javelin (I Samuel 17:5-7). No one in the Israelite camp dares to challenge him—except young David.

A passage in I Samuel says that David, armed with only a slingshot, launches a stone at the mighty giant; struck in the forehead, Goliath falls to the ground, lifeless. Shocked, the Philistines turn and flee (I Samuel 17:41-53). David becomes a hero, and Saul has little choice but to place him at the head of the army (I Samuel 18:5). Saul's son Jonathan, the presumed heir, becomes David's close friend.

David proves an excellent military commander. When he returns from battle, says I Samuel, the women approach "singing and dancing ... with tambourines." Unfortunately for Saul, their songs carry a subtle rebuke: "Saul has killed his thousands," they sing, "and David his ten thousands" (I Samuel 18:5-7). Saul feels pangs of jealousy.

Outwardly, Saul showers awards and accolades on his military prodigy, even promising David the hand of one of his daughters, Michal. But inwardly, he has already begun to plot David's downfall.The royal court, sensitive to Saul's mood swings, take notice. Even Jonathan becomes aware that his father is bent on David's death. David must seek refuge in the Philistine homelands along the coast.

The Philistine plains are full of refugees from the war, David finds. Many of them flock to him. "Everyone who was in distress, and everyone who was in debt ... gathered to [David]," the Bible says; "and he became captain over them" (I Samuel 22:2). Time and again, Saul sends men to kill David—and each time he escapes. In retaliation, the king gives David's wife Michal away to another man. David thereupon takes new wives: Abigail, the widow of a rich herder, and Ahinoam, a woman from the Jezreel. Throughout this period, David keeps his eyes on his destiny—cultivating ties with tribal elders, proving himself a loyal Israelite—even as he continues to operate in Philistine-held territory.

Fate comes to his aid. The Philistine armies are moving again and, according to I Samuel, Saul mobilizes his forces to meet them near Mount Gilboa, in the Valley of Jezreel. But Saul's Israelite ranks soon give way. Saul's sons, including his heir Jonathan, succumb to the Philistines. The king himself comes under heavy fire from enemy archers. Badly wounded, Saul pleads with his armor-bearer to finish him off, but the man refuses. Saul then falls upon his own sword. The Israelite army is soundly defeated (I Samuel 31:1-7).

The next day, the Philistines find the bodies of the king and his sons. The soldiers cut off the king's head and later prominently display the corpses on the fortress walls of Beth Shan. This act indicates that the Philistines now control the fortress, which improves their strategic position in the north immeasurably.

When the citizens of Jabesh-gilead (the town that Saul had saved from the Ammonites) learn of the desecration, they organize a party to recover the bodies during the night. The first king of Israel and his sons are cremated and buried, a last kindness performed by the grateful people of Jabesh-gilead.

LEFT: David stands victorious over the head of the slain Goliath in this 1476 work by Renaissance sculptor Andrea del Verrocchio (1436–1488).

OPPOSITE: Mount Gilboa rises 1,660 feet in the Samarian hills. According to the Bible, Saul and his sons perished here doing battle with the Philistines.

THE KINGDOM OF DAVID

Viewed from the Kidron Valley, lush green hills surround the remains of the City of David in Jerusalem.

ISRAEL NOW FACES A DIRE military situation. The Philistine armies have penetrated deep into Israelite territory, yet there is no one to rally the tribes. Israel is leaderless, traumatized by the image of its first king hung upon a fortress wall like a common criminal. Grief-struck, David pours his heart out in one of the most beautiful elegies in biblical literature: "Your glory, O Israel, lies slain upon your high places! How the mighty have fallen!" (II Samuel 1:19-20). Scholars believe that these haunting words, "How the mighty have fallen," are among the oldest literary fragments in the Bible.

The Philistines have every reason to rejoice. Saul's battered army, now under the command of Saul's uncle, Abner, is in full retreat across the Jordan River. The army sets up camp in Mahanaim (meaning "two camps"), which is located in the Transjordan, on the dividing line between the tribe of Gad and eastern Manasseh. The exact site is uncertain, though some have identified it with Tell edh-Dhahab on the Jabbok River. Abner's decision to place his main camp on this remote spot may signal to the Philistines that he has all but given up on the highland territory.

Desperate to retain Israelite unity and anxious to safeguard Saul's dynasty, Abner turns to Saul's surviving male offspring—40-year-old Ishbaal, Saul's fourth son.

ca 1120–800 B.C.E.
"Dark Age" of Greek civilization is marked by little development in literature and culture

ca 1070–712 B.C.E.
Egypt's power wanes, the New Kingdom ends, and the Third Intermediate period begins

ca 1050 B.C.E.
City of Damascus is founded in Syria

ca 1000–970 B.C.E.
King David conquers the Jebusites and establishes Jerusalem as his capital city

So all the elders of Israel came to the king at Hebron; and King David made a covenant with them at Hebron before the Lord, and they anointed David king over Israel. (II Samuel 5:3)

Ishbaal means "man of Baal," but at this stage in Israel's history the word "Baal" (lord or master) did not have a pejorative association with the god Baal. Later, however, some biblical scribes changed the name from "Ishbaal" to "Ishbosheth," meaning "man of shame." The background for this change is not clear, though a verse in Jeremiah suggests that at the time, the word *la-bosheth* (shameful) was associated with Baal (II Samuel 2:8-9). All the tribes, except Judah in the south, support Abner's choice of Ishbaal as leader.

David, anticipating such a move, retreats to his power base of Hebron, the center of Judah, where he is warmly welcomed by tribal elders. Soon thereafter David is anointed "king over the house of Judah" (II Samuel 2:4). Now there are two Hebrew kings: one ruling from Hebron, and one from Mahanaim; after less than a decade or two, the dominion of Saul has split along a tribal fault line. The inevitable result is a civil war between the House of David and the House of Saul, which further drains tribal resources and strengthens the position of the Philistines.

The civil war ends, the Bible says, only when King Ishbaal discovers that Abner has availed himself of one of Saul's concubines, a woman named Rizpah. If Abner marries her, he will assume guardianship of the children that Rizpah has borne to Saul, who are legitimate heirs of Saul's house. Ishbaal chastises Abner, whereupon the general transfers his allegiance to David, promising his support to "bring all Israel over to you" (II Samuel 3:12). David accepts with one proviso: He wants his wife Michal, Saul's daughter, restored to him. No doubt, this condition is prompted by more than romantic motives. Once restored, David and Michal's marriage legitimizes David's rule in the eyes of the northern tribes. Their reunion, and the merger of the Houses of David and Saul, will symbolize a nation restored.

At long last, "all the tribes of Israel" come to Hebron. Here, they pledge their fealty to David, saying, "We are your bone and flesh" (II Samuel 5:1). Scholars say that around 1010 B.C.E., King David's reign over a unified Israel begins.

The Conquest of Jerusalem

SOME MAY HAVE expected David to marshal the tribal militia and ride out to face the Philistines forthwith. David, however, marches to the city of the Jebusites, with an entirely different purpose in mind (II Samuel 5:6). The king's most pressing objective is to solidify the fragile tribal federation into a nation. Israel's greatest handicap is the lack of a political and administrative center. For the new nation to survive and defeat the Philistines, it must be able to recruit and train a national army, levy national taxes, organize the nation's economy, feed the hungry, and rally the people behind a national ideal that supersedes local and regional concerns. The tribes, however, do agree on one thing—the cult of YHWH. Just as the Moabites worshipped Chemosh and the Edomites venerated their chief god, Qaus, so too did the Israelites find common ground in their worship of the

Clay figurines of Asherah, a Canaanite goddess also referenced in the Bible. Found in the City of David, they date to the ninth and eighth centuries B.C.E.

ca 1000 B.C.E.
Phoenicians dominate Mediterranean trade

ca 1000–930 B.C.E.
Unified kingdom of Israel and Judah dominates Palestine

ca 1010–970 B.C.E.
Hebrew alphabet emerges, based on an earlier Semitic script

ca 978–960 B.C.E.
Reign of Pharaoh Siamun

god of Abraham, Isaac, and Jacob. It is arguably the only factor that sustained them as a distinct people throughout their 200 years in Canaan. Israel needed a seat for its government and a sanctuary to centralize the nation's cult. It needed a capital.

During the period of the judges, the priesthood maintained a shrine for YHWH in Shiloh, just north of Bethel, in the high country; the Ark had once been kept here. But Shiloh was destroyed by the Philistines, probably in about 1050 B.C.E.—an event that was corroborated by excavations at the site near modern Seilun. What's more, Shiloh had been firmly in the northern sphere of influence. For the capital to be acceptable to all tribes, it had to lie in neutral territory—a region as yet unconquered by either Israelites or Philistines. David's choice fell upon the stronghold of the Jebusites, a city known as Jerusalem.

The Book of Joshua claims that Joshua captures the king of Jerusalem during the "conquest" (Joshua 10:1-15), but that he ignores the city proper. Some scholars dispute this account; Jerusalem sat at the highly strategic crossroads of the east-west road between Jericho and the coast, and the north-south routes connecting Beth Shan and the northern valleys with the south and the Negev beyond. The city itself, perched on a high ridge, was all but impregnable. It offered a commanding view of three surrounding valleys—Hinnom, Kidron, and Central—thus providing clear fields of fire against all attackers. This position, no doubt, was why the town was still in Jebusite hands after more than a century of warfare.

In David's eyes, however, the city is an irresistible prize. Jerusalem straddled the traditional boundary between Judah and the northern tribes. It had its own source of fresh water in the form of the Gihon Spring in the Kidron Valley, which allowed it to withstand protracted sieges. What's more, it was neutral ground.

And so, David mobilizes his troops and marches on Jerusalem. When he appears before the city walls, the inhabitants address him with derision. "You will not come in here," the Jebusites declare, "even the blind and the lame will turn you back" (II Samuel 5:6). David, however, has a plan. The biblical narrative suggests that he sends his soldiers up "the water shaft," arguably a tunnel that connects the Gihon Spring with the citadel (II Samuel 5:8). The idea of such a tunnel seems plausible; it would have allowed the Jebusites to reach water during a siege without being pelted by enemy fire.

During excavations between 1864 and 1867, British archaeologist Charles Warren discovered a passageway under the ancient city that led to a 43-foot shaft. From here, the citizens of Jerusalem might have lowered their buckets into a basin fed by the Gihon Spring. This shaft, now called Warren's Shaft, survives; visitors can walk in the spring's water before it releases into the Jehoshaphat Valley, on the eastern slope of the citadel. But is Warren's Shaft the passageway by which David's commando forces penetrated

the city? New excavations in the 1990s showed that this tunnel was created after 800 B.C.E., after David's reign, during the era of the divided monarchy. Regardless of which tunnel the soldiers may have used, however, David's capture of Jerusalem is a rather bloodless affair; there are no references to protracted battles or massacres in II Samuel. The Jebusite population is left in peace, to live alongside the court of David. In fact, several illustrious Jebusites will appear later in the biblical narrative.

Word of Jerusalem's conquest spreads quickly. The Philistines are justifiably alarmed, for David's capture of the stronghold threatens Philistia from the east. Determined to evict David before he can consolidate, the Philistines march from the coastal plain to the Refa'im Valley, close to the foothills leading to Jerusalem. According to the Book of Samuel, David lays ready. His armies defeat the Philistines twice in succession, and the hated enemy retreats to the coast.

JERUSALEM

THE NAME "JERUSALEM" FIRST APPEARS IN Egyptian records dated to the second millennium B.C.E., as well as in the 14th-century diplomatic dispatches known as the Amarna Letters, where the city is referred to as Uru-Salim ("foundation of Salim" or "Shalem," a figure who is sometimes identified as a Canaanite god of twilight). The Book of Genesis calls the city by the name of Salem (Genesis 14:18). The Hebrew name, Yerushalayim (Jerusalem), has been alternatively been translated as "heritage of Salem" *(yerusha shalem)* and "abode of peace" (*yerusha shalom* instead of *shalem*).

Excavations suggest that the area south of Temple Mount was inhabited as early as the third millennium B.C.E., possibly by Canaanites of unknown origin. Egyptian records show that in the Late Bronze Age, the rulers of Jerusalem paid tribute to the Egyptian crown. The Amarna Letters refer to Abdi-Heba, a king of Jerusalem, who fought Shechem for control of the highlands and asked Egypt for military aid. Though the Book of Joshua claims that the Jebusite king of Jerusalem is vanquished by Joshua during the conquest, the strategically located city is not occupied, and its citizens are left undisturbed until David sets his sights on the Jebusite hill.

Jerusalem, a city held sacred by the followers of three religions—Judaism, Christianity, and Islam—has long been referred to as the "City of Gold" (*Yerushalayim Shel Zahav*). In rabbinic sources, the phrase "city of gold" is also used to denote an ancient and quite expensive piece of hair jewelry.

From the Mount of Olives, a sweeping view of Jerusalem shows the eastern wall of the Old City with the Dome of the Rock rising behind it.

This 15th-century Flemish tapestry depicts scenes from the story of David and Bathsheba. Today, it hangs in the Palazzo Davanzati in Florence, Italy.

Once this clash is over, Jerusalem is named the capital of a unified Israel. With great rejoicing, the Ark of the Covenant is brought from Kiriath-jearim and placed in a large tentlike shrine (II Samuel 6). David now focuses on building his capital city, which will henceforth be known as the City of David. He asks Hiram, the king of Tyre (in modern Lebanon), to send him architects and skilled workers. These specialists bring with them the precious cedar wood from Lebanon with which they will build David's palace.

At this moment, II Samuel introduces a prophet named Nathan to the story. His appearance will set the precedent for the long line of Israel's prophets, messengers of YHWH, to serve as advisers to Israel's kings—regardless of whether their counsel is ultimately heeded or not. The Book of II Samuel tells us that "when [David] was settled in his house ... [he] said to the prophet Nathan, 'See now, I am living in a house of cedar, but the ark of God stays in a tent' " (II Samuel 7:1-2). In response, Nathan receives a vision. "The Lord," the prophet tells David, "declares to you that the Lord will make you a house"—holding forth the promise of a Davidic dynasty. But, the Lord says, it will be up to David's "offspring"—his son—to "build a house for my name" (II Samuel 7:11-13). Only David's successor will be able to complete a temple dedicated to YHWH.

The exact location of "David's house," long destroyed, is greatly disputed. Most scholars agree, however, that Jerusalem developed across two ridges or "spurs," oriented along a north-south axis and separated by the so-called Tyropoeon Valley. Jerusalem's earliest settlement probably began at the southern end of the eastern spur, in close proximity to the Gihon Spring, the city's main source of water. Here, scholars believe, stood the Jebusite stronghold, which after its capture became the core of David's new residential and administrative center, known as the City of David.

After the Six Day War of 1967, Israeli archaeologists excavated a series of terraces here that, they believed, may have served as the original foundation for David's residential complex. The king may then have extended the city north, covering the area known as Ophel. The Book of II Samuel also tells us that near the end of his reign, David purchases a piece of land on the northern end of the ridge, in order to build an altar to the Lord. This site is used by the Jebusites as a threshing floor—a place where harvested wheat was thrown high so that the wind could separate the chaff from the grain kernels. These threshing floors often serve as assembly places (I Kings 22:10) and sometimes acquire sacral significance. On this spot, identified by many scholars as the Temple Mount, Solomon's Temple would later be built.

David's army, however, is again heavily engaged. The king is determined to drive the Philistines from isolated pockets throughout the country. Slowly but inexorably, II Samuel says, Joab, the commander of David's forces, pushes the Philistines out of Israelite territory until their presence is contained to the thin coastal strip of Philistia itself. All of the regions in Canaan that had previously eluded capture, including the full breadth of the Valley of Jezreel, the Shephelah, the Galilee region, and the stronghold of Beth Shan, are now in David's hands.

The king is not satisfied by this great victory. For his domain's future security, he wants to remove the threat from all surrounding kingdoms by conquering Aram-Damascus (today's Syria) in the north, the territories of Ammon and Moab (today's

MARRIAGE AS POLITICS

To secure his power, David, the Bible says, takes a bride from each of the 12 tribes of Israel and also marries the daughters of foreign potentates. Using marriage for political gain was common in the Near East. King Zimri-Lim of Mari wed his daughters to the rulers of all bordering kingdoms. In Egypt, pharaohs married the daughters of foreign vassal kings to forge alliances. David begins taking wives before even becoming king, to secure tribal support for his bid for the throne. Solomon, the Bible claims, takes the practice to extremes with a harem of 700 princesses and 300 concubines (I Kings 11:3), though this statement is almost certainly an exaggeration.

Transjordan) in the east, and Edom (roughly today's Negev) in the south.

According to the biblical narrative, while the army is heavily engaged, David's eye falls on the wife of one of his commanders, a beautiful woman named Bathsheba (II Samuel 11). He invites her to his palace and seduces her. In due course, she becomes pregnant. Anxious to avoid a scandal, David orders Joab to place Bathsheba's husband, Uriah, on the battle front line, where he will be most vulnerable. Joab complies, and Uriah is killed. David then marries Bathsheba in time for her to give birth to his son.The Prophet Nathan sternly rebukes David for his evil scheming and predicts that the child born from their affair will not live, and indeed, the infant dies (II Samuel 12:1-19). But Bathsheba bears David a second son. His name is Solomon.

Meanwhile, the biblical account describes how Joab, David's general, completes his mission. Buffer states now surround Israel on all sides. With these vassal territories, the Bible tells us, the new kingdom of Israel is a powerhouse that stretches from the Mediterranean Sea to Jordan, from Damascus to the Negev. The capture of Edom is particularly important, for it gives David access to the Red Sea—thus setting the foundation for Solomon's future maritime routes.

Some scholars question these claims, since no archaeological evidence of Israel's control over such a vast territory during this period has been found. The question, therefore, is to what extent the House of David exercised actual control over Aram-Damascus, Ammon, Moab, and Edom. Did David's forces actively patrol these nations and exact an annual tribute, or were these lands merely under David's political influence? The Bible claims that "David put garrisons among the Arameans of Damascus," but it is unclear whether he maintains his troops in the country proper or merely along the border (II Samuel 8:6).

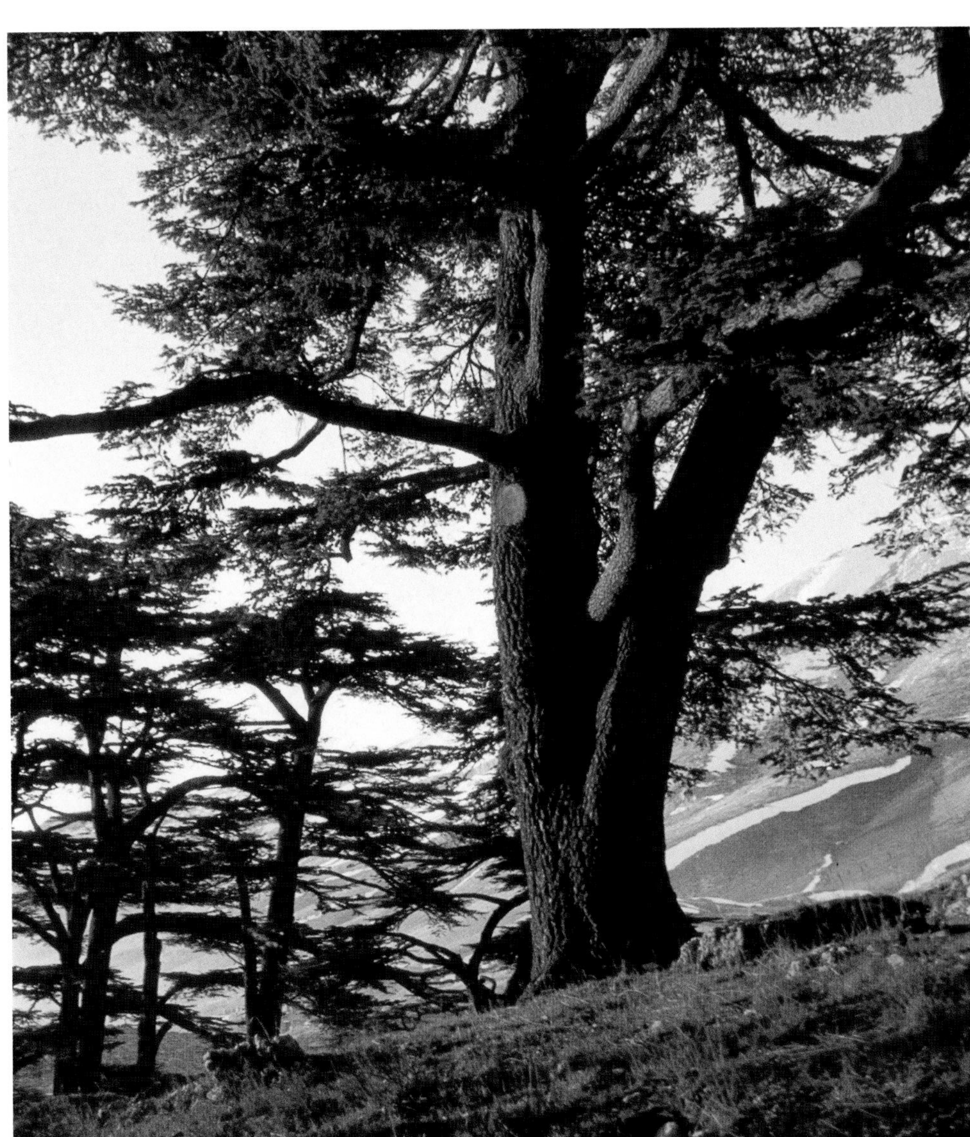

According to the Bible, David's new city in Jerusalem is built with wood from cedar trees in Lebanon, like this majestic tree in today's Bcharre Valley.

The same types of problems attend the description of David's elaborate palace in Jerusalem. During a five-year excavation, the Israeli archaeologist Yigal Shiloh failed to uncover any evidence of significant construction in the City of David during the early tenth century B.C.E.—indeed, no evidence of any habitation during Middle Iron Age II whatsoever. It is possible that these traces were wiped out by successive strata, though archaeologists did find convincing evidence of extensive settlement during the Middle Bronze Age.

One conclusion may be that David's Jerusalem—and David's kingdom—were less far-flung than the Bible suggests, and that the Deuteronomistic editors of the Judges-Samuel-Kings narrative may have overstated some of David's political achievements. This possibility does not, however, diminish the cardinal importance of David's place in Israel's history. In the Bible's telling, he creates a functioning monarchy in a land where no unified polity had existed before. He fuses the quarrelsome tribes into a national identity under the cult of YHWH, and sufficiently demonstrates his military prowess to Israel's enemies to secure peace for the remainder of his

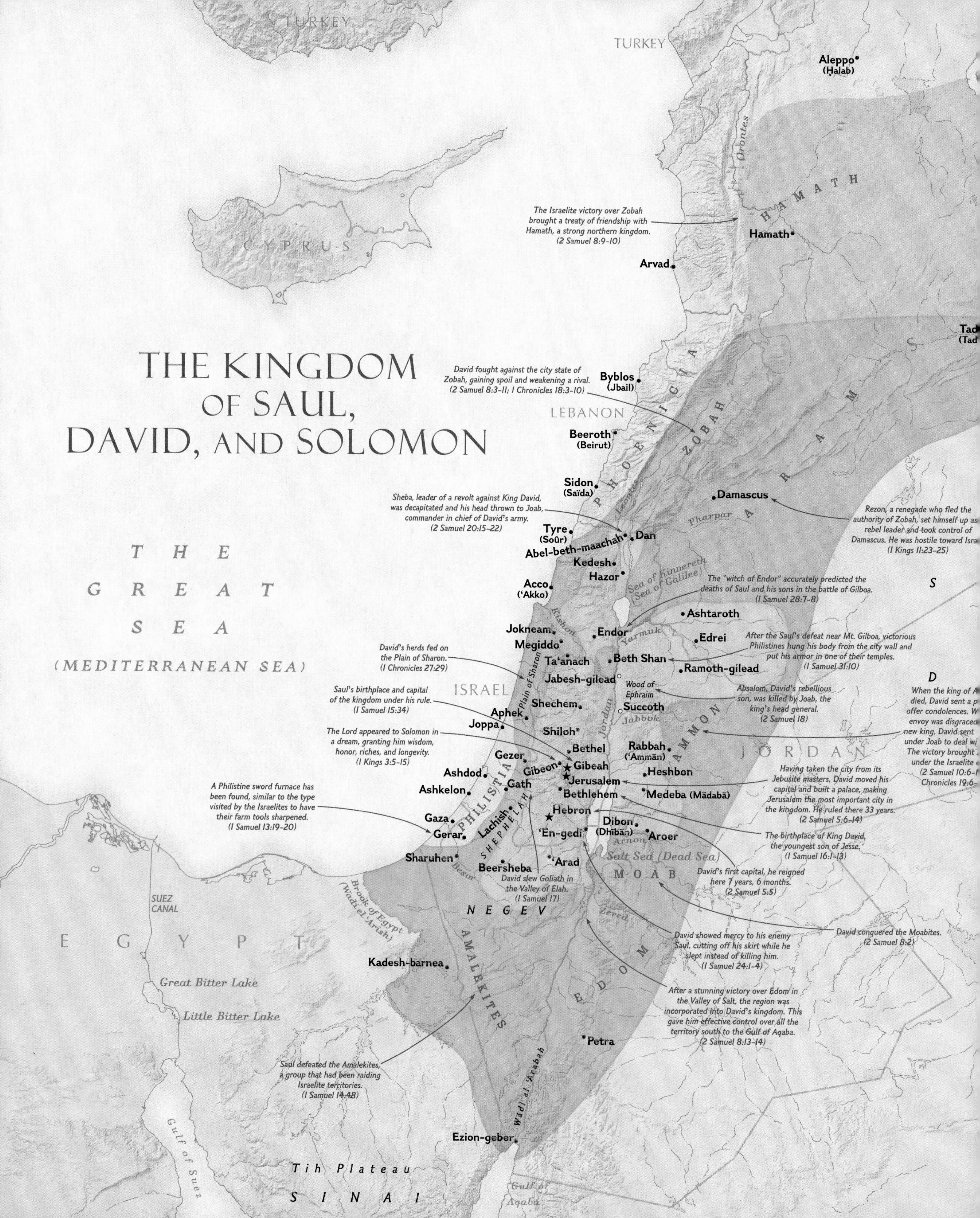

THE KINGDOM OF SAUL, DAVID, AND SOLOMON
TURKEY
CYPRUS
THE GREAT SEA (MEDITERRANEAN SEA)
LEBANON
ISRAEL
JORDAN
EGYPT
SINAI
Tih Plateau
NEGEV
Aleppo (Halab)
Hamath
Arvad
Byblos (Jbail)
Beeroth (Beirut)
Sidon (Saïda)
Tyre (Soûr)
Damascus
Abel-beth-maachah
Dan
Kedesh
Hazor
Acco ('Akko)
Ashtaroth
Jokneam
Endor
Edrei
Megiddo
Ta'anach
Beth Shan
Ramoth-gilead
Jabesh-gilead
Shechem
Succoth
Aphek
Joppa
Shiloh
Bethel
Rabbah ('Ammān)
Gezer
Gibeah
Gibeon
Jerusalem
Heshbon
Ashdod
Gath
Ashkelon
Bethlehem
Medeba (Mādabā)
Hebron
Gaza
Gerar
Lachish
Dibon (Dhībān)
Aroer
'En-gedi
Sharuhen
Beersheba
'Arad
Kadesh-barnea
Petra
Ezion-geber
HAMATH
PHOENICIA
ZOBAH
ARAM
AMMON
MOAB
EDOM
PHILISTIA
SHEPHELAH
AMALEKITES
Orontes
Pharpar
Yarmuk
Kishon
Jordan
Jabbok
Arnon
Zered
Besor
Sea of Kinnereth (Sea of Galilee)
Salt Sea (Dead Sea)
Plain of Sharon
Wood of Ephraim
Brook of Egypt (Wadi el 'Arish)
Wādī al 'Arabah
SUEZ CANAL
Great Bitter Lake
Little Bitter Lake
Gulf of Suez
Gulf of Aqaba
The Israelite victory over Zobah brought a treaty of friendship with Hamath, a strong northern kingdom. (2 Samuel 8:9-10)
David fought against the city state of Zobah, gaining spoil and weakening a rival. (2 Samuel 8:3-11; 1 Chronicles 18:3-10)
Sheba, leader of a revolt against King David, was decapitated and his head thrown to Joab, commander in chief of David's army. (2 Samuel 20:15-22)
Rezon, a renegade who fled the authority of Zobah, set himself up as rebel leader and took control of Damascus. He was hostile toward Isra (1 Kings 11:23-25)
The "witch of Endor" accurately predicted the deaths of Saul and his sons in the battle of Gilboa. (1 Samuel 28:7-8)
After the Saul's defeat near Mt. Gilboa, victorious Philistines hung his body from the city wall and put his armor in one of their temples. (1 Samuel 31:10)
David's herds fed on the Plain of Sharon. (1 Chronicles 27:29)
Saul's birthplace and capital of the kingdom under his rule. (1 Samuel 15:34)
Absalom, David's rebellious son, was killed by Joab, the king's head general. (2 Samuel 18)
The Lord appeared to Solomon in a dream, granting him wisdom, honor, riches, and longevity. (1 Kings 3:5-15)
Having taken the city from its Jebusite masters, David moved his capital and built a palace, making Jerusalem the most important city in the kingdom. He ruled there 33 years. (2 Samuel 5:6-14)
A Philistine sword furnace has been found, similar to the type visited by the Israelites to have their farm tools sharpened. (1 Samuel 13:19-20)
The birthplace of King David, the youngest son of Jesse. (1 Samuel 16:1-13)
David's first capital, he reigned here 7 years, 6 months. (2 Samuel 5:5)
David slew Goliath in the Valley of Elah. (1 Samuel 17)
David conquered the Moabites. (2 Samuel 8:2)
David showed mercy to his enemy Saul, cutting off his skirt while he slept instead of killing him. (1 Samuel 24:1-4)
After a stunning victory over Edom in the Valley of Salt, the region was incorporated into David's kingdom. This gave him effective control over all the territory south to the Gulf of Aqaba. (2 Samuel 8:13-14)
Saul defeated the Amalekites, a group that had been raiding Israelite territories. (1 Samuel 14:48)

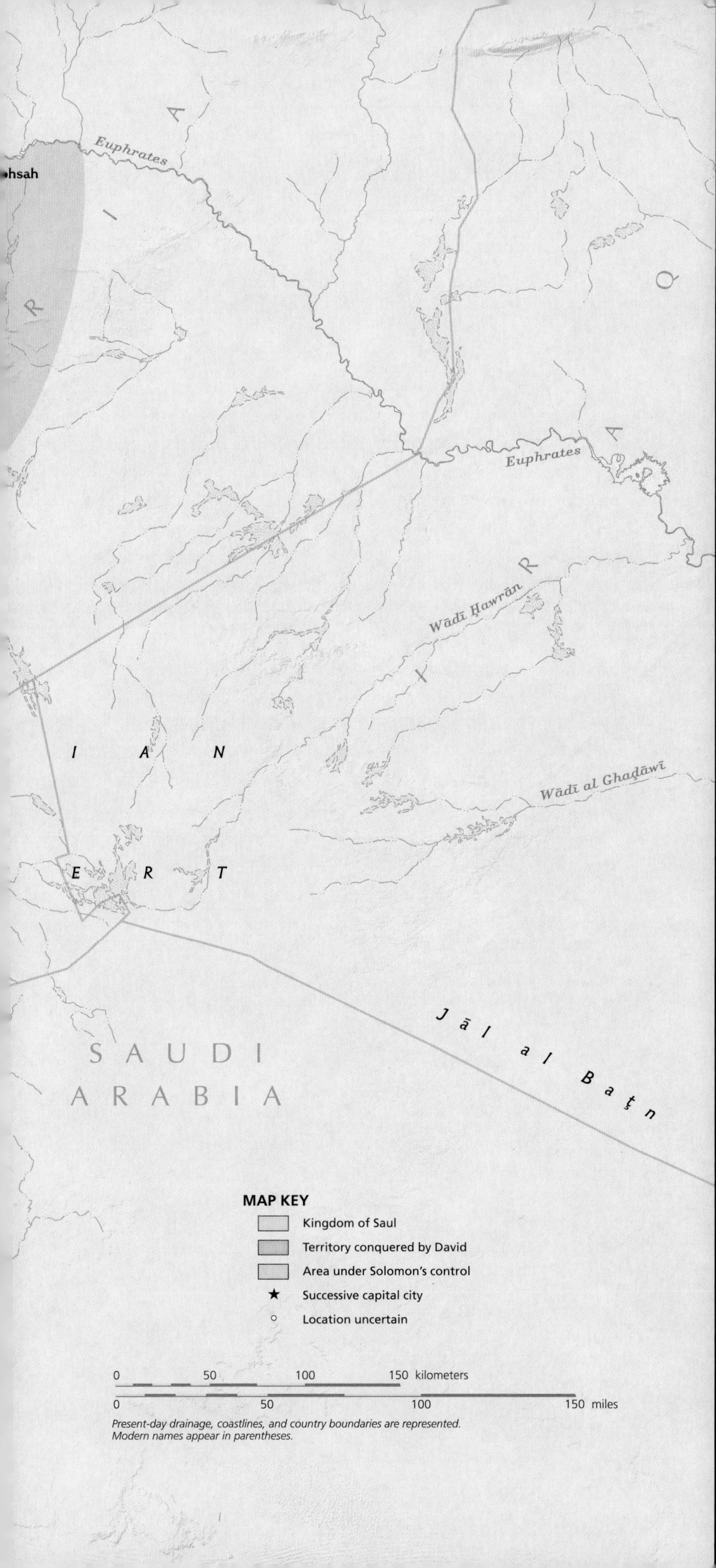

hsah

Euphrates

Euphrates

Wādī Ḥawrān

Wādī al Ghadāwī

I R A Q

S Y R I A

I A N

E R T

Jāl al Baṭn

SAUDI ARABIA

MAP KEY

- Kingdom of Saul
- Territory conquered by David
- Area under Solomon's control
- ★ Successive capital city
- ○ Location uncertain

0 50 100 150 kilometers

0 50 100 150 miles

Present-day drainage, coastlines, and country boundaries are represented. Modern names appear in parentheses.

The strategically important citadel of Aleppo (or Halab in Arabic) was located on the crossing of the two main trade routes between Mesopotamia and Egypt.

The Phoenician city of Tyre (today's Sur in Lebanon), an ally of both David and Solomon, was the principal outlet for trade throughout the Mediterranean.

Megiddo, an important fortress in Northern Israel, guarded the caravan routes between the King's Highway from Damascus and the coastal trade route to Egypt.

These terraced foundations may have belonged to David's palace in the City of David in Jerusalem, which under Solomon became the center of a trading empire.

reign—and that of his successor. He now rules by divine right as "the anointed one," the *moshiach*.

A historical attestation of the rule of David may be provided by a recently discovered and rather controversial basalt stela from Tel Dan, with the tantalizing phrase *"bytdwd"* etched on it. This inscription, many scholars insist, means *BYT DWD*, the House of David. If true, the monument confirms that more than a century after David's rule, the name of his dynasty had become synonymous with the kingdom of Israel.

Family Intrigue

THE TRAGEDY OF DAVID, as the Bible portrays it, is that his great achievements are offset by turmoil in his private life. Eager to buttress the legitimacy of his crown, David takes a wife from nearly every tribe. Like a Babylonian satrap, he surrounds himself with a harem—much to the disgust of the conservative tribal leaders. Jealousies are rampant in David's house. Arguably, the strength of family, the very backbone of the Hebrew patriarchal tradition, is threatened.

The strain in David's polygamous household is evident in the tragic story of his third son, Absalom, borne by his wife Maacah. Absalom's sister Tamar is raped by her half-brother Ammon, David's firstborn son by Ahinoam. Although angry, David refuses to punish Ammon "because he loved him, for he was his firstborn" (II Samuel 13:21). Two years later, Absalom takes revenge by having Ammon killed during a sheep-shearing festival. David tears his clothes in grief and anger, and Absalom must flee into exile. The relationship between father and son is irreparably damaged.

First Absalom secures the support of various tribal leaders (II Samuel 15:10) and then initiates a revolt in Judah's old capital of Hebron with the assistance of David's chief councilor, Ahithophel. The rebellion grows so rapidly that David is forced to leave Jerusalem and flee across the Jordan to Mahanaim. Ahithophel urges Absalom to pursue David and kill him, but Absalom hesitates. By the time Absalom's army finally decides to cross the Jordan, David has gained sufficient strength to strike back and defeat the rebels. Absalom flees, but his hair catches in the branches of a low-hanging oak. David's commander Joab discovers

This work by Florentine artist Francesco di Stefano Pesellino (1422–1457) depicts the killing of David's son Absalom after his hair tangles in the branches of an oak.

him and promptly kills him, even though David gave instructions not to harm the young man. When David hears the news, he cries out in grief: "O my son Absalom, my son, my son Absalom! Would I had died instead of you, O Absalom, my son, my son!" (II Samuel 18:33).

Not all the tribes support the restoration of the House of David. Soon, Sheba, a member of the Benjamite tribe, instigates another revolt with the cry, "We have no portion in David!" "All the people of Israel," says the Bible, "withdrew from David ... but the people of Judah followed their king steadfastly from the Jordan to Jerusalem" (II Samuel 20:1-2). David's able militia, led by Joab, springs to the king's defense and pursues the rebel leader "through all the tribes of Israel" before killing him in northern Galilee. The relative speed with which these two rebellions came about, however, suggests that underneath the veneer of a unified monarchy, tribal enmity between Judah and the northern constituencies continued to fester.

Palace intrigue flourishes as well, the Bible says. As David grows old, different parties align themselves with the ambitions of David's sons. By rights, the crown is destined for David's oldest surviving son, Adonijah. Scholars infer, however, that Adonijah favored a decentralized state, and planned to restore some measure of power to the original tribes. This plan would have inevitably disintegrated David's young kingdom.

This 11th-century Romanesque ivory, originally from the treasury of St. Denis in France, shows David dictating psalms to his scribes.

There is another son of David—the son of his beloved wife Bathsheba. Intelligent, highly educated, Solomon is a staunch supporter of a strong and centralized monarchy. One evening, when an ailing David lay in bed and Adonijah is hosting a party celebrating his upcoming rule, the Prophet Nathan urges Bathsheba to slip into the room of the aging king. She tells him that Adonijah plans to seize the crown—an assertion that Nathan himself corroborates (I Kings 1:11-27). Possibly haunted by visions of another coup, David orders that Solomon be taken to the Gihon Spring and anointed king without delay by Zadok the priest (I Kings 1:34). His command is fulfilled, and "Solomon now [sat] on the royal throne" (I Kings 1:46).

David dies a short while later. Thus passes "the anointed of the God of Jacob" (II Samuel 23:1). According to a Talmudic legend, the old king dies on Shabuoth, the Jewish festival of first fruits and bread, held seven weeks after Passover. On that day, Jewish pilgrims can often be seen entering an old Romanesque complex just outside the Zion Gate of the Old City, where they pray in front of a richly adorned cenotaph called the Tomb of David. The attribution is almost certainly legendary. As the Bible recounts, the king is buried in the "city of David," where his remains have yet to be found (I Kings 2:10). Regardless of where his mortal remains rest, for Jews, "*David melekh Yisrael chai vekayam*—David, the king of Israel, lives forever."

THE PSALMS

THE BOOK OF PSALMS (*TEHILLIM*, PRAISES IN Hebrew) is a collection of hymns and poems. The psalms probably were accumulated over many centuries of Israel's history. The book became a national anthology of songs to be sung during religious rites, festivals, weddings, national feasts, and important events. Organized into five distinct collections (analogous to the Five Books of Moses), the dominant theme of the psalms is the power of God as Savior. There are frequent pleas for divine redemption from enemies, gratitude for peace and prosperity, and expressions of anxiety (laments) over the present or the future. The prayerful character of Psalms is exemplified by what is perhaps the most famous verse of all: "Even though I walk through the darkest valley, I fear no evil; for you are with me" (Psalms 23:4). Musical notations found in ancient manuscripts indicate that many of the psalms were meant to be accompanied by instruments. Of the 150 psalms, 73 claim to be directly linked to David. Though some of these betray the influence of later poetry, there is no reason to reject the notion that David, an accomplished musician and vocalist, would have composed a number of psalms.

Solomon's Realm

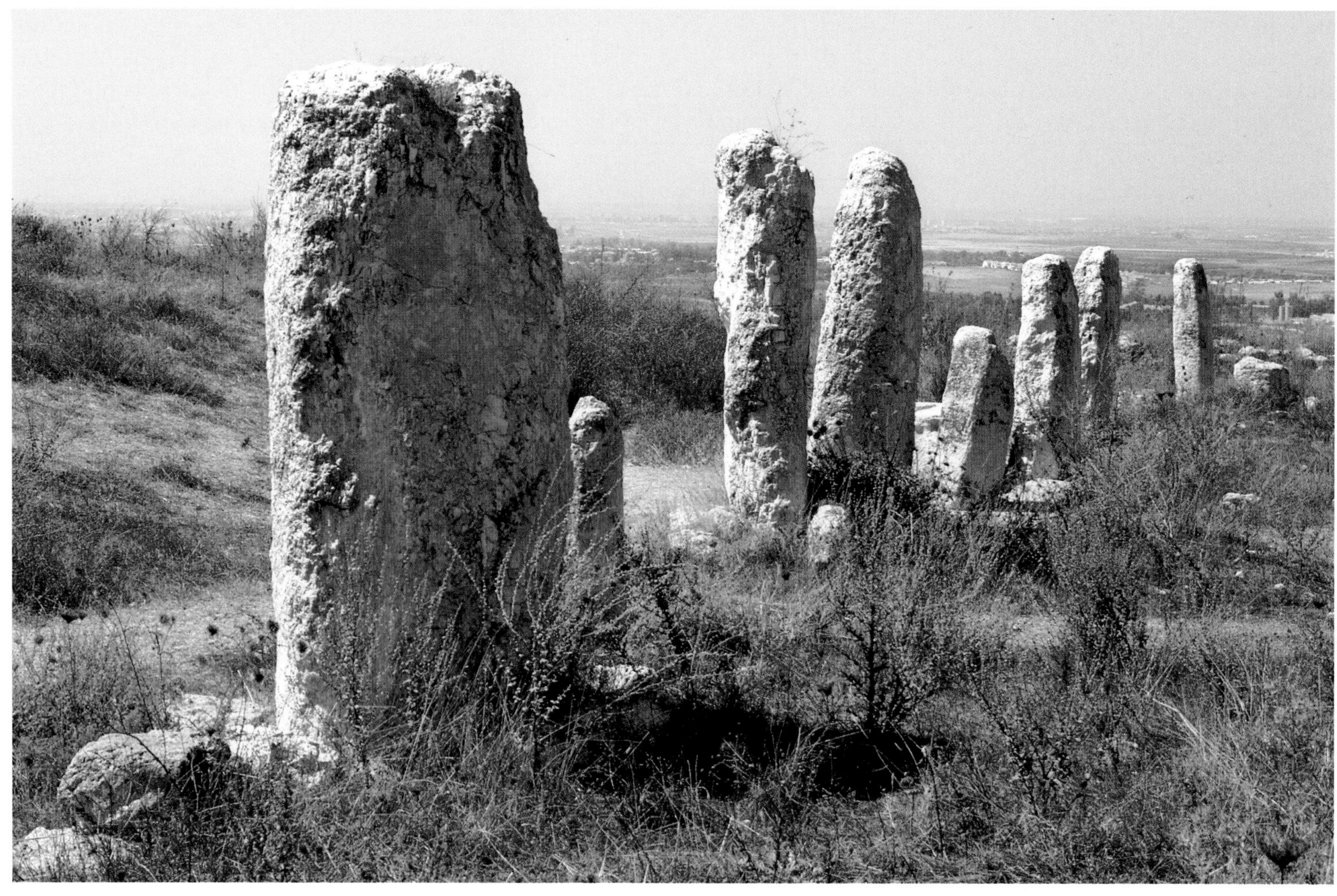

Stelae of the Canaanite sanctuary at Gezer, 1400–1200 B.C.E. According to the Bible, Pharaoh conquers Gezer and presents it and his daughter to Solomon.

Unlike his father, who rises to power from humble beginnings as a shepherd's boy, Solomon is educated, sophisticated, and urbane. Where David is earthy, intemperate, and effusive, Solomon is portrayed as cool and dispassionate—an aloof figure whose elegant exterior hides a sharp brain and a ruthless determination.

Solomon's reign is chronicled in the first Book of Kings, a work that forms part of the Deuteronomistic History of ancient Israel. The division of Kings into two separate books occurred in the Middle Ages; earlier texts treat it as a continuous history that picks up the kingdom narrative where II Samuel ends. The book's sheer detail in describing Solomon's administration has led some scholars to believe that its editors may have used actual palace records from the time of Solomon. Indeed, Kings is one of the first biblical narratives that explicitly bolsters its account with references to other sources, including Acts of Solomon and Book of the Annals of the Kings of Israel, works that are now lost.

According to the Book of I Kings, Solomon moves quickly to consolidate his power. He may have remembered the words of his father, spoken on his deathbed just months after Solomon's

ca 1069 B.C.E.
The Third Intermediate period marks the decline of Egypt's power

ca 1000 B.C.E.
Permanent settlements are present on the hills of Rome

ca 970 B.C.E.
Pharaoh Siamun rebuilds Tanis, capital of the 21st dynasty

ca 960 B.C.E.
Solomon succeeds David as the king of Israel

Solomon was sovereign over all the kingdoms from the Euphrates to the land of the Philistines, even to the border of Egypt; they brought tribute and served Solomon all the days of his life. (I Kings 4:21)

coronation: "Be strong, be courageous, and keep the charge of the Lord your God" (I Kings 2:2). With that in mind, Solomon's immediate goal is to secure the legitimacy of his throne. His most dangerous opponent, naturally, is the official crown prince, David's oldest son Adonijah, who has been robbed of the throne by Nathan and Bathsheba's preemptive maneuver. No one can expect Adonijah to accept this power grab without a struggle. Already, he has secured the backing of two powerful men, David's commander Joab, as well as the high priest, Abiathar. In addition, Adonijah maintains the support of several tribal chieftains anxious to return to the simpler days of tribal federalism.

How to eliminate this looming threat? In the end, Adonijah himself provides a perfect pretext. Shortly after Solomon's coronation, Adonijah asks Bathsheba to petition the young king for permission to marry Abishag, a comely young woman and David's personal nursemaid (and close confidante) in the king's final days. The request immediately raises suspicions. Concubines could wield tremendous power at a Near Eastern court. Any unauthorized attempt to solicit such ladies, even if her original royal suitor were dead, was considered a challenge to the authority of the ruling king. In the biblical narrative, Solomon immediately suspects that Adonijah's request is a thinly veiled attempt at sedition. Why not "ask for him the kingdom as well," he replies sarcastically to his mother (I Kings 2:22). Adonijah is summarily put to death. Other prominent figures of the Adonijah faction, including Abiathar and Joab, are either banished or put to the sword.

Still, the bloody purge affects Solomon deeply. Soon afterward, he goes on a private retreat to a shrine near the Spring of Gibeon. There, he sacrifices and prays for God's guidance. In a dream, YHWH asks what Solomon wishes to have. The young king reflects on this, then replies, "Give your servant ... an understanding mind to govern your people, able to discern between good and evil" (I Kings 3:9). Rather than wealth, power, or a long life, Solomon asks for wisdom.

As we have seen, the paramount attribute of a king in the Near East was wisdom. From King Gilgamesh in Babylon to the Vizier Ptah-Hotep in Egypt, rulers were expected to excel by their superior intellect and judgment. The Code of Hammurabi had set the precedent for a just ruler in Abraham's days, and countless Egyptian kings left detailed instructions for wise governance to their offspring. In striving for wisdom, therefore, Solomon's story followed a long-established tradition.

The Book of I Kings gives us a fascinating example of the king's wisdom. One day, two women appear at the palace. They are, the Bible tells us, prostitutes. Ostensibly, the Mosaic law banned prostitution, but in practice the Israelites (and all of Mesopotamia with them) recognized the inevitable role of prostitutes in society, though these women usually found themselves on the lowest level in society. That Solomon would personally preside over a hearing involving women of such low status speaks volumes about the king's sincere compassion for his subjects.

Each of the prostitutes has recently given birth to a son. One infant died, and now both mothers claim the surviving baby as hers. Solomon listens quietly and says: "Bring me a sword." The women look on as a sword is brought in. And now, says Solomon, "Divide the living boy in two; then give half to the one, and half to the other" (I Kings 3:25). At that moment, one of the mothers cries

Domesticated camels contributed greatly to Solomon's wealth. International trade boomed after their introduction in the 10th century B.C.E.

ca 950 B.C.E. Solomon's Temple is under construction

ca 945 B.C.E. Pharaoh Shoshenq I founds 22nd dynasty of Egypt

ca 931 B.C.E. Solomon's reign ends, and his kingdom splits in two

ca 911–981 B.C.E. The Assyrians, under Adad-nirari II, reemerge as the dominant power in the Near East

THE PROVERBS

In the ancient Near East, wise men were often credited with proverbs, pithy nuggets of wisdom that exemplified a particular philosophy. Jesus espouses his theology of the New Kingdom through a series of sayings known as the Beatitudes. As a king renowned for his wisdom, Solomon, too, is inevitably associated with proverbs. According to I Kings, he writes no less than 3,000 sayings, in addition to composing some thousand songs (I Kings 4:32). These numbers merely serve to exalt the king's sagacity. Solomon is also credited with writing the Book of Proverbs, as the prologue itself suggests: "The proverbs of Solomon son of David, king of Israel." Most scholars accept the view that this attribution is an honorific only and that Proverbs did not reach its current form until after the Babylonian Exile (after 538 B.C.E.). The majority of these sayings were accumulated through the centuries as expressions by prominent sages, officials, and intellectuals in both kingdoms, often under the influence of Mesopotamian and Egyptian texts. In fact, some of the Proverbs bear a remarkable similarity to the Egyptian papyrus Instructions of Amenemopet (ca 8th-6th century B.C.E.).

This miniature of King Solomon reading the Torah is from a 13th-century illuminated manuscript of the Hebrew Bible and Prayer Book.

INSTRUCTIONS OF AMENEMOPET (ca eighth–sixth century B.C.E.)	BOOK OF PROVERBS (ca seventh–sixth century B.C.E.)
Give thy ears, hear what is said, Give thy heart to understand them. (Ch 1:9-10)	*Incline your ear and hear my words, and apply your mind to my teaching* (Proverbs 22:17)
Guard thyself against robbing the oppressed and against overbearing the disabled (Ch 2:4-5)	*Do not rob the poor because they are poor, or crush the afflicted at the gate* (Proverbs 22:22)
Better is bread, when the heart is happy, than riches with sorrow (Ch 6:7-8)	*Better is little with the fear of the Lord than great treasure and trouble with it* (Proverbs 15:16)
At a time when there is a whirlwind of words, They shall be a mooring-stake for thy tongue (Ch 1:15-16)	*For it will be pleasant if you keep them within you, if all of them are ready on your lips* (Proverbs 22:18)

out, "Please, my lord, give her the living boy; certainly do not kill him!" (I Kings 3:26). Solomon nods. He knows that only the true mother would rather give up her own son than to see him killed. "Give [this] woman the living boy," he rules. Before long, all of Israel knows of this amazing judgment, and "they stood in awe of the king" (I Kings 3:27-28)

The Prosperity of Solomon's Reign

Solomon sets out to secure the economic health of the unified kingdom. According to the Bible, he reorganizes the kingdom into 12 districts so as to better control the local governments and improve the collection of taxes. The king makes sure that half of the 12 districts deliberately cut across tribal boundaries. Emulating the Egyptian form of decentralized government, each district has a professional governor, rather than a tribal chieftain, whose performance is judged by the amount of tribute his district yields.

Next, Solomon turns to trade. Over the previous century, Mediterranean trade had gradually recovered from the predations of the Sea Peoples. Even the Philistines now deployed their nautical skills as peaceful sea merchants. Trade was further boosted by the introduction of two revolutionary means of transport in the Middle Iron Age. One was the round, flat-bottomed ship, with either a curved bow or stern, developed by the Phoenicians, masters of the Mediterranean maritime trade. Versatile and light, propelled by sail or oars, these flat-bilged ships could double as cargo ships, coastal vessels, or river barges, thus greatly facilitating the transfer of goods from the Mediterranean to inland waterways. Since their bow ornamentation often featured a horse's head, the ships later became known as *hippoi* ("horses" in Greek).

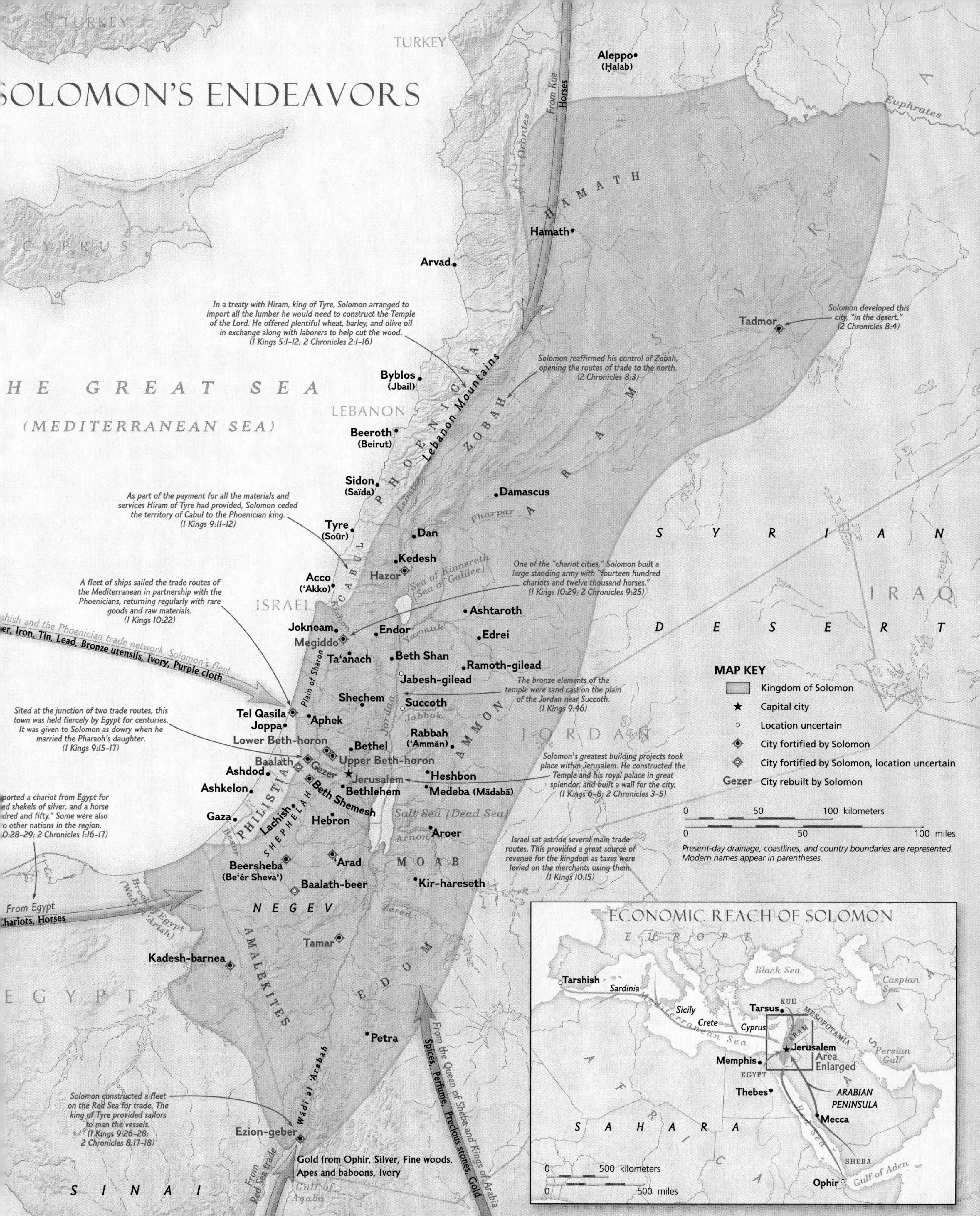

SOLOMON'S ENDEAVORS
TURKEY
Aleppo (Ḥalab)
From Kue Horses
Euphrates
Orontes
HAMATH
Hamath
Arvad
SYRIA
In a treaty with Hiram, king of Tyre, Solomon arranged to import all the lumber he would need to construct the Temple of the Lord. He offered plentiful wheat, barley, and olive oil in exchange along with laborers to help cut the wood. (1 Kings 5:1-12; 2 Chronicles 2:1-16)
Solomon developed this city, "in the desert." (2 Chronicles 8:4)
Tadmor
Solomon reaffirmed his control of Zobah, opening the routes of trade to the north. (2 Chronicles 8:3)
CYPRUS
THE GREAT SEA
(MEDITERRANEAN SEA)
Byblos (Jbail)
LEBANON
Beeroth (Beirut)
PHOENICIA
Lebanon Mountains
ZOBAH
ARAM
Sidon (Saïda)
Damascus
Pharpar
As part of the payment for all the materials and services Hiram of Tyre had provided, Solomon ceded the territory of Cabul to the Phoenician king. (1 Kings 9:11-12)
Tyre (Soûr)
Dan
CABUL
Kedesh
Hazor
Sea of Kinnereth (Sea of Galilee)
SYRIAN DESERT
One of the "chariot cities," Solomon built a large standing army with "fourteen hundred chariots and twelve thousand horses." (1 Kings 10:29; 2 Chronicles 9:25)
Acco ('Akko)
A fleet of ships sailed the trade routes of the Mediterranean in partnership with the Phoenicians, returning regularly with rare goods and raw materials. (1 Kings 10:22)
ISRAEL
IRAQ
Ashtaroth
Jokneam
Endor
Yarmuk
Edrei
Megiddo
Kishon
Tarshish and the Phoenician trade network, Solomon's fleet
Silver, Iron, Tin, Lead, Bronze utensils, Ivory, Purple cloth
Ta'anach
Beth Shan
Ramoth-gilead
Jabesh-gilead
Plain of Sharon
The bronze elements of the temple were sand cast on the plain of the Jordan near Succoth. (1 Kings 9:46)
Shechem
Succoth
Jabbok
Jordan
Sited at the junction of two trade routes, this town was held fiercely by Egypt for centuries. It was given to Solomon as dowry when he married the Pharaoh's daughter. (1 Kings 9:15-17)
Tel Qasila
Aphek
Joppa
AMMON
Rabbah ('Ammān)
JORDAN
Lower Beth-horon
Bethel
Upper Beth-horon
Baalath
Gezer
Ashdod
Jerusalem
Heshbon
Solomon's greatest building projects took place within Jerusalem. He constructed the Temple and his royal palace in great splendor, and built a wall for the city. (1 Kings 6-8; 2 Chronicles 3-5)
Ashkelon
Bethlehem
Medeba (Mādabā)
Beth Shemesh
PHILISTIA
SHEPHELAH
Lachish
Hebron
Salt Sea (Dead Sea)
Gaza
Arnon
Aroer
Besor
Israel sat astride several main trade routes. This provided a great source of revenue for the kingdom as taxes were levied on the merchants using them. (1 Kings 10:15)
MOAB
Arad
Beersheba (Be'ér Sheva')
Baalath-beer
Kir-hareseth
Brook of Egypt (Wadi el 'Arish)
From Egypt
Chariots, Horses
NEGEV
Zered
AMALEKITES
Tamar
Kadesh-barnea
EGYPT
EDOM
Petra
Solomon constructed a fleet on the Red Sea for trade. The king of Tyre provided sailors to man the vessels. (1 Kings 9:26-28; 2 Chronicles 8:17-18)
Wadi al 'Arabah
Ezion-geber
From Red Sea trade
Gold from Ophir, Silver, Fine woods, Apes and baboons, Ivory
From the Queen of Sheba and Kings of Arabia
Spices, Perfume, Precious stones, Gold
Gulf of Aqaba
SINAI
MAP KEY
Kingdom of Solomon
Capital city
Location uncertain
City fortified by Solomon
City fortified by Solomon, location uncertain
Gezer City rebuilt by Solomon
0 50 100 kilometers
0 50 100 miles
Present-day drainage, coastlines, and country boundaries are represented. Modern names appear in parentheses.
ECONOMIC REACH OF SOLOMON
EUROPE
Black Sea
Caspian Sea
Tarshish
Sardinia
Mediterranean Sea
Sicily
Crete
Tarsus
KUE
MESOPOTAMIA
Cyprus
ARAM
Jerusalem
Persian Gulf
Memphis
Area Enlarged
EGYPT
Thebes
ARABIAN PENINSULA
AFRICA
SAHARA
Mecca
Red Sea
SHEBA
Gulf of Aden
Ophir
0 500 kilometers
0 500 miles

The second major innovation was the introduction and domestication of large numbers of camels. This remarkable creature, truly a "ship of the desert," was capable of traveling 14 days without nourishment of any kind. Camels rapidly replaced the donkey as the favored beast of burden in transport over long distances. In almost every respect, the camel was made for desert travel. Its thick coat, often used to make garments, protected the animal from the sun, while its broad feet gave extra purchase on the sand. Its flattened nostrils and long eyelashes protected the head against wind and sand. The English word "camel" may, in fact, be derived from the Arabic word *jamal* or the Hebrew *gahmal.*

In Solomon's time the Kingdom of Israel straddled the crossroads of all the principal trade routes linking Assyria, Egypt, and the Mediterranean. In the past, Canaan had been a mere tollbooth on the caravan route. Israel now became a broker and trade partner in its own right, as "King Solomon excelled all the kings of the earth in riches and in wisdom" (I Kings 10:23).

To facilitate his plans, Solomon strikes an alliance with King Hiram of Tyre, the same royal house that assisted his father David in the construction of his palace. As part of this alliance, Phoenician flat-bottomed ships are built (arguably "under license") at Solomon's main southern port at Ezion-geber, today's Elat. Soon, entire fleets of these tubby ships cut their bows through the azure waters of the Gulf of Aqaba on their way to Africa. There, according to the Bible, Solomon discovers a highly valuable capital resource—the rich gold ores of Ophir, located on the eastern coast of Africa. A regularly scheduled cargo service is inaugurated from Ophir to Ezion-geber (I Kings 9:26). From there it would have been a mere five-day journey to the construction sites of Jerusalem. Crewing these ships is a problem, since the Israelites themselves have little naval experience. Fortunately, "[King] Hiram sent his servants with the fleet, sailors who were familiar with the sea, together with the servants of Solomon"(I Kings 9:27).

The mines of Ophir produce gold at a volume never before seen in the Near East. The first Book of Kings claims that in just one year, Solomon receives gold revenues of 666 talents, roughly the equivalent of 50,000 pounds of gold (I Kings 10:14).

As this new wealth streams into the capital, the royal court grows commensurately. In one day, says the Bible, Solomon's court devours 10 oxen, 20 pasture-fed cattle, and a 100 sheep—not counting the mounds of bread and

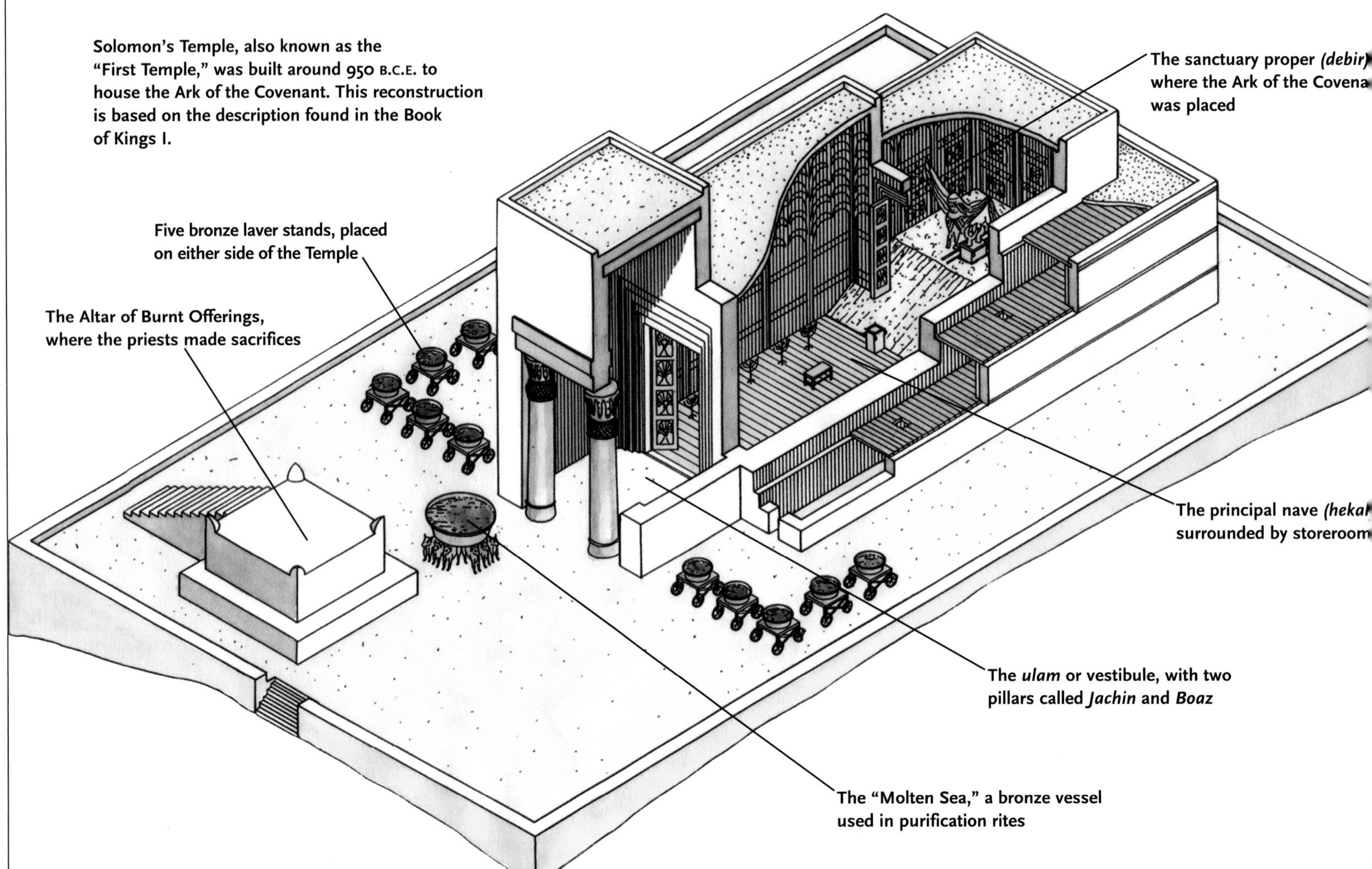

Solomon's Temple, also known as the "First Temple," was built around 950 B.C.E. to house the Ark of the Covenant. This reconstruction is based on the description found in the Book of Kings I.

flour that accompanied this repast. Not only courtiers partake in this largesse. Solomon's harem, too, has grown considerably. The Bible alleges that his women include 700 princesses and 300 concubines, including "many foreign women" (I Kings 11:3).

While these numbers may be exaggerated, there is little doubt that Solomon relies on intermarriage, rather than military force, to strengthen his ties with the "vassal" states nominally added to the kingdom under David. During a stroll through Solomon's harem, one would have found women from Moab, Ammon, Edom, Sidon, and other surrounding areas, as well as daughters from Israelite tribes. Solomon, who "loved many foreign women," also wisely protects his southern flank by marrying "the daughter of Pharaoh" (I Kings 11:1). The father of the bride would have been Siamun (ca 978–960 B.C.E.) of the 21st dynasty.

Siamun is chiefly known for his long reign of nearly 20 years, during which his attention was focused on rebuilding Tanis, the capital of the 21st dynasty (ca 1075–945 B.C.E.). This move to the Nile River Delta was forced by the growing power of the priesthood in Thebes (Karnak) and sealed a split in Egypt's spheres of influence. Upper Egypt was now firmly in the hands of the priests of Amun in Thebes, while the kings controlled Lower Egypt from their new center in the delta. Tanis was entirely rebuilt using monuments, sculptures, obelisks, and other spoils from the old Ramesside cities at Avaris and Pi-Ramses, originally built by Israelite slaves. First excavated by the French archaeologist Pierre Montet between 1929 and 1939, the site yielded many tombs from 21st-dynasty pharaohs. One such find is the silver coffin of Psusennes I, the only pharaonic tomb ever recovered fully intact.

Siamun's decision to send his daughter to marry a foreign king is remarkable. Heretofore, it was Pharaoh who married daughters from foreign potentates, thus sealing their fealty to the Egyptian crown. It is a sign of Solomon's (and Israel's) new status in the Near East that the process would be reversed and that it was Egypt's turn to send daughters for marriage to royal houses abroad. Solomon is, however, not the only one who enjoyed this privilege. Earlier, Siamun had given a daughter named Hadad to the prince of Edom. The prince had been living in exile in Egypt, after King David had driven him from his homeland during the years of David's conquest.

A bronze vessel supported by oxen, similar to the Molten Sea vessel described in the Book of I Kings, found in Susa and dated to around 1500 B.C.E.

These political marriages signaled Egypt's new interest in its former lands in Canaan. The Book of I Kings states that the Egyptian king even undertakes a daring raid on the city of Gezer, in Philistia, during which he defeats the weakened forces of the Philistines. Pharaoh then presents the city to his daughter and Solomon as a wedding gift (I Kings 9:16).

Solomon's Temple

DESPITE THE CHARMS OFFERED by his growing harem, Solomon focuses his attention on construction projects. The biblical account indicates that the king does not engage in military campaigns to extend the kingdom given to him by his father, David; rather, he supplies it with wealth and adorns it with a beauty never before seen by the Israelites.

The focal point is the construction of an all-new sacred precinct for the Ark of the Covenant on the old Jebusite threshing floor. Solomon plans to replace the tabernacle—a tentlike shrine where David placed the Ark—with an Israelite temple for YHWH. With the adroitness of a politician, Solomon appeals to the patriotism of his wealthier subjects by "suggesting" that they donate a generous portion of their income to the building project. His citizens do not disappoint him. In all, Kings tells us with characteristic precision, Solomon raises 5,000 gold talents and 10,000 silver talents (roughly $100 million in today's currency) from public conscription, not counting untold quantities of wood, brass, and iron.

To judge from the description in Kings, Solomon's sanctuary closely follows the Near Eastern archetype of a megaron. First, a pillared *ulam* or portal provides a ceremonial entrance. From

QUEEN OF SHEBA

According to the Bible, Solomon's merchant ships travel all along the Red Sea, including, quite possibly, the southern coast of Yemen, a region associated with the legendary Land of Sheba. "When the queen of Sheba heard of the fame of Solomon," says the Book of I Kings, "she came to test him with hard questions."

The much later Koran also speaks of this event; chapter 27 (Al-Naml) devotes nearly 30 verses to the queen's visit. The Koran recounts how Solomon initiates the meeting after one his advisers arrives with the alarming news. "I have come to you from Sheba with sure tidings," the councilor says; "I have found a woman ruling over all of them; she has been granted everything and she has a mighty throne" (Koran 27:22-23). The observation raises the issue of whose throne was mightier, Solomon's or the queen's. According to the Bible, Solomon's throne is made of ivory and overlaid with gold; "there were stays on either side on the place of the seat, and two lions stood beside the stays" (I Kings 10:19).

The Koran relates how Solomon sends a letter, urging the queen "to come ... in submission" (Koran 27:31). The missive's tone riles the queen's advisers, who protest, "[W]e are strong and we possess great prowess" (Koran 27:33). But the queen counters, "I have decided to send them gifts and will see what answer the envoy brings back" (Koran 27:34-35). Her lavish gifts prompt Solomon to instruct his advisers to "Make this throne even better than her own, so that her own should appear common to her, and let us see whether she follows the right way or remains misguided" (Koran 27:37-38).

The throne of Solomon is a metaphor of God's rule on Earth. A challenge to the seat of the Lord's anointed is a challenge to the Lord himself. If the queen can be brought to admit that Solomon's throne is superior, she will implicitly accept that God is the one and only Creator. And she does. In the Bible, the queen exclaims, "Blessed be the Lord your God, who has ... set you on the throne of Israel" (I Kings 10:9). In the Koran, the queen says: "[L]ike Solomon I submit myself to [God], the Lord of the worlds" (Koran 27:44).

This Ethiopian miniature from the early 20th century depicts the meeting of Solomon and the Queen of Sheba.

The whole earth sought the presence of Solomon to hear his wisdom, which God had put into his mind. Every one of them brought a present, objects of silver and gold, garments, weaponry, spices, horses, and mules, so much year by year. (I Kings 10:24-25)

here, one enters a tall nave (described n the Bible as the "house"), lit by nar-ow clerestory windows and surrounded n three sides by lower administrative vings *(yasia')*. The nave *(hekal)*, covered with "boards of cedar from the floor o the rafters" (I Kings 6:16), leads to the nner sanctuary *(debir)* proper, where he Ark of the Covenant is placed. Solomon then covers the entire buil-ding with "carved engravings of cheru-bim, palm trees, and open flowers" (I Kings 6:29).

The Temple is surrounded by a precinct fronted by a spa-cious courtyard. Here, the king places a sacrificial altar and a huge bronze vessel, known as the Molten Sea. Measuring 10 cubits from one brim to the other and 30 cubits in circum-ference, this vessel rests on 12 bronze oxen in groups of three, each facing the four points of the compass. This magnificent work has not survived, but a similar bronze basin that dates to around 1500 B.C.E., found in Susa, suggests that a vessel borne by oxen was not an uncommon motif in the Levant.

Some 120 feet long and 55 feet wide, Solomon's Temple was certainly not as monumental, nor as sumptuous, as the vast temple districts of Thebes or Nineveh. But by the standards of the young Kingdom of Israel it was grand enough—worthy to be called the dwelling of the Lord. If the biblical description of the Temple is accurate, then the First Temple in Jerusalem emulated a plan that had been used for centuries at other shrines throughout the region. A very similar temple, built by King Jabin during the time of the Israelite conquest, was uncovered by Yigael Yadin at Hazor. This earlier tem-ple, dedicated to the god Hadad, also unfolded along an axis of vestibule, central hall, and inner sanctum. This discovery prompted Yadin to exclaim that he had found a "prototype of the Solomonic Temple."

This detail from a 5th-century sarcophagus provides a detailed impression of the Phoenician ship type introduced in Iron Age II (1000–800 B.C.E.).

It takes seven years to complete the Temple in Jerusalem, the Bible notes. Solomon then spends 13 years creating his own palace as well as a government complex containing administrative, treasury, armory, and storage facilities. In addition, there are dwellings for Solomon's courtiers, staff, servants, and his extensive harem, though Pharaoh's daughter is housed in a separate pavilion for her private use (I Kings 7:8). We know very little about this complex, except that it was placed south of the Temple and adorned with double colon-nades made of cedar wood. When this massive construction project was fin-ished, a new citadel of gold had risen over Jerusalem. It towered high over the horizon, above the stone and mud-brick homes of the surrounding city.

Nothing of Solomon's complex survives; not the precious stones and marble blocks, "sawn instead of hewn," nor the countless vessels, furniture, and candelabra of cedar and wood. Everything was destroyed dur-ing the sack of Jerusalem by Nebuchadnezzar in 586 B.C.E. Though the Temple was rebuilt after the Exile (520–515 B.C.E.), the foundations of Solomon's acropolis were razed for a new, even more stupendous temple complex built by Herod the Great in the first century B.C.E. Nothing of Solomon's Temple remains today, with one possi-ble exception.

The Book of Kings tells us of a remarkable bronze laver stand that Solomon commis-sioned from the Phoenician artist Hiram, who "made the ten stands of bronze ... [which] had borders ... on the borders that were set in the frames were lions, oxen, and cherubim ... Each stand had four bronze wheels and axles of bronze" (I Kings 7:27-37). Apparently, Hiram is so proud of his work that he actually makes 11 such stands: 10 to be shipped to Jerusalem, and 1 to keep for himself—perhaps to show to other prospective clients. A similar bronze stand has survived, and the British Museum has dated it to the

This structure near the fortress of Megiddo is believed by some scholars to be stables and stone troughs built by King Ahab (874–853 B.C.E.), a century after Solomon.

time of Solomon. Conceived as a square cube on wheels with a round base on top, the four sides feature winged sphinxes, lions, and bulls exactly as described in the Book of Kings. It is, quite possibly, the only major work of art from ancient Israel dating to the time of Solomon.

In terms of architecture, however, there may be more physical evidence of Solomon's construction zeal. According to the Book of Kings, Solomon rebuilds the Canaanite strongholds surrounding his kingdom, including Hazor, Megiddo, and Gezer, the city granted to Solomon by Pharaoh Siamun as a wedding present. During excavations at each of these sites, Yigael Yadin and other archaeologists were surprised when they discovered a casemate portal of an almost identical design. All of the monumental city gates feature a long and narrow passageway flanked by three large chambers on either side that could house guards, weapons, or other goods. As archaeologist Amihai Mazar wrote, the "ashlar masonry, stone molding and specificity" of these gates all point to a new, royal style imposed by Solomon's architects.

Inevitably, recent studies have contested these claims. Some have shown that the distinct motif of this city gate is found in places elsewhere in the Near East, notably Phoenicia, though not before the ninth century B.C.E. This suggestion, in the opinion of some, appears to be corroborated by pottery sherds found in the Solomonic strata of each of these sites, as well as by carbon-dated wood fragments. However, other scholars continue to support Yadin's attribution to Solomon.

Another debate concerns the area adjacent to the palace precinct of Megiddo, which Yadin likewise dated to the time of Solomon. It appears to be a vast exercise yard bordered by rows of rectangular shelters or stalls. Each one of these stalls is furnished with hollow stone blocks that may be feeding troughs. The Book of Kings tells us that Solomon has "forty thousand stalls of horses ... and twelve thousand horsemen," enough to outfit a division of 4,000 chariots (I Kings 4:26). Seeing the troughs, the excavators readily identified the Megiddo stalls as stables. Indeed, standing in the center of this marshaling yard, it is not difficult to imagine the hoof beats of hundreds of impatient horses, snorting and straining at the straps of their chariots. New research, however, has shown that the complex served a later monarch, possibly the ninth-century King Ahab. The stalls may have been used as stables, or for the more prosaic purpose of storing supplies for troops stationed in the Megiddo citadel. A very similar storage facility, also from the time of Ahab, has been found in Hazor.

Solomon's architectural feats mark a high point in his reign. Then the inevitable decline did set in. The seeds of political unrest were present long before the end of Solomon's reign. Rather than being part of a unified kingdom, the northern tribes preferred to be recognized as an affiliated territory. Many northern chieftains might also have been repelled by Solomon's luxurious lifestyle and his Asiatic-style harem. The southern tribe of Judah, they felt, had become a ruling urban elite at the expense of the hard-working, agrarian northern tribes. But scholars believe that the real sources of discontent were Solomon's ruthless taxes and his policy of sending press-gangs throughout the provinces to recruit forced labor. These actions ran counter to the largely egalitarian, agrarian spirit that was Israel before the monarchy, and confirmed that Samuel's apprehension about the monarchy had been prescient.

This wall painting, dated to C.E. 244, from a synagogue in Dura Europos, in today's Syria, depicts Solomon's Temple.

According to the Deuteronomistic authors, the waning of Solomon's power is due to his failure to stay truthful to the Covenant Law. "[His] heart was not true to the Lord his God, as was the heart of his father David," the Bible says with surprising frankness. The Book of Kings readily casts the blame on the bad influence of his foreign wives, who continue to worship their ancestral gods: "For when Solomon was old, his wives turned away his heart after other gods" (I Kings 11:4). The king even goes so far as to build shrines to the deities of Ammon and Moab on the hills surrounding Jerusalem. In the eyes of the Deuteronomistic authors, this construction is sacrilege of the highest order. The return of foreign deities, under the king's protection no less, will inevitably despoil the land that YHWH had given to Israel. And the Lord's punishment for Solomon's hubris will not be long in coming.

EGYPT	MESOPOTAMIA	ISRAEL
ca 1187–1156 B.C.E. Reign of Ramses III in Egypt	ca 1168 B.C.E. The Elamites sack Babylon and come to dominate the region for a short period	ca 1200–1025 B.C.E. Israel is ruled by a series of judges
	ca 1125–1104 B.C.E. Under Nebuchadnezzar I, the Babylonians soundly defeat the Elamites	ca 1005–970 B.C.E. During his reign over a unified Israel, King David conquers the Jebusites and establishes Jerusalem as his capital city
ca 1075–715 B.C.E. The rule of Egypt's Third Intermediate period begins	ca 1114–1076 B.C.E. King Tiglath-pileser I rules Assyria	
ca 970 B.C.E. Pharoah Siamun rebuilds Tanis, capital of the 21st dynasty	ca 1050 B.C.E. The Aramaeans found the city of Damascus in Syria	ca 950 B.C.E. Construction on Solomon's Temple begins
ca 945 B.C.E. Pharaoh Shoshenq I founds 22nd dynasty of Egypt	ca 1000 B.C.E. In Mesopotamia, animal and plant wastes begin to be used as fertilizer	ca 931 B.C.E. Solomon's reign ends, and his kingdom splits in two
	ca 930 B.C.E. Expansion of Neo-Assyrian Empire under Ashur-Dan II	

CHAPTER SEVEN

The Fall of the Two Kingdoms

NO SOONER HAD SOLOMON BEEN LAID TO REST than his storied empire broke apart along tribal fault lines. Scholars believe that the principal reasons for the rift were Solomon's policies of coercive tribute and forced labor, and the resentment among the northern tribes toward what they perceived as his bias in favor of the tribe of Judah. The kingdom of Solomon then split into the Northern Kingdom (Israel) and the Southern Kingdom (Judah), each portion competing to be the rightful heir to YHWH's Covenant with the people of Israel. Each kingdom, particularly the north, had the fortune—or misfortune—of straddling the crossroads of the booming caravan trade. This strategic location emboldened the rulers in both north and south to engage in dangerous power politics, hoping to recover the glory of David's kingdom through alliances or conquest. According to the Bible, however, what ultimately doomed both kingdoms was the growing attention paid to pagan idols, including deities such as Baal and Asherah. Though strenuously resisted by prophets, these "abominable practices" provoked the Lord's wrath. The instrument of his vengeance, say both Books of Kings, is the aggressive militarism of the colossus to the east: the Assyrian Empire.

The Judean desert stretches east of Jerusalem along the Dead Sea and the Jordan River Valley.

THE MONARCHY DIVIDES

Seen from above, this site is associated with ancient Shiloh, where, according to the Bible, the Ark of the Covenant was kept until taken to Jerusalem.

INDICATIONS OF TROUBLE were evident in the kingdom long before Solomon breathed his last. Absalom's attempted coup d'état against his father, King David, nearly succeeded because of the wide support he enjoyed among tribal elders of the north. David's great achievements as a military leader notwithstanding, the tribal chieftains in the north only reluctantly accepted the trade-off of their autonomy and never agreed to the idea that the monarchy would draw its kings exclusively from the tribe of Judah.

In addition, the northern tribes were affronted by the selection of Jerusalem as the locus of national worship. Long-established sacred precincts in the north, in places like Bethel and Shiloh, were now superceded by Solomon's Temple in Jerusalem. The economy in the north had suffered as well. Solomon's arrogation of forced labor stripped the fields of sowers, reapers, and harvesters. Most of Israel's workers had grown totally dependent on Jerusalem's domination of the kingdom's economy.

The ultimate break with Solomon's regime was precipitated by Jeroboam, Solomon's "minister" of forced labor in the tribal region of Ephraim. According to the Book of I Kings, Jeroboam is

ca 1200 B.C.E.
Use of domesticated camel becomes widespread

ca 950 B.C.E.
The Aramaean kingdom emerges in Syria

ca 931 B.C.E.
Israel and Judah divide into separate kingdoms after Solomon's death

ca 931 B.C.E.
Rehoboam's reign in Judah and Jeroboam's in Israel begin

[T]he Lord said to Solomon, "Since ... you have not kept my covenant ... I will surely tear the kingdom from you ... I will not, however, tear away the entire kingdom ... I will give one tribe to your son, for the sake of my servant David." (I Kings 11: 11-13)

urged to do so by the Prophet Ahijah, who conveys a warning from "the Lord, the God of Israel: 'See, I am about to tear the kingdom from the hand of Solomon, and will give you ten tribes. One tribe will remain his, for the sake of my servant David and for the sake of my city Jerusalem.' " The reason, says the Bible, is because Solomon "worshipped Astarte the goddess of the Sidonians, Chemosh the god of Moab, and Milcom the god of the Ammonites" (I Kings 11:31-33). Jeroboam thereupon begins to plot against Solomon, who discovers the conspiracy and condemns his former official to death. Jeroboam, however, is able to escape to Egypt, where King Shishak grants him political asylum. Shishak has been identified with Pharaoh Shoshenq I (ca 945–925 B.C.E.), the founder of the 22nd dynasty of "Libyan" kings (ca 945–715 B.C.E.).

If Solomon's successor had been a figure of strength and conviction, the kingdom might well have been saved. But the opposite was the case. Solomon's son and heir, Rehoboam (931–913 B.C.E.), was an insecure and vacillating man, overwhelmed by the duties of the monarchy. After his accession to the throne, Rehoboam set out to renew the treaty of unification with the northern tribes and journeyed to Shechem, where all the tribal leaders had gathered. Among them was Jeroboam, who had slipped back into the country upon the death of Solomon.

In the biblical account, the tribal leaders take their measure of Rehoboam and state their conditions. "Your father made our yoke heavy," the tribal elders plead. "Lighten the hard service of your father and his heavy yoke that he placed upon us, and we will serve you" (I Kings 12:4). The northern tribes, evidently, want a moratorium on Jerusalem's recruitment of forced labor, a reduction in taxes, and possibly a greater autonomy in local government. Rehoboam stalls. He asks for three days to think it over. The tribes agree to give him more time.

Rehoboam's advisers beg him to accept the terms, but the young king brushes their arguments aside. At the end of the three days, he gives his answer. "My father made your yoke heavy, but I will add to your yoke," he tells the people. "My father disciplined you with whips, but I will discipline you with scorpions" (I Kings 12:14). The people are stunned by the arrogance of the young king. As with one voice, a cry goes up:

What share do we have in
David?
We have no inheritance in the
son of Jesse.
To your tents, O Israel!
Look now to your own house,
O David.

(I Kings 12:16)

And so, the northern tribes break their treaty with Jerusalem and anoint Jeroboam (931–910 B.C.E.) as king of a new state—a northern kingdom, which according to the Bible appropriates the name "Israel." Rehoboam flees back to Jerusalem. His own kingdom has now shrunk to little more than the territory of the tribes of Judah and Benjamin (which Judah had absorbed). It will from now be known as the kingdom of Judah.

And thus began the period of the divided monarchy. The Northern Kingdom would last for only 200 years; 7 of its 19 kings would die violent deaths. Judah, the Southern Kingdom,

Found in 1904, this Megiddo seal's inscription says "servant of Jeroboam." It possibly belonged to a minister of Jeroboam II (786–746 B.C.E.).

ca 928 B.C.E.
Pharaoh Shoshenq I invades Judah and Israel. Reliefs in the Egyptian city of Karnak record his activities

ca 925 B.C.E.
Shoshenq I dies, and Egypt's resurging power begins to wane

ca 890–884 B.C.E.
Under Tukulti-Ninurta II, the Assyrians consolidate their dominance in Mesopotamia

ca 850 B.C.E.
Greek city-states form around commercial centers, such as Athens

THE KINGDOMS OF ISRAEL AND JUDAH

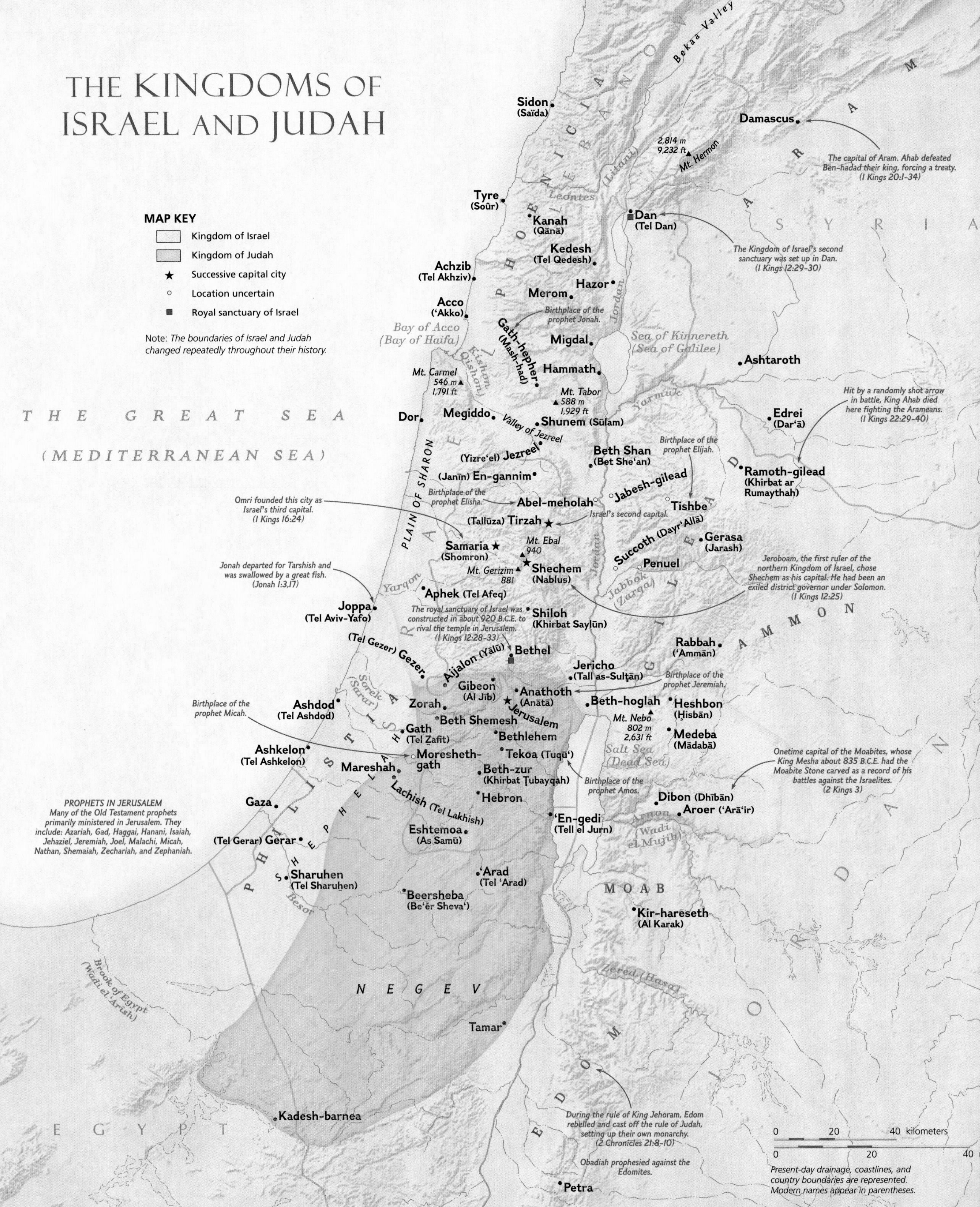

MAP KEY
Kingdom of Israel
Kingdom of Judah
Successive capital city
Location uncertain
Royal sanctuary of Israel
Note: The boundaries of Israel and Judah changed repeatedly throughout their history.
THE GREAT SEA
(MEDITERRANEAN SEA)
Sidon (Saïda)
Damascus
The capital of Aram. Ahab defeated Ben-hadad their king, forcing a treaty. (I Kings 20:1-34)
Bekaa Valley
LEBANON
PHOENICIA
ARAM
SYRIA
2,814 m 9,232 ft
Mt. Hermon
Litani
Leontes
Tyre (Soûr)
Kanah (Qānā)
Dan (Tel Dan)
The Kingdom of Israel's second sanctuary was set up in Dan. (I Kings 12:29-30)
Kedesh (Tel Qedesh)
Achzib (Tel Akhziv)
Hazor
Merom
Acco ('Akko)
Birthplace of the prophet Jonah.
Bay of Acco (Bay of Haifa)
Gath-hepher (Mash-had)
Migdal
Sea of Kinnereth (Sea of Galilee)
Ashtaroth
Kishon Qishon
Mt. Carmel 546 m 1,791 ft
Hammath
Mt. Tabor 588 m 1,929 ft
Yarmuk
Hit by a randomly shot arrow in battle, King Ahab died here fighting the Arameans. (I Kings 22:29-40)
Dor
Megiddo
Valley of Jezreel
Shunem (Sūlam)
Edrei (Dar'ā)
PLAIN OF SHARON
(Yizre'el) Jezreel
Beth Shan (Bet She'an)
Birthplace of the prophet Elijah.
Ramoth-gilead (Khirbat ar Rumaythah)
(Janīn) En-gannim
Jabesh-gilead
Birthplace of the prophet Elisha.
Abel-meholah
Tishbe
Omri founded this city as Israel's third capital. (I Kings 16:24)
Israel's second capital.
(Tallūza) Tirzah
GILEAD
Samaria (Shomron)
Mt. Ebal 940
Succoth (Dayr 'Allā)
Gerasa (Jarash)
Mt. Gerizim 881
Shechem (Nablus)
Penuel
Jordan
Jonah departed for Tarshish and was swallowed by a great fish. (Jonah 1:3,17)
Jeroboam, the first ruler of the northern Kingdom of Israel, chose Shechem as his capital. He had been an exiled district governor under Solomon. (I Kings 12:25)
Yarqon
Aphek (Tel Afeq)
Jabbok (Zarqa)
Joppa (Tel Aviv-Yafo)
The royal sanctuary of Israel was constructed in about 920 B.C.E. to rival the temple in Jerusalem. (I Kings 12:28-33)
Shiloh (Khirbat Saylūn)
AMMON
Rabbah ('Ammān)
(Tel Gezer) Gezer
Aijalon (Yālū)
Bethel
Jericho (Tall as-Sulṭān)
Birthplace of the prophet Jeremiah.
Sorek (Sarar)
Gibeon (Al Jib)
Anathoth (Anātā)
Birthplace of the prophet Micah.
Ashdod (Tel Ashdod)
Zorah
Jerusalem
Beth-hoglah
Heshbon (Ḥisbān)
Beth Shemesh
Mt. Nebo 802 m 2,631 ft
Gath (Tel Ẕafit)
Bethlehem
Medeba (Mādabā)
Ashkelon (Tel Ashkelon)
Moresheth-gath
Tekoa (Tuqū')
Salt Sea (Dead Sea)
Onetime capital of the Moabites, whose King Mesha about 835 B.C.E. had the Moabite Stone carved as a record of his battles against the Israelites. (2 Kings 3)
Mareshah
Beth-zur (Khirbat Ṭubayqah)
Birthplace of the prophet Amos.
Lachish (Tel Lakhish)
Hebron
Gaza
PROPHETS IN JERUSALEM
Many of the Old Testament prophets primarily ministered in Jerusalem. They include: Azariah, Gad, Haggai, Hanani, Isaiah, Jehaziel, Jeremiah, Joel, Malachi, Micah, Nathan, Shemaiah, Zechariah, and Zephaniah.
Dibon (Dhībān)
Aroer ('Arā'ir)
'En-gedi (Tell el Jurn)
Arnon (Wadi el Mujib)
Eshtemoa (As Samū)
(Tel Gerar) Gerar
SHEPHELAH
PHILISTIA
Sharuhen (Tel Sharuḥen)
'Arad (Tel 'Arad)
MOAB
Beersheba (Be'ér Sheva')
Besor
Kir-hareseth (Al Karak)
Brook of Egypt (Wadi el 'Arish)
Zered (Hasa)
NEGEV
Tamar
EDOM
JORDAN
During the rule of King Jehoram, Edom rebelled and cast off the rule of Judah, setting up their own monarchy. (2 Chronicles 21:8-10)
Kadesh-barnea
EGYPT
Obadiah prophesied against the Edomites.
Petra
0 20 40 kilometers
0 20 40 m
Present-day drainage, coastlines, and country boundaries are represented. Modern names appear in parentheses.

This stepped "high place" in Tel Dan may have been erected by the Northern Kingdom's King Jeroboam I (931–910 B.C.E.), according to the Bible.

would fare marginally better: it lasted for 350 years, ruled consistently by monarchs from the House of David. Then, it too descended into chaos.

Northern Kingdom Sanctuaries

TO SECURE THE LEGITIMACY of his rule, Jeroboam's first priority was to create a national shrine to YHWH in the north, to spare his subjects from having to travel to Jerusalem to offer sacrifice. There was no sanctuary in his new capital of Tirzah, some seven miles east of Shechem, so Jeroboam revived the cult centers of Bethel in the south and Dan in the north. He created his own priestly caste and instituted a special religious festival to compete with the ones celebrated in the south. Jeroboam did not have the Ark of the Covenant for his new YHWH cult. Instead, he commissioned two golden calves to be placed in the sanctuaries of Bethel and Dan.

The scribes of the Deuteronomistic History (the historical narrative comprised in the Books of Joshua, Judges, Samuel, and Kings) saw this act as idolatry of the highest order. But biblical scholars continue to debate the motive behind Jeroboam's actions; they suggest that he may have wanted to return to the original worship of the Abrahamaic El. The Canaanite El had traditionally been represented as a bull, a symbol of strength and fertility, as had the Canaanite god Baal. The calves may not have been intended as the representation of the deity but rather as his symbolic attendants—much in the same way that the Ark of the Covenant was guarded by winged, golden cherubim. In Ugaritic depictions, for example, the gods are often shown standing on top of a bull. By the same token, the close association of calves with traditional Canaanite deities would doubtlessly have appealed to those Israelites who continued to complement their worship of YHWH with native gods.

The Bible describes how a "man of God," displeased with Jeroboam's rival shrines, comes from Judah to rebuke the king. He finds the king officiating in front of his new altar at Bethel and cries "O altar, altar, thus says the Lord: 'A son shall be born to the house of David, Josiah by name; and he shall sacrifice on you the priests of the high places who offer incense on you, and human bones shall be burned on you' " (I Kings 13:2). The Deuteronomistic redactors, writing during or immediately after the reign of

Even after this event, Jeroboam did not turn from his evil way … This matter became a sin to the house of Jeroboam, so as to cut it off and destroy it from the face of the earth. (I Kings 13:33-34)

King Josiah, spoke with authority, for Josiah did kill the apostate priests of Bethel in about 620 B.C.E., burning their bones on the altar so as to defile the shrine forever.

The sanctuary of Bethel is today buried under the West Bank city of Baytin. As the city where Abraham had built an altar (Genesis 12:8) and where God had confirmed his covenant with Jacob in a dream (Genesis 28:13-19), Beth-El (literally "house of the Lord") was the preeminent religious center of the north. Dan, shaded by Mount Hermon in the far north, was a smaller sanctuary that largely served the locals who could not afford the long journey to Bethel. In 1992, during a cleanup of the archaeological site of Tel Dan, workers by chance discovered a paved courtyard, measuring some 195 by 145 feet, in the center of which stood an elevated stone platform. This structure may have been the high place (or *bamah*) erected by Jeroboam (I Kings 12:31) to serve as the base for the golden calf. Excavators also found a horn from the main altar, as well as a smaller horned altar that was still intact.

Egypt Intervenes

THE BREAKUP OF SOLOMON'S kingdom had not gone unnoticed by the outside

King Jeroboam I sacrifices to the idols in this 1752 painting by the French Rococo artist Jean-Honoré Fragonard (1732–1806).

world. Shoshenq I (ca 945–925 B.C.E.), a pharaoh of the 22nd dynasty and a former chief commander of the Egyptian forces, was plotting to restore Egypt's glory. Already, he had used the army to force a reconciliation of Tanis and Thebes, reunifying the twin kingdoms of Egypt in the process. Now, the path to the restoration of Egypt's empire led to its former possession of Canaan.

As the pharaoh's hieroglyphics on the Temple of Amun in Karnak proclaim, Shoshenq decided to launch an attack on Judah's southern border. The biblical Book of Chronicles attests to Shoshenq's military superiority, listing his "twelve hundred chariots and sixty thousand cavalry," and more soldiers than could be counted (II Chronicles 12:3). This formidable army brushes past Rehoboam's border forces and lays siege to Jerusalem. In desperation, Rehoboam sues for terms and watches helplessly as the Egyptian pharaoh makes off with "the treasures of the house of the Lord and the treasures of the king's house" (I Kings 14:25).

From the north, Jeroboam observes Shoshenq's movements closely, hoping that the man who once offered him sanctuary in Egypt will refrain from attacking the Northern Kingdom. But Shoshenq does continue north, raiding all the principal cities of his former guest until he has destroyed Jeroboam's most formidable fortress, the stronghold of Ma-ke-thu, or Megiddo.

Almost 3,000 years later, archaeologists working on Megiddo found fragments of a victory slab dedicated to Shoshenq's triumph. After the pharaoh victoriously returned to Egypt, he ordered the construction of a monument, the Bubastite Portal, in the Temple of Amun in Karnak, insisting that the artists try to imitate the style of Ramesside triumphal reliefs as closely as possible.

EGYPT STRIKES BACK

Beset by turmoil in the Third Intermediate period (ca 1075–715 B.C.E.), Egypt's pharaohs had relinquished their erstwhile control of Canaan, and the armies of David and Solomon had formed a strong deterrent to Egyptian advances in the region. But when the Davidic empire crumbled, Pharaoh Shoshenq I (Shishak in the Bible) saw an opportunity. The immediate cause of war may have been the presence of Solomon's fortresses in the Negev. The hieroglyphics on Shoshenq's Bubastite Portal of the Temple of Amun in Karnak claim that the king was provoked to action by "Asiatic attacks on Egyptian frontier settlements."

Egyptian forces marched through Sinai along the Way of the Philistines, passing through Philistia for an attack on Gezer. Shoshenq then turned eastward, following the route of Philistine raids during the time of Saul, which led to Aijalon, Gibeon, and the foothills of Jerusalem. Having exacted a punishing tribute from Rehoboam, Shoshenq continued his campaign northward, plundering and looting as he went.

The hieroglyphics from the Bubastite Portal proudly list the Israelite cities that yielded to the Egyptians: Ra-bi-tha (Rabbith), Ta-an-kau (Ta'anach), She-n-mau (Shunem), Beith-Shanlau (Bet She'an), Re-ha-bau (Rehob), Ha-pu-re mau (Hapharaim), A-dul-ma (Adullam), Ma-ha-ne-ma (Mahanaim), Qe-be-a-na (Gibeon), Beith-Huaron (Beth-horon), Qa-de-moth (Kedemoth), A-ju-lon (Aijalon), and Ma-ke-thu (Megiddo). Archaeological excavations have shown, however, that the "destruction" of these cities was cursory and haphazard. The fortresses were swiftly rebuilt.

The Bubastite Portal (920–930 B.C.E.) in the Temple of Amun in Karnak celebrates the victory of Pharaoh Shoshenq over the Israelites.

THE NORTHERN KINGDOM FALLS

In the ninth century B.C.E., King Omri and his son King Ahab built Samaria, the capital of the Northern Kingdom, on the Hill of Shemer, visible here in the distance.

FOLLOWING THE INCURSION by Shoshenq, the twin kingdoms found themselves in a time of major power shifts in the Near East. Egyptian power was on the wane after Shoshenq's death in 924 B.C.E. Because of this opportunity, new Eastern empires rose in Egypt's place, driven by aggressive rulers determined to conquer as much land as they could, including Anatolia, Persia, Syria, Canaan, and Egypt.

Poised between the grinding forces of these giants, tiny Israel and Judah embarked on a dangerous game of power politics. Many Hebrew kings attempted to recapture the glory of the Davidic kingdom by making aggressive alliances for the sake of territorial expansion. At the same time, the growth of trade brought great wealth to the region, widening the divide between a wealthy urban elite and the rural peasantry.

Tensions increased further by the adoption of foreign religious cults, particularly the worship of Baal. These crises became the principal focus of the Major Prophets who ministered to Israel and Judah during the time of the divided monarchy. The biblical narrative follows the developments of the political and spiritual debates that arose between the Hebrew kings and the prophets. More often than not, the prophets' advice to

ca 885–874 B.C.E.
Omri becomes king of Israel. The Northern Kingdom begins a period of prosperity

ca 883–859 B.C.E.
King Ashurnasirpal II expands the Assyrian Empire. He moves the Assyrian capital from Ashur to Kalhu

ca 883–859 B.C.E.
Ashurnasirpal II may be the first to use cavalry units to mask infantry movement

ca 853 B.C.E.
Israel allies with the kings of Tyre and Damascus and defeats the Assyrians at the Battle of Qarqar

[Ahijah said,] "The Lord will strike Israel, as a reed is shaken in the water; he will root up Israel out of this good land that he gave to their ancestors, and scatter them beyond the Euphrates." (I Kings 14:15)

heed the words of YHWH was ignored, and the Jewish kingdoms plunged headlong toward self-destruction.

The House of Omri

ARCHAEOLOGICAL excavation at settlements of this period (Iron Age IIB, 900–800 B.C.E.) suggests that after its break with Judah, the Northern Kingdom emerged as the dominant monarchy of the region. The north was far more populous and covered a far larger territory than Judah. The northern tribes also possessed the best farmlands and fertile foothills, including the Valley of Jezreel. With its manpower restored, the Northern Kingdom could now begin to exploit these rich agricultural lands in earnest—including the production of olive oil, wine, figs, dates, and grains. The agricultural surplus could be used for barter against commodities from abroad. The resulting wealth led to a more sophisticated and centralized administrative structure that, by the mid-ninth century B.C.E., would produce a "state" in the true sense of the word.

The principal architect of this newly centralized commonwealth was King Omri (885–874 B.C.E.), who had been a general commanding the forces of the Northern Kingdom during one of its periodic military campaigns against the Philistines. Omri seized power after a usurper, Zimri, had toppled King Elah. This power struggle prompted the ruler of Aram-Damascus—the former vassal state of David and Solomon—to mobilize his forces toward Israel's northeastern border. Located at the crossing of two principal trade routes, the King's Highway and the coastal trade route known as the Way of the Philistines, the oasis city of Damascus was Israel's natural rival in seeking to control the flow of trade through the region.

To avoid a threat on two fronts, however, King Omri first made peace with the kingdom of Judah. He then struck a pact with King Ittobaal of Sidon on the Phoenician coast (known as Ethbaal in the Bible), thus securing his eastern borders. The alliance was sealed with the marriage of Omri's son, Ahab, to Jezebel, daughter of Ittobaal.

Omri now turned to the offensive. Seeking to outflank Aram-Damascus, he conquered the land of Moab, east of the Dead Sea, which also had been part of the Davidic kingdom. He then defeated Aram-Damascus itself, thus gaining some of Solomon's former possessions in the Transjordan.

A New Capital

THE KING WAS NOW able to focus on creating a new capital for the Northern Kingdom—one that would rival Jerusalem in the south. Omri settled on a spot in Ephraim, strategically located on a summit in the hills just northwest of Shechem. He called it Samaria, "after the name of Shemer, the owner of the hill" (I Kings 16:24).

The site overlooked the road that linked the Transjordan and the King's Highway with the important coastal trade routes along the Mediterranean Sea—including those leading to the port city of Tyre, located in modern Lebanon.

This ivory plaque (ninth or eighth century B.C.E.) of a palm tree carved in the Phoenician style was found in the royal enclave of Samaria.

ca 830–715 B.C.E.
Egyptian cohesion breaks down during the 23rd dynasty, when different royal lines are recognized in various cities

ca 823 B.C.E.
Assyrian astronomers record the first of three solar eclipses

ca 745–727 B.C.E.
Tiglath-pileser III annexes the Northern Kingdom, except for the vassal state of Samaria

ca 721 B.C.E.
Samaria, the capital of Israel, falls to the Assyrians led by Sargon II

Today, the remains of Samaria are still visible just outside the village of Sebastiya, located about eight miles north of Nablus. The views are breathtaking; just beyond the escarpment, the hill plunges to a valley of endless groves and fields, bordered on the horizon by the rising majesty of Mount Ebal.

As a further sign of the growing rapprochement between Israel and Phoenicia, Omri enlisted the help of Phoenician artisans to adorn his palace with their work in ivory and other semiprecious materials, which had become highly prized throughout the Near East. Omri died however in 871 B.C.E., well before the new palace was finished.

Ahab as King

OMRI WAS SUCCEEDED by his son Ahab (874–853 B.C.E.), who continued work on the royal palace. Today, the remains of this acropolis are still visible, stretched across a vast terrace buttressed by a thick, fortified wall that ranges from 15 to 30 feet in width. The fine ashlar masonry (large building stones worked to smooth faces), occasionally supported by columns, all point to the experienced hands of Phoenician architects and sculptors.

It is likely that these same craftsmen also brought along other things besides architecture. They also brought their culture. Phoenicians worshipped the ancient Mesopotamian divinities, such as Asherah (Astarte) and the chief god Baal Melkart. These gods found fertile soil in Samaria. King Ahab did little to deter this influx of pagan gods, possibly for fear of insulting his Phoenician queen, Jezebel. Worse, the king himself "erected an altar for Baal in the house of Baal, which he built in Samaria" (I Kings 16:32). Scholars debate whether the Bible refers to the Phoenician, Baal Melkart, or the

The Prophet Elijah appeals to YHWH on Mount Carmel. Wall painting (C.E. 244) from the synagogue at Dura Europos, located in today's Syria.

Canaanite god, Baal Hadad, who had long been revered in the region as the god of storm, dew, and rain—key prerequisites for the northern agriculture.

The worship of the Canaanite Baal deity had probably survived in rural areas throughout the preceding centuries. But Ahab now took the unprecedented step of elevating Baal to the status of an officially recognized deity in his kingdom. Not surprisingly, the Bible states that "Ahab did more to provoke the anger

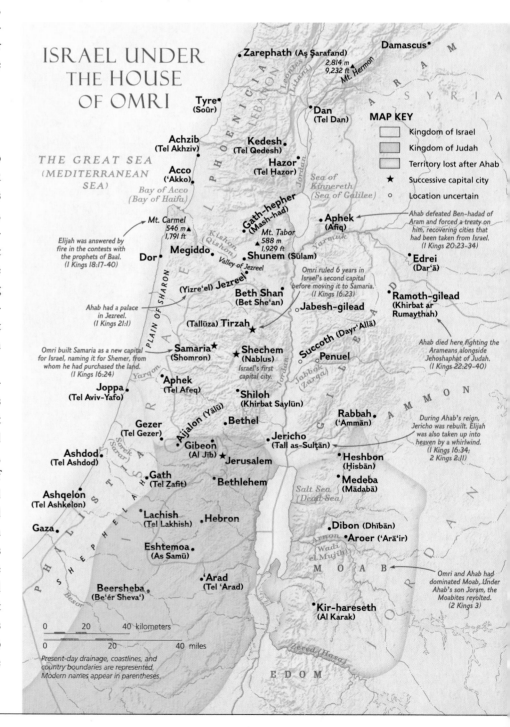

ISRAEL UNDER THE HOUSE OF OMRI

MAP KEY
Kingdom of Israel
Kingdom of Judah
Territory lost after Ahab
★ Successive capital city
○ Location uncertain

Elijah was answered by fire in the contests with the prophets of Baal. (I Kings 18:17–40)

Ahab had a palace in Jezreel. (I Kings 21:1)

Omri built Samaria as a new capital for Israel, naming it for Shemer, from whom he had purchased the land. (I Kings 16:24)

Omri ruled 6 years in Israel's second capital before moving it to Samaria. (I Kings 16:23)

Israel's first capital city.

Ahab defeated Ben-hadad of Aram and forced a treaty on him, recovering cities that had been taken from Israel. (I Kings 20:23–34)

Ahab died here fighting the Arameans alongside Jehoshaphat of Judah. (I Kings 22:29–40)

During Ahab's reign, Jericho was rebuilt. Elijah was also taken up into heaven by a whirlwind. (I Kings 16:34; 2 Kings 2:11)

Omri and Ahab had dominated Moab. Under Ahab's son Joram, the Moabites revolted. (2 Kings 3)

0 20 40 kilometers
0 20 40 miles

Present-day drainage, coastlines, and country boundaries are represented. Modern names appear in parentheses.

of the Lord, the God of Israel, than had all the kings of Israel who were before him" (I Kings 16:33).

Some scholars, however, have argued that Ahab did not intend to displace the cult of YHWH, but to facilitate worship for those people—local farmers as well as Phoenician expatriates—who wished to sacrifice to Baal in addition to YHWH. For the redactors of the Book of I Kings, however, this was not an option, and the subsequent narrative portrays a struggle between adherents of YHWH and Baal to determine which deity should be recognized as the sole national god.

The Prophet Elijah

THE PRINCIPAL ACTOR in this struggle is a prophet called Elijah—meaning "YHWH is my God." He is the first of a line of prophets who ministered during the days of the divided monarchy. Not much is known about his background and family, other than that he was a native of Gilead, the hilly region east of the Jordan River.

Elijah is furious at the renewed interest in pagan worship. He predicts a prolonged period of drought, in which "there shall be neither dew nor rain these years, except by my word" (I Kings 17:1)—a direct challenge to the legitimacy of the Baal cult. According to the biblical narrative, the Lord then directs Elijah to flee to a riverbed (or wadi) east of the Jordan, outside of Israel's territory, where the prophet will be assured of water as well as food, brought by ravens (I Kings 17:3-6).

Later, God tells Elijah to go to the house of a widow in Zarephath, where the prophet uses a small vial of meal and olive oil to sustain the widow's family and himself for many months (I Kings 17:8-16). Zarephath has been identified with the Phoenician city of Sarepta (or As Sarafand in today's Lebanon), located midway between Sidon and Tyre. When the widow's son falls ill and dies, Elijah revives the boy (I Kings 17:17-24).

It is not until the drought enters its third year that the Lord sends Elijah back to Ahab to confront the cult of pagan idols, which has grown considerably. The Book of I Kings claims that the court is now ministered by "four hundred fifty prophets of Baal and four hundred prophets of Asherah, who eat at Jezebel's table" (I Kings 18:19).

THE STONE OF OMRI

In 1868, the Reverend F. A. Klein discovered an inscribed stela of black basalt near Dhiban (in modern Jordan) that confirms the biblical story of King Omri's conquest of Moab. It reads in part: "I am Mesha son of Chemosh ... king of Moab. Omri king of Israel had oppressed Moab for many days, as did his son." The Mesha Stela, however, claims that Mesha later routed Omri, which is yet to be confirmed. The text also provides what is perhaps the first reference to the name YHWH outside of the biblical text: "(Mesha) took ... the vessels of YHWH and dragged them before Chemosh."

Elijah challenges the people to a test to determine who was the true God, YHWH or Baal. Each faction will cut up a bull and lay the pieces on a pyre of firewood. Whichever deity first ignites the sacrifice with a lightning strike will be recognized as the true god. Elijah's proposal is a shrewd move, for in the ancient Near East lightning was well recognized as a symbol of a god's strength and power. A fork of lightning was the favored attribute of Baal in his capacity as god of storms; according to one myth he used heavenly fire to build his house. Fire was likewise a divine attribute of YHWH, for his first manifestation to Moses had been in the form of a burning bush.

The great confrontation takes place on the summit of Mount Carmel overlooking the Mediterranean Sea, on the frontier, appropriately, between Israel and Phoenicia. The priests of Baal begin their rituals first. All day long they dance and sing, but Baal's lightning does not appear. Elijah mocks them, saying "Cry aloud! Surely he is a god; either he is meditating ... or perhaps he is asleep and must be awakened" (I Kings 18:27). They continue their invocations, but Baal does not respond.

When evening falls, it becomes Elijah's turn. He sets up his altar and drenches everything with water—making it even more difficult for the pyre to ignite. He has hardly finished his preparations before fire rains from the sky, exploding the altar in a burst of flame. The crowd falls to the ground in awe and says, "The Lord indeed is God." Seizing the moment, Elijah orders all the priests of Baal to be put to death (I Kings 18:38-40). A deluge follows, and the drought ends. Elijah tells Ahab, "Go up, eat and drink; for there is the sound of rushing rain" (I Kings 18:41).

Furious, Queen Jezebel plots to kill Elijah, giving the prophet no choice but to flee for his life. Shortly thereafter, however, Elijah makes one last and terrible prophecy: All of Israel and Judah will be destroyed, except for those people who remain faithful to YHWH, "all the knees that have not bowed to Baal, and every mouth that has not kissed him" (I Kings 19:18). Later, the prophet also curses the House of Ahab, after the king arrests and executes a man named Naboth, whose vineyard Ahab wants to acquire. Elijah says, "Because you have sold yourself to do what is evil in the sight of the Lord, I will bring disaster on you" (I Kings 21:20-21).

Elijah's prophecy against Ahab is fulfilled when the king is killed during a war against Aram-Damascus, Israel's old enemy. Ahab is wounded by an arrow during battle. He tells the driver of his chariot to take him from the field, but he continues to watch the battle, "propped up in his chariot facing the Arameans, until at evening, he died" (I Kings 22:25).

This statue representing King Ashurnasirpal II (883–858 B.C.E.) was found in the shrine of Ishtar in the city of Nimrud, which became the capital.

Ahab's son, Ahaziah, succeeds him (853–852 B.C.E.). He is also denounced by Elijah and ultimately dies after a fall from his window. Ahab's second son, Jehoram, is toppled by an army commander named Jehu, after which Ahab's queen Jezebel is ignominiously thrown from a window to her death. Because she is a king's daughter, Jehu asks that she be given a burial. When his servants go to seek her body, they find that nothing remains but her skull, feet, and the palms of her hands (II Kings 9:34-35).

GOLDEN AGE OF THE PROPHETS

In the Bible, prophets are sent by God to convey his will and words to the people of Israel. Some early prophets, like Samuel, were seers attached to a particular sanctuary. During the period of the monarchy, the prophets gravitated to the royal court to advise the king and uphold a faithful observance of the Covenant. In the Hebrew Scriptures, the division of Nevi'im (Prophets) usually distinguishes between the former prophets (the historical Books of Joshua, Judges, Samuel, and Kings) and the individual books of the latter prophets, who were active in the period of the divided monarchy. These prophets—Isaiah, Jeremiah, Ezekiel, as well as the Minor Prophets—were active in what has been called the golden age of biblical prophecy, spanning a range of some 400 years.

The Minor Prophets include 12 prophets who worked in both the Northern and Southern Kingdoms. In the mid-eighth century B.C.E., Hosea operated in the north, while Amos prophesied in Judah. Jonah may have been their contemporary. Micah worked in the latter part of the eighth century around Jerusalem, coinciding with the early activity of Isaiah. Seventh-century prophets include Nahum, who acclaimed the fall of the Assyrian Empire; Zephaniah, who worked in Judah during the reign of Josiah; and Habakkuk, whose oracles dealt with the fate of Babylonia during the reign of Jehoiakim. The sixth-century period following the Babylonian Exile was the time of Obadiah, whose book suggests he lived in Judah after the fall of Jerusalem, and Haggai and Zechariah, who both urged the rebuilding of the Temple so that Jerusalem would prosper once again. The fifth century had Joel, whose oracles include a vision of locusts swarming over Judah, heralding the "day of the Lord"; and that of Malachi, who urged a faithful observance of the Covenant Law, possibly coinciding with Nehemiah's activity in Jerusalem.

Painted by Italian artist Giotto (1226–1336), the Prophet Malachi appears in this detail from the ceiling of the Scrovegni Chapel in Padua, Italy.

Elijah, already advanced in age, is directed by YWHW to find a young man named Elisha and groom him as his successor. While living in a community of holy men and prophets in Jericho, Elisha performs many miracles, including the feeding of hundreds with just 20 loaves of barley bread (II Kings 4:42-44). The prophet also revives a dead child, as his mentor Elijah had once done (II Kings 4:34).

Even after his own death, Elisha's powers remain. In one account, when a corpse is accidentally thrown into Elisha's tomb, the dead man is revived (II Kings 13:21). As such, Elijah and Elisha are among the few prophets from the Old Testament credited with miracles. But the prophets' lessons go unheeded, for as the Deuteronomistic History tells us, Ahab's successors continue to do "what was evil in the sight of the Lord" (II Kings 3:2).

When Jehu came to Jezreel,
Jezebel heard of it;
she painted her eyes, and
adorned her head, and looked
out the window … [Jehu]
looked up to the window and …
said, "Throw her down."
So they threw her down …

(II Kings 9:30-33)

King Jehu of Israel prostrates before King Shalmaneser III of Assyria in this detail from a black stela (ca 841 B.C.E.) from Nimrud.

Assyria's Power

In the Bible, the destiny of the Northern Kingdom is spelled out in II Kings, which originally formed a single work with the first Book of Kings. The second Book of Kings picks up the story of the north from the reign of Ahab's son Ahaziah to the destruction of the capital of Samaria by Assyrian forces. It also provides an overview of the history of the kingdom of Judah, during the time of King Jehoshaphat's reign (870–848 B.C.E.) to the period immediately following the destruction of Jerusalem in 586 B.C.E. In both books, the threat posed by Assyria plays a prominent role.

Assyria had been a mere client state of the old Babylonian Empire back in the days of Abraham. By the 15th century B.C.E., it had developed into a large, independent kingdom bordered by the Euphrates and the Tigris Rivers, from Carchemish in the west to Ashur (its capital city) in the east, and Hit in the south. Prodded by the growth of its population, the Assyrian kings looked to expand their territory.

By the ninth century B.C.E., after the kingdom of Solomon had divided, Assyria already dominated the northern half of Mesopotamia, from the north of today's Baghdad to Haran (Harran), in today's southern Turkey, the location where Abraham's father, Terah, had settled and where Jacob went to find a wife. Assyria thus controlled most of the trade between its homeland and the northern coast of the Mediterranean—but its sphere of influence ended on the border between Syria and the northern kingdom of Israel.

By 883 B.C.E., a new Assyrian king named Ashurnasirpal II (883–858 B.C.E.) was ready to make his mark on the world. His official motive for initiating this conquest was religious: He wanted to convert foreign peoples to the enlightened faith of the Assyrian god Ashur. For new "converts," this privilege also called for a heavy tribute. Henceforth, kings from Assyria would invariably be depicted in the company of Ashur as their patron god.

To realize his dream of territorial expansion, Ashurnasirpal first pushed the Assyrian border south to the Persian Gulf, conquering all of Babylonia. He then moved southwest through Syria, reaching Mount Lebanon and the Mediterranean region in 877 B.C.E. Tribute poured into the Assyrian coffers. Ashurnasirpal used these plentiful, new funds at home to restore ancient Babylonian temples and ziggurats. He also used them to construct a vast new palace complex in the city of Nimrud, or Kalhu (Calah in the Bible), which later became his capital.

DEPORTATION AS POLITICS

The Assyrian kings appear to have been the first rulers to use deportation as a strategic political tool. The populations of Samaria (in 721 B.C.E.) and Judah (in 587 B.C.E.) were not the only peoples to meet that fate. People from Urartu (Armenia), Persia, as well as Medes and Arabs, were likewise forcefully moved to other regions. Recent studies suggest that the primary motive was not to destroy the social infrastructure of a conquered region but to discourage revolt. By unmooring captive peoples and placing them in a relatively unpopulated area, the Assyrians may also have sought a more equitable distribution of population centers in proportion to the available natural resources—in effect "colonizing" areas with relatively low habitation. It also enabled Assyrian economic planners to exploit highly fertile regions, such as the Valley of Jezreel in Israel, using skilled, agricultural labor imported from Mesopotamia. The deportations seem anything but haphazard: the Israelites were moved to Iran and Babylon, the Arabs and Persians were relocated to Syria-Canaan, and the Chaldeans were deported to Armenia.

The Assyrians were careful not to break up families and clans, so that, once the refugees arrived at their destination, they were free to rebuild their communities, till the land, and practice their faiths as they had done before. Eventually, skilled craftsmen, scribes, scholars, and other highly trained Jews were able to attain prominent positions in Babylon's polyglot and racially diverse society—one reason why, when Cyrus II granted the Jews permission to leave, only a part of the community of exiles took him up on his offer, sometimes reluctantly.

Limestone relief showing a prisoner family with their two children. Palace of Ashurbanipal, Nineveh, seventh century B.C.E.

British explorer Austen Henry Layard first uncovered Ashurnasirpal's palace in 1845. When the sand and dirt had been cleared away, Layard was stunned to see vast interior walls covered from top to bottom with numerous reliefs and paintings depicting the king's glorious victories. This striking form of decoration and commemoration would be emulated by many of Ashurnasirpal's successors.

Ashurnasirpal died in 858 B.C.E. His son Shalmaneser III (858–824 B.C.E.) continued to search for land to expand the empire. These additions, inevitably, were the lands of Aram-Damascus, Phoenicia, the Northern Kingdom, Judah, and Egypt. Shalmaneser enjoyed great success initially at the battles of Carchemish in northern Syria and at Aleppo farther south, but then the king ran into determined resistance. Assyrian aggression so alarmed the Phoenicians, Syrians, Egyptians, and Arab Bedouin that they put age-old differences aside and formed the first comprehensive coalition in the region's history.

The Northern Kingdom of Israel and its archenemy, Aram-Damascus, also joined the alliance of Canaan-Syria-Egypt. Together they met the Assyrian

ASSYRIA'S MILITARY MACHINE

Several military inventions enabled the Assyrians to make rapid conquests. Ashurnasirpal II was arguably the first to use cavalry units to spearhead and screen the infantry and its chariot forces. He is also credited with developing a siege machine. This large wooden framework placed on wheels was equipped with a heavy metal-clad ram suspended from chains, which soldiers could swing against the walls or gates of an enemy city. If necessary, slaves would build a large earthen ramp to bring the ram close to the city walls. The Romans adopted the machine and updated it. The Roman-built ramp used to drive the siege towers of the Tenth Legion to the walls surrounding the fortress of Masada, on the Dead Sea, is still visible today.

army in 853 B.C.E. near Qarqar, located some 150 miles north of Damascus and 25 miles east of Hamath.

The Bible does not cover this battle, but, fortunately, a detailed report is provided by a large stela recovered in the city of Kurkh, in southeast Turkey, in 1861. Adorned with the profile of Shalmaneser III, surrounded by the symbols of Ashur, Ishtar, Anu, and Sin, the stone confirms that the Assyrians faced a determined enemy. Damascus fielded 1,200 chariots, 1,200 cavalry, and 20,000 infantry; Hamath appeared with 700 chariots, 700 cavalry, and 10,000 infantry; and Israel's forces joined the battle with 2,000 chariots and 10,000 horses commanded by "Ahabbu," no doubt the biblical Ahab. The figures were greatly exaggerated, as was the custom, so as to make Shalmaneser's inevitable victory seem even more glorious. But scholars tend to believe that the battle ended in a draw because, for a decade or more, Assyrian soldiers were prevented from setting foot in Syria and Canaan.

The Assyrian Invasion

NEVERTHELESS, Assyria did recover and eventually struck back. Within a few years, during the reign of King Jehu (841–814 B.C.E.), Assyria had succeeded in forcing the Northern Kingdom to pay tribute. A large black obelisk, discovered in 1846 by Austen Henry Layard near the ancient city of Nimrud, clearly shows Shalmaneser with the winged god Ashur in the act of receiving tribute from a king accompanied by an inscription that reads: "*ia-ú-a mar hu-um-ri-i*—The tribute of Jehu son of Omri." Elsewhere, Assyrian records refer to the Northern Kingdom as *bit humri*—the house or dominion of Omri. Obviously, the legend of the earlier king had sufficiently endured for the name of his dynasty to become synonymous with the kingdom.

Shalmaneser III died in 824 B.C.E. He was laid to rest in the Temple of Ashur. More preoccupied with internal politics than with distant vassal states, succeeding Assyrian kings loosened their grip on the Northern Kingdom.

Phoenician gold and ivory inlay of a lioness attacking a Nubian shepherd. Nimrud, late eighth century B.C.E.

About a half century later, however, a new king took charge of Assyria. Tiglath-pileser III (745–727 B.C.E.) was convinced that Assyria should do much more than receive tribute from the surrounding states.

The new king wanted to annex these subject lands and incorporate them into a vast new empire that would stretch from the Tigris River to the Nile River. Ten years after assuming the throne, Tiglath-pileser was close to realizing his goal. His armies had moved down the Mediterranean coast, capturing all the ports up to Gaza and were now approaching the borders of Egypt. The local kingdoms were thoroughly alarmed. Once again, the monarchs agreed that regional quarrels had to be put aside in order to form a strong defensive force.

At the time, the Northern Kingdom was ruled by King Pekah (737–732 B.C.E.), who swiftly formed a defensive alliance with the king of Aram-Damascus as well as with the remaining city-states, such as Ashkelon and Tyre. But the monarch of southern Judah, King Ahaz (736–716 B.C.E.), interpreted Pekah's alliance as an attempt by the north to isolate and ultimately overrun the south.

Distraught, King Ahaz appealed for help to Assyria's King Tiglath-pileser, who readily obliged him. To demonstrate his good faith to his new ally, the Bible tells us that Ahaz imported effigies of Assyrian gods and placed them in Solomon's Temple. His southern flank thus secured, Tiglath-pileser struck hard against the coalition, and, in quick succession, the Assyrians defeated the states of Syria, Tyre, and Ashkelon.

Tiglath-pileser then moved on the Northern Kingdom of Israel, conquering, "Kedesh, Hazor, Gilead, and Galilee, [and] all the land of Naphtali, and he carried the people captive to Assyria" (II Kings 15:29). Kedesh was a city in eastern Galilee; the tribal region of Naphtali stretched along the northwestern banks of the Jordan River. Tiglath-pileser, in other words, had taken possession of all Israel's important agricultural centers, as well as a substantial section of the Transjordan. King Pekah, utterly defeated, was killed by

An Assyrian cavalry pair, one rider wielding a bow and he other controlling the horses, charges the enemy lefenses in this relief from Nimrud, ca 860 B.C.E.

n this panel from ca 860 B.C.E., a massive Assyrian siege-engine batters the walls of a city, while defending rchers fire a volley of arrows.

Dating from ca 730 B.C.E., this relief shows Assyrian oldiers, led by King Tiglath-pileser III, as they occupy a town and carry away the city's idols.

This panel, from ca 695 B.C.E., shows the presentation of prisoners and the heads of dead enemy soldiers to King Sennacherib, so that he may rule on their fate.

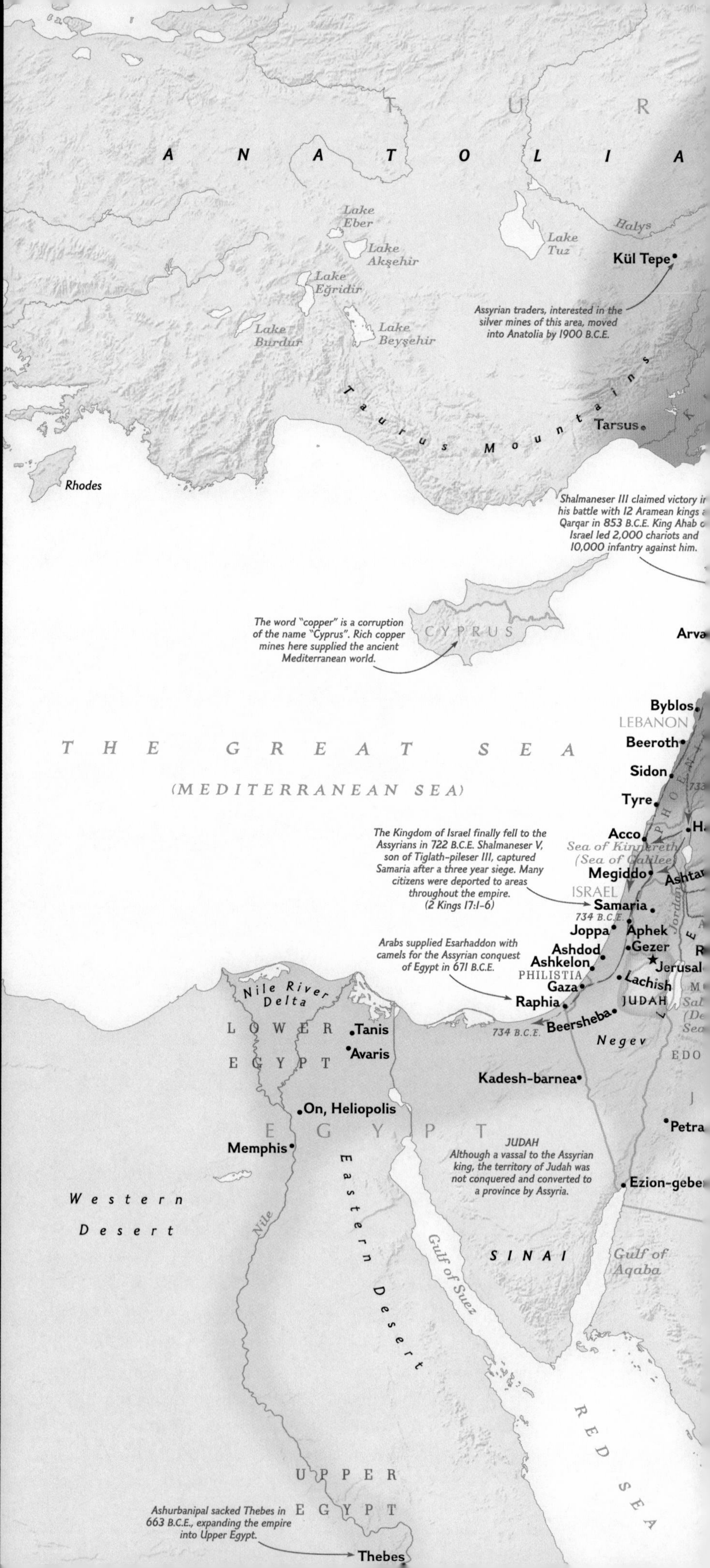

ANATOLIA
TUR
Lake Eber
Lake Akşehir
Lake Eğridir
Lake Burdur
Lake Beyşehir
Lake Tuz
Halys
Kül Tepe

Assyrian traders, interested in the silver mines of this area, moved into Anatolia by 1900 B.C.E.

Taurus Mountains
Tarsus
Rhodes

Shalmaneser III claimed victory ir his battle with 12 Aramean kings a Qarqar in 853 B.C.E. King Ahab o Israel led 2,000 chariots and 10,000 infantry against him.

The word "copper" is a corruption of the name "Cyprus". Rich copper mines here supplied the ancient Mediterranean world.

CYPRUS
Arva
Byblos
LEBANON
Beeroth
THE GREAT SEA
(MEDITERRANEAN SEA)
Sidon
Tyre
Acco
Sea of Kinnereth (Sea of Galilee)
Megiddo
Ashtar
ISRAEL
Samaria
734 B.C.E.
Joppa
Aphek
Ashdod
Gezer
Ashkelon
Jerusal
PHILISTIA
Gaza
Lachish
Raphia
JUDAH
734 B.C.E.
Beersheba
Negev
EDO

The Kingdom of Israel finally fell to the Assyrians in 722 B.C.E. Shalmaneser V, son of Tiglath-pileser III, captured Samaria after a three year siege. Many citizens were deported to areas throughout the empire. (2 Kings 17:1–6)

Arabs supplied Esarhaddon with camels for the Assyrian conquest of Egypt in 671 B.C.E.

Nile River Delta
LOWER EGYPT
Tanis
Avaris
Kadesh-barnea
On, Heliopolis
EGYPT
Memphis
Petra

JUDAH
Although a vassal to the Assyrian king, the territory of Judah was not conquered and converted to a province by Assyria.

Ezion-gebe
Western Desert
Nile
Eastern Desert
Gulf of Suez
SINAI
Gulf of Aqaba
RED SEA
UPPER EGYPT

Ashurbanipal sacked Thebes in 663 B.C.E., expanding the empire into Upper Egypt.

Thebes

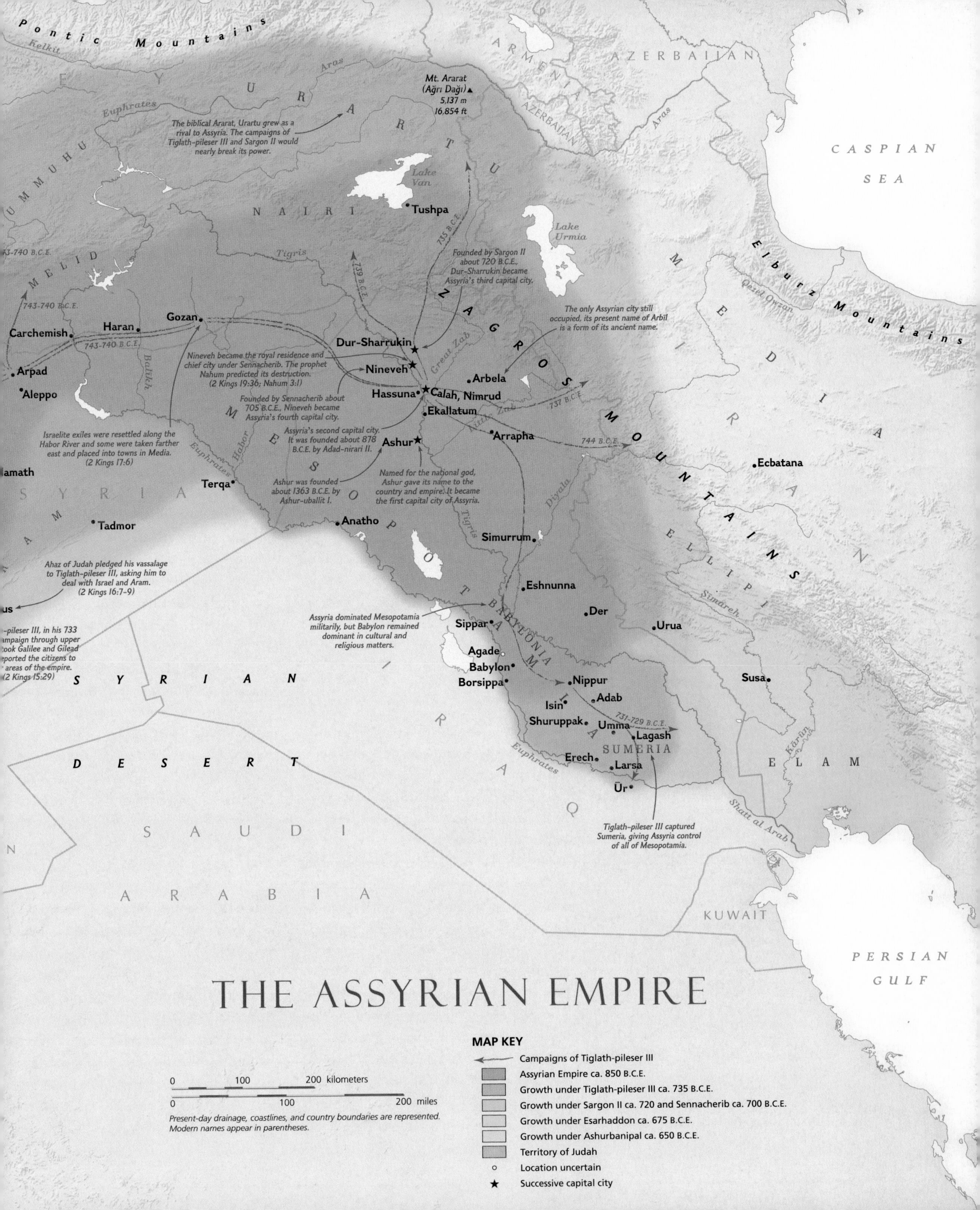

THE ASSYRIAN EMPIRE
MAP KEY
Campaigns of Tiglath-pileser III
Assyrian Empire ca. 850 B.C.E.
Growth under Tiglath-pileser III ca. 735 B.C.E.
Growth under Sargon II ca. 720 and Sennacherib ca. 700 B.C.E.
Growth under Esarhaddon ca. 675 B.C.E.
Growth under Ashurbanipal ca. 650 B.C.E.
Territory of Judah
Location uncertain
Successive capital city
0 100 200 kilometers
0 100 200 miles
Present-day drainage, coastlines, and country boundaries are represented. Modern names appear in parentheses.
The biblical Ararat, Urartu grew as a rival to Assyria. The campaigns of Tiglath-pileser III and Sargon II would nearly break its power.
Founded by Sargon II about 720 B.C.E., Dur-Sharrukin became Assyria's third capital city.
The only Assyrian city still occupied, its present name of Arbil is a form of its ancient name.
Nineveh became the royal residence and chief city under Sennacherib. The prophet Nahum predicted its destruction. (2 Kings 19:36; Nahum 3:1)
Founded by Sennacherib about 705 B.C.E., Nineveh became Assyria's fourth capital city.
Assyria's second capital city. It was founded about 878 B.C.E. by Adad-nirari II.
Israelite exiles were resettled along the Habor River and some were taken farther east and placed into towns in Media. (2 Kings 17:6)
Named for the national god, Ashur gave its name to the country and empire. It became the first capital city of Assyria.
Ashur was founded about 1363 B.C.E. by Ashur-uballit I.
Ahaz of Judah pledged his vassalage to Tiglath-pileser III, asking him to deal with Israel and Aram. (2 Kings 16:7-9)
-pileser III, in his 733 ampaign through upper ook Galilee and Gilead eported the citizens to areas of the empire. (2 Kings 15:29)
Assyria dominated Mesopotamia militarily, but Babylon remained dominant in cultural and religious matters.
Tiglath-pileser III captured Sumeria, giving Assyria control of all of Mesopotamia.
Pontic Mountains
Kelkit
Aras
Euphrates
URARTU
ARMENIA
AZERBAIJAN
Mt. Ararat (Ağrı Dağı) 5,137 m 16,854 ft
CASPIAN SEA
UMMUHU
Lake Van
Tushpa
NAIRI
Lake Urmia
735 B.C.E.
739 B.C.E.
Tigris
MELID
743-740 B.C.E.
MEDIA
Elburz Mountains
Qezel Owzan
ZAGROS MOUNTAINS
Carchemish
Haran
Gozan
Dur-Sharrukin
Nineveh
Great Zab
Arbela
Arpad
Aleppo
Balikh
Hassuna
Calah, Nimrud
737 B.C.E.
Ekallatum
Little Zab
Arrapha
744 B.C.E.
Ashur
Habor
MESOPOTAMIA
Ecbatana
amath
Terqa
SYRIA
Diyala
Tadmor
Anatho
Simurrum
ELLIPI
Eshnunna
BABYLONIA
Der
Urua
Simareh
Sippar
Agade
Babylon
Borsippa
Nippur
Susa
Isin
Adab
Shuruppak
Umma
731-729 B.C.E.
Lagash
SUMERIA
Kārūn
ELAM
Erech
Larsa
Ur
SYRIAN DESERT
IRAQ
SAUDI ARABIA
Shatt al Arab
KUWAIT
PERSIAN GULF

a usurper named Hoshea (732–724 B.C.E.), perhaps with the tacit support of the Assyrians.

The First Exile

THE PROUD NORTHERN Kingdom of Israel ceased to exist. It was broken up into the separate Assyrian provinces of Dor, Megiddo, Gilead, and Karnaim. Only the district around the capital of Samaria remained. However, it would later be tossed to Hoshea to rule as a puppet king under Assyria.

As was Tiglath-pileser's practice, the king next indulged in wholesale deportation. Entire villages were forcefully removed to Assyria. Dating from the eighth-century B.C.E., reliefs found in the palace in Nimrud illustrate these exiles and their tragic fates. Tiglath-pileser then returned to his kingdom, just in time to put down a rebellion in Babylonia in 729 B.C.E.

Tiglath-pileser could now proclaim himself the ruler over all of Mesopotamia and the Levant. He was the undisputed master of an empire unprecedented in scale and scope. But Tiglath-pileser did not live to enjoy the fruits of his labor. He died a short while later, around 727 B.C.E.

Unlike Tiglath-pileser, the new Assyrian king, Shalmaneser V (726–722 B.C.E.), was little interested in having foreign adventures and capturing new lands. Raised at the Assyrian palace in Ashur, he was more concerned with palace and political intrigue in the Assyrian capital itself. Samaria's ruler, King Hoshea, took note of this lack

Possibly representing the legendary King Gilgamesh, this heroic man tames a lion. Dating to the eighth century B.C.E., this statue was found in the palace of Sargon II in Khorsabad.

THE SAMARITANS' ORIGINS

When Assyria captured Samaria, much of the population was exiled and its property handed over to Babylonian "settlers," many of whom hailed from Cuthah. In time, these settlers assimilated with the remaining inhabitants of Samaria, married, and adopted Jewish customs, including the worship of YHWH. The mixed-race Israelites were called Samaritans, but were still ostracized by the Judeans. The Jewish historian Josephus, writing in the late first century C.E., scathingly called them Cuthaeans (*Antiquities* XI:2). The negative attitude toward Samaritans continued into the time of Jesus, as attested by the Gospels.

of attention. Outwardly he remained a loyal vassal to the new Assyrian king and "paid him tribute" like everyone else (II Kings 17:3).

Behind the Assyrian king's back, Hoshea began to plot "treachery," possibly a full restoration of the Northern Kingdom. To form an alliance with Egypt, he sends "messengers to King So," arguably to enlist him in a rebellion (II Kings 17:4). There is no agreement over who this pharaoh was, though quite possibly "So" refers to Osorkon IV (ca 775–750), who ruled the delta region after Egypt had split into various competing monarchies. Hoshea then made the decision to withhold his tribute from Assyria, a move that he would later regret, for it prompted Shalmaneser to undertake a punitive campaign against Samaria (II Kings 17:4-5).

The Assyrian army moved swiftly, and a lengthy siege began. The Book of II Kings claims this offensive stretched into a three-year blockade. During that time, Shalmaneser died and was succeeded by a formidable new ruler named Sargon II (721–705 B.C.E.).

A more incisive leader, Sargon II immediately dispatched additional forces to storm the Samarian citadel. Thus, "the king of Assyria captured Samaria; he carried the Israelites away to Assyria. He placed them in Halah, on Habor, by the river of Gozan, and in the cities of the Medes" (II Kings 17:6). Halah was located northeast of Nineveh; Habor, a tributary of the Euphrates, is today called Khabur, while the "cities of the Medes" lay to the east of the Assyrian heartland.

In his annals, Sargon proudly boasts of having uprooted no less than 27,000 Israelites. In their stead, the Assyrians moved various other subject peoples, mostly Babylonians and people from Aram-Damascus, into settlements in Samaria. The groups included settlers from Babylon, from Cuthah (possibly Tell Ibrahim, northeast of Babylon), Avva (or Awa in eastern Babylonia), Hamath (a major Syrian trade city on the Orontes River), and Sepharvaim (possibly Shabarain in Aram-Damascus) (II Kings 17:24).

The Deuteronomistic authors of II Kings go into great detail to explain the reasons for the Northern Kingdom's ignominious defeat.

"This occurred because the people of Israel
had sinned against the Lord ...
They had worshiped other gods and
walked in the customs of the nations ...
They did wicked things, provoking
the Lord to anger"

(II Kings 17:7-11).

Even though the Lord warned them through the agency of prophets and signs, the people "would not listen but were stubborn, as their ancestors had been, who did not believe in the Lord their God" (II Kings 17:14).

As scholars have pointed out, this accusation was no doubt colored by the political outlook of Judah, where the Deuteronomistic authors were living and writing. An argument can be made that the Northern Kingdom considered itself no less a nation of YHWH than Judah. The Northern Kingdom strayed from Covenant Law and was punished. The ultimate purpose of this theological object lesson was to warn the people of Judah that a similar fate awaited them too unless they returned, exclusively, to observing the Covenant Law.

Rolling hills surround the acropolis of Samaria, capital of the Northern Kingdom, which was vanquished in 721 B.C.E. by the Assyrian King Sargon II.

THE SOUTHERN KINGDOM'S FATE

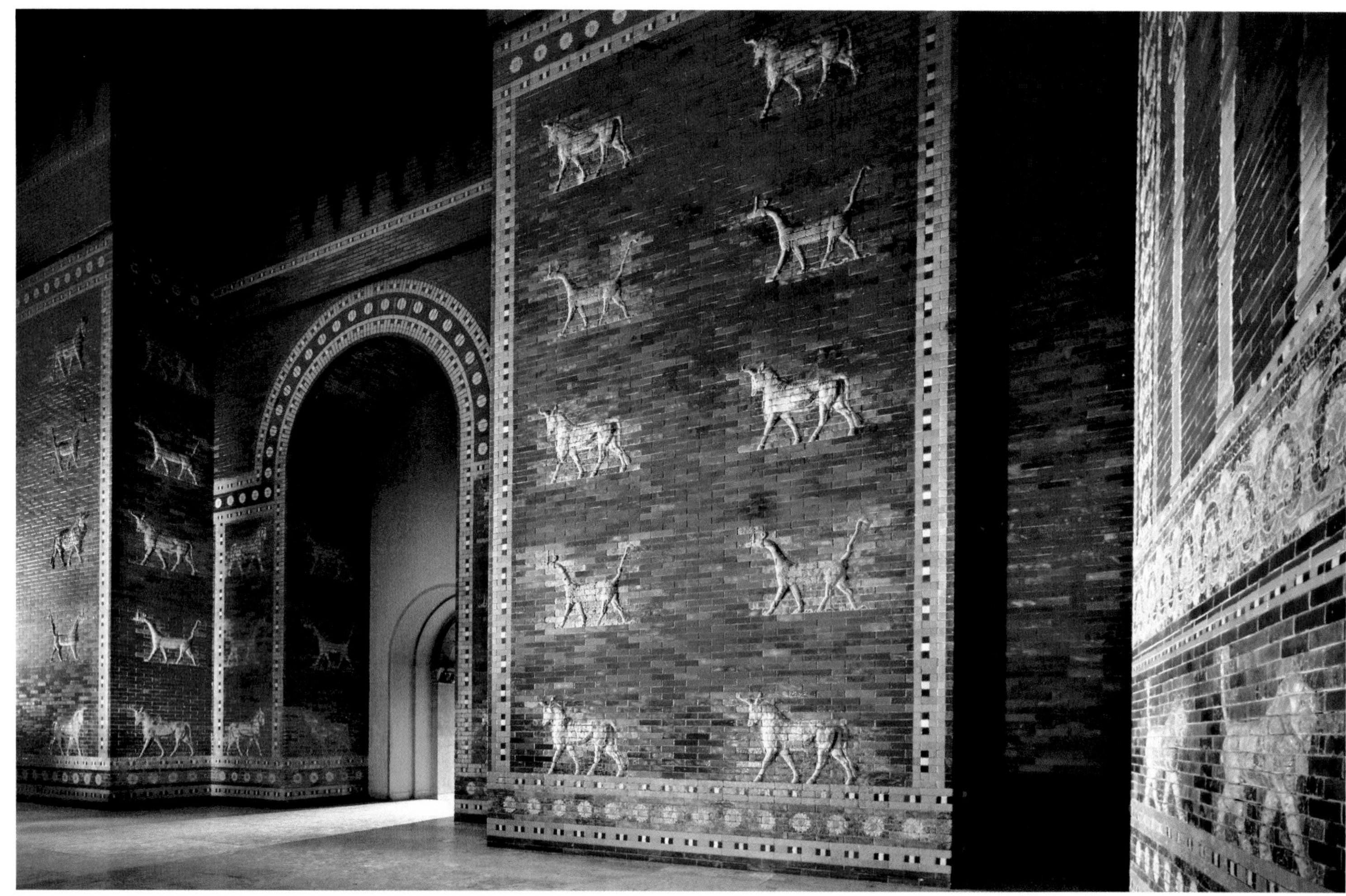

The reconstructed Ishtar Gate features glazed bulls and dragons on molded brick. It once stood over the Processional Way of Babylon, leading to the Temple of Marduk.

AS WE HAVE SEEN, JUDAH was a much smaller realm than the Northern Kingdom, limited to the tribes of Judah and of Benjamin, which Judah had absorbed. Judah's economy was also more modest in scope, with agricultural activity essentially limited to the Shephelah Valley west of Jerusalem and orchards and fields of dry farming in the southern highlands. According to the Book of Chronicles, however, the eighth-century King Uzziah (783–742 B.C.E.) is able to wrest control of the strategic port of Elath on the Red Sea from Edom, its eastern neighbor (II Chronicles 26:2). The book claims the king also succeeds in expanding his kingdom westward at the expense of the Philistine territory of Philistia, "[breaking] down the wall of Gath and the wall of Yabneh and the wall of Ashdod" (II Chronicles 26:6). He then sets about to fortify his reign, building towers in Jerusalem as well as in the wilderness. He hews "out many cisterns, for he had large herds, both in the Shephelah and in the plain, and he had farmers and vinedressers in the hills and in the fertile lands" (II Chronicles 26:10).

The Bible says the Prophet Amos, a herdsman who hailed from Tekoa (a village six miles south of Bethlehem), is

ca 765 B.C.E.
Possible birthdate of the Prophet Isaiah

ca 640–609 B.C.E.
During the reign of King Josiah in Judah, the Book of the Law is discovered

ca 732–627 B.C.E.
Judah continues to exist as an Assyrian vassal kingdom

ca 612 B.C.E.
A coalition of Medes and Babylonians destroys the Assyrian capital of Nineveh

Isaiah said to Hezekiah, … "Days are coming when all that is in your house, and that which your ancestors have stored up until this day, shall be carried to Babylon: nothing shall be left, says the Lord." (II Kings 20:16-17)

active in the Southern Kingdom as well as in the Northern Kingdom of King Jeroboam II (786–746 B.C.E.). Amid the growing prosperity, Amos denounces the power of rich landowners who steadily destroyed the fabric of local land ownership among clans and families. By forsaking social justice and true faith, Amos says, the people of Israel directly violate Covenant Law, and would soon feel the wrath of the Lord. This message is subsequently transferred to Judah as well: "For the three transgressions of Judah, because they have rejected the law of the Lord … I will send fire on Judah, and it shall devour the strongholds of Jerusalem" (Amos 2:4-5).

Amos's criticism of the growing social injustice in Israel and Judah is taken up by the Prophet Micah (or Micaiah, meaning "Who is like YHWH?"). The Book of Micah claims the prophet was active "in the days of Kings Jotham, Ahaz, and Hezekiah of Judah," (Micah 1:1), hence from 742 to 687 B.C.E., though scholars believe a dating during the latter part of the eighth century is more likely. Micah came from Moresheth-gath in the Shephelah and spent most of his time arguing the plight of the poor to officials in Jerusalem, including priests and judges. Like Amos, Micah believes that the kingdom's social ills violate the fundamental precepts of the Law of Moses. Moresheth-gath is a frontier town, from where Micah could readily have detected the growing threat of Assyrian invasion. To the "chiefs of the house of Israel, who abhor justice and pervert all equity," the prophet predicted the destruction of Jerusalem, during which "Zion shall be plowed as a field; Jerusalem shall become a heap of ruins" (Micah 3:9, 12). The instrument of this destruction was the might of Assyria.

Since the reign of King Ahaz, as we have seen, Judah had indeed become a vassal state of Assyria. Perhaps under Assyrian influence, Ahaz had allowed the cult of pagan idols to flourish once again. "The king," says II Kings, "sacrificed and made offerings on the high places," referring to open-air shrines where various cultic practices were performed (II Kings 15:4). As the threat of Assyrian aggression grew, Ahaz was succeeded by King Hezekiah (716–687 B.C.E.), who immediately initiated sweeping reforms, razing the "high places" of pagan worship and purifying the Temple. Hezekiah then set about to restore the economy of Judah, which had been badly affected by Tiglath-pileser's conquest of the north. Assyrian encroachment had reduced Judah to an area ranging from Mizpah (near today's Ramallah) in the north to Beersheba in the south. It was landlocked, deprived of its former access to the Mediterranean (through Philistia) as well as its former port of Elath on the Red Sea.

Hezekiah's priority was to break Judah's isolation and restore Judah's role in the prosperous trade between Egypt and the Assyrian Empire. Shortly after King Sargon's death in 705 B.C.E., Hezekiah was approached by Assyria's vassal king in Babylonia, Merodach-baladan, who was nurturing thoughts of sedition. In the Bible, Hezekiah invites him to Jerusalem to show him the house and its precious things, "the silver, the gold, the spices, the precious ointment, his armory, [and] all that was found in his storehouses" (II Kings 20:13).

Sennacherib's prism details the Assyrian king's (704–681 B.C.E.) military campaigns in Canaan and names King Hezekiah of Judah as a foe.

ca 609 B.C.E.
Pharaoh Necho II leads Egyptian forces against Judah; King Josiah is killed at Megiddo

ca 609–605 B.C.E.
Egypt dominates the former kingdom of Josiah

ca 601 B.C.E.
King Nebuchadnezzar leads the Babylonians against Egyptian forces in Palestine

ca 586 B.C.E.
The Babylonians destroy Jerusalem and end the kingdom of Judah

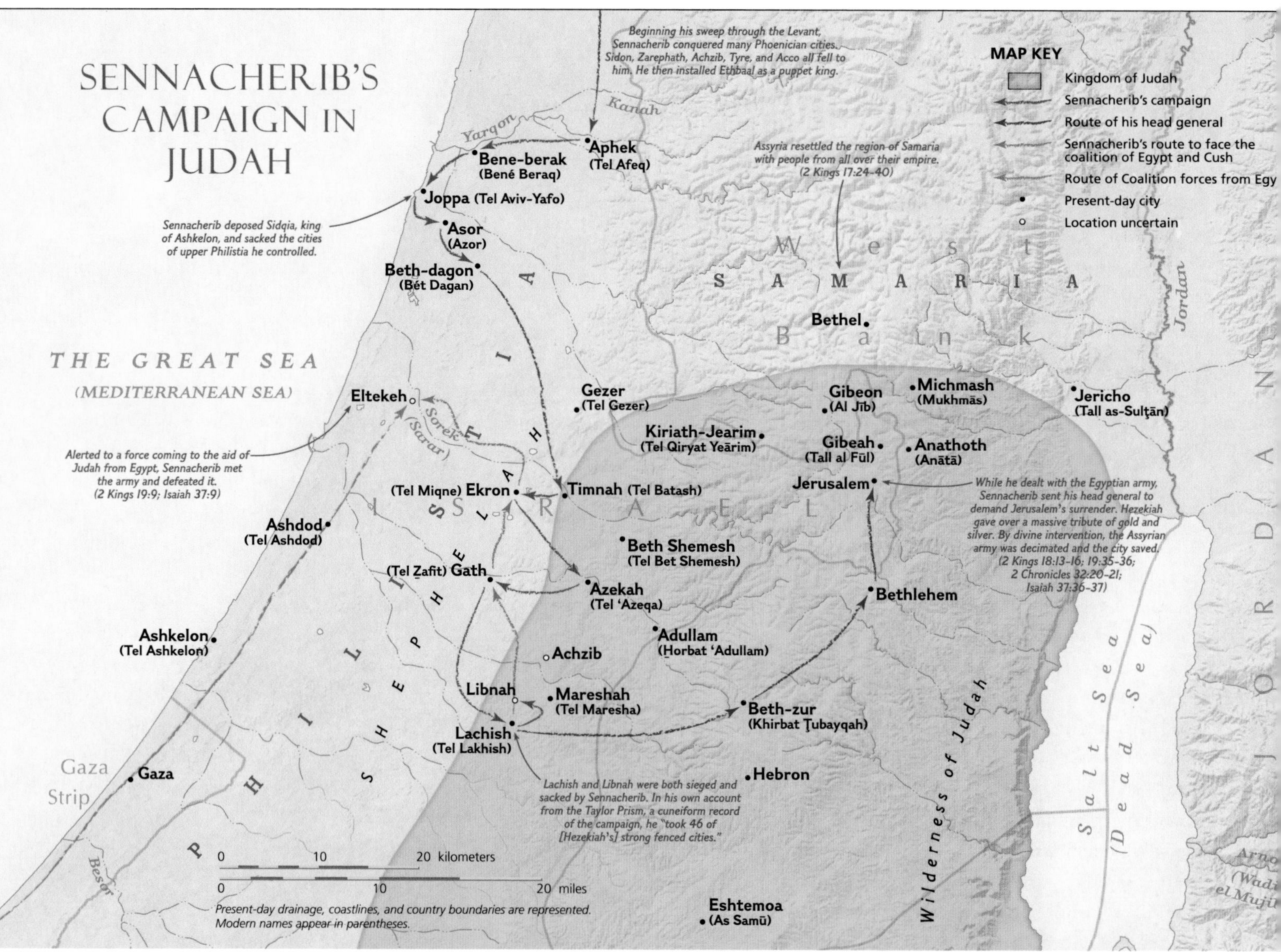
SENNACHERIB'S CAMPAIGN IN JUDAH
MAP KEY
Kingdom of Judah
Sennacherib's campaign
Route of his head general
Sennacherib's route to face the coalition of Egypt and Cush
Route of Coalition forces from Egy
Present-day city
Location uncertain
Beginning his sweep through the Levant, Sennacherib conquered many Phoenician cities. Sidon, Zarephath, Achzib, Tyre, and Acco all fell to him. He then installed Ethbaal as a puppet king.
Assyria resettled the region of Samaria with people from all over their empire. (2 Kings 17:24-40)
Sennacherib deposed Sidqia, king of Ashkelon, and sacked the cities of upper Philistia he controlled.
Alerted to a force coming to the aid of Judah from Egypt, Sennacherib met the army and defeated it. (2 Kings 19:9; Isaiah 37:9)
While he dealt with the Egyptian army, Sennacherib sent his head general to demand Jerusalem's surrender. Hezekiah gave over a massive tribute of gold and silver. By divine intervention, the Assyrian army was decimated and the city saved. (2 Kings 18:13-16; 19:35-36; 2 Chronicles 32:20-21; Isaiah 37:36-37)
Lachish and Libnah were both sieged and sacked by Sennacherib. In his own account from the Taylor Prism, a cuneiform record of the campaign, he "took 46 of [Hezekiah's] strong fenced cities."
THE GREAT SEA
(MEDITERRANEAN SEA)
Aphek (Tel Afeq)
Bene-berak (Bené Beraq)
Joppa (Tel Aviv-Yafo)
Asor (Azor)
Beth-dagon (Bét Dagan)
Eltekeh
Gezer (Tel Gezer)
Kiriath-Jearim (Tel Qiryat Yeārim)
Gibeon (Al Jīb)
Michmash (Mukhmās)
Jericho (Tall as-Sulṭān)
Gibeah (Tall al Fūl)
Anathoth (Anātā)
Jerusalem
(Tel Miqne) Ekron
Timnah (Tel Batash)
Ashdod (Tel Ashdod)
Beth Shemesh (Tel Bet Shemesh)
(Tel Zafit) Gath
Azekah (Tel 'Azeqa)
Bethlehem
Ashkelon (Tel Ashkelon)
Adullam (Horbat 'Adullam)
Achzib
Libnah
Mareshah (Tel Maresha)
Lachish (Tel Lakhish)
Beth-zur (Khirbat Ṭubayqah)
Gaza
Gaza Strip
Hebron
Eshtemoa (As Samū)
Bethel
S A M A R I A
West Bank
P H I L I S T I A
S H E P H E L A H
I S R A E L
J O R D A N
Wilderness of Judah
Salt Sea (Dead Sea)
Yarqon
Kanah
Sorek (Sarar)
Besor
Jordan
0 10 20 kilometers
0 10 20 miles
Present-day drainage, coastlines, and country boundaries are represented. Modern names appear in parentheses.

The Bible describes how this state visit alarms the Prophet Isaiah (or Yeshayáhu), whose name means "YHWH will save." A contemporary of Micah, Isaiah had a vision at age 25, during the last year of King Uzziah's reign, of YHWH calling him to service. From that moment, he embarked on a long career as a prophet, diplomat, and poet, serving three kings as councilor while acting as Judah's religious conscience. Isaiah's easy access to Judah's monarchs has led scholars to believe that the prophet may himself have been related to the royal house.

The prophet firmly believed in the Davidic dynasty's validity as God's anointed rulers of the realm, and that Zion, the city of Jerusalem, had been chosen by God to be his seat on Earth. Consequently, Isaiah was deeply concerned about the danger of Judah being mired in international politics that could only lead to its destruction. One such occasion arose when King Pekah of the Northern Kingdom and King Rezim of Aram-Damascus were plotting to attack Judah.

According to the Book of Isaiah, the Lord sends the prophet to King Ahaz, telling him to "Take heed, be quiet, do not fear, and do not let your heart be faint" (Isaiah 7:4). As a sign of the Lord's protection, Isaiah says, "Look, the young woman is with child and shall bear a son, and shall name him Emmanuel." Before that child is weaned, "the land before whose two kings you are in dread will be deserted" (Isaiah 7:14, 16).

Now, a decade or so later, the pending visit of the Babylonian delegation fills Isaiah with dread. He goes to Hezekiah's palace and warns, "Days are coming when all that is in your house, and that which your ancestors have stored up until this day, shall be carried to Babylon; nothing shall be left, says the Lord" (II Kings 20:17). Hezekiah, his eye on future glory, does not listen to the prophecy. He and his guests sit down to formulate a plan. Together they will launch a rebellion against Assyria; Babylonia will attack from the north, and Judah will strike from the south.

Sargon's successor in Assyria, King Sennacherib (704–681 B.C.E.), learns of Hezekiah's plot against Assyria well before the Babylonian emissaries return home. He mobilizes his forces and defeats the King Merodach-baladan's forces. He then turns west, determined to punish Judah. Knowing he is facing impossible odds, Hezekiah prepares for a long siege and orders a new tunnel dug to the waters of Gihon that will channel the precious water directly into the Pool of Siloam. A detailed account of this campaign, which matches the account of II Kings to a remarkable degree, survives on a delicately carved clay prism (a block with six sides), which was found at Nineveh in 1830. According to these annals, Sennacherib first moved west to strike against the Phoenicians (who, much to their regret, had sided with the rebellion) and defeated them at Tyre and Sidon. He then moved south and accepted the fealty of the kings of Ammon, Moab, and Edom, who each rushed to pledge their tribute.

Having thus isolated Judah from all sides, Sennacherib slowly drew a noose around Jerusalem. According to the biblical account, the protective ring of Hezekiah's fortresses is methodically destroyed, as "King Sennacherib of Assyria came up against all the fortified cities of Judah and captured them" (II Kings 18:13). The text of Sennacherib's prism concurs: "As to Hezekiah [ha-za-qi-a-u], he did not submit to my yoke. I laid siege to 46 of his strong cities, walled forts and to the countless small villages in their vicinity, and conquered them by means of well-stamped earth ramps, and battering rams ... with the attack by foot soldiers."

One of these "strong cities" was the Judean city of Lachish, located just 30 miles southwest of Jerusalem. This battle was so fierce and its aftermath so

THE SECRET OF HEZEKIAH'S TUNNEL

THE BIBLE TELLS US THAT HEZEKIAH ordered a new tunnel dug that would bring water from the Gihon Spring to the Pool of Siloam, providing the citizens of Jerusalem with a protected water source. (II Kings 20:20). This conduit would provide far improved access to fresh water than through the vertical rock opening known as Warren's Shaft, by which thirsty citizens could only hoist one bucket of drinking water at a time.

In 1880, archaeologists discovered an inscription (now in Istanbul) from Hezekiah's time that describes in detail how the king had two teams of diggers start from opposite ends, who then met in the middle exactly as planned, completing the tunnel in half the time. But as excavations show, the 1,750-foot tunnel actually follows a seemingly haphazard course with numerous twists and turns. How were these eighth-century B.C.E. workmen able to reach the midway point underground without benefit of modern geological instruments?

Dan Gill, the geological expert who assisted the Israeli archaeologist Yigal Shiloh during his excavations in 1978, believes he has the answer. He discovered that underneath the City of David lies an elaborate karst system of natural caverns and channels, burrowed through the limestone hill by the sheer pressure of groundwater. Knowing this, Hezekiah's engineers carved channels between these existing cavities to create what is, in essence, a natural channel carrying the water to a large reservoir inside the city walls.

Below Jerusalem, stairs descend to Warren's Shaft and Hezekiah's Tunnel, which connected the Gihon Spring to the Pool of Siloam.

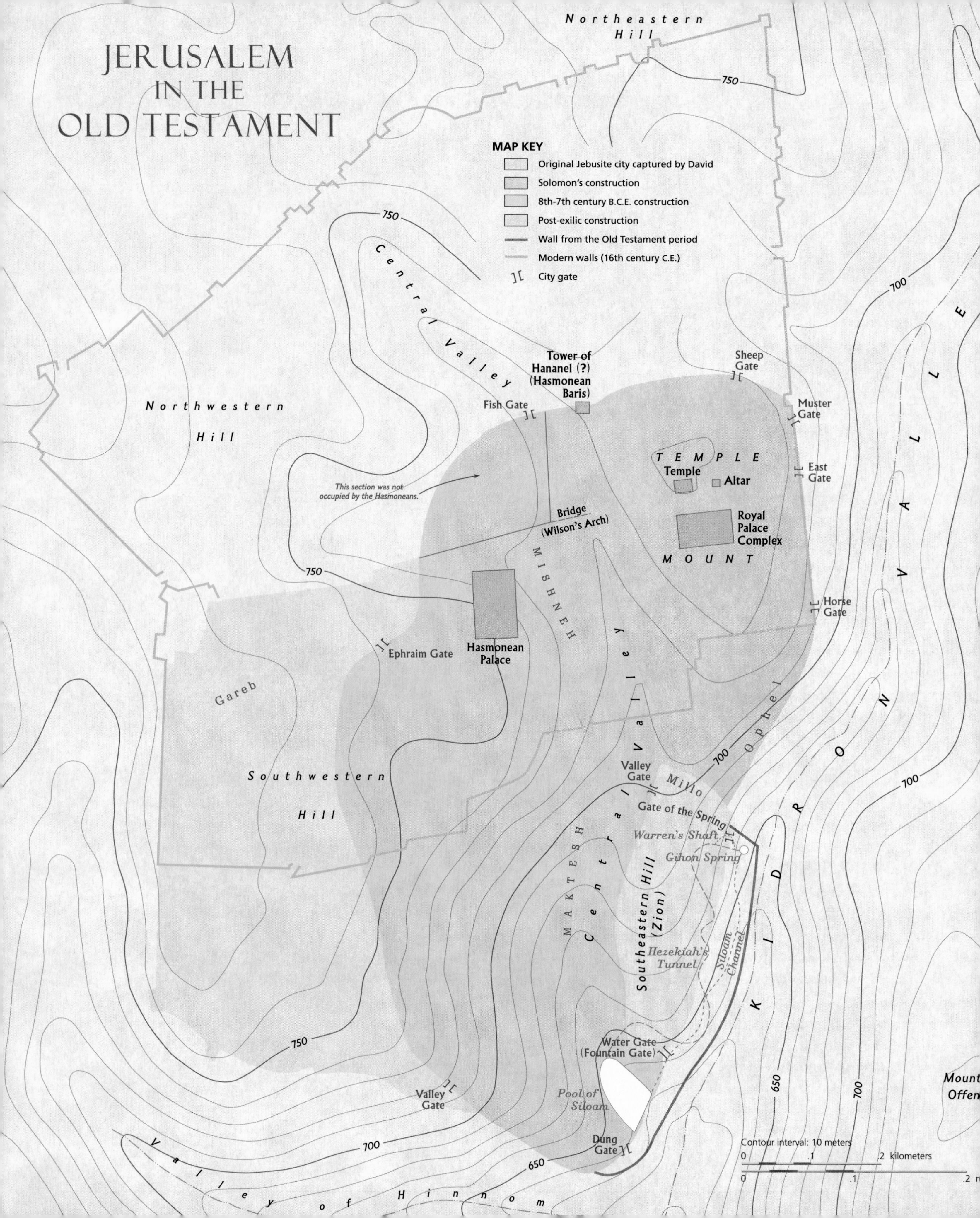
JERUSALEM IN THE OLD TESTAMENT
MAP KEY
Original Jebusite city captured by David
Solomon's construction
8th-7th century B.C.E. construction
Post-exilic construction
Wall from the Old Testament period
Modern walls (16th century C.E.)
City gate
Northeastern Hill
Northwestern Hill
Central Valley
Tower of Hananel (?) (Hasmonean Baris)
Fish Gate
Sheep Gate
Muster Gate
East Gate
Horse Gate
TEMPLE MOUNT
Temple
Altar
Royal Palace Complex
This section was not occupied by the Hasmoneans.
Bridge (Wilson's Arch)
MISHNEH
Hasmonean Palace
Ephraim Gate
Gareb
Southwestern Hill
Valley Gate
Millo
Ophel
Gate of the Spring
Warren's Shaft
Gihon Spring
MAKTESH
Southeastern Hill (Zion)
Hezekiah's Tunnel
Siloam Channel
KIDRON VALLEY
Water Gate (Fountain Gate)
Pool of Siloam
Dung Gate
Valley of Hinnom
Mount Offen
750
700
650
Contour interval: 10 meters
0 .1 .2 kilometers

And Hezekiah prayed before the Lord, and said: "… Truly, O Lord, the kings of Assyria have laid waste the nations and their lands, and have hurled their gods into the fire … So now, O Lord our God, save us, I pray you, from his hand." (II Kings 19:15-19)

Lachish defenders fight the Assyrian onslaught.

Assyrian soldiers impale captured prisoners on stakes.

Captive Judean families are sent under guard into exile.

These 3 scenes from Sennacherib's palace at Nineveh depict the capture of Lachish, ca 701 B.C.E.

gruesome that Sennacherib commissioned his artists in Nineveh to produce four panels in bas-relief with scenes of this unfortunate city.

Siege of Jerusalem

HEZEKIAH, HOWEVER, may initially have believed that the defenders of Lachish were holding firm. Excavators found several pieces of inscribed pottery sherds that were used to convey military signals. One of the clay pieces, in Hebrew, states hopefully: "May YHWH cause my lord to hear news of peace, even now, even now." Before long, however, Hezekiah learns of the true fate of Lachish and fears that the war has been lost. With his forts gone, Hezekiah becomes aware that nothing stands between Sennacherib and Jerusalem itself. The king makes one last desperate gambit. He sends a message to the Assyrian king, still camped at Lachish: "I have done wrong; withdraw from me; whatever you impose on me I will bear" (II Kings 18:14).

Sennacherib responds by demanding a tribute of 300 talents of silver and 30 talents of gold. In the days of Solomon, this might have been a tolerable sum. But for Hezekiah's impoverished nation, the tribute is a staggering burden. Hezekiah raids his royal treasury and even the Temple to come up with the necessary ransom money. But Sennacherib is interested in more than money. With more than 200,000 Jews already in captivity, his army lays siege to Jerusalem. The Assyrian soldiers taunt the defenders on the walls: "On whom do you now rely, that you have rebelled … on Egypt, that broken reed" (II Kings 18:20-21).

The Book of II Kings describes how Hezekiah turns to Isaiah for help. What should Judah do, surrender or fight? Do nothing, replies Isaiah. "By the way that he came, by the same he shall return; he shall not come into this city" (II Kings 19:33). And, says the biblical account, it comes to pass as Isaiah has foretold, for "the angel of the Lord struck down" 185,000 soldiers in the Assyrian camp. Quite possibly, this event may refer to a sudden outbreak of disease. Whatever the cause, the siege of Jerusalem is lifted. The prism of Sennacherib makes no reference to the final outcome, but confirms the tribute required of Hezekiah: gold, silver, precious stones, and furniture, all looted from Hezekiah's palace and the Temple. That fact in itself is telling. There is no report of victory, no reference to Jerusalem's inhabitants being sent into exile. With the tribute paid, the army left.

It seemed as if Jerusalem had been delivered, but Hezekiah paid a heavy price for his insurrection. His proudest cities lay in ruins. The Shephelah, the rolling foothills between the Judean hills

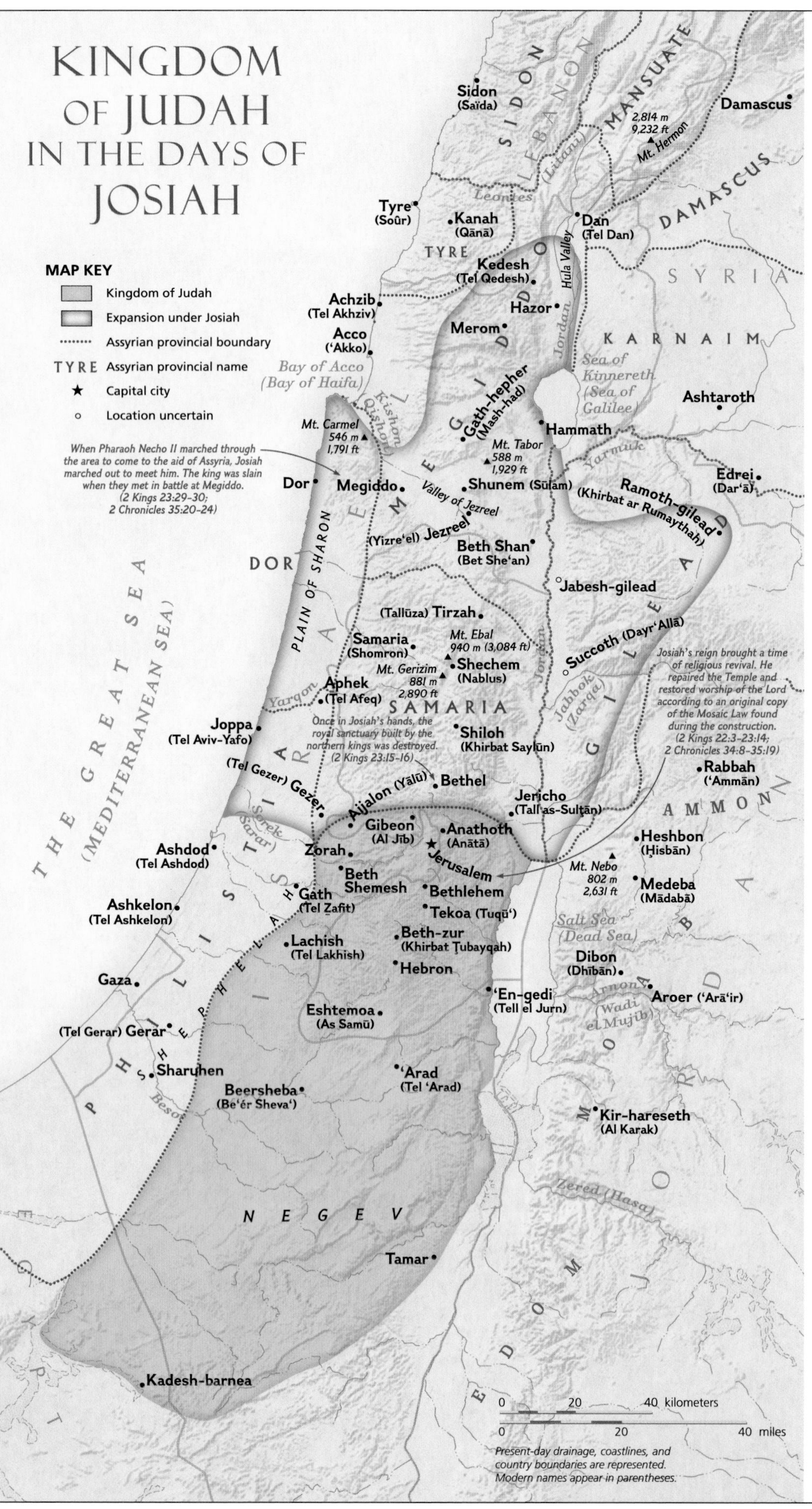
KINGDOM OF JUDAH IN THE DAYS OF JOSIAH
MAP KEY
Kingdom of Judah
Expansion under Josiah
Assyrian provincial boundary
TYRE Assyrian provincial name
Capital city
Location uncertain
When Pharaoh Necho II marched through the area to come to the aid of Assyria, Josiah marched out to meet him. The king was slain when they met in battle at Megiddo. (2 Kings 23:29-30; 2 Chronicles 35:20-24)
Once in Josiah's hands, the royal sanctuary built by the northern kings was destroyed. (2 Kings 23:15-16)
Josiah's reign brought a time of religious revival. He repaired the Temple and restored worship of the Lord according to an original copy of the Mosaic Law found during the construction. (2 Kings 22:3-23:14; 2 Chronicles 34:8-35:19)
Sidon (Saïda)
SIDON
LEBANON
MANSUATE
Damascus
2,814 m 9,232 ft
Mt. Hermon
(Litani)
Leontes
DAMASCUS
Tyre (Soûr)
Kanah (Qānā)
Dan (Tel Dan)
TYRE
Kedesh (Tel Qedesh)
Hula Valley
SYRIA
Achzib (Tel Akhziv)
Hazor
Acco ('Akko)
Merom
KARNAIM
Bay of Acco (Bay of Haifa)
Jordan
Sea of Kinnereth (Sea of Galilee)
Kishon (Qishon)
Gath-hepher (Mash-had)
Ashtaroth
Mt. Carmel 546 m 1,791 ft
Hammath
Mt. Tabor 588 m 1,929 ft
Yarmuk
MEGIDDO
Dor
Megiddo
Shunem (Sūlam)
Valley of Jezreel
Ramoth-gilead (Khirbat ar Rumaythah)
Edrei (Dar'ā)
(Yizre'el) Jezreel
Beth Shan (Bet She'an)
DOR
PLAIN OF SHARON
Jabesh-gilead
THE GREAT SEA (MEDITERRANEAN SEA)
(Tallūza) Tirzah
Mt. Ebal 940 m (3,084 ft)
Samaria (Shomron)
Succoth (Dayr 'Allā)
Shechem (Nablus)
Mt. Gerizim 881 m 2,890 ft
Aphek (Tel Afeq)
Yarqon
SAMARIA
GILEAD
Jabbok (Zarqa)
Joppa (Tel Aviv-Yafo)
Shiloh (Khirbat Saylūn)
(Tel Gezer) Gezer
Aijalon (Yālū)
Bethel
Rabbah ('Ammān)
Jericho (Tall as-Sulṭān)
AMMON
Sorek (Sarar)
Gibeon (Al Jīb)
Anathoth (Anātā)
Ashdod (Tel Ashdod)
Zorah
Jerusalem
Heshbon (Ḥisbān)
Mt. Nebo 802 m 2,631 ft
Beth Shemesh
Medeba (Mādabā)
Ashkelon (Tel Ashkelon)
Gath (Tel Ẕafit)
Bethlehem
Tekoa (Tuqū')
Salt Sea (Dead Sea)
Lachish (Tel Lakhish)
Beth-zur (Khirbat Ṭubayqah)
Hebron
Dibon (Dhībān)
Gaza
SHEPHELAH
PHILISTIA
En-gedi (Tell el Jurn)
Arnon (Wadi el Mujib)
Aroer ('Arā'ir)
MOAB
Eshtemoa (As Samū)
(Tel Gerar) Gerar
Sharuhen
'Arad (Tel 'Arad)
Beersheba (Be'ér Sheva')
Besor
Kir-hareseth (Al Karak)
Zered (Hasa)
NEGEV
EGYPT
Tamar
EDOM
Kadesh-barnea
0 20 40 kilometers
0 20 40 miles
Present-day drainage, coastlines, and country boundaries are represented. Modern names appear in parentheses.

and the sandy coast, and the Negev territories were transferred to Philistia.

The warnings of the eighth-century prophets were ignored by Hezekiah's successor, Manasseh (687–642 B.C.E.), who during his long reign encouraged a return to idolatry and the restoration of "high places," where local deities could be worshipped. Child sacrifice was performed in the Valley of Hinnom. According to II Kings' Deuteronomistic authors, it was this long period of "abominable practices" that would ultimately doom Judah as well as the city of Jerusalem.

Restoration of Josiah

BEFORE THIS phenomenon comes about, however, King Josiah (640–609 B.C.E.) initiated a thorough restoration of the exclusive worship of YHWH. This era of reform coincided with the death of Assyria's King Ashurbanipal in 627 B.C.E., which prompted many vassal states in the Assyrian realm to initiate a rebellion. Josiah joined the revolt as well, hoping to expand his territory and perhaps realize the elusive dream of restoring the former kingdom of David and Solomon. The crumbling Assyrian Empire was unable to resist, and the rebellion met with considerable success. Josiah's forces were able to

AN ANCIENT CANAL

Pharaoh Necho II (Neco in the Bible, 610–595 B.C.E.) of Egypt's 26th dynasty used the tribute levied on Judah and other vassal states to embark on a number of construction projects, including a forerunner of the Suez Canal. This navigable link between the Mediterranean and the Red Sea was accomplished by digging a canal from the Pelusiac branch of the Nile through Wadi el Tumilat (near the frontier city of Pelusium) to the Bitter Lakes, and from there to the Red Sea. A city named Per-Temu-Tjeku was built to guard the waterway and to serve as a storage facility.

steadily extend the kingdom of Judah into the realm of the Assyrian provinces in the north, which previously had comprised the Northern Kingdom.

In 622 B.C.E., the high priest Hilkiah reported to Josiah that he had come across an ancient scroll in the Temple that contained "the book of the law" (II Kings 22:8). Many scholars believe it may have been a version of our Book of Deuteronomy. Josiah and his priests were amazed at the detail and complexity of the Mosaic law and realized how far the people had strayed from the old ways of their forefathers. The king thereupon resolved that the record of Jewish history, and the full scope of the Covenant Law, needed to be revived and codified. Thus began what experts believe was the first attempt to compile the Bible, by drawing together the many (and often conflicting) fragments of oral and written history into a comprehensive set of books.

First and foremost, this probably included an early redacted version of the Torah, based on three separate sources: the J strand, the oldest Pentateuch tradition, which refers to God as YHWH and probably originated in the tenth century during the reign of either David or Solomon; the E text, which refers to God as Elohim and is usually dated to the period of the divided monarchy; and the D source, which is primarily found in the Book of Deuteronomy and may be the book discovered by the high priest Hilkiah. The Pentateuch was later expanded during or after the Babylonian Exile with another source, described by scholars as the P or Priestly source, which emphasizes the priestly role in the communication between the people and God.

In addition, scholars believe, Josiah's scribes redacted what we have referred to as the Deuteronomistic History, the Books of Joshua, Judges, Samuel, and

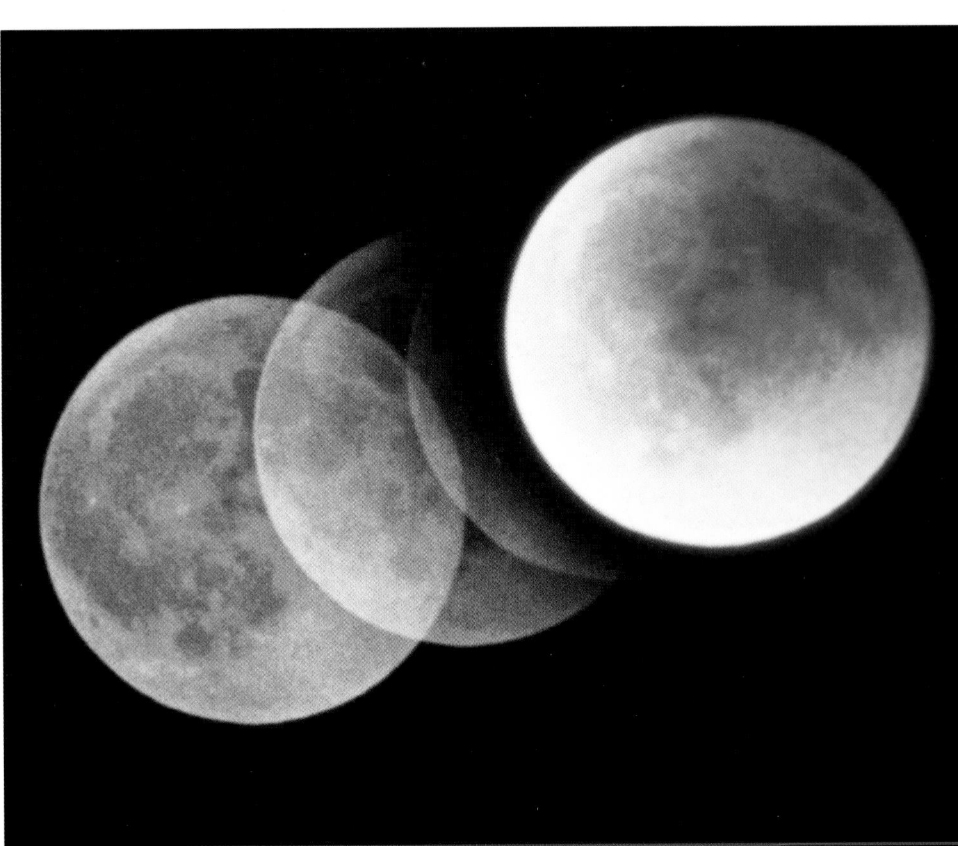

ASSYRIAN ASTRONOMY

Modern astronomers have been able to contribute to the dating of the successive dynasties of the Assyrian Empire by studying the recordings made by Assyrian astrologers of solar eclipses. Computer models show that three solar eclipses could have been observed from the heartland of Assyria (around the capital cities of Ashur and Nineveh): one in 832 B.C.E. (during the reign of Shalmaneser III), another one in 763 B.C.E. (coinciding with the reign of Ashur-dan III), and a last one in 585 B.C.E., just after the capture of Jerusalem by King Nebuchadnezzar.

To observers in Assyria, a solar eclipse was often considered a portent of major events. The library of the Assyrian scholar-king Ashurbanipal also contained a number of tablets with observations of stars and planets for the purpose of divining the future health of the king and the country's prosperity.

Based on their observations of the moon, Babylonian astronomers developed a lunar calendar that was adopted by most civilizations in the Near East. Their records of comets, eclipses, and other celestial observations were studied by Greek and Roman scholars and continued to influence scientists well into the Middle Ages. So pervasive was the pursuit of astronomy and astrology that when King Sargon II (722–705 B.C.E.) built his new palace complex at Dur Sharrukin, a short distance northeast of Nineveh, he ordered a spiral staircase to be built to the roof for celestial observation. Assyrian astronomers may have discovered that Earth is a sphere, since the Greek scientist Pythagoras, who studied at Babylon, also propagated this view.

Astronomers in Babylon studied and recorded many astral events, including comets, solar eclipses, and lunar eclipses, like the one shown.

Kings, greatly influenced by the theme of Deuteronomy: Namely, that the welfare of the nation depends on people's observance of the Covenant, and that all kings of Israel's history should be judged accordingly. The ambition of Josiah to restore the great Davidic realm may have influenced the redactors of this history as well.

Josiah also initiated a thorough purge of the "high places" and other areas of polytheistic worship. The Bible describes how he destroys the shrine of Bethel in Samaria, now under Judah's control, and every other cultic center "from Geba to Beer-sheba"(II Kings 23:8). When the king finally pronounces his realm cleansed of alien gods, he arranges for a great national feast, a Passover celebration in Jerusalem, for "[n]o such passover had been kept since the days of the Judges" (II Kings 23:22).

Josiah further decrees that all of Israel should live in full compliance with the Laws, including the practice of circumcision and all the laws of purity, sacrifice, and worship.

The king's reign coincides with the first biblical appearance of the Prophet Jeremiah, the son of a priest from the village of Anathoth, some three miles north of Jerusalem. Like other prophets before him, Jeremiah often speaks in oracles that reportedly reveal the word of God. He supports Josiah's campaign against idolatry, but remains suspicious of the king's political ambitions. As the kingdom returns to prosperity, Jeremiah heaps scorn on those hoarding riches at the expense of others, as Micah and Isaiah had done before him, and castigates those who "amass wealth unjustly; in mid-life it will leave them, and at their end they will prove to be fools" (Jeremiah 17:10-11). The prophet pours forth his visions in poems and sayings recorded by his faithful scribe, Baruch. "I the Lord test the mind and search the heart," reads one of Jeremiah's verses, "to give to all according to their ways, according to the fruit of their doings."

Rise of Neo-Babylonia

In 612 B.C.E., the kingdoms of the Medes and the Babylonians, former vassals of Assyria, sacked Assyria's capital city, Nineveh, an event that figures prominently in the oracles of the Prophet Nahum, who says that the city "is like a pool whose waters run away" (Nahum 2:8). Fearing widespread chaos, Pharaoh Psamtek I (664–610 B.C.E.) decided to come to the aid of the hard-pressed Assyrian troops. The king's main concern was to guard Egypt's lifeline, the coastal merchant highway that led from the Nile

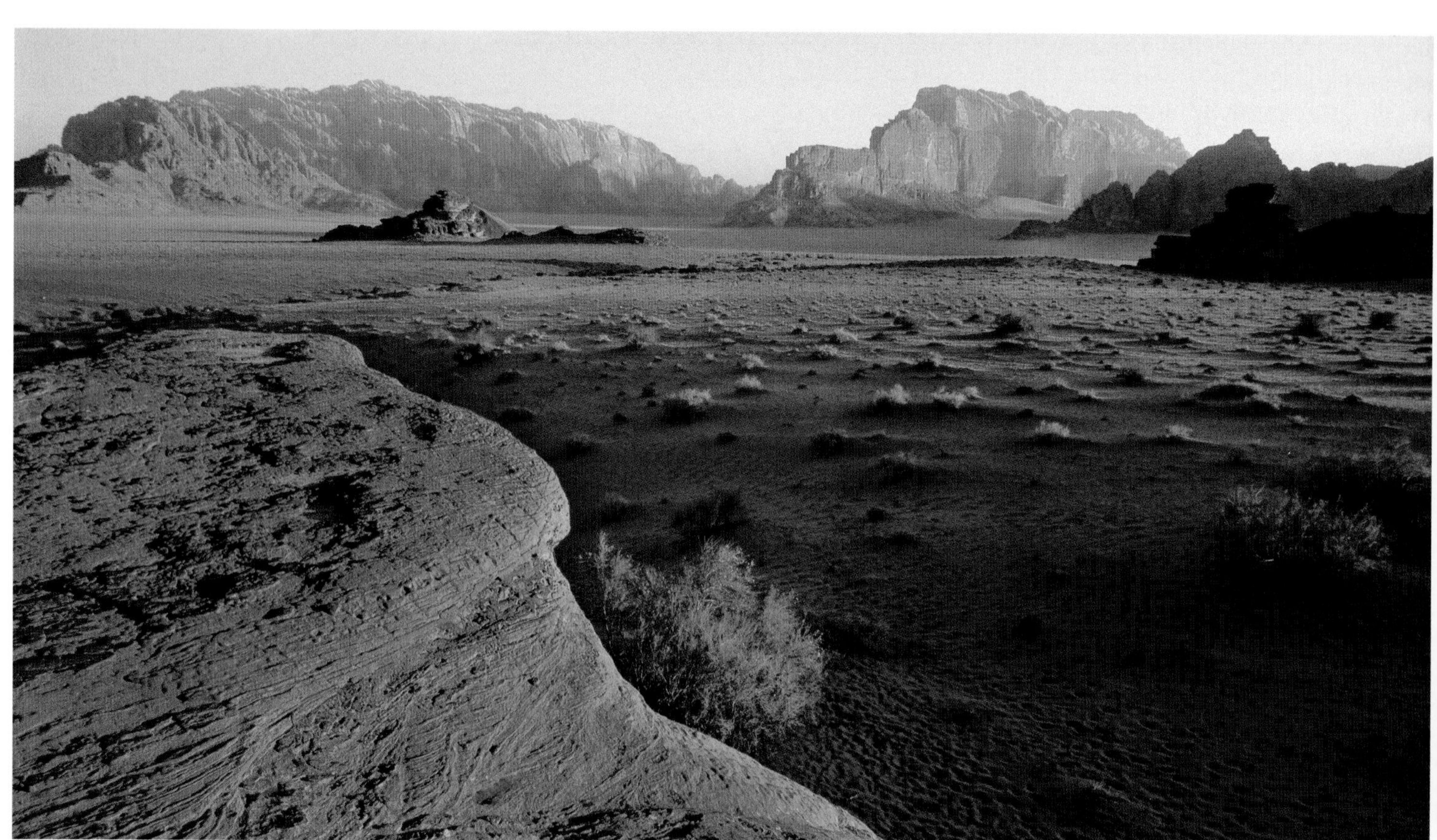

The magnificent desert wasteland of Wadi Rum, in today's Jordan, formed part of Moab in biblical times.

After all this, when Josiah had set the temple in order, King Neco of Egypt went up to fight at Carchemish on the Euphrates, and Josiah went out against him. (II Chronicles 35:20)

River Delta through Philistia to Tyre, Hamath, and Carchemish. It was then that King Josiah made the fateful decision to enter the war on the side of the Medean-Babylonian coalition. He attacked the Egyptian relief forces near the fortress at Megiddo. The Egyptians, however, had far more chariot forces and archers than Josiah expected. A cloud of arrows descended on the attackers, and the king himself was mortally wounded. According to the Bible, he rushes back to Jerusalem in his chariot, where he dies (II Kings 23:29-30).

Josiah's ill-advised attack had dire consequences. The defeat made Judah a vassal state under Egyptian control; Jerusalem had merely exchanged one master for another. The new Egyptian Pharaoh, Necho II (610–595 B.C.E.), made sure that Judah understood who was in charge. When the people of Judah anointed a new king, Josiah's son Jehoahaz, Necho intervened and placed another, more pliable son of Josiah on the throne, named Jehoiakim (609–598 B.C.E.), who ruled as Egypt's puppet king.

In 605 B.C.E., the Medean-Babylonian coalition defeated the Assyrian and Egyptian armies at Carchemish, in one of the pivotal battles in the ancient Near East's history. The region's center of power now shifted from Ashur to Babylon. The Babylonian king, Nebuchadnezzar (604–562 B.C.E.), vowed that a new, Neo-Babylonian Empire would rise from the ashes of the former Assyrian dominions. He called all the ruling kings of the region to a summit, including Josiah's successor Jehoiakim, and forced them to accept a heavy annual tribute.

This gold crown, embellished with rosettes, was found in an Assyrian tomb under the royal palace of Nimrud.

The Bible tells us that Jehoiakim chafes under the new Babylonian yoke, however. Jehoiakim begins talking of an anti-Babylonian alliance, and sends emissaries to neighboring states, including Moab, Tyre, Sidon, and Edom. The Prophet Jeremiah tries to dissuade Jehoiakim from this disastrous course of action, and is incensed when Jehoiakim allows a return of pagan worship, including sacrifice to Baal and Moloch. So pervasive were these cults that people even took idols to their graves, as demonstrated by the contents of a woman's tomb near Bethlehem, dated to the period of Jehoiakim's reign. There, in addition to the usual array of perfume vessels, anklets, and bracelets, archaeologists uncovered the statue of a woman supporting her breasts—a favored fertility symbol at the time.

In the biblical account, Jeremiah warns that God's revenge will be swift and merciless, just as Isaiah had before him. This time, God will use the new, armed might of Babylon to deliver punishment. Judah's only recourse is to return to the faithful, and exclusive, worship of YHWH before it is too late. "For twenty-three years the word of the Lord has come to me, and I have spoken persistently to you," Jeremiah cries, "but you have not listened" (Jeremiah 25:3). If Judah does not change, the Lord will send for "Nebuchadnezzar of Babylon, [his] servant," and "bring [the Babylonians] against this land and its inhabitants, and against all these nations around, [and] ... utterly destroy them." "This whole land," Jeremiah adds, "shall become a ruin and a waste, and these nations shall serve the king of Babylon seventy years" (Jeremiah 25:9-11).

Jeremiah's dire prophecy eventually came to pass in 598 B.C.E., after Jehoiakim had been succeeded by his son, Jehoiachin, and Nebuchadnezzar had embarked on a punitive campaign. A tablet of baked clay, found near the palace in Babylon, tells us that "in the seventh year, in the month of Kislimu [winter 598 B.C.E.], the king of Akkad [Nebuchadnezzar] mustered his troops, marched to the Hatti-land [Syria-Canaan] and encamped against the city of Judah [Jerusalem]."

Jehoiachin was terrified by the appearance of the Babylonian archers, chariots, and siege towers in front of his city. Before matters deteriorated, he capitulated. Jehoiachin was arrested and shipped off to Babylon, along with most of Jerusalem's nobles. Judah was once again burdened with a crushing tribute. Jehoiakim's uncle Zedekiah was put on the throne, to rule at Nebuchadnezzar's behest.

But no sooner had Nebuchadnezzar turned his back than Jerusalem was once again abuzz with rumors of revolt.

HANGING GARDENS OF BABYLON

No ancient structure has so captured the popular imagination as the palace complex of Babylon with its famous Hanging Gardens. According to ancient tradition, the wondrous gardens were built at the order of the Neo-Babylonian King Nebuchadnezzar II specifically to surpass the legendary palaces of his Assyrian predecessors in Nineveh and Ashur.

This vast palace complex featured five courtyards leading to the royal harem, the king's residence, and a magnificent throne room adorned with cedar beams, glazed-brick walls, and decorations of silver and gold. Nearby was a "royal museum," which included precious objects looted from vassal states throughout the Fertile Crescent. The gardens were reportedly built on an elevated terrace covered with soil and planted with every imaginable tree and plant species from the Babylonian Empire. An elaborate system of mechanical pumps, dams, and irrigation pipes ensured that the botanical complex was sprinkled constantly with water from the Euphrates.

Nebuchadnezzar, according to legend, ordered the construction of the gardens to please one of his favorite wives, Amytis, the daughter of the king of the Medes who longed for the lush forests of her native Iran. Ancient writers do not agree on the exact layout of the gardens; some (like the Greek historian Diodoros) claimed the artificial park was built on a ziggurat, while the Roman author Quintus suggested that the gardens comprised a large square base, measuring some 1,600 square feet. Regardless of the specifics, the Greek historian Herodotus claimed that the palace was "the most magnificent building ever erected on earth."

German artist Ferdinand Knab (1834–1902) painted a lush and verdant *Hanging Gardens of Babylon* in 1886.

Jeremiah is beside himself. Jews cannot fight the will of the Lord, he explains. The nation should be wise to be content with the terms imposed by the Babylonian overlord.

In 589 B.C.E., just nine years after the Babylonian siege, Zedekiah felt sufficiently emboldened to act. Abetted by the Egyptian Pharaoh Apries (589–570 B.C.E.), Zedekiah openly declared Judah's independence from Babylon. It did not take long for Nebuchadnezzar to respond to this defiance. Within months, he was back at the city gates. The Bible describes how Pharaoh Apries stages a preemptive strike on a Babylonian frontier garrison, which forces Nebuchadnezzar to move south to the Egyptian border (Jeremiah 37:5). Zedekiah is jubilant. Jeremiah, who has counseled the king to surrender, is promptly thrown into prison. But it is only a temporary stay of execution.

The Prophet Jeremiah ponders in this detail of the Sistine Chapel ceiling by Michelangelo Buonarroti (1475–1564).

The Babylonians soundly defeated the Egyptians and quickly traced their steps back to Judah. "In the ninth year of King Zedekiah of Judah," says the Book of Jeremiah, "in the tenth month King Nebuchadnezzar of Babylon and all his army came against Jerusalem and besieged it; in the eleventh year of Zedekiah, in the fourth month, on the ninth day of the month, a breach was made in the city" (Jeremiah 39:1-2).

This time, the invaders gave no quarter. Jerusalem and its Temple were systematically razed. Virtually all of its inhabitants were either slaughtered or carried off into captivity. Zedekiah fled only to be captured by a Babylonian patrol and executed.

In the biblical account, Jeremiah, however, is spared. Nebuchadnezzar's informants brief the monarch fully about the prophet's strenuous attempts to restrain Zedekiah. The king orders that Jeremiah be set free. In the meantime, the Jewish captives set out on the long road to the rivers of Babylon.

EGYPT	MESOPOTAMIA	ISRAEL-JUDAH
ca 928 B.C.E. Pharaoh Shoshenq I invades Palestine, and his activities are recorded on reliefs in the Egyptian city of Karnak  ca 830–715 B.C.E. Egyptian cohesion breaks down during the 23rd dynasty, when different royal lines are recognized in various cities ca 609 B.C.E. Pharaoh Necho II leads Egyptian forces against Judah ca 609–605 B.C.E. Egypt dominates the region of Syria-Palestine	ca 950 B.C.E. The Aramaean kingdom emerges in Syria ca 883–859 B.C.E. Like his father and grandfather before him, King Ashurnasirpal II continues to expand the Assyrian Empire. He moves the Assyrian capital from Ashur to Kalhu  ca 823 B.C.E. Assyrian astronomers record the first of three solar eclipses ca 612 B.C.E. A coalition of Medes and Babylonians destroys the Assyrian capital of Nineveh	 ca 853 B.C.E. Israel allies with the kings of Tyre and Damascus and defeats the Assyrians, led by Shalmaneser III, at the Battle of Qarqar ca 721 B.C.E. Samaria, the capital of Israel, falls to the Assyrians led by Sargon II ca 640–609 B.C.E. During the reign of King Josiah in Judah, the Book of the Law is discovered ca 586 B.C.E. The Babylonians destroy Jerusalem and bring end the kingdom of Judah

CHAPTER EIGHT

From Exile to Restoration

WITH THE ADVENT OF THE SIXTH CENTURY B.C.E., the people of Israel entered into a new era. Important segments of Judah's population had been forced into exile in Babylon, and Jerusalem lay defenseless, its walls breached, Solomon's Temple destroyed. Nevertheless, prophets such as Ezekiel and Second Isaiah sustained the people's hope that one day the people of Israel would be restored. Meanwhile, the Babylonian captivity gave new impetus to completing the codification of the Hebrew Scriptures (which later would become known to Christians as the Old Testament), a process that was not finished until the first or second century C.E.

In 553 B.C.E., the mighty Babylonian Empire fell to the King of Persia, Cyrus the Great, who took control over all of Mesopotamia, Syria, Judah, and Egypt. Cyrus allowed the Hebrew exiles to return to their homeland, where soon prominent officials including Ezra and Nehemiah struggled to restore an observant Jewish society. Two hundred years later, a young prince from the house of Macedon, based on mainland Greece, crossed into Asia and forced a decisive battle between East and West. The conquests of Alexander the Great would change the world forever. They also cast Judah under the spell of a new pagan culture known as Hellenism: the civilization of the Hellenes, the people of ancient Greece.

A colossal head of Zeus marks the funerary complex of Antiochus I of Commagene at the sanctuary of Nemrut Dagi, Turkey.

OUT OF EXILE

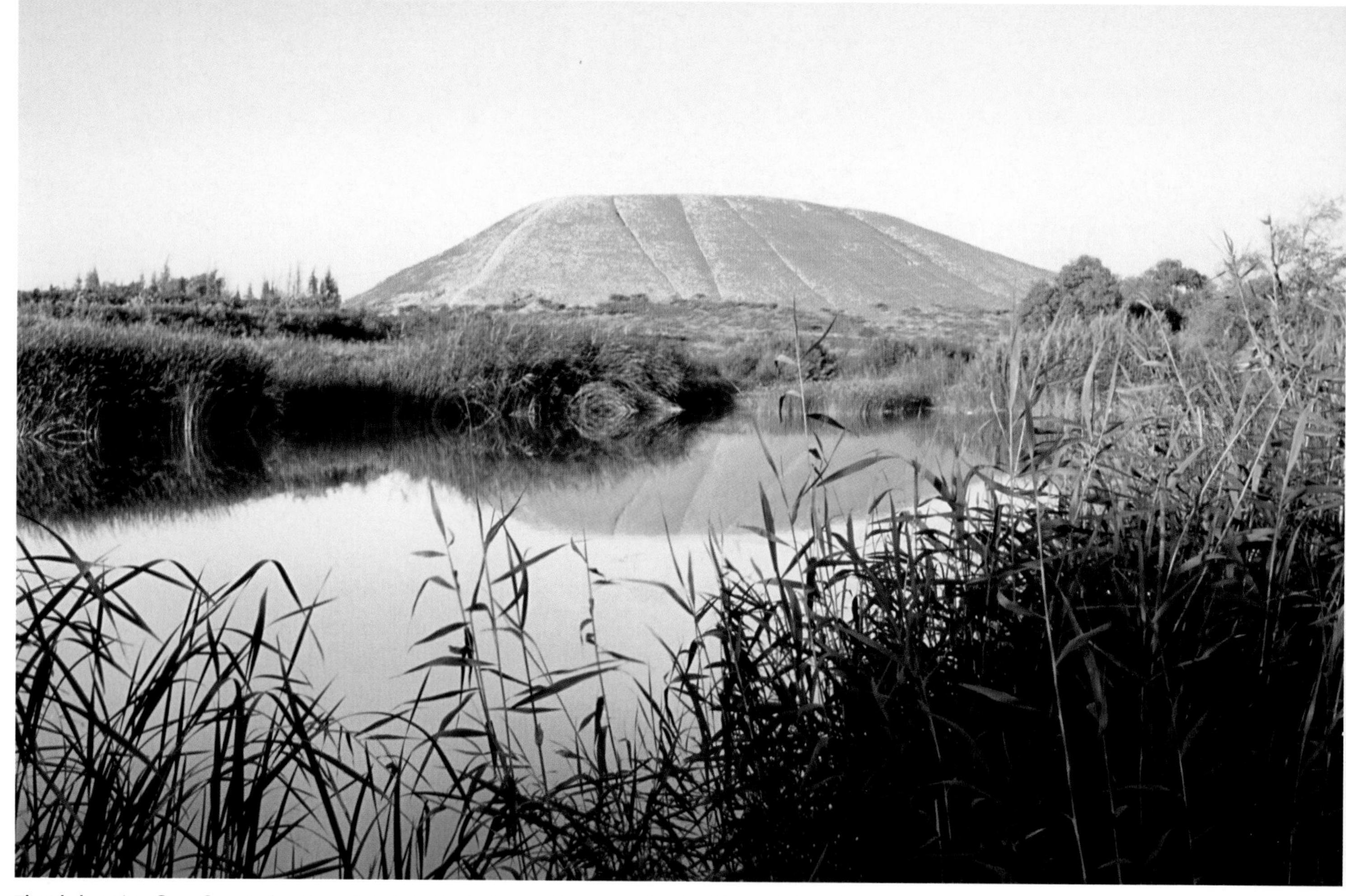

The Khabur River flows from Turkey through Syria to the Euphrates. Some associate it with the Chebar, along which the exiled Israelites settled according to the Bible.

IN A SPAN OF LESS THAN 20 years, Judah suffered four deportations at the hands of Nebuchadnezzar: during the reign of King Jehoiakim in 598 B.C.E., King Jehoiachin in 597, King Zedekiah in 586, and a final exile in 582. Those left behind—farmers and shepherds, and soldiers who had escaped the Babylonian wrath—were governed by a special administration set up in the city of Mizpah, just north of Jerusalem.

In the Bible, the Babylonians install Gedaliah, of the family of Shaphan, to rule as governor of the province of Judah (II Kings 25:22). As various officers and soldiers of the defeated Judean army emerge from hiding, Gedaliah advises them to live peacefully, without thoughts of rebellion. "Do not be afraid of the Chaldean officials," he urges; "live in the land, serve the king of Babylon, and it shall be well with you" (II Kings 25:24). His advice is not heeded. The officers, repelled by Gedaliah's collaborationist policies, assassinate him during his seventh month in office, then flee to Egypt, possibly taking the Prophet Jeremiah with them. According to the Book of Jeremiah, these acts may have prompted a fourth wave of arrests and deportations by the region's Babylonian commander, Nebuzaradan, who sends 745 people into exile (Jeremiah 52:30).

ca 753 B.C.E.
Traditional date for the founding of Rome

ca 687–642 B.C.E.
King Manasseh allows Jews in Judah to worship idols

ca 650 B.C.E.
Greeks ruled by tyrants

ca 553 B.C.E.
Under Cyrus the Great (559–529 B.C.E.), the Achaemenids defeat the Medes and take control of a vast empire

I am the Lord … who says of Cyrus, "He is my shepherd, and he shall carry out all my purpose"; and who says of Jerusalem, "It shall be rebuilt," and of the temple, "Your foundation shall be laid." (Isaiah 44:24-28)

Here the narrative of II Kings ends, and with it the group of books known as the Deuteronomistic History. Like the Northern Kingdom, Judah had been destroyed at the hands of a foreign power. The reason, from the Deuteronomistic point of view, is the neglect of covenant obligations to YHWH. King Manasseh (698–643 B.C.E.) reintroduced the worship of idols, an "evil in the sight of the Lord" that provokes YHWH's anger. The Lord warns in II Kings, "I will wipe Jerusalem as one wipes a dish. … I will cast off the remnant of my heritage, and give them into the hand of their enemies" (II Kings 21:7, 21:13-14). Now this terrible vengeance comes to pass, and Jerusalem lay in ruins. "How lonely sits the city that once was full of people!" cries the Book of Lamentations, a series of poems bemoaning the city's fate; "How like a widow she has become" (Lamentations 1:1-2).

Visions of Ezekiel

MEANWHILE, IN BABYLONIA, refugees arrive. Many find themselves settled alongside the Chebar River, joining the Prophet Ezekiel, who had been forcefully moved there during the first wave of deportations in 598 B.C.E. (Ezekiel 1:1). The Chebar River has alternatively been identified with the Kabar Canal; with the Nahr Malcha, the canal that Nebuchadnezzar ordered dug between the Euphrates and the Tigris; and with the Khabur River, which flows south from Turkey through modern Syria to join the Euphrates at today's Busayrah. Here, in this new land, the Prophet Ezekiel offered succor and spiritual guidance to the grieving exiles.

The Prophet Ezekiel is an enigmatic figure. According to the Bible, he is both priest and prophet: a member of the Temple establishment concerned with outward ritual purity, and a mystic seer focused on man's inner communication with God. As a prophet and "sentinel for the house of Israel" (Ezekiel 3:17), Ezekiel tries to warn Judah of God's pending punishment for its transgressions (Ezekiel 5:7-10). After the destruction of Jerusalem, his message turns to one of hope. Through his ecstatic visions, Ezekiel recognizes that the Covenant nation of YHWH has lost its power as a political entity. If the survivors of Israel and Judah are to continue as a distinct people, they can express themselves as such through religious practice. Ezekiel's prophecy of a valley filled with dry bones resurrected by YHWH's command is a compelling promise that the community of Israel would one day be restored (Ezekiel 37:7-10).

Another prophet, whose name is not known, articulates this same message of hope. He speaks in the name of Isaiah, even though Isaiah died years earlier; scholars refer to him as Second Isaiah or Deutero-Isaiah. His words soothe his people still grieving for their lost homes and land: "Comfort, O comfort my people, says your God." (Isaiah 40:1-2). "Cry out," says the prophet, for God will "feed his flock like a shepherd; he will gather the lambs in his arms, and carry them in his bosom" (Isaiah 40:6-11).

Worship of YHWH gave the exiled peoples a way to preserve their common identity. Unmoored from their homeland, the refugees felt an urgent need to record and propagate Jewish cultic life. This provided a renewed impetus to complete the work begun by King Josiah years earlier: to compile the disparate strands of Jewish history, law, rituals, and dietary customs into one comprehensive set of scripture that would become the

Written in Babylonian cuneiform, the clay, sixth-century B.C.E. Cyrus Cylinder documents Cyrus the Great's conquest of Babylon.

ca 539 B.C.E. Babylon surrenders to the Achaemenids

ca 525–404 B.C.E. Persian kings rule Egypt as the 27th dynasty

ca 515 B.C.E. Jews dedicate new temple in Jerusalem, and the era of Second Temple Judaism begins

ca 508–507 B.C.E. Greeks establish a new, democratic constitution

guidebook for the Jewish nation in exile—the Bible. Scripture would enable the scattered Israelites in Babylon and beyond to celebrate their faith in a consistent and recognizable manner. From this time onward, modern scholars speak of the Hebrew nation as "Jews" (or *Yehudim*, possibly derived from "Judean") and refer to "Judaism" as a distinct community in religious terms, no longer bound to a particular political entity or geographical location.

Cyrus the Great

THE RISE OF A NEW EMPIRE set in motion the prophecies of Ezekiel and Second Isaiah. In 614 B.C.E., Cyaxares (625–585 B.C.E.), King of Media (a territory roughly equivalent to modern Iran), advanced against Babylonia's northern flanks and took control of the adjacent area of Anatolia in modern southeast Turkey. Next, he fought a war of attrition with Lydia, to the northwest of today's Turkey. But Media itself was threatened from within by the ambitions of a vassal state that it all but surrounded, the kingdom of Anshan, also known as Fars or Persia. Anshan had been led from around 700 B.C.E. by rulers who claimed to be descendants of a legendary figure named Achaemenes (later the dynasty would be referred to as the Achaemenid dynasty). In 553, King Cyrus II (559–529 B.C.E.), also known as "Cyrus the Great" rose up against the Medes and defeated them. Cyrus then took control of the vast Median empire, stretching from the Persian Gulf to the Black Sea.

Italian Renaissance artist Raphael (1483–1520) created his version of *The Vision of the Prophet Ezekiel* just two years before his death.

In this great realm, a culture clash seemed inevitable. Media, under King

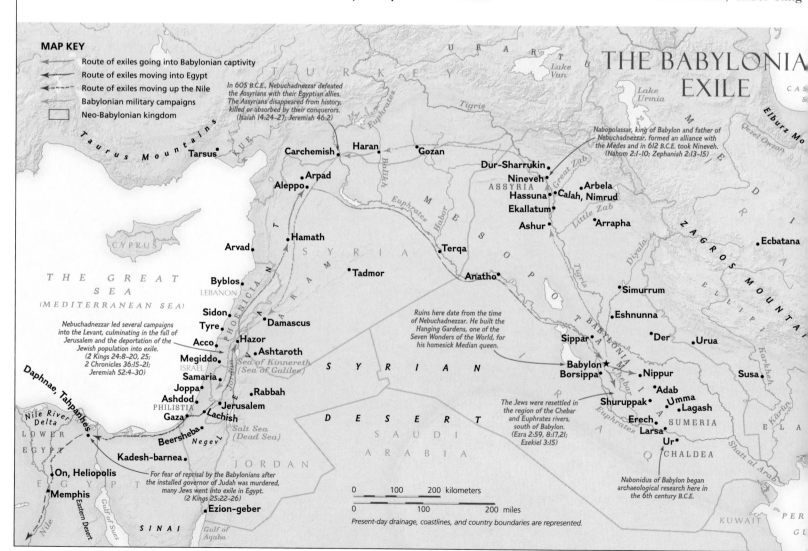

THE BABYLONIAN EXILE

MAP KEY
Route of exiles going into Babylonian captivity
Route of exiles moving into Egypt
Route of exiles moving up the Nile
Babylonian military campaigns
Neo-Babylonian kingdom

In 605 B.C.E. Nebuchadnezzar defeated the Assyrians with their Egyptian allies. The Assyrians disappeared from history, killed or absorbed by their conquerors. (Isaiah 14:24-27; Jeremiah 46:2)

Nabopolassar, king of Babylon and father of Nebuchadnezzar, formed an alliance with the Medes and in 612 B.C.E. took Nineveh. (Nahum 2:1-10; Zephaniah 2:13-15)

Nebuchadnezzar led several campaigns into the Levant, culminating in the fall of Jerusalem and the deportation of the Jewish population into exile. (2 Kings 24:8-20, 25; 2 Chronicles 36:15-21; Jeremiah 52:4-30)

Ruins here date from the time of Nebuchadnezzar. He built the Hanging Gardens, one of the Seven Wonders of the World, for his homesick Median queen.

The Jews were resettled in the region of the Chebar and Euphrates rivers, south of Babylon. (Ezra 2:59, 8:17,21; Ezekiel 3:15)

For fear of reprisal by the Babylonians after the installed governor of Judah was murdered, many Jews went into exile in Egypt. (2 Kings 25:22-26)

Nabonidus of Babylon began archaeological research here in the 6th century B.C.E.

0 100 200 kilometers
0 100 200 miles
Present-day drainage, coastlines, and country boundaries are represented.

THUS SPAKE ZARATHUSTRA

JUDAISM WAS FAR REMOVED FROM traditional Mesopotamian religion, but it had more in common with a new doctrine that originated in the kingdom of the Medes, a nation later absorbed into Persia by Cyrus the Great. This new faith was espoused by a legendary priest named Zarathustra (Zoroaster). Like Moses before him, Zarathustra preached that there was but one God—a Lord of Heaven and Light named Ahura Mazda, or Wise Lord, who ruled supreme over every being—and that life on earth is essentially a struggle between good and evil. To please the Wise Lord, Zoroaster said, one must be honest, ethical, and compassionate; to defy such virtues is to cater to the Devil (Ahriman). Zoroaster also preached that, at the end of time, a new savior named Saoshyans would come to raise the dead, preside over a Last Judgment, and herald eternal life. Little is known about Zarathustra himself. Followers considered him half human and half divine, his birth the result of a shaft of light from God that struck and impregnated a young virgin who lived quietly in the country. After Zarathustra spent a lifetime preaching, he left this earth in a flash of lightning that sent him straight into paradise.

Zarathustra's teachings were compiled in a collection of sayings known as the Avesta. Of this once massive 12,000-page work, only one book, the Vendidad, and a few other fragments have survived.

Zoroastrianism exerted considerable influence on the new Persian Empire, including Jewish scholars in Babylon and Judea, just as the canon of the Jewish Bible was being developed. In espousing ideas such as an afterlife, in which doers of good are rewarded and evil men are punished, Zoroastrianism planted the seeds for the concept of immortality in later Judaism and in Christianity.

A four-winged guardian figure, inscribed with "I, Cyrus the Achaemenid, King," was found in the ruins of Cyrus's palace in Pasargadae, Iran.

Astyages, had become a religious center for a new and fervent monotheism called Zoroastrianism, whereas the court of King Croesus of Lydia was known for its Hellenistic tendencies, even offering sanctuary to Greek exiles. Yet Cyrus was not like other Mesopotamian leaders. He gave strict instructions to allow each occupied people to worship freely, believing that religious observance can be a powerful stabilizing force regardless of political circumstance.

Cyrus next mobilized against the Babylonian Empire, ruled by a king named Nabonidus (ca 556–539 B.C.E.), a monarch more interested in antiquities than politics. A few years into his reign, he allowed his son, Bel-shar-usur, to rule with him as co-regent (ca 553–540 B.C.E.). This person is arguably the "Belshazzar" of the Book of Daniel, which describes the visions of a Hebrew exile at the court in Babylon. Because these prophetic visions reveal various looming crises for Judah in centuries to come, the book is often referred to as an apocalyptic work (from the Greek word *apokalypsis*, meaning "revelation"). Although the Book of Daniel is set in the sixth century B.C.E., scholars believe that it was completed in the second century B.C.E., for the text also refers to events that occurred during the reign of Antiochus IV Epiphanes (175–164 B.C.E.).

According to the Book of Daniel, Belshazzar holds a great feast, served on vessels looted from Solomon's Temple in Jerusalem by Nebuchadnezzar. As Belshazzar, his concubines, and other guests begin to celebrate, "the fingers of a human hand appeared and began writing" on the ornate wall of the banquet hall: "mene, mene, tekel, and parsin" (Daniel 5:5, 5:25). None of the stricken revelers could decipher the text, but Belshazzar's queen suggests that they summon Daniel, who was educated at the Babylonian court. Daniel interprets the words, explaining that "*mene*, God has numbered the days of your kingdom and brought it to an end; *tekel*, you have been weighed on the scales and found wanting; *peres*, your kingdom is divided and given to the Medes and Persians" (Daniel 5:26). The text is Aramaic; on the wall, it would have appeared as *mn*, *'tql*, *prs*. Daniel's prediction is fulfilled. The Bible text says that Belshazzar is assassinated that same evening (Daniel 5:30), although Persian

Detail from the palace at Persepolis highlighting the garb of the Persian Royal Guard. The two Persians wear cylindrical hats and the Mede, the rounded one.

Detail from the palace at Persepolis showing officials from Media ascending the stairs to the Council Hall to offer their tribute to the Persians.

Detail from the Audience Hall of Darius I at Persepolis showing two Babylonians, wearing peaked hats, bringing a Zebu in tribute.

Detail from the palace at Persepolis showing Lydians bearing gifts (vases and textiles) to the Persians as tribute. This relief dates to the time of the Achaemenids.

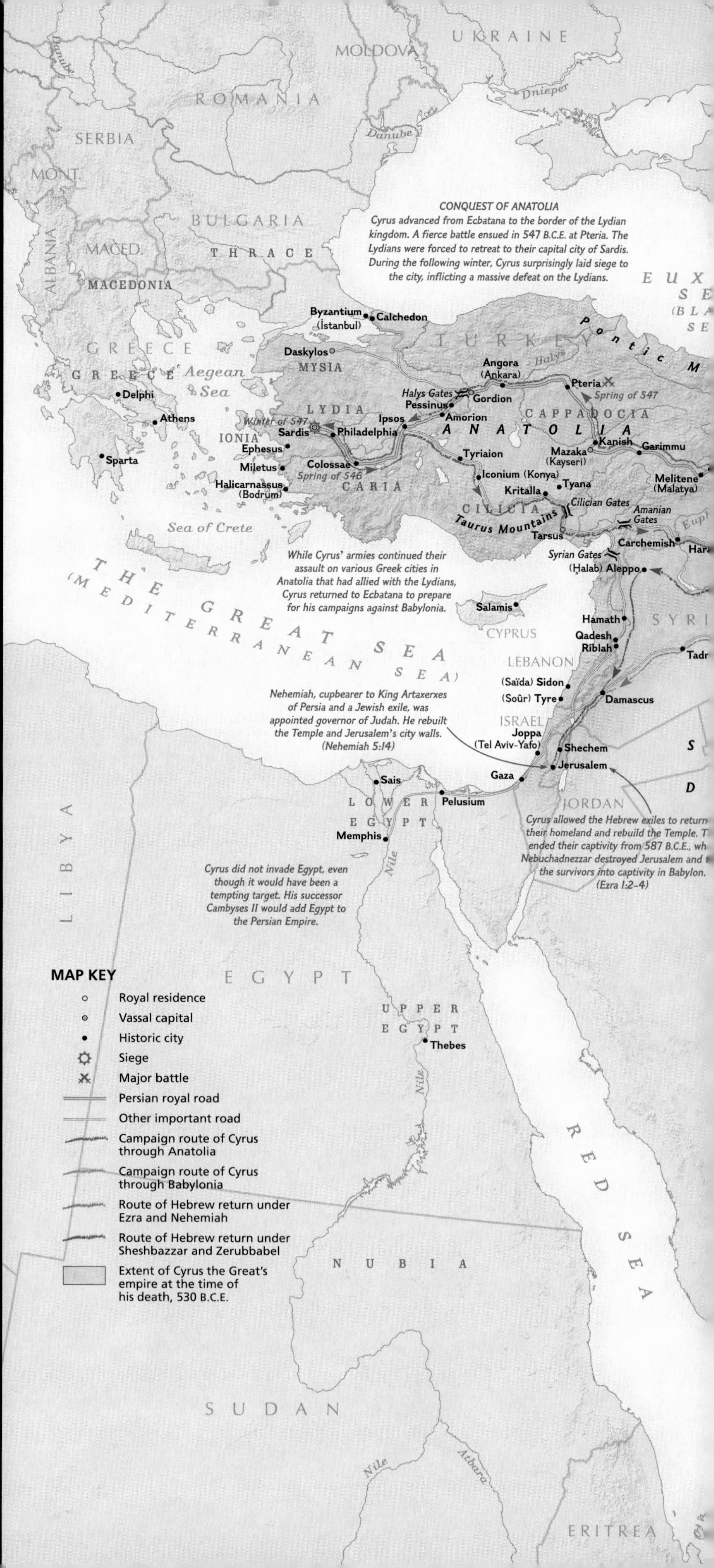

CONQUEST OF ANATOLIA

Cyrus advanced from Ecbatana to the border of the Lydian kingdom. A fierce battle ensued in 547 B.C.E. at Pteria. The Lydians were forced to retreat to their capital city of Sardis. During the following winter, Cyrus surprisingly laid siege to the city, inflicting a massive defeat on the Lydians.

While Cyrus' armies continued their assault on various Greek cities in Anatolia that had allied with the Lydians, Cyrus returned to Ecbatana to prepare for his campaigns against Babylonia.

Nehemiah, cupbearer to King Artaxerxes of Persia and a Jewish exile, was appointed governor of Judah. He rebuilt the Temple and Jerusalem's city walls. (Nehemiah 5:14)

Cyrus allowed the Hebrew exiles to return their homeland and rebuild the Temple. T ended their captivity from 587 B.C.E., wh Nebuchadnezzar destroyed Jerusalem and the survivors into captivity in Babylon. (Ezra 1:2–4)

Cyrus did not invade Egypt, even though it would have been a tempting target. His successor Cambyses II would add Egypt to the Persian Empire.

UKRAINE · MOLDOVA · ROMANIA · SERBIA · MONT. · BULGARIA · ALBANIA · MACED. · THRACE · MACEDONIA · GREECE · TURKEY · MYSIA · LYDIA · IONIA · CARIA · CAPPADOCIA · ANATOLIA · CILICIA · Taurus Mountains · Aegean Sea · Sea of Crete · THE GREAT SEA (MEDITERRANEAN SEA) · EUXINE SEA (BLACK SEA) · Pontic Mountains · CYPRUS · LEBANON · ISRAEL · JORDAN · SYRIA · LIBYA · LOWER EGYPT · EGYPT · UPPER EGYPT · NUBIA · SUDAN · ERITREA · RED SEA

Danube · Dnieper · Halys · Nile · Atbara · Euphrates

Byzantium (İstanbul) · Calchedon · Daskylos · Angora (Ankara) · Pteria · Spring of 547 · Halys Gates · Gordion · Pessinus · Amorion · Ipsos · Winter of 547 · Sardis · Philadelphia · Ephesus · Miletus · Colossae · Spring of 546 · Halicarnassus (Bodrum) · Delphi · Athens · Sparta · Tyriaion · Iconium (Konya) · Mazaka (Kayseri) · Kanish · Garimmu · Melitene (Malatya) · Kritalla · Tyana · Cilician Gates · Amanian Gates · Tarsus · Carchemish · Syrian Gates · (Halab) Aleppo · Salamis · Hamath · Qadesh · Riblah · Tadmor · (Saïda) Sidon · (Soûr) Tyre · Damascus · Joppa (Tel Aviv-Yafo) · Shechem · Jerusalem · Gaza · Sais · Pelusium · Memphis · Thebes

MAP KEY

- Royal residence
- Vassal capital
- Historic city
- Siege
- Major battle
- Persian royal road
- Other important road
- Campaign route of Cyrus through Anatolia
- Campaign route of Cyrus through Babylonia
- Route of Hebrew return under Ezra and Nehemiah
- Route of Hebrew return under Sheshbazzar and Zerubbabel
- Extent of Cyrus the Great's empire at the time of his death, 530 B.C.E.

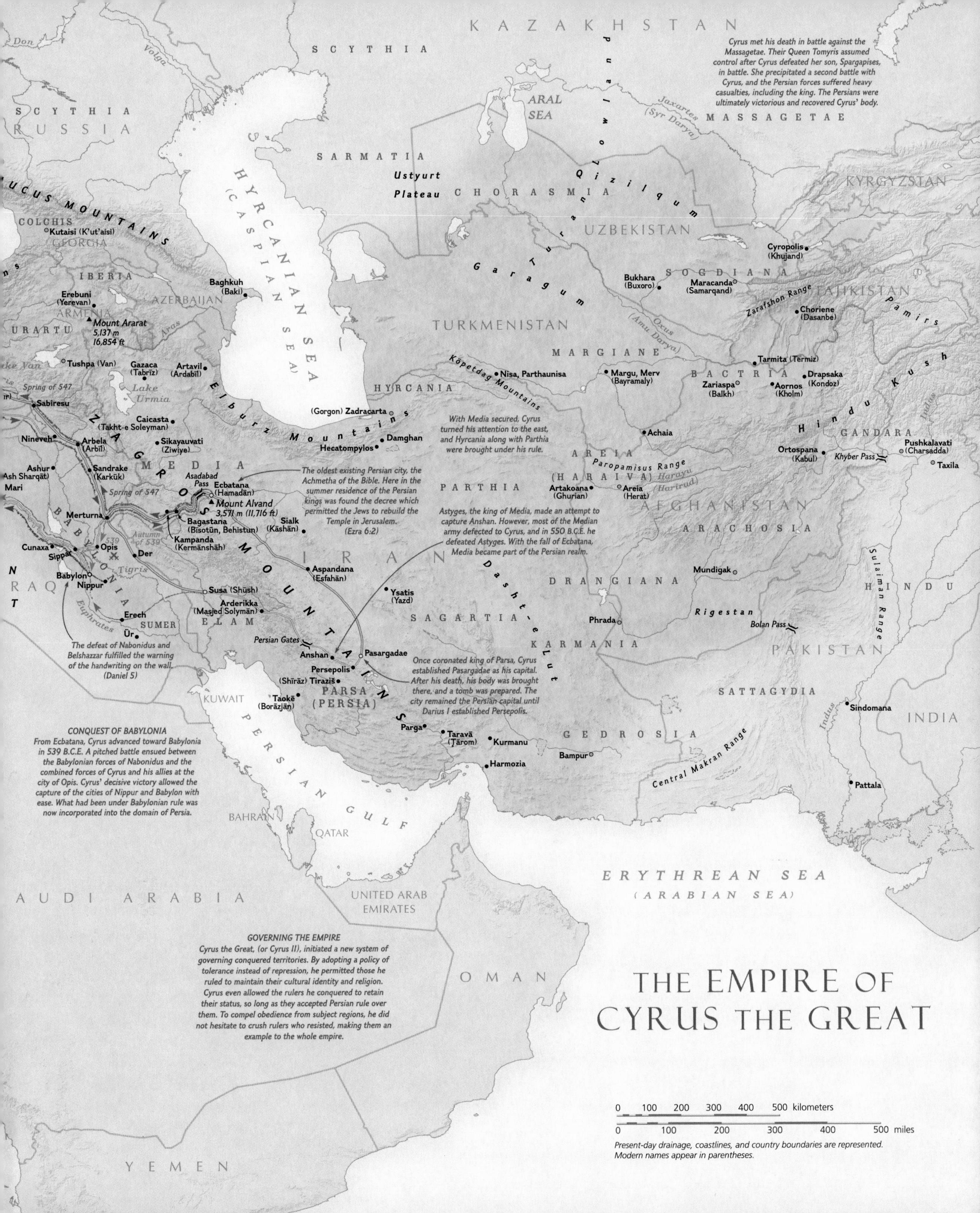

THE EMPIRE OF CYRUS THE GREAT
Cyrus met his death in battle against the Massagetae. Their Queen Tomyris assumed control after Cyrus defeated her son, Spargapises, in battle. She precipitated a second battle with Cyrus, and the Persian forces suffered heavy casualties, including the king. The Persians were ultimately victorious and recovered Cyrus' body.
With Media secured, Cyrus turned his attention to the east, and Hyrcania along with Parthia were brought under his rule.
The oldest existing Persian city, the Achmetha of the Bible. Here in the summer residence of the Persian kings was found the decree which permitted the Jews to rebuild the Temple in Jerusalem. (Ezra 6:2)
Astyges, the king of Media, made an attempt to capture Anshan. However, most of the Median army defected to Cyrus, and in 550 B.C.E. he defeated Astyges. With the fall of Ecbatana, Media became part of the Persian realm.
Once coronated king of Parsa, Cyrus established Pasargadae as his capital. After his death, his body was brought there, and a tomb was prepared. The city remained the Persian capital until Darius I established Persepolis.
The defeat of Nabonidus and Belshazzar fulfilled the warning of the handwriting on the wall. (Daniel 5)
CONQUEST OF BABYLONIA
From Ecbatana, Cyrus advanced toward Babylonia in 539 B.C.E. A pitched battle ensued between the Babylonian forces of Nabonidus and the combined forces of Cyrus and his allies at the city of Opis. Cyrus' decisive victory allowed the capture of the cities of Nippur and Babylon with ease. What had been under Babylonian rule was now incorporated into the domain of Persia.
GOVERNING THE EMPIRE
Cyrus the Great, (or Cyrus II), initiated a new system of governing conquered territories. By adopting a policy of tolerance instead of repression, he permitted those he ruled to maintain their cultural identity and religion. Cyrus even allowed the rulers he conquered to retain their status, so long as they accepted Persian rule over them. To compel obedience from subject regions, he did not hesitate to crush rulers who resisted, making them an example to the whole empire.
0 100 200 300 400 500 kilometers
0 100 200 300 400 500 miles
Present-day drainage, coastlines, and country boundaries are represented. Modern names appear in parentheses.
KAZAKHSTAN
SCYTHIA
SCYTHIA
RUSSIA
Don
Volga
ARAL SEA
Jaxartes (Syr Darya)
MASSAGETAE
Qizilqum
Turan Lowland
SARMATIA
Ustyurt Plateau
CHORASMIA
HYRCANIAN SEA (CASPIAN SEA)
CAUCUS MOUNTAINS
COLCHIS
Kutaisi (K'ut'aisi)
GEORGIA
KYRGYZSTAN
UZBEKISTAN
Cyropolis (Khujand)
IBERIA
Baghkuh (Baki)
Garagum
Bukhara (Buxoro)
SOGDIANA
Maracanda (Samarqand)
Zarafshon Range
TAJIKISTAN
Pamirs
Choriene (Dasanbe)
Erebuni (Yerevan)
ARMENIA
AZERBAIJAN
Mount Ararat 5,137 m 16,854 ft
URARTU
Aras
TURKMENISTAN
Oxus (Amu Darya)
MARGIANE
Tushpa (Van)
Lake Van
Gazaca (Tabrīz)
Artavil (Ardabīl)
Köpetdag Mountains
Nisa, Parthaunisa
Margu, Merv (Bayramaly)
BACTRIA
Tarmita (Termiz)
Drapsaka (Kondoz)
Zariaspa (Balkh)
Aornos (Kholm)
Hindu Kush
Indus
Lake Urmia
Spring of 547
Sabiresu
Elburz Mountains
HYRCANIA
(Gorgon) Zadracarta
Caicasta (Takht-e Soleyman)
Sikayauvati (Ziwiye)
Damghan
Hecatompylos
Achaia
GANDARA
Pushkalavati (Charsadda)
Ortospana (Kabul)
Khyber Pass
Taxila
Nineveh
Arbela (Arbīl)
ZAGROS MOUNTAINS
Ashur (Ash Sharqāt)
Mari
Sandrake (Karkūk)
MEDIA
Asadabad Pass
Ecbatana (Hamadān)
Mount Alvand 3,571 m (11,716 ft)
AREIA (HARAIVA)
Paropamisus Range
Harayu (Harirud)
Artakoana (Ghurian)
Areia (Herat)
PARTHIA
AFGHANISTAN
ARACHOSIA
Merturna
Bagastana (Bīsotūn, Behistun)
Kampanda (Kermānshāh)
Sialk (Kāshān)
Spring of 547
539
Autumn of 539
BABYLONIA
Cunaxa
Sippar
Opis
Der
Tigris
IRAN
Aspandana (Esfahān)
Mundigak
Sulaiman Range
HINDU
IRAQ
Babylon
Nippur
Susa (Shūsh)
Ysatis (Yazd)
DRANGIANA
Dasht-e Lut
Euphrates
Erech
Arderikka (Masjed Solymān)
ELAM
SUMER
Ur
SAGARTIA
Phrada
Rigestan
Bolan Pass
Persian Gates
Anshan
Pasargadae
KARMANIA
PAKISTAN
Persepolis
(Shīrāz) Tirazīš
PARSA (PERSIA)
Taokē (Borāzjān)
KUWAIT
SATTAGYDIA
Sindomana
INDIA
Parga
Taravā (Ţārom)
Kurmanu
Harmozia
GEDROSIA
Bampur
Central Makran Range
Pattala
PERSIAN GULF
BAHRAIN
QATAR
ERYTHREAN SEA (ARABIAN SEA)
SAUDI ARABIA
UNITED ARAB EMIRATES
OMAN
YEMEN

records indicate that Bel-shar-usur lived to defend Babylon after Cyrus launched his offensive.

As the Persian troops led by Cyrus massed on the border in 540 B.C.E., Nabonidus rushed back to reassert his authority. He went so far as to cancel the annual Babylonian New Year's feast, for which he incurred the wrath of the priesthood. By October 539 B.C.E., Cyrus reached the city of Babylon itself.

According to the Verse Account of Nabonidus, a Babylonian tablet recovered in 1924, the citizens of Babylon just opened the city gates to the Persian conquerors. Cyrus's own chronicle, a clay cylinder in the Babylonian tradition, gives credit to Marduk, the Babylonian god, for his victory. This account betrays his shrewd use of claiming divine patronage to legitimize his conquests, a practice also reflected in the biblical account. According to Second Isaiah, the Hebrew exiles anoint him as the "servant of YHWH" (Isaiah 44:21), just as Cyrus will be honored as the "chosen one" of Marduk in Babylon, and his grandson Darius will soon be welcomed in Egypt as the new "son of Ra." In the Book of Ezra, Cyrus specifically credits YHWH for his success, just as he had recognized Marduk in Babylonia: "The Lord, the God of heaven, has given me all the kingdoms of the earth" (Ezra 1:2).

The Return to Judah

CYRUS MIGHT HAVE understood that an occupied people would instinctively transfer their collective aspirations to the national cult. In order for these cults to flourish, they required religious leadership and a central place of worship. Unfortunately, as far as Judah was concerned, the religious elite of Israel lived along the banks of the rivers of Babylon; here were the scribes, the priests, and the scholars, busy finishing the Deuteronomistic History of Israel and the final composition of the Pentateuch. Cyrus's decision to release the exiles in Babylon and sanction a reconstruction of the Temple (Ezra 1:2) was therefore a calculated political move. According to the text of the Cyrus Cylinder the Persian king also returned of the "gods of Sumer and Akkad" and willingly paid for the "repair of their dwelling places."

The exiles were free to return to their homeland. The first caravans duly set out, although many Jews chose to remain in Babylon. According to Flavius Josephus, the first-century C.E. Jewish historian, the Jewish expatriates were "unwilling to leave their possessions." These expatriate communities remained faithful to the Covenant Law and the worship of YHWH and would in the coming centuries develop into important centers for the study of Jewish law.

The Bible does not say how the exiles returned to Judah. One possibility was a 600-mile route that led straight through the Syrian Desert via Tadmor and Damascus, though it was fraught with danger. More likely, however, the Hebrew caravans followed the trade routes that ran along the Euphrates River to the city of Aleppo before turning southward to Qatna, Riblah, Damascus, and ultimately Jerusalem—a 1,000-mile journey.

Some scholars infer from the Book of Ezra that the exiles were accompanied by a "prince of Judah" named Sheshbazzar, possibly a descendant of King Jehoiachin and therefore a member of the house of David. The Persians installed him as governor of Judah, now known as the subprovince of Yehud, part of the fifth Persian satrapy known as 'Abar nahara ("beyond the [Euphrates] River"). Ruling from Mizpah, Sheshbazzar settled the incoming exiles and repatriated the sacred silver treasure taken from the Temple by Nebuchadnezzar (Ezra 5:13-16). He also laid the foundations for a new Temple in

I returned to (the) sacred cities on the other side of the Tigris, the sanctuaries which have been ruins for a long time, the images which (used) to live therein, and established for them permanent sanctuaries.

Cyrus the Great, from the Cyrus Cylinder

MEASURE OF A MAN

Ezra relates how the priests financed the rebuilding of the Temple in Jerusalem with the "grant that they had from King Cyrus of Persia" (Ezra 3:7). In fact, the Persians were the first to introduce a common currency of coins in their empire. Ezra tells us that the priests raised "sixty-one thousand darics of gold" and "five thousand minas of silver" for the restoration. Originally called the Babylonian shekel (equal to two Greek drachmas), the daric was a gold coin of 8.4 grams. This eighth-century B.C.E. weight, cast in the form of a lion, was equal to twice the value of a mina, weighing two pounds, four ounces. The words *mene, tekel,* and *parsin,* which Daniel deciphered on the wall of Belshazzar's banquet hall, are actually units of measure equivalent to the mina, shekel, and half-mina.

A sixth-century B.C.E. clay seal depicts a priest praying before the symbols of Marduk, the chief god of Babylon, and Nabu, the god of wisdom and writing.

Jerusalem. Sheshbazzar's actual domain, however, was much smaller than the former kingdom of Judah. Yehud was now bordered to the north by the tribal boundary just north of Bethel, to the east by the Jordan River (including Jericho), and to the south by a frontier that ran well short of Hebron, depriving the subprovince of Israel's ancient patriarchal city.

According to the Book of Ezra, another of Jehoiachin's alleged grandsons, Zerubbabel, replaces Sheshbazzar (although some scholars believe that they may be the same person). Despite delays and conflicts, notably involving the Samaritans upset by their exclusion from the Second Temple's construction, Zerubbabel continued rebuilding the sanctuary with the financial support of the new Persian king, Darius I (522–486 B.C.E.). But about 20 years after the first exiles' return, the Temple still remained incomplete, provoking the ire of the Prophet Haggai, whose book probably originated during the early years of King Darius's reign. Pointing to poor harvests and drought as signs of the Lord's wrath, the prophet asks, "Is it a time for you yourselves to live in your paneled houses, while this house lies in ruins?" (Haggai 1:4). Dating to the same period, the Book of Zechariah also presses for the Temple's completion. In mystical visions reminiscent of Daniel, Zechariah sees great turmoil ahead, but also the return of a glorious Jewish kingdom. "I will return to Zion," says the Lord in Zechariah; "Jerusalem shall be called the faithful city" (Zechariah 8:3). Under pressure from the prophets, the Temple was finally completed. In 515 or 516 B.C.E., the people of Yehud were finally able to dedicate the new Temple in Jerusalem, beginning the era of Second Temple Judaism (ca 515 B.C.E.–C.E. 70).

Archers, possibly members of the Persian Guard of the Immortals, march on this wall of molded enameled brick from Darius's palace at Susa from around 510 B.C.E.

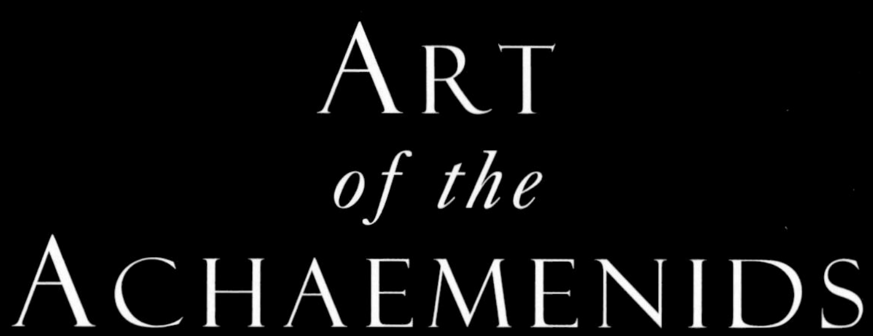

Art *of the* Achaemenids

Gold plaque depicting a priest in Median costume

Handle of a vessel in the shape of a winged ibex

To show its might, the Achaemenid dynasty of Persia built palaces at Pasargadae, Persepolis, and Susa, which today have yielded a wealth of archaeological treasures, including life-size bas-relief sculptures, which purposely aimed to surpass their Assyrian predecessors. Skilled craftsmen of this dynasty also exhibited a virtuosity with precious metals, especially gold and silver. Drinking cups were typically fashioned in the shape of animals—such as the mythological winged lion that is the hallmark of Achaemenid rule. Many of the objects on this page are from the Oxus treasure, a collection of 170 objects from the fifth and fourth centuries B.C.E., now in the British Museum in London.

Gold rhyton or drinking cup in the shape of a lion

Silver bowl with gold inlay, decorated with archers

Top of a staff with lion heads of gold and lapis lazuli

Gold jug with lion-headed handle

Gold bracelet with terminals in the form of griffins

The Persians' might would last until Alexander the Great defeated Darius III (shown above in a mosaic from the House of the Faun in Pompei) in 333 B.C.E.

Ezra and Nehemiah

THE RESTORATION OF JUDAISM in Judah, however, was not without challenge. In the intervening decades, ancestral homes were seized by Assyrian homesteaders or by those who had escaped deportation. The returning refugees had become invaders themselves.

During this period, two prophets figure prominently in restoring full observance of the Covenant Law: Ezra and Nehemiah. The chronology of their activity is a matter of debate. Although the Bible suggests that Ezra came first, scholars believe that Nehemiah preceded him.

According to the Bible, Ezra (active ca 458–428 B.C.E.) is a highly educated scholar and priest who had originally stayed in Babylon as a religious "ambassador at large." He is shocked to learn that, despite the resumption of sacrifice at the Temple, few people in Yehud actually embrace the Mosaic laws. Many of the recent arrivals from Babylonia have married existing settlers, some of whom are not Jews at all. The postexilic land of Yehud threatens to become a melting pot in which the Jewish character might slowly dissolve.

Artaxerxes I (465–425 B.C.E.), the ruling Persian monarch, authorized Ezra's voyage to Jerusalem, also permitting him to return any Temple treasure still held by the Babylonians. The king could have been motivated by revolts in Egypt, first in 488 and then in 461 B.C.E., which made Yehud's stability a matter of strategic importance. The Book of Ezra quotes the king's mandate: "Artaxerxes, king of kings, to the priest Ezra ... Peace. ... For you are sent by the king ... to make inquiries about Judah and Jerusalem according to the law of your God" (Ezra 7:11-14). The Bible describes how, upon arriving in Jerusalem (ca 458 B.C.E.), Ezra orders the Jewish men to "separate yourselves from the peoples of the land and from the foreign wives" (Ezra 10:11). He imposes strict observance of the Mosaic laws and urges obeisance of the priesthood in all matters.

Nehemiah (active ca 445–420[?] B.C.E.), referred to as the "cupbearer of Artaxerxes," also receives permission to enforce priestly rule and observance of the Covenant Law in Yehud. His message also emphasizes the importance of compassion under God's rule. After a famine reduces most of the poor to virtual serfs, who had pledged their land to acquire grain, Nemehiah urges nobles and officials to "stop this taking of interest.

Restore to them, this very day, their fields [and] their vineyards" (Nehemiah 5:10-11). He also supervises the reconstruction of the city walls, a defensive move prompted by unfriendly governors in Samaria and Ammon, who do not welcome a resurgence of Jerusalem's power.

Yehud was now, for all practical purposes, governed by the religious elite of the priesthood. A Jewish theocracy with authority rooted in the sacrificial system of the restored Temple had replaced the ideal of a Davidic monarchy. This idea of the cult system's absorbing and replacing the need for a Jewish political identity would become the dominant theme of the Second Temple period. Ezra and Nehemiah succeeded in preserving Judaism and restoring the worship of YHWH in Jerusalem, but a new powerful threat loomed ahead in the future.

THE EMERGENCE OF ARAMAIC

The idea to rebuild the Temple in Jerusalem led to opposition from non-Jewish settlers in Judea, who wrote to Ahasuerus, or Xerxes I (486–465 B.C.E.). This letter, Ezra specifically notes, was written in Aramaic (Ezra 4:7) and thus had to be translated for Xerxes. Aramaic, the language of the Aramaeans, had originated in Mesopotamia, and shares roots with Semitic languages such as Hebrew. It was already in use in the Assyrian Empire in the eighth century B.C.E., gradually replacing the ancient Akkadian language. In the sixth century B.C.E., the Achaemenid conquerors of Babylonia deliberately chose Aramaic as the new lingua franca of their realm. Aramaic then began to replace Hebrew as the language of Judea.

THE COMPLETION OF THE BIBLE

DURING THE EXILE AND RESTORATION, priestly scribes continued the task of editing and harmonizing the different traditions related to Covenant Law and the history of Israel into a comprehensive set of books—an effort that produced the Hebrew Bible or the Christian Old Testament. Their sources included various oral traditions, documented in scrolls, that contained the stories of the Five Books of Moses, known as the Pentateuch: Genesis, Exodus, Leviticus, Numbers, and Deuteronomy. Then there were the scrolls of Judges, Samuel, and Kings, and the rich tradition of Psalms, which bear the imprint of the sixth century and may have been collated and edited during the Exile proper.

Following extensive research in the 19th and 20th centuries, scholars have been able to tentatively identify the predominant strains of the Pentateuch tradition. The oldest strain is identified by its author, referred to as J (after the German name for Yahweh, spelled Jahveh). J is primarily focused on the role of God (YHWH) as the principal force behind Israel's destiny, and emphasizes the Davidic dynasty and the Messianic tradition as Israel's ultimate source of redemption.

The second oldest strain, usually dated to the period of the divided monarchy, is what scholars refer to as E, based on the author's reference to God as El or Elohim (the Lord). E most likely worked in the Northern Kingdom and therefore did not share J's faith in the Davidic monarchy. Rather, E focuses on the role of the prophets, particularly Moses, and the power of the Covenant.

The D author or authors worked primarily on the Book of Deuteronomy and perhaps the book discovered by the high priest Hilkiah. Their priority is the codification and integrity of ritual worship and sacrifice at the Temple in Jerusalem.

The Pentateuch was later expanded during or after the Babylonian Exile with another source, described by scholars as the P or Priestly source, which emphasizes the priestly role in the communication between the people and God. P is concerned with the practical application of the Mosaic law in everyday life, particularly the laws of purity. The P author is also less concerned with narrative style and drama, which are the superb qualities of the E and J authors.

In addition, scholars believe, King Josiah's scribes redacted what we refer to as the Deuteronomistic History (the Books of Joshua, Judges, Samuel, and Kings), greatly influenced by the theme of Deuteronomy: The welfare of the nation depends on people's observance of the Covenant, and that all kings of Israel's history should be judged accordingly.

Seventh-century B.C.E. silver scroll from Ketef Hinnom containing the "Priestly Blessing," one of the earliest fragments of biblical text found.

THE LEGACY OF ALEXANDER

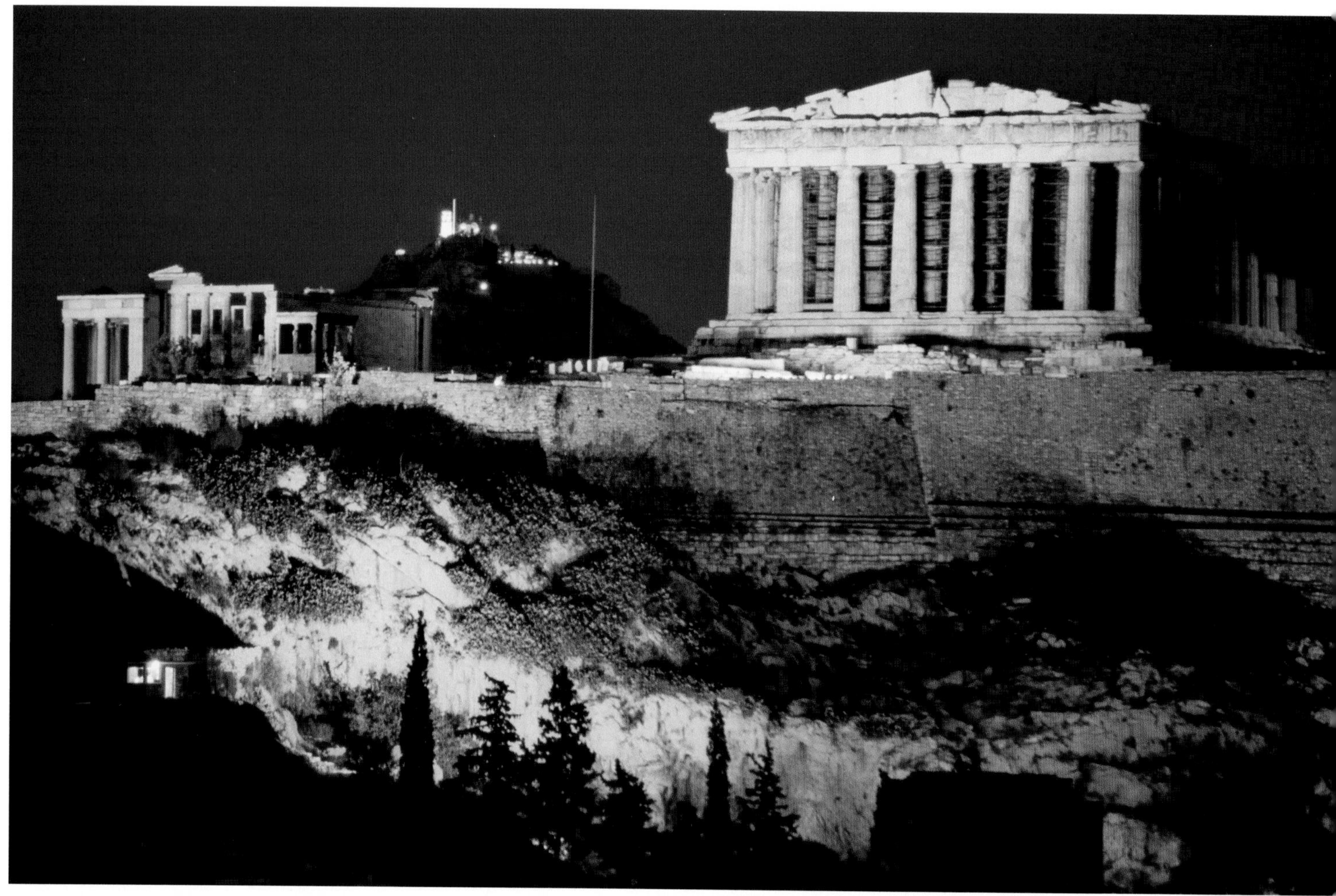

Rising over modern Athens, Greece, the Acropolis is crowned by the Parthenon, a temple dedicated to the goddess Pallas Athena and built in the fifth century B.C.E.

FOR SEVERAL CENTURIES, Greece and Persia had eyed each other warily across the Aegean Sea. Though the separate Greek city-states were often embroiled in civil war, they came together as one when the Persian king Darius I appeared on the shores of the Aegean Sea. They succeeded in rebuffing Darius at the Battle of Marathon in 490 B.C.E., but the clash between the two cultures continued unabated.

Xerxes I, son of Darius, tried again and succeeded in sacking Athens in 480 B.C.E., only to be defeated by a superior Greek naval fleet later that year. Several years later, the Persian Artaxerxes I, distracted by an Egyptian uprising, signed the Persian-Greek Peace Treaty of Callias in 449 B.C.E., which suspended hostilities but did not end the mutual mistrust. Both Greece and Persia were still contesting economic control of the eastern Mediterranean Basin, including the largely Hellenic territory of Asia Minor, which was experiencing explosive growth at the time.

Meanwhile, Greece's culture—its architecture, theater, literature, philosophy, and political concepts such as democracy (literally, "rule of the people")—continued to make its way into the Persian realm. There was not a single Persian soldier who could stop it.

ca 490 B.C.E.
The Greeks defeat invading Persian forces at the Battle of Marathon

ca 480 B.C.E.
During the Second Persian War, Xerxes defeats the Greeks at Thermopylae and destroys Athens

ca 338 B.C.E.
Philip II of Macedon, and his son Alexander, establish Macedonian control over the Greek world

ca 333 B.C.E.
Alexander defeats Darius III, the Persian king, at the Battle of Issus. Two years later, the Persian Empire falls

After Alexander son of Philip, the Macedonian, ... defeated King Darius of the Persians and the Medes, he succeeded him as king ... He fought many battles, conquered strongholds, ... advanced to the ends of the earth, and plundered many nations. (I Maccabees 1:1-3)

Judah was no exception. Hellenistic culture made its way into Yehud through Phoenicia, whose cultural and economic influence both stretched along the Mediterranean coast and across much of Galilee. Throughout this region, pottery with Greek-themed decoration began to appear. The themes, often showing semiclad or nude demigods at sport or in drunken revelry, must have shocked the devout Jews of the region. They remained faithful to the Mosaic edict against "graven images" and would not have approved of these depictions of the human form.

Thus, the seeds for the inevitable conflict between Judaism and Greek paganism had already been sown well before a young and able warrior named Alexander, son of Philip, appeared on the scene. The city of Athens may have shaped Greek thought and culture, but it would be Alexander who would introduce it to the lands of the Middle East.

Alexander the Great

ALEXANDER'S FATHER, Philip II of Macedon (382–336 B.C.E.), had wanted to defeat the Persians with the help of a united Greek army. He achieved the first part of this goal when he conquered Greece's divided city-states in 338 B.C.E. The second half of his dream would not be realized, for an assassin's knife would take Philip's life just two years later. After Philip's death in 336 B.C.E., his 20-year-old son, Alexander, would become king and ruler of Macedonia.

What motivated young Alexander (336–323 B.C.E.) to strive for military glory and fame has never been convincingly articulated. The Greek historian Plutarch, writing in the late first century C.E., credits Alexander's divine parentage as the origin for his ambitions; he reports that Alexander's father was not King Philip, but in truth the Greek supreme god Zeus. Some scholars believe that Alexander's ambitions were nurtured by his mother, Olympias, a native of Epirus, a region located east of Macedonia on the northwestern coast of the Aegean Sea.

Dating to ca 460 B.C.E., this Greek mixing bowl (krater) depicts Heracles, the Argonauts, and other heroes of Greek myths and legends.

In a declaration of war against Persia, Alexander took his army of about 40,000 soldiers and crossed the Hellespont in 334 B.C.E. With the help of his flying cavalry, as well as stout phalanxes of Macedonian hoplites (heavy infantry), Alexander dealt a crushing defeat to the army of King Darius III at the Battle of Issus in 333 B.C.E. Alexander then proceeded to advance deep into the Persian realm, claiming Persian lands and booty for himself and his troops.

One by one, Syria, Phoenicia, Judah, and Egypt were added to the territory of the young Macedonian warrior. Tyre, Gaza, and later, Samaria, offered meaningful resistance, but they too soon became part of his empire. Then Alexander's army turned to the east, capturing the great Mesopotamian cities of Babylon, Susa, and Persepolis before reaching the Upper Indus River Valley. Many cities that had been founded by Greek colonists centuries earlier welcomed Alexander as a liberator. As he moved farther east into territories thousands of miles from his home, Alexander remembered to seek and earn the loyalty of the local peoples. He would worship at their local shrines to win them over to his side.

The young king Alexander championed Hellenism and founded many

ca 323 B.C.E.
Alexander dies, and his successors fight for dominance. The Hellenistic period begins

ca 302 B.C.E.
Mithradates I founds the kingdom of Pontus

ca 301 B.C.E.
Ptolemy I defeats Antigonus and establishes the Ptolemaic dynasty in Egypt and Palestine

ca 285–246 B.C.E.
During the reign of Ptolemy II, the Hebrew Bible is translated into Greek

COIN OF THE REALM

THE CONCEPT OF A MINTED COIN, PART OF an official currency system, was developed in Lydia (western Turkey) in the seventh century B.C.E., but coinage would truly flourish as part of the Greek civilization. Greek coins in the so-called Archaic period (ca 600–480 B.C.E.) were small lumps or ingots of silver, which were stamped with the symbol of the issuing community. Gradually, manufacturing systems improved to the point that a coin could be struck, that is impressed, as a small disk of a more or less consistent radius and density. Later coins continued to be identified with regional symbols, although with the growing power of Athens, the owl, symbol of the goddess Athena, became predominant.

The value of the Greek currency was pegged to the drachma, or drachm, which some experts believe was equal to a day's wage. Based on the drachm, many cities issued a silver tetradrachma (four drachmas) coin, or the even larger decadrachma (ten drachmas). As Greek culture and trade spread, the drachma became the currency of choice in international commerce, with many cities along the Ionian coast minting their own drachmas. From the third century on, particularly in Ptolemaic Egypt amd the Seleucid empire, coins were struck not with the symbol of the city but the likeness of the current ruler. This practice has greatly facilitated the ability of archaeologists to date certain strata in excavations, using coins found in a given layer. The idea of stamping the image of the ruling head of state on coins persists to this day.

This fourth-century B.C.E. Athenian silver tetradrachm (meaning "four drachmas") coin bears an owl, symbol of Athena, goddess of wisdom.

cities based on the Greek model. Chief among them was Alexandria, founded in Egypt on the Mediterranean coast in 331 B.C.E. It became a cosmopolitan learning center for centuries. Thousands of Greeks came to seek their fortunes and became merchants and administrators. As they relocated to new cities, they spread Hellenistic thought and culture throughout the Mediterranean Basin and into western Asia.

Alexander did not live long to enjoy his empire. Some ten years after the Battle of Issus, in June 323 B.C.E., Alexander died of a fever, brought on by an ailment that has never been fully identified. His death at age 32 caused chaos within his empire. After his death, a power struggle ensued among his generals. They fought over control of the new Macedonian empire and its conquered territories. Cassander aimed for control of Greece and Macedonia; Ptolemy, one of Alexander's ablest generals, wanted Egypt; Antigonus took control of Asia Minor, while Seleucus was awarded the heartland of Babylon. Few of these generals were content with their allotments, however, and war erupted among them. Between 315 and 312 B.C.E., Antigonus and Seleucus I (312–280 B.C.E.), who had temporarily aligned himself with Ptolemy I, turned Judah into a battlefield.

In 301 B.C.E., Antigonus was vanquished at the Battle of Ipsus. Ptolemy I Soter (301–285 B.C.E.) then established the Ptolemaic dynasty. His kingdom now ranged from Egypt to Phoenicia and Syria, including Judah. Judah would now serve as a buffer zone against any future encroachment by his rivals. He also moved the capital of his new Egyptian empire from Memphis to Alexandria, the city founded by Alexander, in recognition of the key importance of trade in sustaining his kingdom.

Politically, Alexander's empire had fallen apart after his death. But as a cultural entity it remained largely intact. Although Aramaic continued to be spoken, the Greek language (spoken in a

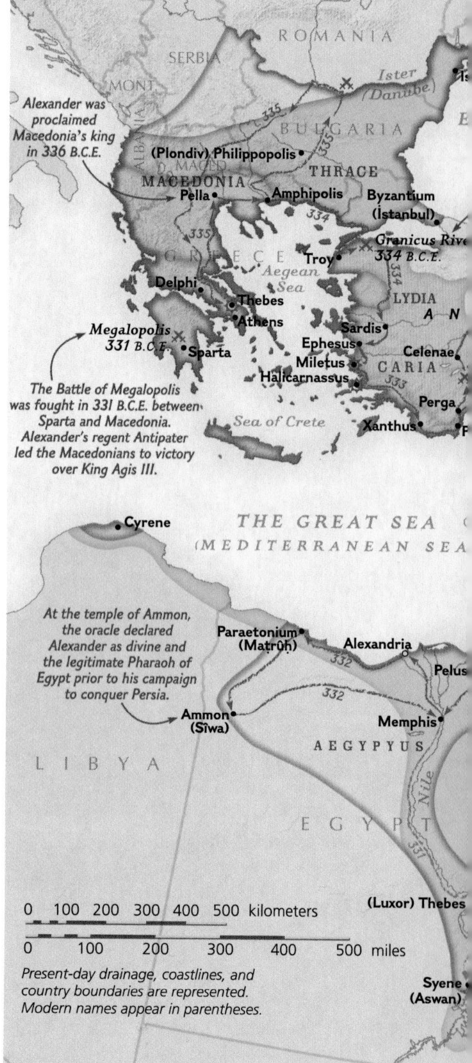

Present-day drainage, coastlines, and country boundaries are represented. Modern names appear in parentheses.

patois known as Koine) now became dominant in the arenas of international trade, politics, and the arts.

New cities sprang up on the Greek model, using the grid pattern developed by Hippodamus of Miletus, with theaters, libraries, temples, and gymnasia, all designed in the Hellenistic style. Greek literature, theater, and philosophy were studied in academic centers throughout the Mediterranean Basin. Literacy rates rose, particularly in coastal areas, as did standards of living.

A currency system was introduced, using coins featuring the Attic owl. Common coins greatly facilitated international trade. This booming trade, in turn, necessitated an expansion of sea routes. New roads needed to be laid as well, while the existing ones were restored and expanded to support the increased economic activity.

All this activity was bound to affect Judah—or Judea, as it became known during the Ptolemaic era. Hellenistic influence was no longer incidental; it became more and more intrusive and, quite literally, the coin of the realm. For the next 300 years, many practicing Jews would try to resist and fight this new cultural imperialism. They would have varying degrees of success, until the arrival of a new and far more brutal imperialism—the reign of the Roman Caesars and their empire.

The Diaspora

NEVERTHELESS, there were many in Judea who welcomed the promise of prosperity and peace in the Alexandrian commonwealth. The Ptolemies actively encouraged a restoration of the region's former agricultural bounty. Since Egypt and Judea were now one political entity, movement between the two realms increased. A number of Jews, eager to participate in and gain from the new regional renaissance, decided to travel and to relocate to Alexandria. There always had been a substantial Jewish community in Egypt,

This portrait of Alexander the Great, created in Alexandria between the second and first centuries B.C.E., presents a youthful, idealized image that became popular after his death.

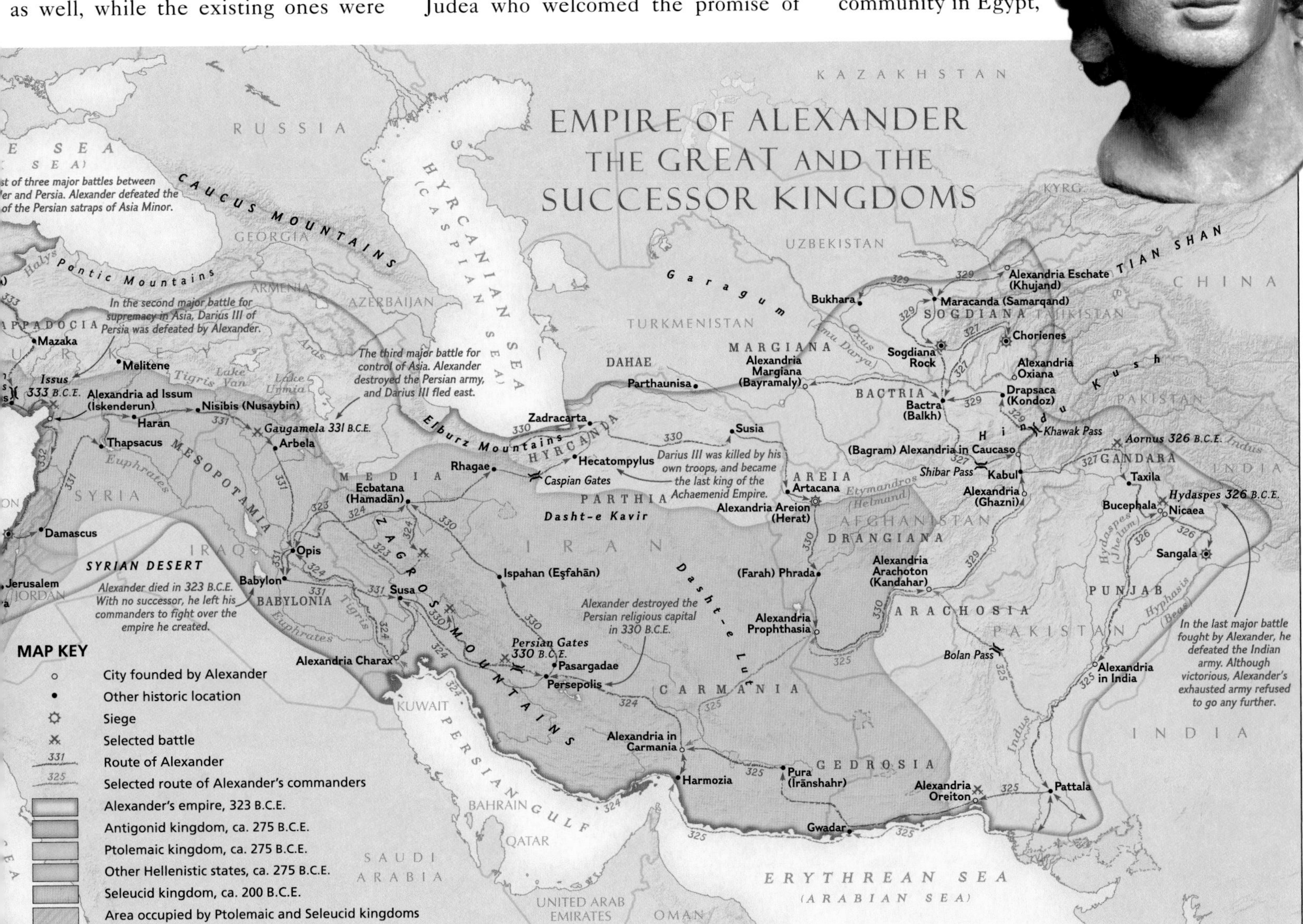

made up of exiles, most of whom had arrived after the destruction of Jerusalem in 586 B.C.E. Egyptian papyri have revealed the existence of a Jewish colony as far south as Aswan.

The Ptolemaic kings lavished such attention on their new capital city that Alexandria became a magnet for Jewish merchants, officials, and scholars, as well as immigrants from throughout the Ptolemaic empire. By the following century, Alexandria had truly become the cultural center of the Middle East, with a university, an astronomical observatory, a zoo, a botanical garden, and, above all, a magnificent library containing more than 400,000 volumes and texts, possibly the greatest concentration of learning in antiquity.

Other Jews—farmers as well as craftsmen—also seized the moment to escape the rural villages of Judea and seek their fortunes among the budding cities of the Ionian coast of western Greece. The Diaspora—an international dispersal of the Jewish community—had begun, a voluntary exile prompted not by war but by economic opportunity.

Created ca 100 B.C.E., this sculpture of two women engaged in conversation reveals the penchant for naturalism in the Hellenistic style.

This Diaspora encountered its share of problems. At nearly every turn, Jewish expatriates were confronted with Hellenistic civilization. However, the resulting tension did lead to stronger adherence to Covenant Law. Exiles continued to observe the laws of circumcision and diet at home, and they honored YHWH by reading the Torah during community assemblies.

The Jewish exiles also began to build small community halls known as synagogues, from the Greek meaning "house of assembly"—or *beit knesset* in Hebrew. Egyptian papyri refer to the construction of a synagogue in the third century B.C.E., but it is possible that such assembly houses had been in use much earlier. Synagogues usually consisted of a rectangular hall, flanked on the long sides by benches, with one end wall facing Jerusalem, where a niche called the ark contained the scrolls of the Torah.

The oldest surviving synagogue, and the only one discovered from the Second Temple period, was found in the northwestern section of the casemate wall surrounding the Herodian mountain redoubt of Masada. This synagogue, built around 31 B.C.E., was capable of holding about 250 people. It was originally divided into two parts by a wall and featured two stone columns supporting the roof. The Zealots, who took over the Masada fortress during the Jewish War (66–74 C.E.), added plastered stone benches, running in four tiers along three sides, facing the wall that held the niche for Torah scrolls. They also built a small attendant's room behind the niche, where excavators found fragments of scrolls containing the Books of Ezekiel and Deuteronomy. The additional discovery of a potsherd inscribed with the phrase *me'aser kohen* (priest's tithe) suggests the presence of a priest on site.

A synagogue was not the same as a temple—no sacrifices were

And after Alexander had reigned twelve years, he died. Then his officers began to rule, each in his own place. They all put on crowns after his death, and so did their descendants after them for many years; and they caused many evils on the earth. (I Maccabees 1: 7-9)

performed—but rather it was a pastoral center. It was to be used for readings and commentary on the Torah, as well as other community events.

Language barriers began to present problems in readings of the Torah. The sacred scrolls were written in Hebrew, but both during and after the Babylonian Exile, an Aramaic translation of the Hebrew Scriptures (known as the *Targum*) had begun to circulate as Aramaic became the dominant language of both Babylon and Judah. In the Ptolemaic kingdom, as elsewhere in the ancient world, people tended to speak Greek. By the third century B.C.E., few of the Jewish expatriates themselves could understand the ancient texts read in the synagogue. This lingustic separation was a concern, for despite their cosmopolitanism, many Jews in Alexandria remained steadfastly loyal to the Law and their faith.

Origins of the Septuagint

THE OBVIOUS SOLUTION was to translate the Hebrew Scriptures into Greek, a vast, and therefore expensive, undertaking. According to the Letter of Aristeas, a document probably written in the mid-second century B.C.E., the idea of a Bible written in Greek was first submitted to King Ptolemy II Philadelphus (285–246 B.C.E.), a book devotee himself, by his librarian, Demetrius of Phalerum. Demetrius, who had a talent for soliciting royal grants, argued to his king that "the laws of the Jews are worth transcribing and therefore deserve a place in your library."

Now on the Mediterranean seabed, this colossal head from the Ptolemaic era once belonged to the royal precinct of ancient Alexandria.

King Ptolemy II Philadelphus then remembered there were still many hundreds of Jewish captives languishing in jail—the result of the military campaigns of the preceding decades. Ptolemy II sent an emissary to the high priest Eleazar in Jerusalem to strike a deal. He offered to set the political prisoners free if the high priest sent him 72 learned scholars (6 from each of the original 12 tribes) to complete the translation of the Hebrew Bible. A deal was struck, and in due course, 72 translators were busy at work converting the Hebrew text into Greek. The result was a work that is known as the Septuagint, its name taken from the Latin word meaning "seventy," *septuaginta*.

It is a charming story, but its historical accuracy is troubled by the fact that the Septuagint contains a suspicious amount of Alexandrian dialect. In fact, most modern historians believe that scribes in Alexandria did most of the translation, with the imprimatur of Jerusalem scholarship maintained so as to lend greater religious authority to the translation. The Septuagint originally comprised the Greek translation of the Pentateuch, but in subsequent centuries translations of other books were also introduced to it. Eventually, the Septuagint would come to include all of the Hebrew Scriptures.

The days of Ptolemaic rule in Judea were numbered, as foreign threats began to emerge. Around 200 B.C.E., Ptolemy V Epiphanes (203–181 B.C.E.) became embroiled in a war with the Seleucid empire, which was ruled by the descendants of the former Alexandrian general Seleucus I. Ptolemy V was ignominiously defeated in 200 B.C.E. during the Battle of Paneion. The victor was Antiochus III (223–187 B.C.E.), and by his decree all of Palestine was annexed to the Seleucid empire.

THE SELEUCIDS

Emperor Augustus of Rome dedicated this temple in Antioch-in-Pisidia, one of the most Romanized cities in Asia Minor, to the mother goddess Cybele.

THE SELEUCID ERA BECAME one of the most turbulent periods in the history of Judea: The incessant power struggles over the Seleucid throne in Antioch were reflected in the competition between Jewish supporters and opponents of Seleucid rule in Judea. The increasing Hellenization of Judea, including the construction of Greek-style cities, which led to a growing polarization of the formerly homogenous Jewish society between those who sought accommodation with Greek culture and those who opposed it, compounded the problem. And, the exploitative economy of the Seleucid regime increasingly divided the Jewish nation between rich and poor, a schism that would deepen after the Roman conquest of Judea. One Jewish family, the Tobiads, used their monopoly on tax collection (or "tax farming") in the Transjordan to amass such a fortune that they were able to influence political developments in Jerusalem, where a never ending struggle had ensued over the position of high priest, with various factions trying to buy their way into office. All these factors resulted in the splintering of the Jewish nation and in the future formation of Jewish dissident groups, including the Pharisees, Essenes, and Zealots, whose influence would extend well into the New Testament era.

ca 200 B.C.E.
Antiochus III defeats Ptolemy V and adds Palestine to the Seleucid empire

ca 225 B.C.E.
Earliest known Jewish synagogue founded in Alexandria, Egypt

ca 218–202 B.C.E.
Hannibal invades Italy in the Second Punic War, but Rome finally defeats the Carthaginians in 146 B.C.E.

ca 190 B.C.E.
Rome defeats Antiochus III at Magnesia, securing Roman control of Asia Minor

He shall be enraged and take action against the holy covenant ... Forces sent by him shall occupy and profane the temple and fortress ... but the people who are loyal to their God shall stand firm and take action. (Daniel 11:30-32)

The turmoil of the Seleucid empire was precipitated by Antiochus III's ill-fated attack on Greece, then a vassal of an emerging new power called Rome. Defeated, Antiochus was forced to remit crippling reparation payments to Rome. By the time his son Seleucus IV (187–175 B.C.E.) acceded to the throne, the Seleucid empire was nearly bankrupt. Seleucus's brother, Antiochus IV Epiphanes (175–164 B.C.E.), responded to the financial crisis by looting temples throughout his realm. A Seleucid high official, Heliodorus, was dispatched to Jerusalem to confiscate the treasure contained in the Temple of YHWH. According to the Book of Maccabees, Heliodorus is about to seize the Temple's coffers when a divine manifestation intervenes: a "magnificently caparisoned horse, with a rider of frightening mien," which "rushed at Heliodorus and struck at him with its front hoofs" (II Maccabees 3:24-25). The theft of the Temple treasure was prevented, but the relations between Jerusalem and Antioch had taken a turn for the worse.

Power struggles began to erupt over who would hold the position of high priest. One contender, a man named Yeshua, or Jesus, who changed his name to the Hellenized "Jason," preempted his opponents by offering the king a princely bribe. He then solidified his position by petitioning the king to turn Jerusalem into a Greek polis or city, including the construction of a gymnasium, an institution detested by pious Jews. Antiochus, who strongly believed that only thorough Hellenization would unify his fragmented empire, agreed to confirm Jason as high priest of the Temple.

Within a few years another priest with a Hellenized name, Menelaus, offered Antiochus IV an even higher bribe, earning him the coveted title. This appointment inflicted further damage on the prestige of the office of high priest, since Menelaus (unlike Jason) was not a member of a Zadokite family. It was a key tenet in Jewish belief that only a man who could trace his ancestry back to Zadok, the high priest of Solomon, qualified for the supreme post. Menelaus was invested, and Jason fled to the Transjordan to appeal for help from the wealthy Tobiad family. Thus the power struggle in Jerusalem continued.

As it happened, Antiochus IV was in the region after being repulsed from Egypt by Egyptian forces assisted by Rome. Eager to assuage his wounded pride, Antiochus turned and marched on Jerusalem to put an end to the strife. The pro-Greek faction warmly welcomed him, but the Seleucid king expended his wrath by rounding up scores of dissidents.

According to the Jewish historian Josephus, writing in the first century C.E., Antiochus IV then decreed that henceforth all non-Greek cults and practices were proscribed under pain of death. The stated aim was to enforce a common culture, language, and religion in Judea. Scholars have argued that this was not motivated by animus against the Jewish God, but by Antiochus's conviction that only a rigorous enforcement of a single state religion could bring peace within the region. As a consequence, worship of YHWH was forbidden; worship of Greek deities such as Dionysus, god of wine, was established. According to Josephus, those who resisted were "whipped with rods, and their bodies torn to pieces, and were crucified while they still lived and breathed."

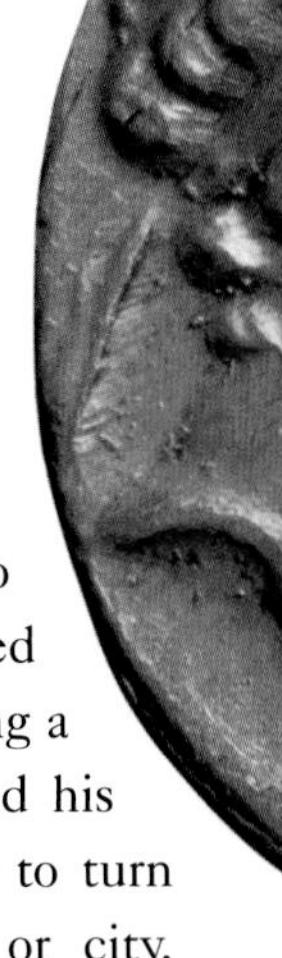

A coin bears a portrait of Antiochus IV Epiphanes (175–164 B.C.E.), the Seleucid whose Hellenization of Judea led to the Maccabean Revolt in 166 B.C.E.

ca 175–164 B.C.E.
Antiochus IV Epiphanes proscribes all non-Greek cults in Seleucid empire; Greek gymnasium built in Jerusalem

ca 167 B.C.E.
Rome conquers Macedonia

ca 166–160 B.C.E.
Judas Maccabeus leads revolt against Seleucid rule and successfully captures Jerusalem

ca 139 B.C.E.
Jews expelled from the city of Rome for "infecting" Roman society with their cultic rites

Horrified by this regime of terror, a priest named Mattathias, from Modein, some 20 miles west of Jerusalem, decided to act. As it happened, a Seleucid officer came to the village to enforce pagan sacrifice. Mattathias refused to sacrifice, and he slew the Jewish apostate who stepped forward to make the offering in his place. Mattathias then killed the Seleucid for good measure. The priest was forced to flee to the safety of the Judean mountains, but his dramatic deed galvanized the Jews into rebellion against the Seleucid rulers. Mattathias and three of his sons—Judas, Jonathan, and Simon—led the revolt and ultimately established the Hasmonean dynasty, named after Mattathias's great-grandfather Asamonaios. After the death of Mattathias, his son Judas Maccabeus (166–160 B.C.E.) took up the torch of the uprising; able-bodied Jewish men throughout the region flocked to his call.

It is believed that the Book of Daniel was compiled in these difficult days of national resistance, and it captures the spirit of a Judaism besieged. The first six chapters recount the trials of the Babylonian Exile, reminding its readers that the Jewish nation survived only by virtue of its observance of Covenant Law and faith in YHWH. The latter half of the book describes the "evil" of the reign of Antiochus IV in symbolic terms, in the form of visions received by Daniel, and foretells the imminent collapse of the Seleucid empire. The book's principal message is that if the Jews are steadfast in their faith, God's sovereignty will triumph in the end. The author or authors of Daniel have been identified with a group called "the wise" described in the book, possibly a group of pious Jews (sometimes associated with Hasidim), who struggled to set an example of religious observance in the face of persecution.

Illustration of Antiochus and the seven Maccabee brothers from a late-15th-century illuminated manuscript of Flavius Josephus's *The Jewish War*.

The revolt of the Maccabees succeeded beyond all expectations. In 164 B.C.E., Judas took Jerusalem, cleansed the Temple, and rededicated it to Jewish worship—an event commemorated by the festival of Hanukkah. The war with Antiochus IV continued uninterrupted, but Judas gave no quarter. In 161 B.C.E., he achieved a spectacular victory over the forces of the Syrian commander Nicanor. Judas was killed in the Battle of Elasa in 160 B.C.E., whereupon his brother Jonathan (160–142 B.C.E.) took over the leadership of the revolt. Jonathan continued to pound the Seleucid armies so severely that King Demetrius I (162–150 B.C.E.) finally sued for an armistice.

Under the terms of the 152 B.C.E. peace accord, Jonathan was invested as governor of the autonomous Seleucid province of Judea. The Jewish populace rejoiced; the first glimmer of freedom had appeared. Two years later, after Alexander Balas (150–145 B.C.E.), Jonathan's ally, toppled Demetrius, the new Seleucid king confirmed Jonathan's assumption of the title of high priest. This precipitous act, however, stunned many pious Jews. The purpose of the Maccabees' revolt had always been to restore full observance of the Covenant Law, including the rules governing the appointment of high priest. Jonathan, however, was not a Zadokite, a descendant of Solomon's high priest. Many Jews were outraged and withdrew their support of the Maccabees.

Later that year, tensions between the Seleucid kingdom and Ptolemaic Egypt escalated, and Jonathan saw his chance. He marshaled his veteran army and captured Ashdod, Joppa, and Gaza, as well as parts of Samaria and Galilee. Alexander

This marble mosaic from Pompeii depicts a satyr dancing with a Maenad, a female worshiper of Dionysus, the Greek god of wine and mystery.

THE HASMONEAN DYNASTY

MAP KEY

- Judea before the Maccabean revolt
- Area conquered by Jonathan, 160–142 B.C.E.
- Area conquered by Simon, 142–134 B.C.E.
- Area conquered by Hyrcanus I, 134–104 B.C.E.
- Area conquered by Aristobulus I, 104–103 B.C.E.
- Area conquered by Alexander Janneus, 103–76 B.C.E.
- [Megiddo] Former name of city or town

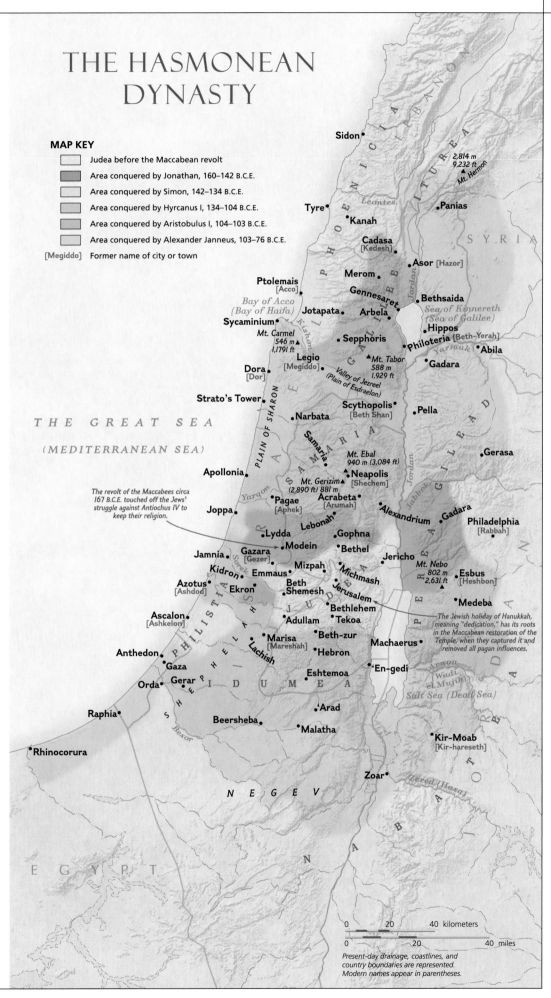

The revolt of the Maccabees circa 167 B.C.E. touched off the Jews' struggle against Antiochus IV to keep their religion.

The Jewish holiday of Hanukkah, meaning "dedication," has its roots in the Maccabean restoration of the Temple, when they captured it and removed all pagan influences.

THE GREAT SEA (MEDITERRANEAN SEA)

0 20 40 kilometers
0 20 40 miles

Present-day drainage, coastlines, and country boundaries are represented. Modern names appear in parentheses.

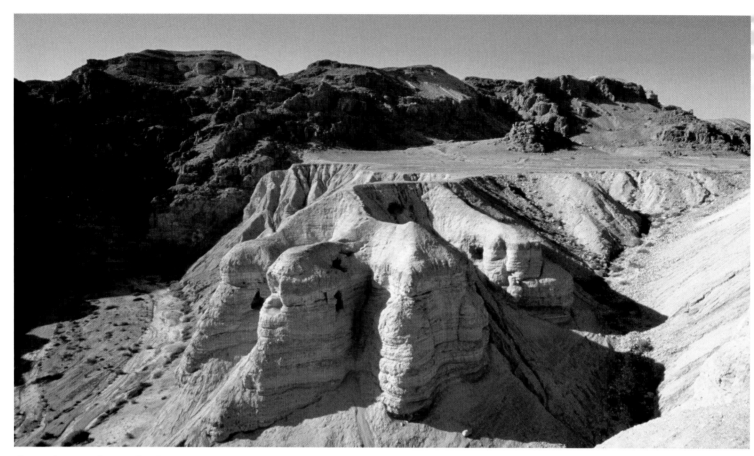

The Dead Sea Scrolls were found in 1947 in this group of caves just outside the ancient settlement of Qumran, close to the Dead Sea.

Balas was too distracted to intervene, for a new power struggle for the Seleucid crown was raging. Jonathan was assassinated by the head of one competing faction, Tryphon, in 143 B.C.E. One year later, Tryphon successfully usurped the throne in Antioch. Jonathan's brother and successor, Simon (142–134 B.C.E.), promptly threw his support behind Tryphon's opponent, Demetrius II (145–140 and 129–125 B.C.E.). By way of cementing this alliance, the deposed king then formally recognized Judea as an independent kingdom.

It was 142 B.C.E., and the glorious moment had arrived, some 445 years after the destruction of Jerusalem by Nebuchadnezzar. The Jews were free—free to worship, free to sacrifice, free to live according to the laws promulgated by Moses. The kingdom of David and Solomon had been restored.

JEWISH FESTIVALS

The cleansing and rededication of the Temple in Jerusalem by Judas Maccabeus in 164 B.C.E. is commemorated each year during Hanukkah, the Festival of Dedication, by lighting the menorah. Other principal Jewish festivals restored after the Babylonian captivity, and continuing to this day, include Rosh Hashanah (the New Year), Yom Kippur (the Day of Atonement), Succoth (the Festival of Booths), the Festival of Passover (which merged the Festival of Unleavened Bread with the Paschal Offering of Spring), and Shavuot (the Feast of Weeks), marking the presentation of the Ten Commandments.

Beneath the veneer of popular exultation, however, disenchantment with the Hasmonean usurpation of the position of high priest continued to fester. Although the successors of Jonathan and Simon expanded Judea to the historical borders of the kingdom of David, from the Negev to Galilee, from the Transjordan to the Mediterranean coast, large portions of the Jewish population were disillusioned and fatalistic. They felt the great success of the Maccabees was based on hubris and as such, doomed to failure.

The mood of the era is captured in a number of religious works by Jewish authors that, for various reasons, were not included in the final canon of the Hebrew Scriptures. Called the Apocrypha by Christian authors, these books include wisdom, sayings, poetry, prayers, and histories that were included in the Septuagint, the Greek translation of the Hebrew Scriptures, and subsequently in the Christian Old Testament. These books depict a nation struggling to come to terms with other cultures, notably Hellenism, prompting a divergence of ideas and beliefs within Judaism itself. The Book of I Maccabees, for example, chronicles the Hasmonean dynasty's achievements, whereas II Maccabees, which covers much of the same history, is primarily concerned with the restoration of the sanctity of the Temple in Jerusalem. The author of the Wisdom of Solomon, tentatively dated to the first century B.C.E., fulminates against Hellenism, arguing that the heathen are sybaritic revelers who "take [their] fill of costly wine and perfumes, and let no flower of spring pass [them] by" (Wisdom 2:7). Even so, the author accepts the Greek idea that the soul is immortal—"the righteous live forever, and their reward is with the Lord" (Wisdom 3:15)—as well as the Greek concept of the creative power of *Logos,* meaning "word" or "reason" (Wisdom 18:15). Both ideas would return in the New Testament. The idea of the resurrection of the dead, first argued in the Book of II Maccabees, will become a central tenet of Christianity.

Continuing dissatisfaction with the priesthood prompted one group, described as "Essenes" by Josephus, to leave the cities and seek solitude in the desert. There they formed what could tentatively be described as a commune, living an ascetic lifestyle focused on the pursuit of the Covenant Law—especially its rigorous rules on ritual purity. They dressed in simple robes, prayed at regular intervals, and worked long hours tilling the desert soil. Physical and spiritual cleanliness were one: They dug an elaborate network of cisterns to catch the rainfall and channel water from nearby springs in order to submit to ritual immersion on a daily basis. The purpose of this lifestyle, practiced in the solidarity of a commune under the leadership of a "Teacher of Righteousness" (significantly, a Zadokite), was to bring them closer to God.

The principal purpose of the Essene community was to enable each member to devote himself wholeheartedly to the study of the Hebrew Scriptures without any outside interference. According to the Essene "Rule of the Community," every evening, after daytime chores were completed, the congregation gathered "to read from the Book, to study Law, and to pray together."

DEAD SEA SCROLLS

THE SECTARIAN GROUP THAT LIVED IN THE community of Qumran included scribes, who copied almost all Hebrew Scripture onto scrolls. When not in use, the scrolls were kept in large clay jars. In C.E. 68, when the Roman army had moved closer to crushing the Jewish revolt, the sect placed the jars in nearby caves. There they remained until 1947, when a young Bedouin shepherd looking for a lost sheep stumbled upon them. Scholars who examined the find, known ever since as the Dead Sea Scrolls, were astonished.

These Hebrew Scriptures were nearly a thousand years older than the oldest complete manuscript of the Bible known at that time, which dated from the ninth century. Of the more than 800 manuscripts, 100 relate to the Hebrew Bible. The scrolls contain all the books of the Old Testament, save the Book of Esther, as well as a Manual of Discipline pertaining to all members of the Qumran sect. The scrolls confirm that across nearly a thousand years, the biblical text remained surprisingly intact and that the canon of the Hebrew Scriptures at the time had not been closed. Scholars have detected only small variations between the Dead Sea version and later manuscripts.

Some scholars have linked the Essenes to the scrolls. Archaeologists uncovered the ruins of an elaborate monastic settlement near Khirbat Qumran. Whether the occupants of this community were the Essenes described by Josephus continues to be a topic of considerable debate.

Early second-century B.C.E. Dead Sea Scroll fragment: Its apocryphal text has embellished versions of the Noah and Abraham stories.

The Roman Conquest

The Roman aqueduct in Caesarea, on the Mediterranean coast of modern Israel, built by Herod the Great between 22 and 10 B.C.E.

THE HASMONEANS RULED for almost a hundred years. In 76 B.C.E., upon the death of King Alexander Jannaeus (104/3–76 B.C.E.), his widow Salome Alexandra (76–67 B.C.E.) took control of the country rather than pass the throne to her eldest son, Hyrcanus II. She assuaged her son's sensibilities by awarding him the mantle of high priest. Before his death, Alexander had advised his wife to favor the party of the Pharisees in her royal appointments, underscoring the growing partisanship under the pseudolegitimate rule of the Hasmoneans.

In Jerusalem, power traditionally rested in the hands of the priesthood, the large body of chief priests, priestly officials, and Levitical assistants who supervised the system of ritual sacrifice in the forecourt of the Temple. Under Hasmonean rule, the priesthood was increasingly associated with a group known as the Sadducees (or *Tzedoqim* in Hebrew). The Sadducees, who claimed to descend from the high priest Zadok, formed a wealthy, archconservative Jewish aristocracy that would welcome the Roman occupation of Judea in the years to come.

By contrast, the Pharisees were not a clerical group as is often assumed, but a coalition of pious laymen. They

ca 73 B.C.E.
King Herod the Great is born

ca 58–51 B.C.E.
Julius Caesar leads military campaigns in Gaul and Britain

ca 44 B.C.E.
The Roman Republic ends with the assassination of Julius Caesar

ca 40 B.C.E.
The Roman Senate declares Herod king of Judea; his reign is characterized by peace and prosperity

Next, Pompey deprived the Jews of the towns they had occupied in Coele Syria, putting them henceforth under a Roman governor especially appointed for this purpose. Josephus, *The Jewish War,* Book 1

scrupulously observed the Covenant Law and distinguished themselves from the Sadducees by their views on cultic purity. The more the Sadducees argued for ritual sacrifice as the only way for man to please God, the more the Pharisees focused on ritual purity as the defining experience of Judaism in virtually every aspect of daily life.

In 67 B.C.E., Salome Alexandra died, and a power struggle ensued between Hyrcanus and his younger brother Aristobulus II (67–63 B.C.E.). However, Hyrcanus lacked the loyalty of the army and therefore had no leverage to enforce his royal claim. Hyrcanus and his followers then appealed to the ruler of Edom for help. Edom, in the postexilic period, had been conquered by an Arab people known as the Nabataeans (ruling over a territory corresponding to the Negev and southern Jordan today). King Aretas III (ca 87–62 B.C.E.) agreed to Hyrcanus's request and laid siege against Jerusalem in 66 B.C.E.

Pompey Invades Judea

THIS POWER STRUGGLE coincided with a decision by Rome's senators to expand Roman influence in the Near East, notably at the expense of the tottering Seleucid empire. The man they chose for this task was one of their ablest commanders, General Gnaeus Pompeius, later called Pompey the Great (106–48 B.C.E.). The reason behind this campaign was yet another war waged by Mithradates VI, the opportunistic king of Pontus (a region identified with the northern coastal region of modern Turkey). Pompey quickly defeated Rome's enemy and established himself in the city of Damascus in 63 B.C.E. There, the Roman general was promptly visited by three separate delegations from Jerusalem, each one lobbying for Roman support: the Aristobulus faction, the Hyrcanus faction, and the Pharisees, who were urging the Roman general to eradicate the Hasmoneans altogether.

Apprised of the power struggle in Jerusalem, and therefore the city's vulnerability, Pompey swung his armies around and resolved to extend Roman rule into Judea, to the very borders of Egypt. That same year, Pompey captured Jerusalem and extinguished the flame of Jewish independence that had flickered for less than a century. Hyrcanus was restored to the position of high priest, but at the cost of reducing his country to a vassal state, ruling under the thumb of Rome.

The maneuvering between Pompey and Hyrcanus was observed with keen interest by a young man named Herod, who hailed from Idumaea, in southern Judea. This region had been settled by Edomites (hence the name "Idumaean") after the conquest of Edom by the Nabataeans. Herod's father, Antipater, was a wealthy Idumaean chieftain who had married the daughter of a Nabataean nobleman.

During the long reign of the Hasmonean King John Hyrcanus (135–104 B.C.E.), Idumaea had once again been annexed to the Judean realm, and the inhabitants had been forced either to convert to Judaism or to leave the territory. As a result, although Arab blood flowed in Herod's veins, the young man grew up in a family that, outwardly at least, had converted to Judaism. In addition, like the Hasmoneans, Herod wholeheartedly embraced Hellenistic culture.

Dating to the second century B.C.E., this imperial Gallic helmet with crossbars of a Roman legionnaire was found in Judea.

ca 31 B.C.E.
Octavian defeats Mark Antony's fleet at the Battle of Actium

ca 27 B.C.E.
Octavian becomes the first Roman emperor; his name is changed to Augustus

ca 22 B.C.E.
Construction of Caesarea, a harbor city dedicated to Augustus, begins

ca 20 B.C.E.
King Herod begins expansion of the Second Temple precinct

[Herod] freely admitted to [Octavian] Caesar that he had fought the greatest friendship for Antony. … and that he had not fought in his army only because the Arab wars had diverted him … [Octavian] Caesar thereupon restored his crown … Josephus, *Antiquities of the Jews*, Book 1

Herod's father, Antipater, observed the rise of Roman power and decided that it would be prudent to cultivate ties with Rome. When Pompey arrived in Judea, Antipater hastened to pledge his support to the general, hoping that Pompey would look favorably on his family's ambitions. With regards to this hope, Antipater was not disappointed. Before much time had passed, Antipater and his son Herod were welcomed into the circle of Pompey's co-consul, a man named Julius Caesar.

At this point, Herod began a lifelong friendship with Mark Antony, one of Caesar's most important supporters. The Roman civil war intervened, however, and Julius Caesar was compelled to chase Pompey to Egypt, where his former friend and ally was killed. Antipater then deftly transferred his allegiance to the Caesar faction. He was rewarded for that act by being named procurator of Judea in 47 B.C.E. Antipater was also given the extraordinary honor of Roman citizenship.

Moving quickly to solidify the position of his Idumaean family, Antipater appointed his son Phasael governor of Judea and Perea, and Herod governor of Galilee. Seven years later, this relatively tranquil state of affairs was thrown into complete disarray when the Parthians, rulers of Persia, invaded Judea in support of a pretender named Antigonus, the son of Aristobulus II. They successfully captured Jerusalem, where Antigonus proceeded to cut off Hyrcanus's ears, knowing that the maiming would make him unfit to continue as high priest. Herod's family was toppled, Phasael committed suicide, and Herod fled, having sequestered his extended family in the safety of a Hasmonean fortress known as Masada, which sat on a high rock plateau near the southern end of the Dead Sea.

Herod made his way to Rome, where he argued that the Parthian invasion threatened Roman sovereignty in the Near East. Invited to address the

OPPOSITE: **The Herodium, about seven miles south of Jerusalem, was built by Herod the Great between 24 and 15 B.C.E. to serve as his palace and mausoleum.**

Roman Senate, he spoke with such eloquence and conviction that the Senate proclaimed him king of Judea. Of course, the title was strictly honorific, for Judea was still firmly in the hands of the Parthians; therefore, the Senate also voted Herod a Roman army to help him recapture his territory. And so, in 39 B.C.E., Herod landed in Joppa at the head of a Roman army, fought his way to Jerusalem, and was able to pacify his kingdom by 37 B.C.E.

The Politics of Herod

THUS BEGAN THE REIGN of Herod the Great (37–4 B.C.E.), a time of peace and unprecedented prosperity during which Herod changed the face of the Holy Land, always walking a fine line between placating the Jewish populace and the Roman overlords so despised by his subjects. Since he was not by birth a Jew, Herod treated his subjects with great circumspection. During his reign, coins minted in Judea, for example, did not show the king's likeness in deference to the Jewish proscription against graven images.

Herod, though already married, was keen to legitimize his rule. This desire probably motivated his marriage to a Hasmonean princess, Mariamne, granddaughter of Aristobulus II, in 38 B.C.E. Herod could have taken her as a second wife, but he may have been anxious to appease the Jews, who were mostly monogamous. The marriage to Mariamne was also calculated to curtail the ambitions of her brother, Aristobulus III, who was the legitimate Hasmonean heir.

Under pressure from his new wife, Herod installed Aristobulus as high priest, even though he was only 17 years old. One year later, during a feast, Aristobulus drowned under suspicious circumstances. Although there was no conclusive evidence pointing to Herod's complicity, the incident did remove Herod's most formidable opponent from the scene. Far from being assuaged of potential threats to his throne, however, Herod grew increasingly suspicious of his entourage as time wore on, with most of the distrust falling on those nearest to him.

Another challenge to Herod's crown arose when Octavian, the great-nephew and heir of Julius Caesar, defeated

THE SADDUCEES AND THE PHARISEES

THE SADDUCEES FORMED THE ARISTOCRATIC upper crust of Jewish society. Deeply conservative, they controlled ritual sacrifice at the Second Temple, including the collection of tithes for the upkeep of the Temple. They also wielded real secular power. Under Hasmonean rule, the Sadducees gained control of the Sanhedrin (priestly council), which exerted jurisdiction over religious and other domestic matters.

During the Roman occupation, the Sadducees were able to preserve their control over the sacrificial cult of the Temple as well as the Sanhedrin. Certain families grew quite powerful, allowing them to maintain their great influence.

The Sadducees did not believe in the concept of an afterlife, which was gaining popularity in Judaism, particularly among the Pharisees. In the Gospel of Luke, the Sadducees question Jesus on this very subject, hoping to ridicule him (Luke 20:28-38).

This sixth-century C.E. mosaic depicts the parable of the Pharisee and the Publican in the Saint Apollinare Nuovo, Ravenna.

The Pharisees were a coalition of pious laymen who observed the Covenant Law but believed that it should be adapted to meet changing needs. As a result, they studied and debated extensively, developing a growing scriptural commentary known as the Oral Law. The Pharisees, under Hasmonean rule, also exerted power in Jerusalem and vied for royal, political appointments.

The Pharisees adhered to a rigid application of the laws governing the Sabbath and ritual purity. An elaborate cleansing system arose from their debates over what was "clean" or "ritually impure." Scholars theorize that the Pharisaic movement became largely limited to urban elites with plentiful water access.

In the New Testament, the Pharisees are presented challenging Jesus on matters involving the Law, including purity and Sabbath observance. Nevertheless, Jesus includes them in his fellowship of the meal (Luke 7:36).

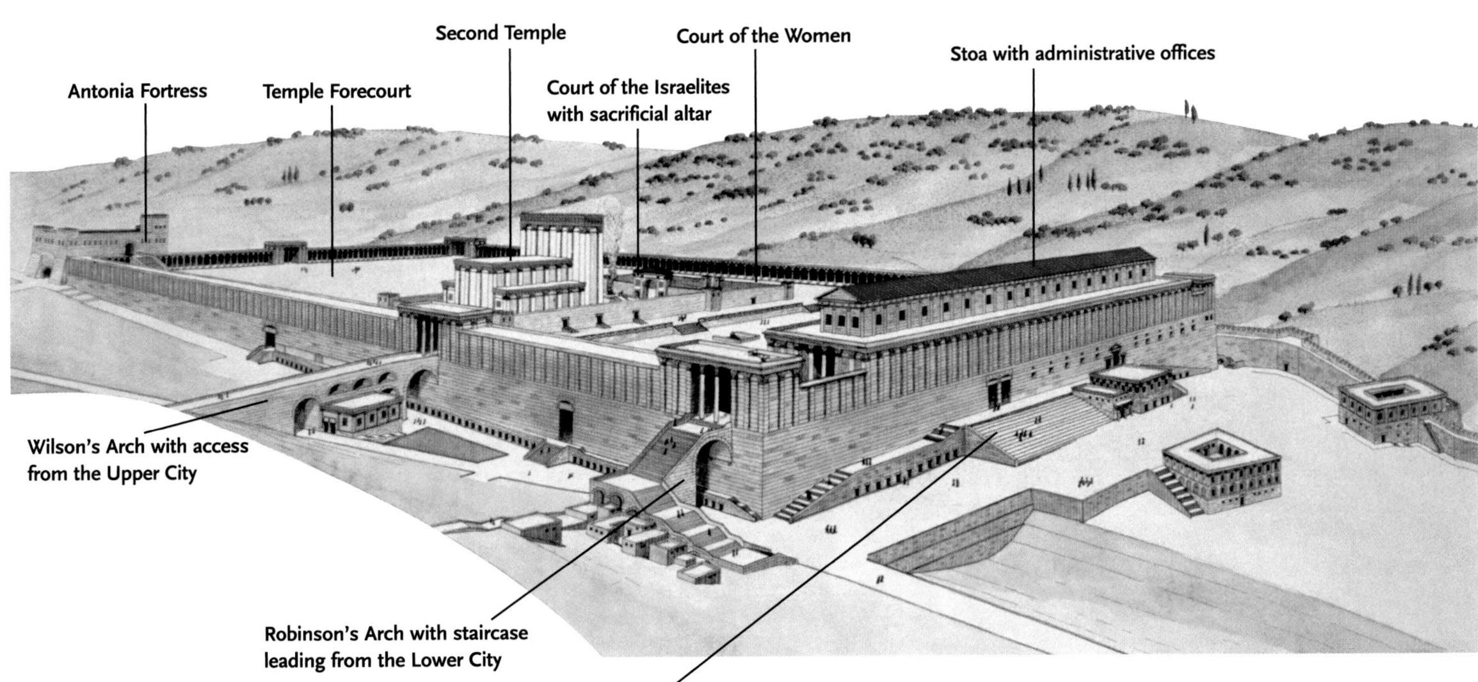

Herod's sanctuary platform, built 20 B.C.E. to C.E. 62, surrounded the Second Temple. This reconstruction envisions its appearance from the southwest.

Herod's great friend and ally, Mark Antony, at the Battle of Actium in 31 B.C.E. In an effort to protect his crown, Herod made haste to Octavian's field headquarters on Rhodes and pledged the man his allegiance. Pleased by the scene of this humble king placing a crown at his feet, Octavian confirmed Herod as king of Judea. Herod then wisely remained on the sidelines while Octavian chased Mark Antony back to Egypt, where he and his lover, the Ptolemaic Queen Cleopatra, committed suicide in 30 B.C.E.

Even though he was now more powerful than ever, Herod continued to suspect treason where there was none. In 30 B.C.E., the king ordered the execution of Hyrcanus II, even though the old man was nearing 80. The following year, his distrust turned to his beloved wife Mariamne, by now the mother of his five children. Mariamne was convicted and ultimately executed. Herod then turned his wrath upon Mariamne's mother, Alexandra, who was executed in 28 B.C.E., followed by Kostobar, Herod's brother-in-law. Many more family members would be put to death in the years to come.

Herod's Achievements

DESPITE THE TURMOIL within his own household, Herod the Great excelled as a builder and organizer. During the great famine of 25 B.C.E., Herod organized a massive aid program, using grain imported from Egypt. At Samaria, the former capital of the Northern Kingdom and the place where he had married Mariamne 11 years earlier, Herod built a large Greco-Roman acropolis on top of the ancient palace of Omri and his son Ahab, former kings of Israel, with little regard for Jewish history or the local sensitivity of the Samaritans. Samaria was renamed Sebaste in honor of Octavian, who, since 27 B.C.E., was known under his new title, Caesar Augustus (or Sebastos in Greek). A new temple was also built, and equally dedicated to Rome's first emperor.

From an economic point of view, Herod realized that Judea could never profit properly from the lucrative seaborne trade between Rome and its far-flung empire as long as the kingdom had no major port outside the modest harbor of Joppa. In 22 B.C.E., the king launched a highly ambitious and technically complex endeavor to construct a state-of-the-art harbor city on the Mediterranean coast. He named it Caesarea, in honor of Caesar Augustus.

The key to his revolutionary design was the construction of a vast breakwater, which, according to the historian Flavius Josephus, was "laid out as a compass towards the land … so that the great ships might lie in safety." Huge blocks of stone, hewn "fifty feet in length, not less than eighteen in breadth, and nine in depth," were dropped into water "twenty fathoms" deep. When it was finally completed, the harbor proper (called Sebastos) became the envy of the entire Mediterranean world. Even today, visitors standing on the white-sand beach still can see the remnants of Herod's vast breakwater system lying just beneath the blue waters of the Mediterranean Sea.

Herod's zeal for construction projects extended to military fortifications. He threw a ring of defensive forts around his realm, the most famous of which still survive: the massive Herodium in the Judean desert and the magnificent palace on the fortress of Masada, overlooking the Dead Sea. In addition, the king rebuilt a military complex, containing an arsenal and troop barracks, known as the Antonia Fortress in the northwestern corner of the Second Temple in Jerusalem, which could be the flash point of any future insurrection. From the Antonia, Roman soldiers could surround the sensitive Temple area in minutes.

Undoubtedly, however, Herod's greatest achievement was the expansion of the Second Temple precinct. He turned it into a magnificent Jewish sanctuary, built on the principles of and to the highest standards of Hellenistic architecture. This project, initiated in 20 B.C.E., was not completed until around C.E. 62.

The original Temple and its forecourt, restored after the Babylonian Captivity, were now fronted by a large courtyard known as the Court of the Women. This complex, in turn, was surrounded by a vast esplanade covering no less than one-sixth the area of the city, accessible through two "floating" staircases on the west, each supported by arches. A small portion of one of these arches, known as Robinson's Arch, is still visible today, as are the monumental stairs that led to the Double Gate on the south.

This aerial view shows the Roman ruins at Herod's port of Caesarea, one of the engineering marvels of the Herodian era.

Josephus, who visited the Temple before its destruction in C.E. 70, describes how it was built with "finely hewn white stones, twenty-five cubits long," while the vast arcade was "four columns deep, their capitals fashioned in the Corinthian order, which amazed visitors with their grandeur." The entire complex was supported on a huge platform, which dwarfed anything that had ever been built on the site. Only the western part of this massive platform, known as the Western, or Wailing, Wall, remains today.

As the last decade before the beginning of the Common Era began, Herod the Great gazed upon a land that had changed beyond recognition. Dusty Jewish settlements had been replaced by splendid cities of marble. New roads crisscrossed the country, their safety secured by frequent patrols of Roman soldiers. Sleek triremes plied the waters and nestled in the magnificent embrace of the port of Caesarea.

These monumental stairs from the first century C.E. led to the Double Gate, with access to Herod's sanctuary platform.

Beneath the veneer of Hellenistic gentility, however, the country seethed with unrest. Herod's boom economy had created a small upper crust of Hellenized Jewish families that welcomed the occupation by Rome, as did the priesthood, whose wealth and power were magnified tenfold by Herod's new Temple. But the majority of Jews, although they may have helped create this new wealth by being pressed into work gangs on Herod's projects, did not share in the wealth.

Wracked by illness, Herod spent his last years in debilitating pain and died in 4 B.C.E. The Herodian kingdom, created at such enormous cost, was carved up between his three surviving sons. Archelaus, the eldest, gained the principal share as ethnarch (ruler of the people) of Judea, Idumaea, and Samaria; Philip became tetrarch (ruler of one-fourth) of the Gaulanitis (the Golan), and Antipas (later known as Herod Antipas) became "tetrarch of Galilee" and the Transjordan, an area known as Perea.

And in that same year, an infant born to a woman in Nazareth was just beginning to walk.

JUDEA	GREECE/MACEDONIA	ROME
ca 687–642 B.C.E. King Manasseh allows Jews in Judah to worship idols ca 515 B.C.E. Jews dedicate new temple in Jerusalem, and the era of Second Temple Judaism begins ca 166–160 B.C.E. Judas Maccabeus leads revolt against Seleucid rule and successfully captures Jerusalem  ca 22 B.C.E. Herod begins the construction of Caesarea, a harbor city dedicated to Augustus	ca 490 B.C.E. The Greeks defeat invading Persian forces at the Battle of Marathon ca 480 B.C.E. During the Second Persian War, Xerxes defeats the Greeks at Thermopylae and destroys Athens  ca 333 B.C.E. Alexander the Great defeats Darius III, the king of the Persians, at the Battle of Issus. Two years later, the Persian Empire falls to Alexander	ca 753 B.C.E. Traditional date for the founding of Rome  ca 218–202 B.C.E. The Carthaginian general Hannibal invades Italy in the Second Punic War and nearly crushes Rome. Rome finally defeats the Carthaginians in 146 B.C.E. ca 31 B.C.E. Octavian (later known as Caesar Augustus), heir of Julius Caesar, defeats Mark Antony at the Battle of Actium. Four years later in 27 B.C.E., he becomes the first Roman emperor

CHAPTER NINE

The World of Jesus

In the last years of the reign of Herod the Great, a son was born to a young mother named Miriam, or Mary. The child, who in the local Aramaic tongue would have been called Yeshua bar Yosef ("Jesus, son of Joseph"), grew up and worked in and around a Galilean hamlet called Nazareth. One day, when he was about 30 to 33 years old, he left Galilee to join a dissident group in the desert led by a preacher named John the Baptist. John's political and religious activism led to his arrest and execution by the Tetrarch of Galilee, Herod Antipas.

Jesus then began his own movement as a teacher, or rabbi, not in the Jordan wilderness but in the towns and villages of Lower Galilee. Jesus himself was arrested, convicted of sedition, and executed on the cross. Shortly after his burial, his tomb was found to be empty, and a number of witnesses claimed they actually had seen the resurrected Jesus.

These are the basic outlines of Jesus' life as reported by the Gospels, but what happened during the two years of his ministry in Galilee is still the subject of scholarly debate. One thing we do know: The words and deeds of Jesus of Nazareth survived his crucifixion and inspired a religion that would soon sweep the Roman world.

This third-century C.E. synagogue of Capernaum may stand on the site of an earlier one where, according to Luke, Jesus taught on the Sabbath.

A Son of Galilee

The green fields of Tiberias (Teverya) stretch out before the southern side of Sea of Galilee as the Golan Heights rises beyond.

Galilee is in the northernmost part of modern-day Israel. Josephus, the first-century C.E. Jewish historian, reported that Galilee in his day was bordered by Akko (Acre) and Mount Carmel in the west; the Jordan River in the east, the Valley of Jezreel and Samaria in the south, and the town of Baca (modern-day Bezet) in the north. The region's most prominent body of water was—and still is—the Sea of Galilee, surrounded by today's Plain of Gennesaret in the north and northwest, the hill country of Lower Galilee in the west, and the slopes of the Golan plateau in the east. Fed by the Jordan, the Sea of Galilee supported a thriving fishing industry and other commerce. Elsewhere in Galilee, the predominant activity was agriculture. The region continues to be the rainiest and most fertile region of Israel. Josephus wrote, "Its soil is so universally rich and fruitful," that all of the land "is cultivated by its inhabitants, and no part of it lies idle."

Because of its natural bounty, Galilee's history was separate from Judah's in the south. Traditionally the territory of the tribes of Naphtali, Zebulun, Issachar, Asher, and later Dan, it formed part of the tribal alliance that broke away from Solomon's unified monarchy in 931 B.C.E., to form the Northern Kingdom,

ca 73–71 B.C.E.
Spartacus and his army of slaves wage an unsuccessful war against the Romans

ca 64–63 B.C.E.
The Roman general Pompey conquers Syria and Palestine

ca 57 B.C.E.
Galilee becomes a Roman province

ca 47 B.C.E.
The Royal Library of Alexandria is consumed by fire

Its soil is so universally rich and fruitful, and so filled with plantations of every variety of trees, that it invites even the most indolent to devote themselves to agriculture because of its very fecundity. Flavius Josephus, *The Jewish War*

or Israel. Galileans, in particular, were resentful of Solomon's rule, for the king had given 20 cities in Galilee to King Hiram of Tyre in payment for cedar and other materials (I Kings 9:11). Galilee was subsequently ruled by northern kings, from Jeroboam I to Pekah, and endured the Assyrian invasion in 733 B.C.E. Galilee then became part of the Assyrian province of Megiddo, and it remained under foreign domination, by varying degrees, until the advent of Hasmonean rule in 142 B.C.E. After the Roman conquest of the Hasmoneans by Pompey, Galilee became a district ruled from the regional capital of Sepphoris, until Herod the Great was given control of the country. The Romans referred to the region as "Palaestina," based on the Greek translation of "Philistines," *Palaistinei.*

In all likelihood, most of Galilee's farmers were spared the deportations of Israel's urban population by the Assyrians in the eighth century B.C.E., probably because their removal would have significantly disrupted the region's agricultural output. During the following 600 years of occupation, the bounty of Galilee attracted a variety of settlers, including Assyrians, Phoenicians, Aramaeans, Greeks, and Persians, who mixed and intermarried with the remaining Jewish farmers. In time, the Jewish element in Galilee became very different from that in Judea, where the Jewish culture and religious orthodoxy were closely guarded during and after the Exile. Galileans also spoke with a different accent, an Aramaic patois that instantly branded them as northerners (Matthew 26:73).

By the beginning of the Common Era, the Galilean community of rural hamlets and villages formed a tight-knit, devoutly Jewish enclave in a region that was all but surrounded by a Hellenistic world. To the northeast lay Caesarea Philippi; to the north, the Hellenized cities of Ptolemais, Tyre, and Sidon on the Mediterranean coast; and to the east, in the Transjordan, the Greek community of the "Ten Cities," or Decapolis.

Many Jewish villages had synagogues, which were simple and modest. Built like most local dwellings, with plastered walls and roofed with branches and mud, most did not survive the passage of time. Of the 204 Galilean cities and villages mentioned by Josephus, archaeologists have only been able to identify three synagogues dating from the first century C.E.

Galilee, in sum, was a rural backwater. When, in the Gospel of John, one Apostle confides to a friend named Nathanael that the Messiah has come from Nazareth, Nathanael looks at him and scoffs: "Can anything good come out of Nazareth?" (John 1:46). Nevertheless, Josephus (a native Galilean himself) asserts that, despite their simple ways, the Galileans were a remarkably proud people who "were always ready to put up a strong resistance during times of war."

Jesus in History

IN THE HEART OF GALILEE, in a tiny hamlet called Nazareth, lived a boy called Jesus. Because of the sometime conflicting information in the Gospels of the New Testament, the exact dates of his birth and death are not known. Furthermore, no historical attestation of Jesus dates from his lifetime: His name does not appear in any cuneiform tablets, papyrus rolls, cylinders, prisms, or ostraca. One reason for the lack of information about Jesus' early life may be that few people

A farmer harvests grain with a sickle on this stone seal, discovered in Israel and dating to the sixth century B.C.E.

ca 37 B.C.E.
Herod wrests control of Judea from the Parthians and his rival, Antigonus, to begin his 40-year reign

ca 30 B.C.E.
Egypt becomes a Roman province and suffers under heavy taxation

ca 21 B.C.E.
Herod Antipas, son of Herod the Great, is born

ca 6 B.C.E.
Judea becomes a Roman province

FARMING IN PALESTINE

THE ACCOUNTS OF THE FIRST-CENTURY C.E. Jewish historian Flavius Josephus tell us that much of the land of Palestine, and particularly Galilee, was used for agriculture. After the autumn rains, Jewish farmers softened the fields and prepared them for seeding using a wooden plow. They either used the family mule to drag the plow or borrowed a donkey from a fellow farmer in the village, as was the custom with poorer peasants. Sowing the Galilean soil required great skill. As Jesus notes: "unless a grain of wheat falls into the earth and dies, it remains just a single grain, but if it dies, it bears much fruit" (John 12:24).

At harvesttime, the wheat would be reaped with an iron sickle, such as the one found near 'En-gedi in 1962, then taken to a threshing floor, where it was beaten or trod upon by cattle. The wheat was then winnowed—thrown up into the air by a fork so that the lighter chaff separated from the grain in the wind; the method is still used today by farmers throughout the Middle East. This same image appears in John the Baptist's description of the coming of the Son of Man: "His winnowing fork is in his hand, to clear his threshing floor and to gather the wheat into his granary; but the chaff he will burn with unquenchable fire." (Luke 3:17).

A field of wheat flourishes on the hills of Galilee in modern-day Israel. In the Bible, agriculture features in many of the parables of Jesus.

in Galilee knew how to write. Jesus' followers, known as the Apostles (from the Greek *apostolos*, meaning "a person sent [forth]"), are described as "uneducated and ordinary men," which makes it unlikely they were literate (Acts 4:13). It is often assumed that Jesus could read (although this is not certain, given that knowledge of the Scriptures was often taught by rote), but no evidence shows that Jesus could write. Jesus was not a prominent official or a king, nor a prophet such as Jeremiah, who could afford a personal scribe such as Baruch. He was a village rabbi, who taught in rural Galilee, far from the intellectual centers of Judea.

In addition, scholars have inferred from the New Testament that Jesus' ministry was short—perhaps less than two years. By contrast, Ezra, Nehemiah, and Jeremiah were active for anywhere from 20 to 40 years, enough time to commit their personal memoirs and sayings to writing. Jesus' career, by comparison, had only recently begun when he was crucified.

Supporting testimony of the existence of Jesus has, however, survived in the works of later Roman writers. The Roman historian Suetonius (C.E. 75–130), in writing about the life of the Roman Emperor Claudius in C.E. 119, mentions that "as the Jews were making constant disturbances at the instigation of Chrestus [*sic*], he expelled them from Rome." Given that this decree occurred around C.E. 49, it follows that there must have been a flourishing community of Christians (many of whom still considered themselves observant Jews) in Rome as early as 20 years after the Crucifixion, which scholars date to between C.E. 29 and 33. Further support appears in the New Testament Book of Acts of the Apostles, written by the author referred to as Luke, which reads: "[A] Jew named Aquila, a native of Pontus ... had recently come from Italy with his wife Priscilla, because Claudius had ordered all Jews to leave Rome" (Acts 18:2). Suetonius also reaffirms the persecution of Christians during the reign of Emperor Nero: "Punishment by Nero was inflicted on the Christians, a class of men given to a new and mischievous superstition."

The Roman historian Tacitus (C.E. 56–117) explains Nero's actions in his C.E. 117 work, *Annals*. Nero needed a scapegoat for the great fire of C.E. 64 that ravaged Rome: "Nero created a diversion and subjected to the most extraordinary tortures those hated for their abominations by the common people called Christians (Christianos)." The originator of this sect, Tacitus adds, "[was] Christ (Christus) who, during the reign of Tiberius had been executed by sentence of the procurator Pontius Pilatus" (*Annals* 15, 44). "Christus" is the Latin version of Christos, the Greek translation of the Jewish title *moshiach* (or *meshiach* in Aramaic), meaning "messiah" or "anointed one," a name for Jesus that gained currency after his death.

Perhaps the most intriguing attestation of Jesus in first-century non-Christian texts comes from the Jewish historian Josephus. His book *Antiquities of the Jews* was faithfully copied in Christian monasteries throughout the Middle Ages. In the process, however, the monks often added more text, which scholars call interpolations. Several studies have tried to isolate these interpolations, though the results remain the subject of considerable debate. Assuming that the kernel of the Josephus account is authentic, the author tells us that "there was about this time Jesus, a wise man" who was "a doer of wondrous works" and "drew over to him many of the Jews and many of the Gentiles." Josephus adds, "[W]hen Pilate, at the suggestion of the principal men amongst us, had condemned him to the cross, those that loved him did not cease to be attached to him."

Creation of the Gospels

TODAY, many Christians believe that the four canonical Gospels and the letters of Paul, all included in the New Testament,

Looking over modern Nazareth, the Church of the Annunciation occupies the center, built on the location where tradition holds that the archangel Gabriel visited Mary.

WHAT DID JESUS LOOK LIKE?

Roman fresco, fourth century

Byzantine mosaic, sixth century

Icon, St. Catherine's Monastery, sixth century

Renaissance painting, 16th century

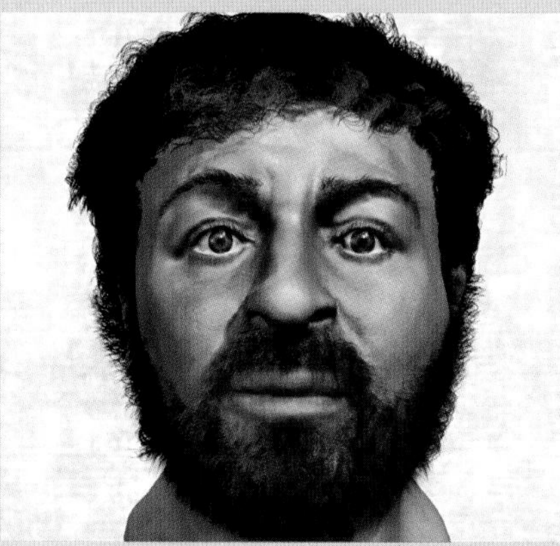
Forensic restoration of first-century Judean skull

Restoration using Shroud of Turin, 21st century

PORTRAITS OF JESUS ARE USUALLY A projection of the times in which they are produced. In Roman catacombs, Jesus is portrayed in the form of a beardless Apollo. As the focus of Christianity shifted toward Asia Minor, Jesus appeared in the guise of a Greek philosopher. Byzantine art emphasized the transcendental nature of Jesus by depicting him in the two-dimensional medium of the mosaic. From this Byzantine paradigm, the Eastern Orthodox Church developed the image of the Pantocrator, or "Ruler of All"—a frontal view of the bearded Christ with stern features and a hand raised in blessing. In northern Europe, the most popular image was the Jesus of the Passion, crucified on the cross. The Italian Renaissance introduced a new motif: a warm, pale-skinned young man with soulful eyes and long flowing hair, an image still with us today.

Despite their popularity, none of these portraits comes close to the probable Jesus of history. Jesus was likely a strong, muscular man, about five feet two to four inches in height—average size for Galilean peasants—with rough, chafed hands; tanned, olive-tinged skin; and dark brown eyes. He would have worn a beard, like most pious Jews. In 2002, British medical artist Richard Neave created a facial reconstruction using a skull from Jerusalem dated to the first century C.E., which press accounts proclaimed as "a new face of Jesus." The use of a skull from Jerusalem, capital of Judea and known for its multiethnic population, might not have yielded the most accurate result. A reconstruction of a skull from Galilee might have been more representative.

On Christmas Day 2004, Italian newspapers printed what they claimed was the face of Jesus as he appeared at the age of 12. The image had been produced by the forensic unit of the Italian police in Rome, which used a computer program to scan the image of the famous Shroud of Turin (traditionally believed to have been used to wrap Jesus after he was taken down from the cross) and reconstitute the face at an early age. What emerged was the visage of a young boy similar to countless Italian devotional paintings of the young Jesus: pale-skinned and blond, with a sweet, angelic expression.

are the most authoritative sources on the life of Jesus. The word "gospel" is derived from the Greek *euangelion* (*evangelium* in Latin), a common word that usually means "authoritative message," which later acquired the implicit allusion of "good news." Nevertheless, it is important to remember that the Gospels are not biographies in the modern sense, but religious testimonials inspired by faith. To ancient writers, history was not an objective, chronological arrangement of facts, but a vehicle for instruction. Historical accounts had no purpose if they taught no a certain philosophy or moral value. Accordingly, the evangelists were not concerned about arranging Jesus' biography in chronological order; their theological argument provided the principal narrative arc. One of the church's earliest leaders, Bishop Papias of Hierapolis (in modern Turkey), noted in the early second century C.E. that "Mark wrote accurately what he remembered the Lord said and did, though not in order."

How far removed are the written Gospels from the historical Jesus? Most biblical scholars accept that the evangelists were not eyewitnesses to the events they describe. The oldest Gospel in the New Testament, Mark, is believed to have been written about 40 years after the Crucifixion. Therefore, Gospel materials likely are based on many oral and written traditions about Jesus, interpreted through a theological prism, although quite possibly some of these strands originated within the circle of the Twelve Apostles. Scholars believe that this original material was quite extensive and may have included sayings, parables, miracle stories, anecdotes, and other accounts about Jesus. The evangelists gathered these strands of information into a unique and cohesive theological argument. Some of these different strands survive in their work, which explains why the Gospels diverge on specific details of Jesus' life.

There is no consensus on the dating of the four Gospels, but many experts believe that their writing was influenced by the hostility between Jews and Romans after the outbreak of the Jewish Rebellion in C.E. 66 and the destruction of the Second Temple in C.E. 70. The Gospels may have served to distance the nascent Christian communities, which included Jewish followers of Jesus, from the Jewish Zealot faction that instigated the costly war against Rome. If this is true, then the author known as Mark may have written his Gospel either during or after the Jewish War, which lasted until C.E. 70.

This depiction of the evangelist St. Matthew comes from the Gospel Book of Archbishop Ebbo of Reims, created in the ninth century C.E.

This interpretation of events also helps us to date the Gospels of Luke and Matthew, for critical analysis has shown that both Luke and Matthew derived major portions of their narrative from the Gospel of Mark. This fact would imply that both evangelists were active after the Gospel of Mark had entered wide circulation, possibly between C.E. 70 and 90. According to Christian tradition, the author of Luke was also responsible for the Book of Acts of the Apostles, and this suggestion is widely accepted.

If Matthew's work was indeed written around C.E. 80 or 90, as many scholars believe, it is unlikely that the author was "Matthew, the tax-collector," who knew Jesus firsthand (Matthew 10:2-4). Jewish authors often attributed theological works to prominent biblical figures so as to bolster their authority and credibility. It is possible, however, that the author had access to original writings or recollections associated with the Apostle Matthew.

Because of their similarity, the works of Luke and Matthew, as well as the original by Mark, are together referred to as the synoptic Gospels (from the Greek *sunoptikos,* meaning "seen together"). These three works are remarkably different from the fourth, and last, Gospel in the Christian canon, written by the author known as John. The Gospel of John places Jesus in a highly developed theological framework, illustrated with lengthy monologues spoken by Jesus. Scholarship tends to place the Gospel of John near the end of the first century C.E. Nevertheless, a lot of material in John does not appear in any of the synoptic Gospels, which suggests that John may have used authentic sources about Jesus to which none of the other evangelists may have had access.

Jesus' Birth and Childhood

The Shepherds Field near Bethlehem is where, according to tradition, the angels appeared to announce the birth of Jesus to local shepherds.

THE GOSPELS OF MATTHEW and Luke each provide a different version of Jesus' birth. Luke states that Mary, a young woman "from a town in Galilee called Nazareth," is betrothed to a man named Joseph. There is no indication of where Joseph resides, except that he descends from "the house of David," thus establishing Jesus' messianic pedigree (Luke 1:26-27). The Gospel of John, by contrast, explicitly refers to Joseph as originating "from Nazareth" (John 1:45).

Luke describes how the archangel Gabriel appears to Mary to tell her that "you will conceive in your womb and bear a son, and you will name him Jesus" (Luke 1:31). This episode follows the scriptural precedent of a divine promise that a childless woman will bear a son, as in the cases of Abraham's wife, Sarah, and of the Prophet Samuel's mother, Hannah. The name Jesus, or *Yeshua* in Aramaic, is a contraction of Yehoshuah, meaning "YHWH is salvation."

When Mary protests that she is still a "virgin," the archangel Gabriel assures her that "the Holy Spirit will come upon you, and the power of the Most High will overshadow you." To substantiate this proclamation, Gabriel reminds her that her "relative Elisabeth, in her old age," had conceived a son (who grew up

ca 7–4 B.C.E.
Jesus is born

ca 5 B.C.E.
Chinese astronomers observe an exploding star

ca 4 B.C.E.
Herod dies; his kingdom is divided among his sons, Archelaus, Herod Antipas, and Philip

ca 4 B.C.E.
Roman forces, sent by Archelaus, slaughter more than 3,000 Jews in Jerusalem

When the angels had left them ... the shepherds said to one another, "Let us go now to Bethlehem and see this thing that has taken place, which the Lord has made known to us." So they went with haste and found Mary and Joseph, and the child lying in the manger. (Luke 2:15-16)

to become John the Baptist); therefore, "nothing will be impossible with God" (Luke 1:34-37). These words are reminiscent of the angel's response to Sarah and Abraham in Genesis when announcing Isaac's birth: "Is anything too wonderful for the Lord?" (Genesis 18:14).

In the Gospel of Matthew, by contrast, the angel appears to Joseph. Mary is "found to be with child," and Joseph, her betrothed, plans to "dismiss her quietly" without making a public spectacle (Matthew 1:18-20). But "an angel of the Lord appeared to him in a dream," telling him "do not be afraid to take Mary as your wife, for the child conceived in her is from the Holy Spirit." According to Matthew, whose Gospel is very concerned with connecting Old Testament precedents to Jesus, this event was a fulfillment of Isaiah's earlier prophecy that "the young woman is with child and shall bear a son, and shall name him Immanuel" (Isaiah 7:14). Matthew's account of Joseph's dream repeats Isaiah's prediction to further emphasize the connection between it and Jesus (Matthew 1:23).

Location of Jesus' Birth

CHRISTIAN TRADITION naturally places Jesus' birth in the first year of the Common Era, but details in the Gospels suggest otherwise. According to both Matthew and Luke, Jesus was born during the reign of Herod the Great, which would place the date no later than 4 B.C.E., the year of Herod's death. Luke adds, "[in] those days a decree went out from Emperor Augustus that all the world should be registered. This was the first registration and was taken while Quirinius was governor of Syria" (Luke 2:1-2). This official has been identified as Publius Sulpicius Quirinius, who was governor of Syria. But Quirinius held office from C.E. 6 to 12, well after Herod's death. Moreover, there is no official record of Sulpicius Quirinius ordering a census.

Matthew adds that the birth of Jesus was attended by a bright star rising (Matthew 2:2). Some have linked this phenomenon to a nova, or exploding star, observed by Chinese astronomers in the year 5 B.C.E. Others have associated it with a striking conjunction of the planets Jupiter and Saturn three times in the same year, which would have been clearly visible to the naked eye. Observing this same phenomenon in 1603, the astronomer Johannes Kepler calculated that it also must have occurred in 7 B.C.E. Based on this information, it is reasonable to assume that by the first year of the Common Era (which is meant to mark the year of Jesus' birth), Jesus was, in fact, a boy of about four to six years old.

The Gospels of Mark and John begin the story when Jesus is a grown man. There is no reference to the annunciation, to Jesus' birth, or to his childhood. The Gospel of Mark opens with John, "the baptizer [who] appeared in the wilderness, proclaiming a baptism of repentance for the forgiveness of sins" (Mark 1:4). Jesus does not appear until chapter 1, verse 9: "In those days Jesus came from Nazareth of Galilee and was baptized by John in the Jordan."

Should it be assumed that Nazareth was the place of Jesus' birth? Neither Mark, the oldest Gospel, nor John give any specific details about where Jesus was born. It was unusual at that time to leave the city of one's birth; however, Matthew implies that Joseph and Mary live in Bethlehem and only move to Nazareth after seeking refuge in Egypt.

This sixth-century Byzantine relief is one of the earliest portraits of the infant Jesus in the Nativity story as described in the Gospel of Luke.

ca 4 B.C.E.
Emperor Augustus adopts as his heir Tiberius, who will become emporer in C.E. 14

ca C.E. 1
Romans formally recognize the Euphrates River as the Parthian border

ca C.E. 6–12
Publius Sulpicius Quirinius serves as governor of the Roman province of Syria

ca C.E. 6
A tax revolt, referred to in the Gospel of Luke, follows a census ordered by governor Quirinius

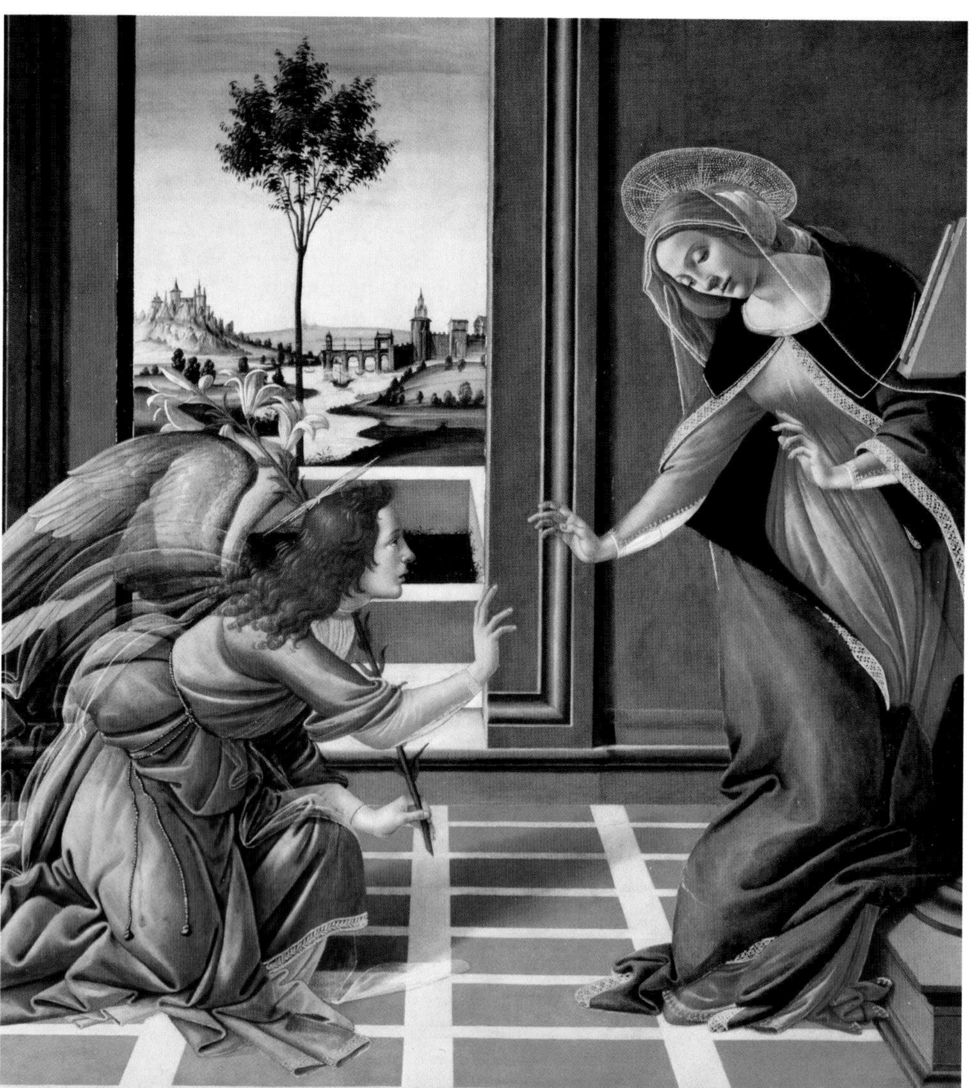

THE ANNUNCIATION

THE STORY OF THE ANNUNCIATION AND THE birth of Jesus to the Virgin Mary appears only in the Gospels of Luke and Matthew. While the annunciation narrative has many precedents in the Hebrew Bible, the virgin birth of Jesus is unique. It does not appear elsewhere in the New Testament, although surprisingly, the Muslim Koran supports the idea (Koran 3:47). Matthew, whose Gospel is deeply concerned with the scriptural precedents of Jesus' ministry, explicitly links the virgin birth to the prophecy of Isaiah: "A virgin shall conceive and bear a son, and shall call his name Immanuel" (Isaiah 7:14). Scholars believe that Matthew took this quotation from the Septuagint (the Greek translation of the Hebrew Bible), where the original word *'almah* was translated as *parthenos,* which in Greek can mean both "virgin" and "young woman of nubile age."

Interestingly, Luke does not use the virgin birth to support his theological argument. The virgin conception by God's Holy Spirit, rather than by Joseph, would also contradict Matthew's lengthy genealogy, the purpose of which is to demonstrate that Jesus, through Joseph, had Davidic ancestry (Matthew 1:1-17).

Sandro Botticelli (1444–1510) created this interpretation of the annunciation, a popular subject with Renaissance artists, circa 1490.

Luke is the only Gospel to state unequivocally that Joseph and Mary travel from Nazareth to Bethlehem in order to be "registered" during the putative census of Sulpicius Quirinius (Luke 2:3-4). The reason for this journey, Luke explains, is that Joseph is a descendant of the house of David, which was based in Bethlehem. This passage does raise historical problems, however. The purpose of a Roman census was to update the mechanism of local taxation. Therefore, the people of Galilee would have been required to appear in their current place of residence, where tax collectors could find them, rather than in the place of their birth or tribal association.

Luke's placement of Jesus' nativity in Bethlehem may have been motivated by the prophecy of Micah that he "who is to rule in Israel" shall come from Bethlehem (Micah 5:2). The New Testament scholar Bruce Chilton has

MARY AS A YOUNG GIRL

Like other girls in Galilee, Mary probably wore simple clothes: a linen undergarment, covered by a long, sleeveless tunic bound by two girdles, one under the bosom and one around the waist. When going out (invariably in the company of a mother or another female relative), a girl covered her shoulders with a long, rectangular cloak and her hair with a veil. These cloaks were often adorned with simple geometric patterns near the shoulders and at the hem. Fragments of human hair found in 'En-gedi suggest that girls braided their hair and used two-faced combs, similar to the one found by excavators in the mountain fortress of Masada, for styling.

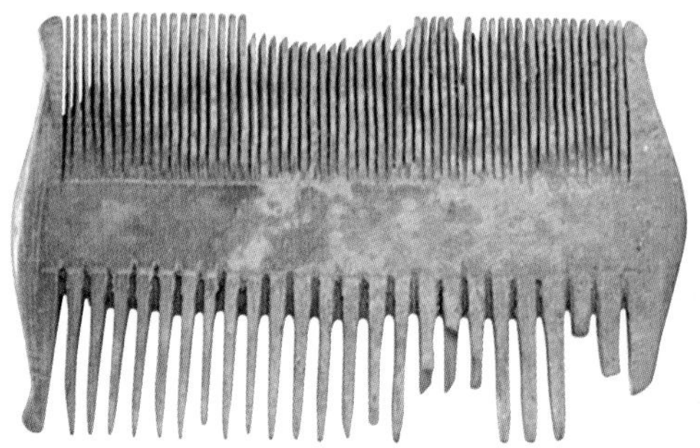

uggested that the reference in Luke nay pertain to a Galilean village called Bethlehem, which archaeological excavations have located just seven miles rom Nazareth.

esus' Youth in Nazareth

ALTHOUGH THE LOCATION of Jesus' birth sn't known for certain, we do know that ne grew up in Nazareth. Tradition holds hat Joseph was a carpenter. If this were rue, then Jesus, as Joseph's firstborn, would undoubtedly have been trained n his father's craft.

But the Gospels give a different mpression. As many of his parables or symbolic stories testify, Jesus is intimately familiar with agriculture and the careful cultivation of Galilean soil. In the Gospel of Mark, Jesus speaks with evident authority about the difficulty of sowing:

> *A sower went out to sow.*
> *And as he sowed, some seed fell*
> *on the path, and the birds came*
> *and ate it up. Other seed fell on*
> *rocky ground, where it did not*
> *have much soil, and it sprang up*
> *quickly, since it had no depth of soil.*
> *And when the sun rose,*
> *it was scorched; and since it had*
> *no root, it withered away.*
>
> (Mark 4:3-6)

Casting a practiced eye on a fig tree that had not borne fruit for three years, Jesus counsels the owner to "let it alone for one more year, until I dig around it and put manure on it. If it bears fruit next year, well and good; but if not, you can cut it down" (Luke 13:8-9). And to emphasize that the goodness of one's heart produces good, Jesus reminds his

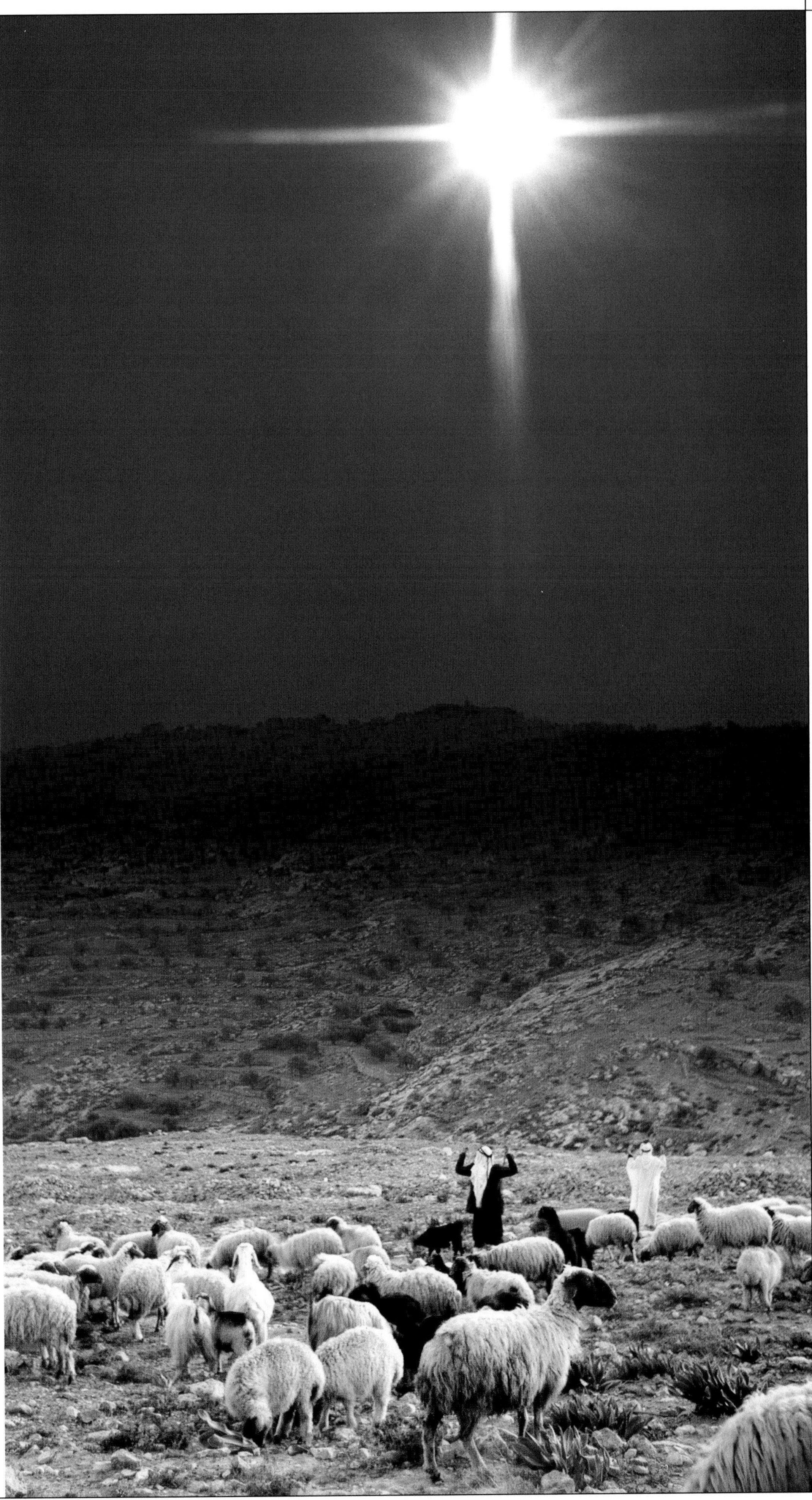

According to the Gospel of Matthew, "wise men from the East" searched for the newborn Jesus, having observed "his star at its rising" (Matthew 2:1-2).

[The master replied:] "Let [the wheat and the weeds] grow together until the harvest; and at harvest time I will tell the reapers, Collect the weeds first and bind them in bundles to be burned, but gather the wheat into my barn." (Matthew 13:30)

audience that "[figs] are not gathered from thorns, nor are grapes picked from a bramble bush" (Luke 6:44).

These words from the Gospels create an impression that Jesus (or Jesus' father, Joseph) was a Galilean peasant. He was a man whose life revolved around the cycle of harvest and nature's seasons, rather than hammer and saw. In his histories Josephus observed that virtually everyone in Galilee was in some way or form involved with farming the land.

Apparently, this fact held true for the small hamlet of Nazareth as well. Beginning in 1955, the Franciscan archaeologist Bellarmino Bagatti spearheaded a series of excavation campaigns directly underneath the Church of the Annunciation in Nazareth—traditionally the site associated with the grotto where Mary received the archangel Gabriel. The area revealed a series of structures built atop each other, the oldest of which may have been an early synagogue, arguably built by Jewish Christians in the third century C.E. Underneath this synagogue, Bagatti found granaries, olive presses, and wells, which attest to the existence of an agricultural village as early as the first or second century C.E.

Revolt in Galilee

WHY, THEN, is Joseph described as a carpenter in the New Testament? The answer may be found in the history of first-century Galilee, since the years after the death of Herod the Great were a period of great upheaval. Galilean farmers were deeply resentful of Herod's crushing taxes. During Passover in April of 4 B.C.E., a number of Jewish dissidents organized a protest in the Temple

MARRIAGE AND BIRTH

JEWISH GIRLS IN FIRST-CENTURY PALESTINE, like Mary, were probably betrothed shortly after puberty began, around age 13 or 14. Both parents would negotiate the marriage contract. Jewish women were expected to make clothes for their family, and learned the art of spinning wool and weaving as young girls. Often they used a loom of threads suspended with small wooden weights. One such loom was discovered in 'En-gedi.

Childbirth was the exclusive province of women. In first-century Palestine, every village had at least one practicing midwife. A physician named Soranus of Ephesus recorded childbirth practices in the time of Jesus. The midwife would rub the stomach of the pregnant woman with olive oil and myrtle, and she was then bathed in sweet water to relax her skin. As dilation approached, the midwife anointed the genital area with herbs and oils and then moved the mother to a "birthing stool," equipped with special arm and back supports and an opening in the seat for the delivery of the child. Two flanking midwives supported the mother, while the midwife in charge crouched in front of her to catch the child. Once the baby was born, the midwife used powdered salt to clean the baby and then rinsed the nose, mouth, ears, and anus with warm water. Thus cleansed, the newborn would be swaddled in wool cloths and laid down on a pillow full of hay or on a mattress with a channel to keep the baby from rolling over. In fact, Soranus recommends using "feeding troughs" for this purpose since they were slightly inclined and could prop up the baby's head. Luke's reference to a "manger" as Jesus' first crib may therefore attest to actual use.

According to the Mosaic law laid out in the Book of Leviticus, a woman was considered "ritually unclean" for the first seven days after giving birth. If the newborn was male, he was circumcised in a ritual known as berith on the eighth day. Then, the new mother was freed from household chores for the next 25 days in order to speed her recovery and allow the mother and child to bond (Leviticus 12:1-8).

This C.E. 19th-century birthing chair, found in the Old City of Cairo, Egypt, resembles those depicted in reliefs from the Roman Empire.

forecourt, then still under construction. A Roman cohort sent to break up the protest was pelted with stones. Convinced that a major revolt was brewing and anxious to protect his inheritance, Herod's son Archelaus sent in Roman troops, including cavalry, who killed about 3,000 Jews, most of them innocent bystanders. The event sent shockwaves throughout the country.

While Archelaus was in Rome to claim the throne of his allotted tetrarchy from Emperor Augustus, a man named Judah instigated a revolt in Galilee, took the provincial capital of Sepphoris, and captured the arms cache stored there. According to Josephus, the Romans retaliated by attacking Sepphoris, enslaving the inhabitants, and burning the city to the ground. The Roman governor Varus, says Josephus, "[then] sent part of his army around the countryside, seeking those to blame for the revolt." The rebellion was quelled, but the farming communities seethed with rage. This anger erupted again ten years later.

In C.E. 6, when Jesus may have been about 12 years old, a man named Judas of Gamala, who would later found the Jewish paramilitary group called Zealots, organized the second Galilean tax revolt. The combined forces of two Roman legions were dispatched from Syria to suppress the rebellion.

Galilean fields were burned, wells were poisoned, and entire villages were destroyed. Two thousand Jews were executed; in addition, some 6,000 young Galileans were deported into slavery. Galilean agriculture was devastated; farmers whose families had tilled their plots for centuries lost everything they had. Perhaps it is with these unfortunates in mind that, in the Gospel of Matthew, Jesus refers to "the lost sheep of the house of Israel" (Matthew 10:6). It may also explain why Josephus

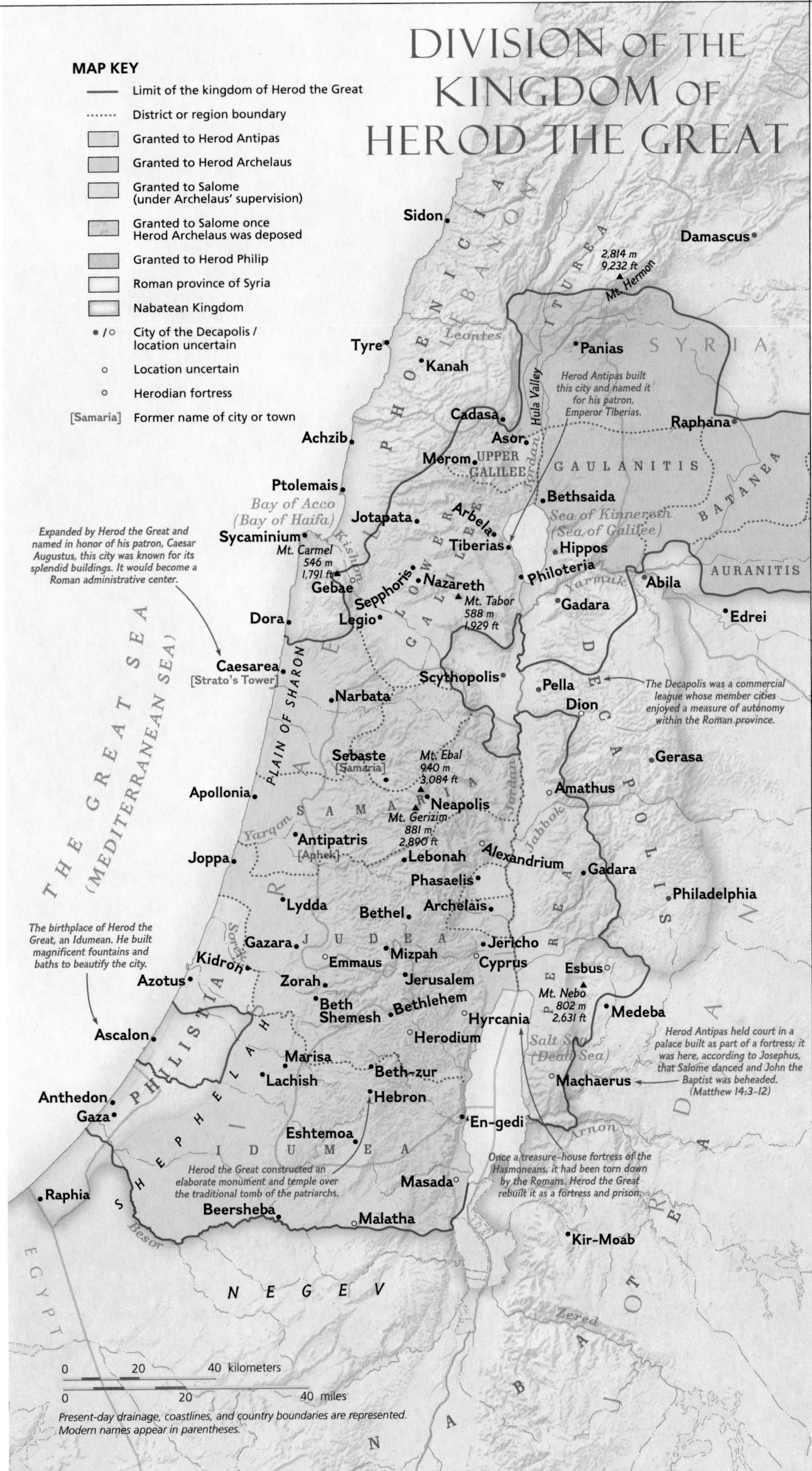

describes Galileans as "inured to war from their infancy."

In the aftermath of this war, many farmers, bereft of harvest and land, would have been desperate to find employment elsewhere. As it so happened, an enormous new construction project was under way, less than half a day's march from the village of Nazareth: the restoration of the city of Sepphoris, the place where the Galilean tetrarch, Herod Antipas, resided. Sepphoris had been destroyed during the first Galilean tax revolt, and Antipas decided to rebuild Sepphoris in the Greek model so beloved by his father.

Sepphoris

THE REMARKABLE FULL story of Sepphoris has come to light only in recent years, following the excavation of the ancient site in the 1980s by Duke and South Florida universities and the Hebrew University of Jerusalem. Archaeologists working at the site uncovered a typical Greco-Roman city that used a street grid anchored on a main north-south axis known as the *cardo* and bisected at right angles by another axis known as the *decumanus*. Each avenue, bordered by the bustle of shops and offices, ultimately led to the commercial and religious heart of the city, the forum.

There was even a sophisticated sewage system underneath the stone pavement. In addition, Antipas indulged in the building of an expensive Roman theater, similar to the famous amphitheater of Jerusalem built by his father. "Sepphoris," writes Josephus, "was the jewel of all Galilee."

The construction of Sepphoris took many years. The project must have dominated commercial activity in Galilee and consumed considerable amounts of manpower, supplies, and foodstuffs from all over the region throughout Jesus' adolescence. It is difficult to imagine that such a nearby undertaking would have left the family of Jesus unaffected. Sepphoris was barely five miles from Nazareth. For a farmer without land, tools, draft animals, or seeds, the booming construction activity would have presented a fortuitous opportunity to earn a living to sustain a growing family.

The "Mona Lisa from Galilee," is a detail from elaborate floor mosaics found in a third-century Roman villa in Sepphoris.

And Joseph's household *was* growing; according to Mark and Matthew, Jesus had four younger brothers and an unspecified number of sisters (Mark 6:3; Matthew 13:55). Several scholars suggest that Joseph and his eldest son may have worked on Antipas's reconstruction of Sepphoris for much of Jesus' teenage years and well into his early adulthood. In fact, the true meaning of the Greek word *tekton* in Mark, chapter 6 verse 3, traditionally translated as "carpenter," is more akin to the Aramaic *naggara'*, meaning "laborer" or "worker."

According to the Gospel of Luke one of Jesus' first public acts was to go to the synagogue of Nazareth and read a verse from the Book of Isaiah (Luke 4:16-20). All in attendance "were amazed at the gracious words that came from his mouth" (Luke 4:22). But if Jesus spent most of his adolescent years on the scaffolding of Sepphoris, how would he have received an education? Did he, in fact, learn to read? How was he introduced to the Scriptures?

Few Galileans spoke or read Hebrew; it is likely that the Nazareth synagogue, like other synagogues in the region, used an Aramaic translation of Hebrew Scripture, later known as the Targum. But who taught Jesus how to read Scripture, as Luke claims, and to develop the scriptural knowledge that would earn him the honorific of rabbi (teacher) in his later years? Some scholars have argued that in the first century C.E., the Pharisees maintained a number of schools, usually attached to synagogues, where children could learn to read and receive instruction in the Torah. It is doubtful, however, that such a school would have existed in a small hamlet like Nazareth. Nevertheless, the young Jesus must have been very articulate, for later it is revealed that his speeches and sermons drew hundreds of people from far and wide. "The Jews were astonished at it," says John, "saying, 'How does this man have such learning, when he has never been taught?' " (John 7:15). The likeliest answer is that Jesus received some form of education outside of Nazareth, though any evidence has so far remained elusive.

OPPOSITE: **The Roman theater of Sepphoris, built by Herod Antipas. Enlarged in the third to fourth centuries C.E., it could seat 4,000 people.**

MINISTRY OF JESUS

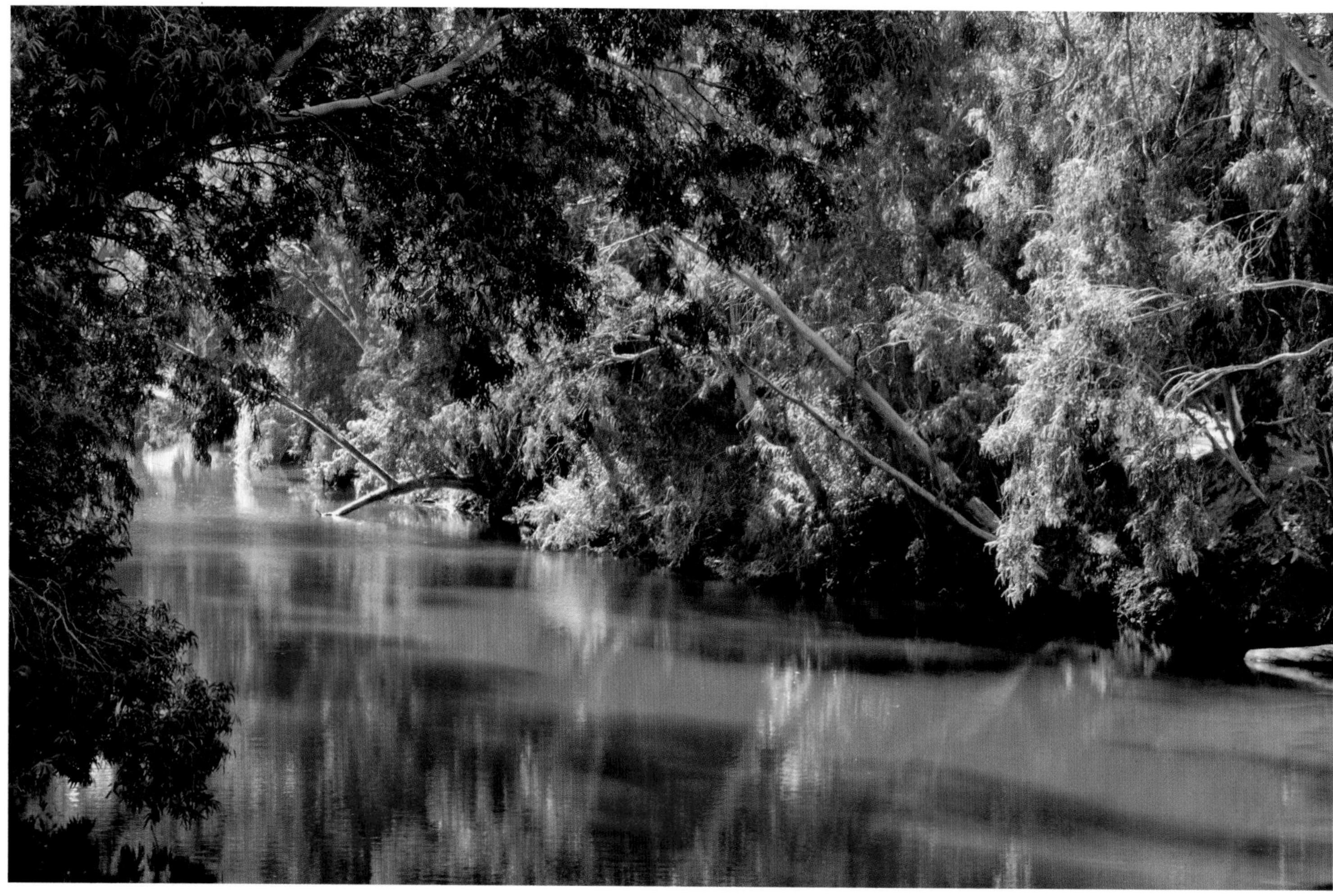

From the Sea of Galilee, the Jordan River begins to descend south and down to the Dead Sea, located at 1,300 feet below sea level.

THE BAPTISM OF JESUS IN the Jordan River by John the Baptist appears in all four canonical Gospels. Mark and John use this critical moment to open their Gospels. Luke even marks the works of John the Baptist with a specific date, namely, the "fifteenth year of the reign of Tiberius Caesar" (either C.E. 28 or 29), and adds that Jesus was "about thirty years of age" at the time (Luke 3:1; 3:23). This fact suggests that the baptism marked a seminal point in Jesus' life. Jesus abandoned his everyday pursuits and devoted himself to the search for God.

The Teachings of John the Baptist

BUT WHY DID JESUS choose to go to John? Why did he travel to the desert of the lower Jordan in search of a hermit, who ate locusts and dressed himself in a tunic made of camel's hair (Mark 1:6)? The answer may once again be found in the works of the first-century C.E. historian Flavius Josephus, who describes John as one of the most charismatic preachers of his day. "John," says Josephus in *Jewish Antiquities*, "was a good man, and commanded the Jews to exercise virtue, both as to righteousness towards one another, and piety towards God, and so to come to baptism."

ca C.E. 6
Following its destruction by Roman troops, Herod Antipas begins rebuilding Sepphoris in Galilee

ca C.E. 9–12
Marcus Ambibulus is appointed procurator of Judea

ca C.E. 12–26
Annius Rufus and Valerius Gratus succeed Ambibulus as Judean procurator

ca C.E. 14–37
Tiberius reigns as emperor of Rome

Jesus came to Galilee, proclaiming the good news of God, and saying, "The time is fulfilled, and the kingdom of God has come near; repent, and believe in the good news." (Mark 1:14-15)

The public response to John was overwhelming. People flocked to him, "for they were very greatly moved by his words." The reason, no doubt, was the prevailing atmosphere in Palestine. The Jewish people felt unmoored from their destiny as God's chosen people. Their land was occupied and crushed by tribute and taxes. The Temple, the traditional center of Jewish religious identity, was run by a collaborationist priesthood wholly focused on maintaining the apparatus of ritual sacrifice and on collecting their tithes. The land itself, given in holy tenure by YHWH, was also contaminated by Greco-Roman symbols, just as it had been in the days of Ahab and Manasseh when the idols set up had angered YHWH. If scripture was any guide, pious Jews believed another catastrophe was undoubtedly on the horizon, another King Tiglath-pileser or King Nebuchadnezzar, sent by a Lord stirred to anger by Israel's sins.

John nurtured these apocalyptic fears by warning his followers that God's wrath would be more devastating than it has been at any time in Israel's history. A messiah would come, John says in the Bible, whose "winnowing fork is in his hand, to clear his threshing floor and to gather the wheat into his granary; but the chaff he will burn with unquenchable fire" (Luke 3:17). Faced with such a terrifying prospect, John the Baptist's followers believed they could do only one thing: break with their sinful past and symbolize their repentance by an all-cleansing immersion in water. Only then will the righteous ones be able to find shelter in the Lord's "granary."

Many scholars have linked John's teaching to that of the Essenes of Qumran, who likewise pursued an ascetic lifestyle in the desert. Like the Essenes, John preached the message that God's retribution was imminent. Nothing but an all-consuming rebirth, symbolized by ritual immersion, could save the Jewish people from destruction.

The Essenes, however, preached a communal life of celibacy, self-negation, and extreme purity—even to the point of withholding one's bodily functions on the Sabbath. Theirs was an exclusive circle, open only to those willing and prepared to abide by the community's rules. John, by contrast, reached out to anyone who was willing to listen and repent. John's *Torah* was a school unto itself, sustained by the urgency of God's coming judgment.

Most scholars agree that the Gospel material relating to John the Baptist is authentic, simply because the apparent success of John's movement posed a subtle challenge to the future role of Jesus himself. John's prominence challenged the orthodox view that Jesus' message was unprecedented. While Jesus merits only one paragraph in Josephus's *Antiquities*, John receives more than a full page. John the Baptist, it would seem, was the star prophet of his day, which is probably why Jesus, together with many other idealistic young Jews, was attracted to him in the first place.

John's Arrest and Execution

AT SOME POINT in time after Jesus joined the Baptist community, however, Herod Antipas arrested John. The Gospels of Mark and Matthew argue that the tetrarch issues the warrant because John has criticized Herod's unseemly marriage to Herodias, the wife of his half-brother Herod Boethus, whom the Gospels confuse with his full brother Philip (Matthew 14:3-4; Mark 6:17-18; Luke 3:19-20). This second marriage for Herod Antipas was politically motivated. Herodias was a granddaughter of Herod the Great's wife Mariamne, the Hasmonean princess, who could thus give Antipas's rule a Hasmonean pedigree.

This pair of first-century leather sandals was found on the fortress of Masada in the Judean desert, close to the Dead Sea.

ca C.E. 18–36
Joseph ben Caiaphas serves as high priest in the Temple in Jerusalem

ca C.E. 26–36
Pontius Pilate serves as prefect of Judea

ca C.E. 26–36
Pilate allows military standards in the Temple precinct, provoking the Jewish population

ca C.E. 26–28
Jesus joins the movement of John the Baptist in the Jordan River Valley

SIMON PETER'S HOUSE

ONE REASON JESUS CHOSE CAPERNAUM as the center of his ministry was that the Apostle Simon Peter had a house in this lakeside city. The archaeologists who excavated the traditional site of Simon Peter's house uncovered several layers of construction, the oldest of which dates to the first century B.C.E. Here, on the plastered wall of one house, excavators found a number of inscriptions mentioning both Simon Peter and Christ, as well as a number of references to *ichthys*, the Greek word for "fish." It was a popular word among early Christians because of its double meaning. The fish relates to the Apostles' being called "fishers of men" (Mark 1:17); the word "ichthys" itself is an acronym in Greek of the phrase *Jesus Christ Son of God Savior.* The inscriptions suggest that the house was already revered by pilgrims within decades after the Jesus' death. Even more telling, archaeologists recovered small fishhooks on the floor, indicating that the house had been occupied by fishermen, some of whom may have been recruited by Jesus as followers (Matthew 4:21-22).

The remains of churches built on top of a first-century house, which according to tradition was the house of St. Peter in Capernaum.

From her first marriage, Herodias also had a daughter, named Salome. According to Mark, Salome dances at one of Antipas's banquets and pleases her stepfather so much that he offers her "[w]hatever you ask [of] me." Salome consults her mother, who clearly has not forgiven John the Baptist for denouncing her new marriage. She tells her daughter to ask for the head of the preacher. Antipas is "deeply grieved," yet he has no choice but to grant her request (Mark 6:21-27). Herod sends a guard to the prison where John is held. The guard beheads John and brings his head on a platter to Salome.

Josephus, however, suggests that there was another reason for John's death. Antipas, he writes, "feared that John's great influence over the people might put it into his power and inclination to raise a rebellion, (for they seemed ready to do any thing he should advise)." Certainly John had uttered strident sentences such as: "every tree therefore that does not bear good fruit is cut down and thrown into the fire" (Luke 3:9). And so, according to Josephus, Antipas put John to death rather than spare "a man who might make him regret it when it would be too late."

In the Bible, John the Baptist is executed (Matthew 14:10) in the Herodian fortress of Machaerus, located in modern Jordan just five miles east of the Dead Sea. Herod decided to execute John without consulting the Sanhedrin, the council of priests based in Judea but endowed with authority over all of Israel. Their approval would have made the execution legal. Herod's decision is surprising, since John's death could well have incited the very insurrection that Antipas was trying to prevent.

After John's death, his disciples "came and took his body, and laid it in a tomb" (Mark 6:29). The followers are shocked, bewildered, adrift. Where should they go? Would Herod's soldiers come for them next? Several scholars have inferred from the Gospel of John that a number of the Baptist's disciples turn to Jesus and anoint him John's successor (John 1:40-41).

A Ministry's Beginnings

THE BIBLE TELLS US that Jesus' first decision is to move the followers out of danger, away from the western banks of the Jordan, which fell under Antipas's jurisdiction. The group might have headed north to Bethsaida, on the shore of the Sea of Galilee, just across the border in the territory of Tetrarch Philip, and later to Capernaum, the territory of Antipas, which also lay on the shores of the great lake.

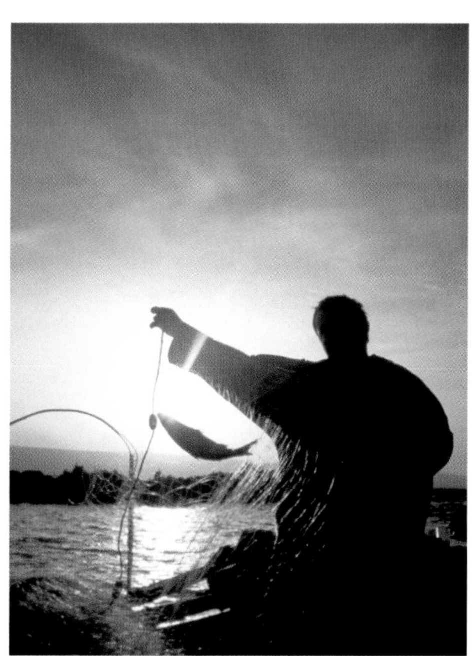

The first rays of dawn shine over the water, as a lone fisherman retrieves his nets on the Sea of Galilee.

Overwhelmed by the responsibility of leadership, Jesus then withdraws into the desert. Mark states that this retreat lasts 40 days (Mark 1:13), but such figures in the Bible often carry a symbolic rather than a literal meaning. The 40 days in the desert, like the 40 years spent by the Israelites in the Sinai, are a time of spiritual cleansing, a period of preparation before moving on to the next stage of Jesus' life.

Upon his return, "Jesus went throughout Galilee," says Matthew, "teaching in their synagogues and proclaiming the good news of the kingdom and curing every disease and every sickness among the people" (Matthew 4:23). Jesus' path did not lead to the solitude of the wilderness but to the heart of Galilean towns, where the sinners,

The craggy peaks and canyons of the Judean desert stretch between the Samarian hills to the west and the Jordan River Valley to the east.

THE MINISTRY OF JESUS IN LOWER GALILEE

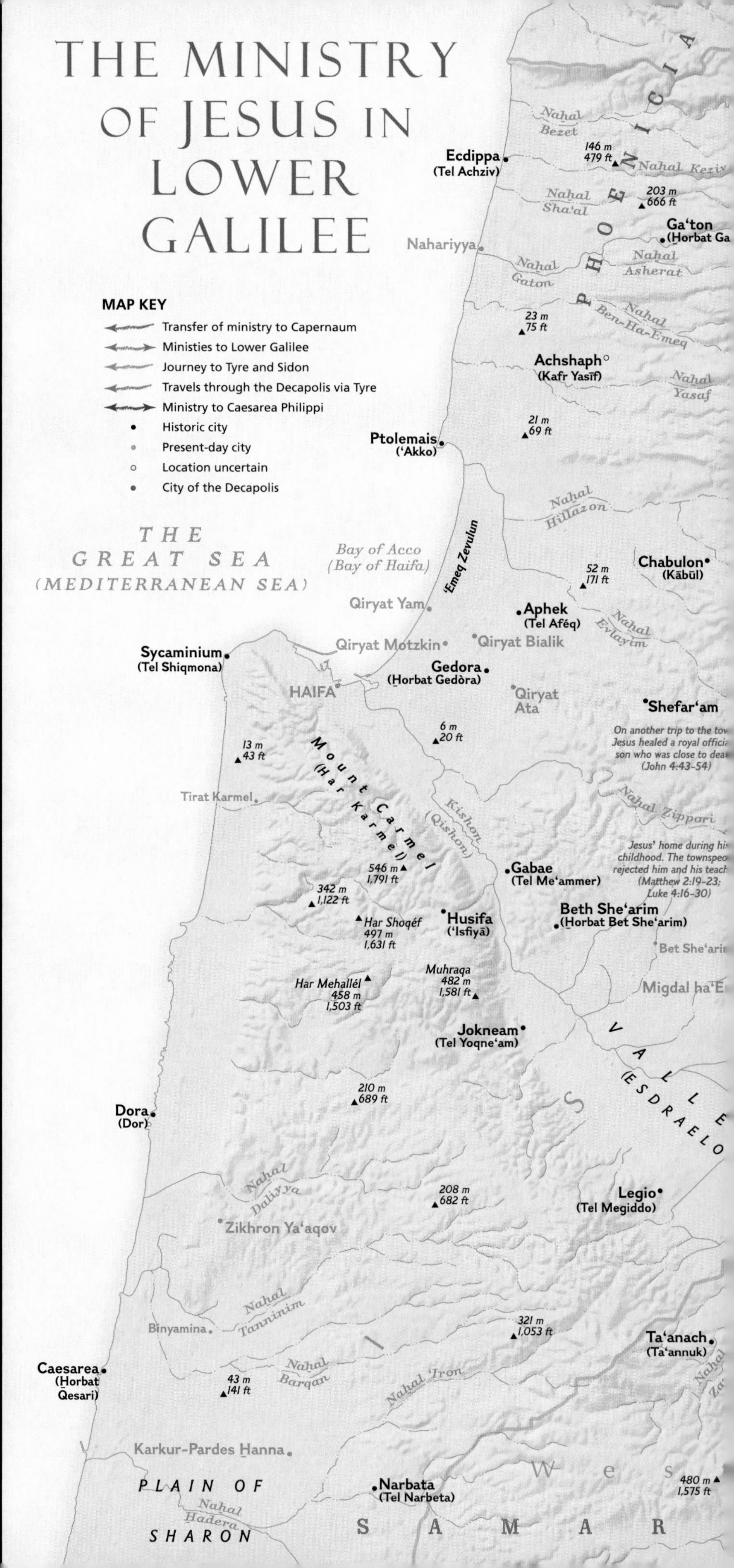

Green fields surround the hillside village of Nazareth, where Jesus lived as a child. There, he "grew and became strong, filled with wisdom" (Luke 2:40).

hese earthenware vessels come from Cana, the location of Jesus' first miracle in the Gospel of John, where he changes water into wine at a wedding.

his Byzantine mosaic in Tabgha, located two miles west of Capernaum, commemorates Jesus' miraculous multiplication of loaves and fishes.

Centrally located on the Sea of Galilee, the ancient city of Capernaum was at the center of Jesus' activity. Here, a Greek Orthodox Church sits by the shore today.

MAP KEY

- Transfer of ministry to Capernaum
- Ministies to Lower Galilee
- Journey to Tyre and Sidon
- Travels through the Decapolis via Tyre
- Ministry to Caesarea Philippi
- • Historic city
- • Present-day city
- ○ Location uncertain
- • City of the Decapolis

PHOENICIA
Nahal Bezet
Ecdippa (Tel Achziv)
146 m 479 ft
Nahal Keziv
Nahal Sha'al
203 m 666 ft
Ga'ton (Horbat Ga
Nahariyya
Nahal Gaton
Nahal Asherat
23 m 75 ft
Nahal Ben-Ha-Emeq
Achshaph (Kafr Yasīf)
Nahal Yasaf
21 m 69 ft
Ptolemais ('Akko)
Nahal Hillazon
THE GREAT SEA (MEDITERRANEAN SEA)
Bay of Acco (Bay of Haifa)
'Emeq Zevulun
52 m 171 ft
Chabulon (Kābūl)
Qiryat Yam
Aphek (Tel Aféq)
Nahal Evlayim
Sycaminium (Tel Shiqmona)
Qiryat Motzkin
Qiryat Bialik
Gedora (Horbat Gedòra)
HAIFA
Qiryat Ata
Shefar'am

On another trip to the tow Jesus healed a royal officia son who was close to dea (John 4:43-54)

6 m 20 ft
13 m 43 ft
Mount Carmel (Har Karmel)
Tirat Karmel
Kishon (Qishon)
Nahal Zippori

Jesus' home during hi childhood. The townspeo rejected him and his teach (Matthew 2:19-23; Luke 4:16-30)

546 m 1,791 ft
Gabae (Tel Me'ammer)
342 m 1,122 ft
Har Shoqéf 497 m 1,631 ft
Husifa ('Isfiyā)
Beth She'arim (Horbat Bet She'arim)
Bet She'ari
Muhraqa 482 m 1,581 ft
Har Mehallél 458 m 1,503 ft
Migdal ha'E
Jokneam (Tel Yoqne'am)
VALLE (ESDRAELO
210 m 689 ft
Dora (Dor)
Nahal Daliyya
208 m 682 ft
Legio (Tel Megiddo)
Zikhron Ya'aqov
Nahal Tanninim
Binyamina
321 m 1,053 ft
Ta'anach (Ta'annuk)
Caesarea (Horbat Qesari)
43 m 141 ft
Nahal Barqan
Nahal 'Iron
Nahal Za
Karkur-Pardes Hanna
PLAIN OF SHARON
Nahal Hadera
Narbata (Tel Narbeta)
480 m 1,575 ft
SAMAR
Wes

Cadasa (Tel Qedesh)
To Caesarea Philippi and returning to Capernaum
To Tyre and Sidon
Lake Hula
From Tyre and Caesarea Philippi
Har Avital 1,204 m 3,950 ft
540 m 1,772 ft
82 m 269 ft
504 m 1,654 ft
160 m 525 ft
Nahal Dishon
Nahal Gilbon
Har Yosifon 981 m 3,219 ft
Har Addir 1,006 m 3,301 ft
885 m 2,904 ft
Gischala (Jīsh)
Har Ben Zimra
Asor (Tel Hazor)
Nahal Hazor
372 m 1,221 ft
GAULANITIS
Nahal Keziv
Har Merom 1,208 m 3,963 ft
Merom
CAPERNAUM
Called, "his own town," Jesus based his ministries from this city and performed many of his miracles there. A frontier town between the lands of Antipas and Philip, the city was astride an important trade route that would have helped spread his message throughout the region. (Matthew 9:1)
As Jesus taught his "good news of the kingdom" and healed multitudes, large crowds from the surrounding regions followed him from place to place. (Matthew 4:23-25)
After his resurrection, Jesus met the disciples in Galilee and commissioned them to "go make disciples of all nations." (Matthew 28:16-20)
Zefat
Nahal 'Ammud
Jordan
Har Ha'ari 1,047 m 3,435 ft
Har Hillel 1,071 m 3,514 ft
Jesus denounced the cities most of his miracles had been performed in because of their lack of repentance. He also included Bethsaida and Capernaum in his judgement. (Matthew 11:20-24)
Nahal Meshushim
Har Peres 929 m 3,048 ft
Bersabe (Horbat Be'er Sheva')
Biq'at Bet Kerem
One possible location where the feeding of the multitude could have taken place. (Matthew 14:13-21; 15:32-39)
Har Kena'an 486 m 1,595 ft
435 m 1,427 ft
A likely location where the feeding of multitude and the multiplication of the loaves and fishes took place. (Matthew 14:13-21; 15:32-39)
Jesus healed many when he and the disciples visited. (Mark 6:53-56)
Har Kammon 598 m 1,962 ft
Hanania (Zomet Hananya)
Chorazin (Korazim)
Gamala (Gamla)
Nahal Daliyyot
Har Hazon 584 m 1,916 ft
Tradition places the Sermon on the Mount here.
Bethsaida (Zomet Bet Zayda)
Capernaum (Kefar Nahum)
Mary Magdalene was from here. She was one of several women who had been healed or cleansed, and who provided support for Jesus and the disciples. (Luke 8:2-3)
Bethsaida was the home town of disciples Peter, Andrew, and Philip. (Luke 1:44)
Jesus healed a blind man by spitting on his eyes and laying his hands on him. (Mark 8:22-26)
Sakhnin
Jesus performed his first miracle here, turning water into wine at a wedding. (John 2:1-11)
Heptupegon ('En Sheva')
Nahal Zalmon
487 m 1,598 ft
Nahal Kanaf
Gennesaret (Ginnosar)
After sending the disciples on ahead by boat, Jesus walked on the water out to them during the night. (Matthew 14:22-33)
Har Netofa 526 m 1,726 ft
Magdala / Taricheae (Migdal)
Sea of Kinnereth, Lake Tiberias (Sea of Galilee)
Nahal Samakh
548 m 1,798 ft
Cana (Horbat Qana)
Gergesa (Kursi)
Biq'at Bet Netofa
151 m 495 ft
Horns of Hattin (Qarne Hittim) 326 m 1,070 ft
A possible site where Jesus cast out demons which entered swine that then rushed down the slope to drown in the water. Another possible place is near the city of Gadara south of the Yarmuk River. (Luke 8:26-39)
Arbela (Horbat Arbel)
261 m 856 ft
Haré Tir'an 548 m 1,798 ft
Tiberias (Teverya)
Aphek (Afiq)
Bethmaus (Horbat Bet Ma'on)
Hippos (Horbat Susita)
Nahal Yiftahel
Hammath (Hammat)
Nahal Raqqad
Taking his ministry to the towns of the region, Jesus cleansed a leper, and his fame spread throughout Galilee. (Mark 1:38-45)
The capital of Herod Antipas, whom Jesus called "that fox." He ruled Galilee and Perea in Jesus' time. (Luke 13:32)
Shaken by a sudden storm, the disciples despaired until Jesus awoke and "rebuked the wind and the waves," quieting the maelstrom. (Matthew 8:23-27)
Sepphoris (Zippori)
Garis (Kefr Kanna)
Biq'at Yavne'el
Gath-hepher (Mash-had)
Har Yona
532 m 1,745 ft
144 m 472 ft
Yarmuk
A possible site of the Transfiguration. Jesus also healed an epileptic boy in the area. (Matthew 17:1-13; 17:14-22)
Philoteria (Tel Bet Yerah)
Sennabris
368 m 1,207 ft
Nazerat 'Illit
Nazareth (Nazerat)
Mt. Tabor 588 m 1,929 ft
Har Yavne'el
DECAPOLIS
Haré Nazerat 397 m 1,302 ft
Exaloth (Iksāl)
368 m 1,207 ft
Emmatha (Hammat Gader)
Abila
Biq'at Kesullot
Jordan
Yarmuk
Gadara (Umm Qays)
Endor ('En Dor)
335 m 1,099 ft
565 m 1,854 ft
'Afula 'Illit
Nain (Nein)
Giv'at Hamore 515 m 1,690 ft
Nahal Tavor
Wādī 'Arab
Afula
Shunem (Sūlam)
147 m 482 ft
Ramot Yissakhar
Jesus brought the dead son of a widow back to life before the whole funeral procession. (Luke 7:11-17)
Kamon (Qam)
Jezreel, Esdradela (Yizre'el)
JEZREEL / 'EMEQ YIZRE'EL
Jesus healed a deaf and mute man in the Decapolis. (Mark 7:31-37)
Arbela (Irbid)
377 m 1,237 ft
Nahal Harod
Wādī Taiyiba
Ephron (At Tayyibah)
JORDAN
SYRIA
The Decapolis was a commercial league whose member cities enjoyed a measure of autonomy.
Haré Gilboa'
497 m 1,631 ft
Scythopolis (Bet She'an)
0 4 8 kilometers
0 4 8 miles
Present-day country boundaries are represented. Modern names appear in parentheses.
Ginae (Janīn)
Pella (Tabaqat Fahl)
Har Malkishua' 473 m 1,552 ft
GALILEE
West Bank
LEBANON

the "publicans" (tax collectors), and the Roman collaborators could be found. Like a physician, Jesus went straight to the place where he could expect to find the sick, waiting to be cured.

The first town, and indeed the center of Jesus' ministry, was Capernaum, the place where Simon Peter, perhaps Jesus' most devoted follower, had a house. Capernaum was situated centrally on the Sea of Galilee, connected by constant maritime traffic to the eastern shore and the Decapolis, the territory of the Greek league of ten cities; and to the western shore and the hinterland of Lower Galilee. Capernaum lay at the heart of what became Jesus' "mission triangle," the area circumscribed by Bethsaida, Chorazin, and Capernaum, where Jesus focused much of his minstry's activity.

During their first excavation of Capernaum in 1905, German archaeologists H. Kohl and C. Watzinger discovered a beautiful, basilica-shaped synagogue. The limestone building featured a central prayer hall, screened from the two flanking aisles by carved Corinthian columns. Could this synagogue be the one in which Jesus taught "on the Sabbath" and where he first revealed his healing power (Luke 4:31-37)? As excavation work continued well into the 1960s, it became clear that the synagogue dated from the third or fourth century C.E. Nevertheless, further digging revealed that the synagogue was built on top of an older and very similar house of worship. This older building could very well date to the time of Jesus.

The synagogue's elaborate facade, with its two consoles carved in the shape of palm trees, leaves little doubt that the city of Capernaum was an affluent place, prosperous from trade in basalt, olive oil, and wine. Evidence of this lucrative trade is everywhere. A few steps from the synagogue are reliefs of vines and grapes; nearby is a delicately carved cornice featuring grapes and figs and a rare depiction of the Ark of the Covenant. Such luxury might have offended John the Baptist, but for Jesus, Capernaum was the perfect symbol of Galilee's precarious balance between Jewish consciousness and Greco-Roman wealth.

Discovered along the Sea of Galilee in 1986, the remains of this first-century C.E. boat show how Jesus' vessel, used in his ministry, might have been built.

In the biblical account, Jesus often travels with his fishermen companions on the Sea of Galilee. Their boats allow him to traverse the lake quickly. Unlike John the Baptist, Jesus does not wait for the people to come to him; instead, he actively courts his growing audience by visiting as many different villages as possible. A small ship was the fastest and most economical means for doing so.

There are some 20 references in the Gospels to the vessel used by Jesus. According to Matthew, "when he got into the boat, his disciples followed him" (Matthew 8:23). The boat is, by implication, a vessel large enough to accommodate at least 10 or perhaps 13 men—Jesus and the Twelve Apostles.

With no physical description of such a boat, no one quite knew what it could look like until the winter of 1986, when a drought dropped the water level of the Sea of Galilee to unusually low levels. The receding waters exposed an ancient boat, fully preserved, at a distance of no more than five miles from Capernaum. Expert restorers used the science of carbon dating to assess the age of the boat. They were astonished to discover that the vessel was built between 50 B.C.E. and C.E. 50, a time span that overlaps the period of Jesus' ministry.

This Galilean boat is an impressive example of ancient craftsmanship. It is 26 feet long and 7.5 feet wide—large enough to comfortably accommodate 10 people with their sacks and nets.

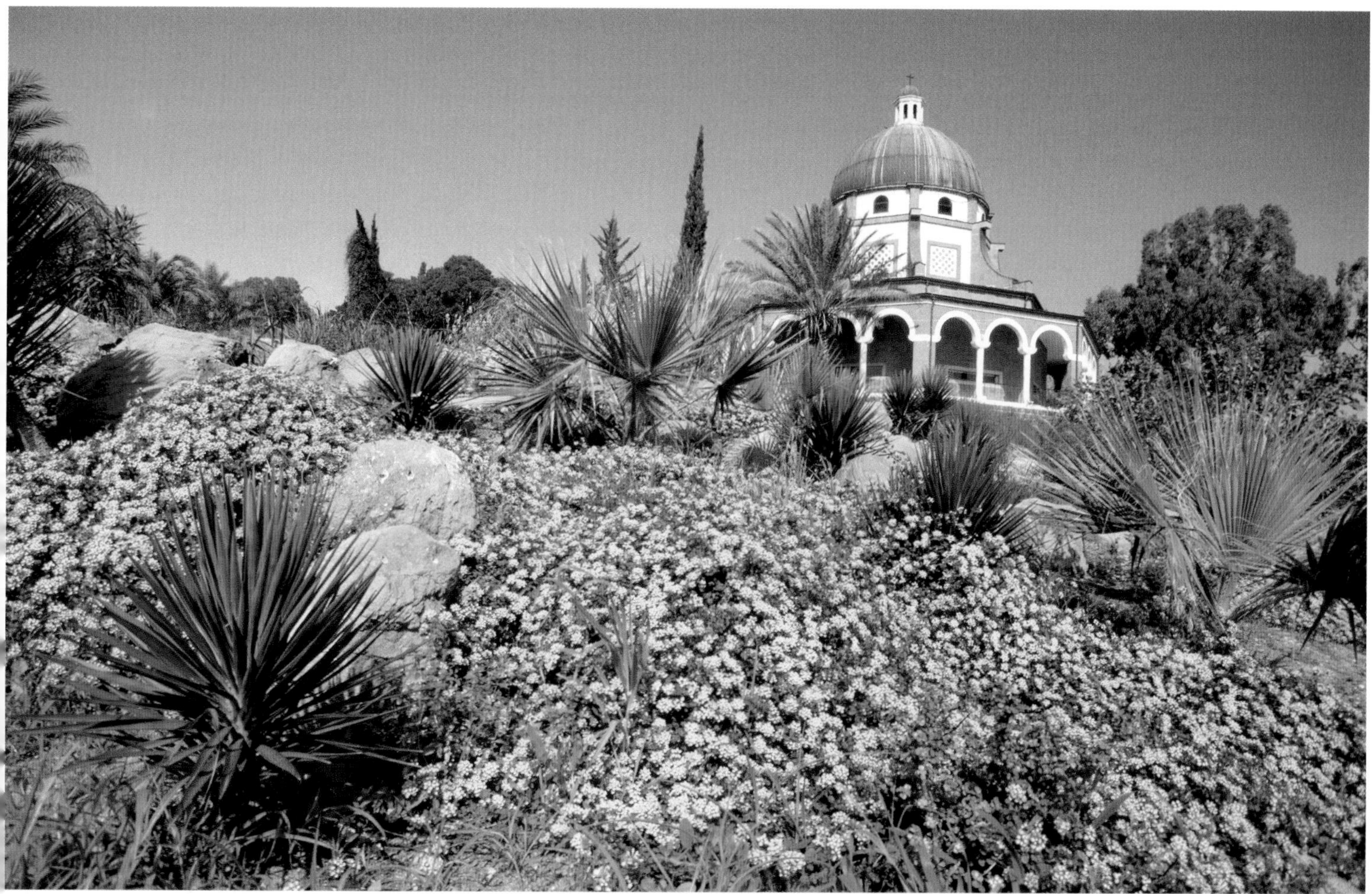

The Mount of the Beatitudes, topped by a Franciscan church built in 1937, marks the place associated with Jesus' Sermon on the Mount.

The planks are bound together with joints fastened by pegs—a construction method favored by shipbuilders throughout the Mediterranean.

During one of his journeys along the shores of the Sea of Galilee, Jesus reportedly teaches on a hill near Tabigha and soon attracts large crowds. Using the gentle slope as his sounding board, Jesus turns to the people and says:

Blessed are the poor in spirit,
for theirs is the kingdom of heaven.
Blessed are those who mourn,
for they will be comforted.
Blessed are the meek, for they will
inherit the earth.
Blessed are those who hunger and thirst
for righteousness, for they will be filled.
Blessed are the merciful, for
they will receive mercy.
Blessed are the pure in heart,
for they will see God.
Blessed are the peacemakers,
for they will be called children of God.

(Matthew 5:3-9)

Scholars believe that of the Beatitudes listed above, the first two and the fourth one are among the oldest quotations attributed to Jesus. As we have seen, such proverbs were the ancient philosopher's preferred oratorical device. The Judaic Scriptures, particularly the psalms, are replete with proverbs that teach the secret of happiness. Beatitudes, also known as macarisms (based on the Greek word *makarios*, meaning "fortunate"), were equally popular among the Egyptians and the Greeks. With Jesus, this familiar motif gained a new meaning by the addition of another favorite Near Eastern formula, the paradox.

Thus, the phrase "Blessed are those who hunger" is a deliberate oxymoron designed to jolt Jesus' audience. As the poor people of Galilee knew only too well, hunger did not make people happy; it made them miserable. And yet, says Jesus, today's suffering is the key to happiness in the new kingdom of tomorrow (Matthew 5:3-10). These proverbs—blessed are the poor, blessed are those who mourn—reveal Jesus' target audience: the poor and the marginalized in Galilean society.

The "kingdom of God" is the central theme of Jesus' teaching. Mark puts it most succinctly: "Jesus came to

Galilee, proclaiming the good news of God, and saying, 'The time is fulfilled, and the kingdom of God has come near; repent, and believe in the good news' " (Mark 1:14-15). Time and again Jesus struggles to explain the kingdom to the Apostles, often reverting to parables: "The kingdom of heaven is like a mustard seed ... the smallest of all the seeds, but when it has grown it is the greatest of shrubs and becomes a tree" (Matthew 13:31-32). "The kingdom of God is as if someone would scatter seed on the ground, ... and the seed would sprout and grow, he does not know how. ... [F]irst the stalk, then the head, then the full grain in the head. But when the grain is ripe, at once he goes in with his sickle, because the harvest has come" (Mark 4:26-29). And, "The kingdom of heaven is like yeast that a woman took and mixed in with three measures of flour until all of it was leavened" (Matthew 13:33).

This colorful 14th-century stained-glass window from the Klosterneuburg Abbey in Austria commemorates Jesus' healing of the leper.

Even so, scholars do not agree on the true meaning of the kingdom doctrine. To some, it is an apocalyptic vision of the world after the end of time, when the dead will rise again and God will resume control over all of mankind. To others, it is a theocratic reign established by the Messiah, rightful heir to the throne of David, whose arrival is imminent. Another interpretation holds that the kingdom of God is life after death, in which the righteous will be received into the grace of God.

A problem that loomed large for Jesus' followers was when and how Jesus thought this theocratic kingdom would come about. Several sayings suggest that Jesus thought it was imminent, and this urgency is precisely what the early Christians believed. The evangelist Paul, who energetically spreads Jesus' message to the Gentile world, is convinced it will happen in his lifetime (I Corinthians 15:51). When the Thessalonians ask him how they would know when the kingdom has come, for example, Paul replies, "[C]oncerning the times and the seasons, brothers and sisters, ... you yourselves know very well that the day of the Lord will come like a thief in the night" (I Thessalonians 5:1-2).

Luke may present it best, however, when Jesus turns to the Pharisees and says, "The kingdom of God is not coming with things that can be observed; nor will they say, 'Look, here it is!' or 'There it is!' For, in fact, the kingdom of God is among you" (Luke 17:20-21). In this interpretation, the kingdom of God is neither a political entity nor a distant reward after the passage of death, but a blueprint for a society based on justice, compassion, and surrender to God.

Then he returned from the region of Tyre, and went by way of Sidon towards the Sea of Galilee, in the region of the Decapolis. They brought to him a deaf man who had an impediment in his speech; and they begged him to lay his hand on him.

(Mark 7:31-32)

Jesus' Travels

ACCORDING TO the synoptic Gospels, Jesus focuses his campaign on the area immediately to the north and west of the Sea of Galilee, in cities like Capernaum, Chorazin, and Bethsaida on its northern shore, and Nain just south of Nazareth. An excursion to the sea's eastern shore leads him to Kursi (Gergasa), while a journey to the region of Tyre and Sidon brings him in contact with a Gentile girl, the daughter of a Syro-Phoenician woman, whom he is persuaded to heal (Mark 7:24-30). At other times, he withdraws to pastoral fields along the Banyas River, in the foothills of Mount Hermon, to rest and pray (Mark 6:45-46). When Jesus visits nearby Caesarea Philippi, Peter proclaims him to be the Messiah (Matthew 16:16). The Gospel of John, however, places much of Jesus' activity in Samaria, Judea, and, particularly, Jerusalem. For example, the healing of a sick man in the Pools of Bethesda only appears in John (John 5:2-9).

Though it is impossible for us to know with certainty, Jesus may have met in Magdala his most important female follower identified by name, Mary Magdalene (which means "of Magdala"). Located on the western shore of the Sea of Galilee, Magdala was a principal center of the rapidly growing fishing industry. Formed by the Jordan River, bordered on the east by the hills of Perea, the Sea of Galilee is really a large lake, some 13 miles from north to south and 7 miles from east to west. At its deepest point, it is only 150 feet deep. Excavations below the coastal water level have revealed no less than 15 different harbors along its shores.

It is possible that, in the early decades of the first century C.E., the ranks of fisherman had swelled with farmers and their sons who no longer had any land to till. The Gospels indicate that incessant fishing threatened the stability of the fish stock in the Sea of Galilee. According to Luke, Simon Peter tells Jesus that the fishermen have "worked all night long but caught nothing" (Luke 5:5). Jesus counsels them to throw their nets one last time. The result is an enormous catch. Luke says that when the nets threaten to tear, "ships from nearby" rush to the scene to help—and to get their share of this unexpected boon.

Israeli scientists have established that, then as now, there were some two or three dozen species of fish in the lake. The Apostles, like most of the local fishermen today, would have been eager to catch three types of edible Galilean fish. The first is the small silvery sardine, possibly the species of the "two fish" mentioned in the story of Jesus' miraculous multiplication of bread and fish (Luke 9:13). Sardines

According to the Gospel of John, Jesus healed a paralytic man by the Pools of Bethesda, one of the few locations attested to by archaeological discovery.

and bread were the staple of the Galilean diet in Roman times. The second species is the barbel, a long, streamlined fish. The third, and perhaps most popular, type of fish is the Galilee tilapia, popularly known as Saint Peter's fish. This fish has a long, comblike dorsal fin and can grow to a length of 1.5 feet. According to Israeli scientists, a stable stock of Saint Peter's fish, which feeds on seaweed, would have been vital in maintaining the ecosystem and chemical balance of the lake.

Fishing on the Sea of Galilee was not without its dangers. For instance, the synoptic Gospels report the onset of a sudden storm while the disciples are on the lake (Mark 4:37; Matthew 8:24; Luke 8:23). Though the Sea of Galilee is usually placid, sudden squalls do occur. During a particularly violent gale in March 1992, for example, waves ten feet high crashed into downtown Teverya, causing significant damage. Subsequent investigations attributed these sudden storms to the east-west topography of Galilee's hill country. The hills act as a funnel, accelerating winds coming down from the north as well as hill breezes off the eastern Golan Heights. The winds, swirling in the lake basin, can unleash sudden squalls that endanger anyone caught on open water.

Miracles Performed by Jesus

THE MIRACLES ATTRIBUTED to Jesus established his credibility as a teacher and prophet of God. He is said to have healed lepers, to have made the blind see, and even to have restored the dead to life. According to other stories, Jesus controlled the elements of nature. Even the first-century C.E. Judeo-Roman historian Flavius Josephus writes that Jesus was a "wise man and a doer of wondrous works." The Gospels contain more than 30 miracle stories, but they are not always consistent. There is also an obvious similarity between the healings reportedly performed by Elijah and Elisha and those credited to Jesus, including the miraculous multiplication of bread and the resuscitation of young children. These common threads among the stories have prompted some experts to dismiss the miracles as legend.

A sixth-century ivory relief from the Cathedral of Maximian in Ravenna depicts Jesus' multiplication of wine during the Wedding at Cana.

Diligent literary archaeology, nevertheless, has uncovered that the healing stories, in particular, belong to the very oldest oral traditions about Jesus. Two elements distinguish the healing accounts from the other miracles. First, Jesus explicitly tells the afflicted person, "your sins are forgiven" (Matthew 9:2). Among first-century Jews, illness and disease were regarded as God's punishment for sins. If a child was born blind or deaf, for example, it was assumed that the infant had been conceived in sin and thus bore the penalty for the immoral acts of the parents. Consequently, those people suffering with chronic disease were ostracized from society and often had to live in squalor on the periphery of villages. Illness was therefore often compounded by great emotional stress. Jesus' deliberate closeness to the patient, and his assurance that any presumed sins are forgiven, must have lifted a powerful mental obstacle to a person's natural ability to heal.

The second thing that distinguishes the healing accounts from the other miracles is that Jesus makes a point of touching those who are ill. To someone bereft of human intimacy for years, or possibly most of his life, the physical touch of Jesus would have been an electrifying experience. Eastern medicine holds that the human mind has far greater power over an individual's wellness than Western tradition would assume. If this were true, then Jesus' affirmation of a diseased person's innate dignity would have been a powerful stimulant to healing.

Some scholars emphasize the symbolic meaning of Jesus' miracles. By blessing and multiplying a humble meal of bread and fish, Jesus may have deliberately seized on the typical staple of a poor man's diet and "multiplied it" to illustrate that those who believe will be rewarded tenfold in the kingdom of God. In this interpretation, Jesus' emphasis on bread goes beyond theology and into the realm of social justice. When Jesus emphatically states, "laborers deserve their food" (Matthew 10:10), he affirms the basic dignity of the Galilean peasant and his right to feed himself and his family.

TWELVE APOSTLES

The Gospels relate that Jesus chose 12 followers "whom he named apostles" (Luke 6:13). The number 12 has been interpreted to symbolize the 12 tribes of Israel, while the name "apostle," based on the Greek word *apostolos*, means "a person sent [forth]." Jesus often sent the Apostles ahead of him to determine if he would be welcome. He instructed the Apostles to avoid the cities of the Gentiles and focus on Jewish villages, the "lost sheep of Israel"; not to carry gold or silver, or luggage with a change of clothes, but to appeal to the charity of villagers (Matthew 10:9-14).

Some of the Apostles were former disciples of John the Baptist; many made a living as fishermen. James and John, sons of Zebedee, hailed from Capernaum; Philip, Simon Peter, and his brother. Andrew, were men of Bethsaida. The other Apostles were Bartholomew; Matthew the "publican" (tax collector); Thomas; James the son of Alphaeus; Thaddeus (or Judas); Simon the Canaanite (or "Zealot"); and Judas Iscariot (Matthew 10:2-4; Luke 6:13-16).

The Gospels often depict the Apostles as plodding, well-intentioned but uneducated men struggling to understand Jesus' teachings; but their loyalty to Jesus is absolute. After the Crucifixion, no one from the original corps of Apostles is heard of again except for Peter, who takes the lead in building the early Church in Jerusalem. James, the brother of Jesus, eventually takes over. Several letters, including one written by Clement to the Christian community of Corinth in C.E. 96, suggest that Peter left Jerusalem to focus on pastoral work. In time, he came to Rome, where the persecutions under Emperor Nero led to his arrest. According to tradition, he was crucified and buried in a dumping ground near a hill called Vatican. At his request, he was crucified upside down: He felt unworthy to die in the same manner as Jesus.

Leonardo da Vinci (1452–1519) sketched this study of the apostles before painting the fresco *The Last Supper*.

THE ROAD TO JERUSALEM

Today, this view from the Garden of Gethsemane on the Mount of Olives looks toward Temple Mount, where the Second Temple once stood.

RECONSTRUCTING THE LAST weeks of Jesus' life with any certainty is difficult because the chronologies of events in the four Gospels do not always agree with one another. The Gospel accounts suggest, however, that Jesus' ministry in Galilee has run its course. Crowds still come to the Sea of Galilee to hear Jesus speak, perchance to see a miracle, but few people actually change their lives in the manner prescribed by Jesus. The people's indifference may be the explanation for Jesus' outburst in Luke: "Woe to you, Chorazin! Woe to you, Bethsaida!," turning his back on the very cities that had been at the heart of his ministry (Luke 10:13). Frustrated by the lack of repentance, Jesus scoffs that if his "deeds of power" had been carried out in the Gentile cities of Tyre and Sidon, "they would have repented long ago."

Jesus may have felt a need to redirect his ministry. Passover is drawing near—a time when Jerusalem overflowed with pilgrims bearing offerings for the Temple. Perhaps he is inspired by the Prophet Jeremiah, whom the Lord summons to go to the Temple and appeal to "all [the] people of Judah," telling them:

> *[I]f you truly amend your ways*
> *and your doings, if you truly act*

ca C.E. 28
Pontius Pilate brutally suppresses a peaceful protest near the Temple in Jerusalem

ca C.E. 30–33
Jesus is crucified at Golgotha on the orders of Pilate

ca C.E. 36
Pilate is recalled by Emperor Tiberius and replaced with Marcellus

ca C.E. 36
High Priest Caiaphas is succeeded by Jonathan ben Ananus

When he entered Jerusalem, the whole city was in turmoil, asking, "Who is this?" The crowds were saying, "This is the prophet Jesus from Nazareth in Galilee." (Matthew 21:10-11)

justly one with another, if you do
not oppress the alien, the orphan,
and the widow, or shed innocent blood
in this place, and if you do not go after
other gods to your own hurt, then I will
dwell with you in this place,
in the land that I gave of old
to your ancestors forever and ever.

(Jeremiah 7:1-7)

"See," Jesus tells his disciples, "we are going up to Jerusalem, and everything that is written about the Son of Man by the prophets will be accomplished" (Luke 18:31).

Jesus chooses a circuitous route, perhaps because friendly Pharisees had warned him that that Herod Antipas is looking to kill him (Luke 13:31). Why Antipas wants to arrest him is not stated, though it is possible that the tetrarch is once again planning a preemptive strike before Jesus' following became too large and powerful. After a sojourn in the region of Gaulanitis in the tetrarchy of Philip, Jesus may have moved south along the Yarmuk River, passing the popular Roman spa center of Hammat Gader, until he and his followers reached the Jordan. From there they would have crossed over the Jordan near Beth Shan in order to avoid Perea, territory ruled by Antipas, until the group reached Jericho, then an important center for the Roman colonial administration. According to the Gospel of Luke, Jesus restores the sight of a "blind man begging" in Jericho (Luke 18:35-43) and stays at the house of a tax collector, whom he urges to change his sinful ways (Luke 19:1-9).

From Jericho, a steep climb would have awaited the group: the long meandering road through the Judean hills to Jerusalem. It is the lunar month of Nisan, arguably the Jewish calendar year of 3790 (early April in the year C.E. 30). Inns and private homes must have been overflowing with the large crowds of pilgrims that already have preceded Jesus and his followers to Jerusalem. So Jesus stays in Bethany, in the house of Lazarus and his sisters, Mary and Martha (Mark 11:11; Luke 10:38; Matthew 21:17; John 11). From Bethany it is only a two-hour walk, less than two miles at most, to the walls of Jerusalem.

The next day the group sets out for the city. Upon entering the city gate, Jesus may have been recognized by Galilean pilgrims, or by Judeans who have heard of him, for the Gospels state that he is welcomed with spontaneous hymns and praise. Here too, the Gospels may seek a deliberate link to Old Testament prophecy, notably that of Zechariah: "Shout aloud, O daughter Jerusalem! Lo, your king comes to you; triumphant and victorious is he, humble and riding on a donkey" (Zechariah 9:9).

A public entry like this one would have attracted the attention of the authorities. During this time, the Roman procurator of Judea (now a Roman province rather than an autonomous region like Galilee) had traveled to the city with a military unit, possibly a detachment of the Tenth Legion (X Fretensis), which was permanently stationed in the port city of Caesarea Maritima, the capital of Roman Judea. The procurator was Pilatus of the house of the Pontii (C.E. 26–36), a minor Roman family of knights with great ambitions. Pontius Pilatus (or Pilate), then in his fourth year in office, was determined to make his term in Judea a model of law and order. Astonished by the news that Jews were exempt from bowing or sacrificing to images of the emperor, Pilate soon after his arrival in C.E. 26 provoked the population of Jerusalem by moving his cohorts into winter quarters in the city, each carrying the standards of

This silver shekel with an Omer cup from Judea dates to the fourth year of the Jewish Revolt against the Romans (C.E. 66–70).

ca C.E. 37
Tiberius dies, and Gaius, also known as Caligula, becomes Roman emperor. Caligula is followed by Claudius

ca C.E. 37–44
Herod Agrippa I rules portions of Judea as tetrarch

ca C.E. 49
Emperor Claudius expels the Christians from Rome

ca C.E. 62
High Priest Ananus strikes against the Jesus movement

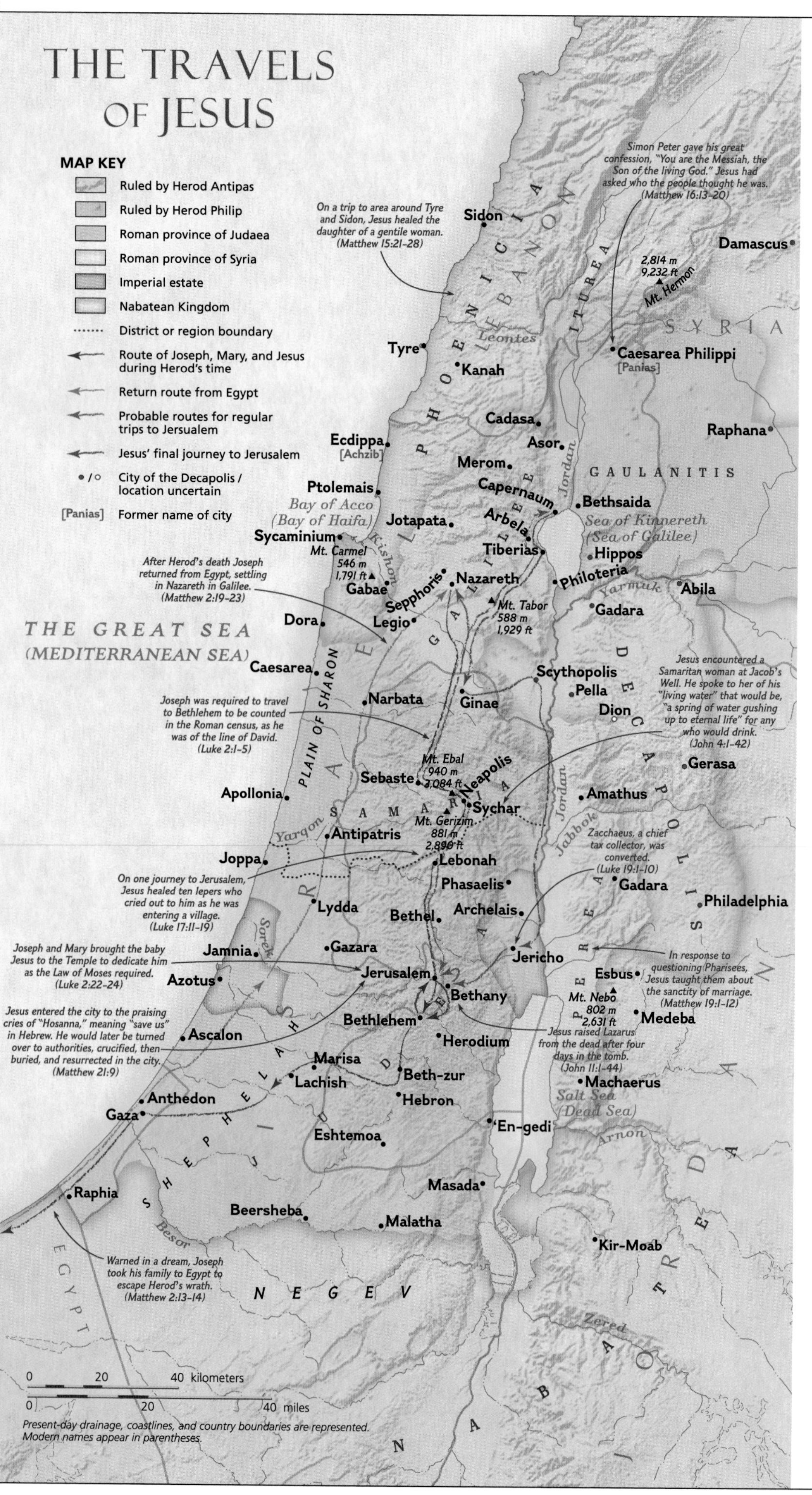

Rome as well as portraits of Emperor Tiberius. Soon thereafter (scholars do not agree on the exact date, but C.E. 28 would appear likely), Pilate arranged for the construction of a new aqueduct to bring water into the Upper City, where the priesthood and other wealthy families resided. Josephus states that this construction was financed out of the coffers of the Temple treasury, an act that, under normal circumstances, should have caused an uproar among the priesthood. After word of this action spread, Judean crowds staged a protest near the Temple, which, according to Josephus, Pilate ordered suppressed without mercy. His soldiers infiltrated the crowds dressed in cloaks and fell on the "rioters and bystanders in equal measure, so that a great number were killed."

Memories of this massacre were probably still fresh in the minds of the Jewish pilgrims who converged on Jerusalem in C.E. 30. Anticipating unrest, Pilate had placed the Roman garrison on high alert, determined to sit out Passover (a celebration of Israel's deliverance from slavery) in the city. In the Gospels of Mark, Luke, and John, Pilate is portrayed as a compassionate man who is vexed by the possibility of Jesus' innocence. Mark, however, wrote for a Roman audience, and he may have sought to exculpate Judea's highest Roman official in his story. The Pilate of history was a different man altogether, detested not only by Josephus but also by the Jewish philosopher Philo, who wrote that his term was marked by "outrageous injustice and ceaseless cruelty."

Following his entry into Jerusalem, the Bible describes how Jesus spends most of the day in the Temple forecourt, teaching and praying. According to the Gospels, it is the eve of Passover (Mark 14:12). In preparation, every male was expected to come to the Temple with a lamb for sacrifice; later, portions of this lamb would be eaten during seder. The Paschal lamb had to be older than eight days, but no older than one year, and free of any blemish. This rule was rigorously enforced, which is why many families bought lambs from the pens in the forecourt of the Temple, since they were guaranteed to pass priestly inspection.

To do so, however, the pilgrims had to "change" their Roman currency into Temple shekels, which were devoid of any graven image. This trade would have turned the Temple forecourt into a scene of frenzied commercial activity, with people pushing through the crowds to change their coins and buy their Paschal lamb (or in the case of the poor, a dove). The Gospels relate that Jesus is shocked by this commerce. According to Matthew, "Jesus entered the temple and drove out all who were selling and buying in the temple, and he overturned the tables of the money changers and the seats of those who sold doves" (Matthew 21:12). Moving from one table to the next, scattering the terrified money changers, Jesus cries: "It is written, 'My house shall be called a house of prayer'; but you are making it a den of robbers" (Matthew 21:13), as Jeremiah had done before him (Jeremiah 7:11). Some scholars suggest that the target of his wrath was not only the money changers, but also the panoply of priestly sacrifice. In this interpretation, Jesus' "cleansing" of the Temple was a symbolic act wholly consistent with his vision of a new and purified kingdom of God.

Later that day, the Bible says the disciples arrange for temporary board in a hall in the Lower City (Mark 14:12-15; Luke 22: 9-11). Tradition states that this hall was located above a synagogue. Today, Christian pilgrims in Jerusalem can visit a room in a complex just outside Zion Gate known as the Room of the Last Supper. Rebuilt by Franciscans in the 14th century, it was turned into a mosque by the Ottomans in the 16th century. During the war of 1948, a Jordanian shell destroyed part of its

The Room of the Last Supper, located on Mount Zion, is traditionally believed to be the place where Jesus and his disciples shared their last meal together.

supporting wall. Subsequent excavations uncovered sections of a stone wall in the Herodian style, built with neatly hewn stones, which could indicate the presence of a first-century ceremonial building, possibly a synagogue.

Jesus and his disciples then share what the synoptic Gospels describe as a Passover meal. Known as the Last Supper, it would become the foundation for the Christian sacrament of the Eucharist (from the Greek *eucharistia*, meaning "thanksgiving"). The fellowship of the meal had been a prominent feature of Jesus' ministry and much of the history of Judaism. Through the essential activity of sharing bread, Jews celebrated life. Abraham offered a meal to the three angels who visited him. Alliances or peace pacts, such as the one between Isaac and King Abimelech, were formally sealed with a celebratory meal (Genesis 26:30). But in the hands of Jesus, the Last Supper with his disciples became a spiritual substitute for the ritual sacrifice at the Temple—an idea that was also current among the Essenes.

A stone from the Roman theater in Caesarea bears the dedication: "[to the gods this] Tiberium [has been dedicated by] Pontius Pilate, Prefect of Judea."

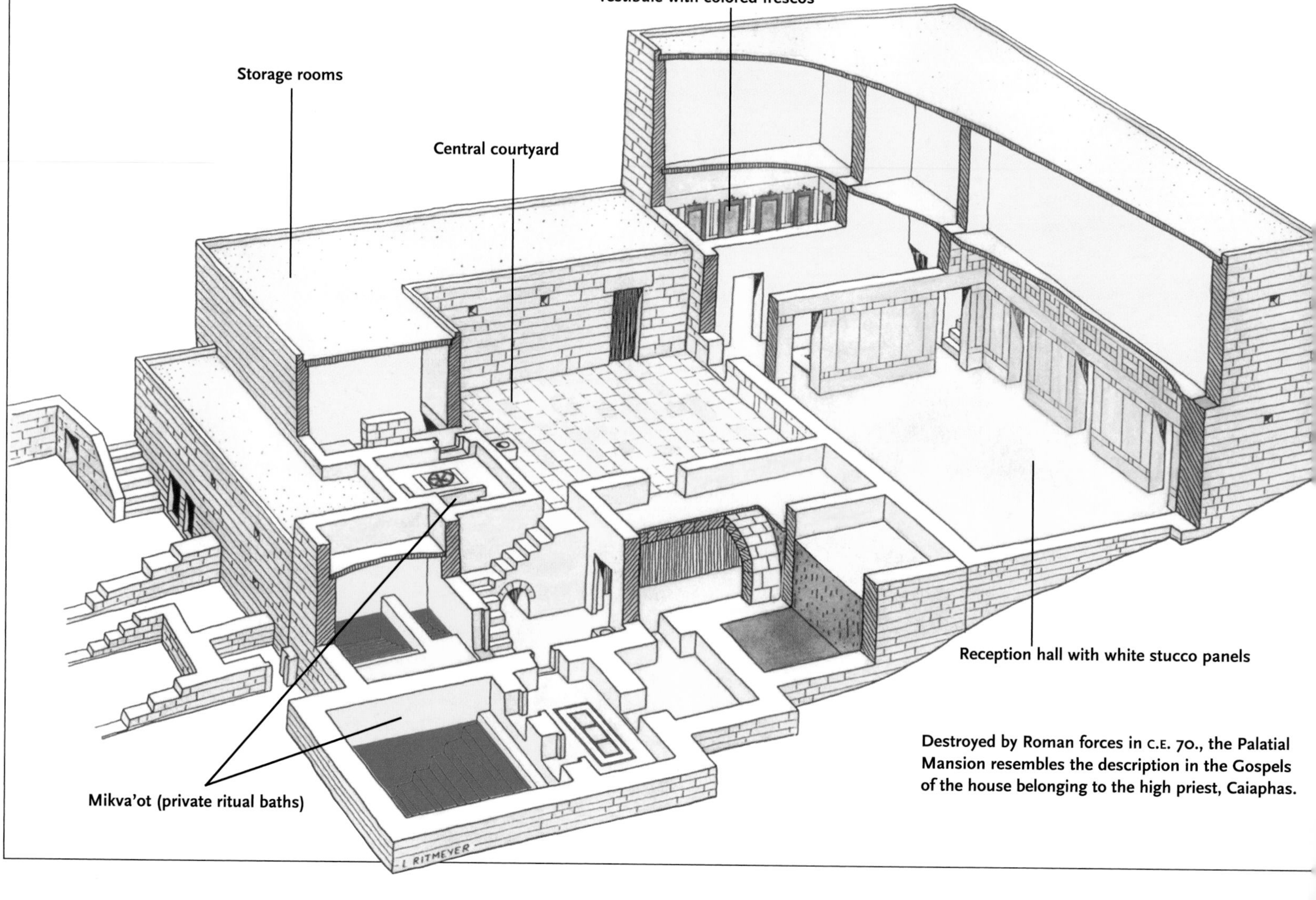

The words spoken during the Christian Eucharist—"Blessed are you, Lord God of all creation, through your goodness we have this wine to offer, fruit of the vine and work of human hands"—are rooted in the traditional Jewish blessing of kiddush: "Blessed are you, O Lord of our God, King of the universe, who creates the fruit of the vine." In the Gospels, Jesus, however, brings an entirely new dimension to the meal by adding, "This bread and this wine is my body and my blood that will be given up for you," thus sealing a new "covenant"

Vestibule with colored frescos

Storage rooms

Central courtyard

Reception hall with white stucco panels

Mikva'ot (private ritual baths)

L. RITMEYER

Destroyed by Roman forces in C.E. 70., the Palatial Mansion resembles the description in the Gospels of the house belonging to the high priest, Caiaphas.

between God and man (Mark 14:22-24; Matthew 26:26-28; Luke 22:17-20).

Most paintings of this meal, including *The Last Supper* by Leonardo da Vinci, depict Jesus with bread that looks like a roll or a loaf. Since this day was the first day of Unleavened Bread, however, Jesus would have broken the thin unleavened bread known as matzo. Wine, too, was and is an important component of the Paschal supper. According to the Mishnah, everyone should drink "at least four cups" to share in the joy of Israel's release, even the poor. If for some reason a poor man lacks the money to obtain it, he should "sell or pawn his coat, or hire himself out for these four cups of wine."

Later that evening, the Bible tells us, Jesus and the Apostles retire to the Mount of Olives, just beyond the city walls and across the Kidron Valley. They do not know that the order has gone out for Jesus to be apprehended. The Gospel of Mark clearly states that the reason for Jesus' arrest warrant is the disturbance he caused in the Temple (Mark 11:18). Midway on the Mount of Olives is a cave used for pressing oil, known as *gat-shemanim*, the origin of the name Gethsemane; in the winter months the cave would have been empty and well suited as a place of refuge. In a nearby garden, Jesus prays while his companions sleep (Mark 14:32-42; Matthew 26:36-46). However, one of the disciples, Judas Iscariot (the group's only Judean) betrays their location to the priestly authorities. What motivated Judas to do so? Some authors have linked the name "Iscariot" to the term *sicarius*, a Zealot "dagger man," but others believe the name simply indicates that Judas was a man *(ish)* from Kerioth, a town in southern Judea.

While in Western Christian civilization the name "Judas" is synonymous with treachery, some scholars have

THE TRIAL OF JESUS

In broad outline, the Gospels' accounts of the trial of Jesus follow Roman precedent. Presumably Pilate, having served as a judge in Rome, would have been familiar with the law. The Roman Empire recognized two legal codes. The *ius civile* applied only to Roman citizens—which is why Paul, a native of Tarsus and therefore a Roman citizen, could insist on a trial in Rome, rather than be at the mercy of a court in Caesarea or Jerusalem. All noncitizens in occupied territory, however, fell under the *ius gentium*, the Law of the Peoples. Under this jurisdiction, major cases, including capital ones, were heard by a *praetor peregrinus*, a foreign prosecutor. When no such official was available, the senior *legatus* was given the task. Since Pilate happened to be in town when Jesus was tried, the burden fell to him.

A trial under the *ius gentium* takes place in three phases. First, the accusers, or *delatores*, state their case. In the Gospels, the chief priests play this role. Then witnesses are called to prove or disprove the charge. Next, the defendant is asked to defend himself. Lastly, the presiding judge pronounces his verdict.

Jesus disrupts the process, however, by refusing to respond to Pilate's questioning. This development is disturbing because, without a proper defense, a verdict could be considered invalid. Jesus' response is particularly evident in the Gospel of John. For example, when Pilate asks Jesus a series of questions during their first interview, Jesus reportedly gives him only cursory and evasive replies (John 18:33-38), except for one telling comment: "My kingdom is not of this world." In the Gospel of Matthew, Jesus does not respond at all (Matthew 27:14).

Located beneath the Church of the Sisters of Zion, the Antonia Fortress is a possible location of Jesus' indictment by Pontius Pilate.

recently sought to exculpate Judas. They argue that as a native Judean, Judas may have believed himself best qualified to seek forgiveness for the Temple disturbance and negotiate a safe return for all to Galilee. According to the Gospel of Judas, a third- or fourth-century C.E. Coptic translation of a now-lost second-century C.E. Greek manuscript, which was translated and published by the National Geographic Society in April 2006, Jesus asks Judas to betray him in order to fulfill the prophecy of his death in Scripture.

Either way, the Gospels state that Judas personally directs a group of Temple guards to the location of Jesus and the Apostles on the Mount of Olives (Luke 22:47-48; John 18:2-12). Seeing the armed men, one of the disciples tries to make a desperate stand by lunging at one of the guards with his sword and cutting off his ear, but Jesus sternly rebukes him (Luke 22:51).

Arraignment and Trial

THE GOSPELS next tell us that Jesus' captors take him to the residence of Caiaphas, the high priest. Since the disturbance occurred on the Temple premises, the matter falls under the jurisdiction of the priestly council, the Great Sanhedrin. Mark implies that Jesus is interrogated in the presence of the full Sanhedrin (Mark 14:53), but this scenario is unlikely. The Great Sanhedrin is believed to have numbered 71 members, made up of both Pharisees and Sadducees, who would have been difficult to summon on such short notice. Moreover, full sessions of the Sanhedrin usually took place in the Lishkat La-Gazit, the Chamber of Hewn Stones near the Temple. Mark explicitly states, however, that Jesus was judged in the private residence of the high priest (Mark 14:66). It is unlikely that a private house could have accommodated a full session of the Sanhedrin. Even the sprawling first-century mansion excavated by Israeli archaeologist Nahman Avigad, a 700-square-yard palace located in the Upper City, featured a reception room that could not have seated more than 30 people at one time.

It is therefore likely that Jesus is arraigned by Caiaphas and a small group

Onlookers mourn as Jesus' body is taken down in *Descent from the Cross* by the Flemish Renaissance artist Rogier van der Weyden (1399–1464), painted around 1435.

of trusted Sadducee priests and scribes. The principal charge is his "blasphemous" claim that he is the "Messiah." Jesus' replies to his questioners are ambiguous (Matthew 26:64; Luke 22:67-68), which prompts Caiaphas to refer the matter to the Roman authorities, in this case the Roman prefect, Pontius Pilate, who is still in the city at the time. For Pilate's benefit, the accusation is cleverly amended to that of sedition against the Roman Empire: Jesus' claim to be the "king of the Jews" changes the nature of the offense from a purely religious matter to a political felony with far-reaching consequences. Given that Pilate was in Jerusalem for one reason only—the immediate suppression of popular unrest—such a case would undoubtedly have had his interest.

During the subsequent trial, the chief priests served as *delatores,* or accusers, charging Jesus with treason in the hope that Pilate would condemn him to death. It is not clear whether this inquest took place in the former palace of Herod the Great, which was located in the western part of the city and could have been requisitioned by Pilate, or in the Antonia Fortress, where Pilate's troops were garrisoned. The Gospels suggest that the trial is held in public and that Pilate, distressed by the weakness of the case, is finally forced to act under pressure of the crowds.

Scholars tend to question this scenario, as well as the suggestion that Pilate offers an amnesty at the occasion of the Passover festival by giving the crowd a choice between pardoning Jesus or a convicted rebel and murderer named Barrabas (Mark 15:6-15). Roman officials did not make a habit of practicing democracy, nor of allowing the mob to rule on highly incendiary cases involving sedition. The idea of releasing a career criminal on the eve of the most volatile day in Jerusalem would not have been consistent with what is known about Pilate. The image of the Jewish crowds crying for Jesus' execution may therefore be a creation of the evangelists, particularly Matthew and John, in their attempt to place collective guilt for Jesus' murder on the Jews. The fateful cry of the crowd, "His blood be on us and on our children!" (Matthew 27:25), would later justify countless pogroms and persecutions against Jewish communities throughout Europe and the Near East, and help to sustain anti-Semitism well into the modern day.

In the end, Jesus was condemned to crucifixion, which Cicero calls "the most heinous of punishments." This form of execution was reserved for wayward slaves and noncitizens who had schemed to overthrow the state. In Palestine, religious offenders were usually punished by stoning, according to the Mosaic laws (as in the case of Stephen, Acts 6-7), while local rulers used beheading for political offenses (as in the case of John the Baptist). Pilate's choice of this form of execution was therefore motivated by sheer cruelty, or by a desire to set an example for the thousands who had flocked to the city for Passover.

Crucifixion usually involved a set sequence of events. First, the condemned man was flogged to draw blood and thus weakened prior to crucifixion. Practice had shown that a healthy man could survive on the cross for two days or more. But Jewish laws demanded that a "hanged man" be taken down before sunset (Deuteronomy 21:22-23). Thus it was important to accelerate death by first causing substantial blood loss. Jesus would have been flogged with a special whip, called a *flagrum.* After this point in the biblical narrative, Roman soldiers throw knucklebones to decide who would receive his garments, probably using a game called *basilinda.* Roman dice from the time of Jesus have been recovered from the excavations of Sepphoris. A basilinda "game board," marked by the letter *B* (for *basileus,* king) is still visible on the pavement of the monastery of the Sisters of Zion, which stands on the probable location of the Antonia Fortress. Recent research, however, indicates that the pavement date from the second century C.E.

The Gospels state that Jesus and two other condemned men are forced to pick up the instruments of their deaths and carry them to the place of execution. Since wood was extremely sparse in Jerusalem, however, it is unlikely that they bore full crosses. Presumably, the Romans made use of permanent upright

Then the high priest tore his clothes and said, "He has blasphemed! Why do we still need witnesses? You have now heard his blasphemy. What is your verdict?" They answered, "He deserves death."

(Matthew 26:65-66)

A crucified man's remains were recovered in an ossuary just north of Jerusalem. Among the bones was this foot bone still pierced by iron nail.

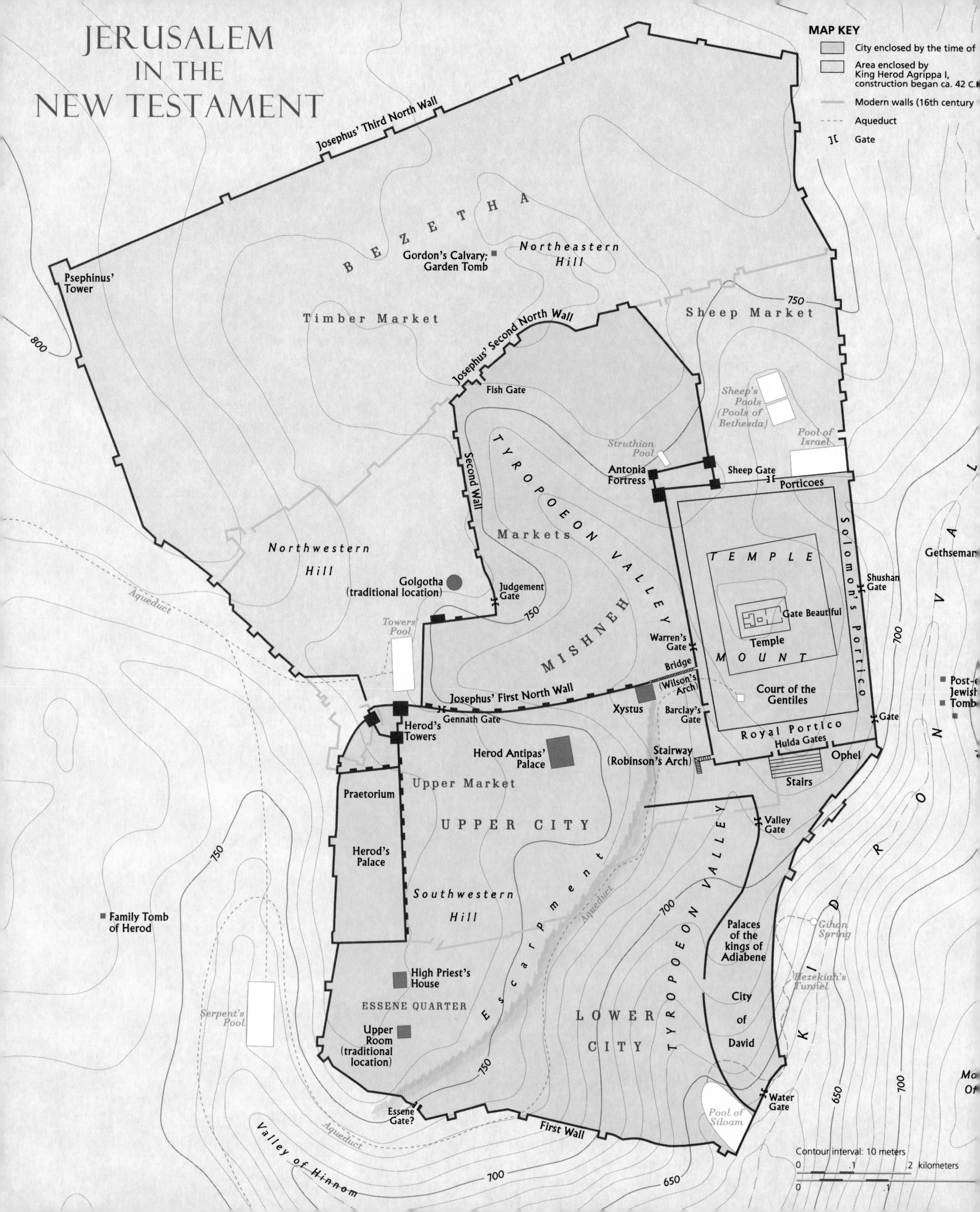

JERUSALEM IN THE NEW TESTAMENT
MAP KEY
City enclosed by the time of
Area enclosed by King Herod Agrippa I, construction began ca. 42 C.
Modern walls (16th century
Aqueduct
Gate
Josephus' Third North Wall
B E Z E T H A
Gordon's Calvary; Garden Tomb
Northeastern Hill
Psephinus' Tower
Timber Market
Sheep Market
750
800
Josephus' Second North Wall
Fish Gate
Sheep's Pools (Pools of Bethesda)
Pool of Israel
Struthion Pool
Antonia Fortress
Sheep Gate
Porticoes
Second Wall
TYROPOEON VALLEY
Markets
Solomon's Portico
TEMPLE MOUNT
Temple
Gate Beautiful
Shushan Gate
Northwestern Hill
Golgotha (traditional location)
Judgement Gate
Aqueduct
Towers Pool
MISHNEH
Warren's Gate
Bridge (Wilson's Arch)
Court of the Gentiles
Josephus' First North Wall
Xystus
Barclay's Gate
Gate
Gennath Gate
Herod's Towers
Royal Portico
Hulda Gates
Ophel
Herod Antipas' Palace
Stairway (Robinson's Arch)
Stairs
Praetorium
Upper Market
UPPER CITY
Valley Gate
Herod's Palace
Southwestern Hill
Escarpment
Family Tomb of Herod
700
Palaces of the kings of Adiabene
Gihon Spring
Hezekiah's Tunnel
KIDRON VALLEY
High Priest's House
ESSENE QUARTER
Serpent's Pool
Upper Room (traditional location)
LOWER CITY
City of David
Water Gate
Pool of Siloam
Essene Gate?
First Wall
Valley of Hinnom
650
Contour interval: 10 meters
0 .1 .2 kilometers

JEWISH BURIAL TOMBS

TRADITION CALLED FOR THE JEWISH DEAD TO be buried within 24 hours of passing away (Deuteronomy 21:22-23). It was the duty of every Jew to assist in the burial of a loved one or friend; to leave a corpse without burial was a disgrace. Once the body was cleaned and covered in linen, it was laid to rest. The bodies of the poor were usually interred in the soil, whereas the affluent placed their dead in caves or tombs hewn in the rock.

These caves were originally unadorned. As the Hellenistic artistic influence increased from the third century B.C.E. on, tombs became more elaborate, with carved niches *(kokhim)*, wall paintings, and carved facades screened by columns, such as those found in the rocky slope of the Kidron Valley, where Pharisaic Jews believed that Judgment Day would take place. These were family tombs where, following decomposition of the flesh, the bones were placed in a small ossuary, enabling the burial of several other family members in the tomb.

In a location just south of Jerusalem, an astonishing discovery was made in 1990: a small family tomb containing several ossuaries from the first century C.E. The most elaborate box bears an Aramaic inscription: Yehoseph bar Qypa—Joseph Caiaphas. This man may have been the high priest Caiaphas who indicted Jesus.

This ossuary contained the bones of Joseph Caiaphas (*Yehoseph bar Qypa*), possibly the same high priest named in the Gospels.

stakes set in a mound known as the Hill of the Skull (Golgotha in Aramaic). Jesus would have carried only the crossbeam, called a *patibulum*, which could weigh as much as 80 pounds.

In Jerusalem today, pilgrims still follow the traditional course from where the Antonia Fortress was located to Golgotha, along a route known as the Via Dolorosa. The actual route that Jesus took is difficult to ascertain, however, since Jerusalem was thoroughly destroyed by the Roman army after the second major Jewish rebellion in C.E. 135. Scholars still debate where Golgotha was located, based on uncertainty about the actual course of the walls encircling Jerusalem in Jesus' time. A third-century tradition argues for the present location of the Church of the Holy Sepulchre, but recent articles have argued that originally the church was located inside the walls of first-century Jerusalem, which would have disqualified the site as an execution ground. Other scholars have dismissed this theory.

After arriving at the place of execution, Jesus would have been stripped and then forced down onto the patibulum. Modern experts have deduced that his arms would have been bound to the crossbeam, after which a nail was driven through the left forearm near the radial bone, hitting the medial nerve and causing immense pain. The procedure was repeated with the right forearm, after which the soldiers raised the crossbar and placed it in a notch on top of the stake. Next, the Romans might have squeezed the ankles sideways into a small U-shaped wooden block. This block was then affixed to the cross. In this posture, sagging from the ropes and the nails, a man would find his chest cavity compressing, and it would become very difficult for him to breathe. This paradox is the essence of the punishment: in order to breathe, the condemned must lift himself up; by lifting himself up, he increases the strain on his nailed limbs, thus inducing further pain. As was

ALOE AND MYRRH

According to the Gospel of John, Nicodemus brings to Jesus' burial "a mixture of myrrh and aloes" (John 19:39). Principally a fragrance agent, myrrh (shown below) was also an adhesive applied during burial preparation before the body was wrapped in linen. John Chrysostom, writing in the fourth century C.E., commented that the "myrrh used was a drug which adheres so closely to the body that the grave-clothes could not easily be removed."

The purpose of aloe in burials is less clear. Powdered aloe was usually mixed with olive oil prior to its application on the body. Aristotle recommended aloe as an anti-inflammatory, and Egyptian texts suggest that aloe was used to stem bleeding. Some scholars have seized on aloe's healing properties to suggest that perhaps Jesus was not truly dead. Others believe that aloe was used simply as another aromatic to cover the odor of decomposition.

MYSTERY OF THE SHROUD

IN NEW TESTAMENT TIMES, A BODY WAS prepared for burial with a cleansing and anointing, after which it was wrapped in linen. This burial cloth consisted, most often, of strips of linen or cotton that easily could be wrapped around the corpse. Typically, the linen strips were cut into no less than three and usually seven separate segments, including a head cloth called the *sudarium*. Alternatively, the body of Jesus could have been wrapped in a large linen shroud. The Gospel record is not clear: Mark speaks of "a linen cloth" (Mark 15:46), while John refers to "linen wrappings" (John 20:6).

In 2000, British archaeologist Shimon Gibson discovered an unexcavated first-century tomb in the Valley of Hinnom. Squeezing through an opening no bigger than about two feet square, he entered a typical rock-cut tomb of the Roman period. Inside one of the niches was a body that still retained a thatch of hair. It was wrapped in a shroud, blackened with age,

The authenticity of the Shroud of Turin remains a subject of controversy and intense scientific debate.

which was carbon-dated to the first half of the first century C.E. This exciting discovery showed that burial shrouds were in use in the time of Jesus, thus bolstering the claim to authenticity of the famous Shroud of Turin, which appears to contain the negative imprint of a crucified man, traditionally held to be Jesus Christ.

Late in the 20th century, the shroud was carbon-dated by three separate laboratories to sometime between C.E. 1260 and 1390, though recent studies suggest these samples may have been taken from repairs made in medieval times. No one, however, has yet proposed a plausible explanation as to how such a detailed imprint could have been created without modern photographic means. Recent studies of shroud samples have detected tiny crystals of travertine aragonite, a rare form of calcite found near the Damascus Gate in Jerusalem, as well as 48 samples of pollen, 7 of which originate from plants in Palestine.

common with crucifixions, the Gospels state that the soldiers affix a placard to the cross that mockingly identifies the condemned as "Jesus of Nazareth, the King of the Jews" (in Latin: *Iesus Nazarenus Rex Iudaeorum*, or "I*N*R*I") (Mark 15:26; Luke 23:38).

The Gospels tell us that Jesus endures this agony for several hours. Then, according to Mark, he suddenly cries out the opening verse of Psalm 22, "*Eloi, Eloi, lema sabachthani*?" which means, "My God, my God, why have you forsaken me?" (Mark 15:34). The use of the original Aramaic in the Gospel may have been intended to underscore the cry's authenticity. Shortly thereafter in the Gospels, Jesus dies, most likely of asphyxiation compounded by shock and blood loss. A few hours later, as the sun sets over the Judean hills, soldiers break the legs of the other condemned men who are still alive (John 19:32). Without the ability to swell the chest cavity by pushing against the wooden block that held their feet, the prisoners can no longer breathe and die of asphyxiation.

These gruesome details were graphically illustrated by a discovery in 1968 in the cemetery of Giv'at ha-Mivtar, near Jerusalem. Archaeologists uncovered several ossuaries (stone containers for bones collected once the flesh has decomposed). One box held the skeleton of an adult Jewish male from the first century C.E., identified in an inscription as "Yehohanan." Forensic research revealed that Yehohanan had been crucified. His anklebones were still held together by a single, seven-inch nail. Injuries to the arms suggested that the man was nailed to the cross through the wrists, rather than through the palms as most depictions of the Crucifixion suggest. But most astonishing was the condition of the condemned man's legs. As Dr. Nicu Haas reported, "the right tibia and the left calf bones were all broken at the same level ... suggesting a single, strong blow." This forensic evidence indicates that details in the Gospels about breaking the legs of the other two condemned are authentic.

Since Jesus dies on the cross, his legs are not broken. After the centurion on site pronounces the prisoner dead, the Gospels say, the lifeless body is washed, draped in cloth, and laid in a tomb owned by a sympathizer, a wealthy man named Joseph of Arimathea, a member of the Great Sanhedrin (Mark 15:43). Tombs were typical burial places for affluent Jews. Usually carved into the rock in the hills around Jerusalem, these tombs were more like small caves, with a stone platform for the body and several niches or loculi for ossuaries. The entrance to such a burial cave was sealed by a round or square stone, called a *golal.*

According to the Gospel of John, another member of the Sanhedrin, a Pharisee named Nicodemus, assists Joseph in his task (John 19:39-40). As Pharisees, however, Joseph and Nicodemus would have been anxious to complete the burial rites before sunset and the beginning of the Sabbath. Allowing for time to secure access to the body from Pilate (Mark 15:43), and to return to Golgotha and remove Jesus' body would have left little leeway to wash and anoint the body properly before wrapping it in linen.

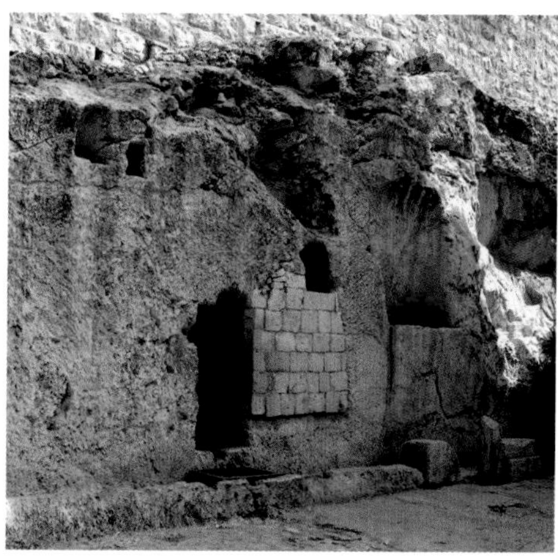

Though no longer considered a possible location for Jesus' burial, the Garden Tomb outside Jerusalem is an example of a Jewish burial chamber from the Second Temple period.

This delay is probably why the women, including Mary Magdalene, have to return to complete the process after the Sabbath—on Sunday. The Gospel of Mark states that they set out at dawn, fretting whether, at this early hour, they will be able to find any men who can help them roll away the heavy golal. But when they arrive at the tomb they find the large stone already rolled aside. Upon entering the tomb, they find a young man in a long white garment sitting to one side. "Do not be alarmed," the man says to them. "You are looking for Jesus of Nazareth, who was crucified. He has been raised; he is not here" (Mark 16:6). The women "fled from the tomb, for terror and amazement had seized them," writes Mark. And although the man had instructed the women to tell his disciples and Peter that they will find Jesus in Galilee, the women "said nothing to anyone, for they were afraid" (Mark 16:8). Here, the Gospel of Mark comes to an end, and the story of Jesus, the Christ, begins.

PALESTINE	ROME	SYRIA
ca 6–4 B.C.E. Jesus is born	ca 4 B.C.E. Emperor Augustus adopts Tiberius, who will succeed him as emperor in C.E. 14	ca C.E. 1 Romans formally recognize the Euphrates River as the Parthian border
ca C.E. 6 A tax revolt follows a census ordered by the governor, Quirinius	ca C.E. 6 Emperor Augustus removes Archulaus as Ethnarch. Judea becomes a Roman province, led by a procurator	ca C.E. 6–12 Publius Sulpicius Quirinius serves as the governor of the Roman province of Syria
ca C.E. 6 Following its destruction by Roman troops, Herod Antipas begins the rebuilding of Sepphoris in Galilee	ca C.E. 37 Tiberius dies and is succeeded by Gaius (also known as Caligula), who is followed by Claudius	ca C.E. 10–38 Artabanus II becomes king of Parthia
		ca C.E. 37 City of Antioch in Syria is shaken by earthquakes
ca C.E. 26–36 Pontius Pilate serves as prefect of Judea		ca C.E. 37–49 The period of peace between the Romans and the Parthians is short-lived
ca C.E. 28 or 30 Jesus is crucified at Golgotha	ca C.E. 49 Emperor Claudius expels the Christians from Rome	ca C.E. 58 Orodes becomes king of Parthia

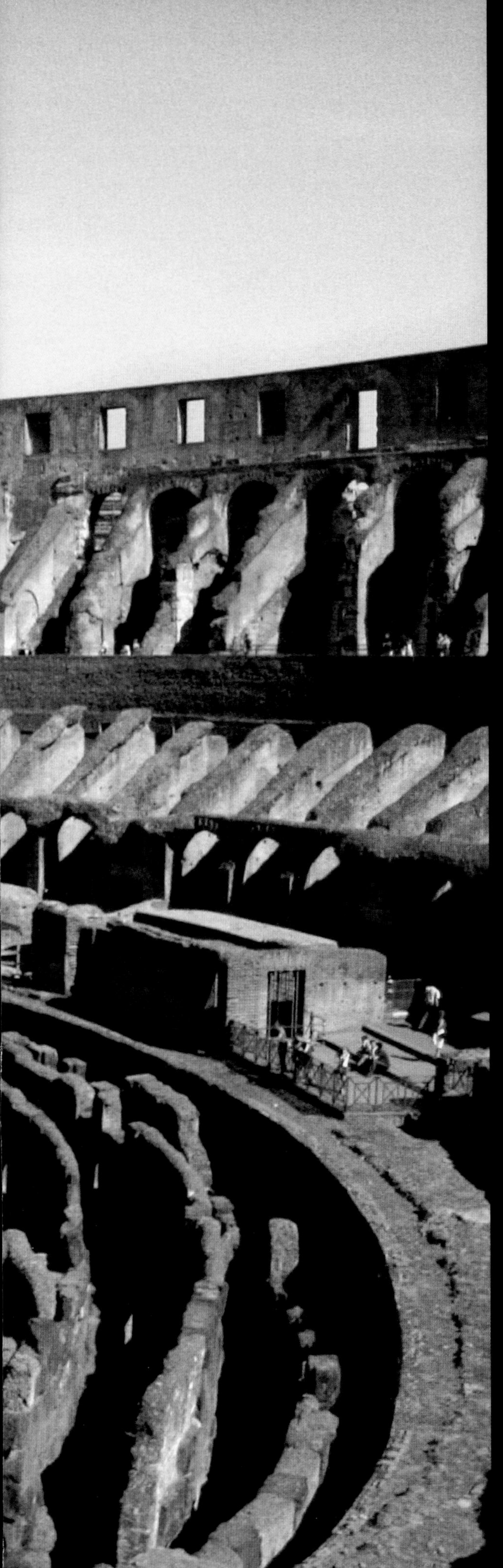

CHAPTER TEN

Early Christianity and Rabbinic Judaism

WITHIN A DECADE OF THE CRUCIFIXION, the teachings of Jesus began to spread throughout the eastern Mediterranean. The Apostle Peter and Paul of Tarsus led the creation of Christian communities outside of Jerusalem and even of Palestine proper. Paul in particular was instrumental in the foundation of both Jewish and Gentile Christian "chapels," specifically in Syria, Asia Minor, and Greece. Over the same period, Second Temple Judaism continued to thrive. In C.E. 62, Herod's vast new Temple precinct was finally completed, even as Roman rule in Judea turned increasingly corrupt. Then came the turning point. After the great fire of Rome in 64, Emperor Nero pinned the blame on Christian communities, leading to the first persecutions. Two years later, Roman misrule in Judea incited a Jewish rebellion, but the Roman General Vespasian and later his son, Titus, brutally suppressed it. In 70, the Roman army entered Jerusalem and destroyed the Second Temple.

The war and the demise of the Temple led to a crisis for early Christianity. It also spelled the end of the highly diverse Judaism of the Second Temple period. Yet, despite rigorous persecutions and oppression, both Christianity and Judaism survived and flourished—both ultimately outlasting the Romans and their pantheon of gods.

The Colosseum in Rome, originally called the Flavian Amphitheater, was commissioned by Emperor Vespasian in C.E. 72.

TEACHINGS OF PAUL

Acts 9 describes how Jesus blinds Saul (Paul) en route to Damascus. This Roman road to Damascus in modern Syria still features paving stones from the Roman era.

ACCORDING TO THE GOSPEL of John, Jesus' Crucifixion leaves his followers demoralized and fearful. The "doors of the house where the disciples had met" are shut (John 20:19). Some flee to Galilee. "We had hoped that he was the one to redeem Israel," a follower notes mournfully on his way to the village of Emmaus (Luke 24:21).

At first, the Apostles do not believe the reports from the women (including Mary Magdalene) that Jesus has risen, dismissing them as "idle talk" (Luke 24:11). The fact that women conveyed the news of the empty tomb is believed by scholars to be an authenticating detail, because a first-century author would, under normal circumstances, have chosen a man to witness so pivotal an event. Thereafter, the Gospels describe numerous appearances of the risen Jesus, but the specifics vary. In some accounts, Jesus appears as a man of flesh and blood; he breaks bread with his companions (Luke 24:30) and invites the disbelieving Thomas to examine his wounds (John 20:27). In other reports, Jesus appears as a transcendent being, capable of moving in and out of rooms without passing through a door (John 20:19), who must warn Mary Magdalene not to touch him because "I have not yet ascended to the Father" (John 20:17). Luke places the sightings of Jesus in

ca C.E. 10
Possible birthdate of Paul (Saul)

ca C.E. 30
Jewish writer Philo active in Alexandria, Egypt

ca C.E. 37
Jewish historian Josephus is born

ca C.E. 38
Jewish pogroms in Alexandira

Paul was occupied with proclaiming the word, testifying to the Jews that the Messiah was Jesus. When they opposed and reviled him, in protest he shook the dust from his clothes and said to them, "Your blood be on your own heads! From now on, I will go to the Gentiles." (Acts 18:5-6)

Jerusalem and Judea (Luke 24:13-49). In Matthew (and possibly Mark as well) the appearances occur in Galilee (Matthew 28:10, 16-17; Mark 16:7). John adds a sighting near the shore of the Sea of Galilee (John 21:1-14).

For Christians, the Resurrection is one of the foundations of their faith. From a strictly historical point of view, what matters about the Resurrection is that the followers of Jesus believed it. According to Acts of the Apostles, the divine spirit descends on Jesus' followers in the form of tongues of flame (Acts 2:2-4) during the Jewish Feast of Pentecost, celebrated 50 days after Passover. At the time, Jerusalem is filled with pilgrims who have come to celebrate the festival. Filled with newfound courage, the apostles burst out of their hiding places and begin to preach, so that, as Acts describes it, their sermons are heard by Jewish pilgrims from Parthia, Media, Elam, Mesopotamia, Cappadocia, Lybia, Crete, and Egypt, as well as many other regions; these listeners will take the accounts back to their native lands and sow the seeds of future Christian communities (Acts 2:9-10).

It is possible that this activity was reported to the priests and Sadducees, for the Bible says that Peter and a number of the Apostles are arrested and brought before the Sanhedrin, the council of priests (Acts 4:1-6). Here began the official opposition to the spread of Jesus' teachings that, in future years, would come close to eradicating the movement in Palestine altogether. Only one member of the Sanhedrin, a Pharisee called Gamaliel, speaks on Peter's behalf, and the Apostles escape with only a beating (Acts 5:34-40). In the months and years to come, however, the official proscription against Christian proselytizing stiffened. Acts tells us how one particularly vocal disciple, Stephen, is stoned to death (Acts 7:54-60). In response, the movement shifted its activity beyond Judea. The Apostle Philip preached in Samaria and the cities of Philistia. Peter went to the coastal cities of Lydda, Joppa, and even polytheistic Caesarea.

Conversion of Saul

DURING THIS TROUBLED TIME, a man named Saul appeared on the scene. Saul was a native of Tarsus, a city in the Roman province of Cilicia. Later known as Paul, this highly educated Jew would exert a decisive influence on the development of early Christianity. Indeed, his letters to Christian communities throughout Asia Minor are generally accepted to be the earliest Christian writings still extant.

Located near the mouth of the Cydnus River in what is today the Turkish province of Mersin, Tarsus came under Roman control in 64 B.C.E. The city so readily submitted its annual tribute to Rome that Augustus granted it the exceptional status of a "free Roman city," endowing its leading inhabitants with Roman citizenship. Within the empire, Tarsus became known as a leading center of learning, where Greco-Roman philosophers could mingle informally with Jewish scholars.

Saul was probably born about C.E. 10 into what was most likely an observant Jewish family. Scholars assume that he was educated in a synagogue school and groomed for the rabbinate, since at the age of 18 he was sent to Jerusalem to study Pharisaic commentary under Gamaliel—quite possibly the same Gamaliel who had defended the Apostles in Jerusalem. Gamaliel was a pupil (and, it is believed, grandson) of the great Rabbi Hillel (ca 30 B.C.E.–C.E. 10), an advocate of a flexible interpretation of the Torah.

The arrest of Paul is shown in this detail from a third-century sarcophagus in the St. Victor Basilica, in Marseilles, France.

ca C.E. 41
Emperor Claudius confirms Jewish right to observe religious practices

ca C.E. 50
Paul begins travels throughout the eastern Roman Empire in an effort to convert non-Jews to Christianity

ca C.E. 64
Nero blames the Christians for a fire that ravaged the city of Rome

ca C.E. 64
Traditional date for the deaths of Peter and Paul in Rome

Apparently, Saul's attitude did not match Gamaliel's tolerance toward dissenters like Peter. He avidly supported the persecution of Jewish followers of Jesus and firmly rejected their claim that Jesus was the Messiah. The Book of Acts places Saul at the stoning of the disciple Stephen and suggests that he may have instigated this action, for while the mob stones the disciple, witnesses "laid their coats at the feet of a young man named Saul"; although this lynching apparently is spontaneous, "Saul approved of their killing him" (Acts 7:58, 8:1).

The stoning launched a "severe persecution against the church in Jerusalem" and beyond, by vigilantes acting with the tacit consent of the Sanhedrin. Saul himself lead one of these groups, and appealed to the high priest for authorization to extend the persecution beyond Judea to cities such as Damascus (Acts 9:1-2). Saul was given leave to do so sometime between C.E. 32 and 35.

According to Acts of the Apostles, Saul then experiences a dramatic and total change of heart on the road to Damascus. The Bible describes how suddenly "a light from heaven flashed around him." He falls to the ground, blinded, and hears a voice calling to him, "Saul, why do you persecute me?" According to Acts, Saul stands up and, now blind, is led by companions into Damascus (Acts 9:4-8).

Interestingly enough, Saul did not refer to this pivotal event on the road to Damascus in his later letters. To the Galatians, however, he confessed that ambition drove his zeal for persecution, raising him "beyond many among my people of the same age" (Galatians 1:14). What changed his mind, says Saul, is that "God ... was pleased to reveal his Son to me." Later, Saul became convinced that the Holy Spirit had chosen him as one uniquely qualified to bring Jesus' message to the pagan world, for he spoke Greek, understood Greco-Roman culture, and could travel throughout the Mediterranean world, as a Roman citizen, under the protection of Roman law.

When they saw that I had been entrusted with the gospel for the uncircumcised, just as Peter had been entrusted with the gospel for the circumcised ... and when James and Cephus and John, who were acknowledged pillars, recognized the grace that had been given to me, they gave to Barnabus and me the right hand of fellowship, agreeing that we should go to the Gentiles.

(Galatians 2:7–9)

A man sails a two-masted, coastal vessel in this marble relief from Carthage, dating to circa C.E. 200.

The Bible says that Saul regains his eyesight and remains "with the disciples in Damascus" for several days (Acts 9:19). He then begins to preach in local synagogues, proclaiming that Jesus is the Messiah (Acts 9:22). But Saul, an intellectual, might have been acutely aware of the young movement's intrinsic weaknesses. The group lacked a cohesive doctrine, an established liturgy, and, most important, a body of scripture demonstrating that Jesus was the Messiah.

Rather than help build the Jesus movement alongside its acknowledged leaders, Peter and James (the brother of Jesus), Saul elected not to "go up to Jerusalem to those who were already apostles before me." Instead, "I went away at once to Arabia" (Galatians 1:16-17). Like Jesus, Saul chose the desert as a place to seek spiritual guidance before launching his mission. There, in the wilderness, he applied all the reasoning skills of a trained Pharisee to the problem of nurturing this fledgling movement to maturity.

Pauline Creed

WHEN SAUL RETURNED from the desert, he was ready to propagate his creed. Jesus' Crucifixion and death were not accidental, Saul taught; rather, they had been divinely ordained. According to Saul, Jesus' resurrection was the ultimate fulfillment of God's covenant with Abraham: Jesus' sacrifice on the cross had expiated all the sins of mankind. This doctrine was notably different from the program of the Apostles, who continued to preach "the good news about the kingdom of God and the name of Jesus Christ." Christ (Christos) is Greek for "the Anointed One" or "Messiah" (Acts 8:12). In his later letters, Saul hardly refers to events in Jesus' life or to his teaching of the new kingdom; for Saul, Jesus' message was defined by his death and resurrection.

Still avoiding the Apostles in Jerusalem, Saul preached the doctrine he had formulated to both Jews and Gentiles, people who are not Jewish. His successful efforts caused a complaint to be lodged with the king in Nabataea, whose jurisdiction included Damascus. The Bible says that Saul must escape the city in a basket lowered from its walls (II Corinthians 11:32-33).

Three years after his first embrace of Jesus, Saul traveled to Jerusalem to meet with James and Peter at last. The Apostles kept their distance, "for they did not believe that he was a disciple" (Acts 9:26). Saul only met briefly with Peter and James (Galatians 1:18-19) then left them for his home province of Cilicia. He did not return to Jerusalem for another 14 years.

Saul (henceforth known in the Bible by his Roman name, Paul) then embarked on the first of many journeys to bring the Pauline gospel of Jesus to the Greco-Roman world. A disciple named Barnabas, who had been Paul's host in Jerusalem, invited him to the Syrian city of Antioch on the Orontes River, where Barnabas had discovered a keen interest in Jesus among the locals. Some of these new converts were Jewish; but a high number of aspirants were, in fact, Gentiles. According to Acts, the people of this city first coin the term "Christians" to denounce Gentile disciples of Jesus. These followers, however, accept the name as a badge of honor (Acts 11:26).

Why were the Gentiles attracted to Jesus' message? Perhaps the simplest answer is that Christian theology was essentially populist and egalitarian; it offered redemption to everyone, regardless of social class or race. For those who were attracted to the monotheism of Judaism, Christianity offered a faith in one God devoid of the more onerous precepts of Covenant Law, including the dietary laws and circumcision. Moreover, the stories of Jesus' healings and exorcisms must have appealed to a world where mystery and magic were basic ingredients of everyday life.

The success of Paul's mission to the Gentiles posed an urgent dilemma for the Apostles, who targeted their conversion efforts at Jews. Jesus himself had always focused on reforming Judaism from within, warning his followers not to "think that I have come to abolish the law or the prophets; I have come not to abolish but to fulfill" (Matthew 5:17). Throughout his Galilean ministry, Jesus had avoided predominantly Gentile cities such as Tiberias and Sepphoris.

Paul is blinded on the road to Damascus in *The Conversion of St. Paul* as painted in 1600 by the Italian artist Michelangelo Merisi da Caravaggio (1573–1610).

But Paul might have sensed an opportunity to create a much larger, more inclusive Jesus movement. To him it mattered little that Gentile followers are not circumcised, do not know Judaic Scripture, or do not abide by Covenant Law. Baptism in the name of Jesus Christ was the spiritual equivalent of circumcision, he taught; faith in salvation through Christ would grant followers the mercy of God regardless of whether they observed the Mosaic laws or not.

The Book of Acts of the Apostles suggests that Paul and Barnabas travel back to Jerusalem between C.E. 45 and 48, during a famine in Judea, carrying desperately needed funds from the Christian community in Antioch (Acts 11:26-29). At this opportunity, the Jerusalem leaders confronted Paul over his decision to convert Gentiles without their acceptance of the Covenant Law, including the need to be circumcised. In a "private meeting with the acknowledged leaders" (Galatians 2:2), Paul stood firm. "[W]hat they actually were makes no difference to me," Paul continues. "God shows no partiality ... those leaders contributed nothing to me" (Galatians 2:6).

Journeys of Paul

For the next 14 years, Paul concentrated on his missionary work among the Gentiles, using Antioch on the Orontes as his base. He wrote many letters (or epistles) to the nascent communities in an effort to bolster their faith, and to adjudicate whenever tensions arose among the different constituencies in these early Christian groups. Some of these letters he dictated himself; others were written on his

The ruins of the Temple of Apollo remain in Corinth, the Greek city first visited by Paul between C.E. 51–52, possibly during the governorship of L. Iunius Gallio.

St. Paul's pillar stands before an early Christian basilica in Cyprus, where Paul was scourged by the Roman governor of Paphos before his conversion to Christianity.

Around C.E. 54, Paul visited Ephesus, a large, coastal city located in Turkey. Today, impressive ruins, like the Gate of Hercules (shown here), can still be seen there.

Paul probably found shelter on the rocky coast of Malta, after his ship bound for Rome was hit by a heavy squall in the Mediterranean Sea.

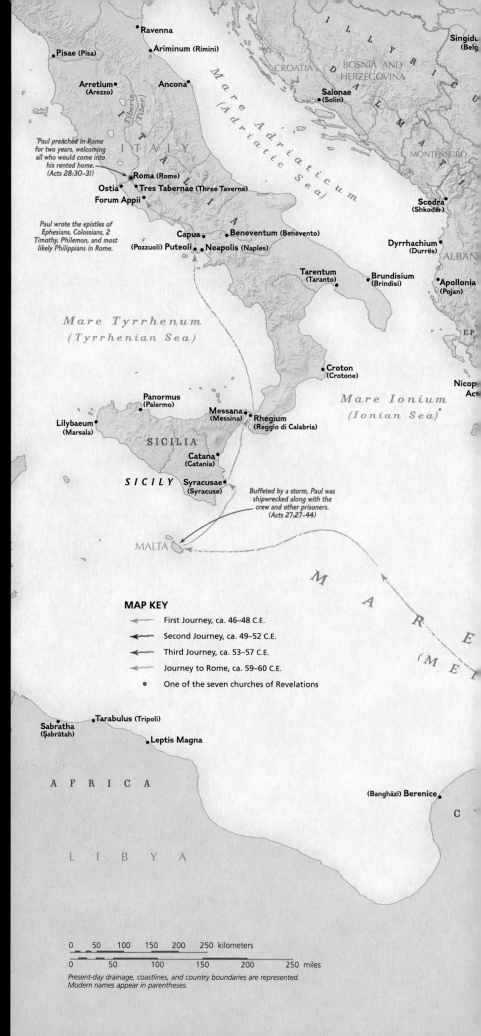

Ravenna
Pisae (Pisa)
Ariminum (Rimini)
ILLYRICUM
Singidu
(Belg
CROATIA
BOSNIA AND HERZEGOVINA
DALMATIA
Arretium (Arezzo)
Ancona
Tiberis (Tiber)
Salonae (Solin)
Mare Adriaticum (Adriatic Sea)
ITALY
ITALIA
MONTENEGRO

Paul preached in Rome for two years, welcoming all who would come into his rented home. (Acts 28:30–31)

Roma (Rome)
Ostia
Tres Tabernae (Three Taverns)
Forum Appii
Scodra (Shkodër)

Paul wrote the epistles of Ephesians, Colossians, 2 Timothy, Philemon, and most likely Philippians in Rome.

Capua
Beneventum (Benevento)
(Pozzuoli) Puteoli
Neapolis (Naples)
Dyrrhachium (Durrës)
ALBAN
Tarentum (Taranto)
Brundisium (Brindisi)
Apollonia (Pojan)
Mare Tyrrhenum (Tyrrhenian Sea)
EP
Croton (Crotone)
Nicop
Act
Panormus (Palermo)
Messana (Messina)
Rhegium (Reggio di Calabria)
Mare Ionium (Ionian Sea)
Lilybaeum (Marsala)
SICILIA
Catana (Catania)
SICILY
Syracusae (Syracuse)

Buffeted by a storm, Paul was shipwrecked along with the crew and other prisoners. (Acts 27:27–44)

MALTA
MARE (ME

MAP KEY

- First Journey, ca. 46–48 C.E.
- Second Journey, ca. 49–52 C.E.
- Third Journey, ca. 53–57 C.E.
- Journey to Rome, ca. 59–60 C.E.
- One of the seven churches of Revelations

Sabratha (Şabrātah)
Tarabulus (Tripoli)
Leptis Magna
AFRICA
(Banghāzī) Berenice
C
LIBYA

0 50 100 150 200 250 kilometers
0 50 100 150 200 250 miles

Present-day drainage, coastlines, and country boundaries are represented. Modern names appear in parentheses.

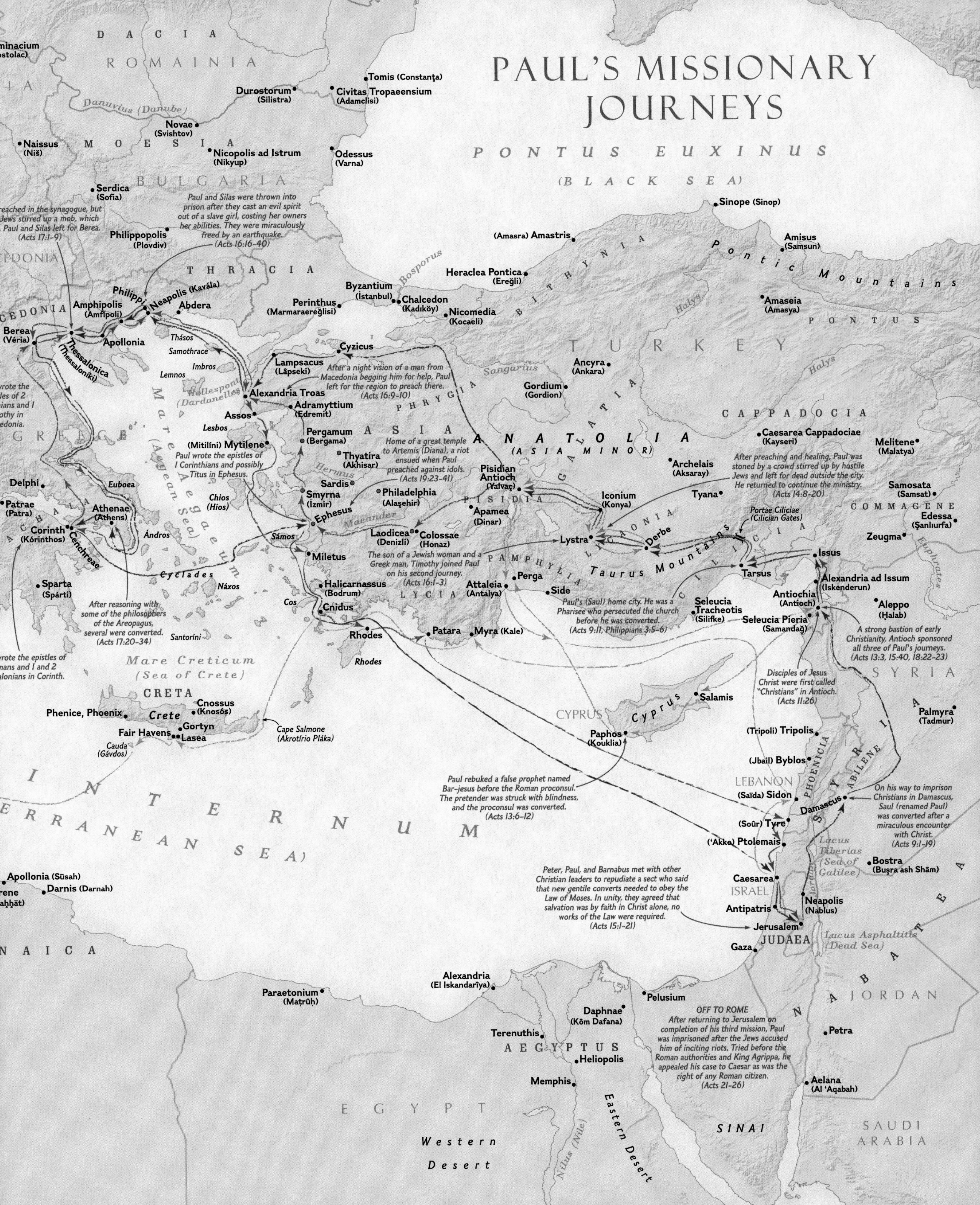

PAUL'S MISSIONARY JOURNEYS
D A C I A
R O M A I N I A
Tomis (Constanța)
Durostorum (Silistra)
Civitas Tropaeensium (Adamclisi)
Danuvius (Danube)
Novae (Svishtov)
Naissus (Niš)
M O E S I A
Nicopolis ad Istrum (Nikyup)
Odessus (Varna)
P O N T U S E U X I N U S
(B L A C K S E A)
Serdica (Sofia)
B U L G A R I A
Paul and Silas were thrown into prison after they cast an evil spirit out of a slave girl, costing her owners her abilities. They were miraculously freed by an earthquake. (Acts 16:16-40)
Philippopolis (Plovdiv)
Sinope (Sinop)
(Amasra) Amastris
Amisus (Samsun)
T H R A C I A
B I T H Y N I A
Pontic Mountains
Heraclea Pontica (Ereğli)
Bosporus
Byzantium (İstanbul)
Chalcedon (Kadıköy)
Perinthus (Marmaraereğlisi)
Nicomedia (Kocaeli)
Philippi
Neapolis (Kavála)
Abdera
Amphipolis (Amfípoli)
Apollonia
Berea (Véria)
Thessalonica (Thessaloníki)
Thásos
Samothrace
Imbros
Lemnos
Amaseia (Amasya)
P O N T U S
Halys
T U R K E Y
Cyzicus
Lampsacus (Lâpseki)
After a night vision of a man from Macedonia begging him for help, Paul left for the region to preach there. (Acts 16:9-10)
Sangarius
Ancyra (Ankara)
Gordium (Gordion)
Hellespont (Dardanelles)
Alexandria Troas
Adramyttium (Edremit)
Assos
P H R Y G I A
G A L A T I A
C A P P A D O C I A
Mare Aegaeum (Aegean Sea)
Lesbos
Pergamum (Bergama)
A S I A
Home of a great temple to Artemis (Diana), a riot ensued when Paul preached against idols. (Acts 19:23-41)
A N A T O L I A
(A S I A M I N O R)
Caesarea Cappadociae (Kayseri)
Melitene (Malatya)
(Mitilíni) Mytilene
Paul wrote the epistles of I Corinthians and possibly Titus in Ephesus.
Thyatira (Akhisar)
Hermus
Pisidian Antioch (Yalvaç)
Archelais (Aksaray)
After preaching and healing, Paul was stoned by a crowd stirred up by hostile Jews and left for dead outside the city. He returned to continue the ministry. (Acts 14:8-20)
G R E E C E
Delphi
Euboea
Sardis
Philadelphia (Alaşehir)
P I S I D I A
Iconium (Konya)
Tyana
Samosata (Samsat)
Patrae (Patra)
Chios (Hios)
Smyrna (İzmir)
Apamea (Dinar)
C O M M A G E N E
A C H A I A
Athenae (Athens)
Ephesus
Maeander
Portae Ciliciae (Cilician Gates)
Edessa (Şanlıurfa)
Corinth (Kórinthos)
Cenchreae
Ándros
Sámos
Laodicea (Denizli)
Colossae (Honaz)
L Y C A O N I A
Lystra
Derbe
Zeugma
Euphrates
Miletus
The son of a Jewish woman and a Greek man, Timothy joined Paul on his second journey. (Acts 16:1-3)
Taurus Mountains
C I L I C I A
Issus
Cyclades
Náxos
P A M P H Y L I A
Tarsus
Sparta (Spárti)
Halicarnassus (Bodrum)
Attaleia (Antalya)
Perga
Side
Alexandria ad Issum (Iskenderun)
L Y C I A
After reasoning with some of the philosophers of the Areopagus, several were converted. (Acts 17:20-34)
Cos
Cnidus
Paul's (Saul) home city. He was a Pharisee who persecuted the church before he was converted. (Acts 9:11, Philippians 3:5-6)
Seleucia Tracheotis (Silifke)
Antiochia (Antioch)
Aleppo (Ḥalab)
Seleucia Pieria (Samandağ)
Santorini
Rhodes
Patara
Myra (Kale)
A strong bastion of early Christianity, Antioch sponsored all three of Paul's journeys. (Acts 13:3, 15:40, 18:22-23)
Mare Creticum (Sea of Crete)
S Y R I A
Disciples of Jesus Christ were first called "Christians" in Antioch. (Acts 11:26)
CRETA
Cnossus (Knosós)
Salamis
Phenice, Phoenix
Crete
Gortyn
CYPRUS
Cyprus
Palmyra (Tadmur)
Fair Havens
Lasea
Cape Salmone (Akrotírio Pláka)
Cauda (Gávdos)
Paphos (Kouklia)
(Tripoli) Tripolis
(Jbail) Byblos
PHOENICIA
ABILENE
Paul rebuked a false prophet named Bar-jesus before the Roman proconsul. The pretender was struck with blindness, and the proconsul was converted. (Acts 13:6-12)
LEBANON
(Saïda) Sidon
On his way to imprison Christians in Damascus, Saul (renamed Paul) was converted after a miraculous encounter with Christ. (Acts 9:1-19)
Damascus
I N T E R N U M
E R R A N E A N S E A)
(Soûr) Tyre
('Akko) Ptolemais
Lacus Tiberias (Sea of Galilee)
Bostra (Buşra ash Shām)
Apollonia (Sūsah)
Darnis (Darnah)
Peter, Paul, and Barnabus met with other Christian leaders to repudiate a sect who said that new gentile converts needed to obey the Law of Moses. In unity, they agreed that salvation was by faith in Christ alone, no works of the Law were required. (Acts 15:1-21)
Caesarea
ISRAEL
Neapolis (Nablus)
Antipatris
Jordan
Jerusalem
JUDAEA
Lacus Asphaltitis (Dead Sea)
Gaza
N A I C A
N A B A T E A
Alexandria (El Iskandarîya)
Paraetonium (Maţrūḩ)
Pelusium
J O R D A N
Daphnae (Kôm Dafana)
OFF TO ROME
After returning to Jerusalem on completion of his third mission, Paul was imprisoned after the Jews accused him of inciting riots. Tried before the Roman authorities and King Agrippa, he appealed his case to Caesar as was the right of any Roman citizen. (Acts 21-26)
Terenuthis
A E G Y P T U S
Heliopolis
Petra
Memphis
Aelana (Al 'Aqabah)
E G Y P T
Eastern Desert
SINAI
SAUDI ARABIA
Western Desert
Nilus (Nile)

behalf, or by anonymous authors eager to claim Paul's authority.

During Paul's first journey with Barnabas and the disciple John Mark, he traveled to Cyprus and preached in synagogues from Salamis to the capital of Paphos, where he succeeded in converting the Roman proconsul, Sergius Paulus (Acts 13:12). Paul and Barnabas then continued to Asia Minor, landing in Perga, from where they set out for another Antioch, in Pisidia. This bold foray deep into Gentile Asia Minor possibly was facilitated by Sergius Paulus, whose family had extensive land holdings and connections in the area of Pisidian Antioch. Fierce opposition from Jewish groups, however, soon put Paul and Barnabas back on the road, traveling to Iconium in Roman Lycaonia. Rumors of a plot to kill them propelled the travelers to Lystra, back to Attalia, and ultimately back to their home base in Antioch on the Orontes, in Syria.

In the process, Paul began to refine his theology—inspired, as he believed, by Jesus and the spirit of God. As he later wrote, "we have the mind of Christ" (I Corinthians 2:16). Paul confronted the challenge of explaining profoundly Jewish tenets, such as redemption by a "messiah," to an audience that had no concept of the Judaic faith and its aspirations. In the process, many scholars believe, Paul developed a Christology uniquely suited to Gentile followers. In Acts of the Apostles, it is Paul who first argues that Jesus is the "Son of God" (Acts 9:20), an idea that—in a biological sense—was difficult to accept for observant Jews but eminently plausible to Gentiles raised in the polytheistic Roman world.

Some scholars argue that in the Gospels Jesus never explicitly declares himself the Son of God. He most often refers to himself as the "Son of Man," a term that first appears in Daniel (and possibly Ezekiel), but one that scholars interpret as a self-deprecating form of speech meaning "this mere mortal" or "son of the people." Jesus also speaks of God as "my Father," but authors debate whether this was meant in a literal or even exclusive sense. The prayer that Jesus teaches his disciples opens with "Our Father, who art in heaven." Elsewhere, Jesus refers to his followers as "children of your Father in heaven" (Matthew 5:45). The Book of Exodus, too, says: "Thus says the Lord: Israel is my firstborn son" (Exodus 4:22).

Paul must have known that in the Greco-Roman world the title "Son of God" imparted an entirely different status. Many mythological figures had been begotten in the union of a god and a mortal being. Gentiles were intrigued by the moral purity of monotheism, but would have struggled with the intangible, amorphous nature of YHWH. Contrary to the Jewish abhorrence of graven images, Greco-Roman religion thrived on visual imagery; indeed, to the Greek mind, physical beauty was proof of divine favor. As a divine being, Jesus could become the visual symbol of the unseen Jewish God. Even Paul and Barnabas were once taken for gods. Acts describes how, after Paul heals a cripple in the city of Lystra, witnesses in the crowds shout "The gods have come down to us in human form!" (Acts 14:10-11).

The Antioch Church and its satellite communities grew rapidly due to Paul's teachings. Encouraged, Paul embarked on a second and far more ambitious voyage, one that will take him to the heart of Greek culture: Athens and Corinth. The exact chronology of Paul's journeys is subject to scholarly debate. Many authors, however, accept that sometime between C.E. 48 and 51, Paul traveled from Antioch to the center of Anatolia and on to Troas (near today's Istanbul). From there he sailed across the Aegean, probably landing at Philippi and continuing along the Via Egnatia, the military highway built by Rome. Traveling through the Greek mainland, he formed Christian communities in Philippi and Thessalonica, until a mob in Thessalonica forced him to flee to Beroea (Acts 17:5-10). He then traveled to Athens, where he debated with Epicurean and Stoic philosophers in the central marketplace.

A warm welcome awaited Paul in Corinth, and he stayed in the city for 18 months. According to Acts, however, a group of Jews brings Paul before a tribunal, accusing him of "persuading people to worship God in ways that are contrary to the law." The presiding judge, named Gallio, "proconsul of Achaia," dismisses the charge, since it is a "matter of questions about words and names and your own law," not pertinent to Roman law (Acts 18:12-17). An inscription from C.E. 52, found in the Greek city of Delphi, containing a decree from Emperor

EPISTLE TO THE ROMANS

Paul steadily sent newly founded Christian communities letters on how to live in imitation of Christ. The Epistle to the Romans, one of seven letters that most scholars unquestionably attribute to Paul, is one of his finest works. The Christians in Rome had been cool to Paul, for they considered their community to be an observant offshoot of the Jerusalem Church. Paul therefore reiterated his principal arguments with great care: baptism in Christ superceded Jewish Law, faith in the Lord was justification in itself, and "just as Christ was raised from the dead by the glory of the Father, so we too might walk in newness of life" (Romans 6:4). The letter reveals ongoing tension between observant Jewish and Gentile Christians.

Claudius (C.E. 41–54) mentions a governor, L. Iunius Gallio, by name. This inscription has been very useful in determining the chronology of Paul's stay in Corinth. He then journeyed back to Asia Minor, landing at Ephesus. All along the way, Paul converted both Jews as well as Gentiles (referred to as "God-fearers") to the message of Jesus as the risen Messiah.

Around C.E. 52, Paul set off on a third major journey, centered on Ephesus, one of the largest cities on the Ionian coast of Anatolia (today's Turkey), where it is believed he stayed for more than two years. Paul then headed back to Corinth for a sojourn that may have lasted until C.E. 56. In his Epistle to the Romans, written in Corinth, Paul conveys the greetings of several followers, including "Erastus, the city treasurer" (Romans 16:23). In 1929, excavators found a first-century limestone fragment in Corinth inscribed with the words "Erastus, in return for his aedileship, laid [this pavement] at his own expense." It is possible that this was the Corinthian official who knew Paul.

Paul's Arrest

EVENTUALLY, Paul did return to Jerusalem, where news of his activity among the Gentiles had preceded him. As Paul entered the Jerusalem Temple, he was arrested on the charge of taking Gentiles past the *soreg*, the wooden fence surrounding the Temple precinct (Acts 21:26-30). He appeared before the Sanhedrin and was remanded to the Antonia Fortress, while various plots were hatched to kill him. Paul appealed on the basis of his status as a Roman citizen, which forced the commander of the Antonia to send him to Caesarea, the capital of Roman Judea. During Paul's two-year captivity in that city, Jewish chief priests demanded his return to Jerusalem to stand trial. Paul thereupon appealed as a Roman citizen to his right of *provocatio*, of being heard by the emperor (Acts 25:10).

Around C.E. 60, Paul and other prisoners were duly dispatched on a ship to Rome. During the voyage, the vessel was hit by a heavy squall, which stranded Paul and a number of other survivors on the beach at Malta. From there, an Egyptian

In C.E. 130, Tiberius Iulius Aquila built the Library of Celsus in Ephesus as a monument to his father and to circumvent the prohibition against building tombs there.

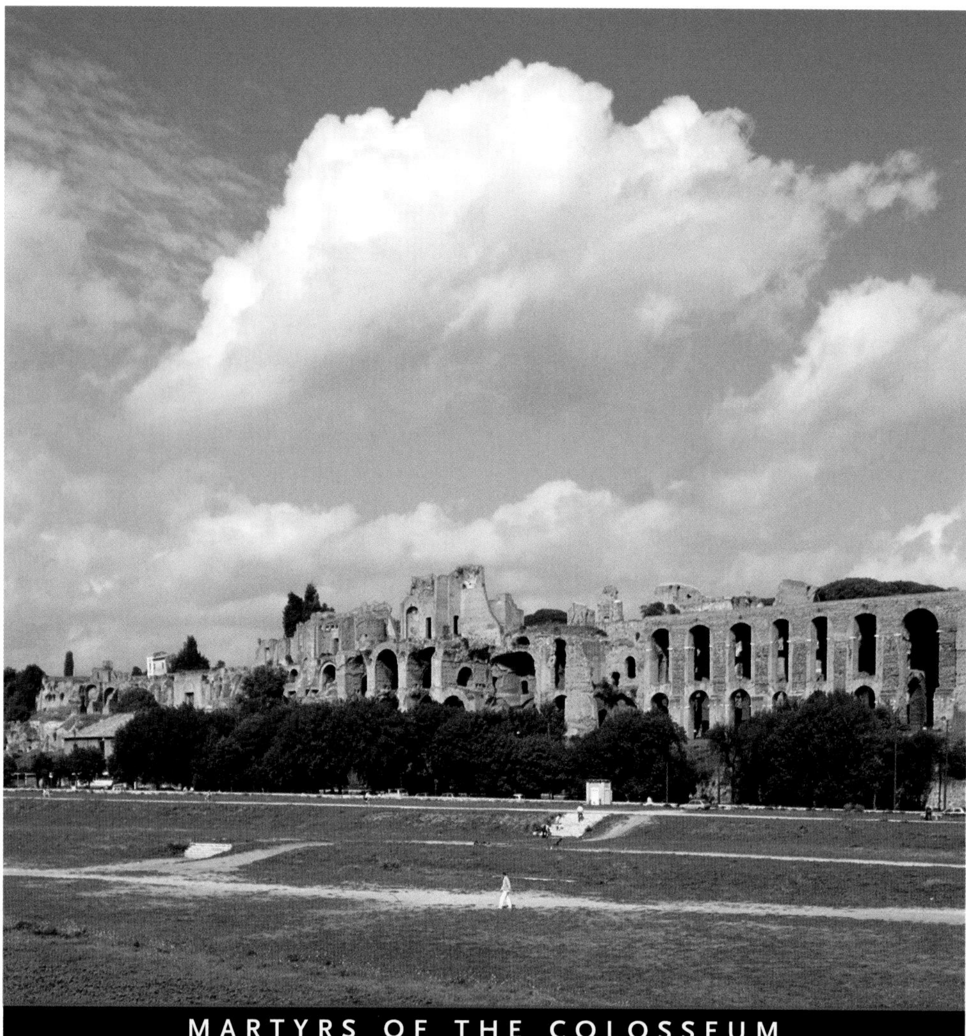

MARTYRS OF THE COLOSSEUM

THE ROMAN HISTORIAN TACITUS STATES that Emperor Nero put hundreds of Christians to death as part of lavish public entertainments staged "in his gardens ... and in the Circus." It is possible that the gardens were located on Nero's property on the Esquiline Hill, where later he would build his sumptuous Domus Aurea, or Golden House. Before the fire of C.E. 64, the former palace of the Esquiline had been the venue for many festive and sometimes outrageous banquets hosted by Nero.

The location of the Circus is more difficult to pinpoint. Today, guides at the Roman Colosseum solemnly point to the spot where they say Christians were thrown to the lions. Yet the Colosseum (more properly called the Flavian Amphitheater) was built some eight years after the fire—not by Nero but by Emperor Vespasian. Tacitus, in fact, may have been referring to the Circus Maximus, which was a favorite venue for chariot racing and boasted a track of some 550 yards. If Nero wanted to make an impact, he would no doubt have chosen to kill Christians in the Circus Maximus, for it would have accommodated the largest possible crowd. After the fire, Nero himself extended the racetrack by about 100 yards.

The outline of the Circus Maximus in Rome is still visible near the ruins of the Domus Augustana, a wing of Domitian's imperial palace on Palatine Hill.

grain ship eventually deposited him at Puteoli, in the bay of Naples. Paul then slowly made his way to Rome, awaiting his hearing at the emperor's court. He remained there under house arrest for two years, writing letters to the faithful and receiving visitors. This is the last we hear of Paul, and the remaining years of his life are cloaked in mystery.

Power of Rome

IN C.E. 64, a terrible fire of suspicious origins swept through the city of Rome. Some believed that Emperor Nero (C.E. 54–68) had it set deliberately to clear space for his grandiose new city plan. The Roman historian Tacitus (ca C.E. 56–117) wrote that Nero needed a scapegoat, and he settled on the Christian community of Rome. Its members were arrested and rigorously interrogated, after which, says Tacitus, "large numbers of others were condemned." A late-first-century C.E. letter of Clement I, bishop of Rome, and an apocryphal second-century C.E. document entitled "Acts of Peter," claim that the Apostle Peter was caught up in this persecution. How Peter would have made his way from Judea to Rome is not clear; the Book of Acts of the Apostles only refers to Peter's missionary work in Palestine, although Paul's letter to the Galatians, written around 53, describes an encounter with Peter in Antioch (Galatians 2:11). According to "Acts of Peter," the Apostle Peter was subsequently crucified in the Roman Circus together with other Christians, though Peter demanded that his cross be turned upside down, deeming himself unworthy to die in the same posture as Jesus.

Tradition holds that Peter was subsequently buried in a rural spot on the right bank of the Tiber River called the Ager Vaticanus. The Christian theologian Tertullian of Carthage (ca 155–220), writing around 200, reported that Paul was

The more often we are mown down, the more in number we grow; the blood of Christians is our seed. Tertullian of Carthage, *Apologia*

also put to death during Nero's pogroms, a claim that was later reiterated by the theologian Origen (ca 185–254). If true, then it is likely that, as a Roman citizen, Paul would have been beheaded.

Jewish Revolt

TWO YEARS LATER, a revolt broke out in Judea, and Rome found itself at war with the Jews of Palestine. In C.E. 37, Emperor Gaius Caesar, nicknamed "Caligula" (C.E. 37–41), had granted to the grandson of Herod the Great, Herod Agrippa I (C.E. 37–44), the former tetrarchy of Philip. After the downfall of Herod Antipas in 39, Agrippa received Galilee and Perea as well. Soon thereafter, however, Caligula declared himself to be a god and that sacrifice should be made to him in temples throughout the empire, including Jerusalem. The Jews refused and prepared for war, which was only preempted by Caligula's assassination in 41. Caligula's successor, Claudius, added Judea, Samaria, and Idumea to Agrippa's territory. For a brief time, Agrippa ruled over a territory that was roughly the size of his grandfather's kingdom, stirring Jewish hopes for a full restoration.

This bust of Emperor Nero (C.E. 54–68) was completed around 150 and can be found today in the collection of the Uffizi Museum in Florence.

In C.E. 44, Agrippa died suddenly in Caesarea. Since the tetrarch's heir was only 17 years old, Emperor Claudius decided to hand Judea back into the experienced hands of a Roman procurator, Felix, in 52 C.E. (the stable parts of the kingdom were eventually handed over to Marcus Julius Agrippa II, C.E. 48-70, who, according to Acts, interrogated Paul). Judea thus became a Roman province once again, now known as Syria Palaestina. Within the span of only 16 years, it would be ruled by 5, mostly incompetent, procurators.

In C.E. 62, the sudden death of Felix's successor, procurator Porcius Festus, created an unexpected power vacuum. According to the first-century-C.E. Jewish historian Josephus, the high priest Ananus won the Sanhedrin's backing to indict both "James, the brother of Jesus known as Christ, and several others on the charge of breaking the Law." Eusebius wrote that James, the leader of the Jerusalem community, was thrown off the Temple parapet and then clubbed to death. With both James and Peter dead, the early Christian movement in Palestine was leaderless. Within a decade, it would all but cease to exist.

Meanwhile, dissident Jewish groups —including the Essenes, the Pharisees, and another more militant group, the Zealots in Galilee—continued to agitate against Roman oppression. Born from the tax revolts of the early part of the century, the Zealots had become a potent militant organization with its own wing of *sicarii* (*sikarioi* in Greek), meaning "dagger men." In C.E. 66, during the regime of Gessius Florus (C.E. 64–66)—who, says Josephus, ruled "like an executioner rather than a governor"—these tensions turned into a revolt.

This limestone fragment from Corinth recognizes a city official named "Erastus." He may be the Erastus referred to in Paul's letter to the Romans.

BIRTH OF RABBINIC JUDAISM

The ruins of ancient Tiberias stand on the southwestern shore of the Sea of Galilee, the center of the Rabbinate after the Second Jewish Revolt.

ROME'S REACTION TO THE outbreak of the Jewish Revolt in C.E. 66 was slow in coming due to Nero's chaotic governance. Rome eventually sent one of its ablest generals, Vespasian, to Palestine to quash the revolt. His troops marched on northern Palestine in the spring of 67 and easily defeated the Zealot troops commanded by Josephus, the historian, in Galilee. In July 69, with Rome caught up in civil war, Vespasian's legion pronounced him emperor (C.E. 69–79), and Vespasian's son, Titus, was charged with prosecuting the war against the Zealot militias.

In C.E. 70, Titus moved quickly to bolster the siege of Jerusalem, which had been in place, with varying success, since 68. His forces dug a trench and breastworks around the walls of the city, and killed any Jews who tried to flee by crucifying them in full view of the defenders. By the summer of 70, Titus finally was able to breach the walls of Jerusalem, and his soldiers steadily fought their way toward the last holdout of the Zealots in the Temple precinct. On August 29 or 30, this enclave yielded to the Roman onslaught. The Temple was burned to the ground (though Josephus claims that Titus had wanted to spare the sanctuary). By eradicating the Temple, the Romans effectively

ca C.E. 66
Outbreak of the Jewish War in Palestine, the first major revolt against the Roman occupation

ca C.E. 66–70
"Mark" writes his gospel, the oldest of the four canonical Gospels in the New Testament

ca C.E. 67
General Vespasian arrives in Galilee to suppress the Jewish Revolt

ca C.E. 70
Titus captures Jerusalem and destroys the Second Temple

Let your house be a gathering place for sages; wallow in the dust of their feet, and drink their words with gusto. Let your house be open wide, and seat the poor at your table.

Yosé ben Yoezer and Yosé ben Yohanan, Mishnah, Tractate Avot I

destroyed the focal point of Jewish worship and sacrifice since the days of King David. This act of revenge all but wiped out the sacrificial priesthood: The Sadducees fled and ceased to exist as a cohesive movement.

Titus then exacted a terrible punishment on the Jewish residents, who had vexed the Roman armies for three long years. Men, women, and children were cut down and left to die in the fire that swept the city. Israeli archaeologist Nahman Avigad uncovered poignant evidence of this massacre in 1969 as he carefully picked through the charred remains of a first-century house, now called the Burnt House and converted into a museum in Jerusalem's Old City. There, under a piece of blackened masonry, lay the bones of a young woman in the position in which she had died, clutching at the steps of the house. Modern estimates have put the toll of the siege at more than 100,000 Jews, and an equal number may have been taken as slaves to Rome.

Judea became a province ruled by a Roman legate who reported directly to Rome, rather than to the Roman governor of Syria. Various agricultural estates were annexed as imperial possessions, so that the proceeds from their harvests went directly to the imperial treasury. Jews were evicted from the city of Jerusalem and forbidden to return, though it is not clear for how long or how often this rule was enforced. The war also forced Jewish Christians to leave the city, and many may have settled in Pella of the Decapolis, a city located just across the Jordan River east of Beth Shan.

The Jewish factions that had flourished in the years before the Jewish Revolt scattered, though a core element of the Pharisees may have survived. Yohanan ben Zakkai, a pupil of Hillel and leader of a rabbinical school in Jerusalem, had strenuously argued for peace with Rome, and had denounced the Zealots of Jerusalem for wanting to "destroy this city and burn the house of the sanctuary." As the Roman siege of Jerusalem intensified, Yohanan was smuggled out of the city in a coffin. According to rabbinic sources, he then successfully petitioned the Romans for permission to establish a new religious school in Jabneh, a village on the Mediterranean coast some 12 miles south of present-day Tel Aviv. In time, the center in Jabneh evolved into an academy of scholars, rabbis, and rabbinical students, who continued the Pharisaic tradition of scriptural debate and legislative commentary. Yohanan also restored the traditional Jewish tribunal, known as the Beth Din ("house of judgment"), to rule on both spiritual and secular issues, as the Sanhedrin once had done.

Yohanan's academy became the cornerstone of Jewish spiritual recovery after the destruction of the Temple. The leader's teachings were captured in his famous quote of Hosea, with which he sought to console his followers after the loss of the Temple: "For I desire mercy and not sacrifice [and the knowledge of God rather than burnt offerings]" (Hosea 6:6). Rabbinic scholars (*tannaim*) supplanted priests now that biblical commentary and prayer had become the principal redemptive practice of Judaism. Engaging in the study of Torah was a restorative effort that, in a way, created a new temple: a spiritual temple, a New Jerusalem no longer bound to the ruins on the Temple Mount. Indeed, the rabbis believed that whenever a group of Jews studied the Law together, the presence of the Lord (Shekinah) was with them. The period of Second Temple Judaism

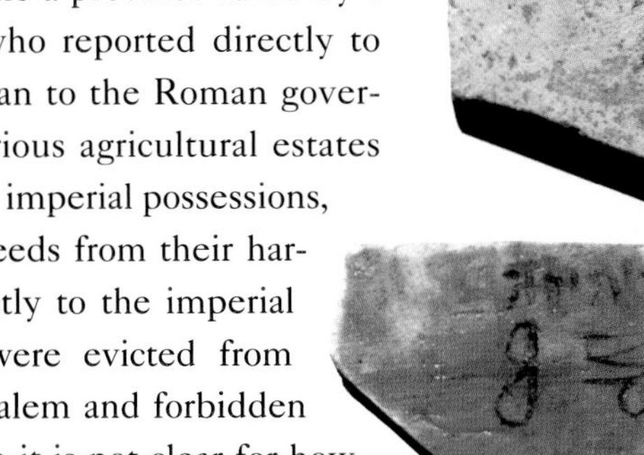

These ostraca found at Masada bear the names Yehuda (left), Yohanan (top), and Simon (right).

ca C.E. 98–117
Besieged by the Roman Tenth Legion, the Jewish Zealots on Masada commit mass suicide

ca C.E. 132–135
A second Jewish rebellion, known as the Bar Kochba Revolt, is successfully repressed by the Romans

ca C.E. 135
Emperor Hadrian decides to raze Jerusalem and erect a new city, Aelia Capitolina, in its place

ca C.E. 135–140
Simeon ben Gamaliel II moves the Jabneh Academy to Galilee and forms a new Sanhedrin

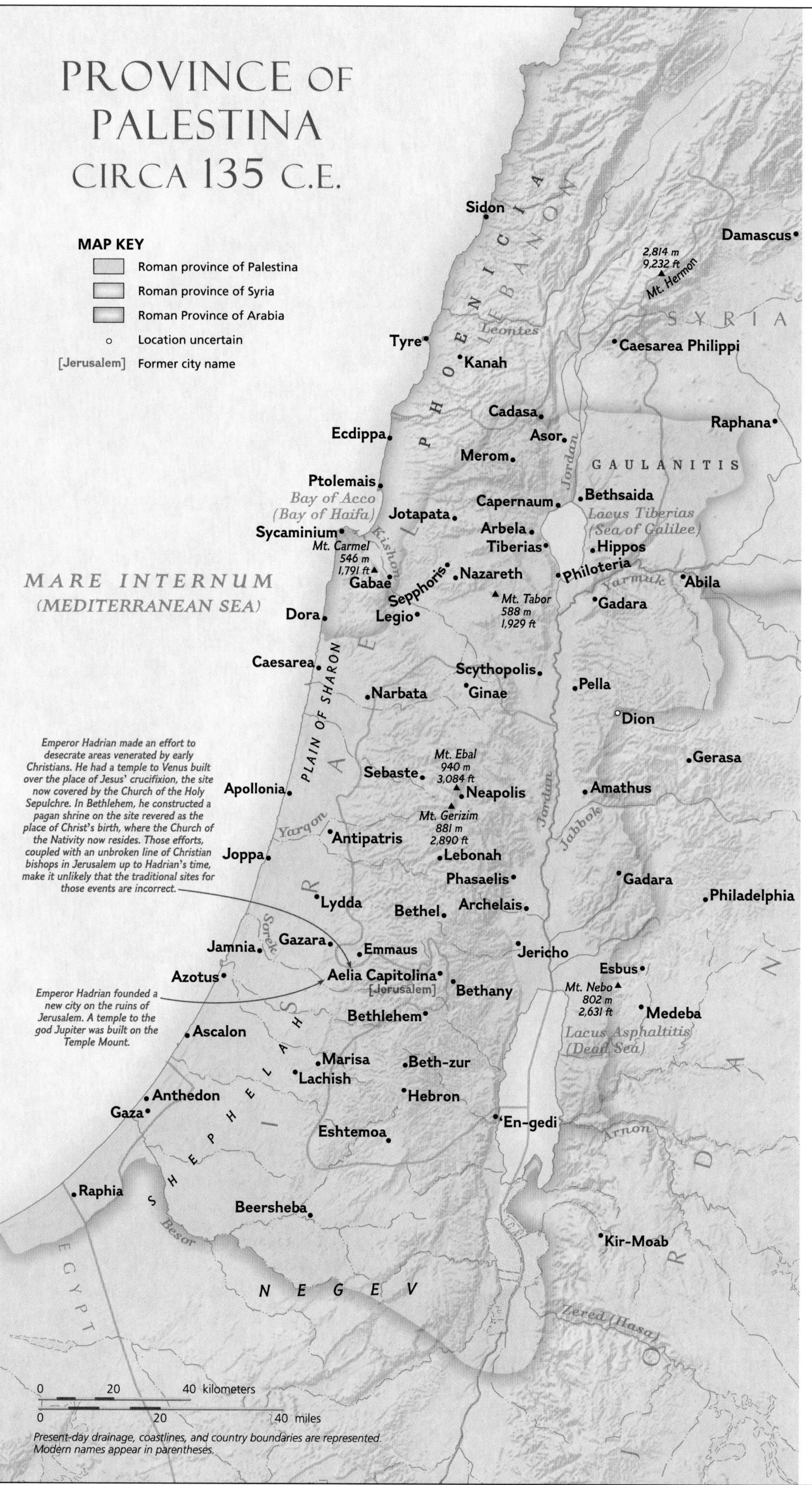

had come to an end; rabbinic Judaism was about to begin.

Jewish Patriarchate

THE TEMPLE'S DESTRUCTION was devastating, but it did not jeopardize the survival of Judaism. Diaspora communities continued to flourish throughout Asia Minor, Greece, and the Italian peninsula, as well as in Egypt, Carthage, and Spain. The growing use of the synagogue as a center of prayer and scriptural study had prepared these communities for the day when the Temple in Jerusalem would no longer figure as the center of their cultic life. Jewish faith now prospered on the strength of its laws, prayer, and ongoing rabbinic study.

Despite the violent suppression of the Jewish Revolt, Roman emperors realized that Diaspora Jews presented little threat to the state. Emperor Vespasian had never revoked Judaism's status as a lawfully recognized religion throughout the empire. However, discrimination against Jewish communities was inflamed once again by a second rebellion known as the Bar Kochba Revolt (132–135), named for its leader Simeon bar Kochba (meaning "son of the star").

DIASPORA OF THE JEWS

The word "diaspora" comes from a Greek word meaning "sowing of seeds" or "dispersal." It traditionally denotes the scattering of Jewish people outside Judea, particularly after the destruction of the Second Temple in C.E. 70. Indeed, the Septuagint, the Greek version of the Hebrew Bible, translates Deuteronomy chapter 28, verse 25 as "you shall be a diaspora in all kingdoms of the earth." In truth, the Jewish Diaspora had already existed for many centuries due to Judea's incorporation into the Persian and Roman Empires. By the middle of the first century C.E., before the Temple was destroyed, Jewish communities flourished throughout Asia Minor, Greece, and Rome, as well as in Egypt, Carthage, and Spain.

Apparently, one of the factors precipitating this rebellion was the decision by Emperor Hadrian (117–138) to raze Jerusalem and build a new Roman city, Aelia Capitolina, in its place. The wholesale confiscation by Roman authorities of Jewish land during the preceding decades may have been a contributing factor as well. Nevertheless, in 138, just three years after the Bar Kochba uprising, Emperor Antoninus Pius (138–161) reinstated the Roman decree allowing the practice of the Jewish religion. Jews were still forbidden from entering Jerusalem, however.

In the aftermath of the Bar Kochba Revolt, the Beth Din, center of rabbinic Judaism, moved from Jabneh to Galilee. It was first established in Bet She'arim; then in the former capital of Galilee, Sepphoris; and finally in Tiberias, on the shores of the Sea of Galilee. Subsequent Roman procurators soon recognized that the Rabbinate could be a stabilizing force, controlling the territory with little political risk. Thus the Rabbinate gained an amount of local autonomy, which sustained the ideal of Jewish self-rule and protected the people from the excesses of Roman power.

This relief from the Arch of Titus depicts soldiers carrying the menorah taken from the Second Temple during the triumphal procession in Rome.

Simeon ben Gamaliel (135–150) was able to secure Roman approval for the formation of a new Sanhedrin in 140. At the head of the Sanhedrin was the patriarch, a position that eventually became a hereditary office for those of Davidic pedigree, endowed with an authority approaching that of the high priest during the Second Temple period. Thus began the heyday of the Jewish patriarchate in Judea.

A very similar process was taking place among the Jewish communities in Persia, which had been conquered by the Parthians. The Parthians had inhabited northeastern Persia, part of today's Iran, and took control of the Persian Empire in the second century B.C.E. Here too, governors had seen the wisdom of delegating local authority to prominent religious figures who understood the unique precepts and cultic practices of Judaism. This empowerment led to the institution of the exilarch, the patriarch of the Jewish community in Babylon. Like his western counterpart, the exilarch claimed Davidic ancestry and held considerable judicial power. In the late third

A CAPTIVE TURNED HISTORIAN

ALTHOUGH LITTLE ARCHAEOLOGICAL EVIDENCE relates to the life of Jesus, two works by the Jewish historian Josephus describe the social and political circumstances of first-century Palestine in detail. Josephus, of priestly descent, reluctantly accepted a commission in the growing Zealot army during the Jewish Revolt of C.E. 66 to 70. He took a post as commander of a regiment in Galilee. Roman legions under the command of Vespasian marched in 67 to quell the rebellion and easily defeated Josephus's troops. Josephus himself surrendered and was brought to Vespasian for interrogation. Josephus then adroitly saved his life (and his career) by prophesizing that the bald, corpulent general would one day become emperor. Vespasian didn't believe him, but decided to call Josephus's bluff and held him captive. Fortunately for Josephus, Rome was now passing through a brief period of civil war that would see no less than 3 different emperors in the span of 18 months. In July of C.E. 69, Vespasian's legions pronounced him emperor, and Josephus was promptly released. He eventually joined the emperor's household in Rome, where he wrote a book about the Jewish Revolt; later he also published a book about Jewish history, entitled *Antiquities of the Jews*. Since the latter features a short paragraph about Jesus, his works were meticulously copied and preserved through the Middle Ages until modern times. Recent scholarship, however, has claimed that the paragraph about Jesus (or parts thereof) were added later.

This 17th-century engraving depicts Josephus, who recorded valuable details of life during the Jewish Revolt of C.E. 66–70.

A tribe, a false prophet, or a high priest can only be tried by a court of seventy-one judges; an aggressive war can only be waged by the authority of a court of seventy-one. Mishnah, Tractate Sanhedrin

century, Judah ben Ezekiel founded a new academy at Pumbeditha that soon emerged as a leading center of rabbinic scholarship; other schools at Nehardea and Sura soon attracted students throughout Babylonia and beyond.

The principal focus of the patriarchate in Palestine was to continue legislating Jewish life based on ongoing discussion of the Law as it applied to everyday practice. In the rabbinic view, this Oral Law had always been part of the Torah tradition, as the cumulative record of debate by generations of scholars steeped in Covenant Law. Most of the Oral Law material was first codified as the Mishnah (which means "teaching") in the early third century B.C.E., possibly by Rabbi Yuda ha-Nasi ("the Prince"). Written mostly in Hebrew, the Mishnah is an attempt to provide a systematic reference for legal arguments and precepts based on the Torah. The Mishnah is organized into six basic orders, or subject areas (subdivided into 63 tractates and 531 chapters): Seeds (agricultural laws), Festivals (Jewish holidays), Women (marriage laws), Damages (civil law), Holy Things (sacrifice), and Purities (issues of cultic purity). On each topic, the Mishnah provides legal commentary illustrated by a rabbinical discussion of actual cases.

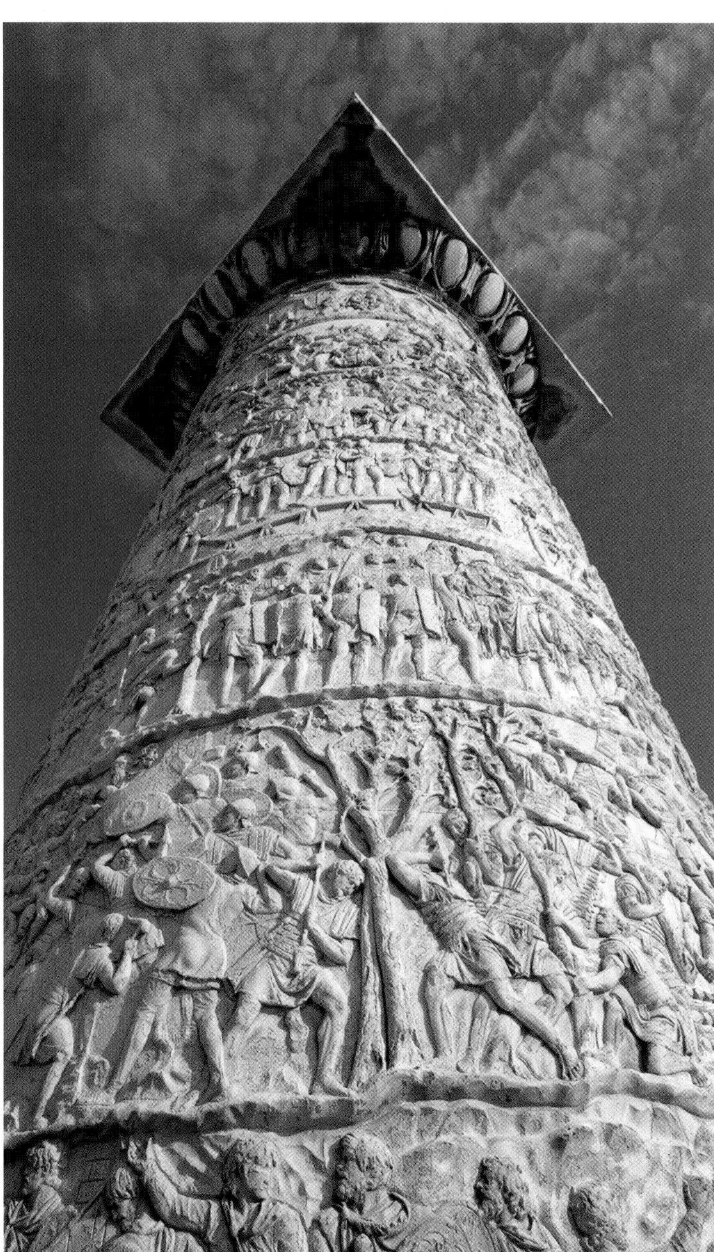

The 108-foot Trajan's Column in Rome, dedicated in C.E. 113, depicts scenes from Trajan's Dacian Wars in one continuous spiral band of carvings.

The Mishnah continued to invite ongoing study and debate. These subsequent rabbinical discussions (redacted in Aramaic as the *Gemara*) were recorded and, together with the Mishnah, included in a series of books known as the Talmud. Typically, the Talmud cites a particular law from the Mishnah, which is followed by a rabbinical discussion of the topic. In Palestine proper, rabbis produced a Palestinian Talmud (*Talmud Yerushalmi*, or Jerusalem Talmud) around C.E. 400. A similar effort to document discussions of the Oral Law and the Mishnah took place among the Jewish scholarly communities in Babylonia. Their texts became known as the Babylonian Talmud (*Talmud Bavli*), which is far more extensive than the Palestinian Talmud and often considered more authoritative. These and other writings, including the Midrash, may reflect a determined effort on the part of the rabbis to respond to the growing power of Christianity, which in C.E. 313 became an officially recognized religion within the Roman Empire.

The Talmud would have become an indispensable guide for Jews in the Diaspora. It offered every Jew, regardless of his background or place of residence, a reliable reference that enabled him to remain faithful to Jewish laws. At the same time, Talmudic scholarship gave the rabbis in Palestine and Babylonia the prestige and authority to adjudicate in virtually all matters pertaining to everyday life, under the protection of their rulers, thus granting local communities a precious sense of autonomy.

TENTH LEGION

The Roman Tenth Legion figured prominently in first-century C.E. Palestine. Judea formed part of the Roman province of Syria, which was protected by four legions: III Gallica, VI Ferrata, X Fretensis (Tenth Legion), and XII Fulminata. Some scholars believe that after the Galilean tax revolts, a detachment of the Tenth Legion was ordered to remain in Palestine, with separate cohorts stationed in Caesarea and Jerusalem. If so, then *immunes* (specialists) from the Tenth Legion may have been involved in the Crucifixion of Jesus. During the Jewish Revolt, the Tenth participated in the siege of Jerusalem and then moved south to the Judean desert in pursuit of the Zealots, who had retreated to the Masada fortress. Along the way, the Romans erased the monastic community at Qumran. The Tenth built a ramp to the fortress of Masada to bring up Roman siege engines, and in C.E. 73 this last Jewish outpost was captured. The Tenth Legion was then stationed in Jerusalem and may have remained there until the third century.

Most infantry in the Tenth Legion were local recruits, primarily from Syria, which was considered more reliable politically. A typical *militis* or "grunt" bore a short sword (*gladius hispaniensis*, or Spanish sword), a spear (*pilum*), a helmet, a shield (*scutum*), a mail shirt, and a cloak (*sagum*). The Tenth's insignia featured a dolphin, a galley, and a bull—the latter a sign that the legion was commissioned by a member of the house of Julius Caesar. The soldier's annual salary of some 225 denarii (about $3,500 today) was given in monthly installments; after deductions for the cost of food and clothing, soldiers were left with about 10 dinarii per month, good for about a jug of local wine per week, with some change to spare. After 25 years of service, a soldier received a bronze plaque or diploma and a pension equivalent to 10 years' pay.

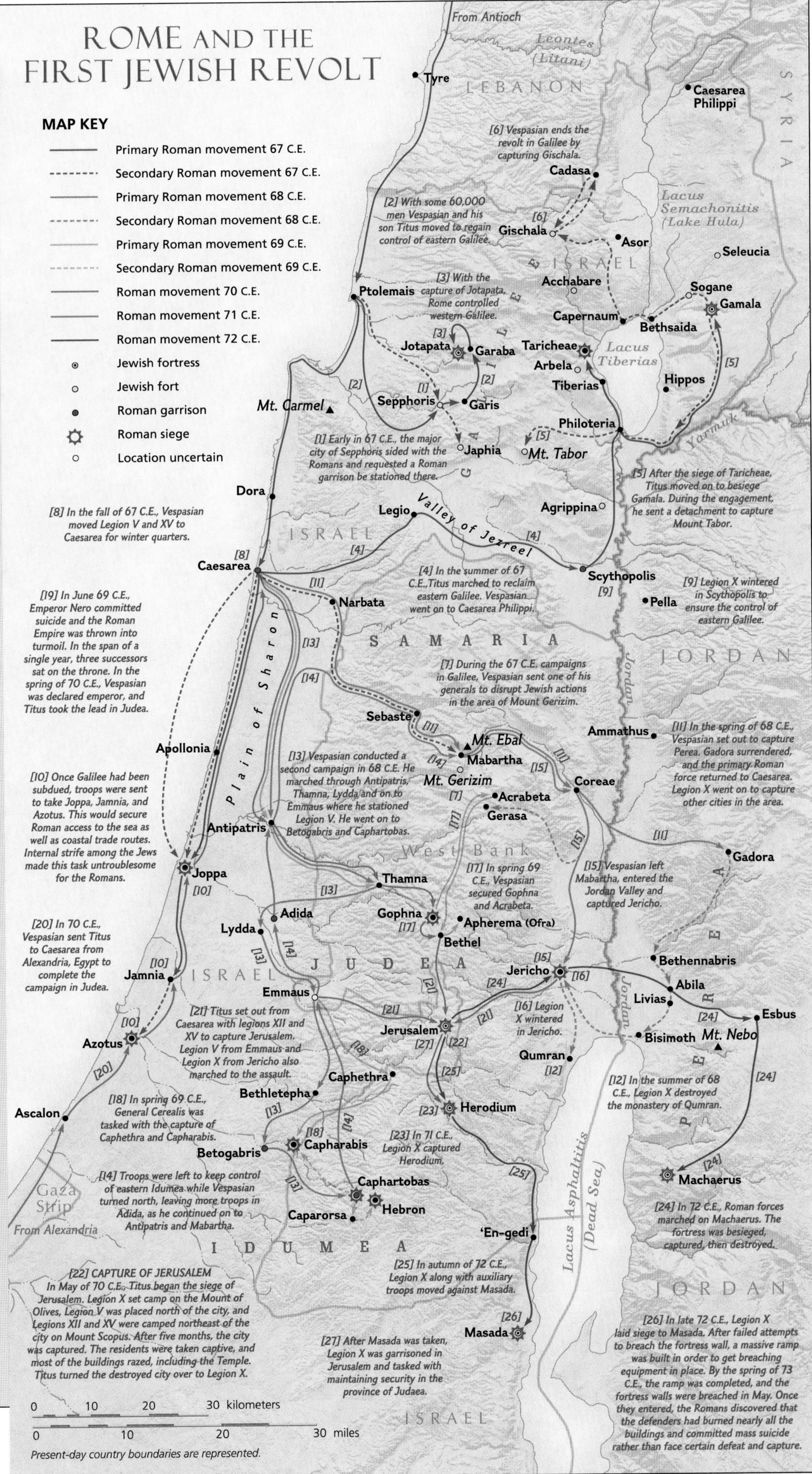

Growth of Christianity

The interior of the early Christian Hypogeum (an underground tomb) in the Catacombs of the Via Latina in Rome dates from the fourth century C.E.

The persecutions under Nero and the subsequent Jewish wars also had a major impact on the Christian movement. In the span of only five years, all of the prominent Church leaders—James, Peter, and Paul—had been put to death. According to one church tradition, Simeon son of Cleopas (Jesus' uncle) took control of the movement in Jerusalem, but any hope of creating a new Christian center in Palestine was gone. Jewish Christians mourned the loss of the Temple as much as their Jewish brethren did, but Gentile Christians in Asia Minor saw the destruction of Jerusalem as God's punishment of a city that had refused to accept Jesus as the Messiah.

Indeed, the war had contributed to the polarization of Jewish and Gentile followers of Jesus. As they sought to further distance themselves from their Jewish brethren, Gentile Christians felt a strong need for a Scripture that was uniquely Christian rather than Jewish—an authoritative source that explained Jesus' teachings and deeds based on the teachings of Paul, now no longer among the living. Growth of dissident Christian sects who disagreed with Paul's Christology also threatened the stability of the young religion. This growing dissidence, scholars believe, was the primary

ca C.E. 146–170
Ptolemy, a scholar in Alexandria, describes the "known world" as stretching from Iceland to Sri Lanka

ca C.E. 185
In Lyon, France, Bishop Irenaeus leads early "canonization" of the New Testament

ca C.E. 193–211
Emperor Septimius Severus allows Roman officials to persecute Christians

ca C.E. 249–251
Reign of Emperor Decius is marked by the "Decian persecution" against the Christians

His disciples said to him, "When will the kingdom come?" [Jesus said,] "It will not come by waiting for it. It will not be a matter of saying 'Here it is,' or 'There it is.' Rather, the Kingdom of the Father is spread out upon the earth, and men do not see it." Gospel of Thomas, 113

impetus for the composition of the Gospels of Mark, Luke, and Matthew, which all appear to have been written some time in the 30 years following the Jewish Revolt.

By this time, early Christianity had begun to expand well beyond the orbit of either Peter or Paul, assuring its survival. Near the end of the first century C.E., growing Christian communities (some Jewish, but more often Gentile) were flourishing throughout the Roman Empire; by one estimate, there were some 300,000 Christians in Asia Minor alone. Many Romans were impressed by the social compassion of Christians. In cities throughout the realm, Christians cared for the sick, the poor, or the unemployed; they tended to those languishing in prisons or helped to bury the dead.

Christianity's growth, however, was haphazard. There was as yet no formal church organization, so "Christianity" in the early second century C.E. was really a collection of local groups focused on the figure of Jesus Christ. Adherents of the Jerusalem Church clung steadfastly to their Jewish roots, Gentile "chapels" were imbued with the theology of Paul. Other communities of people, collectively referred to by biblical scholars as "Gnostic Christians," pursued in various ways the goal of knowing Christ through a life of inner transformation. Gnosticism—derived from the Greek word *gnosis*, meaning "(secret) knowledge"—was influenced by the ancient idea, also postulated in Buddhism, that a complete immersion in the Divine ultimately leads to secret knowledge of the divinity within oneself. This thought was consonant with Greek philosophy, which accepted the premise that each human being carried inside himself a spark of the Divine. In the Gnostic Christian interpretation, Jesus speaks in parables because true knowledge of God is a precious and potentially dangerous secret accessible only to those who prove themselves worthy of that knowledge.

In 1945, the discovery of 13 bound books of papyrus sheets near the Egyptian city of Nag 'Hammadi opened a new window on the world of these early Gnostic Christians, adding to the current body of knowledge based on text fragments recovered in Oxyrhynchus in northern Egypt and elsewhere. These texts, including the gospels of Thomas, Peter, and Philip, indicate that Gnostic congregations embraced both men and women; some Gnostic sects even claimed their apostolic authority from Mary Magdalene, based on the so-called gospel of Mary, discovered in Cairo in 1896.

Gnostic Christians stressed the validity of individual revelation, of becoming, in a sense, an apostle in one's own right. This idea, some scholars believe, may have threatened the hierarchical model of authority that the emerging Church was trying to build. This independence may be one reason why "heresies" such as Gnostic Christianity were persecuted with vigor by the Church.

Other sects, including the one propagated by Marcion from Sinope, saw it as their task to fully uncouple Christianity from Jewish tradition. Marcionites took Paul's dismissal of the Jewish Law one step further and rejected the Hebrew Scriptures altogether. One sage named Tatian went

Jesus is set against the Greek letters *chi* and *rho*, the first two letters of the Greek word *Christos*, in this fourth-century mosaic from Hinton St. Mary, Dorset, England.

ca C.E. 260–340
Bishop Eusebius of Caesarea creates the first canon of the New Testament

ca C.E. 261
Emperor Gallienus issues first decree of Christian toleration

ca C.E. 284
Emperor Diocletian reorganizes Roman leadership in order to face external pressures more effectively

ca C.E. 325
The Roman Empire is increasingly under attack from the Goths and the Persians

so far as to create a single gospel, known as the Diatessaron, which claimed to "harmonize" Mark, Matthew, Luke, and John into one treatise. By contrast, the followers of Theodotus, a wealthy tanner from Byzantium, believed that Jesus was born of the Virgin Mary and that the Holy Spirit was a mortal human being who only became divine after his resurrection. Pope Victor I (187–197) excommunicated the Theodosians and other Gnostic sects near the end of the second century C.E., but other "heresies" continued well into the fourth century and the subsequent Byzantine era.

The proliferation of these different Christian sects forced the early Church to develop a more stringent organization in which the Catholic (or "universal") creed propagated by Paul could be enforced. Since the first century C.E., local leaders, or presbyters, had been chosen to govern Christian communities because of their managerial ability and faith in the Holy Spirit, and not because—like the Apostles—they presumably had been in communication with Christ himself. These presbyters were members of the congregation, not yet ordained priests; many of them were married. By C.E. 96, the presbyters began to argue that their authority should derive from an apostolic source, and so the position of central presbyter, or bishop, developed. This informal structure of delegated authority solidified as dissident sects continued to challenge the Pauline theology in the mid- to late second century C.E.

GNOSTIC GOSPELS

SINCE 1945, SCHOLARS HAVE UNEARTHED many Gnostic treatises, including the Gospel of Peter, the Gospel of Philip, and even the Gospel of Mary Magdalene. One of the most famous is the Gospel of Thomas, a collection of sayings by Jesus that makes no reference to the Passion. In one, Jesus ridicules those who believe that the kingdom of God is a new political order or a physical realm. "If those who lead you say to you, 'See, the kingdom is in the sky,' then the birds of the sky will precede you," he says dismissively. "Rather, the kingdom is inside of you, and it is outside of you. When you come to know yourselves, then you will become known, and you will realize that it is you who are the sons of the living father" (Thomas 3).

Scholars have recently reconstructed the Gospel of Judas, a second-century C.E. Greek text, which was probably translated into Coptic between the third and fourth centuries and first brought to light in 1983. This document claims that Jesus asked Judas to betray him to the authorities so that he might die and fulfill his destiny.

The codices from the Nag Hammadi Library, found in Nag 'Hammadi, Egypt, in 1945, contain some 52 mostly Christian Gnostic texts that were written in Coptic, but which were most likely translated from Greek originals.

Roman Persecutions

UNLIKE JUDAISM, Christianity was not a tolerated religion in the Roman world. Throughout the second century C.E., the Christian movement suffered from Roman hostility, although this did not always manifest itself in active oppression. Emperors Domitian (81–96) and Trajan (98–117) both pursued an anti-Christian policy. However, when the younger Pliny, Governor of Bithynia, reported that Christian sects had spread "not only in the cities, but in the villages and rural areas as well" and then proudly boasted of his persecutory zeal to Trajan, the emperor urged moderation. Despite this advice, Trajan's reign saw the martyrdom of several prominent Church prelates, including Bishop Ignatius of Antioch.

Discrimination was also relatively mild during the reign of Hadrian (117–138), the same emperor who rushed legions to Judea to quash the Bar Kochba Revolt. After the region was pacified in 135, Hadrian proceeded with his plans to demolish Jerusalem and build a new city, Aelia Capitolina, in its place. Most of what remained of Jesus'

Jerusalem was obliterated. A temple dedicated to Jupiter was built near the site of the Second Temple.

Violent outbreaks against Christians sometimes occurred in the provinces, but only Emperor Septimius Severus (193–211) allowed his officials to pursue a policy of persecution, particularly when dealing with the Christian communities in Alexandria and northern Africa. Christian thinkers like Quadratus (writing around 125), Justin of Samaria (100–165), and Tertullian tried to use reason to soften the Roman attitude toward Christianity. They each wrote an "Apologia," or "Defense of the Faith," arguing that there was no intrinsic conflict between the Roman political system and Christian theology. Roman persecutions continued, nonetheless, into the third century, when the Romans, facing a growing number of external threats, returned to pious worship of their gods. In the ensuing religious fervor, sects who engaged in anti-Roman behavior (such as the refusal of military service, as many observant Christians did) risked being accused of treachery against the state. Emperor Decius (249–251) in particular reinstated Christian persecution to bring the "draft evaders" to heel. Bishops and clergy were forced to make sacrifices to the emperor or face death.

Mary Magdalene was a prominant figure in Gnostic as well as mainstream Christian circles. Domenico Fetti painted this picture of her between 1617–1621.

A turning point came in 260 when two emperors—Gallienus (253–268) and Valerian, his father, (b. 200–261)—ruled jointly from 253 until 260. It was an

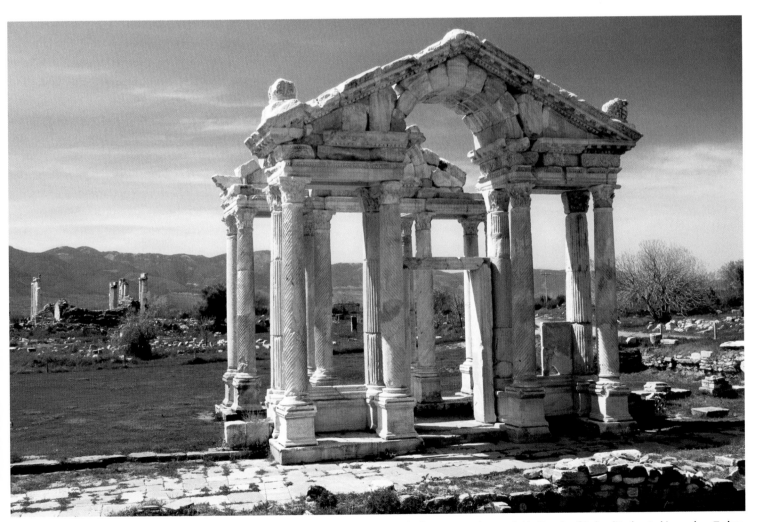

Hadrian (C.E. 117–138) built many cities and temples, including the city of Aelia Capitolina, built over Jerusalem, and this Temple of Aphrodite, located in modern Turkey.

Christian martyrdom was a favorite theme for 19th-century Romantic painters, like Jean-Leon Gerome who painted *The Christian Martyrs' Last Prayer* in 1883.

unusual arrangement prompted by the need to have more than one commander to defend Rome's borders against barbarian invasions. After Valerian was defeated in 260 and taken prisoner by the Persian King Shapur I, Gallienus alone ruled the realm, which in Europe had shrunk to little more than today's borders of Italy and the Balkans.

Under pressure of these outside forces, Gallienus encouraged a revival of Roman arts, poetry, philosophy, and literature to safeguard the integrity of Roman civilization and heal the rifts in its society. The emperor moved in intellectual circles that included the philosopher Plotinus (b. 205–270), who was keenly interested in the different religions of the Roman realm, including Catholic and Gnostic Christianity. It is not certain whether Plotinus' interest in religion was shared by the emperor as well. Nevertheless, it was Gallienus—and not Constantine, as is often thought—who in 261 issued the first Decree of Toleration, an act that made Christianity an officially recognized religion. For the first time since the Jesus' death, Christians could practice their faith publicly. The Church made good use of the opportunity. For the next 40 years, Christians built churches, won converts, and installed bishops in greater numbers than ever before. It has been estimated that by the end of the third century, 10 percent of all people living in Asia Minor were Christian.

Final Scourge of Diocletian

In 284, the continuing pressure of invading hordes demanded a vast reorganization of the Roman Empire. A tetrarchy, or *Dominate*, was established, whereby the supreme power of emperor was divided between two rulers, each of whom were assisted by a subordinate caesar. This foursome now formed, in effect, a military junta with little or no involvement by the Roman Senate. A remarkable sculpture group of red porphyry, located at the southwest corner of the facade of San Marco in Venice, has preserved the likenesses of these four rulers. Frozen in the stylized gestures of a Roman art in decline, the four appear to reach out to one another for support, as if facing a universally hostile world.

As the senior ruler, Diocletian (284–305) divided the empire into four military prefectures. In order to be close to the front, both emperors-in-chief established a forward headquarters: one in Milan and one in Nicomedia in the East, a few miles distant from a city called Byzantium.

Over the years, the external threat of invasions had disrupted trade routes, causing markets to disappear or fall to barbarian conquest. As the Roman economy moved closer to collapse, the Romans sought someone to blame. Once again, the Christians were singled out as a convenient target. A notable example of anti-Christian sentiment is a polemic written in 303, "Against the Christians," by the Greco-Roman philosopher Porphyrius (232–304). This book denounced the "baseness of the Jewish Scriptures" and argued that "though Christ is supposed to have been most pious, the Christians are a confused and vicious sect."

Indeed, Diocletian renewed the persecution of the Christians, an oppression that his caesar, Galerius, applied with alacrity after Diocletian's palace had been destroyed by fire. Churches were either confiscated or razed, including the one abutting the imperial palace in Nicomedia, and all Christian worship was outlawed. Scores of church leaders were arrested, tortured, and put to death. Diocletian, the ablest emperor since Hadrian, who arguably saved the empire from certain ruin, also very nearly succeeded in destroying Christianity.

This Roman coin bears the portrait of the Emperor Diocletian (C.E. 284–305).

BIRTH OF CHRISTIAN ART

Burial became an important ritual for the early Christians, for they believed death was merely a passage to eternal life. In Rome, during the time when Christianity was outlawed, a public, Christian burial was unthinkable. Many followed the example of the poor and began to carve burial niches in the subterranean corridors of the city known as catacombs. Here, Christian families gathered to pray, sometimes to celebrate the Eucharist, and to honor their dead. Today, excavators have uncovered some 40 catacomb networks in Rome. Many contain simple, though moving, paintings that illustrate key phases of worship. In the Via Latina catacomb, discovered in 1955, archaeologists found colorful frescoes, including a scene of Jesus delivering his Sermon on the Mount to a large group of toga-clad followers. The vivid, almost hurried brushwork of these paintings is breathtaking; it tells us as much about first-century Roman portraiture as about the iconography of early Christian art.

After the emancipation of the Christian faith, the wealthy Christian patrons could avail themselves of the best sculptors to create their coffins. These marble sarcophagi became the favorite form of burial for well-to-do people, since Christianity expressly forbade the Roman practice of cremation. One of the earliest examples is the sarcophagus of the Villa Felice in Rome. Carved around C.E. 312, it shows scenes of St. Peter and Christ, including the entry of Jesus into Jerusalem, riding a donkey. Stylistically, the figures betray that the Roman art of sculpture was in decline; the details of folds, beards, and hair had not been sculpted but drilled by a hard metal. Nevertheless, the realistic details of a grazing horse, a child clinging to the folds of his father's tunic, and a man climbing a tree to better witness the entry, all illustrate that, even at this stage, Roman artists had a keen eye for realistic detail.

Created around C.E. 312, this detail from an early Christian sarcophagus, found in Rome, shows Jesus' entry into Jerusalem.

CONSTANTINE'S WORLD

A view of the Bosporus, the narrow strait separating Europe and Asia, with the Hagia Sophia of Constantinople, now called Istanbul, in the background.

IN 305, DECLINING HEALTH prompted Emperor Diocletian to abdicate, forcing his co-ruler, Maximian (286–305), to do the same. The abdications raised the two subordinate caesars—Galerius (305–311) in the East and Constantius I Chlorus (305–306) in the West—to the position of Augustus. These new emperors immediately nominated their own rival caesars, prompting a 20-year period of war between pretenders to the throne. When Constantius, one of the claimants, died suddenly in 306 in York, his troops pronounced Constantine, his son, the new emperor. Not to be outdone, the praetorian guard in Rome elevated Maxentius, son of Maximian, to emperor status as well. Confusion reigned. Eventually Constantine faced the forces of Maxentius in the vicinity of Rome in 312. The two would meet close to a crossing over the Tiber River known as the Milvian Bridge.

The Christian writer Lactantius (ca 240–320) wrote that, the night before the important battle, Constantine had a dream in which he was told to paint "the heavenly sign of God" on the shields of his soldiers. This heavenly sign, the labarum, was the monogram of Christ consisting of the Greek letters *chi* and *rho,* the first two letters of the

ca C.E. 306
Constantine I proclaimed emperor after the death of his father Constantius I Chlorus

ca C.E. 312
The night before Constantine I defeats his rival Maxentius, he has a vision of the Greek letters *chi rho*

ca C.E. 313
Constantine's Edict of Milan guarantees Christians the freedom to worship

ca C.E. 325
Council of Nicea endorses the concept of the Holy Trinity

That we might grant to the Christians and others full authority to observe that religion which each preferred; whence any Divinity whatsoever in the seat of the heavens may be propitious and kindly disposed to us and all who are placed under our rule. Emperor Constantine, Edict of Milan

Greek word *Christos.* A later book by Eusebius, written after Constantine's death in 337, describes Constantine's vision of a luminescent cross in the sky just above the sun, blazing with the Greek words *en toutoi nika* (by this [sign] conquer). Whatever the case may be, the fact is that Constantine rode into battle, defeated the army of Maxentius, and attributed his victory to the God of the Christians. The following year, in 313, the emperor issued the Edict of Milan, which reaffirmed the Decree of Toleration issued earlier by Gallienus and granted Christians unlimited freedom to worship. Constantine went even further by promising a full restitution of all Christian holdings seized by the state. Christian citizens who had been exiled were invited back.

In 324, Constantine secured his power by defeating his last remaining rival, Licinius, at Chrysopolis in Asia Minor, and Christianity in the Roman Empire was secure at last. It would remain this way—save for a brief reversal under Julian "the Apostate" (361–363)—until the coming of Islam.

Basilica of St. Peter

CONSTANTINE then built a vast Christian sanctuary over the reputed site of the tomb of Peter in Rome. This place was traditionally identified with a rural area called the Ager Vaticanus, today's Vatican City. The question that Constantine's architects confronted, however, was what should a Roman temple dedicated to the Christ look like. Up to this point, Christian shrines had been built on an ad hoc basis, often in secret, and far too small to accommodate the vast increase in the number of converts. The archetype of the pagan temple—a deep portico leading to an inner sanctum, or cella, where the cult statue was placed—was not suitable for mass assemblies during services like the celebration of the Eucharist.

Instead, the architects building the church of St. Peter chose the Roman archetype of a basilica, which already had been adopted in the construction of many synagogues throughout the Roman Empire. The Roman basilica was not a religious building but a large, rectangular hall designed for civic functions, such as court sessions. Because of its secular character, it had no religious overtones. The basilica typically featured a large semicircular apse at either end of the hall for the obligatory statues of the reigning emperor or deities; in the Christian version, only one apse was retained, in order to accommodate an altar.

The massive head is a portrait of Constantine I (306–337) from a colossal statue of the emperor now at the Capitoline Museum in Rome.

The construction of St. Peter's basilica took 25 years, and it would stand for more than a thousand years. It was in this church that Charlemagne was crowned emperor of the Holy Roman Empire in 800. By the dawn of the Renaissance, however, the basilica was beginning to show its age. It was finally torn down in 1506 to make room for the current Basilica of St. Peter's, which took 120 years to build.

Church Confronts Dissident Creeds

IN SPITE OF ITS newfound freedom, Christianity continued to be wracked by debates over the nature of Jesus' divinity. The heresy of Arius, an early fourth-century theologian, claimed that Christ was "begotten by the Father" and

ca C.E. 330
Emperor Constantine I moves capital to Byzantium

ca C.E. 337–331
Emperor Constantius II forbids Jewish men to marry Christian women, and bans the building of new synagogues

ca C.E. 361–363
Traditional Greco-Roman religion experiences a brief resurgence during the reign of Julian

ca C.E. 392
Emperor Theodosius effectively criminalizes the practice of Greco-Roman religion

therefore not of the same divine substance as the Father. Arianism rapidly grew in popularity despite strenuous efforts by Catholic bishops to contain it. Finally, Constantine realized that an intervention was necessary.

In 325, the emperor summoned nearly 300 bishops to a synod in Nicea, located near today's city of Iznik in Turkey, and presided over the meeting himself. Constantine tried to bring the bishops to agreement on language about Christ's divinity that would please everybody. The issue came down to whether Christ's relationship to God the Father was subordinate or consubstantial ("of the same substance"). When a final vote was called, the consubstantiality clause as articulated by Athanasius, the chief advocate on behalf of the bishop of Alexandria, triumphed. It remains so to this day as the Nicene Creed: "We believe in one God the Father ... and in Jesus Christ, the Son of God, one in being with the Father." The synod also discussed the inclusion of another divine substance, the Holy Ghost; however, this concept of the Holy Trinity was only endorsed and accepted by the Council of Constantinople some 55 years later.

Two bishops, including Arius, refused to accept this formula. They were removed from the assembly and exiled by the emperor. Eusebius of Caesarea, who had sympathized with Arianist theology, left under a cloud, boosting the prestige of Makarios, the bishop of Jerusalem (312–335). A decree went out that anyone caught with a book by Arius would be summarily put to death. It mattered little; the ancient dichotomy between faith and reason continued to rile the Church until well into the Middle Ages. Some might argue that it has never been settled to everyone's satisfaction.

Meanwhile, Constantine had moved the new capital of the Roman Empire to Byzantium, now renamed Constantinople ("the city of Constantine"). The choice of this location, poised at the bridge between East and West, was driven by the realization that Rome's destiny lay closer to Asia. While the western empire was besieged by barbaric hordes, and countless farms and villages on the Italian mainland lay abandoned, the population centers of Asia Minor were enjoying robust growth. The Roman Empire itself was now known under the name of its new capital city—Byzantium.

Romans, however, continued to worship their traditional gods. Constantine himself maintained his patronage of non-Christian deities and was not baptized as a Christian until close to his death. This custom changed with the advent of Emperor Theodosius I (379–395), who moved with a vengeance to reassert Christianity after the short reign of Julian the Apostate (361–370). In 380, he issued an imperial decree proclaiming "that all peoples who fall beneath the

ST. PETER'S BONES

TRADITION HOLDS THAT THE ORIGINAL Basilica of St. Peter, built by Constantine in C.E. 324, contained a stairway that descended to a crypt where pilgrims could touch the tomb of St. Peter. In 1942, while World War II raged, Pope Pius XII ordered archaeologists to excavate the area underneath the altar in the current St. Peter's. The excavation was conducted in great secrecy, in case, for some reason, the tomb of St. Peter could not be located. After several years of persistent work, the excavators discovered the remains of a white marble shrine, placed against a red stucco wall. This modest shrine appeared to correspond to a description of Peter's tomb in a second-century letter by a presbyter named Gaius. Over it stood a large marble encasement, which archaeologists dated to the time of Constantine the Great. The grave under the aedicule itself was empty; however, within one of the stucco walls of the shrine, archaeologists discovered the remains of a man approximately 60 years of age. In 1950, Pope Pius XII made a radio broadcast announcing that these could very well be the bones of St. Peter, although the pope admitted that "it is impossible to prove with certainty that they belong to the Apostle." Indeed, recent scholarship has contested the claim that these could be St. Peter's remains.

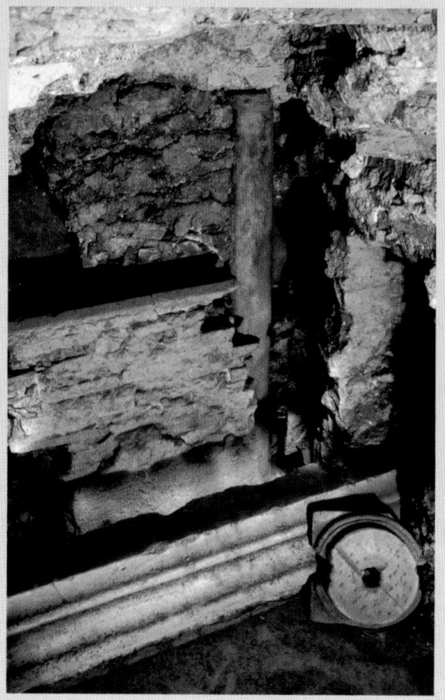

This fragment of a shrine beneath St. Peter's Basilica, excavated in the 1940s, is believed to be a second-century shrine to the Apostle Peter.

sway of our imperial clemency should profess the faith which we believe has been communicated by the Apostle Peter to the Romans." Christianity—based on the Nicene Creed—now became the official religion of the Roman Empire.

Prodded by a militant bishop named Ambrose, Theodosius deposed bishops who were known to be sympathetic to the Arian movement and ordered all Arian churches to be handed over to Catholic priests. He then moved to eradicate the "heresy" of the old Roman religion over the loud protests of the Roman aristocracy. First, blood sacrifice to pagan gods was prohibited. Then, in 392, another decree effectively criminalized all forms of pagan worship. Encouraged by Ambrose, monks throughout the realm enthusiastically broke into the shuttered temples, destroyed countless statues, and made off with votives of silver and gold. Theophilus, the patriarch of Alexandria, personally supervised the looting and destruction of shrines to the Mithras cult and then turned his wrath on the famed Library of Alexandria. In the opinion of many scholars, the culture of classical Rome now effectively had come to an end.

Judaism and Byzantium

CONSTANTINE'S Edict of Milan in 313 also had a profound impact on the relationship between Jews and the Roman Empire. At first, Diaspora Jews were left in peace, and synagogues were not target for destruction. This policy changed when a band of Christians in Callinicum, a city on the Euphrates, felt emboldened to vandalize a Jewish synagogue. Afterward, Theodosius ordered the local bishop to finance the rebuilding of the synagogue. Bishop Ambrose, however, demanded that Theodosius rescind the order, and the emperor complied.

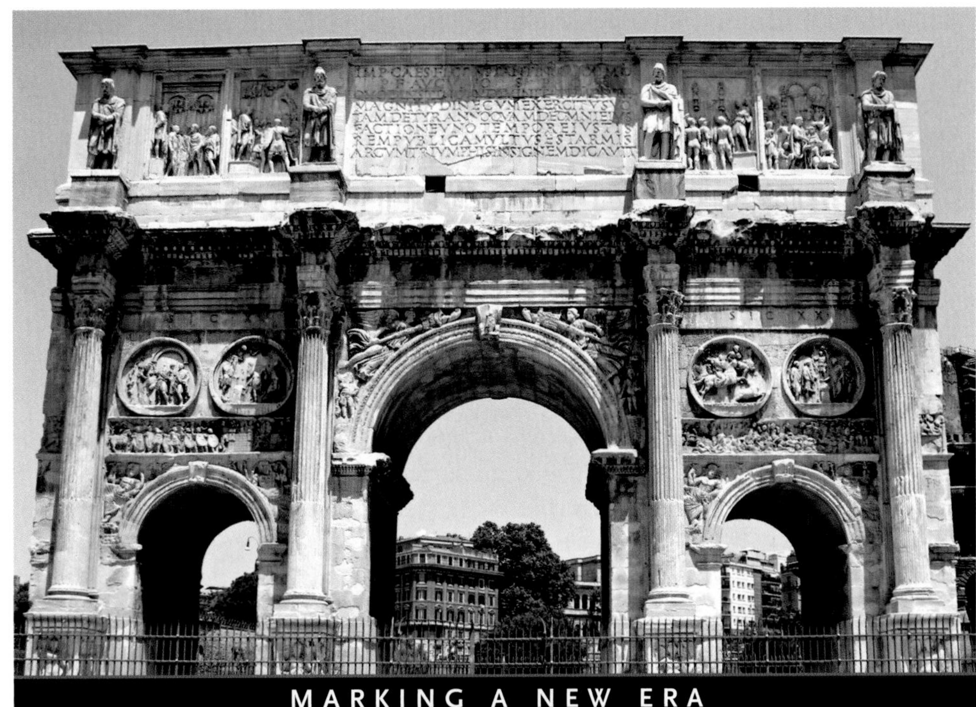

MARKING A NEW ERA

AS IF CONSCIOUS OF THE MOMENTOUS events taking place at the beginning of Constantine's reign, the Roman Senate voted him a triumphal arch. It was built between 313 and 315 in such a hurry that its architects felt compelled to rip sculptural ornamentation from three older monuments to place it on Constantine's arch. Lest anyone detect the fraud, the features of the emperors on these reliefs—notably of Trajan, Hadrian, and Aurelius—were modified to resemble those of Constantine.

The Arch of Constantine is the first official Roman artwork of the Christian era. It is therefore also one of the best preserved of all Roman monuments. The arch still stands in the shadow of the Colosseum at the end of an ancient roadway, now the Via di San Gregorio.

The exquisite proportions of the Arch of Constantine, with a large central fornix for the main traffic and two smaller fornices for pedestrians, was much admired in the Renaissance and imitated many times. On the main facade of the monument, perched over the lateral arches, are superbly chiseled roundels taken from a monument to Hadrian, dedicated to hunting and sacrifice. By contrast, the sides of the arch are decorated with panels from Trajan's times that depict battle scenes with bold, full-length figures carved with complete mastery and confidence—Roman art at its apogee.

Only the narrow frieze beneath Hadrian's roundels is the work of Constantine's sculptors. The stylistic difference is striking. The frieze depicts Emperor Constantine speaking to the people from a rostrum on the Forum. The figures are grotesquely carved, with oversize heads and barely detailed garments. The gestures are stiff and awkward. The Greco-Roman virtuosity of carving three-dimensional figures in the round was by now in full decline and would not be revived until the dawn of the Florentine Renaissance.

Triumphal Arch of Constantine, Rome. It was built between C.E. 313 and 315 to commemorate Constantine's victory over Maxentius at the Battle of Milvian Bridge in 312.

The greatest impact, however, was felt by Jews in Palestine. Suddenly, this Roman territory gained tremendous significance as the Christian Holy Land. The bishop of Jerusalem, Makarios, initiated the excavation of the presumed location of Golgotha and Christ's tomb, a spot that at the time was covered by a Temple of Aphrodite built by Hadrian. Constantine's mother, Queen Helena, also embarked on a campaign to mark the places associated with Jesus with churches and chapels. Thousands of pilgrims, monks, and prelates followed in her wake. This sudden return of Christianity took the Palestinian Jews by surprise. Rabbis watched with apprehension while Jerusalem was reborn, albeit in a thoroughly Christian mold.

Some 25 years after Constantine, Emperor Constantius II (337–361) modified Roman policy on Judaism by proscribing marriage between Jewish men and Christian women, and denying Jews the right to own slaves. Since many Jews were actively involved in the slave trade, this decree had severe economic repercussions. Theodosius II, who made Christianity the only authorized religion in the empire, then decreed that "no Jew ... shall obtain offices and dignities; to none shall the administration of city service be permitted," further marginalizing Jews in Byzantine society. He also reaffirmed a law that banned the building of new synagogues.

The power of the rabbinic court, the Sanhedrin in Tiberias, was thoroughly curtailed, just as the Christian bishop in Jerusalem was elevated to the status of patriarch, placing Jerusalem on a par with the bishoprics of Antioch and Alexandria. Subsequent Roman emperors specifically taxed Jewish communities, including the Samaritans, and plunged many households into poverty. So odious was this tax that in 352, Jews as well as Samaritans rose in revolt. Constantius II sent his son, Caesar Gallus (351–354), to suppress it. The rebellion originated in the city of Sepphoris, which, in the second century C.E., had been the seat of the Sanhedrin and the principal spiritual center of rabbinic Judaism. Up to the fourth century, Sepphoris (which had been renamed Diocaesarea) had prospered as a model of coexistence, with Romans and Jews living in relative harmony even after the Sanhedrin had

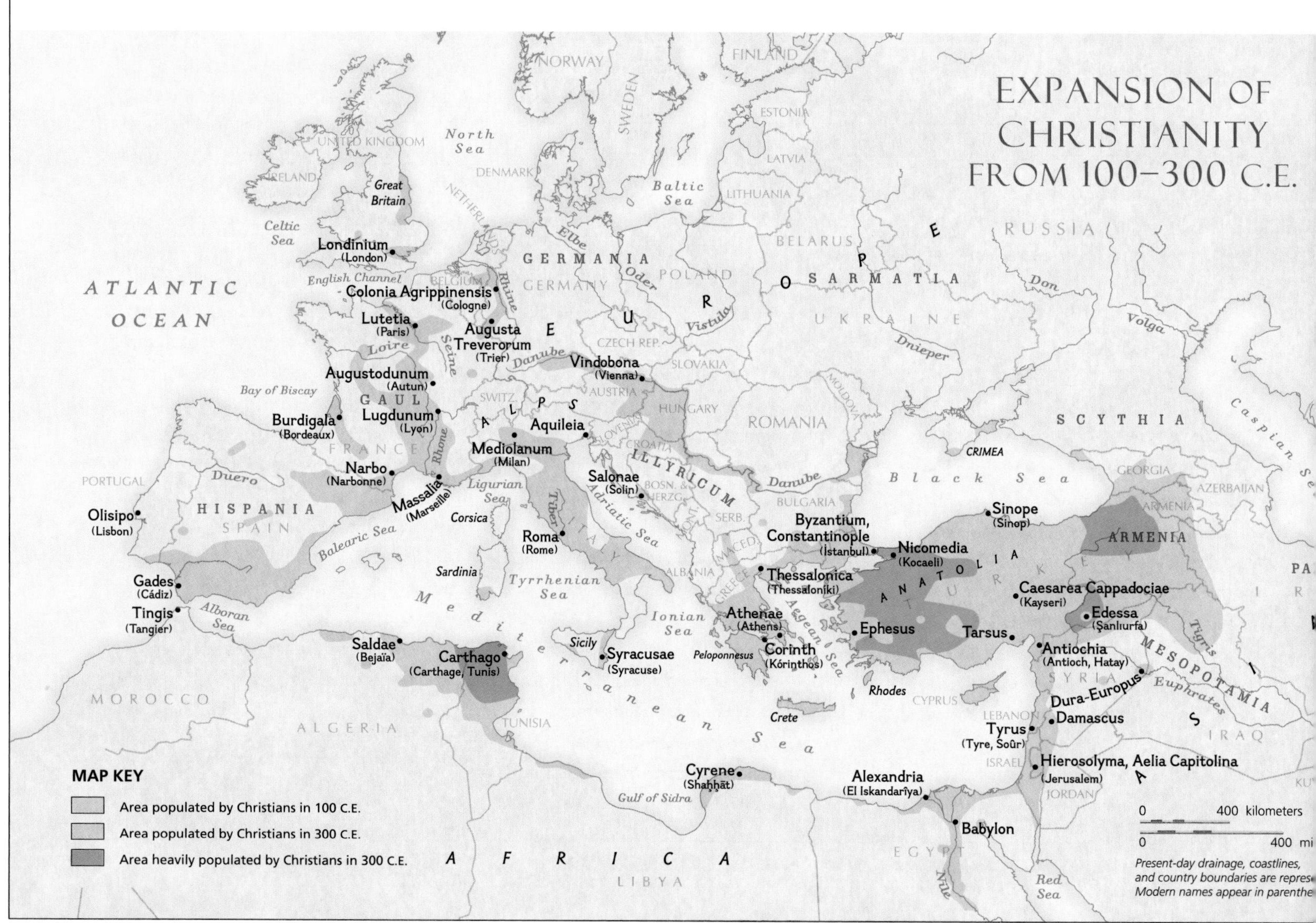

BUILDING THE CHRISTIAN HOLY LAND

CONSTANTINE'S BUILDING FERVOR WAS NOT limited to Rome. He gave permission to Bishop Makarios of Jerusalem to raze the Temple of Aphrodite, which Emperor Hadrian had built on a site traditionally associated with Jesus' tomb. According to Makarios, the excavation not only exposed the presumed location of the grave, but also the hill of Golgotha. Constantine ordered the construction of the first Church of the Holy Sepulchre, including the Anastasis (Resurrection) Rotunda over the presumed tomb site.

Constantine's mother, Queen Helena, endeavored to build new churches in Palestine as well. A legend claims that while visiting the work pits of the new Anastasis church in Jerusalem, Helena discovered the "true cross" used in Jesus' Crucifixion.

She also directed her attention to Bethlehem, where she ordered the destruction of another of Hadrian's temples. In its place, construction began on a new church, which was finished by the time the Christian theologian Jerome (ca 347–420) came to Bethlehem to begin the Vulgate, his translation of the Bible into Latin.

The Bethlehem church was destroyed during the Samaritan revolt of 529, after which Emperor Justinian rebuilt it on the plan of the previous church. It still stands, although portions of the upper nave have been damaged by gunfire sustained in an incident in April 2002.

The Church of the Holy Sepulchre was originally built during the reign of Emperor Constantine. After being destroyed in 529, the church was rebuilt in its current form in the 12th century.

Among the four Gospels, which are the only indisputable ones in the Church of God under heaven, I have learned by tradition that the first was written by Matthew, who was once a publican, but afterwards an apostle of Jesus Christ. Eusebius, Church History

moved to Tiberias. Gallus, however, suppressed the revolt with overwhelming force, "murdering many thousands of men, even those too young to pose a threat." Sepphoris was ruthlessly burned to the ground.

In the years that followed, many Jews moved away from the influence of the Roman-Byzantine Empire. One destination of choice was the Talmudic centers of Babylon. Other Jews traveled along the coast of the Red Sea and settled in Ethiopia, or even as far as Yemen. In time, the links between these far-flung Jewish settlements coalesced into a trade network of their own, so that by the beginning of the sixth century, a good share of Mediterranean maritime commerce was in Jewish hands.

Nevertheless, many Jewish communities in Palestine continued to prosper during the Byzantine era, as is evident from the beautiful mosaics found in the synagogue of Bet Alfa, in the shadow of Mount Gilboa, east of the Valley of Jezreel. The floor mosaic, which among other things depicts the wheel of the zodiac and the sacrifice of Isaac, is dated to the reign of Justinian I, when Byzantium stood at the peak of its power—and would soon face the most significant challenge yet to both Judaism and Christianity.

Creation of the Bible

THROUGHOUT the period of Christianity's stupendous growth, unattested Christian scripture—including gospels, acts, and apocalypse writings attributed to prominent members of Jesus' inner circle (though written much later)—

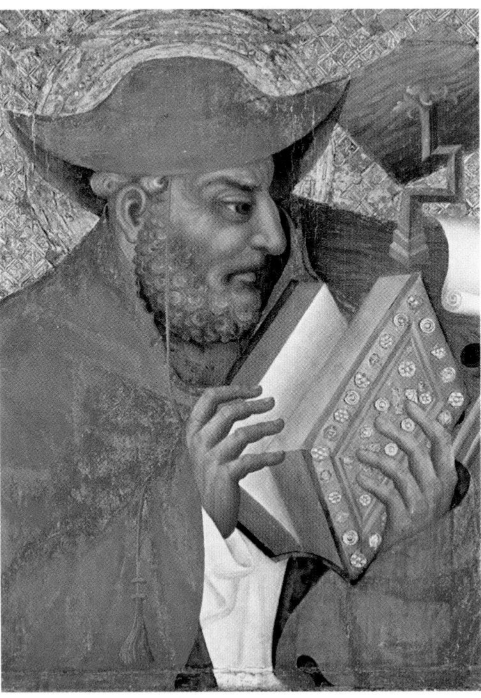

Depicted here in a 14th-century panel from Prague, Saint Jerome is credited with creating the first Latin translation of the Christian Bible, called the Vulgate.

continued to proliferate in the Roman Empire. This wealth of material made it difficult for Church leaders to identify which sources should be considered authoritative in guiding the growing Christian population. An official canon of Christian writings, similar to the canon of the Hebrew Scriptures, was urgently needed. Around C.E. 180, Bishop Irenaeus of Lyons (140–ca 203) argued that only the Gospels of Mark, Matthew, Luke, and John should be considered authoritative, calling them the "four pillars" of the Christian Church. Irenaeus also included the Epistles (Greek for "letters") of Paul in his collection of scripture, believing that the letters were equally inspired by the divine spirit. The theologian Tertullian agreed with Irenaeus's suggestion and coined the phrase "New Testament." He claimed that since Jesus was the living proof of God's New Covenant with mankind, Christian Scripture had in effect replaced or "fulfilled" the "Old" Testament enshrined in the Hebrew Bible.

Almost a century later, Bishop Eusebius of Caesarea created the first formally authorized canon of the New Testament. It was comprised of the four canonical Gospels, the Acts of the Apostles, the Epistles of Paul, the Epistles of Peter, and the Apocalypse of John (known today as Revelation). He explicitly rejected Gnostic documents, such as the Gospel of Thomas and the Gospel of Peter (now known from the cache discovered at Nag 'Hammadi), as the works of "heretics." Other writings, including the Acts of Paul, the Apocalypse of Peter, the Epistle of Barnabas, and the Didache (or the "Teachings of the Apostles"), were branded as "disputed" books of questionable authority. Debate over the New Testament's final composition continued well into the Middle Ages, with much of the attention focused on the authority of the Letter of James and the Book of Revelation, until the Council of Trent (1545–1563) by and large affirmed Eusebius's compilation. Nevertheless, it is safe to say that by the end of the fourth century C.E., both Christianity and Judaism had arrived at the final canon of their Scripture, including an updated version of the Septuagint that was adopted as the Christian Old Testament, thus presenting the world with the Bible as we know it today.

JUDEA	ROME	EGYPT
ca C.E. 10 possible birthdate of Saul/Paul  ca C.E. 37 Jewish historian Josephus born ca C.E. 50 Paul begins travels throughout the eastern Roman Empire in efforts to convert non-Jews to Christianity ca C.E. 66–70 "Mark" writes his gospel, the oldest of the four canonical Gospels in the New Testament ca C.E. 70 Sent by Emperor Vespasian to stop the First Jewish Revolt in Palestine, Titus destroys the temple in Jerusalem  ca C.E. 132–135 Second Jewish rebellion, known as the Bar Kochba Revolt, is repressed by the Romans during the reign of Hadrian ca C.E. 135 Emperor Hadrian decides to raze Jerusalem and erect a new city, Aelia Capitolina, in its place	ca C.E. 64 Nero blames the Christians for a fire that ravaged the city of Rome  ca C.E. 64 Traditional date of the death of Peter and Paul in Rome ca C.E. 79 Pompeii and Herculaneum destroyed after the eruption of Vesuvius ca C.E. 117–138 Hadrian reigns as emperor of Rome ca C.E. 185 In Lyon, France, Bishop Iraneus leads early "canonization" of New Testament ca C.E. 193–211 Emperor Septimius Severus allows Roman officials to persecute Christians  ca C.E. 330 Emperor Constantine I moves capital to Byzantium 	ca C.E. 30 Jewish writer Philo active in Egypt ca C.E. 38 Jewish pogroms in Alexandria ca C.E. 62 Heron of Alexandria, a mathematician and inventor, describes a steam engine, water clock, water fountain, and odometer ca C.E. 146–170 Ptolemy, a scholar in Alexandria, writes about geography and astronomy, describing the "known world" as stretching from Iceland to Sri Lanka ca C.E. 155–117 Diaspora Jews in Egypt revolt against Rome  ca C.E. 200 Coptic Gospel of Judas is composed ca C.E. 286 Anthony of Egypt, a Christian monk, begins 20-year period of solitude in the desert; he is believed to be the founder of monasticism  ca C.E. 296–297 An Egyptian rebellion breaks out against Roman rule. Emperor Diocletian travels to Alexandria and takes the city to quash the revolt

EPILOGUE

Three Faiths in the Holy Land

As the foundations of Christianity began to consolidate, the Roman Empire itself began to crumble. Enemies threatened the empire on every geographic front, from Persian phalanxes on the Tigris River to Visigoths descending from the Danube. Recognizing that no ruler could defend all borders at once, Emperor Valentinian (364–375) split the empire into two realms, one in the West, centered on Rome, and the other in the East, centered on Byzantium. A separate emperor was to govern each realm, but the split ultimately failed to stem the barbarian tides in the West. By 476, Rome had fallen to the Visigoths, and the Western empire was no more. In the East, the Byzantine emperors warred with Persia while trying to recapture parts of the former empire in the West, though with little success.

As these battles raged, a new monotheistic faith, Islam, arose within the Arabian Peninsula. Islam would unite the manifold peoples of Arabia into a powerful military and political force, and come to control, for much of the next twelve centuries, the lands and sites sacred to all three faiths. Nevertheless, the Holy Land would continue to fascinate and attract legions of the faithful, all drawn to its storied locations for centuries to come.

Built by the Umayyad caliph Abd el-Malik (685–705), Jerusalem's Dome of the Rock is one of Islam's greatest artistic achievements.

The World After Rome

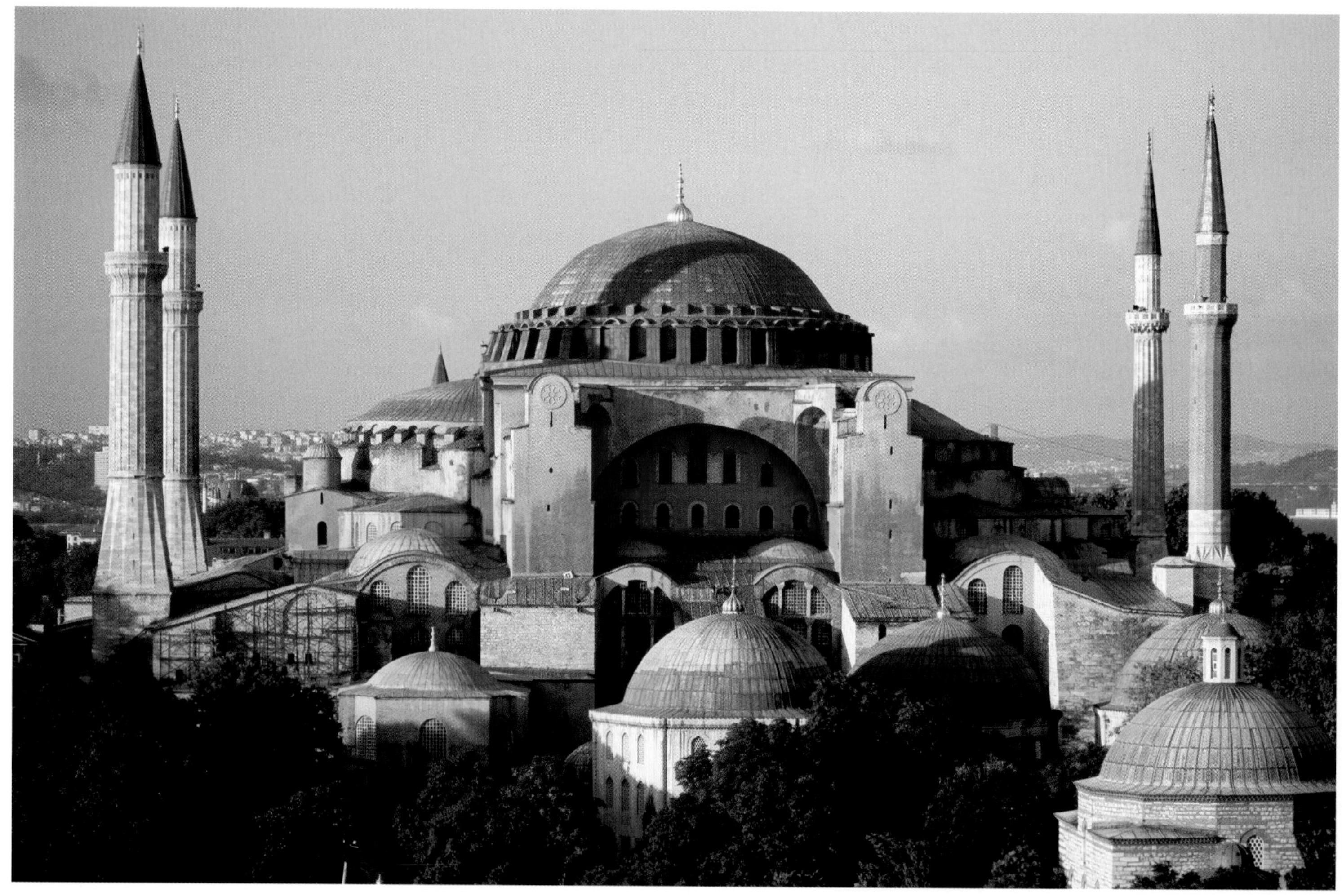

Commissioned by Emperor Justinian I in the sixth century, the Hagia Sofia in Istanbul was first a church and later converted to a mosque. Today it is a museum.

CONSTANTINE CHOSE WELL when he sited the heart of the Christian Roman Empire on the Bosporus. Surrounded on three sides by the sea, Byzantium not only controlled the land route from Asia Minor to Europe, but also the sea route from the Mediterranean into the Black Sea. The Western empire had ceased to exist when Rome fell in 476, but the Eastern empire would last for another thousand years.

By the sixth century, the economy of Asia Minor was on a rebound. Caravans were once again dispatched to the East, in search of silk and spices for the wealthy patrician clients of Constantinople. The recovery of the spice trade inevitably led to an escalation of tensions between Byzantium and Persia over control of the main trade routes to the East.

The emperor at the time, Justinian I (527–565), was using the empire's funds to regain the glory of Rome, both artistically and militarily, a move that would threaten the financial stability of the empire in years to come. In 532, after a Christian church in Constantinople, the Hagia Sophia, had been destroyed, Justinian charged his finest architects to erect a new one that would surpass anything built by Rome. Although conceived as a basilica, the nave of this new church was given the shape of an ellipse, anchored by four semicircular chapels and surmounted by a vast dome. When Justinian entered the church for the first time, he reportedly cried out: "O Solomon, I have surpassed you!"

In matters of state, Justinian tried to recapture the lands of the Western empire. Though initially successful, this campaign devolved into a war of attrition that not only strained the Byzantine treasury, but also provoked Khosrow I, the king of Persia, to attack Byzantium from the East, capturing Antioch in Pisidia in the process. Byzantium suffered another terrible setback in an outbreak of bubonic plague that killed, by some estimates, 40 percent of the population. Then in 557, an enormous earthquake struck Constantinople; the great dome of the Hagia Sophia collapsed and had to be rebuilt completely. When Justinian died in 565, he left his successors, Justin II (565–578) and Tiberius II (574–582), with empty coffers.

Persia Takes the Holy Land

MILITARY CONFLICTS CONTINUED AS Tiberius II attacked the Persian-occupied lands bordering the former Byzantine territory of Armenia. This attempt to restore Byzantium's wealth and prestige led to a prolonged period of warfare between the two powers, until a new Persian king, Khosrow II, faced a rebellion within his own realm. Uncertain of the quality and loyalty of his troops, Khosrow II, in an unexpected move, turned to Byzantium, his former enemy, for help. Emperor Maurice (582–602) sent troops to support the king, and received Persia's agreement to cede Armenia to Constantinople. This peace did not last long, however. In 602, Maurice was overthrown by a commander named Phocas, an act that prompted the Persian king to launch a "war of revenge" against the Byzantine usurper. Persian forces captured Armenia, Syria, and the Caucasus kingdom of Lazica. In 614, Persian General Shahrbaraz entered Palestine, looting and burning his way toward Jerusalem.

During the previous 300 years of Christian control, the Holy City had changed considerably. Roman temples and shrines had been demolished, their columns and capitals recycled for use in the construction of Christian churches. The city center had shifted from the Temple Mount, where the Second Temple had once stood, to the Church of the Holy Sepulchre (then called the Martyrium), the presumed site of Golgotha. Even Jerusalem's city walls had shifted. Streets once filled with Jewish worshippers were now crammed with monks, prelates, and pilgrims from all parts of the Byzantine Empire.

When the Persian troops arrived at Jerusalem's gates to besiege the city, they first destroyed every Christian structure on the surrounding hills, including the possible location of the Garden of Gethsemane. The city walls finally gave way on the 21st day of the siege. An eyewitness, the monk Antiochus Strategos, reported, "the evil foemen entered the city in great fury, like infuriated wild beasts and irritated serpents." More than 65,000 Christians were killed, and survivors were rounded up and dispatched into exile. Churches were burned to the ground, including the Church of the Holy Sepulchre. The "True Cross" identified by Queen Helena was carried back to Persia in triumph. General Shahrbaraz then handed control of Jerusalem back to the Jewish patriarchate. In 616, however, the Persians reneged on their promise of Jewish autonomy, and Palestine was incorporated into the local Persian satrapy.

Persia's rule would be short-lived, however. Heraclius, another Byzantine commander, overthrew Phocas and seized power as the new emperor (610–641), vowing to reclaim Christian territories. In 622, Heraclius and his forces plowed through Asia Minor to restore it to Byzantine sovereignty. They then moved into Mesopotamia and dealt Khosrow II a stinging defeat at the Battle of Nineveh in 627. The triumph was complete when in 630 Heraclius solemnly returned the True Cross to Jerusalem. It appeared as if Heraclius had restored the vast reach of the Roman Empire. But appearances were deceiving, for soon another and far more powerful army would appear on the borders of the Byzantine Holy Land.

A New Faith Rises

WHILE PERSIA AND BYZANTIUM fought over territory and trade routes, a new religion had taken hold in the lands of Arabia. Annexed by Rome in the second century C.E., the province of Arabia Petraea stretched from Damascus in the north to Sinai in the south and to the mountain chain of Harrat al 'Uwayrid in the east, a territory roughly equivalent to today's Sinai, Jordan, and the northernmost corner of Saudi Arabia, including a slice of Syria and Lebanon. Governed from Petra and later Bostra, Arabia was at the edge of civilization, as the Romans knew it; beyond this frontier the Arabian Peninsula fell away to the southern desert, controlled by a number of smaller fiefdoms and tribes. Here was the Hejaz, a region of small cities such as Al Madinah (Medina), then called Yathrib,

The ivory Mughira Pyxis was carved in Cordoba, in Muslim-held Andalusia, in 968 and dedicated to Al-Mughira, son of 'Abd al-Rahman III (912–961).

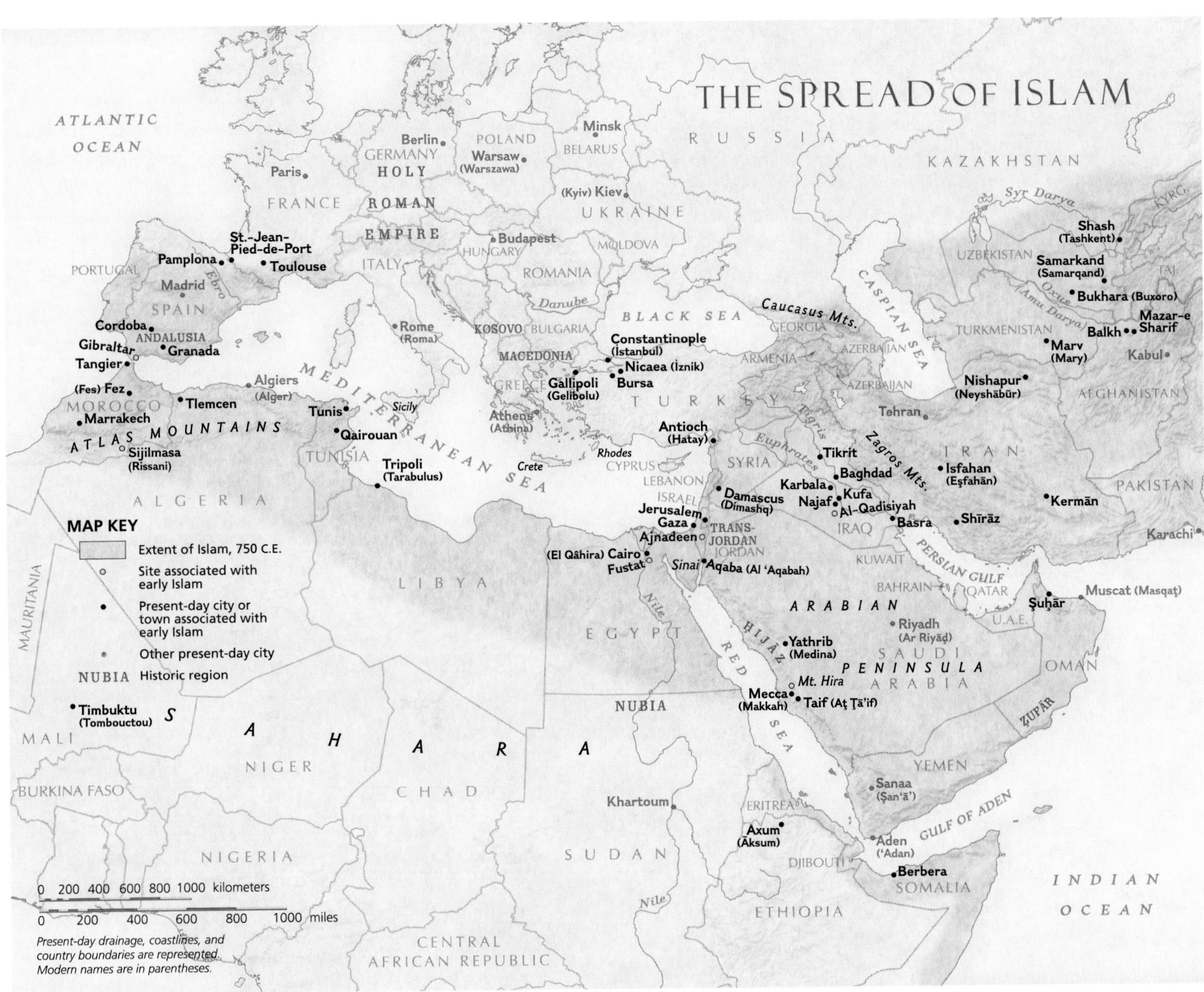

and Mecca, perched along tributaries to the principal caravan routes of the spice trade, all of which eventually connected to the Roman road network. The Arabian peoples lived either in settlements around oases or caravan posts, or were wedded to a nomadic, Bedouin lifestyle focused on the herding of sheep, camels, and goats. Animosity between settlers and nomads ran deep, borne by a history of violent strife, which would continue well into the Islamic era.

OPPOSITE: **The interior walls of the Dome of the Rock majestically rise over the sacred Rock of Abraham at its center.**

Islam holds that in 610, shortly before the Persian conquest of the Holy Land, a man named Muhammad from the city of Mecca began to receive divine revelations. As Muhammad's biographer describes it, the word of God came to him in dreams through the angel Gabriel. Muhammad would continue to experience these revelations for the next 25 years, first in Mecca and later in Al Madinah. In the process, he began to understand that these revelations were the makings of a book of Holy Scripture, which would become the Koran (Qur'an). Muhammad told others of his visions, reciting them as they had been told to him. Soon, a community of believers began to grow up around his teachings; one that in time would represent a new religion for the Arab world, the faith of Islam, which recognizes Muhammad as its Prophet.

Muhammad's teachings were not embraced by the citizens of Mecca, where traditional religion had always centered around a pantheon of local deities, presided over by a supreme god named Allah. Mecca itself was already a pilgrimage destination; in its center stood an ancient cubelike structure, known as the Kaaba, dedicated to the worship of Allah and other, local gods. Threats against Muhammad and his followers grew, and they left the city in 622 for Yathrib. Muhammad's sojourn in this city, now renamed Madina-al-Nabi (the "City of the Prophet," or "Al Madinah"), would transform him into a statesman of considerable renown and ability.

In Al Madinah, Islam grew and attracted large numbers of converts, all the while taking on a more distinctly Arab character. During daily prayer, Muslims had once faced Jerusalem; now the faithful turned in the direction of Mecca, home to the Kaaba, the historical shrine of Allah, which had been revealed to Muhammad as having been built by Abraham and Ishmael. The Prophet conquered Mecca in 630 and rededicated the Kaaba to the worship of Allah as the one and only God.

The Spread of Islam

After Muhammad's death in 632, the influence of Islam would continue to expand. His successor Abu Bakr (632–634), the first caliph, suppressed tribal revolts throughout the Hejaz and southern Arabia and pushed eastward to unify all of the Arabian Peninsula under the banner of Islam. The next caliph, 'Umar (634–644), took the movement beyond the borders of the peninsula and brought the Islamic conquest into Byzantine and Persian realms. Long years of conflict had exhausted both empires. Khosrow II had died in 628, succeeded by a string of weak and inept rulers. Byzantium's financial and military resources were strained, leaving Palestine and Syria vulnerable to attack. 'Umar's forces first plunged into these territories in 634. When the Byzantine and Muslim armies clashed at last in the Battle of Yarmuk in 636, Muslim forces emerged victorious. Some sources maintain that Emperor Heraclius was able to retrieve the True Cross from Jerusalem before the Muslim armies reached the city. Afterward, the Cross—or rather, pieces of it—entered the realm of legend, with many churches in East and West claiming to possess fragments.

Muslim forces took over Jerusalem in 638. But unlike in earlier sieges, the city's residents, including Christian and Jewish citizens, were not persecuted. A special treaty, know as the "Pact of 'Umar" granted Christians "safety for their persons, their goods, churches, crosses—be they in good or bad condition—and their worship in general." The Jews were accorded religious freedom as well. It soon became Islamic policy throughout the empire to treat the "People of the Book" with a circumspection befitting their status as co-believers in God's revelation, even though their beliefs differed from Islamic interpretation. Scholars believe that this policy of tolerance was as much a matter of politics as religion. Military success had the effect of overwhelming the Arab armies. Stretched all over the Middle East, 'Umar and his successors had no choice but to govern by proxy, relying on local systems of government already in place.

The Dome of the Rock

According to a Muslim historian, upon entering Jerusalem 'Umar toured the city and visited the Temple Mount. In Islamic tradition, it was from there that Muhammad, in a dream, had briefly ascended into heaven. Under Christian rule, the site had fallen into disrepair, literally becoming the city's garbage dump. In the Muslim account, 'Umar was stunned when he saw the pitiful state of this holy ground. He unfastened his

This Islamic ivory panel is intricately carved with detailed scenes of the hunt and wild animals. It was created in Egypt in the 11th or 12th century C.E.

THE KORAN

THE WORD "KORAN" (QUR'AN), derived from the Arab verb *qara'a*, literally means that which is "recited" and "rehearsed." Muhammad had to memorize and repeat every revelation, so that each could be shared with his followers and then ultimately written down. The oral tradition of the Koran endured, as many of Muhammad's later followers could recite the entire book by heart, as do many scholars and imams today.

There are a total of 114 chapters, all of varying length, form, and substance. Each contain prophesies, admonitions, or instructions. Modern scholars distinguish between the revelations given to Muhammad in Mecca and those given in Medina: The earlier Mecca verses are short and straightforward, while the Medina segments are much longer and legislative in tone. Unlike the chronological arrangement of the Hebrew Bible, or the biographical arc of the Christian Gospels, the Koran's revelations are organized by length, starting with the longest and ending with the shortest.

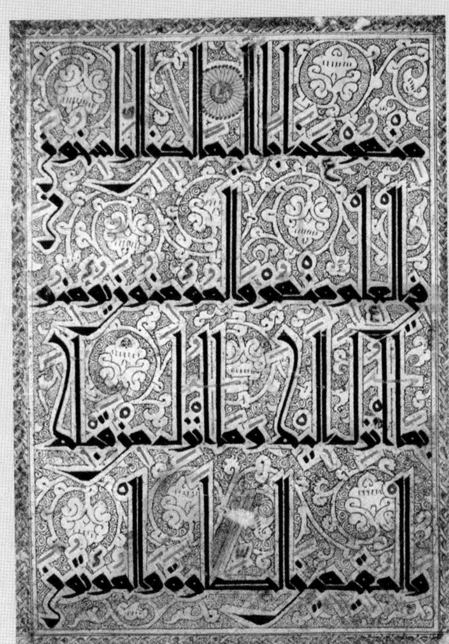

Calligraphy became one of the most revered forms of Islamic art. This illuminated leaf from the Koran dates to the early 11th century C.E.

The Koran holds that God made his will known throughout history, beginning with Adam and ending with Muhammad, who is considered the "Seal of the Prophets" (Koran 33:41). The Koran does accept the Hebrew Bible and New Testament as authentic revelations, calling Jews and Christians the "People of the Book" (Koran 4:54). Both Moses and Jesus are treated as prophets—together, they are the most important individuals after Muhammad. But the Koran also argues that Jews and Christians have misinterpreted these revelations. Islam sees itself as a return to the simple faith of Abraham (Koran 3:66).

cloak and filled it with debris, urging those who were with him to do likewise. They worked to remove the trash until the whole area was cleansed. 'Umar then ordered that a wooden mosque be built on the sacred spot.

This original mosque has not survived, but 'Umar's rededication of the Temple Mount led to what is perhaps the greatest achievement of early Islamic art, the seventh-century Dome of the Rock. Built by the Umayyad caliph Abd el-Malik (685–705), the Dome of the Rock weaves three central elements into one unit: a ring of piers supporting the dome, which itself embraces an ambulatory in the form of an octagon, which in turn is surrounded by a larger exterior octagon. Each of these elements has a symbolic significance: the outer ring represents the world, the ambulatory is the intermediate sphere between earth and the divine, and the inner space evokes the spiritual perfection of heaven itself.

The Dome of the Rock marks a spot revered by Jews, Christians, and Muslims to this day. Inside its muted interior, surrounded by 56 stained-glass windows, is a bare outcropping known as the Holy Rock. Here, legend tells us, God seized Abraham's arm as he was about to sacrifice his son. Islam holds it is also the very spot from where Muhammad ascended for his brief journey to heaven. Below is a cave called the Well of Souls, where Muslims believe the souls of the dead will gather in anticipation of the Last Judgment. According to tradition, David, Solomon, Elijah, and Muhammad all prayed to God at the two altars here.

The smooth pavement outside the Dome covers what was once the Jebusite threshing floor that David chose as the site for the tabernacle. Later, Solomon's Temple stood here, as did, many centuries later, the magnificent Temple precinct of Herod the Great. According to the New Testament, on the eve of his arrest, Jesus preaches to the people from this location.

Relations among the three faiths deteriorated in the centuries following 'Umar's reign. Periods of tolerance alternated with periods of persecution against both Jews and Christians. In the 11th century, the mistreatment of Christian pilgrims and the destruction of the Church of the Holy Sepulchre by the Fatimid caliphs prompted Pope Urban II to call for a reconquest of the Holy Land. Launched in 1096, the knights of the First Crusade conquered Jerusalem and slaughtered its Jewish and Muslim populations. The crusaders controlled the territory until 1187, when Saladin, the Muslim sultan of Egypt and Syria, defeated the crusader army.

The crusaders regained control of Jerusalem, Nazareth, and Bethlehem by treaty in 1228, but the Egyptian Ayyubid army retook Jerusalem in 1244. The city remained under the sway of Islam until the British conquest during World War I.

MAPPING *the* HOLY LAND

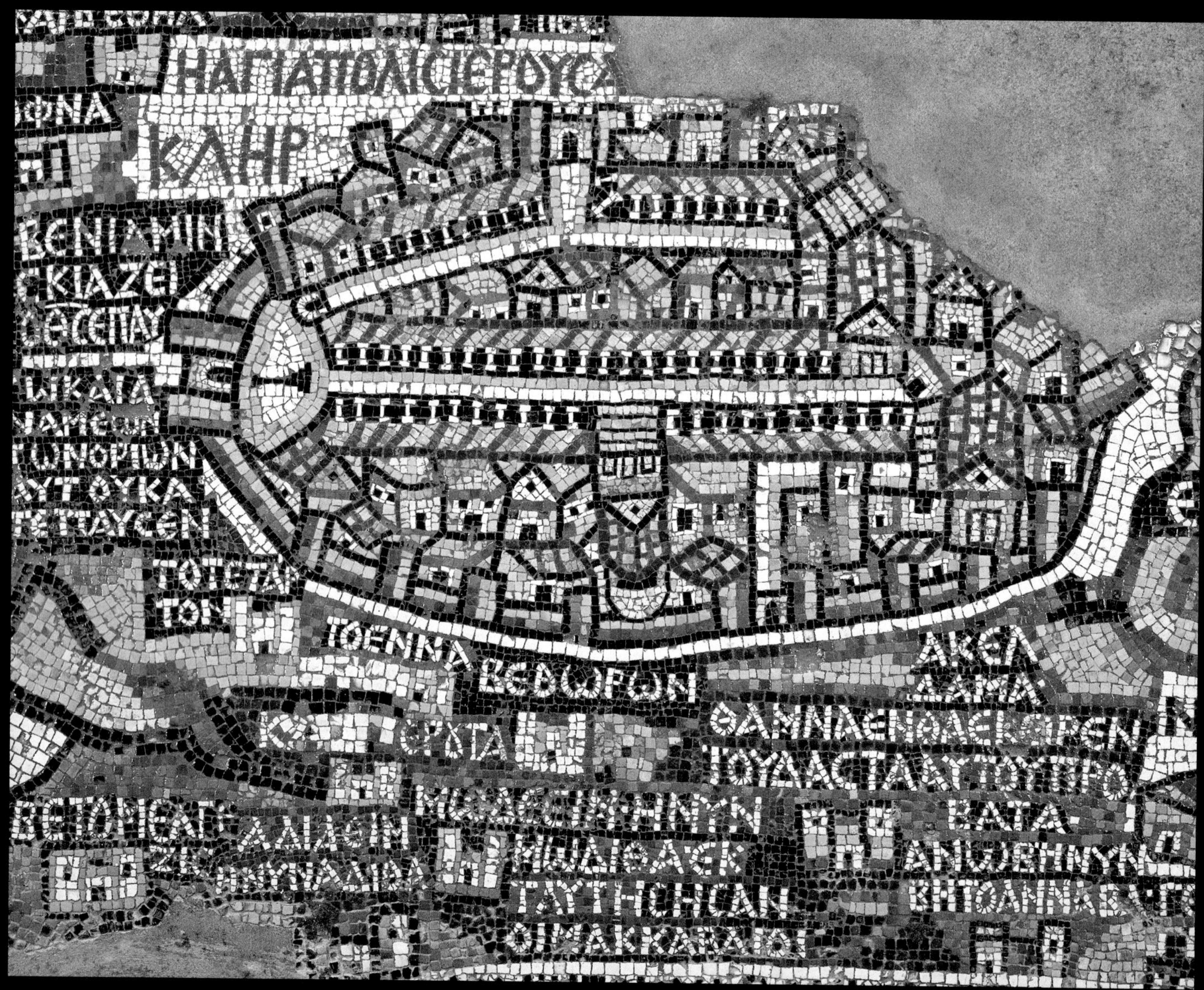

This detail comes from a sixth-century mosaic schematic representation of Jerusalem found in a Byzantine church in Madaba, Jordan.

DURING THE ERA OF THE MAMELUKE RULERS (1261–1516), Palestine became increasingly isolated, visited by only the most determined Christian pilgrims. This remoteness enhanced Jerusalem's almost mythical status as the holy city, and soon maps began to circulate, drawn from biblical narrative and an artist's imagination, rather than actual observation. The oldest extant map of Israel, however, is set in stone. A Byzantine church in Madaba, Jordan, has an impressive sixth-century mosaic with a schematic representation of Byzantine Jerusalem surrounded by the principal regions of the Nile Delta, the Negev, the Transjordan, as well as the Holy Land proper. The Roman-Byzantine *cardo*, the colonnaded road running north–south, is plainly visible (the Madaba Map is oriented toward the east, rather than the north). Remnants of the cardo were discovered during excavations near Temple Mount in January 2007, exposing the full 33-foot width of the street for the first time.

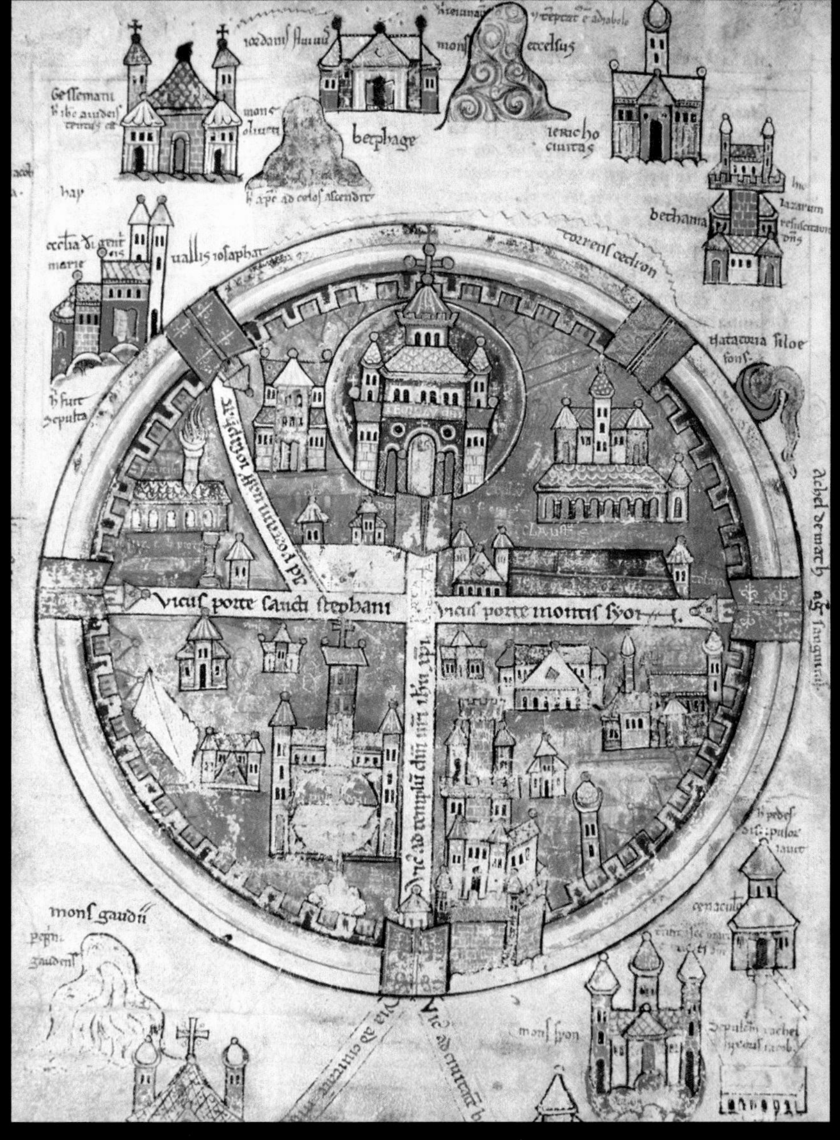

Showing key monuments of Jerusalem, this 12th-century crusader map resides today in the University Library of Uppsala.

The Crusader conquest of Jerusalem in 1099 allowed Westerners to observe the city firsthand. The crusader maps they produced, including the Uppsala Map shown above, typically enclose the city in a circle, representing the city walls, and bisected by the *cardo* and *decumanus*, Roman thoroughfares. The walls show five gates, including the Golden Gate, painted in gold, which, according to legend, Jesus entered through on the back of a donkey. However, the placement of shrines and churches is strictly symbolic. The church near the top, depicted in a blue roundel, is the Dome of the Rock, which was used as a church during the Crusades period. Nearby are the Al 'Aqsa Mosque, which crusaders believed was Solomon's Temple, and the rebuilt Church of the Holy Sepulchre. Just outside the city's circle are schematic representations of places such as Mount Zion and the Room of the Last Supper, the church of Gethsemane, and the Mount of Olives.

The Peutinger Map was engraved and published in Amsterdam in 1653. This detail shows the Nile River Delta, the Sinai, and southern Judea.

Shortly after the Uppsala Map was created, an unknown cartographer produced one of the most remarkable maps of the Holy Land: It became known as the Peutinger Map. Though drawn around 1200, the map appears to be a copy of a Roman map of the empire as it appeared around the fourth century C.E. The multisegment map includes 3,500 place-names as well as the Roman roads connecting these cities, offering a traveler a detailed road map of the empire. The Peutinger Map, which was only discovered in 1506 by Conrad Peutinger (1465–1547), hence its name, uniquely compresses the north–south axis to provide as much topographical information on the parchment as possible; major bodies of water are thus represented as mere slivers. In the above segment, Palestine is shown with all of its main cities and roads identified by their Roman names. The map is oriented toward the east, with the north of Palestine shown at the right.

Ezechielis. V.
Hæc est Ierusalem, Ego eam in medio Gentium
posui, et in eius circuitu terras.
HIEROSOLYMA VRBS SANCTA, IVDEAE, TOTIVSQVE ORIENTIS LONGE CLARISSIMA, QVA AMPLITVDINE AC MAGNIFICENTIA HOC NOSTRO ÆVO CONSPICVA EST.
1 Ager Acheldemach
2 Domus mali consilij
3 Natatoria Siloe
4 Coenaculum
5 Turris David
6 Via quę ducit in Bethleem
7 Domus Caiphę
8 Hic B. Ma: nutrita est
9 Sepulchrum V. Marię
10 Locus, vbi David septē com: posuit Psalm:
11 Domus Annę.
12 Torrens Cedron
13 Porta aurea
14 Templum Salomonis
15 Sepulchrum Domini
16 Locus Caluarię
17 Hic Christus flagellatus fuit
18 Probatica piscina
19 Vallis Josaphat
20 Lazarus
21 Hic S. Stephanus est lapidatus
22 Hoc loci Christus orauit
23 Domus diuitis epulonis
24 Domus Pilati
25 Domus Herodis
26 Palatium equitū peregrinor.
27 S. Veronica
28 Locus decollationis S. Ioannis Baptistę.
29 Castrum Pisanor.
30 Locus in quo Petrus amare fleuit.
31 S. Martha.
32 Arcus Pilati.
33
34 Hic Esaias serra dissectus est.
35 Fons Rogiel.
36 Mons Oliuetj.
37 Mons Sion.
38 Cemiterium Abassanorum.
39 Turris Syloë.
40 Vbi B. Maria nata.
41 Porta S. Stephani.
42 Porta Damascena.
43 Porta Ioppensis.
44 Porta Iudaica.
45 Turris Josaphat.
46 Hic se fugę commiserunt Apls.
47 Domus S. Marię Magd.
48 Masquee.

KARTE VON JERUSALEM
und seiner nächsten Umgebungen
geometrisch aufgenommen
von
F. W. Sieber
im Jahre 1818.
PRAG
Bey Martin Neureuter Buchhändler
Leipzig bey Friedrich Fleischer.
Berg Moria
Tempel Salomons
Thal Cedron
Thal Josaphat
Thal Siloah
Untere Stadt
Judenstadt
Berg Acra
Berg Sion
Weg nach Bethlehem
Maasstab
Norden
M. Olivarum
Valle et Torrens Cedron
M. Moria
Templum
Ophel
Siloe
M. Bezetha
Turris Antonia
Urbs superior
Calvarius locus
Acra urbs
M. Sion
Turris Hippicus
nach Chateaubriand.

David Roberts (1796–1864) created this hand-colored lithograph of the *View of Jerusalem, or Church of the Purification* during the 1840s.

Napoleon's highly publicized conquest of Egypt in 1798 greatly increased the interest of European artistic circles in the Middle East. Inspired, the 42-year-old Scotsman David Roberts embarked on a voyage to Egypt and the Holy Land to draw the places associated with the Old and New Testaments. In 1839, Roberts produced some 300 drawings that not only betray the romantic influence of Orientalism but also offer a tantalizing glimpse of the condition of major historic sites in the mid-19th century. The popularity of Roberts's drawings contributed to the establishment of the British Palestine Exploration Fund in 1865, tasked with the development of a systematic, cartographic survey of Palestine. This project was completed and published in a 26-page volume in 1880. The staff of General Edmund Henry Allenby used these very maps when the British Army took control of Jerusalem in 1917, inaugurating the 20th-century history of the Holy Land.

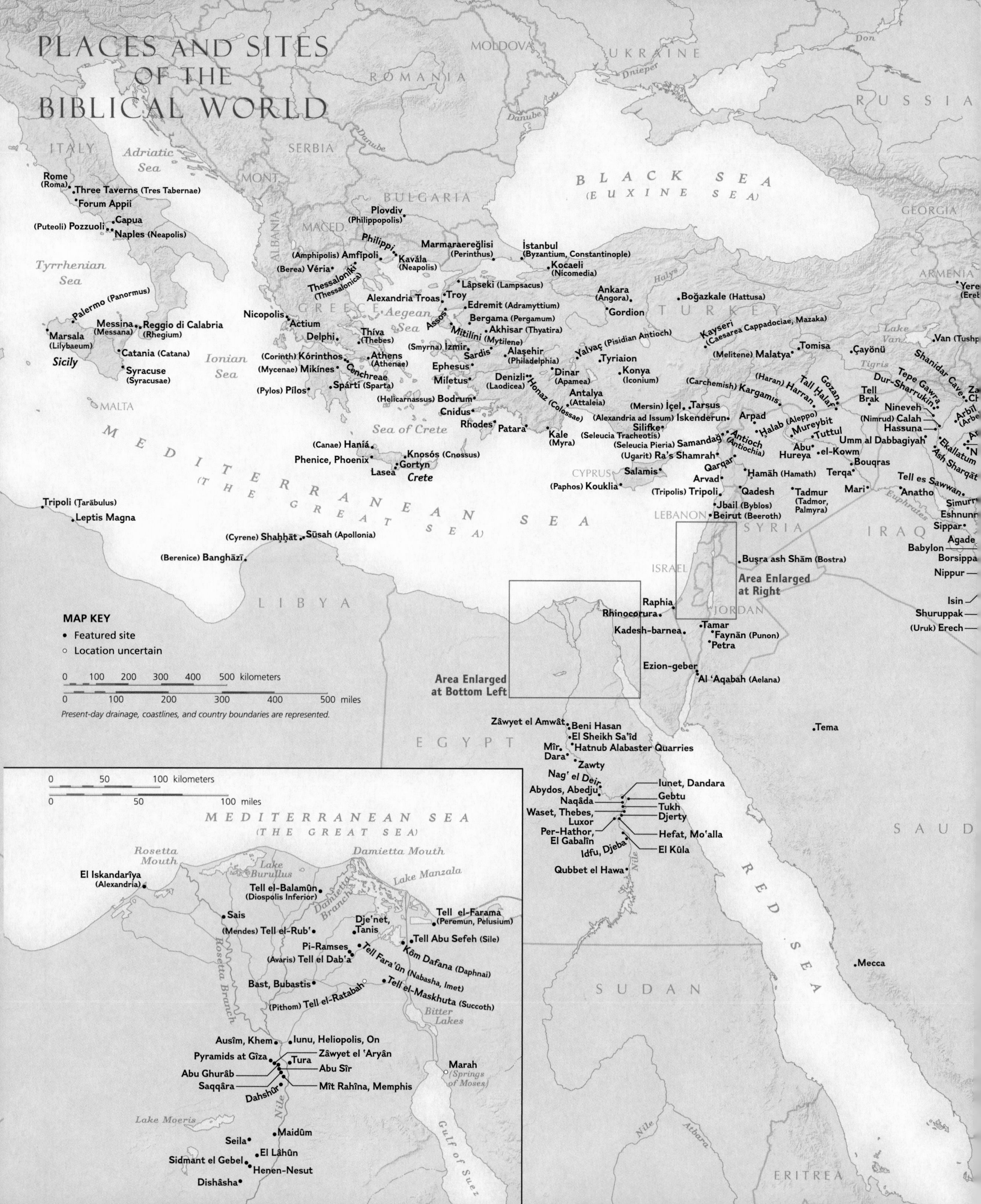

PLACES AND SITES OF THE BIBLICAL WORLD
MOLDOVA
UKRAINE
Dnieper
Don
RUSSIA
ROMANIA
Danube
SERBIA
ITALY
Adriatic Sea
MONT.
BULGARIA
MACED.
ALBANIA
BLACK SEA
(EUXINE SEA)
GEORGIA
ARMENIA
Rome (Roma)
Three Taverns (Tres Tabernae)
Forum Appii
Capua
(Puteoli) Pozzuoli
Naples (Neapolis)
Plovdiv (Philippopolis)
Philippi
(Amphipolis) Amfípoli
Kavála (Neapolis)
(Berea) Véria
Thessaloníki (Thessalonica)
Marmaraereğlisi (Perinthus)
İstanbul (Byzantium, Constantinople)
Kocaeli (Nicomedia)
Halys
Tyrrhenian Sea
Palermo (Panormus)
Marsala (Lilybaeum)
Sicily
Messina (Messana)
Reggio di Calabria (Rhegium)
Catania (Catana)
Syracuse (Syracusae)
Ionian Sea
MALTA
Nicopolis
Actium
GREECE
Aegean Sea
Delphi
Thíva (Thebes)
(Corinth) Kórinthos
Athens (Athenae)
(Mycenae) Mikínes
Cenchreae
(Pylos) Pílos
Spárti (Sparta)
Lâpseki (Lampsacus)
Alexandria Troas
Troy
Assos
Edremit (Adramyttium)
Bergama (Pergamum)
Mitilíni (Mytilene)
Akhisar (Thyatira)
(Smyrna) İzmir
Sardis
Alaşehir (Philadelphia)
Ephesus
Miletus
Denizli (Laodicea)
Honaz (Colossae)
(Helicarnassus) Bodrum
Cnidus
Rhodes
Patara
Sea of Crete
Ankara (Angora)
Gordion
Boğazkale (Hattusa)
TURKEY
Kayseri (Caesarea Cappadociae, Mazaka)
Yalvaç (Pisidian Antioch)
Tyriaion
Konya (Iconium)
Dinar (Apamea)
Antalya (Attaleia)
Kale (Myra)
Lake Van
Van (Tushpa)
Yerevan (Erebuni)
Tomisa
Çayönü
(Melitene) Malatya
Tigris
Shanidar Cave
Tepe Gawra
Dur-Sharrukin
Tell Brak
Gozan
Tall Halaf
(Haran) Harran
(Carchemish) Kargamış
(Mersin) İçel
Tarsus
(Alexandria ad Issum) İskenderun
Silifke (Seleucia Tracheotis)
Arpad
Halab (Aleppo)
Mureybit
Tuttul
Abu Hureya
el-Kowm
Nineveh
(Nimrud) Calah
Hassuna
Arbil (Arbela)
Umm al Dabbagiyah
Ekallatum
Ash Sharqat
(Seleucia Pieria) Samandağ
Antioch (Antiochia)
(Ugarit) Ra's Shamrah
Bouqras
Terqa
Mari
Euphrates
Tell es Sawwan
Anatho
Simurru
Eshnunna
Sippar
Agade
Babylon
Borsippa
Nippur
Isin
Shuruppak
(Uruk) Erech
IRAQ
(Canae) Haniá
Phenice, Phoenix
Knosós (Cnossus)
Gortyn
Lasea
Crete
CYPRUS
Salamis
(Paphos) Kouklia
Qarqar
Arvad
Hamāh (Hamath)
Qadesh
(Tripolis) Tripoli
Tadmur (Tadmor, Palmyra)
Jbail (Byblos)
LEBANON
Beirut (Beeroth)
SYRIA
MEDITERRANEAN SEA
(THE GREAT SEA)
Tripoli (Tarābulus)
Leptis Magna
(Cyrene) Shahhāt
Sūsah (Apollonia)
(Berenice) Banghāzī
LIBYA
ISRAEL
Buşra ash Shām (Bostra)
Area Enlarged at Right
Raphia
Rhinocorura
JORDAN
Kadesh-barnea
Tamar
Faynān (Punon)
Petra
Ezion-geber
Al 'Aqabah (Aelana)
MAP KEY
Featured site
Location uncertain
0 100 200 300 400 500 kilometers
0 100 200 300 400 500 miles
Present-day drainage, coastlines, and country boundaries are represented.
Area Enlarged at Bottom Left
EGYPT
Tema
Zâwyet el Amwât
Beni Hasan
El Sheikh Sa'îd
Hatnub Alabaster Quarries
Mîr
Dara
Zawty
Nag' el Deir
Abydos, Abedju
Naqâda
Waset, Thebes, Luxor
Per-Hathor, El Gabalîn
Idfu, Djeba
Qubbet el Hawa
Iunet, Dandara
Gebtu
Tukh
Djerty
Hefat, Mo'alla
El Kûla
Nile
RED SEA
SAUDI
Mecca
SUDAN
Nile
Atbara
ERITREA
0 50 100 kilometers
0 50 100 miles
MEDITERRANEAN SEA
(THE GREAT SEA)
Rosetta Mouth
Damietta Mouth
Lake Burullus
Lake Manzala
El Iskandarîya (Alexandria)
Tell el-Balamûn (Diospolis Inferior)
Damietta Branch
Tell el-Farama (Peremun, Pelusium)
Sais
(Mendes) Tell el-Rub'
Dje'net, Tanis
Tell Abu Sefeh (Sile)
Pi-Ramses
(Avaris) Tell el Dab'a
Tell Fara'ûn (Nabasha, Imet)
Kôm Dafana (Daphnai)
Rosetta Branch
Bast, Bubastis
Tell el-Maskhuta (Succoth)
(Pithom) Tell el-Ratabah
Bitter Lakes
Ausîm, Khem
Iunu, Heliopolis, On
Pyramids at Gîza
Zâwyet el 'Aryân
Tura
Abu Ghurâb
Abu Sîr
Saqqâra
Mît Rahîna, Memphis
Dahshûr
Nile
Marah (Springs of Moses)
Lake Moeris
Maidûm
Seila
El Lâhûn
Sidmant el Gebel
Henen-Nesut
Dishâsha
Gulf of Suez

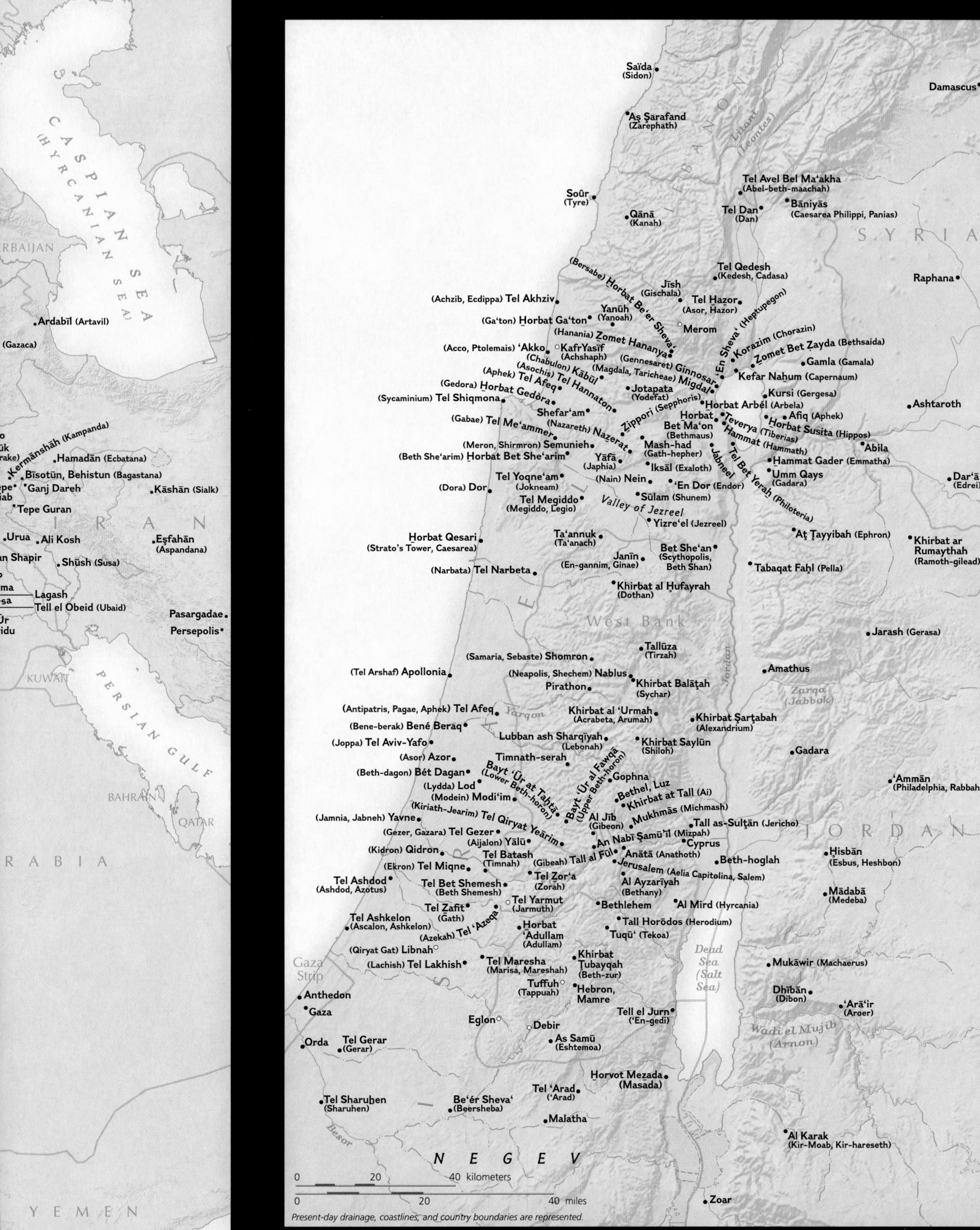

CASPIAN SEA
(HYRCANIAN SEA)
Ardabīl (Artavil)
Kermānshāh (Kampanda)
Hamadān (Ecbatana)
Bīsotūn, Behistun (Bagastana)
Ganj Dareh
Kāshān (Sialk)
Tepe Guran
Urua
Ali Kosh
Eşfahān (Aspandana)
Shūsh (Susa)
Lagash
Tell el Obeid (Ubaid)
Pasargadae
Persepolis
KUWAIT
PERSIAN GULF
BAHRAIN
QATAR
YEMEN
Saïda (Sidon)
Damascus
Aş Şarafand (Zarephath)
LEBANON
Lītanī (Leontes)
Tel Avel Bel Ma'akha (Abel-beth-maachah)
Soûr (Tyre)
Qānā (Kanah)
Tel Dan (Dan)
Bāniyās (Caesarea Philippi, Panias)
SYRIA
Tel Qedesh (Kedesh, Cadasa)
(Bersabe) Horbat Be'er Sheva'
Raphana
Jīsh (Gischala)
(Achzib, Ecdippa) Tel Akhziv
Tel Hazor (Asor, Hazor)
Yanūh (Yanoah)
(Ga'ton) Horbat Ga'ton
Merom
'En Sheva' (Heptapegon)
(Hanania) Zomet Hananya
Korazim (Chorazin)
(Acco, Ptolemais) 'Akko
KafrYasīf (Achshaph)
Zomet Bet Zayda (Bethsaida)
(Gennesaret) Ginnosar
Gamla (Gamala)
(Chabulon) Kābūl
(Magdala, Taricheae) Migdal
Kefar Nahum (Capernaum)
(Asochis) Tel Hannaton
(Aphek) Tel Afeq
Jotapata (Yodefat)
Kursi (Gergesa)
(Gedora) Horbat Gedora
(Sycaminium) Tel Shiqmona
Zippori (Sepphoris)
Horbat Arbél (Arbela)
Ashtaroth
Shefar'am
Horbat Bet Ma'on (Bethmaus)
Afiq (Aphek)
(Gabae) Tel Me'ammer
(Nazareth) Nazerat
Teverya (Tiberias)
Horbat Susita (Hippos)
Hammat (Hammath)
(Meron, Shirmron) Semunieh
Mash-had (Gath-hepher)
Abila
(Beth She'arim) Horbat Bet She'arim
Yāfā (Japhia)
Jabneel
Tel Bet Yerah (Philoteria)
Hammat Gader (Emmatha)
Iksāl (Exaloth)
Umm Qays (Gadara)
Tel Yoqne'am (Jokneam)
(Nain) Nein
'En Dor (Endor)
Dar'ā (Edrei)
(Dora) Dor
Sūlam (Shunem)
Tel Megiddo (Megiddo, Legio)
Valley of Jezreel
Yizre'el (Jezreel)
Aţ Ţayyibah (Ephron)
Horbat Qesari (Strato's Tower, Caesarea)
Ta'annuk (Ta'anach)
Khirbat ar Rumaythah (Ramoth-gilead)
Bet She'an (Scythopolis, Beth Shan)
Janīn (En-gannim, Ginae)
Tabaqat Fahl (Pella)
(Narbata) Tel Narbeta
Khirbat al Hufayrah (Dothan)
West Bank
Jarash (Gerasa)
Tallūza (Tirzah)
(Samaria, Sebaste) Shomron
Jordan
Amathus
(Tel Arshaf) Apollonia
(Neapolis, Shechem) Nablus
Khirbat Balāţah (Sychar)
Pirathon
Zarqa (Jabbok)
(Antipatris, Pagae, Aphek) Tel Afeq
Yarqon
Khirbat al 'Urmah (Acrabeta, Arumah)
Khirbat Şarţabah (Alexandrium)
(Bene-berak) Bené Beraq
Lubban ash Sharqīyah (Lebonah)
Khirbat Saylūn (Shiloh)
(Joppa) Tel Aviv-Yafo
Gadara
(Asor) Azor
Timnath-serah
Bayt 'Ūr al Fawqā (Upper Beth-horon)
Gophna
(Beth-dagon) Bét Dagan
Bayt 'Ūr at Taḩtā (Lower Beth-horon)
'Ammān (Philadelphia, Rabbah)
(Lydda) Lod
Bethel, Luz
(Modein) Modi'im
Khirbat at Tall (Ai)
(Kiriath-Jearim) Tel Qiryat Yearim
Al Jīb (Gibeon)
Mukhmās (Michmash)
(Jamnia, Jabneh) Yavne
Tall as-Sulţān (Jericho)
JORDAN
(Gezer, Gazara) Tel Gezer
(Aijalon) Yālū
An Nabī Şamū'īl (Mizpah)
Cyprus
(Kidron) Qidron
Anātā (Anathoth)
Ḩisbān (Esbus, Heshbon)
Tel Batash (Timnah)
(Gibeah) Tall al Fūl
Beth-hoglah
(Ekron) Tel Miqne
Jerusalem (Aelia Capitolina, Salem)
Tel Ashdod (Ashdod, Azotus)
Tel Bet Shemesh (Beth Shemesh)
Tel Zor'a (Zorah)
Al Ayzarīyah (Bethany)
Mādabā (Medeba)
Tel Yarmut (Jarmuth)
Tel Zafit (Gath)
Bethlehem
Al Mird (Hyrcania)
Tel Ashkelon (Ascalon, Ashkelon)
Tall Horōdos (Herodium)
(Azekah) Tel 'Azeqa
Horbat 'Adullam (Adullam)
Tuqū' (Tekoa)
(Qiryat Gat) Libnah
Dead Sea (Salt Sea)
(Lachish) Tel Lakhish
Tel Maresha (Marisa, Mareshah)
Khirbat Ţubayqah (Beth-zur)
Mukāwir (Machaerus)
Gaza Strip
Tuffuh (Tappuah)
Hebron, Mamre
Dhībān (Dibon)
Anthedon
'Arā'ir (Aroer)
Gaza
Eglon
Tell el Jurn ('En-gedi)
Debir
Wadi el Mujib (Arnon)
Orda
Tel Gerar (Gerar)
As Samū (Eshtemoa)
Horvot Mezada (Masada)
Tel 'Arad ('Arad)
Tel Sharuhen (Sharuhen)
Be'ér Sheva' (Beersheba)
Malatha
Besor
Al Karak (Kir-Moab, Kir-hareseth)
NEGEV
0 20 40 kilometers
0 20 40 miles
Zoar
Present-day drainage, coastlines, and country boundaries are represented.

THE HEBREW SCRIPTURES *(TANAKH)*		
THE LAW *(TORAH)*	**THE PROPHETS *(NEVI'IM)***	**THE WRITINGS *(KETUVIM)***
Genesis Exodus Leviticus Numbers Deuteronomy	*Former Prophets:* Joshua Judges Samuel (I and II) Kings (I and II) *Latter Prophets:* Isaiah Jeremiah Ezekiel *Twelve Minor Prophets:* Hosea Joel Amos Obadiah Jonah Micah Nahum Habakkuk Zephaniah Haggai Zechariah Malachi	Psalms Proverbs Job Song of Solomon Ruth Lamentations Ecclesiastes Esther Daniel Ezra-Nehemiah Chronicles (I and II)

THE BOOKS OF THE OLD TESTAMENT		
Genesis Exodus Leviticus Numbers Deuteronomy Joshua Judges Ruth I Samuel II Samuel I Kings II Kings I Chronicles II Chronicles Ezra Nehemiah Esther Job Psalms Proverbs Ecclesiastes Song of Solomon	Isaiah Jeremiah Lamentations Ezekiel Daniel Hosea Joel Amos Obadiah Jonah Micah Nahum Habakkuk Zephaniah Haggai Zechariah Malachi	*Deuterocanonical/Apocryphal* Tobit Judith Esther (additions) The Wisdom of Solomon Ecclesiasticus Baruch Letter of Jeremiah Daniel, *including*: • Prayer of Azariah • Song of Three Jews • Susanna • Bel and the Dragon I Maccabees II Maccabees I Esdras Prayer of Manasseh Psalm 151 III Maccabees II Esdras IV Maccabees

THE BOOKS OF THE NEW TESTAMENT

THE GOSPELS	TRADITIONAL ATTRIBUTION	POSSIBLE WRITING DATE
Matthew	Matthew (Levi)	75–90 C.E.
Mark	Mark, Peter's interpreter	66–70 C.E.
Luke	Luke, Paul's attendant	75–90 C.E.
John	John (disciple)	85–100 C.E.
ACTS	**TRADITIONAL ATTRIBUTION**	**POSSIBLE WRITING DATE**
Acts of the Apostles	Luke, Paul's attendant	80–90 C.E.
PAULINE EPISTLES	**TRADITIONAL ATTRIBUTION**	**POSSIBLE WRITING DATE**
Letter to the Romans	Paul	56–57 C.E.
First Letter to the Corinthians	Paul	54–55 C.E.
Second Letter to the Corinthians	Paul	55–56 C.E.
Letter to the Galatians	Paul	50–56 C.E.
Letter to the Ephesians	Paul (pseudonymous)	80–95 C.E.
Letter to the Philippians	Paul	54–55 C.E.
Letter to the Colossians	Paul	57–61 C.E.
First Letter to the Thessalonians	Paul	50–51 C.E.
Second Letter to the Thessalonians	Paul	50–51 C.E.
First Letter to Timothy	Paul (pseudonymous)	90–110 C.E.
Second Letter to Timothy	Paul (pseudonymous)	90–110 C.E.
Letter to Titus	Paul (pseudonymous)	90–110 C.E.
Letter to Philemon	Paul	54–55 C.E.
Letter to the Hebrews	Paul (pseudonymous)	60–95 C.E.
GENERAL EPISTLES	**TRADITIONAL ATTRIBUTION**	**POSSIBLE WRITING DATE**
Letter to James	James, brother of Jesus	50–70 C.E.
First Letter of Peter	Peter (pseudonymous)	70–90 C.E.
Second Letter of Peter	Peter (pseudonymous)	80–90 C.E.
First Letter of John	John (disciple)	ca 100 C.E.
Second Letter of John	John (disciple)	ca 100 C.E.
Third Letter of John	John (disciple)	ca 100 C.E.
Letter of Jude	Jude, brother of Jesus	45–65 C.E.
PROPHECY	**TRADITIONAL ATTRIBUTION**	**POSSIBLE WRITING DATE**
Revelation	John (disciple)	70–100 C.E.

Further Reading

Chapter 1. The World Before Abraham

Baines, John and Jaromír Málek, *Cultural Atlas of Ancient Egypt.* Abingdon, England: Andromeda Oxford, 2000.

Bertman, Stephen, *Life in Ancient Mesopotamia.* New York: Oxford University Press, 2005.

Collon, Dominique, *Ancient Near Eastern Art.* London: Trustees of the British Museum, 1995.

Murnane, William, *The Penguin Guide to Ancient Egypt.* London: Penguin Books, 1983.

Roaf, Michael, *Cultural Atlas of Mesopotamia and the Ancient Near East.* Abingdon, England: Andromeda Oxford, 2004.

Shanks, Hershel, *Ancient Israel : From Abraham to the Roman Destruction of the Temple.* Washington, D.C.: Biblical Archaeology Society, 1999.

Chapter 2. The Journey of Abraham

Cline, Eric, *From Eden to Exile: Unraveling Mysteries of the Bible.* Washington, D.C.: National Geographic Society, 2007.

Finkelstein, Israel and Neil Asher Silberman, *The Bible Unearthed: Archaeology's New Vision of Ancient Israel and The Origin of its Sacred Texts.* New York: The Free Press, 2001.

Hallo, William and William Simpson, *The Ancient Near East: A History.* Forth Worth, TX: Harcourt Brace, 1998.

Lewis, Jon E., *Ancient Egypt.* New York: Carroll & Graf Publishers, 2003.

McCurley, Foster R., *Ancient Myths and Biblical Faith: Scriptural Transformations.* Princeton: Princeton University Press, 1969.

Thompson, T. L., *The Historicity of the Patriarchal Narratives: The Quest for the Historical Abraham.* Berlin/New York: De Gruyter, 1974.

Chapter 3. Joseph in Egypt

Bietak, M., *Avaris, the Capital of the Hyksos: Recent Excavations at Tell el-Daba.* London: British Museum Press, 1996.

Clayton, Peter A., *Chronicle of the Pharaohs.* London: Thames & Hudson, 1994.

Gardner-Wilkinson, J., *The Ancient Egyptians: Their Life and Customs, Vols I-II.* London: Studio Editions, 1994.

Greenberg, M., *The Hab/piru.* New Haven, CT: American Oriental Society, 1955.

Rainey, Anson F., *Egypt, Israel, Sinai: Archaeological and Historical Relationships in the Biblical Period.* Tel Aviv: Tel Aviv University, 1987.

Redford, D. B., *A Study of the Biblical Joseph Story.* Leiden, Netherlands: E. J. Brill, 1970.

Rohl, David M., *Pharaohs and Kings: A Biblical Quest.* New York: Crown Publishers, 1995.

Chapter 4. The Exodus

Coogan, Michael D., Ed., *The Oxford History of the Biblical World.* New York: Oxford University Press, 2001.

Coote, R. B. and K. W. Whitelam, *The Emergence of Early Israel in Historical Perspective.* Sheffield: Almond Press, 1987.

Davies, W. D. et al., *The Cambridge History of Judaism (Vols. I–III).* Cambridge: Cambridge University Press, 1999.

Frerichs, E. S. and L. H. Lesko, Eds., *Exodus: the Egyptian Evidence.* Winona Lake, IN: Eisenbrauns, 1997.

Gottwald, N. K., *The Tribes of Yahweh.* Maryknoll, NY: Orbis, 1979.

Chapter 5. The Settlement in Canaan

Fritz, Volkmar et al., *The Origins of the Ancient Israelite States.* Sheffield, England: Sheffield Academic Press, 1996.

King, Philip J. and Lawrence E. Stager, *Life in Biblical Israel.* Louisville, KY: Westminster John Knox Press, 2002.

Levy, T. E., Ed., *The Archaeology of Society in the Holy Land.* London: Leicester University, 1995.

Mitchell, T. C., *The Bible in the British Museum: Interpreting the Evidence.* London: British Museum Press, 1988.

Steinsaltz, Adin, *Biblical Images: Men and Women of the Book.* New York: Basic Books, Inc., 1984.

Chapter 6. Kingdom of David and Solomon

Finkelstein, Israel and Neil Asher Silberman, *David and Solomon: In Search of the Bible's Sacred Kings and the Roots of the Western Tradition.* New York: The Free Press/Simon & Schuster, 2006.

Handy, L. K., Ed., *The Age of Solomon.* Leiden, Netherlands: E. J. Brill, 1997.

Mare, W. Harold, *The Archaeology of the Jerusalem Area.* Grand Rapids, MI: Baker Book House, 1987.

Silberman, Neil Asher et al., *The Archeology of Israel: Constructing the Past, Interpreting the Present.* Sheffield, England: Sheffield Academic Press, 1997.

Vaughn, Andrew G. and Ann E. Killebrew, eds., *Jerusalem in the Bible and Archaeology: The First Temple Period.* Atlanta: Society of Biblical Literature, 2003.

Yadin, Y., Hazor: *The Discovery of a Great Citadel of the Bible.* London: Weidenfeld and Nicholson, 1975.

CHAPTER 7. THE FALL OF THE TWO KINGDOMS

Ackerman, Susan, *Under Every Green Tree: Popular Religion in 6th-Century Judah.* Atlanta: Scholars Press, 1992.

Becking, B., *The Fall of Samaria: A Historical and Archaeological Study.* Leiden, Netherlands: E. J. Brill, 1992.

Cline, Eric, *The Battles of Armageddon: Megiddo and the Jezreel Valley from the Bronze Age to the Nuclear Age.* Ann Arbor, MI: University of Michigan Press, 2002.

Eynikel, E., *The Reform of King Josiah and the Composition of the Deuteronomistic History.* Leiden, Netherlands: E. J. Brill, 1996.

Vanderhooft, D. S., *The Neo-Babylonian Empire and Babylon in the Latter Prophets.* Atlanta: Scholars Press, 1999.

CHAPTER 8. FROM EXILE TO RESTORATION

Bosworth, A. B., *Conquest and Empire: The Reign of Alexander the Great.* New York: Cambridge University Press, 1988.

Carter, C. E., *The Emergence of Yehud in the Persian Period.* Sheffield, England: Sheffield Academic Press, 1999.

Harrington, Daniel, *The Maccabean Revolt: Anatomy of a Biblical Revolution.* Collegeville, MN: Michael Glazier, 1991.

Maier, Paul L., Ed., *Josephus: The Essential Works; Translation;* Grand Rapids, MI: Kregel Publications, 1994.

Schiffman, Lawrence H., *Reclaiming the Dead Sea Scrolls: The History of Judaism, the Background of Christianity, and the Lost Library of Qumran.* New York: Doubleday, 1995.

Stemberger, Günter, *Jewish Contemporaries of Jesus: Pharisees, Sadducees, Essenes.* Minneapolis: Fortress Press, 1995.

CHAPTER 9. THE WORLD OF JESUS

Borg, Marcus J., *Jesus: Uncovering the Life, Teachings and Relevance of a Religious Revolutionary.* San Francisco: HarperSanFrancisco, 2006.

Charlesworth, James H. et al, *Jesus Jewishness: Exploring the Place of Jesus in Early Judaism.* New York: Crossroad Publishing Company, 1991.

Chilton, Bruce, *Rabbi Jesus.* New York: Doubleday, 2000.

Crossan, John Dominic, *Jesus: A Revolutionary Biography.* New York: HarperCollins, 1994.

Ehrman, Bart, *Jesus: Apocalyptic Prophet of the New Millennium.* New York: Oxford University Press, 1999.

Fredriksen, Paula, *Jesus of Nazareth, King of the Jews.* New York: Alfred A. Knopf, 1999.

Mitchell, Stephen, *The Gospel According to Jesus.* New York: HarperCollins, 1991.

Neusner, Jacob, *Judaism When Christianity Began: A Survey of Belief and Practice.* Louisville, KY: John Knox Press, 2002.

Pagels, Elaine, *Beyond Belief: The Secret Gospel of Thomas.* New York: Random House, 2003.

CHAPTER 10. EARLY CHRISTIANITY AND RABBINIC JUDAISM

Berlin, Andrea and Andrew Overman, *The First Jewish Revolt: Archaeology, History, and Ideology.* New York: Routledge, 2004.

Chilton, Bruce, *Rabbi Paul.* New York: Doubleday, 2004.

Ehrman, Bart D., *Lost Christianities: The Battles for Scripture and the Faiths We Never Knew.* Oxford: Oxford University Press, 2003.

Elsner, Jas, *Imperial Rome and Christian Triumph.* New York: Oxford University Press, 1998.

Freke, Timothy and Peter Gandy, *The Jesus Mysteries.* New York: Harmony Books, 1999.

Grant, Robert M., *Augustus to Constantine: The Emergence of Christianity in the Roman World.* New York: HarperSanFrancisco, 1970.

Neusner, Jacob, *Introduction to Rabbinic Literature.* New York: Doubleday, 1999.

Pagels, Elaine, *The Gnostic Gospels.* New York: Random House, 1979.

Peters, Frank, *The Children of Abraham: Judaism, Christianity, Islam.* Princeton: Princeton University Press, 2004.

EPILOGUE: THREE FAITHS IN THE HOLY LAND

Armstrong, Karen, *Muhammad: A Biography of the Prophet.* New York: HarperCollins, 1992.

Hitti, Philip K., *History of the Arabs.* New York: Palgrave MacMillan, 2002.

Holt, P. M., Ed., *Cambridge History of Islam, Vol 2B: Islamic Society and Civilization.* Cambridge: Cambridge University Press, 1970.

Kaegi, Walter, *Byzantium and the Early Islamic Conquests.* New York: Cambridge University Press, 1992.

Lings, Martin, *Muhammad: His Life Based on the Earliest Sources.* Vermont: Inner Traditions Society, 1991.

Mehler, Carl, *Atlas of the Middle East.* Washington, D.C.: National Geographic Society, 2003.

Nebenzahl, K. *Maps of the Holy Lands: Images of Terra Sancta Through Two Millennia.* New York: Times Books, 1985.

Peters, Frank E., *Jerusalem: the Holy City in the Eyes of Chroniclers, Visitors, Pilgrims, and Prophets from the Days of Abraham to the Beginnings of Modern Times.* Princeton: Princeton University Press, 1985.

Tishby, Ariel, Ed., *Holy Land in Maps.* New York: Rizzoli Press and The Israel Museum, 2001.

ABOUT THE AUTHOR

Jean-Pierre Isbouts is Professor of Culture and Media Studies at Fielding Graduate University in Santa Barbara, California. He studied art and archaeology at Leyden and Columbia Universities. He has written numerous works on ancient, Renaissance, and 19th-century art. In addition to authoring a book about the origins of Judaism, Christianity, and Islam, he is the writer and producer of four programs on the Bible's legacy: *Charlton Heston's Voyage Through the Bible* (1998), *A Children's Guide to the Bible* (1999), *On Common Ground* (2002) and the Hallmark television mini-series *The Quest For Peace* (2005), which won the 2005 Gold Aurora Award and the 2005 DeRose-Hinkhouse Award.

BOARD OF ADVISERS

Barry J. Beitzel is professor of Old Testament and Semitic Languages at Trinity Evangelical Divinity School in Deerfield, Illinois. His areas of expertise include mapmaking and its history, geography, and archaeology. Dr. Beitzel's publications include *The Moody Atlas of Bible Lands* (Moody, 1985). Most recently he served as chief consultant for *Biblica* (Global Publishing, 2006). He has also contributed chapters to several works, including *Orient and Occident* (Butzon & Bercker Kevelaer, 1983), *Major Cities of the Biblical World* (Nelson, 1985), *The Anchor Bible Dictionary* (Doubleday, 1992), and *Crossing Boundaries and Linking Horizons* (CDL, 1997). His maps have appeared in *Ancient Israel* (Biblical Archaeology Society), the *Holman Bible Atlas* (Holman), the *Logos Electronic Atlas of the Bible* (Logos), the *Ryrie Study Bible* (Moody), the *NIV Study Bible* (Zondervan), the *Thompson Chain Reference Bible* (Kirkbride), the *Life Application Bible* (Tyndale), and the *New Living Translation*. He has also published in NATIONAL GEOGRAPHIC, *Biblical Archaeologist*, *Biblical Archaeology Review*, *Bible Review*, and *Archaeology in the Biblical World*, among others.

Bruce Chilton is the Bernard Iddings Bell Professor of Religion at Bard College, Chaplain of the College, Executive Director of the Institute of Advanced Theology, and Rector of the Church of St. John the Evangelist. His books include *Rabbi Jesus: An Intimate Biography; Pure Kingdom; Rabbi Paul: An Intellectual Biography; The Isaiah Targum; Mary Magdalene: A Biography; Trading Places, Jesus' Prayer and Jesus' Eucharist; Abraham's Curse; Jesus' Baptism and Jesus' Healing;* and *The Cambridge Companion to the Bible*. He is the founding editor of *Journal for the Study of New Testament, the Bulletin for Biblical Research*, and of the monograph series, *Studying the Historical Jesus* (E. J. Brill and Eerdman's).

Eric H. Cline currently serves as Chair of the Department of Classical and Semitic Languages and Literatures at The George Washington University in Washington, D.C., where he holds a joint appointment as Associate Professor in both the Classics/Semitics and the Anthropology departments, with additional appointments in the History department and the Judaic Studies Program. He is also the Associate Director (USA) of ongoing excavations at Megiddo (biblical Armageddon) in Israel. A prolific researcher and author, Dr. Cline is perhaps best known for his book *The Battles of Armageddon: Megiddo and the Jezreel Valley from the Bronze Age to the Nuclear Age* (Ann Arbor 2000), which received the 2001 Biblical Archaeology Society (BAS) Publication Award for "Best Popular Book on Archaeology."

Steven Feldman is Web Editor and Director of Educational Programs for the Biblical Archaeology Society, a non-sectarian, educational organization in Washington, D.C. Previously he served as Managing Editor of both *Biblical Archaeology Review* and *Bible Review*, published by the Society. Feldman holds a Masters degree from the University of Chicago Divinity School.

Jacob Neusner is the Distinguished Service Professor of the History and Theology of Judaism at Bard College and also Senior Fellow of the Institute of Advanced Theology at Bard. A Member of the Institute for Advanced Study, Princeton, New Jersey, and Life Member of Clare Hall, Cambridge University, he has published more than 900 books and unnumbered articles for both academic and popular audiences. Dr. Neusner served, by appointment of President Carter, as Member of the National Council on the Humanities and, by appointment of President Reagan, as Member of the National Council on the Arts. He is editor of the *Encyclopaedia of Judaism and its Supplements;* chairman of the Editorial Board of *The Review of Rabbinic Judaism*, and Editor in Chief of the *Brill Reference Library of Judaism*. He is editor of *Studies in Judaism* (Brill), the *Dictionary of Religion* (Harper/AAR), and of the *Encyclopaedia of Religion* (Britannica/Merriam Webster).

F. E. Peters is professor of Middle Eastern and Islamic Studies at New York University. A native of NYC, he was trained at St. Louis University in Classical Languages (AB, MA) and in Philosophy (Ph.L.), and received his Ph.D. from Princeton in Islamic Studies. His interests have since broadened into the comparative study of Judaism, Christianity, and Islam and the history of Muslim Spain. His most recent books are *The Monotheists: Jews, Christians and Muslims in Conflict and Competition* (2 vols.); *The Voice, the Word, the Books: The Scriptures of the Jews, Christians and Muslims;* and *The Creation of the Quran: The Making of the Muslim Scripture*, all from Princeton University Press.

ACKNOWLEDGMENTS

This book would have been unthinkable without the contributions of many people. First and foremost, I must thank Lisa Thomas of the National Geographic Book Division for developing the concept for this book in the first place, and for her unerring support during the editorial process. Also, I wish to thank Amy Briggs for her editorial guidance throughout the manuscript; Steven Feldman for his erudite comments on Near Eastern archaeology; art director Cinda Rose and designer Sanaa Akkach for their imaginative design and layout; Kate Griffin for her excellent photo research; Mary Stephanos for her detailed fact review; and Walton Rawls for his incisive style edit.

Special thanks are due to the panel of distinguished scholars who reviewed the manuscript, specifically Jacob Neusner, Research Professor of Religion and Theology at Bard College in Annandale-on-Hudson, New York; Frank Peters, Professor of Religious, Middle Eastern and Islamic Studies at New York University, New York; Eric Cline, Chair of the Department of Classical and Semitic Languages and Literatures at the George Washington University in Washington, D.C.; and my dear friend Bruce Chilton, Bernard Iddings Bell Professor of Religion at Bard College, New York. Other scholars who kindly gave their time during my research include Peter Awn, Dean of General Studies at Columbia University, New York; Elaine Pagels, Harrington Spear Paine Professor of Religion at Princeton University; Khaled Abou El Fadl, Professor of Islamic Law at UCLA; Dr. Afaf Marsot, Professor Emeritus of Middle Eastern Studies at UCLA in Los Angeles; Sheikh Abdul Aziz Bukhari in East Jerusalem; Bernard J. Luskin, Executive Vice President at Fielding Graduate University; and Rabbi Reuven Firestone, Professor of Medieval Jewish and Islamic Studies at USC in Los Angeles. It goes without saying that any errors in the narrative are mine and mine alone.

I would also like to thank my agent, Peter Miller, and his wonderful staff at the PMA Literary Agency in New York. And finally, I must express my gratitude to my family for their patience and understanding, and particularly to my wife Cathie, my muse and indefatigable companion during our many journeys through the Middle East.

—Jean-Pierre Isbouts

ILLUSTRATION CREDITS

All interior photographs by Pantheon Studios, Inc., unless otherwise noted:

1, Fol.319v The Dream of Nebuchadnezzar, from the 'Bible Mozarabe' (vellum), Spanish School, (10th century)/Church of San Isidoro, Leon, Spain, Giraudon/The Bridgeman Art Library/The Bridgeman Art Library; 2-3, Richard T. Nowitz/NG Image Collection; 4, Eitan Simanor/Alamy Ltd; 8, Jonathan Blair/NG Image Collection; 10, Richard T. Nowitz/NG Image Collection; 16-17, Hanan Isachar/CORBIS; 18, Nik Wheeler/CORBIS; 21 (A), David Keaton/CORBIS; 21 (B), Kenneth Garrett; 21 (C), Richard T. Nowitz/CORBIS; 23, Erich Lessing/Art Resource, NY; 24, Jon Arnold Images/Alamy; 25, Erich Lessing/Art Resource, NY; 27 (UP), Georg Gerster; 28, Erich Lessing/Art Resource, NY; 29, HIP/Art Resource, NY; 30, Nik Wheeler/CORBIS; 31, Scala/Art Resource, NY; 32, HIP/Art Resource, NY; 32-33, Scala/Art Resource, NY; 33, Eye Ubiquitous/CORBIS; 36 (UP LE), Scala/Art Resource, NY; 36 (UP RT), HIP/Art Resource, NY; 36 (LO RT), Scala/Art Resource, NY; 37 (UP LE), Erich Lessing/Art Resource, NY; 38, Christie's Images/CORBIS; 39, Erich Lessing/Art Resource, NY; 40, Tony Craddock/zefa/CORBIS; 41, Werner Forman/Art Resource, NY; 42, The Art Archive/CORBIS; 43, RF/CORBIS; 45 (UP LE), Werner Forman/Art Resource, NY; 45 (LO LE), RF/CORBIS; 45 (LO CTR), Erich Lessing/Art Resource, NY; 45 (UP RT), Erich Lessing/Art Resource, NY; 48, Boris Kester; 49, Erich Lessing/Art Resource, NY; 50 (LO), Dean Conger/CORBIS; 52, Gianni Dagli Orti/CORBIS; 54, Zev Radovan; 55, Scala/Art Resource, NY; 60 (UP), The Art Archive/CORBIS; 60-61 (LO), Erich Lessing/Art Resource, NY; 62, Richard T. Nowitz/Corbis; 63, Art Resource, NY; 64 (UP), A Royal Palace in Morocco, Constant, (Jean Joseph) Benjamin (1845-1902)/Roy Miles Fine Paintings/The Bridgeman Art Library; 64 (LO), Gianni Dagli Orti/CORBIS; 65, Jonathan Blair/CORBIS; 66, Hosul Kang; 67, Shai Ginott/CORBIS; 70, Erich Lessing/Art Resource, NY; 71, Zev Radovan; 72, Alinari/Art Resource, NY; 75, Giraudon/Art Resource, NY; 76, Art by Marc Burckhardt; Calligraphy by Julian Waters; 77 (UP), Jewish rug depicting the Tomb of the Patriarchs, Machpelah, Hebron, made by the Bezalel workshop in Jerusalem, before 1914 (cotton and wool)/Private Collection/The Bridgeman Art Library; 77 (LO LE), The Art Archive/CORBIS; 77 (CTR), Gianni Dagli Orti/CORBIS; 77 (LO), Erich Lessing/Art Resource, NY; 77 (LO RT), Erich Lessing/Art Resource, NY; 78-79, Richard T. Nowitz/NG Image Collection; 80, REZA; 81, Erich Lessing/Art Resource, NY; 82, Dean Conger/CORBIS; 84 (UP), Erich Lessing/Art Resource, NY; 84 (LO), Erich Lessing/Art Resource, NY; 85, Museum of Fine Arts, Boston; 87, Erich Lessing/Art Resource, NY; 88, Joe Baraban/CORBIS; 89, Philippe Maillard; 90 (A), Nimatallah/Art Resource, NY; 90 (B), Scala/Art Resource, NY; 90 (C), Erich Lessing/Art Resource, NY; 90 (D), Erich Lessing/Art Resource, NY; 92, Erich Lessing/Art Resource, NY; 94, Werner Forman/Art Resource, NY; 95, HIP/Art Resource, NY; 96 (UP), HIP/Art Resource, NY; 96 (LO), Stuart Westmorland/CORBIS; 98, Zev Radovan; 99, Joseph, Overseer of the Pharaohs, Alma-Tadema, Sir Lawrence (1836-1912)/Private Collection/The Bridgeman Art Library; 100, Bernard Annebicque/CORBIS; 101, Metropolitan Museum of Art/Art Resource, NY; 102 (LE), Bojan Brecelj/CORBIS; 102 (RT), Scala/Art Resource, NY; 104, Erich Lessing/Art Resource, NY; 105 (UP), British Museum; 105 (LO CTR), Philippe Maillard; 105 (LO RT), Zev Radovan; 106-107, Nathan Benn/CORBIS; 108, Jose Fuste Raga/CORBIS; 110, Richard T. Nowitz; 112 (UP LE), Scala/Art Resource, NY; 112 (LO LE), Erich Lessing/Art Resource, NY; 112 (LO RT), Scala/Art Resource, NY; 113 (UP RT), O. Louis Mazzatenta/NG Image Collection; 113 (LO LE), Richard T. Nowitz/NG Image Collection; 113 (LO RT), Erich Lessing/Art Resource, NY; 114, Jose Fuste Raga/CORBIS; 116, Nathan Benn/CORBIS; 117, Nebamun hunting in the marshes with his wife an daughter, part of a wall painting from the tomb-chapel of Nebamun, Thebes, New Kingdom, c.1350 BC (painted plaster), Egyptian, 18th Dynasty (c.1567-1320

BC)/British Museum, London, UK, /The Bridgeman Art Library; 118, Robert Stacey/WORLDSAT International, Inc.; 119, The Finding of Moses by Pharaoh's Daughter, 1904, Alma-Tadema, Sir Lawrence (1836-1912)/, Private Collection/The Bridgeman Art Library/The Bridgeman Art Library; 120, Erich Lessing/Art Resource, NY; 121, Dave Bartruff/CORBIS; 123, Martin Gray/NG Image Collection; 124, Aladin Abdel Naby/Reuters/CORBIS; 126, Erich Lessing/Art Resource, NY; 127 (UP), REZA; 127 (LO), Remi Benali/CORBIS; 130, Alain Keler/Sygma/CORBIS; 131, Erich Lessing/Art Resource, NY; 134 (LE), The Art Archive/CORBIS; 134 (RT), Robert Maier/Animals Animals; 135, National Gallery Collection, By kind permission of the Trustees of the National Gallery, London/CORBIS; 136, Erich Lessing/Art Resource, NY; 138, Erich Lessing/Art Resource, NY; 139, Israel images/Alamy; 140 (LE), O. Louis Mazzatenta; 141 (LE), Scala/Art Resource, NY; 141 (RT), Erich Lessing/Art Resource, NY; 144, Erich Lessing/Art Resource, NY; 145, Zev Radovan; 146 (UP), Zev Radovan; 146 (LO), Erich Lessing/Art Resource, NY; 147, Ms Fr 247 f.89 The Fall of Jericho, from the French translation of the work of Flavius Josephus (c.37-110 AD), c.1470-76 (vellum), Fouquet, Jean (c.1420-80)/Bibliotheque Nationale, Paris, France/The Bridgeman Art Library; 148 (b), Erich Lessing/Art Resource, NY; 148 (C), Richard T. Nowitz/CORBIS; 150, Hanan Isachar/CORBIS; 151, Erich Lessing/Art Resource, NY; 152, Richard T. Nowitz/CORBIS; 153, Erich Lessing/Art Resource, NY; 155, Shai Ginott/CORBIS; 156, Zev Radovan; 157, Israel Finkelstein; 158, Leen Ritmeyer; 159, HIP/Art Resource, NY; 161, Zev Radovan; 163, Zev Radovan; 164, Erich Lessing/Art Resource, NY; 165, Erich Lessing/Art Resource, NY; 166, Erich Lessing/Art Resource, NY; 167 (UP), Zev Radovan; 167 (LO LE), Zev Radovan; 167 (LO RT), Zev Radovan; 168-169, Annie Griffiths Belt/CORBIS; 170, Hanan Isachar/CORBIS; 171, Zev Radovan; 173, Erich Lessing/Art Resource, NY; 175, Zev Radovan; 176, Erich Lessing/Art Resource, NY; 179, Zev Radovan; 180-181, Gerald L. French/Panoramic Images; 182-183, Scala/Art Resource, NY; 183, Edward Parker/Alamy Ltd; 184 (A), Andrew Watson/Alamy Ltd; 184 (B), Helene Rogers/Alamy Ltd; 184 (C), Jon Arnold Images/Alamy Ltd; 186, The Death of Absalom (oil on panel) by Pesellino, Francesco di Stefano (1422-57)/The Bridgeman Art Library; 187, Reunion des Musees Nationaux/Art Resource, NY; 188, Erich Lessing/Art Resource, NY; 189, The Jewish Museum of New York/Art Resource, NY; 190, Art Resource, NY; 192, Leen Ritmeyer; 194, Giraudon/Art Resource, NY; 195, Erich Lessing/Art Resource, NY; 197 (UP), Zev Radovan; 197 (LO LE), Erich Lessing/Art Resource, NY; 197 (LO RT), The Jewish Museum of New York/Art Resource, NY; 198-199, Erich Lessing/Art Resource, NY; 200, Zev Radovan; 201, Tel Aviv University; 203, Erich Lessing/Art Resource, NY; 204, Erich Lessing/Art Resource, NY; 205, Erich Lessing/Art Resource, NY; 206, Erich Lessing/Art Resource, NY; 207, Erich Lessing/Art Resource, NY; 208, Erich Lessing/Art Resource, NY; 209, Erich Lessing/Art Resource, NY; 210 (UP), Zev Radovan; 210 (LO), Alinari/Art Resource, NY; 211, Erich Lessing/Art Resource, NY; 212, Erich Lessing/Art Resource, NY; 213, Scala/Art Resource, NY; 216, Erich Lessing/Art Resource, NY; 218, Erich Lessing/Art Resource, NY; 219, Erich Lessing/Art Resource, NY; 223 (LE), Erich Lessing/Art Resource, NY; 223 (CTR), Erich Lessing/Art Resource, NY; 223 (RT), Erich Lessing/Art Resource, NY; 225, Roger Ressmeyer/CORBIS; 226, Annie Griffiths Belt; 227, Bill Lyons; 228, The Hanging Gardens of Babylon, from a series of the 'Seven Wonders of the World' published in 'Munchener Bilderbogen', 1886 (colour litho), Knab, Ferdinand (1834-1902)/Private Collection, Archives Charmet/The Bridgeman Art Library; 229 (UP), Sistine Chapel Ceiling: The Prophet Jeremiah (pre resoration), Buonarroti, Michelangelo (1475-1564)/Vatican Museums and Galleries, Vatican City, Italy/The Bridgeman Art Library; 229 (LO LE), Erich Lessing/Art Resource, NY; 229 (LO CTR), Zev Radovan; 229 (LO RT), Erich Lessing/Art Resource, NY; 230-231, Vanni/Art Resource, NY; 232, Yokhanna Yacoub; 233, Erich Lessing/Art Resource, NY; 234, Erich Lessing/Art Resource, NY; 235, Giraudon/Art Resource, NY; 236 (A), SEF/Art Resource, NY; 236 (B), Giraudon/Art Resource, NY; 236 (C), SEF/Art Resource, NY; 236 (D), Giraudon/Art Resource, NY; 239 (UP), Erich Lessing/Art Resource, NY; 239 (LO), Erich Lessing/Art Resource, NY; 240 (UP LE), Erich Lessing/Art Resource, NY; 240 (LO LE), Erich Lessing/Art Resource, NY; 240 (UP RT), HIP/Art Resource, NY; 240 (LO RT), Scala/Art Resource, NY; 241 (LE), Erich Lessing/Art Resource, NY; 241 (UP RT), HIP/Art Resource, NY; 241 (LO RT), Werner Forman/Art Resource, NY; 242, Erich Lessing/Art Resource, NY; 243 (LE), Erich Lessing/Art Resource, NY; 243 (RT), Israel Museum, Jerusalem; 244, Richard T. Nowitz/NG Image Collection; 245, Erich Lessing/Art Resource, NY; 246, Erich Lessing/Art Resource, NY; 249, Christoph Gerigk/Franck Goddio/Hilti Foundation; 250, Dave Bartruff/CORBIS; 251, Zev Radovan; 251-252 (LO), Erich Lessing/Art Resource, NY; 252 (UP), Erich Lessing/Art Resource, NY; 254 (UP), Richard T. Nowitz/CORBIS; 254 (LO), Erich Lessing/Art Resource, NY; 255, Dr. John C. Trever, Ph. D./Corbis; 256, Richard T. Nowitz/NG Image Collection; 257, Erich Lessing/Art Resource, NY; 259, Richard T. Nowitz/CORBIS; 260, Erich Lessing/Art Resource, NY; 261, Leen Ritmeyer; 262, Jon Arnold Images/Alamy Ltd; 263 (LO LE), Richard T. Nowitz/NG Image Collection; 263 (LO RT), Erich Lessing/Art Resource, NY; 264-265, Richard T. Nowitz/CORBIS; 266, Annie Griffiths Belt; 267, Erich Lessing/Art Resource, NY; 268, Erich Lessing/Art Resource, NY; 269, Richard Passmore/Stone/Getty Images; 270 (UP LE), Scala/Art Resource, NY; 270 (UP CTR), Scala/Art Resource, NY; 270 (UP RT), Kenneth Garrett; 270 (LO LE), Scala/Art Resource, NY; 270 (LO CTR), BBC; 270 (LO RT), STR/epa/Corbis; 271 (UP), By Permission of the British Library; 271 (LO), Gianni Dagli Orti/CORBIS; 272, Stone/Getty Images; 273, Erich Lessing/Art Resource, NY; 274 (UP), Scala/Art Resource, NY; 274 (LO), Israel Antiquities Authority; 275, Thomas Nebbia; 278, Eddie Gerald/Alamy Ltd; 280, Jon Arnold Images/Alamy Ltd; 281, Zev Radovan; 283 (UP), Shai Ginott/CORBIS; 283 (LO), Steve Kaufman/CORBIS; 286, Zev Radovan; 287, Richard T.. Nowitz/NG Image Collection; 288, Erich Lessing/Art Resource, NY; 290, Scala/Art Resource, NY; 291, Scala/Art Resource, NY; 293, Erich Lessing/Art Resource, NY; 295, Richard T. Nowitz/NG Image Collection; 296 (UP), Israel Museum, Jerusalem; 296 (LO), Leen Ritmeyer; 298, Descent from the Cross, c.1435 (oil on panel), Weyden, Rogier van der (1399-1464)/Prado, Madrid, Spain/The Bridgeman Art Library/The Bridgeman Art Library; 299, Israel Museum, Jerusalem; 301 (UP), Israel Museum, Jerusalem; 302, INST.OPTIQUE/ZOKO/CORBIS SYGMA; 303, Scala/Art Resource, NY; 303, Israel Museum, Jerusalem; 304-305, Melissa Farris; 306, Sonia Halliday Photographs; 307, Erich Lessing/Art Resource, NY; 308, Zev Radovan; 309, Scala/Art Resource, NY; 310 (A), TongRo Image Stock/Alamy Ltd.; 310 (B), Jim Nicholson/Alamy Ltd.; 310 (C), Michael Melford; 310 (D), Michael Melford; 312, Réunion des Musées Nationaux/Art Resource, NY; 313, Melissa Farris; 314, Angelo Hornak/CORBIS; 315 (UP), Scala/Art Resource, NY; 315 (LO), Zev Radovan; 317, Zev Radovan; 319 (LO), Hulton Archive/Getty Images; 320, O. Louis Mazzatenta; 322, Scala/Art Resource, NY; 324, Institute for Antiquity and Christianity, Claremont CA, courtesy of Jean Doresse; 325 (UP), Alinari/Art Resource, NY; 325 (LO), Martin Gray/NG Image Collection; 326, The Christian Martyr's Last Prayer, 1863-83 (oil on canvas), Gerome, Jean Leon (1824-1904)/Walters Art Museum, Baltimore, USA/The Bridgeman Art Library; 327 (LE), Zev Radovan; 328, REZA; 330, James L. Stanfield; 333, Annie Griffiths Belt; 334, St. Jerome (tempera on panel) by Theodoricus of Prague (fl.1359-c.1381)©Narodni Galerie, Prague, Czech Republic/ The Bridgeman Art Library; 335 (UP LE), Erich Lessing/Art Resource, NY; 335 (UP CTR), Scala/Art Resource, NY; 335 (RT), Institute for Antiquity and Christianity, Claremont CA; 335 (CTR CTR), The Christian Martyr's Last Prayer, 1863-83 (oil on canvas), Gerome, Jean Leon (1824-1904)/Walters Art Museum, Baltimore, USA/The Bridgeman Art Library; 335 (LO RT), Zev Radovan; 335 (LO LE), Hulton Archive/Getty Images; 338, Richard T. Nowitz/NG Image Collection; 340, Jon Arnold Images/Alamy Ltd; 343, Burstein Collection/CORBIS; 344, Erich Lessing/Art Resource, NY; 345, Gianni Dagli Orti/CORBIS; 346, University of Southern Maine, Osher Map Library; 347, The Jewish National University Library/Hebrew University of Jerusalem; 348, The Jewish National University Library/Hebrew University of Jerusalem; 349, Erich Lessing/Art Resource, NY.

INDEX

K

L

O

P

Q

R

T

U

V

W

X

Y

Z

THE BIBLICAL WORLD

AN ILLUSTRATED ATLAS

by Jean-Pierre Isbouts; foreword by Bruce Chilton

Published by the National Geographic Society

John M. Fahey, Jr., *President and Chief Executive Officer*

Gilbert M. Grosvenor, *Chairman of the Board*

Nina D. Hoffman, *Executive Vice President; President, Book Publishing Group*

Prepared by the Book Division

Kevin Mulroy, *Senior Vice President and Publisher*

Leah Bendavid-Val, *Director of Photography Publishing and Illustrations*

Marianne R. Koszorus, *Director of Design*

Barbara Brownell Grogan, *Executive Editor*

Elizabeth Newhouse, *Director of Travel Publishing*

Carl Mehler, *Director of Maps*

Staff for this Book

Amy Briggs, Lisa Thomas *Project Editors*

Steven Feldman, Walton Rawls *Text Editors*

Cinda Rose, *Art Director*

Sanaa Akkach, *Designer*

Barry J. Beitzel, *Chief Map Consultant*

Matt Chwastyk, *Map Research and Production Manager*

William Christmas III, Sean C. Finnegan, Steven D. Gardner,

Thomas L. Gray, Michael McNey, Nicholas P. Rosenbach,

Gregory Ugiansky, Mapping Specialists, and XNR Productions, *Map Research and Production*

Meredith Wilcox, *Administrative Director of Illustrations*

Kate Griffin, *Illustrations Editor*

Marshall Kiker, Rob Waymouth *Illustrations Specialists*

Mary Stephanos, *Researcher*

Richard S. Wain, *Production Project Manager*

John Baldrige, *Editorial Intern*

Ken DellaPenta, *Indexer*

Jennifer Thornton, *Managing Editor*

Gary Colbert, *Production Director*

Manufacturing and Quality Management

Christopher A. Liedel, *Chief Financial Officer*

Phillip L. Schlosser, *Vice President*

John T. Dunn, *Technical Director*

Vincent P. Ryan, *Director*

Chris Brown, *Director*

Maryclare Tracy, *Manager*

Nicole Elliot, *Manager*

Founded in 1888, the National Geographic Society is one of the largest nonprofit scientific and educational organizations in the world. It reaches more than 285 million people worldwide each month through its official journal, NATIONAL GEOGRAPHIC, and its four other magazines; the National Geographic Channel; television documentaries; radio programs; films; books; videos and DVDs; maps; and interactive media. National Geographic has funded more than 8,000 scientific research projects and supports an education program combating geographic illiteracy.

For more information, please call
1-800-NGS LINE (647-5463)
or write to the following address:

National Geographic Society
1145 17th Street N.W.
Washington, D.C. 20036-4688 U.S.A.

Visit us online at
www.nationalgeographic.com/books

For information about special discounts for bulk purchases, please contact National Geographic Books Special Sales:
ngspecsales@ngs.org

Library of Congress Cataloging-in-Publication Data
The Biblical World: an illustrated atlas / by Jean-Pierre Isbouts; foreword by Bruce Chilton
p. cm.
Includes bibliographical references and index.
ISBN 978-1-4262-0138-7 (alk. paper)
1. Bible—Geography—Maps. 2. Bible—History of Biblical events—Maps. I. National Geographic Society (U.S.) II. Title.
G2230.18 2007
220.9'10223—dc22 2007061601

Printed in U.S.A.

Roma (Rome)
ITALY
Adriatic Sea
MONTENEGRO
SERBIA
BULGARIA
BLAC
MACEDONIA
THRACE
ALBANIA
MACEDONIA
40°N
İstanbul (Byzantium, Constantinople)
Tyrrhenian Sea
Sicilia (Sicily)
Ionian Sea
GREECE
Aegean Sea
Athina (Athens)
Ankara (Angora)
LYDIA
TUR
Tuz Gölü (Lake Tuz)
ANATOLI
(ASIA MINOR)
Toros Dağla
(Taurus Mountains)
MALTA
Sea of Crete
Ródos (Rhodes)
MEDITERRANEAN SEA
Kríti (Crete)
CYPRUS
Bey
LEBA
Khalīj Surt (Gulf of Sidra)
West B
ISRAEL
Jerusale
Gaza Strip
El Iskandarîya (Alexandria)
30°N
LOWER EGYPT
Suez Canal
Neg
El Qâhira (Cairo)
Munkhafad el Qaṭṭâra (Qattara Depression)
LIBYA
Western Desert
Gebel el Tîh (Tih Plateau)
SINAI
Nile
Eastern Desert
Gulf of Suez
Gebel Mû 2,285 m 7,497 ft
Libyan Desert
UPPER EGYPT
EGYPT
EUROPE
ASIA
AFRICA
Nile
Aswân
Lake Nasser
20°E
SUDAN
30°E
Nubian Desert